WOODROW
WILSON

The stage is set,
    the destiny disclosed. . . .
The light streams upon the path ahead,
    and nowhere else.

        —To the U.S. Senate, July 10, 1919

WOODROW WILSON

August Heckscher

COLLIER BOOKS
MACMILLAN PUBLISHING COMPANY
NEW YORK

MAXWELL MACMILLAN CANADA
TORONTO

MAXWELL MACMILLAN INTERNATIONAL
NEW YORK   OXFORD   SINGAPORE   SYDNEY

Collier Books
Macmillan Publishing Company
866 Third Avenue
New York, NY 10022

Maxwell Macmillan Canada, Inc.
1200 Eglinton Avenue East
Suite 200
Don Mills, Ontario M3C 3N1

Macmillan Publishing Company is part of
the Maxwell Communication Group of Companies.

Library of Congress Cataloging-in-Publication Data
Heckscher, August, 1913–
    Woodrow Wilson / by August Heckscher.—1st Collier Books ed.
       p. cm.
    Includes bibliographical references and index.
    ISBN 0-02-003871-2
    1. Wilson, Woodrow, 1856–1924. 2. Presidents—United States—
Biography. I. Title.
E767.H44   1993
973.91′3′092—dc20   92-33698   CIP
[B]

Illustrations are from the photographic collection of the Library of Congress, the National Archives, and the Princeton University Library.

Macmillan books are available at special discounts for bulk purchases for sales promotions, premiums, fund-raising, or educational use. For details, contact:

Special Sales Director
Macmillan Publishing Company
866 Third Avenue
New York, NY 10022

First Collier Books Edition 1993

10 9 8 7 6 5 4 3 2

Printed in the United States of America

Contents

8. War Leader

9. World Spokesman

10. Peacemaker

11. Fighter for the League

12. Embattled Invalid

13. Into History

WOODROW
WILSON

CHAPTER ONE

Youth

———◆———

PRINCETON, 1875

In September 1875, a young man of eighteen known to family and friends as Tommy Wilson arrived from the South at the College of New Jersey. This seems a good place, and a good moment in time, to introduce the subject of this biography, the future twenty-eighth President of the United States. Several years later, at the prompting of his mother, Tommy Wilson would adopt the first name of Woodrow. The College of New Jersey, its ambitions enlarged and its reputation growing, would in 1896 rename itself Princeton University. Under whatever names, Wilson and Princeton were to be inseparably linked.

In the autumn when this narrative begins, Wilson entered on four undergraduate years that saw him emerge from diffidence and awkwardness into a young man recognized beyond the circle of his college peers as being of unusual promise. In due course he would return here to teach and write, gaining a high reputation in his day as political scientist and historian; he would become the university's thirteenth president, an educator setting forth with rare eloquence, in terms as relevant to a later generation as to his own, the ideals and structure of liberal learning. Here, as it was to be later on a larger stage, he saw resounding successes followed by equally resounding defeats. The mature Wilson would say, a little sardonically, that he learned at Princeton all he needed to know about practical politics. Bitter memories of his Princeton reversals followed him to the White House and to the Washington house on S Street where he spent his retirement. An invalid in his last days, broken in all but faith, he meditated on the place where he had experienced so many early hopes, as well as what appeared to him such inexplicable defeats.

Wilson's lifetime bridged the two great wars by which Americans continue to define their history. Born shortly before the Civil War (only thirty years after Thomas Jefferson's death), he survived five years after the close of World War I. The first he witnessed through the wondering eyes of a child; in the other he mobilized huge armies and set the terms on which the carnage ended. Between these milestones he lived through the turbulent eras of Southern Reconstruction, the consolidation of the West as a political force, industrial and corporate growth, and the emergence of the United States as an imperial power. Observer, commentator, interpreter of events, the younger Wilson absorbed all that he saw, and most of what he saw left residues to sharpen his perceptions as a statesman and world leader.

His claim to fame seemed well founded while he lived. As the first southern President since the Civil War, he initiated and carried through a program of domestic reform unprecedented in American history. He mobilized a war effort of unparalleled scope and complexity. At the end of World War I he led the European powers in establishing the first modern organization of sovereign states. As a person he was in his prime vigorous and attractive, and he brought to American life one of those sunny periods when political action seems genuinely important. Yet along with his gifts less inviting qualities wove themselves into a personality of apparent inconsistencies. Success was repeatedly shadowed by failures. The man whom Princeton students regularly voted their most popular professor could present a dour image to the public. Affectionate in private life, he could be harsh and vindictive toward adversaries. A man of clear integrity, he too often crossed over the narrow line separating the righteous of this world from the self-righteous.

All that was in the future when the young Tommy, as recorded in a notebook, descended on Princeton with "Ten (10) new shirts" and "One (1) old shirt," as well as an assortment of cuffs, collars, handkerchiefs, and "Two Night Shirts."[1] Finding no room available at the college, he lodged and took his meals for the sum of ten dollars weekly at Mrs. Wright's on Nassau Street. A fellow lodger, Robert H. McCarter, recalled many years later finding in his next-door room "a hungry-looking young man named Tommy Wilson who knew no one else in the class." McCarter adds that Tommy was "very full of the South" and sat up late to discuss its cause.[2]

"Hungry-looking" the lad may well have been, and lonely as well. He was in a strange place, at a journey's end. Besides he was naturally somewhat cadaverous in appearance, with a long face, large ears, grey eyes, and sandy-blond hair. In figure he was, as he remained, tall and slim. But McCarter's reminiscence is certainly erroneous insofar as it implies that the young Wilson was an ardent devotee of the South. Though born in Virginia and reared in the states of Georgia, South Carolina, and North Carolina, he kept from youth a cosmopolitan point of view. He was early a nationalist, as he was later an internationalist; and very probably on this first journey north of the Mason-Dixon Line he was delighted to find himself in a new atmosphere.

Minutes of the American Whig Society, one of the college's two debating societies founded in the eighteenth century, note on September 24 that "whereas etc S. [sic] W. Wilson of N.C." desired to become a member, it was therefore resolved that he be admitted.[3] That is all we know of Wilson's first months at the college, until in the spring of that year he began a diary whose revealing entries will be discussed later.

Princeton was at this time a small country town, as the college was still a country college, its faculty dominated by Presbyterian ministers and its student body made up largely from youths of poor or middle-class families planning to enter the ministry. A dusty road, down which troops of the Revolution had marched, divided the line of shops on the one side from the few college buildings on the other. Of the latter, Nassau Hall was the chief, famous for having served briefly during the Revolution as the seat of the Continental Congress. The twin debating halls of the Whig and Clio societies stood behind it; more recently a few other structures, notably a library and a chapel, had been added. At the fringe of the campus a rectangular declivity in the earth, known locally as Cloaca Maxima, protected such sanitary facilities as the college possessed from recurrent student attempts to vandalize them.

A bird's-eye view of Princeton, engraved in the year of Wilson's arrival, shows the general aspect of the village very much as it remained into the twentieth century, except that wheatfields extend where residential housing would soon be constructed. The spur of the railroad from which young Wilson debarked can be observed running up to the heart of the college.[4] Newly completed, it provided the town's principal link with the outside world.

The college in its earlier days had counted on southerners to supply a major part of its student body. Handsome mansions, most of them now fallen to decay, spoke of bygone southern landlords arriving yearly in summer to enjoy what they considered to be New Jersey's cooling airs. The Civil War cut off the college from this constituency and left it disorganized and enfeebled. In 1868 James McCosh, arriving from Scotland as its eleventh president, toiled to reconstitute the college, add to its revenues, improve its faculty, and restore a semblance of order among the perennially riotous students. McCosh did not succeed in fulfilling two principal aims, to make the college into a university and to transform it into a national institution. Yet he laid the foundations, and he had the satisfaction of seeing the most famous of his successors complete the work.

In its ritualized disorders, in its modest campus and narrow curriculum, in the general tendency of the students to taunt and belittle the faculty, the College of New Jersey was indistinguishable from many such small institutions of the time. But under McCosh an innovating force had been at work, and the college was now ready to enter the modern age. The class of 1879 into which Tommy Wilson entered, the largest in the history of the college, benefited from this transition from old to new and also contributed to it. Not only did its members set standards for an active, vigorous student life, but in later years they remained outstandingly loyal. Unprecedentedly large gifts marked their anniversaries and reunions, and six of their number served as trustees. No one of them as a student profited more than Wilson from the breakup of hidebound traditionalism, or did more, eventually, to make the Princeton of the future a world-famous institution.

The path leading Wilson to his arrival at Princeton winds out of an ancestry rich in colorful and strongly marked individuals, through a childhood of slow maturing, not without its severe difficulties. We look at the ancestry first.

LANDSCAPE WITH FIGURES

Wilson's family was not southern, nor were its origins deep in America. His mother and his four grandparents were born overseas. His father was the son of a first-generation immigrant. Among American Presidents before and since, only Andrew Jackson had roots so newly planted in the New World; Jackson's ancestors, like Wilson's, were Scotch and Scotch-Irish. This quite special immigration, arriving in the New World in the early nineteenth century and spreading out through the middle Atlantic states into the Midwest, came speaking the native tongue and bearing strong natural affinities to the earlier settlers. With their independent spirit and habit of freedom they made themselves quickly at home. The Presbyterian faith to which they were bred fitted easily into a society where Puritan moralism still held sway and preaching and rhetoric were open avenues to success.

Wilson himself was convinced, at least half-jokingly or for the purposes of St. Patrick's Day oratory, that somewhere along the line he had inherited Irish traits. How else, he asked, could he explain those moods when his Scotch conscience seemed to be at rest and he experienced "a most enjoyable irresponsibility"?[1] Moreover his family on the Wilson side, his grandfather and his grandfather's six brothers (including most notably his own father), seemed in their boisterous charm very unlike the typical Scotch-Irish. Documentary evidence which might cast light upon the matter is lacking, for nothing of Grandfather James's lineage has been uncovered, his line losing itself among the myriad other Wilsons in northern Ireland during the eighteenth century. But the idea of an occasional intermixture with Irish blood is not implausible and may account for the strain of pleasant good humor that manifested itself so persistently in Woodrow Wilson's younger years.

Certainly on his arrival in America in 1807 at the age of twenty, Grandfather James Wilson carried himself with the exuberant self-confidence, the brash cheerfulness, traditionally associated with the Irish. Had he remained in his native country he would probably have lived an obscure life like the rest of his family; but something in the airs of the New World, combined with an original bent in his nature, liberated the young immigrant and set him on his way to becoming a successful journalist and local politician. James Wilson behaved, indeed, very much as an immigrant was supposed to behave according to classic American theory. He worked harder than those already established, showed himself more enterprising and resourceful, and quickly won the rewards of his industry.

A year after landing he had a job on William Duane's newspaper, *Aurora*, in a printing office in Philadelphia on the site of Benjamin Franklin's home, and felt sufficiently secure to marry. For his bride he chose a young woman of seventeen, Anne Adams, who had crossed the sea on the same ship with him. In later years she would recall that from her childhood home in Ireland she could look across the Irish Sea and on clear days see linen flying from the clotheslines in Scotland. She must therefore have come from either County Antrim or County Down—she could never be quite sure which. But there was never any doubt about her religious convictions. The faith of her Scotch forbears was in her blood and was written upon the hard lines of a face with piercing eyes and downward-drawn mouth.

The family objected to her marriage with the hearty extrovert who was advancing rapidly in a secular career. She bore James ten children and somehow got him to be an elder in the Presbyterian Church, but the two must have seemed an ill-matched pair—she with the primness of her race and upbringing, he expansive and optimistic, eager for worldly success. A visitor to America in 1829, advised to seek out James Wilson, found him "a man of great size ... with a round full face and fine full hazel eyes; his countenance ... cheerful and pleasing and his manners gay, candid and friendly."[2] The account says nothing of his wife, Anne.

From Philadelphia the Wilson family moved in 1815 to Steubenville, Ohio, part of the wave of western migration which gathered force after the Treaty of Ghent, ending the War of 1812, had set the terms of peace with England and had spurred the building of roads across the Alleghenies. Ohio was becoming the third most populous state (after Massachusetts and Pennsylvania), and Steubenville was a bustling river town with a population of twenty-five hundred, five churches, and several mills. Here James Wilson became the proprietor of the *Western Herald*, was elected justice of the peace (which entitled him to be known as "Judge"), and became a one-term member of the state legislature. In 1832 he established the *Pennsylvania Advocate* in Pittsburgh and thereafter divided his time between the two cities. He was a man known for his extraordinarily strong convictions and for the picturesque forcefulness with which he expressed them. Yet these convictions changed with the times and, like those of many newspaper publishers after him, with the prevailing views of his readers. A Jeffersonian in the late afterglow of the Revolution, James Wilson became an exponent of the nationalism of John Quincy Adams and Henry Clay.

Of Judge Wilson's ten children, the three daughters married well; two of his sons, identical twins, became generals in the Union army. The oldest son, named William Duane after the publisher who had given Wilson his start, rose to be a prominent newspaper figure in Pittsburgh and Chicago and a leader of the Grange movement in Iowa. The youngest, Joseph Ruggles Wilson, born in 1822, became a widely known churchman and the father of Woodrow Wilson.

In the midst of a busy family and professional life, Judge Wilson was adding business interests to his role in politics and journalism, when in 1850, in his sixty-fourth year, he died suddenly from an attack of cholera. According to the *Western Herald*, he had been seen in the streets of the city the day before his death "in his usual health and fine spirits. His conversation was as lively, and his step as firm as has been his wont."[3] He was never to know his famous grandson, whose birth was still six years in the future.

If the Wilsons seem to have sprung, original and youthfully energetic, onto the American scene, the Woodrows, on Woodrow Wilson's maternal side, come to this country trailing a long train of notable progenitors, men of position and learning, scholars, churchmen, lawyers. One branch of the family, according to family tradition, could be traced back to Robert Bruce. The maternal grandfather of Woodrow Wilson, Thomas, who originally spelled his last name "Wodrow," was born in 1793 in Paisley, Scotland. He became the first of his line in hundreds of years to cross over the Leeds River to England—as his father, a maker of Paisley shawls, had been one of the first to go into business. Established on English soil, Thomas changed the spelling of his surname to "Woodrow" and settled down to a long pastorate of the Presbyterian church in Carlisle. Seven children were born to him and his wife, Marion Williamson. Of these the fifth, Janet—always called Jessie—was to become the mother of the American President.

After sixteen years in Carlisle, Thomas Woodrow, with his wife, his children, and his sister-in-law Isabella Williamson, embarked for the United States. It was not the ordinary immigrant family. Thomas was then a mature man and was answering a call to a missionary church in Brockville, Canada. The journey, by packet ship from Liverpool, was a fearful one and was long remembered by the family. The ship weighed anchor on November 10, 1835, and reached New York two months later, on January 12. On the way Jessie, then nine years old, was narrowly saved from being washed overboard in a storm. Battling their way through heavy seas, the voyagers sighted the shores of the New World, and were then swept eastward again until the Irish coast was in view. The winter that greeted them on debarkation was one of the coldest in years. The Hudson was frozen over and the newcomers were prevented from proceeding northward from New York.

A month after landing, Thomas Woodrow was preaching[4] upstate when he received news that his wife, fatally weakened by the sea voyage, had died in New York City. With the children under the care of Isabella, their aunt, the family set out for Canada in April, as soon as the river was open to navigation. In Canada the cold climate continued to be a problem. Thomas Woodrow was required to ride ten or fifteen miles several times a week on preaching engagements in temperatures that fell to twenty-five degrees below zero. A further move was decided upon, and the following April the father and two of his sons set out toward the south. Lake Ontario was still covered by ice so thick that horse-drawn sleds laden with wood could cross the seven miles of its expanse at Kingston. The travelers proceeded to Cleveland and thence by canal into the interior.

At Chillicothe, Ohio, the pulpit of the Presbyterian church was found
to be vacant. After preaching there for several months, Thomas Woodrow was installed as pastor. In the autumn the rest of the family, including the nine-year-old Jessie, were summoned.[5]

Chillicothe was a pleasant town, priding itself on its residential character and on the absence of manufacturing. Here Thomas Woodrow
served for twelve years, in 1843 being married a second time, to Harriet
L. Renick. He resigned his pastorate while still a relatively young man,
on what early Wilson biographers declared to be grounds of health. In
fact, his departure from Chillicothe probably was due more to the unpopularity of his conservative theology and his narrow Calvinist views.
His later years were neither happy nor successful. The spirit of enterprise
that in his youth had carried Thomas out of his own country to England,
and thence to the United States, wore itself out. The marriage to Harriet
Renick soured his relations with the children of his first wife. After
leaving Chillicothe he served two rural parishes of less than fifty members
each, and in 1877 he died in obscurity, in a small community north of
Columbus, Ohio.

In 1919, Woodrow Wilson immortalized this grandfather in a famous
speech in Carlisle, England, leaving a memory of the man larger than
life. The grandfather was indeed learned, with a library of books in
Greek and Latin, and himself the complete master of Hebrew. Short in
stature, bearded, with a heavy Scotch accent, he was a picturesque figure
in the pulpit. Yet he seems never to have grown under American influences, and he remains in the family history a rather crabbed, reactionary
figure. During Woodrow Wilson's youth he made occasional visits to
the family, the old man's somber Calvinist admonitions producing not
altogether happy memories, and his idiosyncrasies—his singing of Scotch
hymns in a high, thin voice or his appearance at the breakfast table with
his nose buried in a Bible—were what was chiefly recalled.

When the child Thomas Woodrow Wilson was born, the mother
informed the grandfather four months after the event. News of the old
man's death, when Woodrow Wilson was a sophomore at Princeton,
was conveyed by the daughter in a brief, cryptic phrase. Children of the
second marriage, of whom there were six, were alone remembered in
the grandfather's will.

The Woodrow side of the family was nevertheless to play an important
role in Wilson's formative years. Not only was his mother, Jessie Woodrow, a more than usually dominant influence, but several of the brothers
and sisters with their children—the generation of first cousins—remained close. When James Wilson had been forgotten except for the

survival of his exuberance and charm in Woodrow Wilson's father, and when his children had been separated from one another by sectional or ideological differences, the Woodrow cousins stood together as a mutually supportive band. Though Jessie Wilson's relations with her father cooled, she cultivated—rather more assiduously than seemed required —the myth of the family's outstanding intellectual and moral qualities. As he grew up, the young Woodrow was given the sense not only of being part of a clan but of having sprung from superior people.

The youngest of James Wilson's sons, Joseph Ruggles Wilson, was marked as the scholar of the family. After learning the trade of printer, he attended the academy in Steubenville and Jefferson College in Canonsburg, Pennsylvania. From the latter he graduated as valedictorian in 1844. He started his career as a teacher, went to theological school at Allegheny, Pennsylvania, and for a year to the Princeton Theological School in New Jersey.

The college at Princeton was not connected with the seminary, but Joseph Wilson, a bright lad with a love for learning, came to know many of the professors in the college which his son was later to attend. In particular, he studied under Joseph Henry, pioneer in electrical science. Returning to Steubenville, still the family home, he taught at the boys' academy. A separate academy for women existed nearby, where the young Jessie Woodrow, daughter of Thomas Woodrow of Chillicothe, was studying. The two met, fell in love, and were married in June 1849. Two weeks afterward Joseph was ordained.

Several further years of teaching—as "professor extraordinary" of rhetoric and then of chemistry and natural science—occupied him before he undertook the full work of the ministry. The first of these professorships was important because it developed the concern for literary composition and for public speech which were to be so marked in both him and his son; the second was important because it brought him out of the Midwest into the South—to Hampden-Sydney in Virginia, seventy miles west of Richmond. It was in the South that he would spend the rest of his professional life. Here his children would put down their roots.

While still at Hampden-Sydney two daughters were born to Joseph and Jessie Wilson: Marion in 1851 and Annie in 1853. Some years later Jessie gave a pleasant picture of the young pair awaiting their first child. "We were among entire strangers," she wrote, "—were utterly inexperienced—had to depend upon 'chance' for everything—not a relation near us. In spite of all this we were the lightest hearted, and the happiest pair in the whole world, from first to last."[6] The passage speaks for Jessie Wilson as she must have been in her youth, before recurrent illnesses and fits of nervousness encouraged her husband to go off regularly on journeys of his own, and created for her son the image of an overprotective mother.

Dr. Wilson's preparatory years came to an end in 1855 when he was called to his first pastorate in Staunton, Virginia. He had begun his career as a teacher; he returned to teaching in later years, and indeed sometimes he considered that to be his true vocation. In the meanwhile he had before him the many-sided institution of the Presbyterian Church. Within it he found a test of his abilities and scope for his natural gifts.

GROWING UP

The town of Staunton, to which the Wilson family moved in 1854, stood in the hills of western Virginia, at a crossroads where travelers passed into the rapidly developing lands of the West. The time spent here was a happy one for the family. In his first pastorate Dr. Wilson revealed his gift for preaching and soon was acting as principal for the nearby women's seminary, overseeing a considerable expansion of its plant as well as in numbers of students. The manse was a brick building erected a decade earlier, imposing for its time and place. On the rear porch, when the weather was fair, the young minister could be seen writing his sermons, with the church and the seminary visible across a little valley.

Here, on December 28, 1856,* the first son was born. He was christened Thomas Woodrow, not, as might be assumed, after Jessie Wilson's father, but after her brother, who had taken care of her and financed her education when the father's second wife had divided the family. The infant was pronounced by an uncle to be "dignified enough to be moderator of the [Presbyterian] General Assembly."[1] "A fine healthy fellow," the mother described him in a letter written to the grandfather several months after the child's birth: "God has been very good to me." She could be thankful, as well, because Joseph's church was prospering in every respect: "He has fine congregations and they are steadily increasing." She expressed the wish that they might live in Staunton for many years, "for our situation could not be more pleasant elsewhere."[2]

---

*In so many ways a transitional figure, bridging two centuries and two great wars, Wilson was actually born between December 28 and 29. The family Bible records his birth as being "on the 28th December, 1856 at 12 3/4 o'clock at night." The twenty-eighth was always celebrated as his birthday.

But Dr. Wilson's career took a different turn. He was a go-getter, as his father James Wilson had been, and he was at the stage of life when a young man finds unforeseen opportunities opening up. In the summer of 1857 he journeyed to Augusta, Georgia, to officiate at brother-in-law James Woodrow's wedding. While there he preached at the First Presbyterian Church, evidently making a strong impression, and soon afterwards was called to be its minister. It was a large parish, a prestigious post, and Dr. Wilson responded affirmatively. He went on alone, to be installed in January 1858. His family followed in the spring. The stay in Staunton had been short, a mere two and a half years, but long enough so that the future President would always refer to himself as "a Virginian." The family would now reside for twelve years in Augusta, through the Civil War and its aftermath.

Thackeray, the English author, visited Augusta at about this time and described it as "a queer little rustic city," with "a happy, dirty tranquility generally prevalent."[3] For the South of that period, however, it was a considerable metropolis. Some twelve thousand inhabitants lived along its wide streets shaded by elms and oaks. Situated upon a bend of the Savannah River, at the highest point of its navigable waters, the city was an active trading center drawing its prosperity from cotton mills and warehouses. The business district stretched three blocks along the present Broad Street; balconied houses faced the river on Bay Street, while to the south, parallel with Broad, lay Green and Telfair streets, two of the most handsome boulevards in the country. Three miles from the center of town rose what were known as the Sand Hills. When the Wilsons moved to Augusta, the richer families were building homes in this area, to escape the summer heat and the threat of malaria hanging over the riverbanks.

On a large plot in Telfair Street, adjoining the Richmond Academy, stood the First Presbyterian Church. Two years after Dr. Wilson assumed his pastorship, a new brick manse was built diagonally across the street, with a barn for Dr. Wilson's horse and carriage out back and enough ground for a vegetable garden. Here the young Wilson spent the formative years of his youth.

The Civil War first touched Augusta in an incident that appeared to its more militant citizens as a dismaying anticlimax. The federal arsenal in the nearby Sand Hill was considered by the local Confederates to be a major Union resource, and amid the general excitement raw recruits prepared to attack it. They expected, perhaps even hoped for, a stiff resistance. However, the general in charge, choosing discretion as the wiser course, promptly abandoned it. Afterwards Augusta had its few glorious moments when Southern battalions, with flags flying and accompanied by brass bands, marched off to the then unimagined holocaust. Mostly the war was endured by its citizens in more prosaic ways.

Older men enrolled in the Silver Greys, organized for service and defense on the home front; women took up needles and sewing machines. A city unlikely to be attacked, Augusta became a center for refugees from Savannah and then from New Orleans and other southern points. Crowds jammed the city, with food growing scarce and lodging unattainable. The chief Confederate powder works, housed on the Savannah River in buildings romantically conceived as medieval Norman forts, performed what were considered miracles of production, guarded by young boys against the possibility of Northern warships coming up the river.

Although Dr. Wilson managed to adapt himself comfortably to the Confederate cause, he was basically a midwesterner, and never became wholly assimilated as a southerner; after the war his natural propensity was to journey whenever possible toward the north. Yet now he backed the war effort by various means. He found slavery to be sanctioned in the Bible.[4] He spent one summer in army service at Columbia, South Carolina. After the Southern victory at Chickamauga he turned his churchyard into a military camp and, with his wife's help, the church into a hospital. On a Sunday morning in 1863 he announced from the pulpit that women were needed at the arsenal to wrap cartridges for General Lee and without further religious ceremony dismissed the congregation. His most far-reaching act, however, was an invitation extended to the southern presbyteries in 1861 for a meeting where the formation of a separate General Assembly would be discussed. The result of that meeting was a division between northern and southern branches of the church.

For two weeks churchmen met in Augusta's First Presbyterian Church to debate the issues of separation. Wide public approval greeted so decisive an ecclesiastical and political proposal. In the hushed and crowded church, as Dr. Wilson recalled the scene years later, Dr. James H. Thornwell, the Calhoun of southern theology, the Calvin of the new cause, rose to set forth with what seemed irrefutable logic the necessity for the breach.[5] At the close of the meeting Dr. Wilson was made recording clerk of the General Assembly. He was elected stated clerk in 1868, and in this important administrative post he exercised for many years his wit and eloquence, as well as his capacity for making and keeping a large circle of friends.

*   *   *

Woodrow Wilson was four when the Civil War began, eight years of age at its close. He recalled very little of its actual events, though his first memory was of standing at the gate of the family house in 1860 and hearing a passerby say that Lincoln had been elected and there would be war.[6] During much of the conflict he was too young to have clear recollections, and was shielded by his family from its more harrowing or unpleasant scenes. Nevertheless, the war persisted as a major influence in Wilson's life and thought. Not only did he struggle with its implications in his early writings, but at a deeper level a sense of the war's encroaching chaos remained with him in later life, less in the form of conscious memories than of impulses to create unity and stability in the world around him. Against the tendencies of his time he fought at Princeton for a focused curriculum and for a college community resistant to the prevailing fragmentation; later he fought for an integrated world order.

The young Wilson was diffident and shy, and often appeared lazy to his contemporaries. He seemed determined to keep his thoughts to himself, refusing to be nudged prematurely into the world of adult preoccupations. In his maturity he championed discerningly a child's right to isolation and privacy. "Absorbed by no interest," he wrote, the child "stands upon a place apart, a little spectator of the world." Before his gaze, Wilson continued, "men and women come and go, events fall out, years open their slow story and are noted or let go as his mood chances to serve them. The play touches him not. He but looks on, thinks his own thought, and turns away, not even expecting his cue to enter the plot and to speak. He waits—he knows not for what."[7]

Along with a youthful tendency to reject the real world of facts, and a few years later to prove more than normally immune to pedagogical learning, Wilson created for himself an imaginary existence peculiarly tenacious and vivid.[8] Again the later Wilson speaks from the depths of his earliest experience: "the age of childhood," he declared, was inhabited by those who with delight live out their own imaginings, who "pursue persons and objects that never existed; they make an Argosy laden with gold out of a floating butterfly."[9] Writing in less literary style to a friend while absorbed in political activities, he confessed that his whole life seemed to be rooted in dreams. "I lived a dream life (almost too exclusively, perhaps) when I was a lad and even now my thought goes back for refreshment to those days when all the world seemed to me a place of heroic adventure, in which one's heart must keep its own counsel."[10]

"I suppose that nothing is more painful in the recollections of some of us," Wilson declared when a college president, "than the efforts that were made to make us like grown-up people." When parents and pedagogues had done their worst, he continued, "the delightful follies that we had to eschew, the delicious nonsense that we had to disbelieve!" Like Robert Louis Stevenson, another Scot, who also read late and was a desultory pupil, Wilson never lost the feeling of what it was to be a child.* He never ceased to amuse and humor children. Of Wilson as of Stevenson it could be said that he prolonged and protected his own childhood in dreams, in fancies; that in the early years as in the later his heart kept "its own counsel."

Wilson's inclination to a dream life seems certainly related to the fact that he was late in reading, not knowing his letters until he was nine nor being fully at home with the written word until he was eleven or twelve. Various causes have been adduced to explain this backwardness, in most of which the retreat into a dream world plays little part. Early biographers, encouraged by Wilson himself, explained that no good schools or schoolmasters were to be found in the postbellum South. Later psychological interpretations have attributed Wilson's slow development to unconscious resentment of his father. Pictured as constantly pressing his son, teasing him, and making no effort to conceal dismay at the boy's slow progress, the father, it is argued, evoked resistance and silent rebellion. His ego damaged, the son first refused to read, and in later life compensated for the slights by inordinate ambition and a relentless drive for success.[11]

Evidence to support this thesis is not found in any of Wilson's overt acts. Far from appearing to resent his father, or to rebel against him, he showed himself to be a devoted son, and throughout his life testified to the father's having been an affectionate guide and counselor. Though much under his father's influence, he gradually, and without pain on either side, established his independence. Admittedly his father was a rather overwhelming man. His teasing humor could be laced with unkindness. He must indeed have goaded Tommy, pushing him to the

---

*There is also a resemblance to the case of Albert Einstein, who did not talk until he was nine. Although admitting that a developmental defect may be suspected, Erik Erikson suggests on the basis of Einstein's total character that the behavior is that of a child who "wished to preserve some playfulness and peacefulness at whatever pace of progress"; one who succeeded "in saving the child in himself even when, increasingly, he had to accept, with a kind of non-violent resistance, isolation and even punishment." (In G. Holton and Y. Elkana, eds., *Albert Einstein: Historical and Cultural Perspectives* [Princeton, 1982].)

point of wanting secretly to resist his instruction. But the youth seems
to have been able to take care of himself. And when things became
difficult, he could always retreat into his private world of story and
imagination.

Another interpretation of the youthful Wilson's behavior and personality is based on the hypothesis that he suffered from dyslexia.[12] Certainly
dyslexia would explain his late reading. However the obvious symptoms
of this dysfunction—reading difficulties, poor spelling—do not show up
in his mature years, and attempts to adduce evidence to this effect are
unconvincing. More subtle signs nevertheless point to some form of
dyslexia as having been present. That Wilson wore spectacles as a child,
that he was close to being ambidextrous later in life, and that he always
had difficulties in mastering foreign languages are suggestive. The shaping of a dream world and the withdrawal into a prolonged childhood,
so marked in Wilson's case, often accompany dyslexia.

Perhaps most persuasive of all is the undoubted fact that the young
Wilson was himself conscious of some unnamed handicap, and that he
strove by his own devices to surmount it. At the age of sixteen he
embarked on the taxing study of shorthand; a little later he became a
devotee of the newly invented typewriter. Both of these are methods
now recognized as helping the dyslexic to overcome an innate tendency
to transpose letters. If Wilson by himself sensed this fact it is a remarkable
tribute to his acumen, and that he then applied himself to mastering the
unfamiliar techniques shows him to have had a strong will even as a
youth.

A scholar recently characterized Wilson's early period as having been
of equal "heroism" with that of his great contemporary and rival, Theodore Roosevelt.[13] As the latter fought successfully to overcome physical
weakness, so Wilson, it is suggested, fought with equal success to overcome his neurological handicap. The two leaders thus developed lifelong
habits of self-discipline and inner strength fitting them for the public
stage. It is a tempting parallel, and certainly the image of Tommy Wilson
is a moving one—the bright and spirited youth immured by a severe
dysfunction, struggling with growing energy and perseverance to fight
his way out.

Yet another view of Wilson's childhood may be advanced, not altogether at odds with such a period of struggle as sketched above. Outwardly, and later in his own reminiscence, the early years appeared placid
and happy. Through the eyes of contemporaries we perceive the slow
uncoiling of a complex personality in an atmosphere of love and family
supportiveness. The world of the imagination faded, rather more slowly

than with the average child; reality came to take its place, perhaps more subtly resisted than could be considered quite normal. Yet the young man in due season and without any grave crisis of maturation put away childish things. There remained of that other world, of that former existence of reveries and dreams, of the child, of the detached and passive onlooker, traces distinct and lasting, to be overlaid in time by the stern disciplines of training and inheritance. Unless one perceives these elements, one is unprepared for the Wilson who was always something of a dreamer, the Wilson of the happy successful years, before public travail and failing health brought out the grimmer side of his nature.

By the end of the Civil War, Tommy Wilson at the age of eight began to take his place in the activities of the family and of the wider scene. The war had left Augusta, as it had most of the cities of the South, exhausted and depleted, providing harsh glimpses even for a sheltered youth. The city was occupied by federal troops and for a time citizens were forbidden to go out at night without a pass. Jefferson Davis, president of the fallen republic, was brought in as a prisoner. General Robert E. Lee passed through, to be received with subdued pride and respect. It is significant that Wilson remembered standing by his father's side and looking up into Lee's face, perhaps his first intimation of what defeat meant and of how it could be borne.

At the core of the child's inner life Jessie Wilson presided. She was described by a niece as "a typical gentlewoman, delicate, refined"[14]—which is perhaps a way of saying that, in addition to many admirable qualities, the lady had her faults. The hypochondria and self-pity that later marked her may not have been evident at this time. But she was inclined to snobbishness; she was certainly of the worrying sort, over-indulgent and possessive toward her son. "Extremely kind, but too anxious," was the way Boswell described his own mother; and the young Wilson suffered from having a similar parent. His two sisters, Marion and Annie, reinforced the mother's encompassing care. They read to him constantly, and in the war years when social amusements were few they must have made of him a kind of family pet. At the least, they strengthened Tommy's tendency to dream and to postpone facing realities. The circle of siblings was completed by the birth of Joseph R. Wilson in 1866. Ten years Tommy's junior, the brother came too late to play the role of rival and tomboy opponent that could have counteracted the sisters' influence.

Wilson's father towered over the other family members, formidable not only in their eyes but also in the eyes of his congregation. His preaching was a blend of learning and of direct, almost blunt, communication, his phrases tuned and honed until they struck close to the heart of everyday concerns. His theology, emphasizing the less intimidating aspects of Calvinism, promoted a geniality that spread into his daily life. He was full of humor. Loving the play of words, he seemed to be bursting in his prime with zest and self-confidence. He acted as if conversation were a chief end of life and puns one of its major diversions. He enjoyed billiards and was not averse to taking a nip of whisky—good Scotch whisky—now and then.

Yet for all his outward brilliance and his many beguiling qualities there was a dark side to the man, an inconsistency that kept him just outside the innermost circle of his congregation's affection. Even members of the family sometimes spoke of him as one not entirely lovable. As he grew older, his jokes became increasingly wounding. Bitterness accumulated as disappointments clouded his earlier achievements, while pride showed itself in an irascibility only partly shaded by wit. In later years he was often depressed and admitted to an underlying want of self-esteem.

Foundations of the mutual admiration of father and son were laid in these Augusta days. In spite of hindrances on both sides—the father must have been baffled by the son's seeming aloofness as was the son by the parent's overenthusiastic prodding—the two came to understand each other. A relative later recalled the tall, frock-coated minister, his Sunday chores behind him, leading the bespectacled youth through the city's mills and warehouses, explaining their arcane workings. Afterwards he was said to have quizzed the boy, insisting upon replies in literate sentences. It seems a forbidding way for any parent and son to enjoy an afternoon together, but Tommy took it in his stride.

For his formal schooling Tommy was placed under Professor Joseph T. Derry, a returned Confederate officer. Derry may not have been the greatest of instructors, but he had before him, in his small schoolroom, a future President of the United States, a future Justice of the Supreme Court, and a future minister to Switzerland.* The future President, unfortunately, did not turn out to be a very good pupil. Nevertheless the

* The future Justice of the Supreme Court was Joseph R. Lamar Hardy, whose family house was directly next door to the parsonage; the future minister to Switzerland was Pleasant Stovall, appointed by Wilson. The Lightfoot Baseball Club in this paragraph was recalled by Wilson many years later in a speech to the Federal Council of Churches. (Dec. 10, 1915, PWW, 35:333).

boy began to find friends and to make his first adjustments to the world of reality. Tommy loved baseball, at least its organizational and ceremonial aspects. His team, known as the Lightfoots, played informally on the grounds of the nearby Richmond Academy; but for Tommy Wilson the most enduring impressions derived from meetings of the Lightfoot Baseball Club in the loft of the family barn. He had never seen a public meeting, nor had any of his comrades, yet he remembered afterwards making rules and regulations according to motions properly proposed and seconded, acting in general as if a man was born to be a parliamentarian.

The extended family of aunts and uncles, and a rapidly growing circle of cousins, led to adventures beyond the confines of the manse. In the Sand Hills area of Augusta lived one of his mother's sisters, Marion, married to James W. Bones, a businessman and a Sunday school principal in Dr. Wilson's church. On weekends Tommy rode his horse over the log road to spend Sunday with the Bones family, and made longer visits during the summer when his family went north to find cool weather. Wilson was devoted to this aunt, who shared the family interest in reading and in the discussion of words and ideas; and he found in her daughter, Jessie Woodrow Bones, an inseparable companion of his own generation.

He became enamored of James Fenimore Cooper's books, particularly the *Leatherstocking Tales*. The two young cousins acted out, in costumes "the most abbreviated . . . decency would permit," the role of hunter and hunted in a forest frequented by Indians. Unsuspecting small "darkies" were attacked by toy bows and arrows as they passed through the wood. On at least one occasion Jessie was prevailed upon to play the role of victim; she fell from a tree on being hit by the toy weapon and was carried home by the stricken Tommy, who thought he had killed her. "He was more like a brother than a cousin to me," Jessie Bones commented long afterward.[15]

Jessie had a younger sister, Helen, who trailed along on these expeditions. Helen would reappear in Wilson's life, withdrawn, unmarried, assistant to the First Lady, and then the President's self-effacing companion in bereavement.

As conditions of peace made travel possible, long-separated family members sought renewed contact. On the Wilson side, within that strong-willed and combative generation, the reunion was not a success. Hungry for the clan at the war's end, Dr. Wilson made a trip northward to find his brothers. Two of these, Edwin Chilton and Henry Clay, had served as generals in the Union Army; the others, too, were fully assimilated northerners. A political and ideological argument left Dr. Wilson so exasperated that he took the next train home. He did not seek out his family again until, footloose after his wife's death, he attempted to establish relationships with the younger generation.

On the Woodrow side of the family it was a different story. A brother of Jessie's, James Woodrow, and a niece, Marion Woodrow, lived in Columbia, South Carolina. Renewed bonds were quickly forged, as affectionate as the unbending exteriors of these diehard Scots allowed. James, in particular, played an important role in the family, as mentor and as exemplar of stubborn rectitude; and he became as close as a brother to Dr. Wilson. In Chillicothe, Ohio, lived another brother, Thomas Woodrow. With the remarriage of Jessie's father, Thomas had assumed the role of head of the family, taking responsibility for his sisters' education. Among his children was the talented Hattie, to become Woodrow Wilson's first love, and her articulate brother Wilson Woodrow, who with his vivid memories would prove a valuable source of information about those early times. At Chillicothe or at other reunions in Augusta or Columbia the white-bearded old grandfather Thomas Woodrow would occasionally be present, with his toddy beside him while he read his Bible in Greek or Hebrew, along with various sons and daughters of the clan and their in-laws, and a cluster of small babies with their nurses.

The uncles usually remained only a day or two before returning to their occupations, but often Dr. Wilson would linger at these Woodrow enclaves, playing chess with any who would take him on and entertaining the company with his stories and puns. "That early period," wrote the self-designated family historian, "possessed a beauty, a glow, that must have dwelt in the heart of Woodrow Wilson as long as he lived."[16]

In the summer of 1870, when Wilson was fourteen, his father was named professor of pastoral theology in the seminary at Columbia, South Carolina. For Dr. Wilson, already known in the South as a preacher of cogency and force, and as stated clerk of the church's General Assembly a figure of wide influence, the call to the prestigious seminary in the state capital was a climactic event in his career. With regret the large Augusta congregation saw him depart. He had been a force in their lives, a charismatic presence, a powerful orator, and, as they noted, a man of literary tastes—"always a student."[17]

Columbia had been laid out in 1787, a model town with broad streets and boulevards and with an ample site for the capitol on the highest point of ground. In contrast to Charleston's coastal site, a location at the precise geographical center of the state had been selected. It had been conceived as a beautiful and spacious city, belying the traditional view that Americans of earlier generations cared little for the urban environment.

In 1870, however, Columbia was a burnt-out shell. A raging fire left standing at the war's end only a forest of chimneys, though the capitol and most of the churches had escaped. Local historians still debate whether Sherman in his march northward from Savannah had set torch to the city, or whether the Southern troops started the fire by igniting bales of cotton to impede the enemy. In either case the scene was a desolate one when the Wilson family arrived five years later. The federal occupation of the city, not to be lifted until 1877, weighed heavily. However future historians might judge the rights and wrongs of Reconstruction, to the defeated whites it appeared the imposition of an alien rule, carried out by freed slaves and supported by so-called carpetbaggers from the North.

Life centered for the Wilsons on the seminary, a fifteen-minute walk down wide and forlorn streets from the capitol. Their first home in Columbia faced the seminary, as did also the house of Professor Charles H. Barnwell, in whose barn at the rear of the property the young Wilson continued his schooling. The family built their own house two years later on a large plot a block away. By any standards it was a substantial structure, and must have seemed imposing to the depressed Columbians. Dr. Wilson was then one of the city's better-off citizens, receiving a salary both as a professor and as the stated supply (or interim) minister of the First Presbyterian Church. In addition, his wife came into a bequest at that time, following the death of a younger brother, William Woodrow, who had made profitable investments in western lands.

Surrounded by gardens laid out by Jessie Wilson, its entrance shaded by a wide porch, the house of white clapboards stood on a conspicuous corner. Within, giving off a central hall, the several spacious rooms included Dr. Wilson's study, where tall windows provided direct access for students. This was a house not only large enough for the four children but one able to receive visiting relatives from far and near. Jessie and Joseph Wilson anticipated a long and prosperous sojourn in Columbia.

An intense intellectual life flowered within the theological seminary. Dr. Wilson was only one of the first-rate minds contending with ancient religious dilemmas and facing up to the new issues presented by advances in science and by evolutionary theory. Among the outstanding scholars was George Howe, a northerner, a graduate of Andover and of Middlebury College, who had remained with the little group of southerners through the war. "It is necessary," he wrote at the time, "whatever the fate of our beloved country, that this seminary should live." His leaving, he realized, could be a near-fatal loss. "If I remain, though the field of my effort must be small, and I must live in obscurity, we may yet transmit to the men of this next generation an institution which will bless them and the world."[18]

Also teaching at the seminary was the brilliant and abrasive James Woodrow, another brother of Jessie Wilson, admired for having studied (though briefly) under the famed natural scientist Louis Agassiz at Harvard, and for having gotten his doctorate at Heidelberg. In the running dispute between conservative Presbyterians and those who made room within their faith for the doctrine of evolution, James Woodrow stood firmly with the modernists. He was in due course rebuked by the church and dismissed from the seminary. When he died in 1907, Woodrow Wilson in a moving letter referred to his uncle as one of the noblest figures he had known: "A man of many small failings, I am glad, for my own comfort, to remember. . . . He followed duty to obscure places and kept himself in mere faithfulness from the eye of fame."[19] The then-president of Princeton University acknowledged the helpful influences he brought into the life of a nephew "who never told him how much he owed to him." Dr. Woodrow's letters to his nephew, it must be said, were not precisely of a kind to encourage intimacy.

The noble scholar and battler for the truth had, like many of the Woodrows, a very practical side to his nature, and succeeded as a businessman, publisher, and banker after retiring as a teacher.

In Columbia the young Wilson, between the ages of fourteen and seventeen, went through the crises of adolescence, not without putting a good deal of strain on the patience of parents and relatives. Under Professor Barnwell he continued having trouble with his studies. He still seemed indolent and vague in manner, as one who had not yet come to grips with life. Uncle James Woodrow was at hand to reinforce his father's influence, admonishing and instructing the nephew in ways the mature Wilson was to remember "painfully."[20] One can imagine the elders wagging their heads and wondering whether Tommy would ever amount to anything. When Uncle James in a family letter remarked that "Tommy Wilson is improving,"[21] he conveyed the distinct impression that the need for further improvement was not lacking.

Yet, as was to be the case throughout his education, Wilson applied himself unreservedly in pursuing what really interested him. While still scoring poorly in Professor Barnwell's Greek and Latin, he became fascinated with the Graham system of shorthand, a refinement of the more popular Pitman system. A series of articles in Frank Leslie's *Boys and Girls Weekly* beginning in November 1872 when Wilson was still short of his sixteenth birthday aroused his intense interest, and as he pasted in a scrapbook all forty-six of the articles, he resolved to become himself a shorthand expert, or "phonographer."[22]

To master the system was a work requiring exceptional discipline and concentration, and these qualities Wilson displayed in a high degree. He began his laborious exercises in 1873, to be interrupted when he went off to Davidson College in the autumn, and resumed when he returned home after a year to prepare himself for the College of New Jersey in Princeton. As a freshman he was proficient enough to produce shorthand lecture notes, a diary, and a commonplace book of selected readings. He began using shorthand for first drafts of speeches and articles, a practice he continued throughout his career as scholar, administrator, and political leader.

What were the reasons for his undertaking to learn this intricate and now obsolete script? "To save time is to lengthen life" is an aphorism appearing several times in his shorthand notebooks. But at this stage of life the young Wilson does not appear to have been inclined to hurry or to have been moved by any drastic urge toward efficiency. It is tempting to think he used this shorthand as a kind of password into his private kingdom of secrecy and fantasy; it was, moreover, an accomplishment all his own, not forced into being by well-intentioned tutors or judged in its progress by a worrisome father or uncle. More profoundly, the immense intellectual effort he engaged in seems to have been prompted by a half-conscious realization that through shorthand he could overcome the troubling symptoms of dyslexia. Coincidentally with his meeting this challenge, at the age of sixteen, his handwriting took the form of the flowing Spencerian script that was to remain with him all his life. He had evidently achieved a new level of self-confidence and a practical mastery of the tools of learning.

Yet with Wilson, lines of growth and development are seldom simple; and at the same time that he was reaching a fresh stage of maturity, he began what can only be called a love affair with ships and the sea, particularly with naval warfare in its most picturesque and fanciful forms. He had never seen a large ship, nor known an expanse of water wider than the Savannah River where it flowed past Augusta. Yet now, fleeing from the real world of his admonitory elders, he made himself an expert in the construction and rigging of various types of vessels. In his notebooks he recorded abstruse details and floated an armada of which the highest commands were given to friends and relatives from Augusta or Columbia. Admiral Thomas Wilson was in charge, sending out daily reports to the Navy Department. A cousin, watching him draw sea and river craft complete to the last line of their rigging, the sea beneath shaded by pencils of various degrees of hardness, observed a framed portrait above the desk.

"That is Gladstone, one of the greatest men that ever lived,"[23] said the young Wilson. He added that when he grew up he intended to be a statesman, too.

In this same summer he underwent a powerful religious experience, or "awakening." He had been up to then a Christian more by routine or emulation than by inner compulsion. In Augusta his father's church had been a focal point of community and family life, where the youth, seated with his relatives in the fourth pew, looked up with awe as his father preached; or with apprehension watched his grandfather Thomas in the course of an energetic sermon, his eyeglasses slipping perilously down his nose. But now, under the influence of a young seminarian, Francis J. Brooke, religion took on a personal meaning and became a part of his intimate life. Prayer meetings were held in Brooke's rooms or in the chapel of the seminary, and on July 5, 1873, the young Wilson took the decisive step of applying for membership in Columbia's First Presbyterian Church. After an examination during which he and two friends evidenced "a work of grace begun in their hearts," all three were admitted.[24]

The "work of grace" continued in Wilson throughout his life. He railed at the church when he thought it displayed narrowness or bigotry, particularly in its opposition to the liberal views held by his uncle, James Woodrow; but its essential doctrines remained unquestioned. "My life would not be worth living if it were not for the driving power of religion," Wilson told a friend visiting the White House in 1915. Although then mourning deeply the death of his wife, he spoke of having "*faith* pure and simple." Never for a moment, he said, had he had in his trial one doubt about his religious beliefs. "There are people who *believe* only so far as they can *understand*—that seems to me presumptuous and sets their understanding as the standard of the universe."[25] Throughout his life, wherever he was, personal prayer and regular reading of the Bible formed part of his daily existence.

At the root of his Calvinist faith was the conviction of being one of God's elect, a state unconditionally granted, but justified by unremitting efforts and the accomplishment of good works. Wilson's God was the

Calvinist God, stern, absolute in his judgments, responsible for every event in history and in the lives of individual men and women. To him, and not to any worldly powers, the believer owed a total obedience. But he was still a merciful God, and as interpreted by liberal theologians like Wilson's father, his love was as unquestioned as his authority. Indeed he was fatherly, in almost the precise way Joseph Wilson aimed to be fatherly toward his son: severe, but prepared in all circumstances to stand behind him.

The strict Calvinist creed could lead to hardness and narrowness, and indeed in Wilson these qualities were evident in later years. But there was another Protestant strain derived from the Scotch Enlightenment, from the University of Edinburgh in its classic age, and associated with the humane philosophy of men like Adam Smith and David Hume. From this source Wilson drew freely. His father was part and parcel of the Scotch Enlightenment, and the son personified at his best the qualities which a modern scholar has associated with it: "its cultivation of reasonableness, its obsession with social and civic virtue, its concern for improvement and faith in progress; its confidence in human nature and its generally benevolent spirit."[26] Along with other factors causing contradictions in Wilson's personality may be placed the opposing schools of Presbyterianism. On one side was the Calvinist orthodoxy personified by his grandfather, Thomas Woodrow; on the other, the more genial faith identified with James McCosh at the College of New Jersey and exemplified vividly in his father's preaching and philosophy.

Approaching seventeen, his learning difficulties largely surmounted, the young Wilson left home for the first time in the autumn of 1873, to begin a new stage in his education. His parents chose Davidson College in North Carolina not only because of its sound academic reputation but because it was a Presbyterian college many of whose students entered the ministry. They probably were hoping that their son would pursue this path. Situated twenty miles north of Charlotte, the campus was dominated by Chambers Hall, a massive, pillared edifice, considered to be one of the most impressive of southern architectural achievements. The structure commanded views of the surrounding countryside; around it nestled a few smaller buildings, including, most prominently, the quarters of the two rival debating societies.

The newly arrived student settled himself in a room in the main building with furnishings that might be termed sparse but adequate. A list in his handwriting itemizes the various pieces: a wardrobe, bookcase, washstand, bowl, two chairs, and two buckets—one old and one new. The clothes in the young scholar's wardrobe (also carefully noted in a memorandum) were more elaborate, and comprised 103 pieces, among them a pair of pearl-colored trousers, a blue vest, and two pairs of gaiters.[27] The students of the college carried their own water and firewood, but if Wilson's dress was typical, life at Davidson was not at that time altogether Spartan.

In formal courses Wilson achieved a good standing, undoubtedly to his family's relief. In English, rhetoric, and composition his marks in the second term were all in the upper nineties; Latin and Greek were only a little lower, and in mathematics he scored 88. A fellow student recalled him as being "witty and genial."[28] The additional adjective "languid" in the description suggests that Wilson had not ceased to convey an impression of aloofness, often mentioned in connection with his childhood. He played baseball, and he made friends with whom he would afterwards correspond in boyishly frank and affectionate terms.

His major interest, however, was debating. A few weeks after arriving at the college he was elected to the Eumenean Society, and the minutes for the ensuing academic year repeatedly show the name of T. W. Wilson as speaker, member of a committee to transcribe the society's constitution, and occasionally as subject to a disciplinary fine for such an offense as "sitting on the rostrum." He was withdrawing from the college library books providing instruction on extemporaneous public speaking and examples of classic English oratory.

By every outward sign the year was a success, and in June Wilson was planning for what would lie in the future after graduation from Davidson. It is surprising to find that far from thinking of entering the ministry, he was considering a college of business training. In a brief item labeled "Important Memorandum"[29] he reminded himself to write home about going to such a college and ask his parents what they thought of the idea. *"Beg hard,"* he added—the italics are his. The phrase suggests his own new-found determination and also his essentially sweet disposition and ultimate submissiveness to his parents' will. At about the same time he made a list of the books he would carry home with him for the summer vacation: his singing book, scrapbook, and photographic album, along with a Greek lexicon and "Dr. Phillips' Lectures on Math."

Yet when he left Davidson that June, it was to be for good. The reasons for this abrupt change in the young student's plans and expectations are obscure but probably derived from several overlapping causes. Wilson said later it was because of ill health.[30] He may well have had periods of homesickness or low spirits, and a long scrapbook entry on ships and naval affairs, written in early April, suggests that he turned from college preoccupations to reenter for a spell the world of private fantasies. Yet apart from his having been absent from several meetings of the Eumenean Society, no evidence of any serious illness exists. A letter from Jessie Wilson in May, the first of those to her son that has been preserved, gives a more meaningful hint. It suggests that a subtle parental pressure was being exerted to bring Wilson home from Davidson and that whatever dark moods he experienced were being exploited for this purpose.

"My darling Boy," Jessie Wilson wrote, "I am so anxious about that cold of yours. . . . Surely you have not laid aside your winter-clothing? Another danger is in sitting without fire these cool nights. Do be careful my dear boy, for my sake. You seem depressed, but that is because you are not well." The mother proceeds with assurances that everyone likes and admires him, and that many young friends await him in Columbia. The letter ends, "I have had a head-ache this morning dear—and wont attempt to write you a letter. My chief object in writing is that I love my absent boy—oh so dearly—and to enclose $5.00 If that is not enough be sure to let me know dear."[31]

A student prone to homesickness or the "blues" could not avoid having his mood reinforced by this subtle plea. The mother's worry over his health, the suggestion that he is not well, the insinuation that her own headache is due to his absence, these themes (undoubtedly repeated in other letters that have not survived) would have weighed heavily on any youth, and must surely have depressed one so sensitive and devoted as Tommy Wilson. Looking back, he not surprisingly assumed that a mysterious disability had enforced his permanent departure from Davidson. Additional factors, moreover, contributed to the family's decision to bring him home.

In this same spring Dr. Wilson suffered a crisis in his professional career, making the son's presence the more needed. The ecclesiastical fracas in which Dr. Wilson became involved is important, not only because it affected Tommy's education, but because it displayed the combative and self-righteous style, the refusal to compromise or surrender, that in later conflicts Woodrow Wilson made his own. Dr. Wilson's troubles began when the First Presbyterian Church voted the appointment of a regular minister. This put in jeopardy his role as supply minister, one in which he took pride and satisfaction and which, not least, provided an important supplement to his professorial salary. To spare the church embarrassment, he resigned. But a short time afterwards, he led the faculty in a move to compel the seminary students to attend Sunday services in their own chapel. This had the effect of depriving the First Presbyterian Church of a considerable portion of its regular congregation.

The timing of Dr. Wilson's move put his motives under suspicion. The situation worsened when students rebelled at what seemed an infraction of their right to worship where they chose. The case came before the General Assembly of the Presbyterian Church, where for three days the debate raged fiercely. On the third day Dr. Wilson took the floor. "I know, I know, I know that I have done right," he cried out defiantly—"and by that right I will stand to the end."[32] The vote went against him by a narrow margin. He and several faculty colleagues resigned; the seminary was demoralized; its enrollment fell by half. Subsequently three men refused to take the chair vacated by Dr. Wilson, and, amid financial difficulties, the institution temporarily closed its doors.

While he was in the midst of these controversies, the First Presbyterian Church of Wilmington, North Carolina, issued an opportune call to Dr. Wilson. "God seems to indicate by his providence," he wrote, "that it is my duty to accept." Though outwardly submissive, Dr. Wilson had suffered a bitter disappointment. He had been compelled to tear his roots from a community where he was comfortably settled, to leave cherished associates and his beloved brother-in-law James Woodrow. For Jessie Wilson it must have been a sad day when she abandoned the house and garden she had planned with such care. She had forebodings, moreover, about the constricted intellectual life of Wilmington. In this state of family affairs the desire to have their son back home is not surprising. Disillusionment with the conduct of the church authorities may, in addition, have dissuaded Dr. Wilson from any strong inclination to have his son enter the ministry.

Another event perhaps contributing to the departure from Davidson had occurred during the Christmas recess, when the family received an important visitor, James McCosh, the president of the College of New Jersey. McCosh was on one of his regular southern jaunts in search of students as well as money for what, in his good Scotch way, he referred to as "me college." The little institution in Princeton was then struggling to reassert itself after the depredations of the Civil War and a succession of reactionary and ineffectual presidents. Joseph Wilson had known the college when he was a student at the Princeton Seminary, and now the presence in his house of the liberal, fighting Scot must have greatly stirred him. Seeing the young Wilson, then on his vacation, McCosh is said to have remarked that he seemed to be good college material.[33] The idea of having their son abandon Davidson and prepare for entrance to McCosh's college may well have taken root at this date.

So it was that when Tommy Wilson packed up his belongings at Davidson in June 1874, he was, without being aware of it, not to return. A year and several months in Wilmington, where his family had just moved, lay unexpectedly before him. Cut off from the college community where he had begun to realize his powers, deprived of newly formed friendships, he confronted the lonely prospect of preparing himself for Princeton. In these unpromising circumstances he was thrown back to a stage of dreamy abstraction. Adolescence was prolonged; traits of withdrawal and self-sufficiency were confirmed in him.

From his point of view, Wilmington at least had the satisfaction of being a port. The town stood at a bend in the Cape Fear River, twenty miles from the open sea, with ships lining its busy docks. During the Civil War, Wilmington had been the principal port for Confederate trade with foreign countries. In the 1870s stories were told of the Confederacy's swift and silent blockade runners, on moonless nights slipping out of the river's mouth where ships of the Northern fleet waited a few miles offshore. The beaches were still strewn with wrecks of vessels that had been sunk, or run aground to elude capture. It was a place to stir the imagination of anyone with a love of the sea in his blood.

The young Wilson haunted the docks with their forest of masts, seeing for the first time in real life the ships he had drawn so meticulously in Columbia. He talked with the sailors and even formed a vague project of going off to sea, or at least enrolling in the Naval Academy. Of this his mother, recalling her fearful Atlantic crossing when she first came to America as a child, would hear nothing; and besides, the college in Princeton now loomed clearly on the horizon.

A notebook dating from Wilson's first summer in Wilmington shows the bent of his dreaming mind. It contains a careful listing of thirty yachts of varying tonnage, Scotch, English, and Irish in their nationality, with "Lord Thomas W. Wilson, Duke of Carlton" now playing the role of commodore. An elaborate table of "rules and regulations" provided another opportunity for constitution-making.

The youth's imagination took flight. In an extended fictional account, written probably at this time, he told of the admiral's discovery and destruction of a mysterious fleet which had been causing unaccountable losses to American interests.* Ships would set out from western ports never to be heard from again, or would disappear on their way home. No reported storms explained the phenomenon; no known wars were being waged. A piratical-looking craft repeatedly eluded the admiral as he sailed the Pacific in his search. Eventually his fleet was led to a hitherto uncharted island, where an inlet was found to open to a spacious bay. "Here lay the ships of the outlawed enemy and the dismantled hulls of many of their victims."[34] Retribution under Admiral Wilson was swift and complete.

The leisurely days of that seaport town provided for Wilson the opportunity to complete his study of shorthand, interrupted during the year at Davidson. "I do not think that there could be a better system than yours," he wrote to the master, Andrew J. Graham, inquiring whether he could enlist as an active pupil. "Friend Wilson," replied the great man, in shorthand, of course, "I am sorry to say that the state of my health is such that it does not answer for me to take any more pupils." But he assured the young devotee that he was "going on very nicely," and would in short time become a first-rate reporter.[35]

He was indeed gaining marked skill, as a consequence of painstaking and apparently inexhaustible practice, and in correspondence with friends he proselytized shamelessly for his cause. His former roommate at Davidson, John W. Leckie, promised in successive letters to begin seriously learning shorthand, and as regularly he postponed the date. John Dooley of Columbia also promised to begin—"which I suppose you are beginning to think will be never," he added. "I see it is only necessary to say 'shorthand' to you and you prick up your ears like the war horse at the sound of a trumpet."[36]

Wilson and his friends did not neglect other subjects, including love and future careers. On his side of the correspondence Wilson wrote promptly and voluminously. "I like nothing so well as writing and talking," he remarked.[37] He begged friends still at Davidson for news of the college and especially of activities in the debating society. His correspondents replied with requests for a description of what they conceived to be the dazzling social life of Wilmington. "You are a miserable moth fluttering around the flame of beauty" wrote Leckie; "the first thing you

---

*Strikingly similar is the imaginary world of another twentieth-century leader. At the age of fifteen, in 1905, Charles de Gaulle wrote a precise description of a Europe of the year 1930 making war upon France: *"Le Général de Gaulle fût mis à la tête de 200,000 hommes et 518 canons."* The subsequent campaign is detailed in daily dispatches from "General de Gaulle." (Charles de Gaulle, *Lettres, Notes et Carnets—1905–1918* [Paris: 1980], pp. 5–29.)

know you will get your wings scorched."[38] Wilson, according to a short-hand draft of his reply, said there was no such danger "yet a while," because of the infrequency of his "visits to [the] fair sex."[39] From Douglas McKay, a friend of Columbia days, came a delightfully sophomoric note: "Never mind Tom you just wait till you and me get to be members of the US Senate and then we'll teach the young Ideas how to shoot. . . . And if we never reach that high estate of honor, it will all be the Same in a hundred years hence. Won't it."[40]

In Wilmington Wilson found at least one congenial spirit of his own age. John D. Bellamy, later a member of Congress, shared his taste for Walter Scott. Together they lay under the trees, reading to each other by turns, on mounds that a decade earlier had covered ammunition magazines of the Confederate Army.

As the spring of 1875 turned to summer, the student was put under increasing pressure of work. He was now seriously preparing for his entrance into the new world at Princeton. From Marion, his older sister, married to a clergyman, Anderson Ross Kennedy, and from Annie, married to a physician, George Howe, Jr. (son of the George Howe who had stood so valiantly by the little seminary in Columbia), came letters inviting visits, inquiring about his health, wondering at the decisive journey that would take him north in the autumn. They seemed to feel they hardly knew this brother. Indeed his time of being fancy-free was almost at an end. The slowly developing young man had completed one phase of his education.

Years of uncertain initiatives and recurrent withdrawals lay ahead before Wilson would find himself as a scholar and teacher and then as a political leader. Seasons of secure accomplishment, like his junior year at Princeton and his second year at Johns Hopkins, were still to alternate with groping and self-doubt. Nevertheless when he left Wilmington for New Jersey he had developed certain permanent attitudes and ambitions. Formal education might have taught him little. More important than what Professors Derry or Barnwell had been able to cram into the head of the unreceptive youth, or anything the faculty at Davidson had imparted, were family and regional values coloring all his later career. The father had set a clear mark upon him. The wit of the conversationalist, the literary polish of the preacher, the believer's faith in a genial and supportive deity: all were to be characteristics of the son throughout his life. Another side of the family influence remained: the memory of Uncle James Woodrow's intransigent rectitude; of Dr. Joseph Wilson's defiant outcry, "I know, I know that I have done right." Nor was the mother's example without its lasting effect. Jessie Wilson had revealed to her son an ideal of womanhood, dutiful, cultivated, self-effacing but deceptively strong, that largely determined Wilson's later relations with her sex.

All these years had been spent in the South, and though the South failed to make Wilson truly one of its own—he had lived too much by the values of his Calvinist inheritance to imbibe its traditions or absorb the sentiments of the landowning aristocracy—it left its mark upon him. Here he had learned the anguish of war, and in its aftermath had observed the pains of postwar settlement. Here, amid easygoing southern ways, he had dreamed and idled and made his first significant contacts with reality. He would boast of being born a Virginian, and return as to a homeland. But it was not his home. His home, if it was anywhere, was in the mid-region where Princeton increasingly colored his life, at that geographic juncture lying below the rationalism of New England and north of Virginia's romantic predispositions.

"MAGICAL YEARS"

This narrative thus circles back to the freshman arriving in Princeton in the autumn of 1875, to take his place in the College of New Jersey. Very probably over the next months (like freshmen before and since) Tommy Wilson had alternating moods of dejection and of growing self-confidence; had moments when he hated the college and then when he slowly became aware of its spell. He must have reached out tentatively toward new friendships, surprised to find that others, equally shy, responded slowly. But all this is conjecture, no letters having survived from this period. What we know of his daily activities at the college comes from a diary begun in the late spring of that freshman year. A chart of his intellectual interests begins earlier, in an *Index Rerum*, a collection of passages from his reading which he began copying out soon after arriving at the college.

All of the diary and much of the *Index* are in shorthand, the former set out beneath an elaborate pencil drawing paying tribute to his teacher Andrew J. Graham. "I am now 19 years old," the diary begins, "and am by the blessings of God in the enjoyment of excellent health."[1] That June 3 was scarcely notable: "I have not employed the day to very much advantage having spent most of my time in loafing." His only reading has been in the works of that other eminent diarist, Samuel Pepys. In subsequent entries he records playing baseball, adding Macaulay to his regular stint of reading, and of grieving over the college's defeat on the diamond by Amherst. He takes a long walk in the woods and holds conversation with a classmate "on different forms of government, especially the relative merits of a limited monarchy and Republic."

As time approached for examinations he felt, in the immemorial way of students, "less and less like preparing for them." The entry for June 13 reads: "Well, another day has passed, and I am $13.80 poorer than I was when it dawned." (He had paid out thirteen dollars to the treasurer's office at the college, and in addition had spent eighty cents for a ticket to the oratorical exercises of the junior class.) Despite his impoverishment he once again, like his mentor Pepys, gives thanks for health and strength. A few more such days and he was thinking of home, and of summer with the family in Wilmington.

The *Index Rerum* shows the young Wilson leaving prescribed courses behind, to wander far and wide in literature and history. His father had introduced him to favorite authors of the contemporary English public, to Carlyle, Goldsmith, Swift. Now, under topical heads listed alphabetically, he adds favorite passages from such political favorites as Burke and Chatham. Often the subject matter is revealing. "The past is in my mind soon constructed into a romance" is quoted from Macaulay,[2] a point of view that would recur, sometimes to his detriment, when Wilson started on his own historical writing. From Francis Jeffrey he copied the observation that the consequences of living in "a refined and literary society or community" are "nearly of the same kind with those of a regular education." The later Wilson would often insist that the influences of the intellectual environment were as important as assigned courses. Continuing the above quotation, Wilson may well have been thinking of his own humble situation as a freshman: "There are so many critics to be satisfied—so many qualifications to be established—so many rivals to encounter, and so much derision to be hazarded, that a young man is apt to be deterred from so perilous an enterprise."

One other illuminating quotation may be added, from Goldsmith, coming under "Passions, Strength of." The man whose youth has been passed "in the tranquility of dispassionate prudence" is compared to "liquors which never ferment, and consequently continue always muddy. Passions may raise a commotion in the youthful breast, but they disturb only to refine it." This is an unexpected thought to find picked out by a young Presbyterian, trained in self-control and in the submergence of natural appetites. But as one in whom the sexual drive was always to prove strong, Wilson may well have chosen the quotation because it assuaged feelings of guilt.

*   *   *

Traveling home at the end of June, he went by train to Baltimore, took the night boat to Portsmouth, Virginia, and spent "a very hard day's travel" on a dusty railroad before arriving, dirty and tired, at Wilmington.[3] He would pass easygoing, rather aimless months in a town where he felt he was a stranger, without close friends of his own age. But his parents were overjoyed at his return, and he is shown in his diary entries to have been an attractive, guileless, and devoted son. He helped his father repair the back fence of their yard, or in the cellar they played a game referred to as "mystery"—no doubt a form of billiards thought not entirely suitable for a Presbyterian household. When Dr. Wilson left for his regular summer visit to Saratoga, Tommy attended to his father's correspondence and worked on the minutes of the church's General Assembly. He accompanied his mother to the market and helped with chores about the home.

The family was busy moving into the manse, a new house built just behind the church, when Joseph Wilson made his timely departure for the North. The tasks of arranging furniture and laying carpets fell upon Tommy and his mother. The second son, Josie, was now at the interesting age of eight, and his older brother showed him how to draw ships—"It delights the dear little fellow so for me to draw with him." On another occasion he made a wooden sword for Josie, "since the dear little fellow wanted one to parade with."[4] Later in the summer sister Annie Howe came over from Columbia, and her young offspring, Wilson Howe, provided further calls on Tommy's patience and ingenuity.

The town of Wilmington is to this day pleasingly laid out, with its main street parallel to the river's shore. Up a slight incline extend shaded residential streets, many of whose ample frame houses were standing when the Wilson family lived there. The church where Dr. Wilson preached was a handsome building situated a few blocks from the business section. Despite the attractions of the place, neither Joseph nor Jessie Wilson was ever really happy in Wilmington. They missed the intellectual life of the Columbia Seminary and felt isolated in their coastal location. They felt, too, that they were not appreciated by their parishioners.* To Tommy, however, Wilmington offered the continuing pleasure of ships and the sea. He would bathe in the Cape Fear River (never learning to swim and always accompanied by a watchful family servant), and occasionally make an expedition down to the river's mouth for a

---

*When it was remarked (according to a much-quoted story) that Dr. Wilson's horse appeared to be in better physical condition than his owner, Dr. Wilson replied, "That is because I care for my horse—my parishioners care for me."

day of boating and fishing. But he was lonely in Wilmington; the weather was often oppressively hot, and besides, as he complained in a letter to the Wilmington *Journal*, the streets were dirty. "Weeds of the rankest and most unhealthy kind," he asserted, "are allowed to grow, and filth of every description to accumulate."[5]

During the summer, under a pen name, he began writing brief articles for the North Carolina *Presbyterian*, a church paper edited by his father. The first of these—also his first.appearance in print—was a homily on everyday religion, calling for something more than "Sunday-piety."[6] The theme was not original; the prose, conventional and pedantic; yet the faintly sounding trumpet, with its emphasis on enlightened action, struck a note to which the mature Wilson would often return. More interestingly, he used the columns of the journal to wrestle with a problem that must have bothered him often during the long summer at home. After a first taste of freedom in Princeton, he found himself restored to family constraints, and what even so good-hearted a youth must occasionally have considered minor oppressions. From acting as household aid to his mother, or tutor to his brother, he would be called to serve as secretary to his father. Perhaps, also, he sensed strains between his parents, driving the father northward to vacation alone in Saratoga. In any case, on returning to Princeton, he wrote for his father's journal a piece on the duty of a son to his parents.

In his diary he recounts having trouble in writing it. Words did not come easily and he suffered from severe headaches. That he was struggling to come to terms with the overpowering influence of his family seems clear. Presently he would surmount that influence, gracefully and without damaging mutual affections; for the moment his only recourse was to reaffirm, though evidently at a certain cost, his absolute submission. "I only speak what I feel from the depths of my heart," he wrote, "when I say that I could not respect myself . . . if I should . . . wittingly do anything to pain those to whom I owe everything in the world, and to whom I am everything."[7]

On the way back to Princeton in September he joined his father, then returning from Saratoga, and the two visited the Centennial Exposition in Philadelphia. Dr. Wilson found his son less enthusiastically responsive than he would have desired. But these traveling theologians took joint pleasure in Machinery Hall, which exhibited the machines that made the other objects in the exposition. Revisiting the exposition the following day, Tommy found of absorbing interest a particular machine, "certainly very wonderful," that was forming stamped envelopes at a stroke. Afterwards he went to Wanamaker's to buy furniture for his room, and the pair journeyed to Princeton, where Dr. Wilson had a long talk with his friend McCosh and was received with deference by various professors.

Witherspoon, a new dormitory and the largest building on the campus, had just been completed, and was considered a model of luxury and collegiate elegance. Wilson moved into one of its corner rooms where he found himself surrounded by a group of congenial friends, to be known in the history of the class of 1879 as "the Witherspoon gang." He also joined the Alligators, a recently formed eating club.

The autumn was marked by a crisis in national politics that aroused the country, penetrating even into the little community of Princeton. The two Presidential candidates, Rutherford B. Hayes of the Republican Party and Samuel V. Tilden of the Democratic, failed to get the requisite majority in the Electoral College. With the election thrown into the House of Representatives, the outcome hung in the balance for days, while partisans on both sides expressed themselves vehemently. On Nassau Street bonfires were lit and rival parades formed. "In consequence of the excitement which was something overwhelming," Tommy wrote in his diary, "I did no studying in the evening and went to bed . . . tired out with shouting and excitement."[8]

To his parents he evidently expressed even more freely his ardor for the Democratic cause. His mother addressed him in a characteristic tone of nervous solicitude. "If I did not know what a prudent good boy you are, dear, I would be anxious for you during these days of excitement. It is a source of great comfort that I know you are able to be so prudent & forbearing in your intercourse with those infatuated people who are your associates in college." She wrote again of her fear that he might be "provoked beyond endurance . . . by those Radical companions of yours. . . . I trust you have been brave enough to disregard their insolence. Tommy dear don't talk about knocking any body down—no matter what they do or say. . . . Some people are beneath your notice."[9] There can be no question where Wilson got the notion, expressed a generation later at a climax of his own and his country's fate, that there is such a thing as a man's being "too proud to fight."

In November of his sophomore year Wilson abruptly stopped making regular entries in his diary. "Discontinued for want of time to do it *justice*," he later added to the neglected pages.[10] The fact that he closed his diary is significant. Wilson was emerging from the doldrums of his freshman year to engage himself busily in college activities. The change was from a state of relative passivity to a role of leadership striking in its energy and mature sense of command. From this time he was increasingly recognized by his friends as an outstanding figure on campus. He was elected to major student offices. His debating, his public speaking, his polished essays won him the awed respect of his classmates. The child who once waited in the wings for "his cue to speak" now, as a young man, stepped out on the stage with complete confidence to act and to lead.

The "magical years" (as Wilson later described the undergraduate experience)[11] began for him at this time. Afterwards there would be moods when he thought he might fall short of his goals. But from this autumn of 1876 there was never any real doubt in his mind that he would make himself a person of note in the world. Probers into the mysteries of Wilson's development have speculated endlessly on the block that kept him from reading at the normal age; they have scarcely questioned the extraordinary release that changed him from a diffident youth into a person who appeared naturally and effortlessly to exercise power.

Inherited abilities, the training of his father, the reading and observations of a leisurely southern boyhood, came together in the Princeton years. Hitherto unfocused elements of his personality fell into place. The college faculty played relatively little part in this intellectual and spiritual awakening; its members are seldom mentioned in his diaries. Having chosen to recognize his father as the great teacher of his youth, he dismissed other teachers as bores. He prided himself on taking his education into his own hands, and he absorbed knowledge enthusiastically from his peers. The group of friends in Witherspoon provided him with precisely the stimulation and support he needed. Together they enjoyed the play of ideas, the liberation of good talk, the easy companionship of the college environment.

"It was a little group of youngsters," one of them later recalled, "ignorant, critical of and merciless to each other."[12] They had their special qualities. One was a Latinist, one a Greek enthusiast, another a mathematician. Wilson was acknowledged the historian and political economist. They shared these interests, taught one another, felt the zest of growing abilities. In a phrase he later put to good use, Wilson in their company "came to himself."

An organization known as the Liberal Debating Club was formed to canalize their endless discussions. Wilson, a prime mover, sought training in a less ponderous form of persuasion than was currently in fashion. He was already learning to speak in the conversational tone, unpreten-

Wilson's birthplace, Staunton, Virginia, 1856

Jessie Woodrow Wilson

Joseph Ruggles Wilson

The Alligator Club,
Princeton, 1877. (Wilson at
center, holding his hat)

President McCosh, on
his daily walk

Thomas W. Wilson, 1879: his class picture

Ellen Louise Axson, about 1883, the time she met Wilson

tious, unaccompanied by dramatic gestures, that was later to be his hallmark. In the speeches of English parliamentarians he saw an ideal model. He had read the works of Pitt, Burke, John Bright; and now his mind was set afire by an understanding of how the parliamentary system of government formed their style.

For the Liberal Debating Club he shaped a constitution based on English practice, with a secretary of state, a sort of prime minister, expressing opinions freely and holding office only so long as he could maintain the support of the majority. This concept of responsible government he would elaborate in his first published writings; but it was the mark of his being a born leader that he embodied it first in a constitution. He acted—and only afterwards did he write about it.

In January 1876 he was made managing editor (the next year he would be made editor) of the recently founded *Princetonian*. He directed its business affairs, wrote news stories and reviews, and then many of its editorials. A fresh note—occasionally juvenile but conveying a brisk sense of authority—came into the pages of the journal. The editorialist's role Wilson described as that of inviting "bold, frank, and manly discussion of College opinion";[13] and then proceeded to express views on promoting public speaking, higher standards of scholarship, more seemly undergraduate conduct, more effective organization of students' extra-curricular activities. To college athletics he devoted at least as much attention as to intellectual and social issues.

The young Wilson's involvement in sports derived from the value he placed on competition and disciplined excellence. He tended to view sports as akin to political rivalry at its most adventuresome. Not a skilled player himself, he won his offices in the athletic associations by applying his intelligence as well as his natural enthusiasm to the strategy and organization of the teams. Football was then only beginning to be played on American campuses; Wilson mastered its intricacies so that by his advice, and by his occasional coaching, he was given part of the credit for the college's undefeated 1878 season. *"Everything,"* he counseled— and he might as well have been describing the ideal leader of the republic—"depends upon the character of the captain and president [of the team.]. . . . The president must, above all things else, be a man of unbiased judgment, energy, determination, intelligence, moral courage, *conscience.*"[14]

In a speech at Whig Hall in this sophomore year he did indeed give his prescription for "The Ideal Statesman." "No doubt many of us hope in future to have some hand in the government of our country," he began; and he claimed that success would come only to those who "so live as constantly to approximate the ideal." The governing of a great country was not a work to engage "the idle moments of petty lawyers or make the fortunes of shallow-minded politicians." The legislator must be in advance of his age—gifted with "something . . . more than foresight and less than prophetic knowledge." "Across the mind of the statesman flash ever and anon the brilliant, though partial, intimations of future events."[15]

The new cheerfulness and confidence of mood conveyed itself to the family in Wilmington. Dr. Wilson responded with joy, seeing a relationship between his son's success and the deepening of his religious convictions. There was no better way to be lifted up than through cheerfulness, the father wrote, adding that a principal use of "our wonderfully humane religion is to promote buoyancy of disposition." With an easy conscience one could live under "the smile of God."[16] Indeed, the religious faith the young Wilson derived from his father's teaching was not the sort manifesting itself only in dark moments, but grew stronger in times of confidence and elation when God's watchfulness seemed to be validated by outward experience. The coming together of worldly good fortune with a feeling of inner blessedness could make the Presbyterian of liberal faith, as it made Wilson in his happiest periods, a charismatic figure.

Through this critical period of Wilson's development his father kept in close touch, offering advice and encouragement, occasionally adding characteristically astringent judgments. The mother, in keeping with an habitual overindulgence, could dismiss disappointments or blame others for being harsh and unfair; but it was not so with Dr. Wilson. Thus he warned his son against being "puffed up," a danger he had apparently manifested in his letters. "Let the esteem you have won," the father urged, "be only as a stimulant to fresh exertion."[17] And when the young Wilson asked whether he should continue with his wide outside reading or give closer attention to his courses, the father responded with stern (and perhaps not altogether expected) good sense: "It is certainly your duty to improve yourself in *all* ways," he wrote, "but it as certainly [is] your *first* duty to conquer your text-books."[18]

Competing in the junior oratorical contest of the Whigs, Wilson gained an early taste of defeat. He sent home "a somewhat despondent letter." "Don't be too ambitious, dear," his mother consoled him, "for that kind of ambition brings *only* worry."[19] His father, as usual, gave more challenging advice. "To *deserve* distinction," he wrote, "is a far worthier thing than distinction itself. To deserve it you have only patiently to plod on, doing with your might what your hands find to do, making the most of opportunity, and, letting the vast clouded future *wait*." One could not "jump into eminency" all at once. Above all, his son must not be depressed. "Dearest boy, do not allow yourself to dwell upon *yourself*. Self-consciousness is a torment: was mine at your age: has, often, since then, been such."[20]

This frank communication between father and son is echoed amusingly on the young Wilson's side in a letter to his father (the only one surviving from this period),* who was then busy fulfilling his duties as stated clerk at a session of the General Assembly. "The son of the said Stated Clerk is a queer fellow," Tommy Wilson wrote.

> He is entirely free from anything like his father's clear-sightedness and altogether his mind seems to be remarkably bright and empty. You could easily distinguish him in a crowd by his long nose, open mouth, and consequential manner. He is noted in college as a man who can make a remarkably good show with little or no material. But, after all, he is a good enough sort of fellow and what he lacks in solidity he makes up in good intentions and spasmodic endeavors.[21]

Evidently the young Wilson was trying to follow the father's advice to take the ups and downs of college life a little less seriously.

In the summer of 1878 he returned to Wilmington for a brief spell, during which he occupied himself by reading Carlyle, writing speeches, and playing croquet. Then he went off with his mother to Rome, Georgia, in the far western part of the state. Here his aunt Marion Bones, the joy of the Sand Hill days in Augusta, had moved with her family. Wilson rode horseback with Jessie Bones, his childhood playmate, and found the kind of friends he lacked in Wilmington. A particular young person, the daughter of the minister of Rome's Presbyterian church, whom in the not-too-distant future he would discover here and would ardently court, was at this time vacationing in Savannah.

The essays Wilson wrote during his last two years in Princeton might be classed as *juvenilia*, yet they set a high standard for undergraduate

---

* An unsolved mystery—considering how much else has been preserved—is what happened to Wilson's letters to his parents. They would unquestionably have been saved by them, and yet, except for this and four others, none have been found. Probably Wilson's father in his last years carried them about with him as he moved from one city to another, depositing them in a trusted household. It is tempting, but no longer entirely reasonable, to believe they may yet be discovered in some attic trunk.

work. Making no pretense to scholarship, derivative in style and given to some rhetorical excesses, they are important for what they reveal of their author. They make good reading as well, for even as a student Wilson had a gift for vivid prose, and he could identify closely with public men and events. They suggest qualities he would aim to acquire, and in an extraordinary way they predict his fate. It was almost as if in later life he would be compelled to follow out the lines of a drama first sketched as a college student.

An essay on Bismarck, his first full-dress piece, shows a grasp of realpolitik unexpected in a young man, particularly in one nourished on the ethical imperatives of a Presbyterian upbringing. It was to be expected that Wilson would be at home in the literature of British politics; here he mastered a new field and showed himself to possess an almost instinctive grasp of leadership based on authority and intrigue. "Beside great intellect," he wrote, "the English statesman must have eloquence and tact; in the Prussian statesman eloquence and tact are nothing unless accompanied by marked administrative and diplomatic talents and a controlling influence over the royal mind."[22] Wilson is at pains to explain, if not quite to justify, Bismarck's "occasional breach of honor." That he quickly and skillfully availed himself of "all the golden opportunities . . . for the aggrandizement of Prussia" is cited as the essential virtue of a breed of statesmen: "men of independent conviction, full of self-trust, and themselves the spirit of their countries' institutions."

The essay on William Pitt (the Earl of Chatham), published a year later, is to an even greater extent self-revealing and prescient. "His mind was strong and clear," Wilson writes of his hero, "his will was unswerving, his convictions were uncompromising, his imagination was powerful enough to invest all plans of national policy with a poetic charm." The description fits the leader Wilson aimed to be. But for Pitt, as for the future Wilson, disaster lay in store. "Disease had unmanned him. . . . In a moment of folly, [he] well nigh [undid] the work of a memorable lifetime." And then the fearful summary, well describing the Wilson felled in 1919 by a major stroke: "William Pitt was a noble statesman; the Earl of Chatham [Pitt after becoming a peer] was a noble ruin."[23]

The major achievement of Wilson's senior year was not in academic courses (his ranking in the class fell); nor was it in college activities. It was the composition of a long article published in *The International Review*, an important journal of wide circulation. Entitled "Cabinet Government in the United States," the article was on a theme which he had already tried out in the Liberal Debating Club and which was to become the substance of his first book. The United States was then still in the post-Reconstruction period, its institutions weakened by corruption on all levels of government. Wilson discerned the essential trouble as being a lack of clear and consistent policies and of leaders capable of articulating them. "Congress is a deliberative body in which there is little real deliberation," he wrote, "a legislature which legislates with no real discussion of its business."[24] As a remedy against the tyranny of congressional committees he proposed an adaptation of the British form of parliamentary government, with members of the President's cabinet leading the debate and with the government falling if it failed to maintain support. The proposal had already been suggested by others, but Wilson put it forward with striking lucidity and force. The circumstances of its publication are historically interesting. The junior editor of *The International Review*, who approved the article and saw it through the press, was a young man named Henry Cabot Lodge, who as a senator would be one of his chief critics and ultimately his nemesis.

As suggestive of the future as the young Wilson's essays on history and politics was a pact he made with a classmate, Charles Andrew Talcott, at some time during senior year. Talcott was an intimate friend, a member of the Whig Society and the Witherspoon group, and like Wilson was possessed of a strong moral commitment to a career in public life. Wilson later made reference to the pact on several occasions, the most precise description being in a letter to Ellen Louise Axson, then his fiancée, four years after his graduation. He told her that he had made "a solemn covenant" with Talcott. They would train all their faculties to advance the political principles they held in common; they would drill themselves in the arts of persuasion; they would "acquire knowledge that [they] might have power." Wilson added in this letter to Ellen Axson that he had, and that he retained, "very pronounced political ambitions."[25]

That the pact was, on Wilson's part, something more than a collegiate gesture is evident. On a more modest scale Talcott also played a part in public life. After studying law he was elected mayor of Utica, New York, and then a U.S. congressman. The two men kept in touch, and in a pathetic effort, when he was stricken and power was falling away, Wilson endeavored to have his friend appointed a federal judge.[26] Wilson's Attorney General argued that Talcott was then too old, and in fact he died before any action could be taken.

Commencement 1879 saw Wilson a little apart from the central events. The honors of the day went to men who had achieved the highest grades, and Wilson paid the price for having chosen to pursue his studies in an independent, slightly disdainful, manner. In the *Princetonian* he had suggested that the faculty change the rules so as to give recognition to students who acquired skills in writing, speaking, and debate, and he was undoubtedly piqued on observing the results of a system that attached so much importance to regular coursework. Nothing, however, could mask from him the sentiment of the season, or lessen its inevitable pain.

"The parting . . . went harder than I had feared even," he wrote his friend Talcott. Beyond the expected wrench of farewells there was for Wilson the sense of having played out a part the last lines of which were now spoken. In a cryptic note written at about this time in a copy of *Hamlet* the feeling of moving upon a stage was expressed. Hamlet, in assuming the role of a madman, had made his life a play; and the actor, in taking the part, had added a further level of unreality. "This player played but for a season," Wilson wrote; "he [Hamlet] was to play perpetually."[27]

Tommy Wilson had had his hour. But another Wilson—or would it be the same one?—was to play an enduring role.

LAW AND LOVE

"Here am I perched on the Blue Ridge. . . . We have horses to ride and picturesque mountains to explore," wrote Wilson to his classmate Robert Bridges soon after graduation. Unfortunately, at his summer retreat in Horse Cove, North Carolina, there was also endless bad weather. "The clouds have crowded down close upon us, almost on our very roofs . . . soaking us with their continuous rains." Later that summer, hoping for sunshine, he tried a second retreat, at Walhalla in South Carolina. Here he was conscious of a different sort of hardship. There was an absence of young women. It possessed "every advantage of *situation* that a lover might desire," but there was, sad to report, "no one to love."[1]

The concern for young women appears to strike a new note; but in fact Wilson had not been immune to their appeal. The adolescent years in Columbia, which saw his awakening to religion, not surprisingly saw as well his awakening to the opposite sex. He referred to the place as "the home of pretty girls," "the scene of many of my old love scrapes."[2] The description was considerably colored, to impress the classmate he was writing to; but in the last, languorous year at Wilmington, as in the summer vacations that followed, he must have felt the sexual frustrations of a youth strongly driven but repressed by a particular religious and social upbringing. The monastic atmosphere in Princeton can scarcely have helped. But the next three years, as he moved through false starts to a serious commitment to his vocation, would also lead him through affairs of the heart.

Despite the summer's disappointments, Wilson resumed his studies and his writing, preparing himself to enter law school in the autumn. He read J. R. Green's *History of the English People*, which one day he would aim to match in a history of the American people. He composed an eleven-thousand-word essay entitled "Self-Government in France."[3] Overlong, the piece did not find a publisher. The author dismissed it as one that burned feebly: "It has not" he wrote, "enough *glow* about it."[4] But the straightforward style of the essay and the measured step of its argument were not to be equaled until Wilson passed through many less successful literary experiments. The foray into the French national character, like the earlier essay on Bismarck, showed him reaching out beyond the Anglo-Saxon tradition. He grasped the deep sources and lasting effects—social and political—of the French Revolution; and this insight remained to guide his judgment on the great revolutions during his time as President—those in China, in Mexico, and, above all, in Russia.

The precise time that Wilson decided to take up the study of law is uncertain, though when he left Princeton he had probably decided on legal studies as his next step. His pact with Talcott had fixed public service as the ultimate aim; law was not only a traditional pathway to politics but would provide in the interim an essential means of livelihood. "A statesman who is unacquainted with the law," he had written as early as his sophomore year, "is as helpless as the soldier who is ignorant of the *use of arms*."[5] The University of Virginia's law course was a natural choice. He would be returning to the state of his birth and entering an institution with a long record of preparing men for leadership.

Arriving at Charlottesville in October 1879, Wilson found that his reputation as author and speaker had preceded him. His article in the summer issue of *The International Review* was being read by faculty and students. Embarking on his studies with intensity, he found like most beginners in the field that the going was difficult and the intellectual fare restricting. "The Law is indeed a hard task-master," he wrote to his Princeton friend Talcott after the first few months. "I am struggling hopefully, but not with *over*-much courage." The injection of a little literature might have made the student's work tolerable. "But when one has nothing but Law, served in all its dryness, set before him from one week's end to another . . . this excellent thing the Law, gets as monotonous as that other immortal article of food, *Hash*."[6]

He missed his Princeton friends. "The memory of that dear old crowd can never die," he wrote Bridges. "To know that we must all change and, because of the change in ourselves, cease to know one another [is] as sad a thought as ever I had." He found the atmosphere of the university cold in comparison to what he had known of undergraduate life. "It's a splendid place to educate the mind," he continued, "but no place to educate the man." Here were no class ties to hold students together. "You meet and know a man just as you might meet and know a fellow-merchant on some Great Corn Exchange. The tendency in such a community as this is toward *disintegration*."[7] Later, as president of Princeton, Wilson would defend his plans for the social reorganization of the university in just these terms. The education of the whole man, not the education of the mind alone, would become a constant refrain in his educational philosophy.

In the law department Wilson was one of seventy-nine students, many of whom were to become well-known in their profession.* The major figure on the faculty, John Barbee Minor, was an unchallenged authority on the English common law, a charming Old World figure, and a teacher of rare gifts. Wilson asserted that, after his own father, no teacher had affected him so deeply.

The freeedom permeating the university held attractions that Wilson began to discover once his homesickness for Princeton passed. The spirit of Jefferson, its founder, lived on in a scholarly community lacking many of the restrictions that still characterized most American colleges. The curriculum was loosely organized. Students moved at will from department to department, determining for themselves their speed of advancement and their mixture of courses. Wilson's closest friend at the university, Richard Heath Dabney, was, for example, younger than Wilson and an undergraduate, yet in his courses and social contacts was not barred from being one with the law students. Jefferson's architectural concept for the university placed the houses for professors at intervals along the rows of student rooms; it shaped the whole into a green (known as "The Lawn") and closed its higher end by a domed and pillared

---

* The class included John Bassett Moore, later a prominent international lawyer; Richard Heath Dabney, who became dean of the University of Virginia; and William Cabell Bruce and LeRoy Percy, both of whom served in the Senate.

library. Here teachers and students lived together in the closeness and freedom of an academic village.

The reference to "Hash" in the letter quoted above indicated a subject of much concern to Wilson's mother. "You tell us nothing about one thing that is of great importance," she wrote shortly after her son's arrival in Charlottesville. "What sort of *eating* have you? I am anxious to know. Is your food wholesome?" Or again, striking another plaintive domestic note: "I am considerably disturbed at what you tell me of your room. You cannot be comfortable in such a place as that. I want you to give me all particulars as to your *bed*. . . . Have you any carpet?"[8]

Wilson was living in a boardinghouse, off academic grounds, and conditions were undoubtedly spare. As for the food, his friend Dabney reported many years later that he himself stood it all right—but then he had "the stomach of an ostrich."[9] Wilson unfortunately did not, as his later history would prove. His mother's concern, though expressed with what seems an exaggerated solicitude, was not unreasonable. By the spring Dr. Wilson was worried by the fact that his son seemed to have a persistent cold, and suggested that he might like to try studying for a year at home. "With the impulse you shall have received, might you not be prepared," he asked, "to profit by a private course?"[10] Wilson resisted the suggestion and the next autumn moved from the boardinghouse into one of the regular student rooms. Conditions were hardly improved. The rooms were heated by smoky fires and opened directly onto exposed walkways. The food was still execrable.

Wilson spent his first Christmas vacation in Staunton. The town where he had been born, and where many of his relatives were now living, lay forty miles west of Charlottesville, accessible by a railroad that seems to have run with exemplary speed and frequency. The seminary over which Dr. Wilson had once presided numbered among its students five female cousins—children of the Bones family and of two uncles, Thomas Woodrow of Chillicothe, Ohio, and James Woodrow of Columbia, South Carolina. The Christmas visit warmed Wilson's heart after the rather barren first term at the law school. He basked in family affection and in the admiration of the young relations who even before his coming had heard much about their male cousin's accomplishments. But the return to Charlottesville and to the lonely uphill struggle with the law put him in a depressed mood which he found difficult to cast off. He began dreaming of a literary, rather than a legal, career.

Wilson's father was deeply concerned. "*Far, far* better conquer the law," he wrote, "than suffer *aught* to turn attention away from this which is probably to be yr. meat & drink. And, to say the truth, I love to think of your grappling with those difficulties."[11] When the son confessed that he was suffering from "that imp, 'the blues,'" the father, who himself suffered from recurring depressions, gave him characteristically blunt advice. "Let [that imp] not again enter. He is from beneath ... his exorcist is found in the cultivation of a hopeful disposition." One had to strive against despondency as against a deadly foe: "Aye, pray against it as you would for some great salvation." Analyzing one's feelings or weighing one's abilities should not become an indulgence. "The true method for knowing oneself and what he is fit for, is to grapple with things outward—it is to attack and conquer difficulties." Added to such strictures would be the assurance of affection upon which the son so largely depended. "I need not explain that I am not in the least blaming you.... I *could not* do so, my precious son, my precious friend."[12]

Wilson followed the father's advice in his own quixotic way. He immersed himself in work—but the work was in fields other than legal studies. He had been elected to the Jefferson Society, a debating and literary group, soon after his arrival on campus. He joined a Greek letter fraternity and as one of the two representatives of its chapter journeyed to Washington for its national convention. The discussions and the chance to meet delegates from many parts of the country gave him unexpected satisfaction. In the university literary magazine he published biographical essays on his favorite British statesmen—on John Bright and, a little later, on Gladstone. Above all, he gave attention to the art of public speech.

The essay on Bright, the Liberal orator, was first delivered as an address before the Jefferson Society. Wilson's reputation as a debater had already spread, and "several young ladies" expressed a desire to hear him speak on this occasion. As a result, the doors were opened for the first time to outsiders. Wilson was in Washington when, much to his "surprise and dismay," he heard this piece of news. "I'm thoroughly scared," he wrote. "I'm fairly entrapped."[13]

On the night of the meeting the hall was crowded, and the speech was Wilson's best up to that time, the subject permitting him to deal with political principles in an effective rhetorical style. The high point came when he dwelt upon Bright's well-known opposition to the Confederate cause. Even at this distance one can imagine a hush falling over that audience of southerners. "Will you think that I am undertaking an invidious task, if I endeavor to justify him in that opposition?" Wilson asked. "I yield to no one precedence in love for the South. But *because*

I love the South I rejoice in the failure of the Confederacy." He went on to picture a region inferior to the North in resources, industry, and maritime power, while suffering from the "irritation abroad and agitation within" which continuation of slavery would have caused. "Even the damnable cruelty and folly of Reconstruction," he concluded, was preferable to helpless independence.[14]

The occasion was important for Wilson. In the university community it confirmed his reputation as an outstanding speaker. It marked him as a man of courage—challenging, in the very heart of the old Confederacy, beliefs still held as articles of faith by most of his audience. It undoubtedly appeared as a new stage in his own thought and development. Yet in fact Wilson had never been an orthodox southerner. He was by temper remarkably free of any parochialism; he had been reared in a household where the Presbyterian ethic, and the Scotch culture, were more powerful influences than the faded romanticism of a slaveholding aristocracy. Dr. Wilson, had he been present, would probably not have been shocked by his son's remarks, but would have seen them as confirming his own views. Though he had accommodated himself during the war years to the prevailing opinion, he shared with his son a reluctance to enshrine and idolize the southern past.

The notoriety gained by the speech prepared the way for one of Wilson's most severe disappointments at Charlottesville. Assured of a numerous audience, the students arranged for a debate between the university's two outstanding orators, Wilson and William Cabell Bruce, the latter a brilliant youth who was to become a Senator and winner of a Pulitzer Prize for biography. The subject: "Is the Roman Catholic element in the United States a menace to American institutions?"

Wilson chose the negative side, indicating at this early stage his lifelong freedom from sectarian bias. (He would have a Catholic as secretary when he was President of the United States and would appoint the first Jew to the Supreme Court.) Now he argued that Catholicism was to be dealt with not as a religion but as a political phenomenon. He proceeded to defend this view with old-fashioned rhetorical fervor. The liberties of the country were safe, he said, "until the memories and experiences of the past are blotted out and the Mayflower with its band of pilgrims forgotten; until our public-school system has fallen into decay and the nation into ignorance; until legislators have resigned their functions to ecclesiastical powers and their prerogatives to priests."[15] It was a grand peroration; but when the judges came to make the award, they voted Bruce the better debater, and (in way of a consolation prize) named Wilson the better orator. Wilson was chagrined. He cared everything for being a debater; the role of orator was one he then and afterwards eschewed. His first reaction was to refuse the prize.

His position was understandable in the light of long-held beliefs and ambitions. As a sophomore in college he had resolved to develop the style of the best English parliamentarians, learning to speak informally and extemporaneously without the flourishes of contemporary platform and pulpit oratory. His powers growing through training and practice, he rarely deviated from this ideal style. In his later career he could address audiences of thousands, his light tenor voice projected without seeming effort to the rear of the largest hall, giving each individual the impression of being personally spoken to. As a student he was already convinced that in lucid argument, in rational appeal illumined by a poetic imagination, lay the basis of democratic leadership. To have been singled out as an "orator," with all this implied of sentiment or bombast, was a blow at the root of his pride.

Wilson's friends persuaded him to accept the award, and at the year's final meeting of the society, the hall again crowded by outsiders including members of the press, Wilson turned the tables on his judges. If on the earlier occasion he had been betrayed into oratorical flourishes, he now spoke with striking modesty and in conversational tones. On being presented with the medal, he possessed, he said, a "lively sense of the delicacy of his position." The assemblage no doubt was present to hear oratorical speakers. But, he said, he did not indulge in oratorical effects. He was just learning to speak; he would only present some thoughts which had perhaps not occurred to his auditors. Proceeding to describe the anomaly of college debating societies, he said they discussed year after year the same subjects—"Did Mary, Queen of Scots, deserve her fate?" "Which was the greatest general, Napoleon or Caesar?"—while the world outside was full of pressing issues, and college students, formerly being graduated at sixteen, were now mature men.[16]

The reporter said that the speech, "from which artificial declamation was conspicuously absent," was judged by many present to be the best which had been heard from a college student in many a year, and far better than that of the first medalist. Wilson never wholly forgot the lesson, and although in later extemporaneous utterance he could become diffuse, or include highly emotional passages, his strength as a speaker and lecturer consisted in a rigorously cultivated simplicity.

During the spring and winter terms following his Christmas visit, Wilson journeyed frequently to Staunton. Taking a train on Saturday, he claimed he could return early Monday morning without having missed any classes. But in fact he must have missed a considerable number; by June, because of repeated absences, he was listed among the delinquents "in the several schools." Wilson concealed nothing of the blow from his family. "Now, dearest," wrote his father, "do not think that I am . . . heaping coals of fire upon your already ashes-covered head"; but he went on to reprove his son for being too independent and forgetting the need for authority. "Your head went agog," he concluded. Wilson's mother, characteristically, found the threat of expulsion to be "wrong and cruel."[17]

That the young man's head had gone "agog" hit nearer the mark than his father perhaps knew at the time. For in the course of that winter Wilson had fallen in love. The previous summer he had written light-heartedly that he was reserving "all my powers of charming" for the Virginia girls. "Do you think that Law and love will mix well?"[18] He was now discovering that they did not.

The object of his affections was not one of the sophisticated Charlottesville beauties, whom he serenaded in the glee club or met on Sundays at Professor Minor's teas. It was a cousin in Staunton's Female Seminary, Hattie Woodrow, a daughter of his uncle Thomas Woodrow. Hattie was in many ways a remarkable young woman, a skilled musician with a fine singing voice, as much at home in the French language as in mathematics, and the envy of all her classmates. Though the ardent Wilson pleaded on more than one occasion for her picture, she does not appear to have been particularly pretty. A liveliness of spirit, or a delicacy of coloring beyond the capacity of faded photographs to convey, must have compensated for what appear to have been rather heavy and cheerless features. In any case she exerted upon the young law student a bewitching spell.

"I would have given a great deal for another glimpse of you today," Wilson wrote after his Christmas visit to Staunton, contenting himself instead with sending a note "with as much love as it can carry and another good-bye."[19] By April he was writing to "My sweet Rosalind" and averring (while still concealing his particular affection) that he learned to love his "sweet cousins" more and more warmly with every visit. When Hattie performed in a musicale he applauded with an enthusiasm that the young lady thought to be not quite proper.

The offense that finally evoked a rebuke from the law school faculty was an absence while attending her graduation in the spring of 1880. Hattie's letters are missing, but it is evident from Wilson's side of the correspondence that he mistook (as young men often do) her reticence for coyness and remained happily unaware of the embarrassment his attentions were causing.

This first love was doomed from the start. Although encouraged by Wilson's mother, the two cousins were of an awkwardly close blood relationship; and besides, as would be made painfully clear in the denouement of this affair a year later, Hattie was quite indifferent to Wilson's advances.

After a summer passed amid a family reunion in the foothills of western Virginia, Wilson returned to Charlottesville resolved to work hard at the law. To his mother's delight the single word "never" appeared after "Absences" on his report. It seemed so "emphatic," she wrote him, "—triumphant in fact."[20] But other distractions still tempted him. He was elected president of the Jefferson Society and immediately informed its members that a new constitution would be prepared. The document, bearing the clear marks of Wilson's authorship, was strongly supported by him in debate and came up for adoption in January 1881.

Meanwhile an abrupt change took place in Wilson's life, and by the time the constitution was adopted he was no longer a student at the university. It will be recalled that in April of the previous spring Dr. Wilson had suggested that because of uncertain health his son spend the next year at home. A pitying, pleading letter came from his mother in early December: "I *have* been very anxious about you—and your letter received this morning . . . reveals to me, more fully, how very serious your cold has been. How did you take the cold dear? Had the want of your new flannels anything to do with it, I wonder?"[21]

A more serious assault on Wilson's resolution to stay the course came less than a week later in a joint letter from his two parents. "We both think . . . that it is *your duty to come home.*" His father, reported Jessie, "does not say you *must*—but he *urges* you to do so."[22] Even this did not shake Wilson, and in a letter of December 21 his mother accepted his decision to stay on. "*Pride* leads you to the determination to sacrifice your health rather than give up the contest"; but she added in a somewhat better spirit that if he could continue at the university "*without* endangering your health, it will certainly be of advantage to you in every way."[23]

About four days later—it appears to have been on Christmas Eve—Wilson capitulated. He was spending this particular Christmas neither at home nor with his relatives in Staunton, but in Charlottesville; he had been overworking and was alone as the festive day drew near. He made up his mind quickly. He withdrew from the university without delaying to say good-bye to his friends and teachers.

Wilson explained this precipitate departure wholly on grounds of health; but other factors were involved and undoubtedly contributed to, if they did not cause, the cold and digestive upsets which were the ostensible cause. A passage in one of his mother's letters suggests that because of troubles with the faculty he might not graduate. Was Jessie Wilson applying subtle pressure, as several years earlier she had induced her son to come home from Davidson College? Was the son apprehensive about his success at Charlottesvile? Was he perhaps truly bored with the law, or did he perceive his endless extracurricular activities as leading him into the dead end of schoolboy triumphs and defeats? All these elements may have played a part in the decision. Wilson was himself reluctant to probe too deeply and seemed reassured, rather than the contrary, when his doctor at Wilmington told him he would have suffered permanent damage to his digestive tract had he remained at the university.

The sudden ending of his law school days undeniably shook the young student and raised doubts in his mind about the future. Yet a few easily ignored considerations make the departure somewhat less traumatic than it at first appears. The law school course at Virginia was then two years in length, so that by resigning at Christmas he was only missing six months. For an ambitious student to complete his studies by systematic reading at home was not an unusual way to gain admission to the bar. And so Wilson again settled in for a long stay with his parents. Contemplating the months ahead he admitted in a letter to Hattie that he had some regret at having once and for all left college life behind. That life, he said, is "about the happiest, because the freest from care, that one can lead."[24]

The weather back home was dismal. It rained for weeks on end in Wilmington, until at last the sun reappeared and Wilson found a sense of health and strength returning. His law books arrived from Charlottesville and he resumed his studies, confident that with the instruction already received he would soon be able to pass the bar examinations. Over the next months he somewhat reluctantly accompanied his mother on calls in the parish and instructed his young brother Josie in Latin, while pursuing his unflagging outside interests. He practiced elocution and, as he told Bridges, was making frequent extemporaneous addresses to the empty benches of his father's church.[25] He was also reading widely and trying his hand at various styles of writing.

During this period Wilson completed a change in his name that had been in the making for some time. "Thomas W. Wilson," his signature up to the end of the Princeton years, gave way to "T. Woodrow Wilson" in the first autumn at Charlottesville. He emphasized the "Woodrow," he told Bridges, at his mother's request.[26] Jessie had always been proud, inordinately proud, of her Woodrow side of the family, and she was now intent on giving it prominence. By the following spring Wilson's sister Marion wrote that she was teaching her children to say "Uncle Woodrow," because she had heard from her mother that this was what he preferred.[27] (One wonders!) It was still to be a year before all vestiges and variations of the original "Thomas" disappeared. In June 1881 we find him practicing on the back of an envelope the signature "Woodrow Wilson," and on August 22, 1881, while lingering in Wilmington, he signed a letter for the first time with the name by which he was to be known to history. No longer was he to be "Tommy," he announced to Bridges in a postscript, *except to my old friends.*[28]

The question of where he would begin the practice of law was discussed at length in the family. Dr. Wilson busied himself with inquiries, and by the spring of 1881 Atlanta seemed the best choice. The city represented the gathering forces of economic development and social progress in the post-Reconstruction South, and Wilson, as he wrote Talcott, hoped "to grow up with a new section."[29] Here Wilson intended to establish himself by the end of the year.

Before he settled down to his profession, however, events occurred that changed his schedule and caused him, a victim of unrequited love, to drag out additional months in Wilmington. In the summer of 1881 he made a round of visits to his family, ending in Chillicothe, where he served a brief legal apprenticeship in the office of an uncle, Henry Wilson Woodrow, and—more important from his point of view—visited his cousin Hattie Woodrow.

In that Ohio city which took pride in having set more fashions than Newport, considering itself an oasis of civilization in the burgeoning Midwest, a busy social season was under way. For the young—with the accomplished Hattie always at the center of attention—a series of picnics, boat rides, and balls filled the time. Wilson was ill at ease in the social whirl (he never did learn to dance), but the hospitality of his uncle and the charms of his cousin beguiled him. His serious intentions toward Hattie, which he had harbored over the past year while she was studying music at Cincinnati, could no longer remain unexpressed. One evening during the visit he took Hattie off the dance floor, confessed his passion, and told her that he could not begin his career in the law unless she reciprocated his love. Hattie summarily rejected him. She gave as her ground a belief that first cousins should not marry; but actually, as was soon to be evident, she did not feel she loved this earnest young man.

The next scenes contain unexpected elements of melodrama. Wilson left the party abruptly, spent a sleepless, anguished night in a hotel, and at dawn on a scrap of torn paper wrote a note imploring Hattie to reconsider. He had a talk the next morning with his uncle Thomas, who voiced no objections to a marriage between cousins. Then he took the next train for home. At the depot Wilson met Hattie's brother, Wilson Woodrow, in the company of a young rival, Edward F. Welles, the man Hattie would presently marry. Welles expressed regret at Wilson's departure. "If he [had] *any* feeling at seeing me go away," wrote the rejected suitor, "it [was] probably a feeling of relief."[30]

As he journeyed back east, and in a long delay as he waited for connections in Kentucky, Wilson brooded on the classic predicament of thwarted love. Hattie was left to cancel engagements in Chillicothe and to make excuses for his impetuous departure. In October Wilson wrote again from Wilmington: "My love for you has taken such a hold on me as to have become almost a part of myself, which no influences I can imagine can ever destroy or weaken."[31] Alarmed by his desperation (and perhaps by now committed to Welles as her future husband), Hattie broke off the correspondence. The father expressed, as he so often did, the pithy truth of the matter. She "would have made you happy," he wrote, "only for a very little while."[32]

Wilson and Hattie nevertheless continued to see each other. He met her again in Rome, Georgia, a year later (on the anniversary of his proposal) at the funeral of his aunt Marion. In a curiously erroneous recollection, perhaps springing from a suppressed sense of guilt, Hattie later convinced herself that while in Rome on that visit she had introduced Wilson to Ellen Axson, the girl he ultimately married. Years afterward, on his first visit to Colorado where Hattie was then living, he stayed with her, and she attended the inaugurations for each of his two terms as President of the United States. To complete the tale: a granddaughter of Woodrow Wilson's, Faith Wilson McAdoo, in the course of time married Hattie's grandson, Donald Wilson Thackwell.

Even after Hattie had stopped writing, her suitor harbored the forlorn hope that she in fact loved him and was only put off by an unfounded suspicion against marriage between close cousins. The following March Wilson wrote to his friend Robert Bridges of the suffering he had been through; his work, he declared, had been "considerably broken in upon."[33] Partly for this reason he stretched out his stay in Wilmington, not arriving in Atlanta until the end of May 1882.

It was a peculiarly aimless and frustrating time. Wilson wrote some inexcusably poor verse and under a pen name engaged in a heavy-handed polemic with a local editor. He wrote articles which he sent to the New York *Evening Post*, where the father of his classmate Harold Godwin was in charge. Only one of these, on new southern industries, was printed. Returning to his old interest, the subject of his first major article written in his last year in Princeton, he began what was to be an ambitious book-length manuscript on cabinet government in the United States. For many young men these activities might not have appeared a sign of idleness; but Wilson was supposed to be getting on with a career in the law, and he was obviously dawdling upon the threshold.

The move to Atlanta, finally undertaken in mid-May 1882 was greatly facilitated by arrangements made in advance by Edward L. Renick, a fellow student of Wilson's at the University of Virginia Law School. The two had not met while in Charlottesville, but Renick introduced himself by letter and offered to find lodgings for Wilson as well as to set up a joint office. The lodgings were in the home of an eminently respectable widow on Peach Street, Mrs. J. Reid Boylston, whom Wilson described as "a prim little person," one "whose faults amuse and whose good qualities win esteem."[34] In the booming small city the two fledgling lawyers found coveted office space on Marietta Street, directly across from the State House. Here a sign, "Renick & Wilson, Attorneys at Law," was placed discreetly in a window of the second floor.

Wilson's father, familiar with the city from visits on church business, came from Wilmington to show his son around and to introduce him to his acquaintances. At home there were fond regrets. "God bless you, darling boy," wrote his mother; "you have never been anything but a comfort to me all your life!"[35] Little Josie, wondering how he was going to progress in his Latin now that his elder brother, his "dear teacher," had gone away, promised to study faithfully.[36] Such good resolves, unfortunately, seldom lasted long with Josie.

The months Wilson spent in Atlanta, despite a deepening disenchantment with the practice of law, were not without rewards. In June he returned to his triennial reunion in Princeton, basking for three days amid old friends and familiar associations. Renick was turning out to be a congenial spirit. The two found agreeable pursuits outside the law, reading together some of Wilson's favorite authors. Living conditions were not unpleasant, with the landlady's niece, Katie Mayrant, proving an unexpected charmer. The long-deferred bar examinations were passed in a style that the presiding judge described as "not short of brilliant."[37]

When a congressional committee on the tariff visited Atlanta in September Wilson testified at the hearings. A young newspaperman, a friend of Renick's, was instrumental in arranging for Wilson's appearance, and afterwards reported in the New York *World* that "no argument of dignity was made today except by Mr. Woodrow Wilson."[38] The reporter's name was Walter Hines Page. Page lingered that evening in the office of the young lawyer, where a friendship began between the future President and his future ambassador to the Court of St. James's. As for business, it was not coming in fast; but putting the best possible light on the matter, Wilson wrote Bridges that there was just enough to keep him in spirits.

Throughout the Atlanta period, Wilson stubbornly refused to adapt himself to the necessities of his profession. The law as an institution fascinated him—its origins, its growth, its relation to changing ethical standards—and he would make of jurisprudence a major element in his teaching. But the day-to-day processes of the law were alien to him and even abhorrent. It was not only that his principal business was still what he called "the young lawyer's occupation of *waiting*," but that such cases as did come were in the form of efforts to collect basically uncollectible claims. In these the pettiness of the law, its mean competitiveness, were most evident. The atmosphere of the courts, Wilson wrote in despair, was one "of broken promises, of wrecked estates, of neglected trusts, of unperformed duties, of crimes and of quarrels."[39] From time to time he glimpsed the possibility of arguing a case where some large principle was involved; but the hope evaporated and he was left to compete for the dregs of legal practice. It cannot quite be said that Wilson "failed" at law; other young lawyers have had fewer cases, handled them less well, and gone on to make respectable careers. But certainly he did not have the stomach for the kind of work that law in a small city required of those who would gain success.

As a matter of fact, he deigned to think about law only during the morning hours, while keeping the afternoons for reading and writing on subjects that were dear to him. The intense efforts which he applied to these, and which caused young Bridges in New York to scurry about seeking outlets for his friend's manuscripts, were noticeably absent from his legal work. During this period Wilson completed the writing of *Government by Debate*, a book-length essay involving arduous composition and much new research. But despite Bridges's best efforts it found no publisher. It was polemical in tone, a plea for drastic changes in American political practices, and no one was anxious to back the recommendations of an unknown Atlanta lawyer.

Wilson's father showed understandable concern at what seemed to him his son's intellectual waywardness. In a series of letters he brought up once more the big battalions of his rhetoric. "My beloved boy," he wrote, "you have only one thing to do:—to stick to the law and its prospects be they ever so depressing." A week later he wrote again: "It is a source of anxiety to me:—your law-distaste." All beginnings were difficult, he assured his son: "It is hardly like you, my brave boy, to show a white feather before the battle is well joined." And a few months later: "Plodding is almost more than genius. Drudgery is almost more than eloquence."[40]

Wilson's recurrent fits of depression passed and his morale improved, but he continued to be very much a disaffected and part-time lawyer. To his friend Heath Dabney, then studying political science and history at Heidelberg, he confessed his envy. "I have to be content with a very precarious allowance of such good things," he wrote. It was somewhat unsatisfactory to be compelled to master the science of politics "as it were by stealth."[41]

At home the mood was increasingly somber. This was only in part because of worry over the son's progress. Dr. Wilson had passed the zenith of his career and was feeling the pangs of a man for whom the road ahead appears to run downhill. "Discouragement knocks at my door," he wrote to Woodrow: "and, too often, I let him . . . in." His work in Wilmington was done, he felt; what was worse, some in his congregation were making it evident that they shared this view. He had never preached better—that was not the trouble. "The fault they find with me is as to visiting. They want a gad-about gossip."[42] Jessie Wilson shared the torment of such criticism, and she had her special cause for complaint: the congregation was often late in paying Joseph's salary. Besides, she felt cooped up in Wilmington—"this dull place" was the way she referred to it, this "stupid place."[43]

As Christmas of 1882 approached, Jessie Wilson discouraged Woodrow from coming home. "The truth is," she wrote on Christmas Eve, "the holidays here are *not* a specially cheerful time with us—we feel, more than ever, our isolation."[44]

Such messages might have been expected to add to the burdens the young Wilson was carrying, but as that particular Christmas came and went he seemed in unusually good spirits. The holiday, he wrote Bridges in a bantering tone, was "merry in the extreme." A "most wonderful change" came over the city: "such another universal drunk is not on record in this part of the country." The station houses were full to overflowing and "our police-men were crazy with press of business." As for himself, he spent the day quietly in his boardinghouse "where a pretty girl helped me nobly [to] while away the leisure time."[45]

The "pretty girl" was, of course, the landlady's niece. That Wilson should have escaped the toils of Katie Mayrant, lonely as he was in a strange city and on the rebound from his first doomed affair, is remarkable. The next summer he made a considerable journey to visit Katie in Aiken, South Carolina. The young woman, whom Wilson spoke of as having "a frail beauty interesting in itself,"[46] found the day he returned home to be such a one as might mark a death in the family. Always close to tears, she now refrained with difficulty from letting loose a flood. Many years later, during one of the most crowded periods of Wilson's Presidency, a touching letter from Katie (then Mrs. K. D. Simons) arrived at the White House. "Befriend me, friend of my youth," she wrote. She was only seeking aid on an administrative matter concerning the draft; but Katie recalled memories of the time when all life was seen *en couleur de rose*, and when the young Wilson wore a halo to which nothing of his later achievements could add.[47]

He had surely not been immune to Katie's attraction. At least the young woman he was soon seriously courting had few doubts on the point. In July Ellen Axson taunted him wickedly. "Can it be possible," she asked, "that you have been domiciled for nine months with so charming a young lady ... without serious consequences?" Such a thought was "contrary to all precedent," she maintained, and "subversive of all principles."[48] Wilson was not one to take "principles" lightly; he must have enjoyed his fiancée's little joke.

Wilson's decision to abandon the practice of law formed slowly, but in February his mind was more or less made up. By the end of April, not quite a year after his coming to Atlanta, he could write Bridges that "a great change has been wrought in my plans."[49] Bridges was not altogether sympathetic to the news, and Wilson wrote him a long defense of his position, maintaining that he could only be happy in the intellectual life and that his future lay in teaching and writing.

His father seemed reconciled to the move but, as dispenser of the monthly stipend on which his son still lived, questioned him with understandable concern: "Are you certain, *can* you be certain, that this same enemy [discontent] will not attack you again?"[50] He thought Woodrow should come home from Atlanta at once, but this was one of the rare occasions when his mother took a sterner stand. She must have had in mind the series of abandonments marking her son's record. He had left Davidson College after a year, had fled Charlottesville, and now if he quit Atlanta without definite plans it would look very much like a defeat.

Inquiries about a possible post for Woodrow were set on foot among the senior Wilson's friends, including President McCosh of Princeton. Nothing came of them; then Wilson's uncle, James Woodrow of Columbia, South Carolina, suggested that his nephew study at Johns Hopkins University, the recently founded graduate school at Baltimore, Maryland, where standards of scholarship new to America were being introduced. Wilson applied for a fellowship, and, although he failed to receive one, decided to take his chances and to enroll in courses for the following autumn.

By the spring of 1883 the young lawyer's major, and certainly most demanding, client was his mother. Jessie Wilson was involved in an unpleasant family disagreement over the settlement of her brother William's estate, consisting of western lands of considerable value. The estate had been administered by Jessie's brother-in-law James W. Bones, who had mortgaged the properties for the benefit of his hardware business. He was not a good businessman, nor was he frank or communicative in regard to his—and to the family's—affairs. Jessie Wilson was now determined to end what her brother-in-law somewhat disingenuously called a "partnership" and to proceed directly to the sale of the lands. The delicate mission of removing the estate from James Bones's hands and forcing a rapid and conclusive settlement was entrusted to the young Woodrow. The fact that he managed fully to satisfy his mother in this matter, while not alienating the Bones family, suggests that in other cases his skill as a lawyer would have been proven.

As a step in fulfilling his charge, Wilson journeyed in April to Rome, Georgia. It will be recalled that the Bones family had moved there from Augusta and, business apart, Wilson now found himself in thoroughly congenial surroundings. Not only was he amid relatives and acquaintances, but Rome itself was (as it still is) a pleasant city. Situated about a hundred miles west of Atlanta, on Georgia's remote western border, it stands, appropriately, among seven small hills and at a confluence of three sparkling rivers. On his march to the sea, Sherman had burned most of Rome's business section; but by 1883 the city had been rebuilt and was looking toward the future. Its educational and cultural facilities were being restored, its churches revitalized, and its residential sections lay charmingly spread out at the base of wooded slopes.

Wilson spent two or three April days working on his mother's affairs, staying at the home of James and Marion Bones, and on Sunday attended the Presbyterian church. The minister, Samuel Edward Axson, was a handsome figure whom the ladies of the parish never tired of noting. The eyes of the visitor, however, came to rest on the profile of a young woman, her auburn curls visible beneath a mourning veil. "What a bright, pretty face," Wilson recalled thinking. "I'll lay a wager that this demure little lady has lots of life and fun in her."[51]

His first impression was that she must be a young widow. Learning that she was in fact Ellen Louise Axson, daughter of the minister, Wilson arranged for an early call at the parsonage. Dr. Axson treated him with respect as the son of his old friend, Joseph Wilson, discoursing upon such topics as the reason for the decline in evening congregations. When Wilson inquired abruptly as to the health of his daughter, she was invited in to join the company.

Ellen Axson was then twenty-three, a young woman whom experience had matured beyond her age. Her mother had died three years before in childbirth; now Ellen was mistress of the parsonage and the bearer of heavy family responsibilities. Of the four children, her younger brother Edward and the infant Margaret (or Madge) had been parceled out among relatives; Stockton was old enough to be away at school. But Ellen acted in place of a mother to them all, as she would continue to do through later years. Her father's health was precarious, moreover, and the handsome exterior clothed a mind subject to severe mental disorders. Ellen Axson had decided that, burdened as she was, she would never marry. Suitors had lined her father's drawing room since she was sixteen, but among her intimates, along with her reputation as a lover of poetry and painting, she was thought of as being a "man-hater."[52]

Her resolution, however, proved less than unshakable. By the time Wilson left Rome he had decided he was in love with her, and in May on a second visit a formal courtship began. "Miss Axson," read Wilson's first note to her, "I write to beg that you will gratify me by taking a drive with me this afternoon." Ellen replied that she would be happy to take the drive and that she would be ready at the appropriate hour. In June Wilson was again in Rome, with Ellen's friends anxious to encourage the match. Among these, Jessie Bones, recently married to Abraham T. H. Brower, was the most sympathetic. "I am permitted by Jessie," Wilson wrote teasingly to Ellen, "to beg that you will go with us on the picnic which we have planned." He was tempted, he said, to add a request of his own—that she take a walk with him that particular afternoon. Ellen accepted the invitation for the walk, but, with the lament that she was "the most unfortunate of mortals," declined the picnic, having a previous engagement for a boat ride.[53]

In the end the day of the picnic was changed. Ellen and Woodrow met with the other guests at Jessie Brower's house, and they all set out in a wagon and a buggy for the ride of eight or nine miles to an ever afterwards remembered spot, where a stream fed into a small lake. Local and family history record that when the others were ready for lunch, Woodrow and Ellen were off by themselves, looking for four-leaf clovers.

Wilson's mother, who had been strongly supportive of the match with Hattie, now struck another note. She spoke of the "weary waiting" before Woodrow was established in a career; she expressed uneasiness at the long delay in his returning home. "Miss Ellie has seen enough of you to know whether or not she likes you—enough at least to consent to *correspond* with you."[54] Such consent Ellie apparently gave. Over the next months the two exchanged frequent letters. "I've made up my mind to win her if I can," Wilson wrote Robert Bridges of the "dear lassie," describing her as one who had become learned "without knowing it, and without losing one particle of freshness or natural feminine charm." In the same letter he announced that he had left Atlanta for good. "The boats are burnt, and all retreat is cut off."[55]

Wilson spent the remainder of the summer at Arden, near Asheville, North Carolina, while Ellen was visiting a classmate some forty miles away in Morganton. For all practical purposes they might have been separated by a continent. They carried on a correspondence subject to the mischances that traditionally afflict young love: their letters crossed, or miscarried, or at best seemed fatally inadequate to the messages they were supposed to bear. Ellen's letters were long enough to dismay their author (though affording pleasurable astonishment to Woodrow), and in a passage characteristic of her warmth and humor she apologized for their length. "They are indeed a sad spectacle," she told Woodrow. "You must know that they are not written of malice aforethought, but are the result of a long course of high crimes and misdemeanors." The consequences of such indulgences, she told Woodrow, "coupled with the natural diffuseness of womankind, is that we really don't know how to write a short letter; we wander along as though time were no more, and are only beginning to get fairly warmed up and into our subject, such as it is, when we reach the third sheet."[56] Perhaps her letters would have gone on forever, but in September Providence intervened.

On a Friday, the fourteenth of the month, Ellen was passing through Asheville to take the train back to Rome. By coincidence, and unaware of her presence, Woodrow was also in Asheville that day. He saw Ellen's unmistakable profile in the window of the Eagle Hotel, where she was staying between connections. Impetuously he rushed in to greet her. The chance encounter, the unfamiliar place, worked their magic. There was nothing, Ellen said later, like "the joy of a sudden meeting and the pain of an imminent parting" to break down the barriers of shyness and doubt.[57]

For two days the entranced pair lingered in Asheville. On Saturday Woodrow took Ellen out to the resort at Arden where his family was staying, and the next day, just before their parting, he formally proposed to her and was accepted. She was leaving for Rome, where she was to find her father seriously ill; he was en route to Johns Hopkins in Baltimore. "I am more eager than I can tell you to be at my life work," Woodrow had written Ellen a month before.[58] Now he was on his way—and he was beginning as an engaged man.

CHAPTER TWO

Scholar, Teacher

——◆——

BALTIMORE / NEW YORK

The seven years between the fall of 1883 and the fall of 1890 were an immensely important period in Wilson's development. "Long a child," he said of himself, "longer a diffident youth."[1] Aspects of that youthfulness, mixed with solid accomplishments and growing self-confidence, carried over into Wilson's thirties as he moved beyond Johns Hopkins into teaching positions at Bryn Mawr and Wesleyan. When in 1890 he achieved his goal of appointment to the Princeton faculty, he had found his style as a teacher and had completed or had begun the major works that would define his stature as a scholar. By then his own immediate family was fully established and relations with his father were on a solid basis of independence combined with filial devotion. Yearnings for a life in politics, never wholly extinguished, appeared to have been subdued. In short, by 1890 Wilson had matured; by 1894—at the end of his first period at Princeton—he had come into his own as a successful teacher, writer, and interpreter of public events.

Two years as a graduate student at Johns Hopkins provided the first stage for this evolution. Established in 1876 by the bequest of a wealthy Quaker, Johns Hopkins, it was the first American university based directly on German methods of research and scholarship. Its president, Daniel Colt Gilman, combed the scholarly world in the United States and abroad for teachers of independent bent and probing minds, and students came with the knowledge that they would not only be trained in the highest standards of scholarship but would be looked on by other institutions as likely candidates for jobs. Old-line Baltimoreans were disappointed by this new college, housed in a miscellaneous group of buildings, neither employing local talent nor bringing to the city the kind of students and young professors that would add light to the social scene. But in the end Baltimore gained intellectual distinction from a faculty and student body, odd and often unsociable, that knew their scholarly mission and concentrated exclusively on that.

A close friend, Hiram Woods, a member of the Witherspoon group at Princeton, had begun medical practice in Baltimore. Wilson stayed with him and his parents while he conducted a weeklong search for lodgings at once comfortable and inexpensive. He settled on a boardinghouse room on Charles Street, in the historic heart of the city. Here in front of large bright windows he spread out his books and began the long series of love letters to Ellen Axson which, with her replies, constitute a moving documentation of the outward and inner developments of his life.

At the university he felt the excitement and slight bewilderment of being a "new boy," cast in unfamiliar surroundings. Instruction at Johns Hopkins was then partly by lectures, but what was new to America was the "seminary" system. At departmental meetings of students and professors once a week, papers were read and discussed, original research reported on, and new ideas propounded. The seminar in history and political science, of which Wilson was a part, met in the newly created Bluntschli Library, named for the noted Heidelberg political scientist, the gift of whose books was supplemented by the latest journals and scholarly studies in the field. It was a handsome room, donated by a group of German-Americans in Baltimore. In charge of the seminar was Associate Professor Herbert Baxter Adams, with Drs. Richard T. Ely and John Franklin Jameson as his associates.

Far from being carried away by scholarly enthusiasm, Wilson was at first bitterly critical of his teachers and of the Johns Hopkins methods. Ely he judged a poor lecturer, coming often unprepared to his classes. Adams perfectly embodied the university's penchant for Germanic conceptions of scholarship: the search for isolated facts and rigorous textual analysis. High value was attached to everything that Wilson disliked, and for which by training and inclination he was unfitted, so that he found himself beset once more by the frustrations of law school days. Soon after the opening of term he went to Adams and laid bare his disappointments. He did more: he asked that he be permitted a wide latitude to explore his own subjects in his own way. To his surprise, Adams acquiesced.

After that Wilson began to feel more relaxed. From the beginning he was liked by his peers and was soon recognized by Adams and Ely as their most promising student. The conviction that he was on the right course after the setbacks of the Atlanta year encouraged him and spurred his determination. It was inevitable, he wrote his friend Dabney, that he should have turned to history and political science. "I was born with that bent in me; and there was no use trying to force nature to unnatural uses."[2] Of course it helped to be in love. "*I do, for some reason or other,*" he wrote Ellen, "feel merrier and happier than I ever did before." And at a deeper level, looking back over the course of his years, he could say that God had never had "anything but blessings for me. It makes me almost tremble to think of the uniform good fortune that has followed me all through life. . . . I have the heathen's instinctive desire to do for Providence some signal service in token of gratitude."[3]

For Ellen, writing from Rome and then from Savannah, it was a time of stock-taking and of a slowly unfolding recognition of the change that had come over her since the earthshaking encounter in Asheville. In their letters the two went step by step over the incidents through which their love had been awakened and confirmed. They sought out new depths of feeling, frequently expressed with pre-Freudian naïveté in elaborately recounted dreams. They groped for fresh ways of saying old things. Wilson was already a skilled writer, and his letters flowed naturally; "You don't know how willful and headstrong I am," he told his fiancée. "I long to be made your master—only, however, on the very fair and equal terms that, in exchange for the authority over yourself which you relinquish, you shall be constituted supreme mistress of me!" That seems "a fair compact," he added, reflecting in his words his constitutional as well as theological presuppositions.[4]

If love, as he noted, was the "predominant figure" in his letters, in Ellen's—more subtly—it was the "pervading colour."[5] A woman's love, she told her fiancé, was very different from a man's. It was by no means so direct, but full of windings and turnings. It was an underground stream which could not be fully explored, and the very existence of which, indeed, could hardly be suspected. In "the struggles of love with pride and shame . . . it is more like the tide, which, however steadily it rises, seems to be constantly beaten back." Many of her letters she spiced with a quixotic humor. The special characteristic of her handwriting she described as "hopelessly careless, chaotic, and unintelligible"—and then she wondered what mental idiosyncrasies might thus be denoted. It was an old trick of hers, "and a very crazy one," to fly from jest to earnest and back again in a most unexpected, inconsequential manner. "What a preacher I would make," she concluded. "I wouldn't ever remember to 'give out' the text, much less to stick to it."[6]

In his letters Wilson commented frequently on university activities. Top men of the intellectual world were coming regularly as visitors. The philosopher Josiah Royce came; a few years before, he had been a prize student in the first class at Johns Hopkins, "one of those very rare minds which exists in a perfectly lucid atmosphere of thought." The Englishman James Bryce dropped in on his way home from the Sandwich Islands. Wilson and he would establish a lasting friendship which carried over into the Presidential years. Now the student discerned an unmistakable "strength and dash and mastery about the man."[7] Charles W. Eliot of Harvard helped celebrate the eighth anniversary of Johns Hopkins, and although he and Wilson would hold opposing views on education the student listened now with admiration to an address of an hour and a half, "striking and suggestive from beginning to end."[8]

Christmas found Ellen and Woodrow apart. Despite their longing, neither felt able to afford traveling the distance that separated them. In that wintry month Wilson began to find his living quarters, so pleasant under the autumn sun, frigid and also lonely. "We are there such an awfully solemn household," he wrote Ellen. "We eat our meals in sober silence."[9] Shortly afterwards he moved to the boardinghouse of Mary Jane Ashton at 8 McCullough Street, where he was surrounded by fellow students from the university. In this house, or one across the street, he would live over the next year and a half and during all his future visits as a lecturer at Johns Hopkins.

On New Year's Day, 1884, Wilson sat down to the first work on a series of essays in which, as he wrote Ellen, his purpose was to show "our constitutional system as it looks in operation."[10] This was the beginning of *Congressional Government*, to be published eighteen months later as Wilson's first book.

Drafts of these essays, read before the "seminary," confirmed the author's reputation as a top student. He found himself being drawn into activities of different kinds. He delivered a paper on Adam Smith. He took part in a debate with a fellow student, brother of the philosopher John Dewey, upon a bill proposing to distribute federal funds to the states for educational purposes. (Wilson was opposed to it.) Most important, he was asked by Professor Ely to be coauthor with him of a book on American economists.

Wilson was at first inclined to turn down this highly complimentary offer. He suspected that Ely was out to pick the brains of his better students. But with unexpected realism (spurred by his urgent desire to become independent and to get married), he took on the assignment. He told Ellen he had come to Johns Hopkins so that, in addition to learning what he could, he might "advertise" himself for a position. "And the best way to do that," he said, "is to please the professors and get them to push me!"[11]

By the end of the academic term he had pleased them sufficiently so that he was granted a fellowship for the following year. To Robert Bridges he wrote in triumph: "I have done as hard a year's work at the Hopkins as I shall ever do anywhere, and have won as great rewards as they had to bestow."[12]

During this same year the older generation, the parents of both Woodrow and Ellen, were in the midst of troubles that cast shadows over the course of young love. In Wilson's family more than the usual amount of sickness prevailed, with his mother sinking into the chronic ill health of her last years. Dr. Wilson was suffering the humiliation of seeing his salary payments in arrears and his congregation generally unappreciative. Like his son, but in very different circumstances, he was seeking a place to teach: "It may be that you and I will have to organize a school somewhere for ourselves! I think we could make it go." He had thought of the idea a good deal, he told Woodrow, "although with my mind looking through a mist."[13] The aging pastor would in fact become a teacher, at Southwestern Presbyterian University in Clarksville, Tennessee; and father and son, by the autumn of 1885, were both at the beginning of new careers.

But it was Ellen who observed at close hand the full misery of life. In Rome her father was increasingly subject to mental illness and depression, and by November it was evident that he could not continue his pastorate. Amid constant changes of mind and shifts of mood he finally consented to return to his family's home in Savannah. Ellen remained to close the house where she had lived for more than twenty years and where she had seen her mother die; she disposed of many of its possessions and then followed her father to the home of her grandparents. But her father did not improve. Early in the new year, in a state of violence, Edward Axson was committed to the Georgia State Mental Hospital.

For Ellen this was a shattering blow. Woodrow, feeling helpless and remote in Baltimore, questioned whether he should join her. A university friend, Charles H. Shinn, urged him to go immediately to Savannah and lent him money for the trip. (But "How can we survive a week without our dear Wilson?" he queried.[14]) Thus in Ellen's girlhood home, amid shaken relatives and friends, the lovers had their first meeting since the engagement in Asheville.

In May 1884, still in the asylum, Edward Axson took his own life. A cousin of Ellen's gave the news to Woodrow, she being evidently too stricken to write. The intensity of her distress through the period of her father's decline affected Ellen and Woodrow differently. Wilson felt more than ever that they should marry immediately and was determined to take advantage of the first post that might present itself. In Arkansas a land-grant college was being established which seemed to offer him a chance. But Ellen's instinct was to draw back from marriage. Urging him to stay on at Johns Hopkins and finish his two-year course, she was thinking partly of her fiancé's career; but there was also at work a deep, persistent doubt about her fitness to become a wife. Her father's death strengthened an earlier feeling that she should sacrifice herself to taking care of her younger sister and brothers. But the manner of his death, the mental illness and the violent end, spoke to Ellen of something else—a tendency in the Axson family to psychological weaknesses and breakdowns (one to which she herself would not prove wholly immune).

The same reluctance to face the ultimate consequences of her love became apparent in mid-summer 1884, when Ellen at first declined to undertake a long-arranged visit to Wilmington. Woodrow was mystified, the more so as she gave as her only reason a promise made to her grandmother not to risk the impropriety of staying in the same house with her fiancé. Even by the standards of the day that seemed farfetched. In the end, much to Woodrow's relief, she did join him in Wilmington. Jessie Wilson's more humane sense of the proprieties prevailed, and for two weeks she chaperoned (efficiently, it must be presumed) her son and his bride-to-be.

Ellen arrived in Wilmington on September 16, the anniversary of their engagement. A fortnight later the two set out northward, she to spend the winter studying at the Art Students League in New York and he to begin his second year at Johns Hopkins. It seems strange, after all the fuss made over the Wilmington visit, that without complaint from their elders the two should now have traveled together unchaperoned. They spent the night in the same Washington hotel, went sight-seeing, and journeyed to New York by sleeper. Woodrow saw Ellen safely installed in a boardinghouse at 60 Clinton Place and that evening made the return trip to Baltimore.

Ellen was an immediate success among her fellow boarders and the students at the League. She appeared younger than twenty-four; Robert Bridges recalled years later that she might have been taken for seventeen: she was "a very pretty girl, with rosy cheeks and a red tam-o-shanter."[15] The next months were to be crucially important to her development as a woman and as an artist. Always serious about her art—she had continued with her studies after graduation, doing portraits which gained her small fees and winning a medal for a drawing submitted by her teacher to the Paris International Exposition—she now found inspiration and release in the Art Students League. Its free atmosphere and sympathetic manner of teaching enlarged her vision beyond anything she had previously imagined.

Her Rome teacher, a product of the conservative National Academy of Design, had taught her that in painting one must look with wide-open eyes and reproduce all that was observed as carefully as possible. "But at the League," Ellen informed her fiancé, "you must always look at the model with your eyes half shut—you must be BROAD above all things—you must understand the *nothingness* of nature."[16] The first tentative influences of Impressionism, with its liberating emphasis on light as opposed to the solidity of objects, were evidently being opened to the young artist.

Ellen's attitude toward life was undergoing an enlargement comparable to that which she was learning through new techniques at art school. Escaping from the rigid provincialism of her grandmother's house in Savannah, she found herself among young women often "bohemian" by her standards, whose influence she partly resisted and by which she was half seduced. Her engagement was still secret and during this period of apparent freedom she was determined not to play the role of a retiring and dependent Southern belle. She insisted, for example, on paying her share of the expenses incurred in coming north with Woodrow. "You cruel, provokingly proud and prompt little darling,"[17] her fiancé wrote when she itemized her share of the Washington hotel bill. (It was $4.25.) Highly popular, she enjoyed being escorted by young men to theaters, art galleries, and church services. The attentions of one intrusive and insensitive young man, a representative of Houghton Mifflin Company, became so persistent as to alarm Woodrow and to cause Ellen to take decisive steps to rebuff him.

Woodrow was troubled by Ellen's mood; she was uncharacteristically coquettish and occasionally seemed genuinely uncertain about the future. In February he made one of his rare trips north to reassure himself. The visit left them both more than ever in love; yet Ellen remained curiously loath to fix their wedding date. Unnamed obstacles seemed to stand in the way of a June ceremony. "Don't you think we had better leave the matter *unsettled* for the present, and await further developments?" she asked with tantalizing vagueness. When some of her young women friends rented a place in the Hamptons for the summer, where they planned to keep house "Gypsy fashion" next door to their art teacher, she told them she would join them "for a month at least,—*perhaps!*" "Isn't that a lovely plan?" she exclaimed to Woodrow.[18]

He was far from finding it so. "Is it possible," he wrote her, "that second thought has led [you] to prefer Hampton Beach and a little longer period of freedom? Of course it is *not* possible. . . . But *something* holds [you] back."[19]

Ellen's rather provoking behavior and Woodrow's perplexity must be seen in the perspective of past incidents in Ellen's life. Her teens, as with many of her age, especially in the old South, were marked by strong female attachments. A long correspondence between her and her intimate friend Beth Adams was of a temper so frankly passionate as to appear disconcerting if not viewed in the context of nineteenth-century cultural mores. The young women had their jokes, and one of them, not entirely without its serious side, was that they would establish one day a "hall" exclusively for unmarried women. Early vows of eternal friendship were broken by engagements and then marriages, but something of the original spirit endured. When one of the group learned of Ellen's promise to marry Woodrow, she let out a guffaw. What had become, she wanted to know, of that "grand institution . . . which was to instill into the feminine part of the coming race, contempt of the men, and entire independence?"[20]

Ellen's dream of independence was tied in with her gifts as an artist. Plans for the "grand institution" had been based on her being able to finance it by her painting, and indeed after graduating from college she considered that she was supporting herself by fees from her portraits. Now at the Art Students League she was more than ever tempted by the vision of a career of her own. Teachers and fellow students encouraged her, and her self-confidence increased. It was "barely possible," she told her fiancé, that "my talent for art combined with my talent for work *might*, after many years, win me a place in the first rank among American artists." The pride was tempered by modesty, and then by self-deprecating humor, as she added that American artists "don't amount to much anyhow."[21]

Despite the jocular tone assumed by Ellen, Woodrow seems to have gotten the message. He was learning and changing, as she was, and he was ready at least to reexamine the ideas about women that as a southerner and a Victorian he had held sacrosanct. He never completely gave up the notion that the wife's role is subservient to the husband's, nor that women exist to make life more delightful for men. But he had come to realize that in marrying Ellen he would be asking her to surrender a promising career of her own. In the future, he would often express gratitude for her sacrifice; sometimes he would even feel guilty about it. With touching solicitude he encouraged her to return to painting after years devoted to care of the family. Along with Ellen, he saw that their daughters were, in their turn, prepared to pursue active, independent lives.

Whatever last-minute regrets for lost freedom Ellen may have experienced, whatever the impish desire to tease and tantalize her fiancé, she was at bottom crystal-clear about the commitment she had made in Asheville. On February 15, in response to Woodrow's urging, she declared her surrender: "If you wish you may come to me in June, my love." As for abandoning her career for marriage, she declared it to be no sacrifice at all. "As compared with the privilege of loving and serving you and the blessedness of being loved by you," she wrote in March, "the praise and admiration of all the world and generations yet unborn would be lighter than vanity."[22] There might have been other ways of solving the modern dilemma of marriage versus career; but this was Ellen's way, and it was made tolerable, even made joyous, because the young Woodrow Wilson did not fail to appreciate the importance of what she had abandoned for his sake.

For Woodrow as for Ellen, the year 1884–1885—his second at Johns Hopkins—was a time of change. It was also a time of striking progress in his career. Looking forward to marriage after the last examinations, he was stirred emotionally to his depths. At the same time he saw his first book published and his first post in the academic world secured.

During a final Wilmington summer he worked to complete the last three chapters of *Congressional Government*, and on October 7 he sent off the manuscript to Houghton Mifflin, one of the leading publishers of the day. For six weeks there was silence; then on November 26 came a letter announcing that they would publish the volume on favorable terms. "It is too lovely for anything," wrote Ellen of the news that a first book had thus been accepted by the first publisher to whom it had been submitted. "I don't believe any young man in America ever had such a brilliant triumph."[23] The printers worked fast in this period. On December 10 the first proofs arrived, and bound copies were in Wilson's hand on January 24.

The book was dedicated to his father—"the patient guide of his youth, the gracious companion of his manhood." In sending Ellen a first copy, he wrote that he was renewing the gift of himself. The first reviews were enthusiastic enough to satisfy the most ambitious of young scholars.

"We have no hesitation in saying," wrote Gamaliel Bradford in the New York *Nation*, "that this is one of the most important books, dealing with political subjects, which have ever issued from the American press." "The best critical writing on the American constitution," declared Albert Shaw in the Minneapolis *Daily Tribune*, "which has appeared since the 'Federalist' papers."[24] Wilson's mother was predictably jubilant. "*Do you take it in*, dear boy," she wrote, "that you have made yourself *famous?*"[25]

The substance of *Congressional Government* was not new. The erosion of Executive authority in the post–Civil War federal government, the concentration of power in congressional committees, had been commented on by journalists and scholars and indeed had preoccupied Wilson since his first published article of undergraduate days. What was new to American writing was the method and style. In the summer of 1883 Wilson had reread Bagehot's *English Constitution*, an old favorite of his, and had realized that his opportunity lay, not in advocating reform, but in describing American institutions as they actually worked. "I want to divest them of the theory that obscures them and present their weakness and their strength without disguise,"[26] he wrote Ellen just before setting out for his first term at Johns Hopkins. And later to Robert Bridges: "I have abandoned the evangelical for the exegetical— so to speak!"[27]

The change in point of view brought a fresh note into American political writing, long dominated by legalisms and constitutional dogma. The style, which owed much—perhaps too much—to Bagehot, flowed lucidly in the expository passages and was enlivened by aphorisms. It was the work of a young man, but the work, too, of one who had the gifts of a natural leader. It was as if the author had not only learned but had also sensed in his own being the imbalances within the political system, the inherent confusions and cross-purposes frustrating effective action. Conceived and written within the academy, *Congressional Government* nevertheless seemed part of a larger world. Critics have complained that Wilson never visited Congress before sitting down to describe its workings. They miss the point; the book was in essence a work of the imagination. And the imagination was that of the born statesman.

Wilson himself was aware of this quality in his work. He had given up, for the time being, a role in public life; but in committing himself to a career of writing and teaching he did not forget what had once been his dream. "It turns out," he told Ellen, "that the latent powers of oratory and statesmanship which I possess—if indeed, I possess them at all—

were intended to complete my equipment as a *writer.*" He had limited his field of action in order that he might "*see* as a statesman."[28] This quality of vision helped give *Congressional Government* a long life. The book went into a second edition a few months after publication, and (what can probably be said of no other thesis for the Ph.D.) was still in print a hundred years later.

In the same November when the editors of Houghton Mifflin decided to publish *Congressional Government,* the author was called to Professor Adams's office to meet the president-designate of a projected women's college near Philadelphia. He knew that he was being looked over for a post.

Bryn Mawr College had been provided for, like Johns Hopkins, in the will of a rich Quaker, in this case Joseph Wright Taylor, who aimed to ensure for women the same advanced education that was being given to men at Johns Hopkins. Several of the trustees during the planning stage were members of the Johns Hopkins board, and it was natural that they should look to Baltimore when recruiting faculty. Wilson was pleased by the attention. He was inclined, moreover, to accept a post within the eastern establishment, under the eye of those at Johns Hopkins whom he looked to for future advancement.

There were drawbacks, however. The dean of the new college was to be a woman, a militant feminist named Martha Carey Thomas. Ellen doubted (with good reason) that Woodrow would find her easy to get along with. Dr. Wilson, who on practical grounds was favorable at first, grew skeptical as the negotiations proceeded. Perhaps reflecting doubts about his own forthcoming move to Clarksville, he saw his son being offered a title and salary less advantageous than he deserved. Besides, he grumbled, the new college had "an unpronounceable" name. "How greatly I wish that it had pleased God to open for you a door very different and much larger than this!" Yet perhaps, he consoled himself, his son needed "the discipline of such narrowness."[29]

The appointment was delayed while Wilson's religious views were tested in further interviews; but in February the board acted favorably. Such doubts as Wilson may have had were, for the moment, dispersed, and he looked forward without reserve to a career of teaching. "I accept my new profession with a profound impression of being providentially directed," he wrote Ellen, "and accept it with pleasure, enthusiasm, and hope."[30]

In March an unsettling diversion arose when the University of Michigan began the search for a professor in Wilson's particular field of constitutional law and administration. The rank and salary were higher than they would be at Bryn Mawr, and the courses he was expected to offer would be far more to his liking. Wilson was invited to go out to Michigan to read a paper. He refused. In view of his promise to Bryn Mawr, he told Ellen, he would make no effort, "open or covert," to attain the chair. This should be remembered in connection with Wilson's later problems at Bryn Mawr, where he was accused of breaking a contract in order to accept another post.

While deciding upon his future employment, Wilson wrestled with the question of whether he should complete preparations for the Ph.D. degree. He was carrying for Professor Ely the major share of writing the projected volume on American political economists. Besides, he found reading under pressure, in areas outside his main field, burdensome and debilitating. His letters to Ellen showed alternating moods of resolve to get the Ph.D. and fears lest he imperil his health by overwork. With his father in agreement he finally decided to postpone the acquisition of what, in a somewhat lordly fashion, he considered to be a mere label, of little meaning except for its value in the job market.

With winter's decline, the young man's thoughts dwelt increasingly on Ellen and their future together. He had been with her in New York at Christmas in what he considered the happiest days he had ever spent. But frequent visits were too expensive to contemplate. He was saving up for the wedding; his father, moreover, now ending his pastorate at Wilmington, could no longer be sure of augmenting the allowance of five hundred dollars provided by the Johns Hopkins fellowship. And so the two lovers pined for each other in immemorial fashion, exploring in words the limits of a passion soon to be consummated. At the first touch of spring, pent-up emotions overflowed. "I begin to realize . . . ," Woodrow wrote, "that my long waiting is almost over." "How rapidly," he wrote again, "we are drawing near to the sweet day for which our lives seem to have been made."[31]

Ellen was growing constantly more lighthearted and demonstrative. It amused her that the League's managers, alarmed at the spirit of romance among her fellow students, had made "a new law . . . viz., that there is to be no more falling in love." As for herself, she looked forward to June "with a joy which one year ago I would have blushed to think possible."[32] Woodrow was amazed at the change which had come upon Ellen, a change for which his own influence (he was far more outspoken in his passion than she) was largely responsible.

"Think of the shy little maid who used to confess to hot blushes whenever she so much as wrote a single sentence of her heart's thoughts to me and who found it hard . . . even to *whisper* 'I love you.' " Ellen could now confess eagerly to pleasure in the physical tenderness of love. "You are the only pupil I ever have had or shall have in this delightful study of love-making," Woodrow wrote proudly as the new candor revealed itself. For his part, "I have found out now what it meant that I was once reserved, sensitive, morbid, almost cold. It meant that I had never begun to live." He was at last liberated from "all the dreariness of loneliness, the pains of heart silence." "I am so glad that I am young so that I can give my youth to you."[33]

He was working hard as the end neared at Johns Hopkins, "dishing up" a political economist a day to fulfill his promises to Ely. In classic style the frustrated lover suffered from colds, lost weight, became (in his word) a "pseudo-invalid." Ellen, meanwhile, faced such trying questions as have ever confronted brides-to-be. What color dress should she wear for the wedding? (Her grandmother, with what Ellen charitably referred to as her "Charleston ideas," wanted the bride, as one still in mourning, to wear black.) Where should the honeymoon be spent? And how should Ellen get down from New York to Savannah—by boat or by train? It seemed a grave dilemma. The boat was cheaper, but she longed to go by train so that she could have a "peep" at her love on the station platform as the train passed through Baltimore.

Early in June Ellen arrived (by boat) at Savannah, where she was immediately taken in hand by relatives and friends and immersed in preparations for the wedding. Woodrow, having finished his course at Johns Hopkins, waited out the next weeks in Columbia, in the house of his sister Annie Howe. There he found his parents, en route to Clarksville from their closed-up home in Wilmington. By coincidence Katie Mayrant of Atlanta days was visiting relatives across the street from the Howes. Woodrow recalled their "one-time intimacy, with its romps and its energetic correspondence." Yet he was not, as he put it, "irresistibly inclined to rush over without delay."[34]

On June 24, 1885, in the parsonage of the Independent Presbyterian Church of Savannah, with the bride's grandfather and the father of the groom officiating, Woodrow and Ellen were married. The bride wore white. Afterward they stopped briefly in Columbia, and spent the remainder of the summer in an idyllic cottage in the hills at Arden, outside Asheville, where the two had gone tremulously, two years before, to meet Wilson's family after the first avowal of their love.

BRYN MAWR

When the Wilsons arrived at Bryn Mawr on its opening day, September 21, 1885, the college consisted of thirty-five undergraduates, about half of them Quakers, and seven graduate students. Of the seven professors, all but Wilson had studied in Germany and earned their Ph.D. degrees. The physical scene was not inspiring. Buildings that in time would settle into the Pennsylvania landscape, tree-shaded and vine-covered, stood forth starkly. The library shelves were almost bare of books. In these surroundings women were to be educated to be the equal of men in every way—morally, intellectually, and socially.

To this center of feminism Wilson brought his own attitude toward women, not only shaped by his upbringing but confirmed by his recent marriage to Ellen. At its core was the ideal of chivalry: men existed to make women's lot easier, to protect them in the vicissitudes of life, while women existed to be cherished for their femininity—growing cultivated without being learned and strong without being overmastering. Ellen, it is true, had taught him something of a woman's independent spirit, of her desire for a sense of accomplishment; but as even she had consented to put marriage ahead of art, so he believed that at every crucial juncture the woman should subordinate herself to the husband's career. Throughout his life Wilson would be drawn to women of wit and intelligence. He shone in their presence; but he drew back from signs of what he considered pedantry in the female mind, and he was acutely uncomfortable at any suggestion of rivalry.

At Bryn Mawr Wilson found himself not only at a college founded exclusively for young women but in a circle of strong female militancy. The militancy was personified by the college dean, Carey Thomas. The same age as Wilson, she was of the Quaker aristocracy, her father being on the board of Johns Hopkins as well as one of the first Bryn Mawr trustees. At the age of fourteen she resolved that "if ever I live and grow up my *one aim and concentrated purpose* shall be and *is* to show that women *can learn, can reason,* and *can compete* with men."[1] After attending Johns Hopkins (1877–79) and Cornell, she went abroad to battle her way into top German and Swiss universities and returned to the United States at the age of twenty-five with a Ph.D. from Zurich. Immediately she set about planning for the opening of Bryn Mawr. Her vision was of a college for American women propagating the most advanced ideas of women's rights, while her ambition was to be its president. James E. Rhoads, considered more experienced and more mature in judgment, was put at the head. But Thomas's ambition was fulfilled when in 1894 she succeeded Rhoads in a long tenure lasting until 1922.

For all her formidable credentials, Thomas was not lacking in charm. With a soft voice, well dressed and spirited in manner, she and Wilson might well have become mutual admirers. In later years Thomas would put Wilson among the great American leaders (the other four being Washington, Lincoln, Theodore Roosevelt, and Susan B. Anthony); but while they were associates, friction on both the professional and personal levels could not fail to develop. In accepting his post Wilson had stipulated that he report not to her as dean but directly to the president. Even this precaution did not forestall encounters, inevitably frigid; and when Wilson left Bryn Mawr in the spring of 1888 Thomas would not conceal her conviction that he had acted improperly in his relations with the college.

Wilson and his bride settled into two upstairs rooms in what was known as the Betweenery—the buildings to left and right being the Deanery and (with its pleasant view) the Scenery. They took their meals downstairs in boardinghouse style with other professors. Wilson's classes the first term were in ancient Greek and Roman history. He also met daily for tutorials in administration and political science with a single graduate student.

Wilson prepared his first lectures—it was part of the prevailing Germanic influence that there should be instruction by lecture even when two or three students were in the class—with meticulous care. The dean let it be known that she did not approve of history, considering it an insufficiently rigorous science. But the young professor in his own way presented its appeal and its essential usefulness. History, he admitted to the young women in his first class, was an acquired taste; but he added that it was one easily acquired. It was not a discipline burdening the mind with dull facts so much as one demanding an act of comprehension. The study of history, he continued, was "full of grave effort; but that effort may be made charming."[2] For his part he helped by leaving a happy impression with his students. He treated them with courteous deference, as he treated women in general; he paid them the respect of being lucid and serious; and he was not averse to an occasional professorial joke.

He had protested at Johns Hopkins against the tendency to treat facts as ends in themselves. Instinctively he felt that history was a humane study, not telling its devotees merely about some particular era of the past, nor teaching them lessons they could rigidly apply to the present; but increasing their understanding of life in all its phases. And so he urged these first students to "look into ancient times as if they were our own times, and into our own times as if they were not our own."[3] The sense of the spirit's being deeply involved and yet detached, of holding free and disinterested some part of the committed soul, was what the later Wilson believed all liberal education should seek to achieve.

These early lectures Wilson set down in a shorthand so sharp as to appear engraved on copper; and thus they slept among his papers until, after almost a century, they were disinterred and translated by scholars. What was revealed was a young teacher almost unbelievably industrious, and unexpectedly wide-ranging in the subjects he treated. Not only the history of ancient Greece and Rome (which later found its way into his published writings), but the Renaissance and the Reformation in art and politics—Dante, Petrarch, Boccaccio; Zwingli, Calvin, Erasmus; Leonardo, Michelangelo—were topics of his carefully laid out courses. Nor were his summaries slight or injudicious. Of Calvin: from 1541 to 1564 "he maintained [in Geneva] under circumstances all of which were of his own making, that remarkable polity which was profoundly to affect Scotland, England and France and which constitutes, even more than his doctrines, his claim to greatness and revolutionary influence." Or this, of Machiavelli: "His book *[The Prince]* is a cold and dispassionate analysis of the politics of that distracted age in dismembered Italy. It recognizes no morality but a sham morality meant for deceit, no honor even among thieves and of a thievish sort, no force but physical force, no intellectual power but cunning, no disgrace but failure, no crime but stupidity."[4] If Wilson, in these buried notes for classroom lectures, was learning to teach, he was also learning to write; and he was giving his students something more than the science to which Carey Thomas would have reduced his field.

Two months pregnant when she arrived at Bryn Mawr, Ellen faced a peculiarly difficult period amid strangers and in cramped quarters. Woodrow was feeling the lack of congenial colleagues in his own field and of adequate library resources. Despite these domestic and professional difficulties, he began upon a body of significant scholarly work. As if preparing his lectures were mere byplay, in December 1885 he drafted a treatise on "The Modern Democratic State." Though not published it was important because it prefigured many of Wilson's later

ideas. His father found that the treatise was, as a whole, "certainly . . .
obscure."⁵ But it broke new ground as it reached beyond the conversational tone of Bagehot for a style that would do justice to the complexity Wilson was discovering in the nature of democracy and its process
of development.

Modern democracy, Wilson wrote, was not a body of doctrine but a
phase in evolution. History alone could explain it, built up as it was by
the growth of habit and accumulated experience. Theoreticians who
endeavored to hasten democracy's development only demonstrated why
it must grow at its own pace. This sense of the organic nature of the
state, with its roots in ancient example and traditional wisdom, deepened
Wilson's political philosophy; but it held the danger of committing him
to a conservative and even negative attitude toward change.

The young scholar, however, was of too activist a disposition to become ensnared in a particular interpretation of history. The same treatise
that propounded the slow, instinctual processes of political growth contains the injunction that "the object of all political thought should be
action." Haltingly Wilson was feeling his way toward a kind of political
free will, rooted in a respect for innate historical forces.

Two months after composing "The Modern Democratic State," he
found the thesis of his *Congressional Government* challenged in the
pages of the *Atlantic Monthly* by a then-unknown political scientist and
lawyer, Abbot Lawrence Lowell. On the basis of a serious critical evaluation Lowell maintained that cabinet government or any form of ministerial responsibility was not suited to the political character of the
United States. Wilson immediately wrote a long article in reply. As was
frequently to be demonstrated, he was at his best when touched by the
polemical spark. In the record of Grover Cleveland, then in his first term,
Wilson found reinforcement for his central argument that, under existing
arrangements, the power of the Executive was dangerously weak. "A
clear-headed, methodical, unimaginative President like Mr. Cleveland
unaffectedly recognizes," Wilson wrote, "the fact that all creating, orig-
inating power rests with Congress." The President's suggestions were
routinely disregarded by Congress, a fact which he took as a matter of
course and did not "even stop to regret."⁶

As a result of the attention paid to *Congressional Government*, requests for articles, and soon for lectures, began to come in. It was a
mark of his growing prestige that the newly established *Political Science
Quarterly* invited Wilson to be a regular contributor. He was encouraged
by such recognition to plan two textbooks in political science—one
(which never matured) intended for grammar schools; the other (which

was to become a major work, *The State*) for advanced students. His
father was pleased by this practical turn in his interests. "Text-books
move the world," he wrote, "to say nothing of their *market-value*."[7]

An invitation from Charles Kendall Adams, president of Cornell University, resulted in one of Wilson's most significant scholarly achievements, a paper delivered in October 1886 entitled "The Study of
Administration." In defining the place of administration within the democratic state Wilson fused much of what he had learned at Johns Hopkins
with original views of his own. The role of administration, he argued,
had been effectively studied only in European countries, where it had
become associated with authoritarian governments. But there was a need
for a scientific approach geared to decentralization and responsive to
the needs and values of the democratic community.

The functions of government had once been simple, because life itself
was simple: "populations were of manageable numbers; property was
of simple sorts."[8] In such an environment the more or less casual interventions of the legislator were adequate for managing affairs. But in the
new order of things the haphazardness and inefficiency of legislation
needed to be supplemented by the continuous processes of administration. Only thus could government deal with an environment grown
complex in structure and multifarious in its needs. In this farsighted and
essentially liberal doctrine, this emphasis on energizing and enlivening
governmental processes, Wilson performed an act of creative scholarship, one that contributed alike to his professional standing and the
development of his political theory. The earlier treatise on the democratic
state had attempted to fathom the underlying, historically conditioned
nature of democracy; here he sketched a science for its management and
reform.

His name was now coming to the fore when openings occurred in the
academic community. Early in 1886 he was approached by Indiana
University about a chair in history. He was tempted, and again his father
encouraged him to consider the post. "Are you in truth . . . tethered
where you are?" he asked.[9] Wilson refused to carry the discussions into
a serious stage, convinced he was under obligation to Bryn Mawr. But
he had begun to chafe at his restricted sphere, and quite suddenly he
became convinced that the lack of a Ph.D. was harmful to his prospects.
With considerable urgency he wrote to Professor Adams at Johns Hopkins, asking whether he could not be granted his degree immediately,
perhaps as the result of a "special arrangement." Adams replied firmly
that a degree without an examination was out of the question, but,
indicating the high regard and affection in which Wilson was held,

promised that he and Professor Ely would conduct the examinations, oral and written. It would be done in a manner "at once considerate & just," and there was no chance of his "being plucked."[10]

Humbled, admitting himself to be "a nervous fellow who can't for the life of him pull in ordinary harness," Wilson began preparing frantically for the examinations. In June, after laborious days in Baltimore, the degree was awarded—"that petty title," Wilson characterized it, but he confessed to enormous satisfaction and relief at having attained it.[11]

In early 1886 the major question affecting Ellen and Woodrow in their private lives was where and in what circumstances the baby should be born. Ellen was having an uncomfortable pregnancy. In Philadelphia she lacked the circle of supportive relatives she instinctively required, while their rooms at the college were hardly appropriate for an accouchement. Wilson's mother felt that whatever the risks or inconveniences, the young couple should be together and in their own home. But after much discussion it was decided that Ellen would go south, to her native state of Georgia, where Louisa Hoyt Brown, sister of her deceased mother, was living in Gainesville.

Aunt Louisa was a picturesque and sturdy character. A rigid Presbyterian, a "tall, angular, unbelievably erect woman whose spine had never known the feel of the back of a chair,"[12] she managed a sizable plantation through the Civil War and then married a heavyset go-getter, a widower, Warren A. Brown, who already had several sons of his own and was soon making money in the manufacture of shoes. Herself homely, Louisa had watched her much younger sister, Ellen Axson's mother, grow into a mature woman of authentic beauty. When the sister married a handsome clergyman, Louisa seemed in her Puritan heart to develop romantic feelings toward him, and her first son was given his name, Edward.

After the death of Ellen's mother, Aunt Louisa was given charge of the surviving child, Madge, five years old. To this household, with its mixed emotions and ill-assorted personalities, Ellen went to wait for her baby's birth.

For the newly married couple it meant a separation of possibly many months. "It will be a cruel parting, but you both know how to *endure*," wrote Wilson's father; and from his mother: "Take courage. God loves you both, and will care for you."[13] Wilson went to Washington with Ellen in early April and placed her aboard the train to Gainesville. She arrived at her aunt's house in the evening, and that night, two or three weeks before expected, the baby was born. Dr. Wilson had spoken of the time when "that ship nears which bears the coming Prince."[14] The ship had arrived, almost disastrously early. It had borne a girl, who was christened Margaret Axson Wilson.

In the midst of his longing and uncertainty Wilson diverted himself as best he could. After leaving Ellen at the depot in Washington he attended sessions of the House of Representatives and of the Supreme Court. Shortly afterwards he made his first visit to Cambridge and Boston. As one who always felt himself a stranger in these northern outposts, he approached the famous scenes, and some of their well-known inhabitants, with considerable awe. "I feel that odd sort of excitement which I imagine the literary adventurers of Sam. Johnson's time used to feel upon reaching London," he wrote Ellen. "It gives one a queer sense of elation to be here."[15]

From his room at the State Hotel, where he was staying for three dollars a day, he sallied forth to the Athenaeum and to the Boston and Harvard libraries. At the latter he introduced himself to the librarian, the well-known historian Justin Winsor. Screwing up his courage he called on Gamaliel Bradford, who had written the highly favorable review of his book. He also called on Horace Scudder, at Houghton Mifflin, with whom he had corresponded. Scudder took him to see the famous author Thomas Bailey Aldrich. Mention was made of Lowell, his *Atlantic* adversary, and "on a sudden impulse" Wilson asked for an introduction. He found Lowell delightful, "a young lawyer of just my age." Many years later, Lowell recalled the visit. "A tall, lantern-jawed young man . . . greeted me with the words, 'I'm Woodrow Wilson. I've come to heal a quarrel, not to make one.' "[16] The two got on well. As presidents, respectively, of Harvard and Princeton, they would later be allied in educational reform.

The proprietors of Houghton Mifflin were still on the list of people to meet. Mr. Houghton turned their young author over to Mr. Mifflin, and the latter showed him through the plant. He must have enjoyed Wilson's company, for he invited him to dine with the family in Cambridge.

Back at Bryn Mawr, he had more than six weeks to go before he would see his wife and the baby. With what he called "desperate regularity" he pursued his correspondence with Ellen. "You would be charmed," he told her, "to see the devotion with which I brave all weathers to carry my letters to you and to the Post Office in season for [the] particular mail." If it was raining he put on rubber boots, rubber coat, and an old hat—a tall figure striding against the elements. Yet he still could not be sure that his letters would arrive on time. If not, he said, "I shall have to go down and strangle the postmaster."[17] In her southern retreat, and under the ministering gaze of her aunt, Ellen was meanwhile feeling the first joys of motherhood. In May, in "the sweet Sabbath peace, the warm sunshine, the cool soft breeze," she sat with the garden full of clove pinks and heartsease, and "the dear little one" asleep beside her. "I used to say she was a very good baby as babies go," she wrote in June, "but now I declare her a perfect cherub."[18]

As the end of the period of separation approached, the young husband found words increasingly inadequate to express his emotions. He looked forward to "that sweet love-making in which there are no words spoken at all." His joy would be full when he counted the last day, he told her; it would be altogether full when he could "count the last moment." Ellen declared she needed her old grandfather to preach her a sermon on calmness. "I will at least try not to let myself be *killed* by excess of love and joy."[19]

The two were reunited at Gainesville in June. The season was one of intense heat, and Ellen's small sister Madge remembered afterwards seeing her "uncle" Woodrow sitting at a table under an oak tree in the backyard garden, working endlessly at his papers. The proud parents took the baby Margaret to visit the grandparents at Clarksville. It would be the last time Woodrow saw his mother. In August he made another family pilgrimage, alone, to stay with his sister Marion and her four small children in Little Rock, Arkansas.

Wilson's scholarly works on the nature of government impressed him with the need to go abroad for an extended period of study. He wanted to see "the constitutions of the Continent *alive*," to observe European politics, and to master the essential languages. "As you know," he wrote Adams at Johns Hopkins, "what I 'go in for' is the *life*, not the texts, of constitutions."[20] Wilson had been wrestling in vain with the German language for two years and now from his friend Dabney came an alluring picture of the life of a wandering scholar. For a total of $450 per annum Dabney had been able to provide himself with a commodious room, ample food, and unlimited beer. Traveling to Switzerland and Italy he had, within the same strict budget, been well supplied with wine. Indeed, he went on, he had not swallowed "one single drop of water" while in those countries, and in Berlin and Heidelberg had "touched this fluid but seldom, save for ablutionary purposes."[21] More than by this enumeration of liquid refreshments available on so relatively scant an allowance, Wilson must have been impressed by the opportunities for study, as well as by Dabney's account of the number of plays and concerts he had been able to attend. In any case, Wilson's mind was soon firmly made up.

From Clarksville Wilson's father encouraged him to make the trip. He was himself discouraged with "ding-donging" theology into dull brains—"Surely," he wrote, "God *does* make use of the weak things to confound the mighty!"[22]—and he probably felt he would enjoy vicariously his son's adventures. Wilson hoped for some remuneration as a correspondent, but his father was ready to foot the bill for as much as two years of his son's *Wanderjahre*.

The family was all prepared to go, but the trip was canceled by the onset of Ellen's second pregnancy. Instead, he was driven back to his teaching, to his Bryn Mawr students, and to his scholarly work. Whatever his subsequent frustration, life at this time was pleasant enough at the college. Wilson was finding his students to be on the whole intelligent and willing. A session of the course was being devoted each week to a discussion of current political developments, and though voluntary, it was increasingly well attended. In his lectures Wilson established the rudiments of his later, highly effective teaching style—seemingly informal but carefully prepared, interspersed with humorous or imaginative passages. An essay on Adam Smith written at this time (based on a paper he had delivered three years earlier to a Johns Hopkins seminar) set forth his image of the good college teacher. The success of Adam Smith's lectures, he wrote (and he might have been writing of his own), "was not altogether a triumph of natural gifts; it was, in great part, a triumph of sedulously cultivated art." "He was no specialist except *in the relation of things*. . . . He took most of his materials at second hand. . . . But no matter who mined the gold, he coined it; the image and superscription are his."[23]

Just at the time when he was mastering the substance and method of his profession, Wilson allowed himself to be diverted into exasperating and futile byways. "Somehow there has come over me of late," he wrote Bridges, "a deep desire to do writing of a distinctly literary sort."[24] It was as if he could not tolerate being classified in any role or limited to the academic scene. If he could not see his way clear to a life in politics, at least he could reach out through other means for a wide public audience, to the great masses of readers who did not "wear spectacles." He was prepared, it seemed, to risk undermining one career in order to keep open the possibility of another.

Having shown he could write direct prose and lucid argument, he began writing short stories and mannered essays, all of which were rejected by publishers. His father sounded a refreshing note: "You have only to appear poorer in order to appear stronger," he wrote; and then, showing that when he wished he could handle words fancily, too, compared Woodrow to a "wealthy marketer": "your golden sentences touch at too many stalls, and fall too broadly upon the laughing pavements."[25] A tendency to jeopardize his reputation as a serious historian and political scientist by becoming "literary" would recur in Wilson's later academic career, again with disconcerting results.

After the final examinations in 1887 the Wilsons left for Gainesville, staying at a boardinghouse and then at the Piedmont Hotel, run by General James Longstreet of Civil War fame, and his wife. Ellen was close to her aunt Louisa as she went through the last stages of her pregnancy, and on August 28 a second daughter, christened Jessie Woodrow Wilson, was born. With the two children, earlier living arrangements at Bryn Mawr were no longer feasible, and the family rented a large house a few blocks from the campus, on Gulph Street, formerly the Baptist parsonage. "Dear child," wrote Wilson's mother, "whatever can you want with *eleven* rooms!"[26] But Ellen and Woodrow were ready to take on a role they would continue throughout their married life, providing hospitality for friends and members of the family, and indeed giving several of the latter the only permanent home they knew.

The first recruit to the new household was Ellen's cousin, Mary Eloise Hoyt, whose long, dreamy letters to Ellen show her to have been a young woman of imagination and humor.[27] Working as a teacher in Athens, Georgia, she ruefully calculated that at her rate of savings she would be seventy-five years old before she could afford to attend college. Woodrow and Ellen invited her to live with them and made possible her education at Bryn Mawr. Not long afterward, the young couple were visited by other members of the family: Ellen's brothers, Stockton and Eddie; Woodrow's father; and his brother, Josie.

Relations with his father were undergoing a significant change. The son had begun to make a name for himself in the teaching profession, which Dr. Wilson had claimed for his own, and in which he had hoped to achieve a fitting climax to his career. In this he was to be greatly disappointed. He kept his position in the Southern Presbyterian Church. He preached occasionally. But the prestige he commanded as head of a large congregation slipped away when he left Wilmington. Southwestern University at Clarksville was not a favorable ground for his kind of learned instruction. The number of his students dwindled. The enrollment of the college, moreover, suffered from the reopening of the seminary at Columbia, South Carolina, which now drained students from the western outpost at Clarksville.

As a preacher Joseph Wilson dazzled his congregations; as a wit and savant he acquired fame in Presbyterian circles. His reputation as a scholar, however, was limited by the fact that he published very little. When at the age of thirty-one Woodrow received his first honorary degree from Wake Forest College in North Carolina, Dr. Wilson expressed congratulations. "Wear it long, my darling, and wear it shiningly,"[28] he wrote; yet, claiming to be the only professor of theology in the country, he felt a pang at not being himself the recipient of such an honor.

He realized now that Woodrow was surpassing him in skills and in accomplishments: "You with your powers all in their spring-time," he saluted his son, "and possessing a truer perspicacity than that with which I was ever gifted! You are assuredly my second edition, 'revised and improved,' as to contents, and with a far superior letter-press and binding." He blessed God that it was even so, adding that "no law of His forbids the pride of your father in his larger son."[29]

Difficult as it may have been for the father to acknowledge being passed by, for Woodrow the change in their relative positions was but one further step in an emancipation long under way. If as a child he had found his father a formidable presence, he had long since outgrown any sense of being dominated. At the start of his professional career Woodrow still counted heavily on advice from his father; he accepted intermittent but generous financial aid. In the White House in after years he would frequently cite his father as having been the most important influence in his life. But he moved freely, in his own chosen way, while the father, often lonely, often depressed or in ill health, accepted his fate with good grace touched faintly with melancholy. Increasingly he found his own fulfillment in Woodrow's growing success. Amid "complex patterns of emulation and concession"[30] the two played out their parts in style.

At the same time Ellen was taking on with assurance her role as head of her orphaned family. Her brother Stockton was continuing his education in southern schools and spending summers with near relatives, but he was a frequent visitor at the Wilson home on Gulph Street and would later become a constant avuncular presence for the Wilson daughters, and a friend and confidant of Woodrow's. For Ellen in the coming years he would become almost another child as she watched over him during the recurrent spells of depression endemic in the Axson family.

The young sister Madge still lived with her aunt Louisa in Gainesville, but Eddie Axson's lot was the most serious. The small child had moved from one relative to another, in one household feeling clearly rejected, and he had developed a distressing stammer. On his arrival at Gainesville for a visit, Ellen found him in rags—"and as for buttons, he has forgotten what they look like, poor little fellow!" It was time for him to have a permanent home. "And of course," Ellen declared, "that home would naturally and properly be with me."[31] Over the next years Eddie became almost the son she and Woodrow never had, and in 1905 would be part of a tragedy that left incurable wounds upon Ellen's psyche.

Jessie Wilson had suffered a fall in her Clarksville house in November 1886, and her health was thereafter increasingly poor. Josie, still living at home, wrote of her worsening condition, news the father could not bear to convey. In April two years later, a telegram came from Josie announcing that his mother had died suddenly. Woodrow immediately took the train for Clarksville, where he found only an empty house and a message that his father and brother had taken the body to Columbia for burial. It was too late for him to follow. For two days, alone in the local hotel, he waited for their return.

Nothing quite explains this harrowing mischance, but one may see in the hurried departure of Dr. Wilson and Josie the expression of emotions previously concealed. Woodrow had been his mother's favorite in every sense, to the point where the younger son, and even the husband, could well have felt excluded from her love. Jessie's letters to Woodrow had been particularly intimate, and not seldom there appear, among the extreme terms of endearment, subtle criticisms of the father. Journeying on the forlorn mission to Columbia, while Woodrow was left to experience the anguish of bereavement alone, those two may indeed have felt a sort of grim, if unconscious, satisfaction at having Jessie at last to themselves.

In this crisis of loss, Woodrow did not conceal from himself or from his wife the degree to which as a child he had been dependent on his mother. He had clung to her apron strings, he confessed; he had been known as "a mama's boy."[32] That she had been an important force in her son's development is plain. Withdrawn but strong, lacking humor but with an encompassing love, she had not only protected him from many of the shocks to which youth is subject, but had left a permanent ideal of womanhood. In his wife he sought and found many of his mother's qualities, her delicacy of sentiment, her unquestioning loyalty. But in Ellen these virtues were edged by wayward humor and by a stubbornly preserved individuality. Even as Wilson mourned his mother he was aware of having shed the maternal influence—or rather of having discovered in Ellen a feminine influence of even greater force. "The life—the home—of my youth is cut off," he wrote her, "and now it is you and me, my sweet one."[33] Whatever his personal grief, he was emotionally prepared for Jessie Wilson's passing.

Dr. Wilson, on the other hand, was left footloose. He stayed on for a while with Josie in the echoing Clarksville home, sold it, and moved to a boardinghouse, then to a hotel. In 1888, in ill health, he resigned his professorship and began years of wandering from city to city. Often preaching as a relief clergyman, he became involved with at least two different women. His final stay would be with Woodrow and Ellen, at Prospect, the official home of Princeton's presidents.

For Josie, then twenty-one but distressingly immature, his mother's death came when he was still much in need of her. He struggled on painfully with his lessons, at once a comfort and cause of concern to his father, and worked on the local newspaper at Clarksville, where his expectations constantly outshone his successes. With his thwarted affections and unfulfilled hopes, he remained a pathetic figure in later years, moving in the shadow of his increasingly famous brother.

By Wilson's third year at Bryn Mawr, discontents had piled up and he was overtaken by a general sense of malaise. Escapes through an extended trip abroad, or through a flight into the stratosphere of belles lettres, had failed to materialize. He was questioning whether he could combine writing with teaching; he was working too hard, and he was feeling a growing hunger to teach men rather than women. It was not that his students at Bryn Mawr were too aggressive—with the exception of three rather stiff graduate students, little of Dean Thomas's fervor seemed to have reached them. Rather it was that they were too docile. He noted a "painful *absenteeism* of mind" in his classrooms. "Passing through a vacuum," he confided to a private journal, "your speech generates no heat." He added, it should be noted, that perhaps some of the trouble was due to "undergraduateism, not all to femininity."[34] In any case, after two years at Bryn Mawr, Wilson was ready—more than that, he was desperate—to find another post.

An invitation to deliver a six-week course of lectures at Johns Hopkins came as a partial release. Rumor spread of a full-time appointment. At the same time Wilson received a serious approach from the University of Michigan and even put his faithful friend, Renick of Atlanta days, to work pushing his name for a vacancy in the State Department. In all these efforts he was in an awkward situation in regard to his commitment to Bryn Mawr.

In March 1887 Wilson had signed an agreement with the college binding him to three years of employment.[35] The extent to which this contract was binding upon Wilson was a question upon which he and the Bryn Mawr trustees came to hold sharply opposed views. The matter was brought to a head when in early June he received from Wesleyan University in Middletown, Connecticut, the offer of a professorship in history and political science. Wilson might not have been anxious to accept. Was it really a promotion? his father queried; and his uncle James Woodrow, seeing him approached by a Methodist college, remarked that it "sounds queer that any one of the blood should be connected in any way with *Wesleyanism.*"[36] But Wilson was by now absolutely determined to move on and would probably have accepted an offer even less tempting than that of Wesleyan.

In the sharp dispute that arose, all agreed that Wilson had accepted the contract with the provision that an assistant in his department be hired by the college "as soon as practicable," the word "practicable" referring expressly to financial and budgetary considerations. In the summer of 1887 Wilson was informed that the college was prepared to meet the expense of the new appointment. He thereupon proposed the name of one whom he judged to be a suitable candidate, but the board refused to act, on the grounds, among others, that the "expense seemed, on final consideration, an unwarrantable one." Wilson thereupon judged the contract to be void and himself free to accept such a post as might be offered him. Six months later, in a conversation with President Rhoads, he first spoke of his attitude in regard to the contract. Rhoads differed sharply and there the matter was left.[37]

When Wilson informed the board of the Wesleyan negotiations, he asked that in formally consenting to his leaving they recognize the contract to have been terminated. This the board refused to do. Accepting grudgingly the fact of his departure, they stood by their view of Wilson's legal obligations. The ensuing controversy raged at Bryn Mawr for many years. On the basis of the documents it is difficult to understand how the college could have failed to recognize that it had seriously breached the agreement. On the other hand Wilson was not candid with President Rhoads and the board of trustees. He appears for an extended period to have supposed he could continue with the security offered by the contract and at the same time feel free to leave when he found it opportune to do so. He was certainly at fault in telling Rhoads only in the spring of 1888 that he considered the contract void.

The real trouble lay in the attitude of the Bryn Mawr administration toward a young teacher whose abilities and obvious ambition marked him for greater distinction. President Rhoads characterized the affair strictly as "the exercise of judgment in a question of business."[38] It was not, however, a question of business alone. It was a question of life and destiny. To attempt to bind professors to employment was a dubious policy, and was so recognized by the college when a few years later it abandoned the practice. A man like Wilson could not but chafe under the restraint, and an underlying bitterness toward the authorities, understandable if not wholly justifiable, is evident in comments made in private correspondence.

President Rhoads, in a final letter, was generous enough to say that he believed Wilson was acting "in accordance with [his] convictions of right" and to add expressions of his warm regard and confidence in the young man's future.[39] An elder of Bryn Mawr's Presbyterian church wrote "regretting [his] departure," as he noted that Wilson's pew rent would not be renewed. There were otherwise no official farewells. To the college where, as he told the board, he had done his first teaching "with so much both of profit and of enjoyment,"[40] he returned only once, alone at vacation time, passing through Bryn Mawr on his way to Johns Hopkins. He had little to say of his visit, except to remark that he approved of his successor.

"A VIVID MIND"

Wilson next turns up in Middletown, Connecticut, settled with his family in a large house—he always liked large houses—at the edge of the Wesleyan campus. They had stayed on at the Gulph Street parsonage with various relatives coming to visit them, and then gone for a few days to New York City and Long Island. In the new home, in addition to the daughters and two servants, there was room for visits from Ellen's two brothers as well as other relatives and friends. Wilson felt himself quickly to be at home, surprised that he should find such warmth among New Englanders. The college grounds were pleasant, the methods of instruction advanced, and the faculty and trustees Wilson judged to be "liberal and progressive" men.[1]

As a teacher at Wesleyan Wilson exceeded the popularity he had first tasted at Bryn Mawr. "He had a contagious interest—his eyes flashed," one student remembered years later. "I can see him now, with his hands forward, the tips of his fingers just touching the table, his face earnest and animated." "He talked to us," said another, "in the most informal, jolly way, yet with absolute clearness and sureness." Phrases he used stuck in the minds of his students. Of one of England's kings, he remarked that, when he came to the age of discretion, it was found that he had none. Or again: "Business is business, which is just another way of saying that it is not Christianity." The college newspaper reported as a news item his comment in class upon the number of students who had indicated being unprepared for a recitation: "Gentlemen," said the professor, "I had hoped you might emulate your Saxon forefathers, who thought it not creditable to be unprepared for anything."[2]

For the first time since his undergraduate years at Princeton Wilson felt himself to be part of a community that encouraged and sustained him, where he was appreciated and thoroughly at home. At the University of Virginia and at Johns Hopkins he had had his circle of friends; at Bryn Mawr he had been absorbed within his own close family. But Middletown provided a larger social environment, congenial and supportive, with men and women of different ages and interests contributing to his growing self-confidence.

It did not take him long to become involved in activities outside his classrooms. He was responsible for organizing a Wesleyan House of Commons, a society closely following the procedures of the British Parliament. For a few seasons this was a center of undergraduate life, outstripping the social clubs in popularity. Unfortunately, the students displayed so much zeal, overturning governments on the least pretense, that the house was ultimately brought into disrepute. Wilson's place in Wesleyan football history was also established. At the start of the 1889 season the college suffered a disastrous series of defeats. He became part of a two-man advisory board, holding coaching sessions in his recitation room, attending practice, and even traveling to a few out-of-town games. The season's early defeats gave way to a series of widely hailed victories.

Of his new friendships, several were to prove long-lasting. The minister of the Congregational church, Azel Washburn Hazen, continued on terms of comradeship with Wilson to the end of his life. Caleb Thomas Winchester, professor of English, who edited Chaucerian texts with the great Harvard scholar George Lyman Kittredge, was a man after Wilson's heart, salty and with the breath of life. Outside the college, the historian John Franklin Jameson, then at Brown University, proved a whimsical correspondent and a delightful visitor. "Talked till midnight," he noted after one visit to the Wilson home, "and had a right good time of it."[3] In a letter of thanks to his host he prayed to be commended to the infant daughters of the household: to "the one with the oval face"

—Jessie, who would always be the beauty of the family; and to the "one with the spherical body"—unmistakably Margaret.

For Ellen, however, nothing at this time seemed to go easily. A third pregnancy brought on physical symptoms particularly harsh. She was haunted by the knowledge that her mother had died after childbirth and the remembrance of her father's decline; at the same time in pitiful dreams she saw herself at last presenting a son to Woodrow. As the months advanced her normally cheerful spirits gave way to an ominous mood of depression. To Woodrow, lecturing at Johns Hopkins, she wrote pathetically, "Oh my darling, what a poor weak creature you are tied to! . . . When I look back over my married life I am oppressed with a sense of failure so great that it seems to me my heart must break. . . . What *has* happened to me? What curse has fallen on me?"[4] Woodrow made a hurried trip north, and after that the depression seemed to lift.

The child, born in October 1889, was a third girl, christened Eleanor Randolph Wilson. Even then Ellen's troubles were not over. The following winter, with the whole family to take care of, she suffered an accident in the kitchen, dropping scalding oil on her feet as she gave instructions to a new cook. Burned painfully, she was unable to walk for three months. Woodrow added baby-sitting to his other chores.

Retreating when he could into his book-lined study, the distractions of the household held precariously at bay, he faced a heavy workload. Besides his scholarly writings and his course lectures, he was soon being asked to deliver talks and addresses outside the college and to write articles for current journals. Fortunately he was no longer facing what he called "an empty barrel," compelled as a novice teacher to compose his regular lectures from day to day. He was served by his meticulously inscribed lecture notes carried over from Bryn Mawr. These lectures supplied chapters for the textbook he was writing, as his ongoing research for this volume provided material for new lectures. The substance of articles and addresses came from earlier drafts of incompleted studies or from manuscripts previously rejected by publishers. In part because he was so prodigious a worker, Wilson set a high store on his literary output. He was not reluctant to convert an essay into an oration or to repeat an address when the occasion permitted.

The writing task engaging him most arduously was a textbook on comparative government. Modestly conceived, the book did not pretend to originality. Wilson based the earlier chapters on his Bryn Mawr lectures on classical civilizations, and his analysis of contemporary European governments largely on a series of currently published German

Bryn Mawr College, about 1885, its opening year

Carey Thomas, the dean

Wilson as a young Princeton professor

The house at Library Place, Princeton, in 1902

Jessie and Margaret

Eleanor

A Princeton snapshot in the early 1890s

Francis Landey Patton, president of Princeto

Frederick Jackson Turner, scholar, whom Wil
tried to bring to Princeton

reference books. The writing was toilsome, the more so because he always had difficulty with foreign languages. Work carried over from Middletown to his winter visits to Johns Hopkins, and out of term-time into vacations. "Catch me undertaking another fact book!" he wrote Ellen from Baltimore. In the future he meant to be an "author," never again a mere "book-maker."[5] Entitled *The State*, the work was published in September 1890.

Coming after *Congressional Government* it established Wilson as a political scientist. In synthesizing German scholarship on comparative government, presenting a large body of knowledge in compact, lucid form, he created a textbook translated into French, Spanish, German, Japanese; it was widely used in university courses until the 1920s. Despite its analytical approach, the book gave its author an opportunity to clarify his own approach to politics.

Wilson was still searching for a position on the political spectrum consistent with a conservatism rooted in his organic interpretation of institutions—the belief that they grew out of customs and traditions and were shaped by historic forces—and his instinctive drive to act. In an address in Middletown on the centennial of Washington's inauguration as President, he reaffirmed the organic view of society. Unlike physics, he argued, politics provides few individual discoveries, few theoretical breakthroughs to a new order. "Society grows as a whole," he said, "and as a whole grows into knowledge of itself."[6] Yet the importance of political action was not to be excluded; and in the concluding chapter of *The State* he made his case fully, even daringly, explicit.

Politics, he argued there, was not to be thought devoid of meaning; government should not be deemed a necessary evil. In advocating the use of governmental power to allay social ills and to advance society's welfare, he verged upon a defense of socialism. If the name had not been restricted to "a single . . . radically mistaken class of thinkers," he wrote, "we ought all to regard ourselves and to act as *socialists*, believers in the wholesomeness and beneficence of the body politic."[7] Wilson upheld the intervention of the state in such broad fields as equalizing opportunity, prohibiting child labor, regulating the work of women, and protecting the consumer. He justified governmental takeover of natural monopolies, including water systems and railways.

Though *The State* was later revised, its author never changed these passages. They contained his fundamental beliefs, notwithstanding swings to conservatism amid the social turbulence of the 1890s; they provided the foundation for his liberalism on entering politics and for the reform programs of the later New Freedom. But Wilson was not content with laying out the field of action. He was prepared to define the political leadership that was necessary to render action effective.

The opportunity came with the invitation to make his first commencement address, in June 1890, at the University of Tennessee in Knoxville. The address, "Leaders of Men," took an hour and a half to read, but it did not daunt the audience of that day.[8] Indeed, according to the local newspaper, it was listened to with close attention throughout. What Wilson said not only put a coping stone on his various political writings, but was to an extraordinary degree self-revealing. Earlier, in biographical essays, he had made clear his relish for action on a grand scale. In more sophisticated studies of institutions he had made place for the free exercise of power. Now in the address on leadership his ambitions stood forth undisguised.

The young professor asked of the leader qualities unexpectedly harsh, inconsistent with his own genial and generally accommodating disposition, yet in keeping with what the world later saw of Woodrow Wilson at Princeton and on the world scene. The leader, he declared, cares little for the "interior niceties" of other people's characters; he cares much —everything—"for the external uses to which they may be put." He sees the mass of men as waiting to be moved. How shall he move them? "He supplies the power; others supply only the materials upon which that power operates."

This Wilson was a realist; not for him the fine points of policy or ethics. "If you would be a leader of men, you must lead your own generation, not the next. Your playing must be good *now*, while the play is on the boards and the audience in the seats; it will not get you the repute of a great actor to have excellencies discovered in you afterwards." In capturing the audience, moreover, leaders of men must be direct and simple. "The motives which they urge are elemental, the morality which they seek to enforce is large and obvious, the policy they emphasize purged of all subtlety."

The leader was thus a man of his time; and yet not of it wholly—as there was always about the later Wilson something not contained within the normal limits of politics. At rare moments the leader must step boldly beyond the habitual boundaries. "One of the great influences which we call a *Cause* arises in the midst of a nation. Men of strenuous minds and high ideals come forward . . . as champions of a political or moral principle." The attacks which such men provoke, declared Wilson with uncanny prescience, are "more cruel than the collision of arms." Friends desert and despise them. They stand alone and often are made bitter by their isolation. "They are doing nothing less than defying public opinion, and shall they convert it by blows? Yes."

Although Wilson delivered the address on various occasions afterwards, it was not included in any of his collected essays or printed in full in his lifetime. He perhaps considered it too personal, too candid, to be subjected to the scrutiny of a wide public. Well he might; for the later Wilson is clearly sketched—both the skill in appealing to the mood of the moment, and the almost brutal disregard of opinion when a "Cause" seemed to be at stake. Apart from its personal significance, the paper is a trenchant exposition of leadership in modern mass democracies.

In the spring of 1889 Wilson was confronted by a more immediate question, testing the scope and direction of his scholarly research. Albert Bushnell Hart, editing in Cambridge an historical series on various American epochs, invited him to contribute a volume on the middle period, covering the years from Jackson through Reconstruction. Wilson was trained as an historian, and history had been a major field of his teaching; but his published work up to that time had been in the field of political science. It was a question of whether he wanted to alter the focus. Besides, as a southerner by birth and upbringing he would find his objectivity challenged.

Wilson's father foresaw the danger of controversy. "What will you say, I wonder, as touching the causes that made our prodigious war inevitable?"[9] Ellen, who had difficulties in transcending her own southern background, and suffered a good deal from what she called her "relapses," assured her husband that he was not a southerner—at least in the old sense; though adding that he was the region's "*greatest* son in this generation and also the one who will have greatest claim on her gratitude."[10] As for Wilson himself, he knew he had outgrown whatever regional prejudices he might once have formed, and he decided to accept Professor Hart's offer. The result was *Division and Reunion*, which was to be published in 1893 and widely recognized as an outstanding contribution to American historical writing.

At the end of 1889 the Wesleyan trustees announced the largest donation ever received by the college, given wholly without conditions. The creation of a chair for Wilson was widely discussed, and it seemed certain he could have it on his own terms. But in the back of his mind other possibilities had long been taking form. While still at Bryn Mawr he had written a paper entitled "Of the Study of Politics," published in the *New*

Princeton Review.[11] It was essentially a plea for the kind of chair Wilson hoped one day to see established at Princeton, with himself as occupant. He set forth his vision of politics as a subject, not of cloistered study alone, but of life and practice. "We are inclined, oftentimes, to take laws and constitutions too seriously," he wrote; "we ought to go in person or in imagination amongst the people whom they command, and see for ourselves whether those people enjoy liberty." The "man of the world" should be merged with the "man of books."

Unhappily he proved something less than a "man of the world" in setting forth these views, for the original version of the paper was delivered as an address before Princeton alumni (during the first of innumerable appearances by Wilson before such gatherings): it bored its slightly inebriated audience, being too long and serious, and as an after-dinner speech was a disaster. But some in Princeton read it as a signal —and a prophecy. After his successes at Wesleyan, Wilson was ready to take a further step. With Bridges as manager, he launched a quiet campaign for a Princeton appointment, supported by four men of his class who would all become trustees and powerful supporters: Cleveland Hoadley Dodge, Cyrus Hall McCormick, Jr., Cornelius Cuyler Cuyler, and Edward William Sheldon.

In mid-summer 1889, Wilson lunched in New York with Francis Landey Patton, the president recently elected as McCosh's successor. Patton suggested Wilson's taking over immediately a chair in economics vacated by the death of the incumbent. Wilson demurred. The authorities at Wesleyan, he told Patton, had been too generous to be left suddenly in the lurch; besides, another year at Middletown would enable him to put a lasting stamp on his department. What he wanted above all was a chair in public law, and he was prepared to play for time. His father backed him in this course. "Your courage in resisting the temptation to accept a position at Princeton at once I greatly prize,"[12] he wrote. But the faithful Bridges was disappointed. He saw his friend missing a chance to throw in his lot with the "new Princeton."[13]

The promised land having been glimpsed, however, Wilson was not really anxious to delay his entry; and Patton, although he was not a man of prompt or decisive action, knew a good thing when he saw it. Within the largely sectarian board of trustees, however, doubts about Wilson were developing. The conservative element was critical because in *The State* he had minimized the "supernatural" element; there was too strong an emphasis on the Darwinian theory of evolution, and on Roman law rather than Christianity as the formative impulse of society.[14] Others complained that the cast of his thought was too British, or that he would be too deep for students to appreciate. The vote of the board was postponed from November to the February meeting, as Patton worked to allay opposition.

Wilson, his desires aroused, was made uneasy by the delay. He would not hesitate, he told Bridges, "to say anything not undignified that would secure me [the] election."[15] He was even prepared to abandon his reluctance to teach economics. But in February, on the thirteenth of that month (Wilson always considered thirteen his lucky number), he was elected to the Chair of Jurisprudence and Political Economy, at a salary of $3,000. The telegram bearing the news was signed by a progressive young trustee, Moses Taylor Pyne, who later would become Wilson's chief antagonist on the Princeton board. Wilson thought the salary inadequate and fretted over the two-year delay before "economy" would be dropped from his title. But Patton encouraged him—"You may count upon me always as your advocate & friend,"[16] he wrote, assuring Wilson he need give himself "no great anxiety" about the future. By March Wilson told his friends at Wesleyan, now putting strong pressure on him to remain, that he had committed himself to Princeton.

The election, when known, brought rejoicing within the Princeton family. Congratulations poured in, particularly from Wilson's classmates of the Class of '79. From McCosh, now in retirement, came a message that must have been particularly heartwarming. McCosh expressed his pleasure that the trustees were bringing Wilson back to his old college: "You will receive a welcome here and will have a wide field of usefulness. You will enter in and possess it."[17] Everyone, Wilson wrote his father, seemed to consider the Princeton election "a sort of crowning success."[18]

At Wesleyan, where it had been realized that their young star was to flash only briefly across its sky, there was inevitable disappointment. But Wilson's departure was very different from the official silence and coldness that had marked his exit from Bryn Mawr. "His work has been an inspiration to the students who have sat under his instruction," declared the campus *Argus* in one of many tributes.[19] He, also, had gained much. At Wesleyan he had come slowly, he wrote, "into such powers as I have." And those powers, he now knew, were of a precise kind. "I *receive* the opinions of my day," he noted in a journal at the end of 1889; "I do not *conceive* them. But I receive them into a vivid mind."[20] The accomplishments of the years ahead, at Princeton and later on the national stage, were chiefly gained as this "vivid mind" took in, assimilated, altered, and gave back the intellectual and political ferment of the time.

To have learned so much about himself and about the world was not a negligible accomplishment for a scholar of thirty-four, on his way to triumphs as well as bitter defeats.

IN ARCADIA

In the fall of 1890 Wilson arrived at Princeton as one coming into his own. He was awaited with anticipation, and caused a sensation when 124 out of the 238 juniors and seniors signed up for his elective course in public law. The faculty and trustees came quickly to regard him as one of Princeton's important assets. When during his first year Columbia's president Seth Low began casting eyes upon him, Patton reacted angrily. "I fought for him against apathy in the Faculty & opposition in the Trustees," he declared with some justice. "I am proud of him. He is a brilliant & unqualified success."[1] The new arrival could only be filled with self-confidence in such an atmosphere. "I feel here in my teaching like a man feeling the bit of a spirited horse," he wrote a friend, "capable of any speed and with wind for any race."[2]

The family rented a house (again a large one) on Stedman Street, later renamed Library Place. Here Wilson began working with his usual intense self-discipline. His chair permitted him to concentrate on subjects within his main field of interest: public law and jurisprudence, American constitutional and international law, and administration. To lectures on these subjects he devoted hardly less care than to his published writings. The course on jurisprudence, which he taught for the first time in 1891, he would continue through the distractions and controversies of his years as university president. It would always be largely attended, considered by generations of students one of the top rewards of a Princeton education.

For the next seven years, moreover, he continued his annual six-week course on administration at Johns Hopkins. He had persuaded the trustees of Bryn Mawr and Wesleyan, as he now persuaded the Princeton board, to give him the required leaves of absence. Before advanced students at "the Hopkins" he taught administration, with particular emphasis on urban and local government, subjects that might have been considered technical and "dry" and which Wilson treated, indeed, with no concession to popular appeal. Yet his lucidity and command of his subject made him a sought-after teacher. In his first year at Princeton he took his family with him to Baltimore; but usually he was alone, painfully cut off from Ellen and the children, working frantically on upcoming lectures. The students remembered him as a striking presence.

"Dr. Wilson is here. Homely, solemn, young, glum, but with that fire in his face and eye that means that its possessor is not of the common crowd."[3] So the future historian Frederick Jackson Turner, writing to his fiancée, described Wilson in the winter of 1890. In succeeding years the students recalled his sharing jokes with them and sitting up late to talk shop in the boardinghouse on McCullough Street.

Putting aside preparation for his courses, he worked during the summers of 1891 and 1892 on the manuscript of *Division and Reunion*. As if this were not enough, he was soon sniffing the air for outside engagements. His friend Winchester at Wesleyan warned him that as a public lecturer he would be in competition with "the itinerant funny man"[4] and facing audiences that "only want to be tickled." But Wilson, ever in need of supplementary income, was prepared for the worst, and soon became a familiar figure on the popular circuit and as a teacher of university extension courses.

The early Princeton years brought important changes in the Wilson family. In the last spring at Wesleyan his brother-in-law, Ross Kennedy, died after a long and painful struggle with tuberculosis. A few months later came news of the death of his widow, Marion, Wilson's older and much-loved sister. The couple left four children orphaned and virtually penniless. Nor was this to be the end of bereavements. In 1895, in Columbia, George Howe, Jr., the family physician and husband of Woodrow's younger sister, Annie, died suddenly, leaving a widow and a young daughter in need of attention and care. During the same period members of Ellen's family—her brothers Stockton and Edward, and soon the much younger sister Madge—began looking to the Wilson household as the one stable point in their homeless lives. Ellen and Woodrow accepted cheerfully their role as heads of an extended family, even though it put heavy strains on their financial resources.

Wilson's father, having resigned from his professorship at Clarksville, moved to New York to live with a reformer and publisher of religious tracts, Elizabeth Bartlett Grannis. He found the environment attractive, he wrote, particularly in view of "the loving ministries of its amiable head."[5] The rest of the family had their doubts, and Woodrow declared Mrs. Grannis to be "about as undesirable a companion as one could find in the ranks of chaste women."[6] Thereafter for many years Dr. Wilson lived a peripatetic existence, a frequent visitor at Library Place, considering and discarding various plans to settle in one city or another. "Perhaps his restlessness," Ellen wrote, "demands several homes."[7]

There would be moments of triumph for the deposed old monarch, as when he returned for an anniversary visit to Wilmington and found, somewhat to his surprise, that he was much loved by his former congregation. But his wit became increasingly touched by malice; his search for affection, by plaintiveness. With advancing years his attention narrowed upon his favorite son, to the annoyance of other members of the family. "A poor old stick," he described himself, apologizing for the "mist of bad humour"[8] that had crept into one of his increasingly somber letters.

Ellen was happy in Princeton. A decision to have no more children allowed her to devote herself to creating a warm family circle within which her three daughters could grow and learn and her adored Woodrow could work creatively. Life there was still simple, a village existence composed almost entirely of members of the college and the theological seminary, along with the local tradespeople. Faculty members lived on $2,500 to $3,500 a year—handsome salaries in those days when a workman, if he was lucky, made $350—and were secure and well off. Food was cheap, and servants were readily available. Entertainments took the form of tea parties in faculty homes, with occasional guests for dinner. Trips to New York or Philadelphia were infrequent, mostly spring or autumn visits for family shopping or for plays and concerts. Ellen was more at home in this comfortable setting than she would be half a decade later, when Princeton became a nascent suburban community with a sudden influx of wealth.

In March 1892, two years after their arrival in Princeton, Ellen set off with the children on a first trip without her husband. She felt removed from southern friends and relatives, and she was eager, in her proud and spirited way, to show off the little family she had produced. The house on Stedman Street was closed; Woodrow moved into hotel rooms, and the couple faced a separation of two months. For both of them the test was important. Ellen renewed her latent sense of independence and adventure, showing that she could flourish on her own. Woodrow learned—if he had not known it already—that he counted for stability and peace of mind on the near presence of his wife.

He was working with something close to desperation to keep up with his Princeton classes; in addition, he had promised to teach a course in the recently established New York Law School. Deprived of familiar surroundings and the supportive environment Ellen provided, he passed through a particularly difficult period. Traveling weekly to New York, he found that the results of haste and inadequate preparation were showing in his lectures. At the same time the sexual deprivation resulting from Ellen's absence drove him to the extremes of physical desire. His letters speak with striking candor of the temptations he found himself undergoing, to the point of almost appearing to taunt her. After delivering one of his lectures, he dared not stay overnight in New York, he told her; he trembled at the thought of what he might do, given "the imperious passions" by which he was driven. At least at Princeton he "*must* keep out of mischief." If he was unfaithful in thought, he added, it meant "not one wit of real infidelity to you—[it] is anatomical and not of the heart."⁹

Ellen refused to get excited by these confessions. It was characteristic of her to deflate Woodrow's emotionalism. "I am very sorry you did *not* stay in New York," she replied. "I am *perfectly sure*, dear, that nothing dreadful would have happened." Yet Ellen appears, at least at this time, to have been responding fully to her husband's strong sexual drive. The correspondence is full of references to the mutuality of their relationship. "*Love's Playmate*," he described her, "led on to all the sweet abandonments and utter intimacies of love."¹⁰

On her sentimental journey through the South, meanwhile, Ellen was revisiting the manse in Savannah where her grandparents had lived. She saw once more the room where she had stayed after her father's death, the parlor where she was married. Crossing the state to Rome, she was much entertained and feted by friends and kinfolk who found her "prettier than ever."¹¹ Thoughts of her father were much on her mind, and she framed an inscription (with suggestions from Woodrow) which was carved in granite over Edward Axson's grave. She sat again in the church where Woodrow had first glimpsed her, walked the pathways of East Rome, rested alone upon a certain "great rock" where their mutual feelings had been first tentatively expressed. "How vividly those dear old days came back to me," she wrote. "The strangeness, the wonder, the doubtful delights of that time, seemed suddenly made real again, and were brought into sharp, sweet contrast with the happy present. . . . Ah dearest love, what a difference between the old and the new,—how sweet was that—how infinitely sweeter this!"¹²

At Gainesville Ellen stayed with her aunt Louisa and finished the tour by visiting Woodrow's sister Annie in Columbia. Her own younger sister Madge, living in Gainesville, was growing into a young girl of unconventional beauty and lively disposition. Ellen immediately formed the desire to take the child north, to make a home for her and to guide her education. She thought she had never seen a more interesting girl or one of more unusual mental promise. But she was dismayed to find Madge slipping into bad grammar, with "all the dreadful Gainesville peculiarities of speech."[13] Her aunt looked so brokenhearted when Ellen proposed that Madge come north that she desisted for the time being. A few years later, however, Madge did make her home with the Wilsons in Princeton and lived with them on and off until her marriage—a breezy and attractive but always slightly abrasive presence.

As a child Madge kept her own counsel, but later she recalled what had seemed to her the comical and faintly threatening appearance of her three small nieces in Gainesville that summer. Unlike herself, they were dressed immaculately in stiff dresses. They walked in perfect order down the town's dusty streets, accompanied by their "colored" nurse.

In that same month of April 1892, as he left his class in Princeton, Wilson was approached by a stranger introducing himself as a trustee of the University of Illinois at Urbana. He had come east to discuss the possibility of Wilson's accepting its presidency. In the circumstances this was a surprising development. Only thirty-seven years of age, Wilson had had no administrative experience, and had only recently been anxiously on the market for a teaching post. He could certainly consider the offer of a presidency as a feather in his cap. This was to be the first of many such offers before he was named president of Princeton in 1902, but with one exception, to be noted later, none was so seriously considered as this approach from Illinois.

The offer caught him at a time when he was restless, when his desire for a life of action was competing with his literary ambitions, and not least, when he thought he needed money. Illinois offered him $6,000 a year, double what he was getting at Princeton, along with secretarial help and the assistance of a competent business manager.

Wilson conferred with Bridges, wrote to his uncle James Woodrow, and talked with members of the Princeton board. He found that he had, as he wrote Ellen, "stirred the best men up very pleasantly."[14] Patton was alarmed at the prospect of losing Princeton's young star, and busied himself seeking private funds to supplement Wilson's salary. Ellen, always practical and businesslike at such a time, urged Woodrow to go out to Illinois, inspect the university, inquire about its endowments; and at the same time to put pressure on the Princeton authorities. She was admittedly tempted by the opportunity. It might give Woodrow power "to mould times and events" to suit himself; and administration might give him more time for literary composition than the constant drain of lecturing. She saw a chance for his intellectual life to flow "in the one great channel, without impediment, whereas now it is divided into numerous small streams."[15]

Wilson was tempted too. He could see a great future for the university, as it turned under his leadership from an agricultural and a technically oriented institution to a leading center for liberal arts in the Middle West. Far from being put off by the fact that the university would be dependent on funds voted by the legislature, he liked the idea of applying to the task the energies of "the latent politician"[16] within him. When he turned down the offer in May it was with a fresh determination to pursue his literary plans, and with visible relief on the part of Princeton, which augmented his salary by $500 in the form of house rent.

Foremost among literary tasks was completion of his historical work *Division and Reunion*. Under the careful editorship of Hart he honed its arguments, strengthened its prose, and reduced its length. Published in February 1893, the volume was well received by reviewers and established Wilson's reputation as an historian. With a degree of objectivity unprecedented at the time he appraised the arguments of Northern and Southern polemicists during and after the outbreak of the Civil War. His conclusion was that the South had been correct in its initial interpretation of constitutional issues—particularly its view that the United States had been formed as a federation, from which a state could not be barred from withdrawing. But later historical circumstances, he contended, created a nation. Time favored the North and in the end justified its stand against secession. Wilson's theme illustrated his belief that the U.S. constitution was capable of growth and change; it reinforced his concept of the state as a developing organism.

Division and Reunion was followed by literary productions bringing Wilson's name before an increasing audience. Collected essays were issued by leading publishers—*An Old Master* by Scribners, *Mere Literature* by Houghton Mifflin—and individual pieces attracted wide attention. In "The Course of American History" Wilson set forth a conception of America more inclusive and more essentially democratic than that which had been the accepted view of New England historians.[17] The latter had seen the western United States as formed by the expansion of northeastern influences; Wilson argued that it was the creation of a new culture, shaped by new men.

He returned to the theme in a discussion of individuals who might be considered most uniquely American. From his "Calendar of Great Americans" he omitted New Englanders because they were essentially parochial; he even excluded Emerson, but for a different reason: because he was a universal genius who might have appeared anywhere at any time. Jefferson he considered too much tainted by doctrinaire French thought to have a place in the pantheon. Calhoun, like the New Englanders, was a provincial. But Jackson, for all his faults, was authentically of the new breed; and Lincoln embodied the essence of Americanism. This view of the nation as not being the transplantation of European civilization to a fresh soil, but one born on native ground and made by hitherto unknown experiences, was a major contribution to American historiography. Wilson shared with Frederick Jackson Turner, his former student at Johns Hopkins, the distinction of having invented it.* But Wilson did not confine his view to a mere academic interpretation. His career as a progressive was to be built in large part on the new forces he had discerned arising in the West.

That, however, was in the future. The 1890s were for much of the country, as they were for Wilson, a time of conservative reappraisal. In reaction to social disorders—the Pullman riots in Chicago, widespread agrarian unrest—he retreated deeper into his study, not so much opposing the tides of Populism as ignoring them. Yet Wilson's so-called conservative period in the 1890s has been overdrawn. His rereading of Edmund Burke in 1894 found him less attracted to Burke's conservatism than to his doctrine of expediency in statecraft—a large-scale expediency justifying compromise and change as adaptations to actual conditions. Burke's defense of the American Revolution and Lincoln's emancipation of the slaves were alike (Wilson believed) in being responses to historical necessities and were not the product of doctrinaire abstractions.

Wilson's systematic concern with educational philosophy began in the same period. It had been stimulated by the Illinois offer. As he observed the influence of major figures at the heads of eastern universities—Eliot at Harvard, Gilman at Johns Hopkins, Low at Columbia—he began to see academic statesmanship as a field capable of engaging a man's best thought and action. In the summer of 1893 at the World's Columbian Exposition in Chicago he delivered a key paper on liberal education as an essential preliminary to professional studies in law, medicine, and theology. In this he presented himself as an opponent of specialization on the one hand, and of scattered electives on the other. That the corpus of ideas and values existing within Western civilization should be transmitted to all serious students and to prospective men of affairs was his overriding belief, then and later. He found himself at odds with Eliot's eclecticism and with the Germanic methods of scholarship then in vogue. He saw literature as embodying truths more significant than the narrow

---

* The editors of the Wilson papers conclude (see PWW, 7:274) that "It is impossible to ascribe the authorship of the theme either to Wilson or to Turner."

generalizations of science, and jurisprudence as being more fundamental than legal rules.

What can the student of law know "but the forms and the tricks of the law," Wilson asked in the Columbian address, "if he know nothing of the law's rootage in society, the principles of its origin and development; how it springs out of . . . elements which run centuries deep into the history of nations?" Without a grounding in history, philosophy, and literature, a man could know only the technical rules, "which must for him be rules dead, inflexible, final."[18*]

A year after this address, Wilson dealt with education more broadly from the point of view of citizenship in a democracy. The aim of education, he argued, was to give the average citizen a comprehension of his own times and of the forces at work in them. "Of all things that a university should do for a man," he said, "the most important is to put him in possession of the materials for a systematic criticism of life."[19] In emphasizing the importance of free and independent critical judgment he set the first stone in the educational philosophy that was to give fire to his major educational addresses, from his oration at Princeton's sesquicentennial in 1896 to his Phi Beta Kappa oration at Harvard in 1909.

In the autumn of 1894 Wilson bought a lot next to the house on Stedman Street that he had been renting for several years. He was ready to build, an undertaking that was to be replete with predictable hopes and heartbreaks. Like many before and after him, he found that the construction of a house involves emotional crises and can leave a burden of debt.

Ellen was by every instinct a homemaker, and she immediately started plans and drawings for her ideal dwelling. A New York architect, Edward Southwick Child, based a design closely on Ellen's ideas and made an estimate of $7,400 for the house of eleven rooms. Dr. Wilson offered to contribute $2,000 of the cost, and the son received indications that Princeton trustee Moses Taylor Pyne would provide a mortgage below the going rate of 5.5 percent. The remainder he expected to pay from a stepped-up schedule of writings and lectures.

What looked like a bright scheme suddenly darkened. The architect's estimate was higher than Wilson had expected and soon was substantially raised. Pyne, it seemed, was not ready to provide a mortgage at the reduced rate. The projected load of literary and scholarly work began

---

* As president of Princeton Wilson later tried to create such a law school as he had envisaged in this striking passage. Caught up in other reforms and controversies, he did not succeed in raising the necessary funds.

to appear crippling. At Baltimore for his annual Johns Hopkins lectures, Wilson came to the conclusion that the house would have to be abandoned. He announced his decision to Ellen in highly emotional terms. He could hardly bear to think of her distress: "I feel as if were thrusting a knife into you," he wrote. "Oh, I don't know how I am to stand this. If ever my heart came near breaking it was this morning."[20]

But Ellen was less given to the tragic mood. She turned with a light heart to face life's setbacks, particularly those which threatened to overwhelm her husband. Now she replied that she had been "a little goose" to attach so much importance to building the house and she gladly agreed to give it up. It made her tremble, she said, to think how the debts might have burdened Woodrow's spirit and kept him from achieving the work for which God intended him.[21]

Steps were taken to put an end to the project. The architect was told to discontinue his work, and the disposition of the lot was discussed. Yet somehow the dream would not go away. On thinking the matter over, Woodrow felt it would be more economical to have the plans completed before being laid aside. Ellen quietly suggested to the architect ways in which the cost of the house might be reduced, principally by slicing several feet off its depth at the rear. Ways of raising money were reconsidered. Wilson discovered that, with less embarrassment than borrowing from Pyne, he could get a mortgage through regular channels. Thus one by one the obstacles were overcome and in the spring of 1895, as if Providence itself were in charge, ground was broken and the cornerstone laid.

In the end, the house and its lot cost more than $14,000, so far exceeding the original estimate that Dr. Wilson was moved to comment caustically on his son's "extravagant mansion."[22] But the investment paid off handsomely. It not only provided a home for a scattered family and a calm center for Wilson's literary labors; it was also financially rewarding. When Wilson moved to Prospect, home of Princeton's presidents, he sold it for more than twice what it had cost him.

The completion of the house, occurring midway in his years as a Princeton professor, found Wilson as close to being a happy man as would ever be the case. He was enjoying, he wrote Ellen from Baltimore in the winter of 1895, "in a certain degree a sense of power,—as if I had gotten some way upon the road I used so to burn to travel."[23] He was as relaxed now as he would ever be. He was a man, as a young colleague remarked, "with a long habit of success."[24] Skills as a lecturer, essayist, political scientist, historian, and orator had been gained by exacting discipline and long self-schooling. These were now paying off in days that appeared uncrowded and in a disposition that struck observers as one of sweetness and generosity.

He kept his mornings for writing, and following an afternoon lecture had time to walk or play tennis, to stop for a game of billiards at the Nassau Club, or to engage in talk with colleagues and shopkeepers along Nassau Street. The tradesmen always liked Wilson and remained his firm supporters in later quarrels and divisions. At evening he worked again; but the family waited for the sound, precisely at nine o'clock, of the rolltop desk being closed and the key turned. Then Woodrow emerged to join in the conversation or the reading aloud, or to lend his tenor voice to the singing of family songs.

In the new house the study at the rear had high windows, eliminating outside distractions. Bookcases contained an extensive library (for several years the family spent more on books than on clothes), and above these were renderings by Ellen of the portraits of English statesmen whom Wilson had never wholly abandoned as heroes. Through a passage this study opened (as did the dining room and formal parlor) into a large square hall, with fireplace and window seat, which formed the heart of the house. On a table in the center of this were spread books and reviews, drawing pads, and often Ellen's sewing; around it gathered the immediate family, stray relatives, and occasional guests.

Bliss Perry, who came to Princeton as a young professor of English in 1892, remembered his first invitation to dinner as coming from "the hospitable Wilsons."[25] The noted British Socialists Sidney and Beatrice Webb came by, having been advised that Woodrow Wilson was one of the country's most promising young men. After dinner Ellen suggested that she and her guest go into another room, leaving the men to smoke. "But I smoke, myself," Mrs. Webb declared as she drew out a cigarette. The Wilson daughters decided that night she was "the wickedest woman in the world."[26]

The three daughters were now at an age where their personalities were distinct and interesting. Margaret was the dominant one, built four-square, intrepid and restless. When the new house was under construction, she was seen, characteristically, climbing over the bare floorbeams, while her anxious sisters begged her to come down. Jessie, with "her long, honey-colored hair, transparent complexion and exquisitely clear-cut profile," was the serene beauty of the family, an unusually appealing and highly intelligent child.[27] Eleanor, the baby, tagged along, given easily to tears but frank and humorous, expressive to the point where a career as an actress later tempted her.

No adequate public grammar school then existed in Princeton, and Ellen took upon herself the task of educating her daughters. This domestic classroom was evidently a vital place, broad-ranging in its field of study. As teacher, Ellen wrote her husband, she was expected to judge between virtues attributed by her pupils to various historical or mythical personages. "Who is the greatest," they wanted to know, "Shakespeare or Homer, Milton or Dante, Themistocles or Miltiades?"[28] Like all healthy children they fought: "Many of our games were fights," Eleanor recalled years later. A favorite game was dividing things among them. "We divided the house. Jessie took the lower porch, Margaret the upper, and that left the front steps—no good at all—and the back steps—not much better—for me. . . . We divided the universe. Jessie took the sun and sunset, Margaret the moon and stars; and I was given the sunrise and rainbow."[29] After that they divided up the Greek gods and goddesses; or they slipped out into the garden behind the house, where a passage under a rotting mulberry tree, redolent of crushed fruit, led into a mysterious dell.

When the girls grew older Ellen engaged a German governess, figuring it would be no more expensive to pay her than to pay three tuitions at the village school. For several years Fraulein Clara Boehm lived with the Wilsons, a figure variously remembered as having been loved and hated. Ellen thought it would help Woodrow to have German spoken at family meals; but Woodrow, who never did master spoken German or French, was made nervous by the experiment and it was soon abandoned. Other members of the family, besides the two servants, Maggie and Annie, included at one time or another nephew George Howe, a freshman at Princeton, along with Eddie Axson, Stockton Axson, and such frequent visitors as Wilson's sister Annie with her daughter, and his father. Madge Axson, who at thirteen came to stay permanently, remembered how crowded the house seemed after her aunt Louisa's empty, high-ceilinged rooms in Gainesville. She was desperately lonely, but she still thought there were too many people in the Wilson house.

Woodrow, guarded in his study during the working hours, did not seem fazed by the comings and goings, but Ellen at least on one occasion tried to impose some sort of order on family visits. She complained that she never knew when somebody might be arriving. "Won't you at least let me know the *day*?" she pleaded in her soft southern drawl. There was a murmur of protest, even from her daughters. "But Mother, we don't always *know* the day!"[30]

Woodrow got on well with children. He treated them with a certain grave courtesy, as equals, and seemed to share with them the secret of how delightful it was being young. "I never knew anyone children liked so much," recalled one elderly lady years afterwards, remembering her own childhood. "He would lift his hat and say, 'How do you do, Thelma?' and then talk to me as an equal."[31] The three daughters worshiped him, and even Madge, the eternal heathen, the bright but slightly alien spirit, found in him an unfailingly sympathetic friend and counselor. Eddie and Margaret typed for him; or in his upstairs room filled with chemical equipment Eddie was prepared to make or to fix almost anything.

Ellen kept the household accounts and Woodrow was left with little in the way of practical chores other than the weekly winding of the tall clock in the hall. This gave him the opportunity to tell regularly, to the children's delight, the story of the Irishman who sought to buy a particular clock. Being informed by the salesman that it would run for a week without winding, "Faith," said he, "and how long will it run if ye wind it?"[32]

He could do no more than tell stories. He had a reputation, he confessed to Ellen when he was still at Johns Hopkins, "as a maker of grotesque addresses . . . as a wearer of all varieties of comic grimaces . . . even as a dancer of the 'can-can!' "[33] Now his gifts were called forth to entertain the family, such routines as the drunken Englishman or the too-sober Scotchman being regularly greeted with calls for an encore. Afterwards he would take the children up to their rooms and sing to them before the nursery fire. Years later Eleanor remembered[34] the dying refrain:

> I had four brothers over the sea
> *Peri, Meri, Dictum, Domini* . . .

The summers of these academic years were often spent writing; or Ellen and the girls were expected to take short journeys to the shore while Woodrow went off to extend his influence—and to augment the ever-growing need for income—by lecturing. Thus in the summer of 1892 he made his first western trip to deliver a series of lectures at Colorado College and in Denver. The West was to play a determining role in Wilson's later political career, and his first visit was of importance. He stayed with his cousin, Hattie Woodrow, her husband now a mining engineer and stockbroker in Colorado Springs. He was, he reported, "affectionately received," and between stints of work he had time to explore with her the surrounding plains and canyons.[35] This "colossal region," he described it, this "abnormal" and then this "wonderful" country. As his lectures drew praise and increasingly large audiences, he was able to write Ellen that he was "excited by new emotions—gradually filling up with new ideas and realization of our continent."[36]

Vacationing a few years later in Front Royal, Virginia, the Wilson family formed a close friendship with a pair of maiden sisters, the Smiths, Lucy Marshall and Mary Randolph, from New Orleans. The relationship was to enrich their subsequent lives. "You don't know how you have both taken hold on our hearts," Woodrow wrote to them in September 1897.[37] The two were daughters of the manse, southern to the core, with the particular brand of sprightliness and wit that appealed to the Wilsons.* The Smiths were to be regular visitors, almost kinfolk within the circle of relatives for whom the latchkey was always out. On one memorable stay with them in 1900, alone, Ellen blossomed and shone in the social whirl of New Orleans, the very image of a coquettish southern belle, a role she could only play when out of the shadow of her dominant husband.

Woodrow was always eager to put down roots—if possible with a house of his own attached. Late in the 1890s the family began going to the Muskoka Lake Region in Ontario, Canada, an "obscure corner of the continent," as he referred to it.[38] He enjoyed the bright waters, the boating, the forested land, and soon was toying with the idea of building. In 1901 he bought an island and adjacent property totaling more than a hundred acres. Wilson's father, now aging and not able to contemplate a wilderness journey, confessed himself "startled" by news of the purchase; but "no doubt," he added, always supportive, "you are right in making this bold venture." The building project did not materialize; Wilson was soon to become president of Princeton and totally absorbed in new duties. But he kept the property, and almost upon his deathbed was still dreaming of constructing a camp, complete (as he had planned so long before) with boathouse, icehouse, bathhouse, and wharf.

At Princeton a small circle of close friends met regularly, exchanging ideas, joking, arguing over the affairs of the world and of the little community whose center was Nassau Street. Henry Burchard Fine lived across the street from the Wilsons; John Grier Hibben, Andrew Fleming West, and Bliss Perry lived a short bicycle ride away. In the afternoons the group would gather for a kind of provincial salon at Henrietta

---

*When he met the Smiths in 1927 Ray Stannard Baker was expecting to find "two rather prim and aristocratic Southern gentlewomen." On the contrary, he found himself talking with "the liveliest-minded, pleasantest, most charming women . . . full of the zest of life."

Ricketts's house on Stockton Street. There Wilson shone, with his clear ideas and vivacious mind—though it was chivalrously noted that when it came to European history, Miss Ricketts had the advantage. The cast of characters that would decisively affect Princeton's future was already on hand—those who would stand together and those who would face each other in implacable hostility. But the controversies were remote. "We were all," said Perry, "living in Arcadia then."[39]

The Woodrow Wilson the students saw was a man who seemed taller than he was, homely when his face was in repose but with grey-blue eyes that lit up changefully when he spoke. He moved with a compact energy, as one sure of where he was going. They rejoiced in his support of causes that involved them, and year by year voted him their favorite member of the faculty. When he went to Johns Hopkins now, he stirred the same kind of anticipation as the heroes of his own student days. At Princeton the young men overflowed his classroom, often crowding the window-sills. "It was not merely a matter of college popularity, of which Wilson enjoyed an enormous amount," wrote one of them, "but that we felt we had been in the presence of a great man." He was Princeton's pride, and he stood familiarly before them, "noble, honorable, and genial."[40]

Building the house had put Wilson under heavy financial strain, increasing still further the need to supplement his college salary by outside lectures and articles. In late June, 1895, while the first timbers of the house were rising, a letter came from the editor of *Harper's*, Henry Mills Alden, with what seemed a beguilingly simple proposal. "Would it be convenient to you to contribute to our Magazine," Alden wrote, "a few articles on General Washington for publication next year?"[41] Each would be about ten thousand words in length; they need not be connected by a continuous theme, and the first would be timed so as to allow two months for preparation. For six articles the editor offered what then seemed the princely sum of three hundred dollars each. Wilson immediately accepted (the total would pay almost a quarter of what the house had originally been expected to cost), and, postponing other projects, went immediately to work. In due course the six articles were gathered in a book and presented, with copious illustrations by Howard Pyle, as a biography of the first President. At least one reviewer recognized it as a lapse from Wilson's usual standard of style and scholarship. "He has produced a very readable sketch," said the *Nation*, "but it is not what was to have been looked for from his pen."[42] The reading public greeted the book warmly, however, and generous royalties were added to the fees already in hand.

George Washington has stood as an embarrassment in the corpus of Wilson's writings. Its incompleteness, its superficiality, its antique and affected style, make it unreadable today. That it was prepared as a series of magazine articles, and undertaken when its author was in need of money, explains much. "I could not be unmindful of the fact that I was building a house," Wilson wrote, rather apologetically, to his old friend Jameson.[43] But other elements that went into its making show significant characteristics of Wilson at this stage of his career. The book was in some measure a revolt against the academy. It was an effort to break through the limits of scholarly discourse to reach the public he had once hoped to influence by political action. As a student at Johns Hopkins he had protested to Ellen against being cast in the narrow role of scholar; at Bryn Mawr he had turned from promising initiatives in political science to mannered essays and even to fiction. *George Washington* was a half-conscious return to the earlier, ill-fated experiments; certainly it expressed a determination not to be confined in an academic mold.

Another explanation lies in Wilson's carefully considered theory of the nature of historical writing. He believed that history should be written as it had been lived—in direct narrative form without the intrusion of criticism or polemics. While at Wesleyan he drew a distinction between two kinds of histories of Rome: the one, he wrote, was "traditional and improbable, the other that which has been produced by treating the traditional with the acids of criticism." The first was the history of Livy; the second, that of Barthold Niebuhr and other German scholars. Without considering a middle ground, Wilson felt drawn to the traditional approach. "Livy's fictions are realities," he declared, "so far as the imaginative, and even the moral and political, writings of subsequent ages are concerned."[44] A consequence of this view was that the historian perceived events, not from a remote elevation or from a perspective in time, but as they were seen and understood by the men who lived through them.

The historian must write of a generation in the air they breathed, Wilson declared in 1895. He must not be in haste to judge; his task must be conceived as radically different from that of the investigator. If you would know the men and women of the past, he urged, "go back to their age; breed yourself a pioneer and woodsman . . . discover and occupy the wilderness with them; dream what may be beyond the near hills."[45] In practice this extended to using the style and the expressions they used—to putting oneself, by an act of the will and the imagination, directly in their shoes. Wilson might have argued, but did not quite, that lighting a candle and taking up a quill pen were necessary to write well about the eighteenth century. In *George Washington* and scarcely to a lesser degree in his *History of the American People*, he was seduced by these attitudes into a lazy scholarship and a cloying style.

The academic year 1895–96 was more crowded than usual with lecture engagements, while work went forward, installment by installment, on the articles for *Harper's*. In October Wilson suffered an attack of grippe, unexpectedly prolonged and severe. It should have provided a warning. He was evidently putting too heavy a strain on a constitution that, while adequate for most purposes, had never been robust. In Baltimore for his annual lectures he was again ill with a lingering fever. "Can we not persuade you to lessen your work?" wrote a sympathetic neighbor in mid-winter. "It is clear, Professor, that you are unduly taxing your strength."[46]

In March he turned down reluctantly an invitation to deliver a series of lectures at the Yale Law School. But the price of overwork was not to go unpaid, and in May he found that his right hand, intermittently subject to what he called "writer's cramp,"[47] was now virtually incapacitated. The combined symptoms from which Wilson suffered during this academic year—the grippe, the lingering fever, and above all the pain in his right hand—can only be seen as premonitory signs (not subject to diagnosis at the time) of the strokes that later were to affect his career decisively. But it was his nature to treat illness lightly; what is striking in his life is as much the way he surmounted illness as the degree to which he was forced to succumb to it.

His response on this occasion was to embark alone for the British Isles, to learn rapidly to write with his left hand (so rapidly, indeed, that the hypothesis of his having had dyslexia is reinforced in the judgment of some by this apparent show of ambidextrousness), and then on his bicycle to take journeys averaging thirty-three miles a day. In fact the trip abroad had been projected before his health problems became acute. The need for rest from intellectual activities seemed plain, and as Ellen was absorbed by family responsibilities it was determined he would go without her. On shipboard he wrote toilsome notes with his left hand and soon informed Ellen that his afflicted right hand was feeling scarcely a twinge. With the impersonal objectivity he assumed toward any part of himself that was injured or ailing, he declared of his arm that it was proving "a most promising patient."[48]

His improvement was certainly rapid. On landing in England he went on to Cambridge in an effort to persuade the noted constitutional scholar Frederic William Maitland to participate in Princeton's forthcoming sesquicentennial celebration. Later, in London, he looked up James Bryce. But the chief joy of the trip was a bicycle tour. The riding, he wrote Ellen, was "exhilarating beyond expression."[49]

On this and on a second trip to England in 1899, Wilson found himself passing through country which his imagination had made familiar to him, associated with literary figures whose works he had read and reread since youth. He stopped at Wordsworth's house at Rydal Mount, traversed the counties Shakespeare knew, and at Langport visited the house where Bagehot had lived and died. He searched for the church in Carlisle where his grandfather, Thomas Woodrow, had served before coming to the United States.

Apart from such shrines and from the changing scenery, he was "in love with touring and life in the open countryside"[50]—the healthy tiredness at the day's end, the lodging overnight in small villages. The weather was often bad—"mists, with some rain" was the routine substance of local forecasts; but it was quite impracticable, he discovered, "to distinguish very nicely between the rain and the mist." His spirits, however, were not dampened. On the second trip he was accompanied by Stockton Axson, and although he was glad to have a bicycling companion, he found that Stockton's was a disposition which had "no exclamation points" in it. Wilson's father had made the same complaint years before about Woodrow, when they visited together the Philadelphia Sesquicentennial Exhibition. But now it was Woodrow who would "find the adjectives and utter the praise." Indeed, he told Ellen, as he grew older he was growing more effusive, more demonstrative.

He seemed to enjoy friends more easily, too. On shipboard on the first trip he struck up an acquaintance with Charles A. Woods of South Carolina. Wilson would one day appoint him a circuit judge; but for the present it was enough that the two join forces for part of the bicycle tour. On the second trip, watching idly one day as passengers disembarked from a ship at Plymouth, he was overjoyed to see his old friends, the Hazens of Wesleyan days, descend the gangplank. Such unexpected meetings gave travel its savor, and he enlarged upon them in daily letters to Ellen.*

---

*On the home voyage, the ship on which Wilson and Stockton Axson were traveling hit an iceberg, ran up on one of its projections, and then slipped back. Wilson's composure in the face of the imminent danger was noteworthy. Axson found him on deck "talking and laughing." Many years later Wilson recalled that, discovering himself unfazed in that incident, he had learned for the first time that he could never be afraid of any physical danger.

Ellen's replies, written from an all-but-deserted college town, give a vivid picture of her personality at this time. She was not "wearing the willow,"[51] she advised her wandering husband; indeed she had become "a devotee of pleasure." Instead of asking herself each morning what she ought to do that day, she would "shamelessly" consult with herself as to what she wanted to do. She took up again her long-neglected painting and drawing. In a hammock on the second-floor piazza of their newly completed house she read the latest novels; through the peace of the Princeton mornings she led the girls in their "literary studies." The girls devoured Scott voraciously and did not even wish to go to the seashore. In one of her letters we see Ellen as she loafs at noon about the empty Princeton campus, "resting on the steps of one building or another . . . enjoying the delicious freshness [of] the long shadows and the golden-green lights."

A rash of burglaries struck the little town in the summer of 1899. Ellen was not exactly afraid of the burglars, but on one occasion it was the visiting Dr. Wilson, always having something Jovian in his aspect, who came thundering down the stairs to scare off an intruder. After that Ellen slept with a pistol beside her bed. When a local artist on their street decided to construct himself a second studio "just as crooked [as the first], but at a different angle,"[52] she declared a crying need for someone to commit not burglary but arson.

As for the novels, Ellen abided by her own judgment—a large ingredient of "Charleston views" combined with a capacity to be agreeably shocked. The "new women," she reported cheerily, ought certainly to take heart, for their cause was prospering, at least in books. The "noble battle for an equal code of morals" had not resulted in making men virtuous—"Heaven forbid! Such a thing is not even dreamed of." Rather did the latest writers "generously, unselfishly, chivalrously . . . contend for the woman's right to be just as bad as the man!"[53]

The summer apart, in this period as well as later, seemed in some ways to be good for both partners. No matter how piteously they complained of the separation, they found themselves enjoying a necessary freedom, and their almost daily letters opened up fresh channels of communication. "I am coming to you like a lover to whom has been revealed the full beauty and sanctity of love," Woodrow wrote to his wife at the end of the journeys of 1896, "with new devotion, new joy, new passion."[54] He was also coming home with his health seemingly restored. But the painful condition of his right hand persisted, and would cast a shadow over the work of many months.

*   *   *

The opening of the academic year 1896–1897 was a turning point for Wilson. During the next five years, leading to his election to Princeton's presidency, he went through familiar routines and lived amid familiar scenes. But the atmosphere subtly changed, and offstage could be heard the sound of approaching events. He was getting ready to face what his ambitions and his labors had aimed at, and what the fates were busily preparing.

CHAPTER THREE

Educator

—◆—

TOWARD POWER

The autumn of 1896 was to be long remembered in Princeton history. Beginning on October 21 and running for three days, a ceremony of academic splendor hitherto unequaled in America marked the one hundred and fiftieth anniversary of the institution, saw it change its official name from the College of New Jersey and lay claim to the status of a university. The proceedings were planned in meticulous detail by Andrew Fleming West, soon to become dean of an embryonic graduate school. Wilson was designated as chief spokesman for the new university and its future.

Surviving alumni of all classes assembled for the ceremonies. Along with them were delegates from American and European universities, the latter garbed in colored robes and hoods that were still a novel sight in the United States. Statesmen of many countries and spokesmen of all religious denominations were on hand. For a little college, in a little town only beginning to emerge from rural ways, it was quite a gathering. Each morning during the convocation a procession formed at Marquand Chapel to march across campus to Alexander Hall. As a climax, President Patton announced Princeton's new name and status, honorary degrees were awarded, and Grover Cleveland, President of the United States, closed the proceedings.

On October 21 Alexander Hall was crowded to its limits. It was Wilson's hour, and he rose to it with assurance. Long practice, combined with the right moment and the right theme, can on rare occasions result in an almost palpable connection between a speaker and his audience. As Wilson recalled on that day the early stages of Princeton's history, as he set forth his vision of its mission and ended with a soaring evocation of "the perfect place of learning," his listeners felt that they had indeed been under a spell. The manuscript copy of the address shows corrections made arduously, because of his stricken hand; but the performance carried all before it. "*Such* an ovation as Woodrow received!" exclaimed Ellen, describing to a friend the "sweet triumph" of that day. "As for the Princeton men, some of them simply fell on his neck and wept for joy."[1]

The oration, "Princeton in the Nation's Service," was a summing up, in a style tempered, at points epigrammatic, yet with the eloquent turns of phrase and the more extended imaginative flights before which an audience, once captivated, rejoices to submit. It expressed what Wilson had been saying whenever he was called on to define a true education. It was a call for the student to be made a critic and interpreter of life. In Wilson's youth he had conceived the college as a training ground for political leadership, with emphasis on debating and party government. But as he matured—and as he came to terms with his own role as educator—he envisioned a new way of serving the nation.

Much noted at the time was his attack on the methods of Germanic scholarship then popular in many American universities, and his attack on the spread of the scientific method from the laboratory into the teaching of literature and history. But he was not against science; his real concern was that men should be educated liberally. Princeton's task, he said, was to provide the country with men "who know the probabilities of failure and success, who can separate the tendencies which are permanent from the tendencies which are of the moment merely."

"We are in danger," he said, "to lose our identity and become infantile in every generation."[2] Men of the world in the best sense were what a college generation ought to be: men who would not be taken in by the world's shows, or misled by fashion or popularity. To achieve this it was not enough merely to have studied the past; it was necessary to have lived it, as it was necessary to be deeply at home in one's own age. That was the characteristically Wilsonian theme, and the way to work it out in practice formed the substance of his later educational reforms.

The sesquicentennial celebration was a dazzling success. It changed decisively the atmosphere at Princeton. It also strongly affected the course of Wilson's next years. The attention his speech attracted—not only within the Princeton community but, reprinted, from a wide public—confirmed his outstanding position in the university world. He could not be an entirely private man thereafter. He was watched; he was sought after for addresses and articles; he was expected to play the role of leader. From 1896 until his election as president six years later he found himself increasingly projected into the politics of his own college.

In a way, from Wilson's point of view, the sesquicentennial had been *too* successful. He was cast in a role of heir-apparent that made him a direct threat to Patton. He had resigned himself to a life of teaching and writing, but now he found that posture undermined. The lure of politics, concealed behind other ambitions, began to reassert itself with troubling force.

For Princeton, too, the aftermath of the sesquicentennial was to prove disturbing. It aroused expectations, both in the faculty and throughout academia, that were difficult to meet. This was particularly true in the light of Patton's well-known reluctance to move with speed on any project. Though pushed by an ardent group of younger professors and by an increasingly modern-minded board of trustees, he was not prepared to take the steps called for by Princeton's newly assumed status as a university. Establishment of a graduate school, the first obligation if the promises of the sesquicentennial were to mean anything, was delayed for four years, and was then achieved over the president's opposition. On being made dean of the school, Andrew West was given semiautonomous powers as a counterweight to Patton's negative attitude. West's prestige had already been inflated by his role in planning the sesquicentennial, and this unusual grant of authority would become a thorn in the side of the next administration.

The hope of bringing in new blood was disappointed as openings were filled from within the existing faculty. Observing all this, Ellen Wilson with characteristic directness wrote her husband that it might have been better had the sesquicentennial never taken place. Princeton had been "a respectable, old-fashioned Presbyterian college; before we were that simply and without pretence; now we have merely made ourselves ridiculous before the whole academic world by making big promises that we have neither the will nor the power to carry out."[3]

Immediately after the autumn celebration, with Patton's apparent support, Wilson made a bold effort to bring Frederick Jackson Turner, then at the University of Wisconsin, to reinforce the history faculty. Wilson vigorously pushed his friend's case while enlisting the support of other Princeton professors and of influential board members. Turner showed himself a rather nervous man, filled with doubts about the opportunities Wilson urged upon him. As he wavered, the board postponed action, and then Patton turned the appointment down, on the grounds that certain monetary gifts might be jeopardized by the naming of a Unitarian to the faculty. "Now I have no evidence that the good Mr. Turner will

do us," Patton wrote privately, "could compensate us for this loss."[4]
Wilson was dismayed by the whole affair. "I am probably at this writing
the most chagrined and mortified fellow on this continent!"[5] he told
Turner. He and Ellen discussed leaving Princeton, taking Hibben into
their confidence and making him privy to their half-formed intent.[6]

Along other lines, the trustees went to great lengths to mollify Wilson.
A chair, financed by Cyrus H. McCormick, Jr., the manufacturer and a
member of the Class of 1879, was created specifically to meet his teaching
preferences, and his courses were revised to put a greater stress on
political, as distinguished from legal, aspects of national development.
Partly as a result of this, Wilson began at this time to break his long-
standing teaching commitments at Johns Hopkins. The university at
Baltimore, in financial straits, had cut back on the number of his lectures,
and then opened them to undergraduates and to the public. "How little
worth while what I am doing seems to be," Wilson wrote from Baltimore
in the winter of 1897. He felt that with the larger and more miscellaneous
audience he was "unconsciously (not altogether unconsciously, either)
spoiling, diluting, confusing the matter by popularizing it."[7]

The annual visits ceased, but Wilson was not forgotten at Johns Hopkins. When his former teacher Herbert Baxter Adams retired in 1901,
Wilson was invited to take his chair; and on the retirement of the university's first president, Daniel Coit Gilman, Wilson delivered the chief
address and was himself greeted with an unprecedented show of affection
and enthusiasm when he received an honorary degree. Visibly moved,
he heard a group of his former students testify to his influence as a
teacher.

Neither outside honors nor the regard shown him at Princeton could
assuage a gnawing sense of discontent. Wilson regretted there was at
this time no opening for the presidency of another university. He meditated on possibilities beyond teaching and university administration. A
man had come to himself, he wrote in this period, when he had arrived
at "the full realization of his powers, the true and clear perception of
what it was his mind demanded for its satisfaction." Wilson had "come
to himself" but he was not certain that his faculties were "stretched to
their right measure, were at last exercised at their best."[8]

National and international events stirred his imagination, and these,
though it was still too early to discern their impact upon him, would
decisively affect his future. In 1898 the Spanish-American War erupted,
inflaming popular passions and creating a sudden mood of jingoism. To
Wilson it meant a revelation of the importance of foreign affairs. With

startling prescience he grasped the moment as a turning point, affecting irreversibly both the structure of American government and also the scope and substance of its policies. It seemed in its way as important as that other historical turning point, the closing of the American frontier. The outbreak of the war increased his resolve to be an interpreter of public affairs. In addresses he commented with a new urgency on the implications of current issues; he was aware of a quickened, if still undefined, ambition to play an active role.

In a kind of private meditation entitled "What Ought We to Do?" set down in mid-summer 1899, Wilson wrote that, whatever might be an individual's judgment or scruples in regard to the origins of the war with Spain (he himself felt it to have been begun upon an impulse of "humane indignation"), the fact of its being an absolutely decisive occurrence was undeniable. "The thing is done," he wrote, "cannot be undone; and our future must spring out of it." When it was over it would be impossible for the United States to return to the place where it had been. "The scenes, the stage itself upon which we act, are changed. We have left the continent which has hitherto been our only field of action and have gone out upon the seas, where the nations are rivals and we cannot live or act apart." The world into which the use of armed force had brought the nation was "a very modern world." "In it civilization has become aggressive, and we are made aware that choices are about to be made as vital as those which determined the settlement and control of North America."[9]

He saw the contenders for new territory and power to be France, Britain, Russia, and Germany, with the two latter America's chief rivals. Wilson was careful to disassociate himself from the extreme expansionists, the jingoists and imperialists. It was his "personal wish," he declared in one public lecture, that the United States had not moved into the Philippines: "I do not know," he said with some courage in December 1899, "but that I wish we did not have them now."[10] That choice, however, was past; and if one of the Great Powers were to occupy the Philippines, it was best that it be the United States, "inasmuch as hers was the light of day."[11] Then and later Wilson favored freedom for the Philippines; but his organic theories of the state raised a large question in his mind. Were the people of the islands, he wondered, in a state of development ripe for freedom?

Wilson was groping at this time for a coherent approach to foreign policy, one recognizing America's predestined world role, affirming its special mission, and adjusting its actions to particular conditions. His approach was a mixture peculiarly his own, a combination of idealism, national interests, and ideas carried forward from his early studies of democratic development. Contrary to what has been generally assumed, he did not enter public life without having given considerable thought to this field.

But the effect of the war with Spain was, from Wilson's perspective, most immediate and notable in changing the constitutional balance of the United States. In 1900 *Congressional Government* was being translated into French, causing the author to reread the book carefully and to write a new preface. The passage of twenty years, he saw, had undermined some of his earlier generalizations. War, and the administration of foreign dependencies, had altered irrevocably the "lodgment and exercise of power." They had "greatly increased power and opportunity for constructive statesmanship given the President." "When foreign affairs play a prominent part in the politics and policy of a nation," he declared, "its Executive must of necessity be its guide: must utter every initial judgment, take every first step of action, supply the information upon which it is to act, suggest and in large measure control its conduct."[12] A self-confidence rings in these sentences that suggests a man not ready merely to judge events, but to take part in them.

In 1897 Grover Cleveland was finishing his second term, and in relation to national events, too, the Presidency began to seem a powerful (and perhaps even a desirable) office. Wilson saw the President, for the first time since Lincoln, commanding the attention of the whole country. Cleveland, he wrote, was not so much a colleague of the two legislative Houses as "an individual servant of the country." Unlike Lincoln, he was "President in ordinary times, but after an extraordinary fashion." He was a leader in spite of himself; he was a man who "made policies and altered parties," as had been done in the earlier stages of American history.[13]

Staying in Washington at this time, where he was composing a series of lectures on Machiavelli, Austin, and Burke, Wilson felt a resurgence of his first ambition for an active political career. In the afternoons he slipped off from his work to sit in the galleries and watch the House and Senate in session. "The old longing for public life comes upon me in a flood," he wrote Ellen; "perhaps I should be safer somewhere else, where I should be kept from a too keen and constant discontent with my calling."[14]

The discontent showed itself when in the spring of 1898 the University of Virginia offered him an opportunity seriously tempting him. Never having fully recovered its position after the Civil War, the university at Charlottesville was in the midst of a major reorganization. Long governed under a system of departmental chairmen, it was prepared to create a presidential office. Wilson was sought as its first incumbent.

This was not, like the earlier offer from Illinois, a call to the presidency of an institution on the make, lacking traditional excellence, but to the leadership of one of the oldest and most famous universities in the country, the beacon light of Wilson's native South. Coming as it did in the midst of his restlessness at Princeton, the offer was not easy to resist. Wilson discussed it with his classmate and benefactor, Cyrus Mc-Cormick. Not surprisingly, McCormick did his best to persuade Wilson against accepting, and cannily advised him to lean upon his wife's counsel, with her "deliberate judgment and intuitive knowledge."[15] Other of his friends were summoned hastily into conference. Patton, who was not consulted, reacted testily when he heard the news and disclaimed any responsibility for Wilson's unhappiness with the general situation at Princeton.

In the end it was a group of alumni, headed by members of Wilson's Class of 1879, who assured his continuance at Princeton. An agreement was drawn up guaranteeing Wilson an annual salary of $6,500 for five years—then the highest in the university—with the amount above his official salary paid for by personal donations. For the next several years Wilson was able to put aside further temptations to leave Princeton. The increased security did not, however, noticeably diminish his positive responses to requests for articles and addresses.

With a new sense of confidence Wilson turned back to a long-simmering project, the writing of a history of the United States. The work had been through many changes of form and scope. Late in 1894 he had written Turner that he was at work upon the history, a major undertaking to require at least six years. Compared to what he was now embarking on, the recently completed *Division and Reunion* had been "child's play." The first chapter, on the Colonial period, was under way: "I pray it may go easier or it will kill me."[16] Turner commented that the full history would be "*the* American history of our time, I believe."[17] The work was interrupted by the writing of *George Washington*, was reshaped as a book designed primarily for schools, and was abandoned temporarily when Wilson rejected *Harper's* sale of the book rights to what he considered an inferior publisher.

Ailing financially but desperately clinging to a tattered prestige, *Harper's* came back to Wilson with a proposition he felt he could not refuse: a major history, to receive first publication in twelve magazine articles, to be paid at the "astronomical" fee of one thousand dollars for each article. In addition, royalties of 15 percent would be paid on publication of the work in book form. The first installment was due in six months. Wilson signed a contract in April 1900 and got strenuously to work.

He was not free of doubts about these arrangements. "The fact is," he wrote Jameson, "that the editors of the popular monthlies offer me such prices nowadays that I am corrupted." He defended the arrangements on the ground that it was work that he wanted to do in any case, and that to suit a popular audience he would "alter the quality not a bit,—nor dilute the stuff, neither." He signed himself, nevertheless, as Jameson's "mercenary" friend.[18] He had doubts again when it became clear that *Harper's* intended to make the first book publication a pretentious, multivolumed work, lavishly illustrated; and he raised questions about the somewhat grandiose title they selected. What had been called in serial form *Colonies and Nation* would become *A History of the American People*.

Notwithstanding his doubts, he struggled with the work to the exclusion of everything else. If he lost a moment, he wrote, the presses would catch up with him. Material written for the earlier school history served him through several chapters, but afterwards he launched into seas not previously crossed. Where he had once determined to consult original documents, he now found himself relying almost exclusively on secondary sources.

As in earlier historical writings, especially his *George Washington*, he planned to let the story tell itself: he would keep "the atmosphere and illusion" of each age as it passed. The result, once again, was an archaic and mannered style, made the worse by the publisher's deadline of twelve months, instead of the four or five years which he had hoped to spend on the work. The book brought him handsome financial rewards, the largest, it was claimed, that any author had previously received for such a commission. In spite of all its faults, moreover, it played a serious role in Wilson's development.

The history takes its place with *Division and Reunion*, and even with the unfortunate *George Washington*, as an attempt to work out in symbolic form his sense of the oneness of the American nation. A wide and varied continent, a composite people shaped in their multifarious pursuits by social and economic forces, was the vision Wilson sought to encompass in his historical works. The first chapter of the *Washington* gives a picture of its hero as a young man mediating between the settled East and a wide-open West; drawn by economic speculation into pioneer lands and then conceiving them imaginatively as part of a new nation. Similarly, the *History of the American People* is at its best in emphasizing the opening of unsettled regions and their consolidation into a national whole. The later Wilson, the political leader in his reformist phase giving expression to what he called "the generous energies of the people," had roots in these historical generalizations.[19]

Toiling through 1901 on the magazine articles forming the basis of the *History*, Wilson laid plans for another project. Conceived in Bryn Mawr days, its outline sketched at Wesleyan, this was to be his *magnum opus*, a "philosophy of politics" crowning his other works. He saw it as being in some ways a companion volume to *The State*, but not a treatise on forms and procedures, not "a fact book"; rather it was to be an analysis of the nature of democracy. It would elaborate his conviction that government by consent of the people is a slow growth, the harvest of all a culture's aspects and characteristics. It would be in the end a witness to the march of civilization, a slow but inexorable march, toward liberty and self-government. If there was a time to begin and to complete such a work, it seemed to Wilson to be within the decade that opened the new century.

With this in mind he asked the Princeton trustees for a leave of absence to begin in the autumn of 1902. He planned to take his family abroad for a year and to concentrate on preparation for the big work. He did not wish to tell even himself too definitely what it was to be, he wrote a prospective publisher, though it had been forming in his mind "these twenty years and more."[20] He knew that he could not begin it without a season of contemplation and without disentangling himself from current modes of life and thought. At Princeton he was immersed in an atmosphere academic and didactic; to his credit he realized that he had formed the teacher's bad habit of talking too much.

The next ten or twelve years of his life "must be devoted to a truly different task." And so he would go his own way for a while and see what he was made of. "After all, I was born a politician," he confided to Turner, "and must be at the task for which . . . I have all these years been in training."[21] It is interesting that being a "politician" was, for Wilson, never entirely separated from being a scholar. He now sought to satisfy both ambitions within a single crowning literary work.

Circumstances, however, intervened. In the early winter of 1901 word came that Dr. Wilson was seriously ill in Wilmington. Woodrow immediately traveled south. The father, Woodrow reported to his uncle James, had four times been stricken "with a kind of rigour" which kept him unconscious for as much as an hour at a time.[22] The doctors diagnosed the attacks as due to an obstruction of the gall bladder, though apparently a progressive arteriosclerosis had set in. Dr. Wilson recovered from the attacks, but in May Woodrow went down to Wilmington again and brought him back to Princeton. Plans for the sojourn abroad were postponed, then abandoned. The patriarch would not leave the Princeton household, nor would the son write *The Philosophy of Politics*.

Other factors, if they did not contribute to keeping Wilson at home, in retrospect made it seem fortunate that he remained at Princeton through this period. Dissatisfaction with the Patton administration, growing since the sesquicentennial, was now reaching crisis proportions. Inevitably Wilson became a central figure in the developments that began to preoccupy the trustees and the faculty.

The hoped-for major changes had not been undertaken, nor had there been any expansion of the university. Morale was low, and standards of work and discipline were declining among the undergraduates. Patton was a deplorably bad administrator, dilatory and vacillating in the most routine tasks of his office; but he was an extraordinarily clever academic politician. No one could be more skilled at blunting criticism, evading issues, or subverting the opposition. The committee on the graduate school, set up at faculty insistence, was rendered ineffectual by his maneuvers, until finally the trustees intervened strongly. The placing of the amiable but indecisive Dean Samuel R. Winans at the head of the discipline committee was too much for the faculty progressives: both Wilson and John Hibben resigned from the committee in an undisguised act of reproof.

Faculty discontent was lodged in a relatively small group, which included, besides Wilson and Hibben, the graduate school dean, Andrew F. West, physics professor Cyrus F. Brackett, and Henry B. Fine, professor of mathematics. On a liberalized and strengthened board of trustees, Grover Cleveland—now retired from the Presidency and settled in Princeton—was an influential member. Between 1896 and 1901 fifteen new figures had come on the board, eight of whom had known as students the bracing airs of the McCosh administration. Before 1896 Moses Taylor Pyne and Cyrus H. McCormick, Jr., had been made trustees at a relatively youthful age, both leaders of the new forces, businessmen direct and practical in their efforts to improve the college they had loved since student days. In the figure of a midwesterner, born in Wales and educated at Leipzig, the first of the trustees elected by the alumni body came to the board: David B. Jones, hungry for action and outspoken to the point of tactlessness.

Just before the regular trustees' meeting of March 1902, Jones entered into conversations with three leading faculty members, Wilson, Brackett, and Fine. Jones became convinced that Princeton was in a serious situation and needed immediate reform. McCormick proved a ready ally. A conference following the board meeting was held at the Princeton Inn, resulting in a proposal to form a committee to oversee the affairs of the university, composed jointly of trustees and faculty. This was immediately set before Patton. He heard it in silence. "Will the president be a member of this Executive Committee?" he asked.[23] The answer being in the negative, he caught the drift of what was up. Nevertheless, with the wily patience that had so often served him well, Patton agreed to consider the proposal.

The next months were consumed in discussions between the cabal of dissident trustees and dissident professors. No plot against a king could have been laid with more circumspection or secrecy. At the request of the trustee group, the professors prepared a memorandum defining the sweeping powers which they believed the committee should wield, and strongly urged that Patton should not be a member. Later they compromised. They proposed that Patton be a member if Grover Cleveland consented to serve as chairman.

"Our plans must be well made before too many people are taken into consultation," McCormick advised a colleague in April.[24] But one of the more conservative members of the board, getting wind of what was in train, declared himself unable to acquiesce to such "a revolutionary measure."[25] Patton, confronted with the developing situation, was described as being "in a very disturbed state of mind."[26] As in all such plots, disagreements broke out within the group. Finding his name associated with the proposals, Pyne attacked Jones; Jones denounced the "contemptible poltroonery" of Pyne and other eastern members of the board. "They act," he declared, "as if they were trustees of Patton's feelings and position, and not trustees of Princeton University."[27]

Patton talked of remaining another six years at the helm, but in private he began to show himself ready to compromise. He agreed to resign if he were given a payment covering the difference in salary between that of president and of a professor over the next six years. He added, as a condition, that his son also be taken care of with an appointment to the Princeton faculty.

So it came about that at the board meeting of June 9, 1902, Patton expressed an emphatic desire to be relieved of his duties. The trustees immediately proceeded to the choice of a successor. Unanimously, on a single ballot, without any other name being presented, Woodrow Wilson was elected. A delegation of trustees from his own Class of 1879 was dispatched to notify him at his home.

*   *   *

Wilson's triumph was unshadowed. The trustees had never been able to agree on anything before, remarked one member of the board. The press greeted the election as major news, with glowing tributes to Wilson in the editorial columns. From far and near came a flood of touching congratulations. "It makes me homesick and blue," wrote Bliss Perry's wife to Ellen Wilson, "to think that the event we had so often talked about and wished for has come to pass, and we are outsiders, not there to enjoy it."[28] From his youthful love, Cousin Hattie, came congratulations, as from Charles Shinn, his ever-affectionate classmate of Johns Hopkins days. Theodore Roosevelt, recently installed in the White House following McKinley's assassination, wrote enthusiastically.[29] The Class of '79 assembled in Princeton "violently and vociferously" to congratulate their Tommy. And when Wilson went to New York to have his portrait sketched for the cover of a popular monthly, nothing less than a coach-and-four was dispatched to meet him at the ferry.

This was no ordinary election to a college presidency. Wilson was a beloved figure within the whole Princeton community, among townspeople no less than among faculty and students. He was widely respected in the scholarly world and known to a broad public as an inspiring writer and speaker. His style and his presence had made a wide mark. He was in his prime, vigorous, apparently in perfect health. Nothing that came afterwards can be seen in its true light unless set against the image of the man as he stood in this spring of 1902. It was possible (all things being possible) that he should fail; or that he should succeed in ways that were paradoxical and ambiguous. The future, as Wilson himself would have said, was in the hands of Providence. But for the moment clear success seemed to be certain, and the general rejoicing was unmixed.

TIME OF ACCOMPLISHMENT

The president-elect and his family lingered in the house they were all soon to leave, and as summer quiet descended on the campus, Wilson brought to completion the book version of his *History of the American People*. He wrote methodically, thirteen hundred words a day, and early in July closed his rolltop desk and put the key away with the task done. It was "a heartbreaking thing," he wrote his friend Mrs. Edith Gittings Reid, to give up literary work. Yet acceptance of the Princeton presidency had been "a singularly plain, a *blessedly* plain, case." Had he never had any doubts? "You must help me to succeed," he wrote, "by being glad that I did not hesitate."[1]

He and his wife had decided to take their vacations at different times, so that one could be at home to care for the ailing Dr. Wilson. In mid-July Ellen set off to Clifton, Massachusetts, to visit her girlhood friend, Agnes Vaughn Tedcastle of Rome days. There Woodrow would take her place a month later.

Staying on at Princeton, he wrote his inaugural address, slowly now, for he was working out for the first time his full argument upon the significance of the various liberal arts studies—of literature, history, mathematics, the sciences—in the education of the civilized man. He was in a peaceful, happy mood. "I often marvel at the circumstances of my life," he wrote Ellen; "there has been so much sweetness and un-marred good fortune in it, so much love and deep content, so much quiet delight."[2]

By August it was his turn to stay with the Tedcastles. They remembered afterwards his happy good humor. On some days he went in alone to Boston, rejoicing in his idleness and freedom from care. His friend Heath Dabney was doing research in the Boston Public Library; Wilson would wait for him outside in the square until the lunch hour, or go in to perform such a chore as looking up a Greek word. One afternoon he decided to call upon an old and reputedly very wealthy bachelor, Isaac Chauncey Wyman of the Class of 1848. Wyman (of whom more will later be heard) was not at home, and Wilson went instead to Keith's vaudeville theater, where for three hours he enjoyed the music, songs, dances, and gymnastics.[3]

A little later, he experienced the largesse of trustee hospitality, visiting the Junius S. Morgans on Mount Desert Island in Maine. He bore up under receptions and dinners; but it was sailing that "saved the day." He borrowed old clothes from his host, fished for cod, picnicked on the boat, and "rejoiced in the fine air of the open sea."[4] But the summer was all too soon coming to an end. With the recurrent sense of taking part in a play not of his own devising, "I must turn away," he wrote, "to the masquerade that lies before me."[5]

On October 18, with the Stedman Street—now Library Place—house sold, the Wilson family moved into Prospect. Designed in 1849 in the Italianate style by John Notman of Philadelphia, the spacious building had been given to the college in 1878 for the home of its presidents. Ellen had spent much of the summer, after the Pattons moved out, vigorously overseeing its renovation and furnishings. Heating, lighting, and plumbing were renewed. Antiques were selected, and when all was finished the somber tones of high Victorianism had given way to Ellen's favorite greys and pinks.

Prospect stood at the southeastern corner of the campus, accessible to students, the border of its grounds defined by the walkway where James McCosh had regularly taken his afternoon exercise. Within, the principal feature was a large square hall, crowned by a glass rotunda with a balcony surrounding it at the bedroom level. Opening off this hall on the first floor were a large dining room and living room looking toward a terrace and the garden that Ellen was soon to redesign. Smaller living rooms and a large book-lined study completed the reception area. At the top of the mansion, above the bedroom floor, was a tower looking far across the New Jersey countryside. Here Wilson made for himself a safe retreat.

Three days after the family's move, the new president met formally with the trustees for the first time. The educational reforms with which Wilson later became involved, the preceptorial system and the abortive "quad" plan, were to overshadow the less dramatic, but highly significant, modernization of the university which he now set on foot. With the support of the board he proceeded to create, in place of relative anarchy that had reigned, an efficient administrative structure, with the heads of departments responsible to the president. He began a major enlargement of the science program. Putting Princeton's fundamentalist past behind, he made biblical studies a scholarly pursuit, appointed the first Jew and the first Roman Catholic to the faculty, and helped liberate the board from domination by conservative Presbyterians. By 1906 a board resolution would formally declare Princeton a nonsectarian institution.

At his first meeting with his trustees the new president shook them out of whatever complacency they had in regard to the Princeton of their day. Wilson declared that the condition of the college was, "in many respects, critical," with needs that were "great and numerous."[6] The college was well behind Yale and Harvard in its capacity and repute, while newer colleges—Johns Hopkins, the University of Chicago—surpassed it. The principal problem, as Wilson defined it, was an inadequate financial base. The kind of contributions that McCosh had sought yearly were used to pay a substantial portion of fixed, recurring expenses, while endowments were pitifully inadequate. Meanwhile the faculty was overworked and underpaid, and glaring deficiencies existed in the equipment of almost every department. Wilson proceeded to specify the financial resources he considered necessary to put the institution on a sound basis. These included sums for a system of instruction putting more reliance on individual tutorials and less on lectures to large classes; a graduate college; a school of jurisprudence, a school of electrical engineering, and a museum of general science. The capital necessary for these purposes totaled the then immense sum of $12.5 million.

Four days later, on October 25, 1902, the inauguration, planned by Dean West, was marked by elaborate ceremony. The great men of the day were present, J. P. Morgan, Mark Twain, and Booker T. Washington among them. President Theodore Roosevelt had planned to attend, but was prevented by an injury suffered when his carriage collided with a horse-drawn trolley. The weather was fair, down to the setting of an orange sun over a victorious game on the football field.

Wilson's inaugural address put the ideal of a liberal arts education squarely at the center of Princeton's task. He was not talking platitudes or attacking a straw horse. The idea that science had made the classic humanistic tradition irrelevant was held by outstanding educators and scientists. At the opening of Johns Hopkins in 1876, Thomas H. Huxley had been the speaker, maintaining that "mere literary education and instruction" were hostile to the pursuit of true knowledge.[7] In the great debate which saw Huxley on one side and Matthew Arnold as his chief opponent, Wilson took his stand with the latter, on the side of humanism. The thesis of the inaugural had been foreshadowed in earlier addresses and writings; but it stood forth with the freshness imparted by a man called to put beliefs into action.

After the ceremony Wilson greeted an exuberant crowd on the steps of Nassau Hall. He had come from a place, he said, where he told "what the ideals of Princeton are"; he was a man asking "the privilege of leading you and being believed in by you while he tries to do the things in which he knows you believe."[8] There was one more speech, late in the evening of that memorable day, to his comrades of the Class of 1879.

One of the most significant acts of Wilson's first year was the appointment of Henry Fine as dean of the faculty. The two had known each other well as undergraduates and had renewed their friendship when Wilson returned to Princeton, where Fine was already serving as an assistant professor of mathematics. They lived across the street from each other, shared the pleasures of the relatively carefree days of the 1890s, and together had dreamed of a Princeton taking its place in the forefront of American universities. Fine, almost alone among his associates, still addressed Wilson as "Tommy." They had sharp differences over the next years, but their friendship was never shaken. Fine served Wilson well, not only by his cool administrative gifts but by spearheading the major advances that put Princeton in the first rank in science and mathematics. The appointment was a fortunate one from every point of view and gave a strong underpinning to the new administration.

As president, Wilson immediately embarked on a tour of alumni gatherings. Under McCosh the alumni had become an organized and highly vociferous group, and since his days as a young professor Wilson had been one of the most sought-after speakers at their dinners. Now he looked upon these Princeton loyalists as his constituents and upon himself as their prime minister. Wherever he went, they turned out in unprecedented numbers. Reaching St. Paul on a first western tour, he found that a number of them had traveled from the Dakota frontier to hear him speak. The Chicago alumni gave him a rousing welcome, and afterwards in New York, where a few years later he was to face sullen hostility, he delivered his most eloquent evocation of the new Princeton. That night Ellen made one of her rare appearances off the campus. Women were not invited to the dinner, but before the speeches she was admitted with other wives to sit in a state box, from which she beamed down proudly on her husband.

In this address Wilson outlined his plans for new professional schools, for a new museum of natural history, for a tutorial system that would "transform the place . . . where there are youngsters doing tasks to a place where there are men doing thinking." "All of that, gentlemen," he declared, "costs money." They whistled when he mentioned the sum of $2.25 million. "I hope you will get your whistling over," he protested, "because you will have to get used to this, and you may thank your stars I did not say four millions and a quarter."[9] The audience applauded this bold sally. They applauded even more vigorously when he put at $12.5 million the sum that Princeton would ultimately need to accomplish its purposes. In that hour, under the spell of the new leader's eloquence, everything seemed possible.

Dr. Wilson, having moved with the family into Prospect, declined in health through the autumn of 1902. A guest at the inauguration had found him "in his serene old age, casting the benediction of his presence upon the family circle."[10] But by December he was as feeble as a child. Coming out of his ever-more-frequent stupors, he moaned and even screamed for hours. Ellen, constantly at home, bore the brunt of it. Many nights she lay silently holding herself to keep her despair from her husband. By January the end was evidently near.

A deathbed scene, recorded by Stockton Axson, perfectly sums up the character of the old man, with his wit and with a sardonic twist to his humor. The assembled family was expecting him to die at any minute when suddenly he opened his eyes. "Stockton," he said, "what are you doing here?" "I just dropped in," was the reply. "I'm a little dropsical myself," said the old man instantly. Then he gazed around: "And where is the sage of Clarksville?" he inquired.[11] Unfortunate Josie! One sees him standing a little apart, always taking second place to Woodrow, and now the butt of his father's last joke.

The funeral service was held in the parlor at Prospect, and Woodrow accompanied the body to Columbia, South Carolina, where it was laid in the churchyard beside Jessie Wilson's. "My life-long friend and companion," Woodrow described him in a letter to Mrs. Reid,[12] and in early February, when he went to Washington for a speech at an alumni dinner, he begged off spending the night with Theodore Roosevelt at the White House. "I feel . . . that I am relieving you of a sad guest," he said.[13]

Dr. Wilson, living into his eighty-first year, had seen his son step into the place of power he had so long been convinced he would hold. For this he had instructed the boy in his youth, had chided him, and through his later development counseled him with rugged good sense, until without envy he had seen the son surpass him in worldly success. Nor did he doubt that even greater things were in store. On a last visit to Wilmington he instructed the former family servant, David Bryant, a black, to cast his vote for Woodrow when he should be a candidate for President of the United States.

He had seen, in his way, the best and the worst of what was to come. "The ambitious man trusts to the people to lift him into the eminence of position," Dr. Wilson had preached in a sermon years before. "They raise him as high as he wished, higher even than once he had dreamed. They lavish upon him their honors and their stations. They place him at the very top." But what is the use of all this? "Elevation has not made him happy; it has only made him cold and lonely, and envied—maybe hated—by some."[14] Joseph Ruggles Wilson, who had known defeat and disappointment in his own life, could not avert it from his son's.

Wilson had twice been frustrated in efforts to travel abroad (except for walking tours in England), and at the end of his first academic year as president he took steps at least to have a quick view of the Continent. The trip was conceived as a "second honeymoon" for Ellen, one which he hoped would make up "for many, many things," not least the burden of fulfilling her official duties as mistress of Prospect. The three daughters and Madge were sent off to pass the summer of 1903 with Annie Howe in North Carolina, and Charles Williston McAlpin, the new secretary of the university, was left in charge of business.

For the first month the travelers visited sites in England and Scotland, many of which were familiar to Woodrow. In Paris, like any tourists, they took in the grand attractions. Ellen spent so much time at the Louvre that she mastered the local omnibus, going often alone, lest her husband be worn out from accompanying her. After Paris they toured Switzerland and were briefly in northern Italy. No details of Wilson's impressions remain (we have only his careful day-to-day expense account); but this was evidently a different sort of journey from that which he had envisaged in his days as student and scholar.

Returning for the official opening of the college on September 23, 1903, Wilson stood as the focus of all its affairs. He was himself in a confident mood, energetic and commanding, a man knowing precisely what he wanted to accomplish. A tightening of discipline, aimed at countering Princeton's record of easygoing and often disorderly student life, alarmed a minority but was generally recognized as being a necessary prerequisite to other reforms. Scholarly standards were raised, with some of the college's best athletes among those dropped after the midyear examinations. The faculty caught the sense of a fresh wind blowing, and many of them were found reworking their lectures for the first time in years.

In his goal of putting Princeton on a sound financial basis, Wilson faced a short-term disappointment. In 1903 a growing panic in the country's financial markets made the start of an endowment drive unpropitious. The university was forced back on annual donations to meet current needs. An appeal was made to a small circle of wealthy alumni to donate a special fund, the sum of $100,000 for each of three consecutive years. To that end Wilson became, resignedly but cheerfully, what he called the university's "official beggar." The drive started slowly but was ultimately successful.

At the same time Wilson spurred himself to inordinate efforts in making off-campus addresses. In addition to wanting to reach out to alumni, he was responding to mounting invitations from the public, the more numerous because his *History of the American People* was by then in the bookstores, five volumes handsomely printed and illustrated. He welcomed the opportunity provided by these invitations to preserve his long-established role as interpreter and commentator beyond the regular college circuit.

The *History* was being favorably reviewed. Old friends among historians and academicians were inclined to be gentle toward this work, by a colleague of whom most of them were personally fond, and which—however its deficiencies might be weighed—shed luster on their profession. The volumes, wrote George McLean Harper, stood among histories that "are really essays on a large scale"; they constituted, said Charles McLean Andrews, a sketch; but as a sketch they were "brilliant and profound." A familiar story was being told "with all the genius of a clear thinker, a sound historical student and a stylist of unusual powers."[15] Thus fortified and encouraged, Wilson was not averse to seeing their sale promoted by his frequent appearances on the public platform.

The larger business before him, however, was at home, on the Princeton campus; and this he tackled with as high a degree of tact, determination, and effective leadership as he was ever to show. His first aim was a profound and far-reaching revision of the Princeton curriculum. To touch the curriculum of a college—then, as ever since—is to risk becoming involved in stratagems and prolonged infighting. The departments defend their territories with all the latent power that entrenched and determined chieftains can muster. It is greatly to Wilson's credit— as it is a testimony to the spirit which his "almost romantic disinterestedness" had fostered in the university—that the 1903–1904 reform at Princeton was carried through almost without opposition.

The faculty, the trustees, the alumni, and even the wider public were brought into an understanding of what was at stake, and ultimately into agreement upon essential steps. Through the winter a small group of the faculty met at Prospect and hammered out a report; when this was presented to the full faculty in April, Wilson himself took the floor to explain in an hour-long speech the details of the proposal. Thereafter there were nightly meetings, conducted under strict parliamentary procedures, until the measures were adopted. At the spring meeting of the board, the new course of studies was approved with some unimportant reservations.

This was not a contest for narrow ends. At issue was Wilson's basic concept of a liberal education. He had long been a critic of the elective system whereby students had almost entire freedom in choosing their courses and shaping their own education. At Harvard, since Charles W. Eliot's election as president in 1869, the elective system had been powerfuly advocated and then put into effect. "A well instructed youth of eighteen can select for himself . . . a better course of study than any college faculty, or any wise man who does not know him and his ancestors and his previous life, can possibly select for him,"[16] Eliot believed.

Wilson, in contrast, addressed the need for order and principle in a youth's college education; for the student's obligation to lay his mind "alongside of the mind of the world."[17] The age as Wilson saw it was like a new thirteenth century, a new epoch of discovery, where the voyage was not "by the old seas or across unknown continents . . . but out upon the great shadowy main of the mind's life."[18] Without some guidance, without a mixture of the old and the new, of literary studies and of science, the search for values could not be fruitful.

In practical terms this meant a curriculum offering the student after freshman year a choice among roughly a dozen fields of specialization, with each field "a well-considered liberal curriculum"[19]—every scientific group rounded by prescribed literary and philosophical studies, every literary or philosophical group rounded by prescribed scientific courses. Thus a student might focus his interest upon classical studies, on history and politics, on English language, natural or physical science, but always with supplementary courses to complete his picture of the world.

The effectiveness of Wilson's approach—a compromise between free electives and the earlier prescribed curriculum—was widely acknowledged. Elsewhere similar changes were taking place, as the tide of the elective approach began to ebb slowly in the early 1900s. Princeton's was not the first, but in symbolic terms its reform was the most significant, made the more so by its president's eloquent and profoundly based exposition of the curriculum change.

Not less important was the change in the form of college teaching that quickly followed. Wilson had long been dissatisfied with the traditional method of classroom instruction, relatively large classes with the students being given no opportunity for participation. To supplement it, he conceived the idea of introducing into the faculty a group of instructors acting as guides and interpreters to young men passing through the thickets of learning. Ironically, he was himself at his best in college lecturing. "I have to lecture a great deal," he admitted to an audience of schoolmasters, "and my conscience is . . . damaged on that account."[20] But he was not bewitched by his popularity or by the students' rapt attention.

In his third year as president he organized a fund-raising drive to provide support for an experiment in a different kind of teaching, one that would be tuned to the needs and interests of the individual student—that would tantalize him, as necessary, into new fields of knowledge. Favorable response to the fund drive was a signal for the college to start defining, department by department, the operation of what was to become famous as Princeton's "preceptorial system."

Wilson played a direct role in the countrywide search for promising talent. Most of the prospects he met with personally. As several of them later testified, it was the president's strong impact that tipped the scales in favor of their coming to Princeton.

More than forty preceptors arrived in the autumn of 1905. No college faculty has ever received at one stroke so dramatic an infusion of new blood. In the social circles of Princeton these young men, most of them unmarried, created a stir, and the undergraduates found a new interest in their studies. By December the president could report to his board that the system was functioning smoothly; it had entered into the life of the university almost as much as if it were already long established. For him, he told his board, it was a moment of "great happiness."[21] For twelve years he had seen the reform of the curriculum and the reform of the teaching system as two essential steps in vitalizing the college. Now both steps were accomplished. Even a year previously he had not dared to hope that the preceptors could begin their work so quickly, or would be introduced at Princeton with such "ease and enthusiasm."

To be fully appreciated, these educational changes must be seen in the light of Wilson's basic conception of undergraduate life. His own happy experiences as a student made him aware of the growth and maturing taking place in the crucial years between eighteen and twenty-two. He knew that aspirations formed at this time—though often overlaid in later life—did not wholly disappear. It was essential, therefore, that the undergraduate be placed in an environment where time unfolded slowly, and where a rich substance of curricular and extracurricular choices invited the soul. He set himself against tendencies then afoot to abbreviate the college years, as he did against anything that oriented them toward technical or overly practical concerns. The college experience he saw as one requiring "a certain seclusion of mind preceding the struggle of life, a certain period of withdrawal and abstraction." The student must be prepared to be "an actor on the stage and stand in the midst of life," and yet "must walk apart and reflect upon the permanent and universal elements that lie within the transactions he takes part in." If experts, they must be "experts in the relations of things."[22]

The seniors in this college year of 1903–1904 took the unprecedented step of inviting the president to deliver the baccalaureate address at their commencement. Wilson accepted gladly, gave much pains in the preparation, and thereafter made his address to the graduating class an occasion for some of his most enlightening appeals to students. To the Class of 1904 he described the Princeton he had himself loved as a youth as "this little world, this little state, this little commonwealth of our own."[23] Here a man's later life was rehearsed in four short years. "It is chiefly what we have learned here, of whatever kind it be, that we are to carry with us as our make-up and capital into the world where we are to trade for success and happiness and power."

On the campus occur the first tests of diplomacy, of statesmanship, of politics. The young man, facing the world, begins to move on a small stage under his own initiative. All too soon "the play of life is on, and we are in the thick of it. Our thoughts take shape, our passions play along the line of action; our hopes and fears lay hold upon actual experience." But it is during the college years that values have been set and objectives shaped; and there the student must be as much a philosopher as a contender for the measurable rewards of life.

Like every college president, Wilson was vexed by troubles among the students and within the faculty. In these early years of his tenure the incidents were met without severe disruptions or lasting bitterness. One such arose from something as absurdly predictable as the erection of a fence around the grounds of the president's house. Its purpose was to avoid having the garden invaded and trampled—not so much by students, it was said, as by "excursionists from Trenton" who took advantage of the recently laid interurban trolley to come down to picnic in spring and summer months. The students, however, felt their immemorial rights curtailed. They professed, too, that the path where old James McCosh had taken his afternoon walks, head bowed in thought, had been profaned.

Sections of the fence were physically removed one dark night, and a little later, after seniors had demonstrated with placards in front of the president's house, the newest college dormitory was damaged by acts of vandalism. Wilson was furious. He interpreted the attack as being upon his own highly prized right to privacy and against a garden that had been lovingly created by his wife. His sister-in-law Madge remembered afterwards the set jaw and the steel in his eyes as he ordered the fence rebuilt.[24] But a compromise between students and the administration resulted in some part of the offending fence being moved; and the trustees assumed responsibility for having erected it in the first place.

The second incident was potentially more damaging, but compromise and good sense again came into play. Wilson formed a determination to remove from the faculty a professor of French, Arnold Guyot Cameron. Cameron's father had taught at the college for fifty years and the son was highly popular with the students. His best friends admitted, nevertheless, that his manner in the classroom was bizarre. When he pronounced women to be good only for "raising bread, babies and hell,"[25] the president decided he was beyond the pale.

The roots of the affair went deeper. As an undergraduate Wilson had disliked the father, and later had been enraged at the way he treated his son. But the son, who buckled under, presented in Wilson's eye an even more lamentable spectacle. Unconsciously, he must have known that by standing up before the teasing of his own father, he had forged respect, and love, where there might have been humiliation. The younger Cameron failed the test, and Wilson denounced him in private as "a mimic man," a "mountebank."[26]

Informing Cameron that he must leave, the president gave him a year's grace. But in an explosive outburst Cameron insulted Wilson, who ordered him from his office and called for his immediate resignation. As the spring of 1904 approached, support for Cameron developed among alumni and undergraduates and a demonstration at commencement was threatened. Intervention by one of Cameron's friends, Wilson Farrand, resulted in the former's apology and the renewed offer of an additional year. For Cameron the break with Princeton was a personal disaster; but Wilson showed that he could compromise even where his personal emotions were strongly engaged.

To compensate for such debilitating controversies, college life provided its high moments, picturesque and ceremonious. These Wilson enjoyed to the full. He was always the orator, when oratory was required; and his presence filled the public stage. In December 1905, the Army-Navy game was played at Princeton. Theodore Roosevelt, then President of the United States, let it be known he would attend, and accepted Wilson's invitation to lunch at Prospect. Roosevelt was accompanied by a considerable retinue, including Elihu Root, the Secretary of State, and a number of army and navy officers. The president of Princeton met the President of the United States at the railroad depot; to the cheers of students and townspeople, the two rode in a carriage up Nassau Street.

This was not the first time the two men had met. At a mass meeting in 1890 the visiting lecturer on politics at Johns Hopkins had spoken with the then–police commissioner of New York on the subject of municipal reform. Through subsequent years Roosevelt looked on Wilson as an interesting—and perhaps ultimately useful—young man, inviting him to meet with him at Sagamore Hill, at Albany, and in Washington.

(Only the first of these occasions worked out.) In 1900 the two engaged
in a lengthy correspondence on choosing a professor of politics for
Princeton. Their orbits were tending to overlap, though none could
foresee their confrontation in the 1912 Presidential race.

Now, as they broke bread together at the long luncheon table of
Prospect, Roosevelt seemed to have eyes only for Ellen's sister Madge.
Several times he called across intervening guests to catch the attention
or solicit the opinion of that enchantress. The Wilson daughters, huddled
upstairs around the lightwell of the mansion's rotunda, deplored among
themselves the noisy behavior of the President of the United States. They
decided that he was "undignified, much too noisy and not to be compared with [their] father."[27]

Andrew Carnegie was a visitor almost equally noteworthy, particularly since he arrived in town to make formal presentation of a large
artificial lake carrying his name. Wilson, harboring the vision of future
gifts, played skillfully on the magnate's native sympathies. Princeton had
been "largely made by Scotsmen," Wilson wrote him in advance; she
was "thoroughly Scottish in all her history and traditions." He was
himself, he added, of "pure Scots blood"—omitting, on this occasion,
the hint of something Irish in his ancestry that could happily beguile a
St. Patrick's Day audience. As the first of what he hoped might be greater
benefactions, more attuned to the new intellectual life of Princeton, he
made the best of the proffered lake. His speech for the occasion was
carefully prepared, bestowing on his guest the honor of being "an
adopted son of Old Nassau." Carnegie responded with a pleasant and
witty speech of his own, and was suitably cheered by the undergraduates.[28]

In March 1904 Ellen Wilson fulfilled one of her oldest longings, to pay
a leisurely visit to Italy and view at first hand the art of the old masters.
Accompanying her and her daughter Jessie, then sixteen, were family
friends, Lucy and Mary Smith of New Orleans. Later the party was
joined by cousin Mary Hoyt, whom the Wilsons had helped put through
Bryn Mawr and who spoke fluent Italian. Woodrow was left in charge
of the mansion and the remaining daughters. No sooner had the voyagers
embarked than illness took over Prospect. First Eleanor and then Margaret developed measles. The daughters were quarantined, and Wilson
was compelled to cancel a carefully planned speaking tour through the
South.

For the family abroad, harsher tests were in store. The travelers passed through Naples and Salerno; at Rome Ellen submerged herself in Michelangelos and Raphaels. Leaving the city April 26, she wrote ecstatically of her joys; and Jessie, she added, was "the very picture of health."[29] Later that same day, as they stopped at Assisi on their way to Florence, the girl developed a severe case of diphtheria.

A doctor was hastily summoned from Rome; the crisis passed; and in the little Italian hill town a slow recovery set in. But Ellen was in mortal dread for several weeks, as Jessie's pulse fluctuated and the possibility of heart failure persisted. That winter in Princeton Grover Cleveland's twelve-year-old daughter, Ruth, had died of diphtheria, as had the daughter of Professor John Huston Finley a few years earlier. Jessie, always beautiful, was a child almost angelic in her appeal, who as she got better wept pathetically at the thought of keeping her mother from continuing through Italy. By June the patient was well enough to travel and the little group went on to Perugia and Florence. Ellen even seized a few days to make a visit to Venice, where the Smith sisters were now in residence.

The return to America had been postponed, and Wilson faced the events of commencement week with Madge as his official hostess. In addition to the usual ceremonies, Wilson's Class of 1879 was holding its twenty-fifth reunion, with the core of the old group staying at Prospect. All signs were propitious for the college. The trustees having approved the reformed course of study, Wilson explained its significance in a speech at the alumni luncheon. The drive for special funds was declared to have exceeded its immediate goal. Finally, a new dormitory, long in the planning stage, was presented to the university by the Class of 1879. The tower room was turned over to the president for his own use as an office, supplementing the study in Prospect from which the university's affairs had been managed.

The group of youngsters who passed through Princeton in the seventies had made good in the world. Their contributions to the university since graduation, it was announced, totaled $425,000, an unprecedented sum for those days. Three of its members—Cleveland Dodge, Cyrus McCormick, and Cornelius C. Cuyler—sat on its board of trustees. The tall man called to look forth from the tower of "79" was making a unique contribution of his own.

Successful, and apparently happy in his job, Wilson thought seriously once more about a life outside of Princeton. A career in politics still tempted him, to the point that he looked around for openings. He was very much a neophyte in the field. His first moves were blunders, leaving false impressions which the future politician would be at pains to erase.

The signal of Wilson's enlarged perspective was a misguided effort to assert leadership in the Democratic Party. The Democrats had been in the wilderness since the end of Grover Cleveland's second term. Twice, in 1896 and 1900, William Jennings Bryan had been their candidate, his program strongly populist in nature. To Wilson, Bryan's appeal was demagogic, as his plans for the free coinage of silver were chimerical and destructive. In late 1904, before the New York Society of Virginians, Wilson gave vent to these feelings in a speech identifying himself with the conservative wing of the party.

The Democrats, Wilson asserted, had fallen under the sway of radical theorists, contemptuous alike of principle and of experience—men who could never have played any role in national politics but that of a noisy minority. What the country needed was not a party of "discontent and of radical experiment" but "a party of conservative reform, acting in the spirit of law and of ancient institutions."[30] Where but from the South could such impulses derive?

The speech, reported the New York *Sun*, "was greeted with one of the most remarkable demonstrations of approval that has been manifested at a public dinner in this city for a long time." But Wilson paid for the applause of that night. Several years later he was still perceived as a conservative southerner, out of touch with new currents of thought. In most quarters this view prevailed when he entered New Jersey politics in 1910.

Seeming to confirm this estimate of Wilson's political and social leanings was his being hailed, two years later, as a possible Presidential candidate by Colonel George Harvey, editor of *Harper's Weekly* and spokesman for eastern moneyed interests. At a dinner in Wilson's honor at the Lotos Club in February 1906, Harvey launched his trial balloon. The suggestion was widely commented on. Wilson was at first inclined to pass it off as without significance and as of no interest to him. That he took the suggestion more seriously than he professed is indicated by the fact that at a lunch with Harvey in the Century Club a few days later he asked about the prominent men that Harvey had suggested were ready to support him. Wilson was not convinced that a political career was feasible, but he was by then plainly willing to be tempted.

In this same period he made his peace with the patron saint of the Democratic Party. Wilson had always been faintly derisive of Thomas Jefferson for being too much influenced by French theoretical doctrines.

But in a speech at a Democratic dinner Wilson discovered there were actually two Jeffersons, the eighteenth-century theoretical philosopher and the practical man of action. The philosophizing he saw as mere literary dress. The basic convictions on which Jefferson acted—the individual's right to free opportunity and the people's right to unmonopolized benefit of the nation's development—Wilson accepted as thoroughly American. As an abstract thinker, he maintained, Jefferson was a child of his age; in action, he was "a child of his country."[31]

A further, potentially disastrous step brought Wilson to the threshold of politics in his own state. In the autumn of 1906 James Smith, Jr., a powerful figure within the New Jersey Democratic Party, was prompted by his friend George Harvey to promote Wilson's name for nomination to the U. S. Senate. Election at that time was by the state legislature, where the Republicans held undisputed control. The nomination of a Democrat appeared, therefore, to be a purely honorary gesture and Wilson saw no reason to discourage his friends from proceeding.

It happened, however, that another Democratic nominee was in the field—Edwin A. Stevens, a classmate of Wilson's and a spokesman for the liberal wing of the party. Stevens strongly urged Wilson to withdraw on the grounds that the fight was not an empty compliment but a question of party control. Did Wilson really wish to be the stalking horse for the conservative element? Somewhat reluctantly Wilson removed his name from the Democratic caucus. This was not the last time Harvey and Smith would jointly promote his name, but to have succumbed to their blandishments at this juncture could have been a costly, and perhaps irreparable, political blunder.

At the height of his popularity and in the season of his greatest achievements at Princeton, Wilson suffered a physical blow that threw his family into confusion, altered all his immediate plans, and had long-range effects on his future course at Princeton. He awoke on May 28, 1906, to find himself blind in his left eye. Hibben accompanied him to Philadelphia, where he consulted two of the leading physicians of the day, Dr. George Edmund de Schweinitz, an ophthalmologist, and Dr. Alfred Stengel, an internist. The reports of the doctors were alarming, though at first softened for the benefit of the family. The loss of vision was attributed to a burst blood vessel in the left eye, with an ensuing clot, and this, in turn, was diagnosed as a symptom of general hypertension. Later medical authorities have judged the incident as ranging from a severe stroke to an early revelation of the high blood pressure that was to cause a succession of lacunar infarctions leading up to the collapse of 1919.

Whatever the evaluation, the contemporary prognosis was grave enough, with a prescription of total rest and with warnings that the patient might not be able to resume an active career.

Wilson took these warnings seriously. He canceled a Harvard commencement address as well as lectures scheduled for the summer at Columbia. He withdrew from Princeton's traditional June events, appointing Hibben to represent him at the trustees' meeting, and sending a brief, elegiac message of farewell to the graduating class. To avoid disturbances during the busy weekend, he slept at the house of a neighbor, Professor John H. Westcott. Ellen found him in an uncharacteristically irascible mood—annoyed by things he usually enjoyed, and even making uncomplimentary references to the confusion caused by "seven women in a house." (His sister Annie and her little daughter were staying at Prospect, adding to the normal complement of wife, daughters, and sister-in-law.)

To her cousins Mary and Florence Hoyt, Ellen poured out her anxieties. She quoted the doctors as saying it was "impossible to exaggerate the critical nature of the situation"; and described what she understood to be the nature of the threat to her husband: "It is hardening of the arteries, due to prolonged high pressure on brain and nerves." Having recently endured at close hand the torture of Dr. Wilson's death, she added with poignancy: "It is, of course, the thing that killed his father." A letter from Dr. Stengel, evidently intended to be reassuring, Ellen took without too much comfort, finding some parts of it to be contradicted by others.[32]

By the end of June, nevertheless, the outlook appeared brighter. The clot was being absorbed with what the doctor termed "extraordinary rapidity" (though Wilson never fully recovered the sight in his left eye). Change of scene and a rest of three months seemed the first, essential steps, and with his wife and three daughters, preparations were made for a stay in England. The family settled in a tiny, rose-bowered cottage in Rydal, close to the homes of Wordsworth and Matthew Arnold in the Lake District. In spite of the grim events that had caused it, the stay turned out to be idyllic. Wilson found his energies returning and was soon walking as much as fourteen miles a day through the surrounding hills. Rydal seemed to him the most beautiful spot on earth, and with his recurrent urge to own property he looked for a house to buy.

One day on the bridge over the Pelter River he was approached by a tall Irishman who introduced himself as Frederic Yates. "We are poor," said he of himself and his family, "but, thank God, not respectable."[33] Wilson was enchanted by the new acquaintance, who was found to live but a short distance from his cottage, and a friendship was formed lasting to Yates's death in 1919.*

Yates was an artist of talent whose portraits and landscapes were hung regularly in the Royal Academy. Adding to the attractions of his household were a charming wife and a daughter, Mary, who "looked like a goddess," and walked "with easy wild grace."[34] When Ellen, with Jessie and Eleanor, went off for a two-week tour, Wilson remained in his little cottage with Margaret. They dined almost daily with the Yateses, and he sat long hours for his portrait.

As autumn approached, the question of Wilson's immediate future presented itself. He was being urged by Princeton friends on the faculty and board to remain in Europe for the winter. But two doctors whom he consulted in Edinburgh encouraged him to resume a normal life, only observing certain restrictions on his schedule. With his family he sailed for home on October 6. "I want to vindicate my prudence by beginning very leisurely and sedately to pull the load again," he wrote, adding that the doctors would have "no indictment" against him this time.[35] He canceled his autumn lectures to the undergraduates, fixed limited working hours, and arranged to withdraw for a rest in the afternoons.

Despite these good resolves, Wilson was meditating plans that would call out all his energies and put his endurance to the test. While still at Rydal he had sketched a physical reconstruction of the Princeton campus which joined the buildings into quadrangles, or separate colleges, such as he had seen at Oxford and Cambridge, and on the basis of which he foresaw a social and educational renewal of undergraduate life. The idea had been long dormant in his mind; the time for its realization, he was convinced, had now come. He felt secure in his leadership and confident of the board's support. "How delightful it is that we should be a group of friends," he wrote Cleveland Dodge, as he headed for home, "who are working heart and soul for the University which has in it the making of the best and most distinguished institution of its kind in the world; that we should believe in each other, and should feel the same enthusiasm for the same ideals. I have indeed fallen upon a happy fortune to be the leader in such an enterprise, so backed and so conducted!"[36]

In this euphoric mood Wilson headed for home. His ship encountered heavy gales in mid-Atlantic, as if symbolic of the changed atmosphere

---

* As his death drew near, while Wilson was negotiating the peace treaty in Paris, Yates wrote a last, touching letter to his friend: "You have lifted us all up, dear Great Man." (Feb. 4, 1919, PWW, 54:488) Wilson contributed to the support of Yates's widow.

he would find developing in Princeton. The alarming illness of June coincided, indeed, with an abrupt change in his fortunes as president, to a degree that raises the question of whether or not the illness caused personality changes and was, in effect, a cause of future setbacks. For four years Wilson had led the university through a series of basic reforms, maintaining an unchecked pace while infusing the institution with a sense of heightened unity and purpose. During the next four years Princeton would undergo a time of fierce division and travail, with Wilson displaying not only a different side of his character but at critical moments making painful errors of judgment.

Neurological illness, following the June attack, certainly contributed to these reversals. In part they are to be explained, also, by changes in Wilson's outlook and work habits. He had been through a shattering ordeal, confronted by the threat of having to abandon his career, and faced with the possibility of an early death. Not surprisingly, he showed himself a man in haste, impatient of obstructions and delays. He had been told it was imperative that he have rest. Not surprisingly, again, he sheltered himself from unnecessary drains on his energy, forgoing many of the meetings, consultations, and personal encounters to which the successes of the first years could be partially attributed.

Beyond such prudential measures, his conduct was conditioned by the situation at Princeton, bound to be frustrating to a leader who had relied for his first victories upon a common enthusiasm. Wilson's idealism had subdued opposition; but the atmosphere it had created could not last. After 1906, rivalries and jealousies within the board and the faculty asserted themselves. To innocent forces of conservatism, desiring nothing but that the old college should never change, were added the menacing voices of the new rich, resolved to take matters into their own hands. To all this Wilson reacted as a man for the first time facing antagonists who could not be charmed by eloquence or brought to share in his own vision. His life up to that point, as he told Ellen, had been full of "sweetness and unmarred good fortune." Now there was bitterness, not altogether of his own making.

Wilson responded to the growing opposition in ways surprising to many. Intimates like Hibben and Axson had thought of him as essentially gentle, the courtesy of his everyday manner reflecting a disposition genial and affectionate to its core. But there was another side to Wilson, betrayed in an occasional irascibility or, more profoundly, in the revelation of his religious faith. He never forgot that he was the son of Presbyterians. Dr. Wilson crying out before the elders of his church that he was "right, right, right!," James Woodrow carrying to ultimate rejection before the highest church court his pro-Darwin views, were alive within the son and nephew. An unexpected sentence in the sesquicentennial oration of 1896 was spoken in more than jest. "Your thorough Presbyterian," Wilson said, "is not subject to the ordinary laws of life,—is of too stubborn a fibre, too unrelaxing a purpose, to suffer mere inconvenience to bring defeat." Woodrow Wilson was a "thorough Presbyterian," and after 1906 felt called to prove it.

Some aspects of Wilson's conduct admittedly remain puzzling. But no great life is ever wholly explicable, and in Wilson's the elements of light and darkness, the ambiguities and the dualisms, are particularly tantalizing. This mixed aspect of the man was brought out especially in crises or temptations. Of these there were to be many in the years immediately following the 1906 illness.

GATHERING CLOUDS

Wilson arrived back from England, rested but still suffering from the effects of his illness, to face what was to become a major crisis in his career, a prolonged, bitter, and ultimately devastating confrontation with Dean West. The two men had been friendly but never intimate. They had watched with common dismay the growing decline of discipline and scholarly standards during the last years of Patton's rule. They had shared hopes for a reborn Princeton. As the graduate school came to be West's special preoccupation, Wilson desired its success no less than West. Both were of similar background, children of the manse brought up in the Presbyterian faith. Wilson admired West's literary imagination and was, like him, a devotee of the classics. With other members of the faculty, among whom West was held in high regard, Wilson recognized as exemplary West's private life, conspicuous for acts of kindness and for devotion to a mentally disabled wife.

By the autumn of 1906 the conflicts between the two men, shortly to wrack the university, had not become generally apparent. Yet scoffing remarks on West's part, combined with a tendency to form alliances among doubters, might have put Wilson on guard. Divergent views on the nature and location of the graduate school were, moreover, already developing. They had earlier agreed that its place was at the center of the campus, West seeing this as a way of giving it prominence and assuring it an impressive architectural setting, Wilson seeing it as vital to his educational theories. Only if the graduate school were placed at the heart of the university, he believed, could it provide the stimulus to scholarship which he sought, with its example and comradeship being "for the benefit of young men and old, for the novice as well as the graduate." The alliance between West and Wilson, based on divergent rationales and values, was obviously fragile.

Indeed during his illness of the previous spring, Wilson had seen how the wind was blowing. The graduate school was then installed temporarily at Merwick, a handsome estate removed from the college, and West was finding the situation to his liking. His autonomy over its affairs, a heritage of the last Patton days, seemed to be reinforced by physical distance; and the luxury of the surroundings was gratifying. Wilson instructed Hibben, his representative at the spring meeting of the board, to declare any suggestion of a remote site to be "out of the question."[1]

There matters rested until, in the autumn, Dean West was offered, quite unexpectedly, the presidency of the Massachusetts Institute of Technology. No one seems to have been more surprised than West himself, the Latinist and classical scholar, by this call to the citadel of New England technical training. Tempted, perhaps, as much by the incongruous challenge as by any conviction of his fitness for the job, he spent sleepless nights mulling over the offer. The Princeton community awaited the outcome with considerable interest. For the trustees at their autumn meeting, Wilson drafted a resolution, enthusiastically endorsed, urging West to stay and declaring that his departure would be "quite irreparable."[2]

This action on Wilson's part is difficult to understand. The storm signals were sufficiently clear to have made it appear preferable for West at that point to move on. Wilson could have taken advantage of the M. I. T. offer to have a frank talk with the man already subtly revealing himself as the adversary. That he should instead have played a leading role in keeping West at Princeton must be attributed, in part, to the aftereffects of the spring illness—Wilson had neither the physical nor psychic strength to face a painful confrontation. In part, also, the explanation must lie in the sort of romantic chivalry marking Wilson's leadership up to this point. He preferred to keep his adversary on the stage, to defeat him in a joust of principle, than quietly and firmly to act the role of practical administrator.

West, in any case, was not appeased. Even before the board resolution, he had arraigned Wilson for failure to cooperate on development of the graduate school; and when, late in October, he turned down the M. I. T. offer, it was after "a stiff and wearing strain," he wrote Wilson, adding rather ominously, "Now for team work"—as if one local chieftain were acting on terms of equality with another. The further appendage of a

Latin tag, *ora pro nobis* (pray for us), was characteristic of a certain strain of pedantry in West, but carried a message that could not have been exactly pleasing to even so confirmed a classicist as Wilson.[3]

One of Wilson's strongest supporters on the board, Melancthon W. Jacobus, an experienced educator who had been acting president and dean of the Hartford Theological Seminary, warned Wilson of West's growing air of independence. Was he remaining, Jacobus asked, "on the basis of a thorough understanding of the position which he occupies in relation to your Presidency of the University?"[4] Wilson replied in a confidential letter. It has not been preserved, but its substance was such that Jacobus found his "suspicions and . . . fears" fully confirmed.[5]

Wilson, however reluctant at this time to admit it, had missed the opportunity of ending a confrontation which was soon to bedevil him and to drive a wedge into the board. He condemned himself to a debilitating warfare between himself and a man who fought shrewdly and in a style totally the opposite of his own. Where Wilson in a situation of conflict elevated issues to the status of ideals and fought for them with the intolerance of a true believer, West was devious, subterranean, and knew instinctively where vanity or spite could be played upon. Not until he faced Henry Cabot Lodge in the struggle over the League of Nations would Wilson again find an opponent so like himself in tenacity and yet so different in choice of weapons, and so utterly implacable.

The character and placement of the graduate college were only a part of much larger plans that Wilson was turning over in his mind in the autumn of 1906. "We are studying *an organic problem*," he had written in his draft to Hibben the previous June, ". . . and the Grad. College must be treated as part of it."[6] Now the nature of the "organic problem" was made clear. In a long report at the December board meeting, Wilson set forth his concern for the way the democratic spirit long characteristic of Princeton was being undermined. The villain was the upper-class eating clubs, which had increased in numbers and become more prominent within recent years. By their exclusiveness, he argued, they were dividing the college and causing a deep disintegration of undergraduate life. For a remedy Wilson suggested dividing the undergraduate college into residential quadrangles, each with its own dining hall and its intimate social contacts. The upper-class eating clubs would either fade away or, democratized and reborn, would become part of the quadrangle plan.

Within the context of this social reorganization the proposed graduate college would have an important place. It would stand among the other collegiate units but with its own privacy and walled seclusion, a reminder to undergraduates of the ultimate values of scholarship. The concept of the quads, moreover, was closely connected in Wilson's mind with reforms he had already introduced. "We have put teacher and pupil into a new relation of comradeship almost forgotten elsewhere," he wrote. "We must now provide a new comradeship for pupil and pupil."[7]

The board, having listened to this report with the respect they were accustomed to give to the ideas of their president, appointed a committee with Wilson as chairman to consider the next appropriate steps. Jacobus referred to it as "one of the most significant measures ever taken under the thought of the Board."[8] There were, nevertheless, a few premonitory rumblings. Grover Cleveland, prompted by his friend West, was reported to be "a good deal worried"[9] about the plan, thinking it would supplant the priority of the graduate college. In the same letter, Dodge, Wilson's faithful supporter, warned that implementation of the quadrangle plan would take a vast sum of money and that expectations of carrying it out immediately were unrealistic.

Thus matters rested until June 1907, when the "quad" plan was made public and the dogs of war were loosed.

For Ellen Wilson the years as president's wife had not been serene. The breaking up of the Library Place house and the move into "big, stately, troublesome Prospect" had been particularly hard for her. Her daughter Eleanor, moving at night through the mansion, recalled hearing her mother's sobbing at the change and being comforted by her father. Yet Ellen faced her new tasks with a mingling of pride and a sense of duty, running Prospect with a firm hand and presiding gracefully at endless receptions and the comings and goings of official visitors.

Life in the mansion marked a break in the family circle that at Library Place had been so intimate and delightful. Ellen suffered the inevitable pain of seeing her children grow up and leave the nest; the sense of loss was the more acute because an extended family had been scattered and was going its own ways. Her brother Stockton was off on his own, teaching; her nephews Edward Axson and George Howe, Jr., who, while students at Princeton, had brought high spirits to the household, both graduated in the late nineties and were making careers of their own. The youthful male contingent of the family had thus been depleted.

Of the three Wilson daughters, Margaret and Jessie went to The Woman's College of Baltimore (later Goucher College), and Eleanor went to St. Mary's School in Raleigh, North Carolina. But they were often at Prospect, as was Ellen's sister Madge. Woodrow's widowed sister Annie and her small daughter were regular visitors. Ellen worried about Woodrow's being surrounded by "petticoats," and she must herself sometimes have wished for the hearty masculine company of earlier days. For Woodrow she craved the sort of intimate gaiety she could not always provide.

Misfortunes of family life fell with particular severity upon Ellen. She had borne the brunt of Dr. Wilson's last illness, and seen Woodrow through an operation for hernia in 1904, complicated by phlebitis. The journey to Italy, which should have been an unmarred delight, became a nightmare as Jessie lay stricken with diphtheria. Her husband's terrifying illness in the spring of 1906 had confronted her with the prospect, almost too painful to be borne, of his permanent disability or imminent death. A year later, Eleanor had to be nursed through an extended convalescence following a dangerous operation for tubercular glands.

From within the Axson family came blows that further shook Ellen's composure and cast a cloud over her normally resilient disposition. In the winter of 1904–1905 Stockton Axson, whose psychological state had long been delicate, went through a severe stage of melancholia. All that autumn Ellen watched him "struggling desperately to keep out of that pit, yet slipping steadily down inch by inch."[10] From Philadelphia, where he remained hospitalized for three months, he returned for particularly harrowing visits. He depended entirely upon Ellen at such times; and Ellen was haunted by the curse which had brought her father's career to an end.

Worse, however, was in store. On April 26, 1905, Edward Axson, his wife, Florence, and their two-year-old son were drowned in a tragic accident. Their carriage was being taken on a flatbed ferry across the Etowah River in Georgia when the horses bolted, plunging them into the turbulent waters. A man standing on the opposite bank of the river last saw the father holding his wife in one arm and his child in the other, until the waters submerged them all.

Edward had been more than a brother to Ellen; he had been as dear as her own child, and to Woodrow he was as the son he had always longed for. He had suffered in childhood from being farmed out to various relations after his mother's death, and had developed a stammer devastating to his self-esteem. His sister worked tirelessly with him, according to the best methods of the day, but the handicap was never wholly overcome. With Ellen and Woodrow he found his first secure home, growing to a handsome youth with strong interests in science and engineering, and graduating with distinction from Princeton. Because of his stammer, however, he felt himself disqualified from marriage. A young woman, herself handicapped by a childhood attack of polio, overcame his shyness. They had been united in affliction, and "in their death"—so read the poignant inscription chosen by Ellen and Woodrow for the common grave—"they were not divided."[11]

Ellen suffered a shock from which she did not soon recover. Her daughter recalled that months afterwards she could rarely be induced to go out of the house even for carriage rides, and then was sunk into a silence which solicitous questions failed to penetrate. Woodrow was deeply, at first helplessly, concerned about her. He began to feel that it was not misfortunes alone that were responsible for her state, but that he had neglected her interests amid the pressures of his career. Ellen had largely given up the painting that had been her means of expression, and indeed once her hope for fame. Now Woodrow encouraged her to take it up again. The summer of 1905 was the first of several summer vacations spent at Lyme, Connecticut, where, in the congenial surroundings of an artists' colony, Ellen could have art lessons and renew her skills.

This helped, but it did not avert the worst aftereffects of her depression. Through the winter of 1906 Ellen suffered from severe pains in her back and limbs. Submitting to frequent massages, she gave up many of her normal activities. In the social life of Princeton, she now began to be thought of as a difficult dinner guest, her attendance a price to be paid for her husband's scintillating presence. The tints in her hair and her complexion that had given her beauty in her younger years had faded; her charmingly diminutive figure had begun to grow rotund. She was the kind of woman that a man might find it awkward to be placed next to at a formal dinner, and yet in whom, if he were sympathetic and intelligent, he would find an originality of mind and a fund of humor which not even low spirits could mask.

Woodrow in this same period was going through changes and stresses in his personal life, not unrelated to the mounting turmoil in university affairs. The winter of 1907 found general agreement that for his health's sake he must take a winter vacation. He chose Bermuda where he hoped not only to get ample rest, but to draft, away from distractions and interruptions, the series of lectures he had promised President Nicholas Murray Butler of Columbia. On a cold day in January he set sail for the south. Bermuda would prove a choice of far-reaching consequences, as would the fact that Ellen did not accompany him. She liked to say that she was the one who remained, like the fixtures, in the house.

This first visit to Bermuda afforded Wilson a blissfully happy escape.

Cares of the college president fell away at once, and his January turned to a metaphorical June. "I find a very strong feeling of strangeness on me," he wrote Ellen soon after arriving; he sensed in his surroundings "everything to disturb one with sweet thoughts of all persons and places loved and longed for."[12] He missed Ellen desperately, yet into his letters to her (her own of this time have not been preserved) there crept for the first time an indication that all was not smooth in their marriage. It seems evident that in her grief and depression Ellen had withdrawn even from him. "Ah, my darling, my darling! how I wish you *knew*! How I wish my love availed. . . . May God show it to you, through your own heart, if I cannot." The gentle reproof was accompanied by expressions of self-blame. He had been thoughtless and absorbed in his career, he suggested; "I get to taking you for granted as a sort of part of my individuality. I cannot in any other way account for the suffering I cause you."[13] In this mood of estrangment he advanced toward an encounter that was to affect his life deeply and that, in the future, might well have cut short his political career.

On shipboard, Wilson fell in with a young couple, the David A. Reeds from Pittsburgh, who took him under their wing and introduced him to the delights of the island. They were "almost like affectionate children to me,"[14] he wrote home. In the mornings he worked on his forthcoming lectures, went on short expeditions on foot or bicycle in the afternoons, and in the evenings enjoyed, if somewhat aloofly, the gay, intellectually unpretentious company at the Hamilton Hotel, where he was staying.

"This land of repose and enchantment," he wrote, "seems for the time being to strip me of all but the essential elements of my life and consciousness."[15] Princeton began to seem far off, and he wondered why men like himself should be so preoccupied with the details of constitutional government. Notes he made for an address at the local church include a rather surprising reference to the "unhappy formality of morals."[16] "I try to be as irresponsible as possible, and so renew my youth," he wrote in the same vein to Ellen.[17]

The month passed rapidly, as vacationers arrived and departed. "I am a little lonely since the last boat left," Wilson wrote at the end of January. "It took away practically everybody I knew. There is almost nobody left to keep my thoughts from missing you, my Eileen."[18] Yet someone who would help him do just that was fated at this juncture to make an appearance.

He first saw her across the hotel lobby as she made her way, fluttering in silken shawls, to a dinner for which she was characteristically late. A few days later he made her acquaintance. The woman was Mary Allen

Hulbert Peck, six years younger than Wilson, born in the Midwest and brought up in Michigan and Minnesota. A first marriage had ended with the death of her husband, a mining engineer; and a second, to a woolen manufacturer of Pittsfield, Massachusetts, had been unhappy from the start. Aiming to make a life of her own, Mrs. Peck had come to Bermuda regularly since 1892, where she had a large house and entertained all the better-known visitors to the island.

Before returning to Princeton on February 6, Wilson wrote her that he did not "like to go away without saying good-bye. Last evening I only said good night." It was not often, he added, that he could have the privilege of meeting anyone whom he could "so entirely admire and enjoy." In their first talks, he had evidently whetted her appetite for his favorite author, Walter Bagehot, and on returning to Princeton, he sent her a volume of Bagehot's essays along with one of his own—"that you may know me a little better."[19] Mrs. Peck, despite her superficial gaiety and her reputation for brilliant entertainments, was not a happy woman, and was facing at that time the question of a legal separation from her husband. In thanking Wilson for the two books he had sent her, she added that in her meetings he had given her "strength and courage in a moment when my spirit faltered and the struggle seemed not worth while."[20]

After this initial exchange, the acquaintance lapsed. But the web of circumstance had been woven, and a year later, on Wilson's second visit to Bermuda, the two would meet again. In Ellen's depression, in Mary Peck's faltering spirit, in Woodrow's emotional isolation existed elements to bring these three into a complex human relationship.

As for the lectures he had drafted during the Bermuda visit, and which were delivered at Columbia in the months following his return, they were to be his last sustained piece of scholarly work; they also cast light upon the road ahead. Spoken from notes and afterwards rewritten, the lectures keep a vivid, unaffected style and show the author at his best. The most significant in the series, covering the various aspects of the American constitutional system, was Wilson's discussion of leadership as it had become focused in the Presidency. The reluctant initiatives of Grover Cleveland had given way to the exuberance of Theodore Roosevelt; and Wilson, however much he might disagree with the Rough Rider's policies, was an admirer of his combative, newsmaking style of action.

The President, Wilson wrote in the lectures published under the title *Constitutional Government in the United States*, was becoming more and more a political, and less and less a merely executive, officer. As a political leader he was the spokesman of the nation, not of a party. "Let him once win the admiration and confidence of the country, and no other single force can withstand him, no combination of forces will easily overpower him. . . . If he rightly interpret the national thought and boldly insist upon it, he is irresistible; and the country never feels the zest of action so much as when its President is of such insight and calibre." His office, he said in another passage, "is anything he has the sagacity and force to make it."[21]

This view would prove important to Wilson's conduct as President after 1912. To a hardly less extent it was important to his role as educator. At Princeton he had won by 1907 the confidence and admiration of the college constituency—of trustees, faculty, alumni, and students. In the largest matters he had correctly interpreted their thought; and now he seemed irresistible. Returning from Bermuda in a mood of liberation and with a sense of renewed youth, he was prepared to move forward with "sagacity and force." Self-confidence bordering on arrogance, a tendency to be urgent and persistent and to personify the issues, might have been predicted by anyone listening carefully to his lectures at Columbia.

The spring of 1907 found Wilson facing head-on the two related issues of the location of the graduate college and the social reorganization of undergraduate life. For the graduate college, West was now firmly committed to a site off-campus, preferably at Merwick, where a small group of students had been living in high style for more than a year. Wilson induced him to put his position in writing. West gave his case away, arguing that Merwick was superior to an on-campus site in part because its location would make it easier to recruit and keep a staff of domestic servants: they would not so easily "roam the streets or hang around the saloons."[22] As for isolation from the college, West stated that his graduate students would be delighted to show the luxurious estate to their undergraduate friends, who might even occasionally be invited to dine.

After such an exposition it was relatively easy for the president to make his case for placing the graduate college on campus, at the center of bustling student life. This had always been important to Wilson but was especially so now, because he was ready to launch full-scale his plan for the physical and architectural reorganization of the university. The graduate college would, as he saw it, be situated among the several colleges where the undergraduates worked and lived. With the construction of the former under way, the quadrangle plan as a whole could be the more convincingly envisioned and promoted.

At the June meeting of the board the plan for these undergraduate residential colleges, first presented by Wilson in December, was formally approved. That the plan was sound the later experience of Harvard and Yale, and finally of Princeton, amply demonstrated. But the trustees acted hastily. They had grown accustomed under Wilson's leadership to accept the wisdom of his proposals, and now they failed to sound out the various constituencies, the faculty, the trustees, the students, which would be directly affected. The plan was made public immediately after the trustee vote, during the days of class reunions and commencement ceremonies.

The peace of that June weekend was shattered as graduates returning to reminisce and observe Princeton's progress found themselves shocked and irate at the radical proposals for reordering the life of the college they had loved. In his official explanation of the quad plan, published in the *Princetonian*, Wilson softened the attack on the clubs and played down his emphasis on democratization of the university. He stressed the plan's purely educational features. The alumni had gone along happily with changes in the organization of the curriculum and methods of teaching. He thought he could count on their support for a crowning reform, which would bring students out of local boardinghouses, so often the source of disciplinary troubles, to submerge them in an atmosphere of reading and study.

He had hoped to disarm the opposition. But a group of powerful graduates saw an attack aimed directly at the heart of their interests. The clubs were threatened, clubs where they had spent exclusive, leisurely undergraduate days and for which many of them had helped financially to build sumptuous quarters. Wilson's offer to transform some of the clubs into parts of the new residential colleges did not appease the organized and vocal groups, though many of the alumni wrote in support of the plan, often reciting harsh experiences suffered under the club system.

A majority of the faculty, when put to the test, would prove supportive of the quads. But Wilson's case suffered from the fact that he had not felt able fully to consult the faculty prior to putting the issue before the board and getting its affirmative vote. A matter affecting so deeply the physical and financial assets of the college he deemed one for the trustees first of all to judge. He was perhaps right. But he forfeited as a result of his scruples the degree of solid faculty support he had won for earlier reforms, and lent credibility to those few who were determined for their own reasons to oppose so radical an innovation.

Among the older men who revolted openly was Henry van Dyke,

declaring the quad plan to be an assault on the cohesiveness of the traditional Princeton structure of classes. West, seeing his vision of a separate and isolated graduate college swallowed up in the general reorganization, was unrestrained in his private attacks on Wilson. "I feel bound to say," he wrote the president in July, "that not only the thing that has been done, but the manner of doing it, are both wrong—not inexpedient merely—but morally wrong."[23]

The defection hurting Wilson most poignantly was that of his friend Jack Hibben. It is impossible to exaggerate the degree of intimacy and trust that had grown between the two men. The easy comradeship of Library Place days had been succeeded during Wilson's years at Prospect by a dependence on Hibben, and on Jenny, his brilliant and attractive wife, for counsel, refreshment of spirit, and the kind of mental relaxation that Wilson constantly needed. A diary begun in 1904 showed scarcely a day passing without his going to see the Hibbens at the close of the working hours, or their coming to see him. In the crises of his personal life—the death of his father, the cataclysmic illness of 1906—Hibben was at Wilson's side, more than a brother in loyalty and solicitude. When Wilson journeyed, it was Hibben who most often saw him off and who first greeted him on his return. On Princeton issues the two men stood as one. Together they had watched apprehensively the disarray of the last Patton years, and together laid the groundwork of Princeton's intellectual regeneration.

It was a shock, therefore, when Hibben first expressed doubts on the collegiate plan, and then admitted to Wilson that he was personally opposed to it. Wilson responded generously. "A struggle is ahead of me,—it may be a heartbreaking struggle," he wrote Hibben, "—and you cannot stand with me in it; but we can see past all that to the essence of things and shall at every step know each other's love. Will not that suffice?"[24]

Wilson was vacationing at St. Hubert's in the Adirondacks that summer, and Hibben was among the many visitors who brought with them echoes of the growing rumble back at Princeton. He and Wilson talked at length and parted on what appeared the old terms of intimacy. But a disastrous break was in the making.

Despite portents of battle, the Wilson daughters remembered the season as relaxed and happy, their father sharing with them mountain walks as well as long and amusing sessions at the pseudomystical Ouija board. In the forenoon Wilson worked at recasting the previous winter's lectures, readying them for publication; at the same time he wrote endless letters of persuasion and appeasement to those who were questioning the collegiate plan. He expressed himself as ready to keep open all the details until further discussion could take place in the fall. "It is our desire to go very slowly with this matter and to consider every opinion,"[25] he wrote to one alumnus. But "very slowly" was plainly a matter of months or seasons with him, not of years. His determination and sense of urgency grew with the rise in the opposition.

Wilson now, almost for the first time, saw himself embattled and at bay. He was engaged, as he had written Hibben, in what might prove a heartbreaking struggle. Up to this time he had not been viewed primarily as a fighter. The long jaw, the Scotch and Presbyterian backgrounds, might have put some on their guard; but until this period he had with few exceptions shown himself princely in courtesy and in the spirit of accommodation; his victories had been won by conveying to others his enthusiasm and the enlightenment of his vision. He had lived in the midst of praise and walked the golden pathway of success. Now suddenly all that was changed. A kind of gaiety still lightened his combativeness: "The fight for the quads is on very merrily," he wrote Jacobus, "and must now be seen through to a finish";[26] the adventure, he told the faculty, was "hazardous, but splendid."[27] Yet beneath joy in the struggle lay the somber, ever-present image of possible defeat, and he saw himself, if he should lose, as standing "isolated and helpless."[28]

A new note of stubbornness found its way into his public addresses. On receiving an honorary degree at Harvard in the spring of 1907, he declared, smilingly: "The beauty about a Scotch-Irishman is that he not only thinks he is right, but knows he is right." And then, more seriously: "I have not departed from the faith of my ancestors." He added that the reason he remained proud of the men who had lost the Civil War was that "they didn't consent to be convinced that they were wrong until they were thrashed."[29] The greatness of George Washington, he said on another occasion, was that he never knew when he was beaten. "He gained but few victories, but he always fought harder after a defeat."

Wilson saw his first task of the new academic year (1907–1908) as that of fully informing the faculty and winning its support for the quad plan. That he was popular with the large majority of them could not be doubted; and the young preceptors, almost without exception, revered him. On September 26, in a faculty meeting with Wilson in the chair, the issue was formally presented. A procedural issue recognized as being adverse to Wilson was moved by Henry van Dyke. Hibben seconded it. For a moment the chamber was silent with an icy chill. "Do I understand

The president

With James Bryce, speaking at a Princeton dedication, October 31, 1907

Dean West, antagonist

John Grier (Jack) Hibben, friend

In Bermuda, with Mary Peck, 1907

Dean Fine, wise supporter

The Wilson family at Prospect—Eleanor, Jessie, Margaret with their parents

that Mr. Hibben seconds the motion?" Wilson asked. "I do, Mr. President," was the reply.[30]

Four days later in a special meeting Wilson defended the quad plan in a speech which many of those present remembered as one of the greatest of his career. In the awed silence that followed it, the van Dyke–Hibben motion was overwhelmingly defeated. From that moment no question existed but that Wilson's concept was endorsed by the faculty. From that moment, too, dated the disastrous break between Wilson and Hibben. Wilson viewed Hibben's hostile initiative as having gone beyond whatever his doubts or reserves required of him. Opposition to the plan, expressed by a negative vote, he would have understood and accepted; but in assuming joint leadership of the dissidents, Hibben was guilty of what seemed an unforgivable betrayal.

Wilson was often accused of demanding loyalty to the extent of complete subservience from those who were close to him. But Wilson remained faithful to Fine despite many disagreements, and harbored no apparent hostility to Henry van Dyke. The friendship with Hibben was, however, of a different and deeper kind. What Wilson was looking for from Hibben was not compliance but something close to love. And the denial of this love, this intimate and brotherly affection, was a blow from which he never recovered. The social amenities might for a time be preserved between the two men, but time only brought greater bitterness and the sense of a wound that would never heal.

In later years Hibben appeared the more generous of the two. Despite rebuffs and humiliations he tried to make up with Wilson, and later as Princeton's president acted without rancor toward his predecessor's friends and former supporters on the faculty. Ellen's brother Stockton Axson testified to Hibben's sincere attempts at reconciliation. Yet it is difficult not to discern in the latter's conduct something wily and even faintly treacherous. Whatever his legitimate doubts about the quad plan, he had no reason to place himself in the forefront of the opposition. Subsequent events, which showed him positioning himself solidly alongside West and Pyne, suggest that he may have felt the balance of power shifting within the university—away from Wilson and toward those on the faculty and on the board of trustees who wanted peace at Princeton and, if possible, a continuance of the old order. That his clever and ambitious wife prompted Hibben to make a strong show of independence is not to be discounted. If he consciously jeopardized a precious friendship with Wilson, and in return won safety and, after Wilson's departure, the Princeton presidency, he could afford to be generous in the aftermath.

Following his defense of the quad plan before the faculty Wilson prepared to consolidate and reaffirm the support of the trustees. For the board meeting of October 17 he prepared a conciliatory statement promising that, in carrying out the plan approved the previous June, he would move forward only after full and free discussion. The statement was never delivered. Frightened by the uproar, the committee in charge of the plan declared it had no report to make. A motion made by Pyne, calling for withdrawal of the quad proposal and dismissing the committee, was then passed. Rarely has a body of men, supposedly rational in their judgment, thus reversed themselves on a large matter, so unaccountably and abruptly.

That Pyne should have made the motion was significant. Here was disloyalty more serious than Hibben's in terms of policy, though less wounding personally. Pyne had long been a close friend and supporter of Wilson. He was the board's most influential member. Respected and loved within the Princeton community for his positive leadership and numerous benefactions, he had withdrawn from business at an early age and devoted himself almost exclusively to the affairs of his alma mater. At a time when trustees did not hesitate to deal directly with faculty members, often assuming responsibility for their appointment and promoting their subsequent career, Pyne was seen as a generous and enlightened friend. But he was a practical man at heart. He had intervened strongly among his colleagues when it appeared that agitation against Patton would weaken the institution; his enthusiasm for Wilson was based not only on long-standing personal ties but also on the conviction that in its dynamic president the college had its greatest single asset. Now the institution was again in danger of being torn apart, and he, Pyne, would call a halt to the discussions that were ravaging it. Besides, he was a confirmed supporter of the club system.

It seemed plain that Wilson could not submit to the board's extraordinary rebuff. No one, however, wanted his resignation—not even Pyne at this juncture. As a means of mollifying him a second resolution, proposed by Dodge and seconded by Pyne, was passed. This stated that the board had "no wish to hinder [the president] in any way in his purpose, to endeavor to convince the members of the board and Princeton men generally that this plan [for the quads] is the real solution."[31]

Wilson indeed considered resigning and drafted a letter to this effect. But as he faced the prospect of abandoning the fight and letting down his supporters, he hesitated, and then began to see a way out of the impasse. He would take seriously the board's consent to his continuing the endeavor "to convince the members of the board and of Princeton men generally" of the merits of his plan. He did not complete the letter of resignation, and the next day he told a reporter from the New York *Evening Sun* that the board had given him "perfect leave" to proceed with a campaign of persuasion.[32]

Pyne reacted in fury. He insisted that the quad plan had been turned down "finally and for good," and that the second resolution had been passed only "to save the feelings of the President."[33] He could well be alarmed at the thought of an aroused and eloquent Wilson loosed among the Princeton constituency and the wider public. As for Wilson, "I thought they meant what they said when they offered to leave me free," he told Jacobus in a mood of discouragement; now he was left with nothing but "complete defeat and mortification."[34] Nevertheless he had made his choice, and at risk of completely alienating Pyne and his supporters on the board, he resolved to go ahead upon the course that had been opened to him.

The defeat, such as it was, Wilson accepted characteristically, with stubbornness and renewed determination. First he plumbed the deep places of his faith. "He that observeth the wind shall not sow; and he that regardeth the clouds shall not reap" was the revealing text for a religious talk to Princeton undergraduates shortly after the board meeting. "The world is not looking for servants," he declared, "there are plenty of these,—but for masters, men who form their purposes and then carry them out, let the consequences be what they may."[35] Then Wilson turned outward to the wider community, in major speeches in Memphis and Indianapolis reaffirming his role as a spokesman on national issues. Finally, very soberly and grimly, but without recriminations, he began the preparation of a series of addresses to Princeton alumni, putting the quad plan in the perspective of reforms already accomplished and of his larger ideals for American education.

The inner turmoil caused by these events took a heavy toll, both physically and emotionally. He had seen friends defecting, crucial support falling away, a cherished vision fading. His continued direction of the university had been challenged. In December he suffered some of the symptoms revealed in 1896 and 1906. Fortunately a second winter vacation in Bermuda lay ahead of him. Again he went alone, as Ellen embarked upon a journey to visit friends and relatives in the South.

For a few days he sat on the verandah of his island hotel, recovered from the December illness but still suffering its lingering effects. He felt sedate and middle-aged, he told Ellen, now that he was removed from the field of action; he looked upon himself "with a sort of half sad amusement."[36]

The mood did not last long. He was seeing a great deal of Mrs. Peck, his friend of the previous winter. Installed in a large house, amid a family consisting of her mother, son, and step-daughter, together with various temporary appendages, she regularly entertained distinguished visitors to the island. Among these was the venerable Mark Twain. Over this assembly the lady of the house presided—"any age by turns, and over-flowing with spirits," Wilson wrote of her. He was perhaps the most frequent visitor of all. "I know that you would like her," he told Ellen, notwithstanding "her free Western manner."[37]

One day Wilson, who then abhorred the automobile, drafted for the local newspaper, the *Royal Gazette*, a protest to be signed by Mark Twain and others against automobiles being permitted on the island roads. On the reverse of the draft he wrote a few words in shorthand, which lay undeciphered until Arthur S. Link and his associates began their work on Wilson's papers. Under the discreet heading of "A Sal-utation" those words now appear in the printed volume for 1908. "My precious one, my beloved Mary," they read.[38]

Wilson drew back from the edge of the precipice. More than a year would elapse, and even greater strains would impose themselves, before he would be fully caught up in the emotions thus furtively expressed. That Bermuda visit, nevertheless, saw Wilson and Mary Peck launched upon a close, if still platonic, friendship. Daily they walked the island roads, lingered on the white beaches, talked in their holiday mood of everything under heaven. One day, watching the sea, Wilson confessed to his dream of a career in politics.

Ellen could not fail to sense what was occurring. She had encouraged her husband's friendships with intelligent and vivacious women, noticing how he bloomed in their company, while feeling herself to be lacking the lightness of tone he required for relaxation. The friendship with Mary Peck was different. Sometime during that spring of 1908 it appears that he and Ellen confronted the issues frankly. He had drawn back with determination from the glimpse of an intoxicating happiness, but it was not with the sense of remorse that Ellen might have expected of him. In his baccalaureate address of that June, with the capacity to express his inner self which he so often revealed in public utterances, Wilson extolled self-denial rather than repentance. "I am not sure," he told the departing undergraduates, "that it is of the first importance that you should be happy. Many an unhappy man has been of deep service to the world and to himself."[39] Leaders of the world's thought, he contin-ued, had sometimes found their joy, not in desires fulfilled but in "triumphs over themselves." Wilson appears to have been saying that he could himself be great while being unhappy, and that even if his desires of the past winter had not been fulfilled, he could find joy in his triumph over them.

In this mood he sailed for a third solitary visit to the British Isles. Jessie pleaded with her mother to accompany him, but Ellen had her own need for separateness. In the artists' colony of Old Lyme, Connecticut, she found health and a restoration of her wounded spirit. She gained admission to the coveted boardinghouse of Florence Griswold, and here, recognized as a painter, she was able to assert herself and cultivate her independence. Woodrow may have felt that she was being perverse, yet he recognized his own grievous faults, his "selfishness and subtle exactions," and he did his best to encourage her and not to complain.[40]

From Scotland came letters professing undiminished ardor, yet with a new note of underlying defensiveness evidently reflecting the candid discussions of the post-Bermuda months. "You are my heart's home and its very life," he wrote to her. "*How* I love you! My happiness depends directly upon the degree in which you comprehend and accept my love for what it is, in spite of all my frailties and absurdities, as they must seem to you." "My sweetheart, my sweetheart! Do you love me? Are you sure?"[41]

He traveled on through scenes he had not known before. It was a new world and he was alone—alone "now, for the first time, in my old age, when I am sombre and *capable* of loneliness." He wrote Ellen of the "depth and intensity and almost tragical strength" of his love for her. "I know I do not give you satisfactory proof of it, my darling, but it is there. . . . Try to believe it and realize it and accept it with a *little* joy!"[42] Ellen's letters from this time are again missing, but Woodrow's with their self-blame, and with their hint of his wife's rejections, speak eloquently of their emotional pains.

The walking and bicycling of these summer months in 1908 were interrupted by a stay of several weeks at a hotel near Rydal where he and Ellen, in their little cottage, had spent the summer two years earlier. Here Wilson found his friends the Yateses once more, arriving at their cottage one evening unannounced. The two men were overwhelmed with delight, and Mrs. Yates "almost embraced" him.[43] Afterwards Wilson walked over regularly from his hotel for long talks and for meals, and sat for another portrait.

Despite these diversions Wilson was burdened by a sense of disorientation. In addition to his troubled relationship with Ellen, he felt doors of the outer world closing against him. Political prospects seemed remote and chimerical. The likelihood of accomplishing cherished Princeton reforms was receding. While abroad Wilson undertook two initiatives, both rather absurd on their face, but explicable in terms of his quandary. The first of these involved his delaying in Edinburgh for several days to be within range of communications while the Democratic National Convention met in Denver. Reading daily the Paris edition of the New York *Herald Tribune*, he confessed to feeling "a bit silly" waiting on the possibility of the impossible happening.[44]

Why Wilson should have thought, even half seriously, that he might be offered a place on the national Democratic ticket is puzzling. It suggests that his political ambitions were running high; it also hints at the stir he was creating wherever he went to speak. Besides, George Harvey, the *Harper's* editor who had discussed Presidential prospects with Wilson two years earlier, had gone out to the convention. Might one not suppose that he had gone there with some purpose in mind?

The Democrats took what seemed endless days in coming to their choice. They nominated William Jennings Bryan, as they had done twice before, while the Republicans prepared to nominate the massive and genial William Howard Taft, handpicked by the departing Roosevelt. That these two particular figures were in the ring would prove of significance to Wilson in the not-too-distant future; but for the moment it was indeed "silly" to be sitting in a hotel bedroom an ocean away, not knowing what he was waiting for. He had left instructions to decline the Vice-Presidential nomination if it should be offered; but the faint and far-fetched idea that he could be nominated as head of the Democratic ticket does less than credit to his political judgment at that time. Even Edinburgh, he admitted with some embarrassment to his wife, grew tiresome when one was obliged to stay there with nothing particular to do.

The second initiative involved Princeton business, and its consequences were equally negative. Wilson realized that, in addition to ideals, some large benefaction was necessary to make the quad plan a reality. He might force the hand of the board by having cash in hand, and perhaps in no other way. In vain he had sought an approach to John D. Rockefeller and to J. P. Morgan; he had failed in his hope to interest the older generation of McCormicks. Andrew Carnegie was another significant possibility, and remembering the pleasant Princeton exchange a few years previously, he arranged a visit to the coal magnate's castle at Skibo on an island off northern Scotland.

For two days he journeyed, resting overnight at Inverness. On arriving, he found the castle full of guests, with anyone of less than cabinet rank welcomed by the servants and introduced to the master only at the next meal, where twenty to twenty-five sat down regularly in the great hall. The American ambassador to the Court of St. James's was there—"a very tiresome person" but with "*some* lucid intervals"; and Lord Morley—John Morley that was, the biographer and man of letters, "an old goose" for having consented to be translated into the House of Lords. The president of Princeton went fishing with Carnegie, where it may be presumed he reminded his host tactfully of the large gift he had made to the college. He acted as boatman and pulled in nets filled with fish; but he did not pull in any promises to sustain the quad plan.[45]

Wilson enjoyed the visit but was more than glad to get back to the hotel at Rydal, with its "wonderland of sweet hills and the magic of sun and shadow."[46] He had done his best, if unsuccessfully; but Carnegie continued to think of "his loch" as his unique benefaction to Princeton.

Wilson was returning to America, Yates noted, "with a new grip of things." The summer's absence from Ellen, with the frank and fervent appeals in his letters, seemed to have restored harmony in his private life. Ellen, who was nothing if not spunky, now accompanied her husband and daughters to stay with Mary Peck in Pittsfield. Mr. Peck's nominal presence lent propriety to the visit, and Wilson had speaking engagements in the vicinity. The daughters were showered with gifts and evidently enjoyed the exotic atmosphere of the Peck home, but Ellen not surprisingly felt indisposed and was unable to attend several of the social functions prepared for her. Whatever the difficulties, calm had been reestablished in the relations between the three chief players in this drama. Wilson resumed his weekly letters to "My Dear Mrs. Peck," no different in tone from those he frequently wrote to women friends whom he found sympathetic or stimulating.

If he had accepted with equanimity the disappointing outcome of the Carnegie visit, it was in part because a way of constructing the graduate college on what Wilson considered a suitable site now appeared practicable, thanks to the bequest of a wealthy widow, Josephine Ward Thompson Swann. Mrs. Swann's will was not entirely clear, and during subsequent controversies would be subjected to varying legal interpretations. But the will *seemed* to say that her money was to be devoted to the contruction of a graduate college on the existing campus. At about the same time the noted architect Ralph Adams Cram was called upon to impose some order on the haphazard growth and eclectic styling of the Princeton campus. Foremost devotee of the Gothic, Cram would not prove immune to a desire to create monuments. But he was capable of common sense, and he and Wilson got on well.

The Swann bequest energized Cram, and he was anxious to proceed with what he considered an exemplary building in the "new" style. He picked a site for the graduate college—what he called "unquestionably the proper site"—between Prospect and the dormitory presented by Wilson's Class of 1879.[47] The board formally agreed, a move coming at a good moment for the president. Here was a chance not only to circumvent West but to frustrate Pyne as well, building a prototype quad whose effects could be expected to stimulate further developments along the same lines.

Unfortunately for Wilson, ground was never broken for this project. The Swann bequest was held up in litigation. Meanwhile, within the Princeton community the atmosphere had worsened, and within the board hard lines were being drawn. On Wilson's side the loyalists were Dodge, McCormick, the Jones brothers, and Jacobus; the opposition, shifting in its composition and the intensity of its feelings, was masterminded by Pyne. Grover Cleveland had died the previous summer. Once the hope of the reformers, he had become in his last phase, as Wilson described him in a private letter, West's "dupe and tool."[48] Other supporters, like Wilson's classmate Cornelius C. Cuyler, were beginning to weaken under the mounting stress. Cuyler died in an automobile accident within the year, his death an emotional blow to Wilson—the loss of an old friend, even though a wavering one. Resentments within portions of the faculty festered, while a wider public tended to be sympathetic, though without a real understanding of what the issues were.

Despite the embarrassment of his Edinburgh vigil, Wilson continued to look to the political stage as a way out of his dilemma. Increasingly his speeches dealt with current issues and were delivered before political audiences. He was taking his stand with the conservative wing of his party, his main target the antitrust policies of Theodore Roosevelt. Wilson saw the trusts as a dangerous threat to economic freedom, but he abhorred the idea of having corporate abuses checked by administrative bodies. The commissions Roosevelt had created set personal power above law, he argued; a more clearly defined legal system would make individuals within the business community accountable for their monopolistic practices. At the same time he opposed such favorite panaceas of the progressive movement as the initiative and the referendum.

While standing with the conservatives of his party on political issues, Wilson was adopting an educational and social philosophy markedly in contrast. In these fields he was revealing a radicalism that would color and in the end dominate his political ideas. Struggles at Princeton might not alter the surface currents of his political thought, but they were stirring the depths of his conviction and faith. Great wealth he began to see as the incubator of selfish interests and narrow views, a barrier cutting off its possessors from sympathy with the mass of the population. Watching the cars speed past the artists' retreat one summer in Old Lyme, he judged them to be filled with "restless, rich, empty-headed people . . . [who] are in the world to deepen all its problems and give it nothing at all that it can profit by." They and their kind, he continued, "are the worst enemies of Princeton, and create for me the tasks which are likely to wear my life out."[49] He began to lace his speeches with references to the narrow base from which American colleges drew their students, urging that they look for recruits to the public schools and to the body of plain citizens.

Early in 1909 he made a significant address on Lincoln, exploring the sources and roots of his strength. Wilson had come to terms with Jefferson as a party deity; now he discovered in Lincoln a model for his own deepening sympathies. Lincoln, he said, was a man of the people; he had felt "that unspoken, that intense, that almost terrifying struggle of humanity . . . to live and be free." Lincoln had participated in that struggle: he had felt beating in him "a universal sympathy for those who struggle, a universal understanding of the unutterable things that were in their hearts and the unbearable burdens that were upon their backs."[50] It was understanding of this sort, not the calculations of the businessman or the nice distinctions of the scholar, that Wilson idealized and saw mounting within himself. With such a yeast at work, conservative political ideas could not long remain unleavened.

He also began to talk more directly to the public about issues which he saw underlying his educational reforms. The Princeton alumni still heard his story with divided sympathies, but on the platforms of other universities and before enthusiastic academic convocations he defined his broad objectives. At Harvard in the early summer of 1909 he found the occasion and the time to put his educational ideas in their most precise and persuasive form.

In the auditorium at Cambridge, when he delivered the Phi Beta Kappa Oration in July 1909, was Charles W. Eliot, recently retired from the presidency, who listened with discreet signs of displeasure as Wilson once more put in question the elective system. There, too, was A. Lawrence Lowell, recently elected, ready to stand with Wilson for a new intellectual integration and for a priority of values. A subdued tension in the audience, an awareness of polite challenge, evoked from Wilson the polemical note that lent an edge to his best speeches.

Harvard had always been for him the home of slightly alien forces, the seat of New England rationalism and religious skepticism. But this was also the place to test a man, its respect worth more than effusive praise from a hundred other institutions. Now at the height of his academic fame, in prose charged with a suppressed passion, Wilson drew an unqualified ovation from the Harvard gathering. Here was an epitome, in a form that was to become classic, of the meaning and value of liberal education.

With a nod to Eliot, Wilson acknowledged that the introduction of electives had imparted a stir to American colleges—"an air of freedom and individual initiative, a wealth and variety of instruction" which the old colleges lacked. But the free choice of courses had led to intellectual disorganization; and (now with a bow to Lowell) it was the task of a new generation to "reexamine the college, reconceive it, reorganize it." Nor was the reorganization necessary only in the field of studies, for along with the intellectual disorganization had come the growth of outside interests, the varied absorbing life of the day, which distracted the undergraduates and dissolved the spirit of learning.

Wilson proposed giving the college one goal, one definite aim: the immersion of the student for a few crucial years in a life where the values of the mind and spirit were predominant. This could not be accomplished in the classroom alone. In fact, very little of it could be accomplished in the classroom. The chief impulse must come from life, a collegiate life, its effect on the young man "habitual [and] continuous," inducing the mind to be at home amid immaterial things. The college must be a place of initiation: "Its effects are atmospheric," he said.

> They are wrought by impression, by association, by emulation. The voices which do not penetrate beyond the door of the classroom are lost, are ineffectual, are void of influence and power. No thought will obtain or live there. . . .
>
> If young gentlemen get from their years at college only manliness, *esprit-de-corps*, a release of their social gifts, a training in give and take, a catholic taste in men, and the standards of true sportsmen, they have gained much, but they have not gained what a college should give them. It should give them insight into the things of the mind and of the spirit . . . a consciousness of having taken on them the vows of true enlightenment and of having

undergone the discipline, never to be shaken off, of those who seek wisdom in candor, with faithful labor and travail of spirit.[51]

Into this oration, Wilson said a little later, he had put "the whole of my academic creed."[52] He had justified his collegiate plan in terms going far beyond the local situation prevailing at Princeton. Now he was set for one climactic effort to establish the conditions in which the ideal might become real.

THE END AT PRINCETON

The year 1909–10, which was to be Wilson's last at the university, was the most charged and stormy of his life up to this time. While he was confronting the defeat of long-held plans for Princeton, he was emerging into dazzling prospects of action on a scale he had not imagined since youth. He was stirred and aroused by these experiences and in his private as well as his public life displayed aspects of his character often at odds with settled patterns. Bizarre coincidences and unexpected turns of fortune accompanied the upheavals.

Some aspects of Wilson's conduct in this period are difficult to interpret or account for. They should perhaps be viewed not as one views in ordinary circumstances the behavior of a college functionary or political aspirant, but rather the behavior of a creative genius in mid-career, tearing things apart and reshaping them in order to achieve his destiny. If Wilson's life had ultimately proved commonplace—if he had compromised, or accepted defeat, or simply failed on entering politics—the year 1909–10 would appear different from the way it does in the light of his subsequent accomplishments and world stature. The prodigious liberation of pent-up forces within him puts events in a perspective beyond ordinary success or failure, even beyond ordinary morality or immorality. The way the story is usually told leaves out a sense of fate. Certainly it leaves out laughter, the sardonic laughter of the gods who in achieving their ends turned the little college at Princeton upside down and made fools of ordinarily grave and solemn mortals. To set forth events precisely, and to be as fair as possible to those involved, should not wholly silence these encompassing echoes.

The last act of the Princeton drama began in the spring of 1909 shortly before Wilson delivered the Phi Beta Kappa Oration at Harvard. He had been disturbed by rumors of large impending donations to the graduate school and in March complained to his friend Jacobus that it was strange that he as president had not been consulted.[1] In April he expressed his fear that many matters of university policy were being taken out of the administration's hands and determined by the Committee of Fifty, charged with raising ever-increasing special funds: "Of late," he wrote, "I have felt this pressure and embarrassment very keenly."[2]

His concern at the rumors of gifts generated outside his knowledge and control was well-founded. On May 10, he was presented with a letter addressed to Dean West from William Cooper Procter of the Class of 1883, offering half a million dollars for the graduate college. The gift, besides calling for matching funds, was conditioned upon the college's being built on some other site than that on the campus formally approved by the trustees at their meeting of April 9, 1908; it was to be a site, Procter added, "which shall be satisfactory to me."[3]

Procter, head of the well-known soap company in Cincinnati, had been tutored by West in his youth and had remained the dean's close friend. He was a practical man, known for having strong opinions and holding to them tenaciously. If devotion to his old tutor suggests an unexpectedly romantic side to his nature, the kind of residue that in older men often lies below a hardened crust, his alliance with Moses Pyne was based on more habitual affinities. He was imperious but not wholly insensitive, and it seems strange that in insisting upon his own choice for the site of the graduate college, he did not perceive how profoundly he was interfering in educational policy.

Despite the dangers implicit in Procter's offer, Wilson at first moved cautiously. He knew that West's autonomy would be confirmed by it; he knew its acceptance on Procter's terms would fatally impair his concept of the graduate college and indefinitely deter the establishment of the first "quad." Yet the gift was "deeply gratifying," he wrote McCormick—"*if we can manage to meet his terms.*"[4] What Wilson could not bring himself to believe was that Procter would prove as stubborn as himself, impervious to persuasion and appeals.

Wilson's conviction that the graduate college must not be placed apart had been strengthened by observing developments at Merwick over the past two years. Whatever indulgence he may have had for ceremony and for quaint academic customs had been dissipated by that experiment. A relative handful of graduate students pursued at Merwick a luxurious and archaic routine. The scholars dined nightly in academic gowns; the master pronounced the grace in Latin. After sumptuous fare the company played bridge and chess, held conversations or occasionally danced, before settling down to work.[5] On Wednesday nights students in evening dress beneath their academic gowns, carrying torches, escorted the dean from his home nearby.

When Ralph Adams Cram revealed the plans for the graduate college to be built on campus, at the site chosen by the board, the impression of luxury was confirmed, as was also the impression that Dean West was introducing characteristic ideas of his own. Wilson submitted the plans to members of the faculty committee on the graduate school, modern-minded men like Dean Fine, and Professors Edward Capps and Winthrop More Daniels, asking for their reactions. They complained of the size of the rooms and the elaborateness of the plumbing: could not the scholars, they asked, bathe in cellar installations as had long been the custom for Princeton undergraduates? They asserted that the rooms would be so expensive as to divide the graduate students into those who could afford to live in the new college and those who could not, thus imparting an undemocratic air to the whole venture. What graduate students sought was a chance to work—to work among their peers and under top scholars in their field; everything else was superfluous and smacked of paternalism or worse.[6]

Pondering these reports, Wilson must have realized how much his own ideas had changed during his presidency. He had come to office with romantic notions about the life of scholars, both graduate and undergraduate; he had seen them dwelling amid ivy-covered walls; he had, himself, indeed, made Gothic the approved style for new campus buildings. "We have dreamed a dream in Princeton of how the charm of that place shall be . . . enhanced,"[7] he told alumni at the beginning of his term. But the dream had passed, and something other than the charm of academia was substituted. Influenced by the brilliant men he had recruited to the faculty, propelled forward by his instinctive mistrust of West, he was thinking by 1909 of severe scholastic standards and of a more democratic community. As he changed, and as West became more than ever enamored of his patrician autonomy, the two men drew irreconcilably apart.

The Procter offer precipitated a fresh examination of West's role. The idea not unnaturally arose that rather than refuse the half million dollars, it might be well to curb his excessive powers, which put him entirely in charge of the graduate school curriculum, of its admissions, and the disposition of its fellowships. The long argument over the site of the graduate college was becoming tiresome and had never appeared an entirely persuasive issue. To several of Wilson's supporters on the board it seemed better that he make a case for administrative reorganization than to argue over real estate. If West's authority was clipped, the location of the graduate college would become relatively unimportant, and the way would be cleared for accepting the Procter gift. For Princeton, this would be an ideal solution. A search was thereupon launched for ways of trimming the lion's claws.

The task might normally have fallen to the president, but Wilson was handicapped by his having urged West to reject the M.I.T. offer. He could neither fire West (as he had once fired Cameron) nor hope successfully to negotiate a reduction of his powers. A plan to have West share power with a faculty committee was discussed, but discarded when it seemed evident that West would dominate and control any such group. A faction of the board suggested that the graduate faculty itself take the initiative in curbing the dean, but the faculty sensibly pulled back. As for the board, it was too divided to act.

The debate, therefore, returned to the issue of site. At the June board meeting, a resolution was offered to rescind the previous decision to erect the graduate college near Prospect. In a victory for Wilson, this was voted down. During the summer Procter visited Princeton and decided to accept a site on the golf links, almost as far as Merwick from the central campus but on university-owned land. Pyne was delighted. Cram now found this to be even more "ideal" than the location he had previously chosen.

Facing the October board meeting, Wilson sought the opinion of the faculty committee on the graduate school. Of the six members, Fine, Capps, Conkling, and Daniels argued against a distant site; West dissented, and with him—now the dean's confirmed ally—was Hibben.[8] The trustees' committee agreed with the majority. But when the full board met the next day, a motion to accept the Procter gift was passed. This carried with it approval of Procter's choice of location, and in a separate motion the board specifically reversed its previously affirmed position that the college be erected near Prospect. Thus twice, on two vital matters—support of the quad plan and support of a central location for the graduate college—this group of well-intentioned but wavering men within a short time made complete turnabouts, in both cases pulling the rug from under their president.[9]

Wilson was understandably angry and discouraged. He again considered resigning; and again decided that out of faithfulness to the men who had supported him, on the board and in the faculty, he could not do so while there remained even a faint chance of achieving his aims. A shred of hope remained in the fact that the board resolution had been hedged by an amendment, proposed by Wilson's supporters, making acceptance of the Procter gift contingent upon a legal determination of the precise meaning of the Swann bequest. But this was small satisfaction, and to Pyne it seemed that the affair had been fully settled. So he reported to Procter. But once again Pyne had underestimated Wilson's capacity to fight on—to fight on "stubbornly and circumspectly," until the game was won or lost beyond any possibility of reversal.[10]

While most aroused over Princeton issues Wilson saw his relations with Mary Peck enter a new phase, in all probability changing from a romantic friendship into a love affair. Later he implied as much. In 1915, during the White House years, in an unpublished, anguished document, he admitted to "a passage of folly and gross impertinence"[11] in his life, during which he had forgotten "standards of honourable behavior." To Edith Bolling Galt, the woman he was courting following Ellen's death, and who later became his wife, he wrote even more explicitly of a "folly long ago loathed and repented of," one bringing him "stained and unworthy"[12] to plead his love. It had been, he told her, "the contemptible error and madness of a few months."[13]

It is possible to place this "madness" within the Bermuda visit of 1908. Certainly at that time, as Wilson's letters to his wife suggest, he had become infatuated with Mary Peck. But the climax of the affair seems to have been delayed by an understandable hesitancy on Wilson's part. A careful reading of the correspondence with Mary Peck over the spring and early autumn of 1909 reveals a mounting fervor, giving the impression that a denouement is approaching, not that one has passed. The explicit limit of "a few months" placed on the duration of the affair by Wilson does not, moreover, fit the Bermuda hypothesis.[14]

The last two months of 1909 and the opening month of 1910 constitute the most likely setting for the self-styled "folly." Mary Peck had decided just then to break definitively with her husband and in November moved from Pittsfield, establishing herself with her mother and son in an apartment in New York at 39 East Twenty-seventh Street, just northeast of Madison Square Park. In her memoir, which is highly discreet, Mary's detailed description of this place is nevertheless suggestive. On the eleventh floor, with "tiny balconies" overtopping the roof of the old Madison Square Garden, with its lightly poised figure of Diana and its flags and banners flying in the breeze,[15] the apartment was well fitted to provide a romantic hideaway. It should be remembered, too, that Wilson had long looked upon New York as a place of dangerous temptation; in earlier years he had written Ellen he dared not stay overnight there, and once asserted that if he succumbed to sexual fantasies it would not mean any real infidelity to her.

"Politics frequently called Mr. Wilson to New York," Mary Peck writes of this time, "and they [sic] often dropped in."[16] The reference to "politics" is characteristic of her vague chronology—at this time it would have been Princeton affairs that brought Wilson to town, and the reference to "they" is evidently an attempt to obscure the fact that Wilson came alone.

Wilson's letters to Mary Peck had been growing increasingly ardent since the time they were last together in Bermuda; in November they cease abruptly, and with the exception of two perfunctory notes do not resume until Wilson went to Bermuda alone in February 1910. It is likely that letters written during these months were destroyed before the "complete" collection was sold to Wilson's official biographer in 1925, or destroyed in some other way; but that letters incriminating in tone and perhaps in substance had at one time existed was indicated by Wilson himself in his 1915 "confession." In any case this sharp break in what had become a heated and frequent correspondence again points to the months November 1909 to February 1910 as the fateful interlude in Wilson's personal life.

The date is worth fixing because of the light it throws upon Wilson's final struggles at Princeton and his subsequent entry into politics. He was not a man to embark upon a conventionally romantic affair simply because he was on a holiday and because the atmosphere of Bermuda seemed made for dalliance. Such an involvement was more likely in his case to occur as part of a much more profound emotional experience in which his private and public lives were inextricably linked. His speeches, nearly always self-revealing, suggest during 1909 a sudden liberation from constraints and cautions that had long bound him, as his actions assumed a boldness, almost a recklessness, quite unlike his earlier deportment. He was a man going though a period of profound change. By some psychological alchemy a subtle fusion of Princeton, politics, and Mary Peck took place. The immense energies released at the time of his campaign for the governorship and the Presidency were generated in the fires that almost consumed his inner and outer lives during this period.

When Wilson went to Bermuda for his third and last regular vacation in February 1910, he went alone. Mary Peck stayed in New York, pleading financial stringency, but they must both have recognized that to have been together at that time and in that place would indeed have been tempting the gods. They were still under the spell of their New

York meetings and their correspondence was full of sentimental references. Wilson mourned her absence, revisited favorite island haunts. Mary recollected the house where she had lived: "Does the bougainvillea fling itself over the cottages as of old?" she inquired of her "best beloved." "Why, *why* can I not be there to fling *myself* where I would!"[17] On returning, Wilson stopped at the apartment on Twenty-seventh Street before going to Princeton.

After that, it would seem, "the few months" had run their course; the "folly" had been played out. Even while it lasted, Wilson indicated in his unpublished document of 1915, he "knew and made explicit what it *did not* mean"—presumably (so far as his intentions were concerned) any breakup of his marriage. He said of his wife at the same time that "She, too, knew and understood and has forgiven."[18] That the end of the affair did not mean a complete break with Mary Peck seems unusual, and can only be attributed to the way Wilson, through an iron self-discipline, felt he could control and manage his emotions, in this case moving from romantic involvement back to friendship in an unbroken chain. (Similarly he kept up a lifelong friendship with Hattie Woodrow after she refused to marry him.) Wilson continued to write Mary Peck well into the White House years, his weekly letters, profuse in their reflections upon daily events, becoming an invaluable resource to future biographers and historians. Far from seeming to want to forget her, he was dismayed whenever she let her side of the correspondence lag; and he continued with expressions of intense sympathy for her endless financial and emotional troubles.

These complex relationships show the dualism that often characterized Wilson. He could appear to be two different men, the one scarcely aware of what the other was thinking. Thus he seems never to have felt the need to make a choice between his wife and Mary Peck. The same post that in 1909 carried from Bermuda letters to Ellen that might have been those of a bridegroom to his bride, carried to Mary passionate assurances of how ardently she was missed. He saw no disingenuousness in the act. Indeed, he was inclined to see others as having two sides also. Ellen was a pair of opposed but equally charming angels. She was for him the essence of unworldly purity, romanticized by all her husband's Victorian predispositions; she was at the same time, at least in her early years, the incarnation of earthly joys—"Love's playmate," full of mischief and fun.

In strange forms the wayward and worldly side of Ellen was personified by her sister Madge, whose attachment to Woodrow was extremely strong. Madge the pagan, the "inscrutable," having grown in the Wilson household from a young child to a woman of exceptional beauty, also felt closest to Mary Peck of any of the Wilson family. "Mrs. Peck was nothing if not smart,"[19] she wrote; and smartness was something Madge admired. She was fascinated by her free ways (Mrs. Peck actually smoked in public!); like Woodrow, Madge, a southerner, could also embrace the breezy independence of this bright character from the West. One day when Madge and her brother-in-law were alone at Prospect he suggested that the two of them take the trolley down to Trenton, where Mrs. Peck was visiting friends. Mrs. Peck was at her best; the afternoon passed splendidly, and Madge remembered how on the way home Woodrow with a sigh remarked that it was not "only the Marthas of the world who help."[20]* One suspects that the two had rarely been closer than at that moment, Madge with her own appreciation of worldly charms and Woodrow with the normally hidden side of his nature briefly exposed.

On another occasion Madge had bought a hat with an unusual amount of "swagger." Ellen remarked that it looked like Mrs. Peck. One can imagine that the remark was made with a certain sharpness in her normally sweet southern drawl; if so, it was a mild enough rebuke from one who must have suffered much from Woodrow's aberration. In her last years Ellen told the trusted physician of the White House, Cary Travers Grayson, that Mrs. Peck was the only cause of unhappiness that her husband had ever given her. No evidence shows Ellen to have seriously resented Madge's admiration for Mary Peck, even though the sister, unconsciously at least, must have formed a bridge between Woodrow and the woman who bewitched him.

What may be called Wilson's "new freedom"—a term applicable to his private life long before he used it in national politics—is revealed with surprising explicitness in the baccalaureate address of June 1909, delivered as his emotional life was approaching its crest. "I write my sermons to myself," he said; "I at least know what *I* need to hear!"[21] And so on this occasion he told the undergraduates that there are things you do for duty, and things you do because your spirit has chosen them for its satisfaction. The latter are things done "with the free spirit of the adventurer"; they are "the inviting by-paths of life into which you go for

---

*See Luke 10:38–42. The famous passage describes Martha as "distracted by her many tasks"; but Mary, her sister, "seated herself at the Lord's feet and stayed there listening to his words." (Translation from the New English Bible.)

discovery, to get off the dusty road of mere duty into cool meadows and shadowed glades where the scene is changed and the air seems full of the tonic of freedom."[22] The year before on the same occasion he had preached a doctrine of happiness through renunciation; this spring he spoke more in the tone of a man who sensed an impending fulfillment.

A similar sense pervades his letters to Mary Peck. On an evening in late June, with the college deserted and himself alone, he basked in the atmosphere of peace and leisure; one's dreams, he wrote to her, were set free. "Surely the time and the place were meant for walks and chats and long loafs in the twilight, and strolls in the garden when the moon is up and the fragrance of the flowers seems enhanced in the lighter air. It is all this that gives me a special heart-ache that I cannot see whom I will."[23] By autumn he was speaking more directly to the woman herself. Underneath the unhappiness and humiliation her second marriage had brought to Mary Peck, he discerned bubbling up "the joy of freedom, of accomplishment, of release, of purification. . . . It is as if you had at last found yourself, after a long nightmare, . . . were just beginning to come to full flower after your own kind." "I expect to see you grow more . . . delightful," he added, "with every passing month."[24]

"You are a veritable child of nature," he told her again. "There is an air about you like the air of the open, a directness, a simplicity, a free movement that link you with wild things that are yet meant to be taken into one's confidence and loved."[25] This letter was addressed to Pittsfield; less than a month later Mary moved to New York.

That summer was a relatively carefree one for Wilson, a lull in the trouble at Princeton when he could relax and let himself enjoy life with a "jolly, irresponsible lot of artists" at Old Lyme.[26] Ellen was staying once more at Florence Griswold's; here Woodrow would join her, and he was prepared to be quite in his element in Bohemia. He was leaving the cool, spacious Prospect for a boardinghouse that did not even have a bath—"We shall have to be very English and very primitive";[27] but Miss Griswold's establishment had its own charms. It had long been a home for artists, many of them subsequently famous; they had left marks of their skill in landscapes and figures in varying styles upon the doors and walls. Meals were taken mostly outdoors, at noontime the men and women eating at separate tables so that they might sit down wearing whatever informal clothes they had been working in. Over the assemblage presided Miss Griswold. "The artists of the Lyme school regard her as their patron saint, and have all in their turns made love to her," Wilson wrote.[28]

Habitués of the establishment had been uneasy at the prospect of the

Woodrow Wilsons coming to live with them; but their doubts were soon resolved. Ellen was at home, an artist among her peers. Woodrow thoroughly enjoyed the company of "the hot air club," the name given to the men's dining table; he joined in the jokes and rituals of the place; he played golf, and summoned "that respectable old hack," his mind, to carry him through an article or two.[29] It was a vacation suiting his mood, and preparing him for events to come.

Conditional acceptance of the Procter gift at the October meeting had left the dispute simmering. The faculty was strongly behind Wilson, but the trustees had divided into two factions and the alumni were growing uneasy at what seemed a highly equivocal attitude toward a would-be donor.* Wilson waited, genuinely puzzled, searching for a solution. On December 22, he arranged one more talk with Procter in New York. Wilson proposed to him that the money from the Swann estate be used to build graduate housing on the campus, while Procter's gift be devoted to the golf course site upon which he had personally been insisting. Rejecting this compromise out of hand, Procter made it apparent that he was dictating not only how the funds given by him be spent, but also the use of other, independently acquired university resources. Wilson left the meeting close to despair, and sitting down in the Jersey City railway station penciled a forlorn note to Pyne: "He [Procter] is unwilling to adjust the terms of his offer to my suggestion. . . . I seem to have come to the end."[30]

The idea of two graduate colleges, one financed by Procter and the other by the Swann estate, was not as farfetched as it has often been pictured. The numbers of graduate students Wilson hoped to generate within the next several years would have made one residential unit either inadequate or else inadvisedly large; and there was, besides, some real legal doubt as to whether the two funds could be combined. If, finally, there were to be several undergraduate quads, why not more than one graduate quad? Wilson seems to have been genuinely anxious to arrive at a compromise acceptable to Procter; and the latter's rebuff not only suggested an invasion of his right to determine academic policy but was also personally humiliating.

A more serious question raised by Wilson's conduct at this juncture

---

* At this same time, on October 27, 1909, the Palmer Physical Laboratory was dedicated, a reminder that Wilson's other accomplishments at Princeton were proceeding, apart from the controversies that consumed the attention of the board and the local community.

is the precipitate manner in which he formulated the proposal of two separate graduate establishments. He had discussed it at length with Pyne before the talk with Procter; he presented it to Professors Magie, Capp, and Daniels. But so far as is known, he did not consult with other advisers, and he later reversed himself, first stating and then denying that the faculty supported the idea. It seems evident that he was groping desperately for some possible solution, and not very sure in his own mind as to the merits of his plan.

On Christmas Day Wilson wrote a long letter to Pyne. The relations between the two men were still outwardly cordial, with some affection lingering from earlier days; and Wilson turned to him in an appeal of somber candor. He admitted for the first time that West's conception of graduate education was at the heart of all other problems, asserting it had completely lost him the confidence of his academic colleagues; "nothing administered by [West]," he wrote, "can now succeed."[31]

He then faced up to an issue even more fundamental, the issue he had found disturbing at the very start of the Procter affair, that of the role being played by wealthy donors. His words fell with the weight of an utterance classically framed. "I am not willing," he said, "to be drawn further into the toils. I cannot accede to the acceptance of gifts upon terms which take the educational policy of the University out of the hands of the Trustees and Faculty and permit it to be determined by those who give money."[32] Copies of this letter were sent to the other members of the board and its thesis was widely discussed.

Wilson had played his trump card. It had the immediate effect of clearing the air. The faction opposed to Wilson was enraged but confounded; Wilson's supporters were jubilant. "It is a stroke," wrote one supporter, "which will rescue Princeton from an intolerable position."[33] The Princeton community had been puzzled by the importance Wilson attached to a particular site for the graduate college. But now all who believed in the independence of private education saw a cause clearly defined. It was a cause, too, that appealed to men and women outside the university. Wilson had raised the issue of the dominance of wealth over social institutions, placing himself squarely within the tide of current progressive ideas.

The next stage of the game was played out at another level, among obscure intrigues and a confusion of personal factors. A meeting of the trustees was scheduled for January 13. Pyne concerted in advance the tactics of the pro-West group. Wilson's supporters, inspired by the position taken in his Christmas letter, were set to do all in their power to reject once and for all the Procter offer. As the board meeting neared, Wilson was in a highly emotional state, not adequately prepared for the outright opposition and the hostile cross-questioning to which the Pyne faction had resolved to subject him.

An hour before the board meeting, the trustee committee on the graduate school came together. A letter from Procter, in part drafted by Pyne, was read. The letter had been deliberately contrived to embarrass Wilson; it indicated that Procter was reversing his position and was ready to accept Wilson's proposal of separating the Swann and Procter gifts so as to create two separate graduate residences. If its motive was to throw Wilson into confusion, it was successful. When he entered the trustees' meeting a few minutes later, he was shaken and unarmed.

What happened at this meeting of January 13, 1910, was the subject of endless gossip at the time and has been lengthily debated since. The facts as we have them, showing Wilson caught in damaging contradictions, derive almost entirely from the accounts of hostile board members; one trustee, identified with neither faction, commented afterwards that Wilson had "made a splendid presentation . . . and acted in a manly way throughout."[34] That Wilson was embarrassed and awkward seems plain, however. Pyne held afterwards that Wilson's conduct at the meeting had fatally alienated him and convinced him that Wilson had to be forced from the presidency. If so, it would appear that Pyne deliberately contrived to be alienated. That he subsequently used every means to displace Wilson is, however, undeniable.

Confronted by Procter's acceptance of the proposal for two graduate colleges, Wilson might well have played for time and refused to be hurried into a decision on so basic a matter of policy. Instead, he rejected the plan he had himself initiated, and declared (as he had done previously to Pyne) that the real issue was West. Without West, a graduate college could be made to work "anywhere in Mercer county."[35] The phrase was later taken up with glee and repeated endlessly by Wilson's detractors. What in other circumstances would have been dismissed as a witty exaggeration, made in confidence to the trustees, was bandied about as something quite literal, the surrender of a position he had supported passionately for years.

In pursuing his argument, Wilson gave further cause for exultation to his opponents. Taking from under a pile of papers before him an elaborately printed promotional brochure prepared for the graduate college by West in 1902, Wilson held it up before the board, declaring it to be proof that West's ideas and ideals were not his. Had he not written for the brochure, he was asked, a highly laudatory preface? Wilson replied he had written the preface before seeing the book. Was the book not accessible, he was asked again, when he urged West to turn down the presidency of M.I.T.? It mattered little in that heated atmosphere that by a strange circumstance Wilson had indeed written the preface before seeing the book, for the preface consisted word for word of a paragraph he had lifted from that year's annual report. The book contained mostly picturesque architectural and landscape details from English universities, and if he had remembered it clearly, Wilson would hardly have taken it as an example of West's peculiar ideas. He had overstated and misstated his case and would suffer bitterly from it in the weeks ahead.

What is usually not noted in the accounts of this famous meeting is that it ended in a victory, at least a victory of sorts, for the cause that Wilson had brilliantly defined and defended. The big issue, the effort of a rich and stubborn donor to impose his will on university policy, could not be downed. A motion that the Procter gift be declined outright was defeated, but a substitute motion succeeded in having the matter referred to a special committee to report back within a month. Within the month, a few days before the committee was to report, Procter withdrew his controversial gift.

Wilson was wary, but immensely relieved. "At least we are free to govern the University as our judgments and consciences dictate!" he wrote Cleveland Dodge.[36] And then he went off alone for his third visit to Bermuda.

Gradually, on that sunlit island, he regained his composure. He had always prided himself on his capacity for sleep and forgetfulness; now he found the nights tormented by dreams. He seemed to move amid "endless debates and slanders, sessions of hostile Trustees, of futile anger and distressing misunderstandings."[37] Pining for Mary Peck, he recalled how two years earlier she had filled the place with enchantment. And he turned over in his mind the means of escape from the Princeton imbroglio. An opening into politics rose as a clear possibility. "It would be rather jolly, after all," he wrote Ellen, "to start out on life anew together, to make a new career, would it not?"[38]

Meanwhile, at Princeton, the firestorm mounted in fury. Procter's withdrawal of his gift was the signal for fresh outbursts of denunciation, with the coals of the January 13 meeting raked over and its minutest details made the subject of abuse or ridicule. Alumni were up in arms, a minority of the faculty sullen and resentful. The latters' wives formed a kind of Greek chorus, repeating and enlarging upon every new charge. From the Princetonian Booth Tarkington, a former student of Wilson's, came the only touch of laughter to lighten the imbroglio, and even that may have been the touch of a later time. It was the kind of bitterness, Tarkington said, that one could find "only in a school, a church, a town meeting, a library committee, or a benevolent society."[39] With her husband away, Ellen found herself a virtual prisoner of Prospect, dreading to emerge into the poisoned air.

The controversy was inflamed by the New York press. The anti-Wilson forces either directly or indirectly fed their views to the *Herald Tribune*, and shortly after several pieces had been printed, the *Times* came forth with a long editorial supporting Wilson. In the heated atmosphere of the day it was widely supposed that he had instigated the editorial and provided the information. In fact, as the editor, Herbert B. Brougham, disclosed many years later, the piece was based on the story as he heard it from fellow Yale men. After it was set in type he had solicited Wilson's opinion, which the latter promptly supplied in a long letter and on the basis of which minor changes were made in the editorial.[40]

In an icy interview with Professor Paul van Dyke in mid-March Wilson submitted to an inquisition by that West supporter.[41] Did Wilson agree with the editorial? he was asked. He replied that he agreed with it in essence but he thought it highly overstated. Van Dyke cross-examined him but did not ask whether he had consulted with the *Times* prior to its publication. Had it been discovered that, even indirectly, Wilson had influenced the piece, the results could have been catastrophic. Given the excited atmosphere of the time, the hate, the manipulated and intemperate gossip, Wilson would have had difficulty surviving the resulting blast.

The "new career" of which Wilson had spoken to Ellen was much in his mind as 1910 opened its stormy course. The deep wounds inflicted at Princeton awoke memories of his earliest ambitions to play a major role in the political life of his times. Besides, there were considerations of a very practical kind. In early January 1910, at Delmonico's famous restaurant in New York, two gentlemen might have been discovered in earnest discourse: one slim, vivacious, his eyes missing nothing of the surrounding scene nor much in the character of men; the other large and portly, one who might have been a banker or a party boss and was in fact both. George Harvey was on that occasion expounding to James Smith, Jr., former U. S. senator and now wealthy boss of the Essex County Democratic machine in New Jersey, the merits of Woodrow Wilson as a candidate in the upcoming gubernatorial election.

It was not only the prospect of a Democratic victory in Smith's own state that Harvey could hold out, but the more dazzling prize of a candidate for the Presidential election of 1912. Jim Smith was noncommittal. He had his own boys (the so-called "Jim-Jim machine") to take care of; moreover, he was not at all anxious to put himself out for a man whose own intentions were so entirely unknown.

Harvey determined to get some light, at least, upon the latter uncertainty. Prior to Wilson's departure for Bermuda, Harvey asked whether, if the nomination were extended to him "on a silver platter," Wilson would be prepared to accept. The Princeton president, according to a contemporary account, walked soberly up and down turning over in his mind all the factors of the situation; at length he replied that in such circumstances he would have to give the matter "serious consideration."[42] It wasn't much in the way of a commitment, but it sufficed; and when Harvey again lunched with Smith at Delmonico's the latter was prepared to set the necessary political forces in motion.

More conjectural than Wilson's acceptance of a possible nomination was the question of his orthodoxy. He was being sponsored by two of the more conservative spokesmen of the eastern Democratic party, representatives of Wall Street and of an entrenched political machine. Would the new boy play their game? With his sober mind and brisk practical approach to problems, Wilson appeared safe enough. His public statements showed him passing muster as a conservative, a confirmed foe of Bryanism and a consistent critic of Theodore Roosevelt.

To those, however, who gave careful attention to Wilson's educational addresses, a radical note, something very close to the progressive arias of the day, was discernible. This note began gradually to creep out and to color the more political utterances. The power of wealth which Wilson saw as a corrupting force at Princeton he declared repeatedly to be at work on the larger scene. Addresses on public issues increasingly called men to rise above their personal interests and to practice statesmanship in their business and professional fields.

All this might have seemed harmless enough, but when Wilson announced to a convention of bankers in January 1910 that their profession rested upon a moral basis, J. P. Morgan, a member of the audience, was reported in the press next day to have puffed vigorously on his cigar while looking "glum."[43] He told Wilson afterwards that he considered the address to be an attack on him personally, to which Wilson replied that he had only been talking "principles." Like Harvey and Smith, Morgan wondered whether principles—or at least Wilson's principles—might not be serious business.

As a political aspirant, Wilson's task was to position himself to the right of Bryan, and yet sufficiently to the left to capture the interest of the powerful progressive movement. He perhaps did not analyze the situation in precisely this way, but with the instincts of leadership he moved consistently toward that posture. Disassociation from the far left was not difficult for him, mistrusting as he did Bryan's sentimentalism and the vagueness of his ideas. To escape the conservative label he had cultivated for himself was more difficult. Yet the ferment at Princeton gave scope to the essentially activist and reformist elements of his nature. The conviction that politics is itself good and that government can be constructive and beneficent—a conviction first set forth in *The State* in the 1890s—was now coming naturally to the surface. No wonder the conservative bosses, his would-be sponsors, felt slightly uneasy.

There was another aspect of Wilson, apart from his political or educational theories, that lent him appeal and made him seem to Harvey and Smith the more valuable a prize. He stood as a man fighting hard for what he believed in. Among the wider Princeton community, often understanding but dimly the real issues at stake—and among the general public, understanding not at all—he was admired for a kind of indomitable courage, superior to programs, issues, or precise goals. He was never altogether a Happy Warrior; he suffered too visibly in defeat, and he had been given by nature a dour look. He was one, he wrote privately, who "fights without a knack for hoping confidently"; he was "simply a Scotch-Irishman who will not be conquered."[44] But to the public that observed him at this time he appeared a brave sort of fighter all the same.

By the winter of 1910 he was, whatever else, a political animal, and old hands at the game so astute as Harvey and Smith knew such an animal when they saw one. Wilson had learned from experience that in the public arena cruel enmities are to be borne; an essentially gentle and vulnerable man, he had perceived the coin of leadership to be wounds given and received. That the most beautiful word in the lexicon of politics is loyalty, and that courage is the highest virtue, were lessons he had fully mastered, and he was psychologically prepared to slip over from academia onto a larger and even more treacherous stage.

Meditating on things of this sort, George Harvey went abroad soon after the crucial meeting with his protégé. He remained there until June. New Jersey politics simmered while Jim Smith bided his time. Wilson, who had promised to give "serious consideration" to an unfettered offer of the governorship, still had business at Princeton from which there was no retreat.

*   *   *

That business was, quite simply, to fight on—to make sure that the Procter gift was not renewed in some still-unacceptable guise; to curb the power of West; with money from the Swann bequest to get the graduate college built within the grounds of the campus. Underlying the other objectives of his program was the election of an alumni trustee neither linked inseparably with the eastern financial interests led by Pyne, nor a confirmed opponent of Wilson's. Adrian H. Joline, a New York lawyer specializing in railways and trusts (and, incidentally, a noted book collector), was the eastern candidate, known to be hostile to Wilson. The Western Association of Princeton Clubs put up John W. Barr, Jr., of Louisville, Kentucky. Barr was president of a Louisville bank and was committed to neither side in the Princeton controversy. The choice between these two men, to be determined by a vote among alumni, was bound to have a decisive impact on the makeup of the board and on Wilson's fortunes.

For Wilson the signals were clear. He must take the issues to the alumni; he must appeal to his constituents in a series of carefully thought-out addresses. Beginning in early March he spoke to alumni in Baltimore, Jersey City, Brooklyn, Hartford, Pittsburgh, and Chicago—as well as in the strongholds of the two opposing camps, St. Louis and New York City. These speeches show Wilson at his most convincing. They represented, said the journalist William Allen White, the pure Scot, the Woodrow side of his nature: they were "full-panoplied, stern, unyielding, cold, and deadly."[45]

Wilson put aside the appeals to sentiment and old loyalties that Princeton audiences expected to hear from their president. He argued for a new Princeton, not the familiar college of the alumni's undergraduate days, but one that was taking its place in the modern world, in competition with the foremost educational institutions of the country for students of the highest caliber: men serious in their professional ambitions, often of small means, their one desire to be free to study and do research without distractions. For such men the graduate college as conceived by West and Procter had no appeal; and indeed the proof was that Princeton enrollment at the graduate level had been almost static, while that of other great universities had been doubling and redoubling. What he asked of Princeton men was not that they cherish fond recollections of undergraduate days, but that they seek for their college the highest distinction of learning. He was listened to with respect, with a kind of awe, and alumni went off in relative silence to ponder his words. It became increasingly clear, moreover, that the western representative, Barr, would carry the forthcoming election to board membership.

In New York, the focus of the opposition, he made his most urgent appeal. Wilson was always at his best when he sensed electricity in the air. He wasted no time in getting to the heart of his message. "I know, of course," he began, "what the question lying at the back of your minds is reducible to. You say, 'It is all very well and very interesting to talk about educational ideals; but it is bad business to refuse half a million dollars.' " He would proceed, he assured his audience, to tell them so far as he could precisely what was the business of a university. He did not spare Dean West—"I speak by the book," he said as he described the almost single-handed control that West had been exercising over the graduate school and college. "I am not speaking by conjecture, but by knowledge, when I say that men looking about for a place to pursue their advanced studies are at present looking askance at Princeton; because they have understood (what is understood throughout the academic world) that we want to do something peculiar with them. They are men, mature men, and they do not choose to have anything peculiar done with them."[46] The audience heard out in silence the grim prophet who would not admit defeat.

A week after this speech the board met for its regular spring session. Its members were divided and obdurate in their opposing views. The Wilson faction lacked one vote and the election of a trustee supportive of its views was deferred. Then Wilson's proposal to refer the question of the graduate school to the faculty for its opinion was defeated. After that there seemed little hope for any kind of accommodation. "Wilson feels that the opposition is now permanent, and is not governed by reason, but simply by orders," Henry B. Thompson wrote to Dodge the next day.[47]

On April 17, three days after the board meeting, Wilson went to Pittsburgh for still another alumni address. As the train journeyed westward his long-suppressed emotions began to translate themselves into the few phrases which the skilled speaker needs to give tone and guidance to his utterance; and that evening, before an audience startled and then abruptly sobered, he let loose one of the most fiery denunciations of his career. Most of what he said that night he had stressed before: the danger of wealth, the selfishness of class, the undemocratic tendencies of American private colleges.[48] Even a sudden arraignment of the exclusiveness of the Protestant churches was of a piece with previous statements. But now all these themes were massed, and were deployed with a consuming passion. To an extent he had never dared before, he identified the struggle at Princeton with the cause of democracy in the country at large. "What we cry out against is that a handful of conspicuous men have thrust cruel hands among the heartstrings of the masses of men upon whose blood and energy they are subsisting." "The universities," he continued,

> would make men forget their common origins, forget their universal sympathies, and join a class—and no class ever can serve America.
>
> The great voice of America does not come from seats of learning. It comes in a murmur from the hills and woods and the farms and factories and the mills, rolling on and gaining volume until it comes to us from the homes of common men. Do these murmurs echo in the corridors of the universities? I have not heard them.[49]

Wilson afterwards characterized the Pittsburgh speech as a "stupid blunder";[50] certainly it gave the opposition a field day. No complete report was available, but a fragmentary text was circulated in a hostile pamphlet, and loud were the outcries against the president's radicalism and irresponsibility. The speech broke the links of rational communication and in the short run made the problems of Princeton more difficult, if not impossible, to solve. Yet within the depths of the Princeton constituency and among a wider public the fiery words seemed to put the president in a new light and to lift the simmering controversy out of its obscure details.

The charge that Wilson was deliberately courting political popularity is certainly not true, but the possibility of his entering upon a new career may well have made him reckless. In a way it also made him more himself; for it was the essence of the Wilsonian style of leadership to push issues to the ultimate level of principle—to convert a controversy into a sacred cause.

In the end it was an outside event, occurring with a devastating finality, that settled the whole matter. On May 18, a month after the Pittsburgh speech, Isaac Chauncey Wyman died in Boston. He had graduated in 1848 from Princeton and was the same ancient alumnus on whom Wilson, newly elected president of the university, had made an unsuccessful effort to call in 1902. West had been more persevering. It now turned out Wyman had left his entire estate, said to be valued at $8 million, to Princeton with West as executor of the will. The size of the bequest (it later turned out to be much smaller than expected), combined with

West's share in its administration, was a clear signal to Wilson. "We have beaten the living," he said, "but we cannot fight the dead. The game is up."[51]

West was jubilant. "I can hardly believe it all! It is so splendid," he purred in a letter to Pyne. He told how he had laid a sprig of ivy on Wyman's grave (well he might!)—and ended with the inevitable Latin tag: *"Te deum laudamus. Non nobis domine."*[52]

Wilson showed himself to be a good loser, no doubt seeing in the event the same providence that had so gratified Dean West. He could convince himself, moreover, that with the prospect of so large an endowment the graduate school could not fail to prosper whoever might be its dean, and whatever might be its disassociation from undergraduate life. In June, at the urging of trustees, Procter renewed his own offer, and at a special meeting of the board a few days later Wilson took the lead in proposing its acceptance.

The commencement season held its pleasant ironies, if no deep spirit of reconciliation. Wilson attended a gathering of West's friends, held in Procter's honor, and made graceful remarks at a ceremony where Pyne was presented with a golden beaker to mark his twenty-five years as a member of Princeton's board. One test of strength waited to be formally resolved, and Wilson won handsomely on that. The election of John Barr and the defeat of Joline as alumni trustee were a signal victory. Wilson considered it a vindication of his administration's policies and a proof that, whatever the mysterious workings of the board, he had maintained the support of the alumni.

He had the support, also, of the students. They had never ceased to crowd his lectures, still given faithfully on Monday and Tuesday mornings; they listened to him (and were almost convinced) when he visited their clubs to explain his plans for reorganizing the social life of the university. In chapel, which he led twice a week, they sat in awe before a man who prayed with simplicity but with such obvious and unquestioning faith. Now they could not imagine that this would turn out to be his last commencement. They responded with more than usual warmth at the senior class dinner, and at the traditional ceremonies in Alexander Hall they cheered until tears started in the eyes of their normally reserved and Olympian president.

In his baccalaureate address Wilson once more revealed his deepest feelings. "This is a turning point in your lives," he told the graduating class, perhaps half-knowing that it was an even more decisive turning point in his own. It was "a day of endings and of beginnings." In a rarely reminiscent mood he looked back on his own years as a student—"the magical years that ran their cheerful course from the exciting autumn of 1875 to the gracious June of 1879." "You are not sad," he said, speaking for himself as much as for them, "because you stand at the threshold of another life, but only because you are at the end of a life you loved. You are conscious of being readier for the things that lie ahead of you because of the days that lie behind."[53]

At almost the same time that Wilson was intimating his readiness for "another life," a group of politicians was lunching in Chicago. Jim Smith of Essex County had journeyed westward, talking with the governors of several states along the way; he had evidently been impressed by the degree of support he discovered for a Wilson Presidential boom. Now a long-time Princeton acquaintance of Wilson's, John M. Harlan,* initiated a conference bringing Smith together with Roger Charles Sullivan, the Chicago Democratic boss, and with Edward Nash Hurley, Chicago manufacturer and bank president. Smith evidently retained some doubts about Wilson, and Judge Harlan offered to be an intermediary in quieting Smith's fears. Would Wilson, if elected governor, set about "fighting and breaking down the existing Democratic organization and replacing it with one of [his] own"? The matter, being referred to Wilson, was quickly disposed of. "The last thing I should think of," he told Harlan, "would be building up a machine of my own." So long as the existing machine backed his policies and he was himself left freedom in the choice of "measures and men," he would consider it "inexcusable" to antagonize the existing organization.[54]

With Smith reassured on this point, there remained the question of whether he could hold his followers in line without an absolute assurance from Wilson that he would accept a nomination. Harvey tried to arrange a conference with Wilson, who was unavailable, being in the midst of moving his family to Old Lyme for the summer. A dinner for Sunday, June 26, was arranged at Harvey's summer home in Deal, New Jersey. It was discovered at the last minute, however, that the only train which could get Wilson down from Old Lyme for an evening occasion did not run on Sunday. An aide was dispatched by midnight train on Saturday and at New London hired a chauffered limousine to fetch the Princeton president. By a complicated travel schedule that would have done credit

---

*Harlan, John Maynard, Princeton 1884, Chicago lawyer and city alderman, was the son and the father of justices of the Supreme Court. His father, John Marshall Harlan, served on the court from 1877 to 1911; his son, also John Marshall Harlan, Princeton 1920, served from 1955 to 1971.

to Phineas Fogg, Wilson was escorted on the return trip so as to arrive in time for dinner. The affair was the more important because it was also attended by the editor of the influential Louisville *Courier-Journal*, Colonel Henry Watterson, who had been found to be visiting nearby. The evening passed delightfully, with the talk lasting until midnight. Wilson was in his best and liveliest form, and Smith was enthusiastic over the support he had found in the Midwest. In the end Wilson still hesitated, insisting he must consult his friends on the Princeton board before making a final decision.[55]

Back in Old Lyme he wrote long letters to the Chicago group—Cyrus McCormick, David B. Jones, and Thomas D. Jones—and made a trip to New York to talk with Cleveland Dodge. He was concerned lest he appear to be abandoning the men who had stood faithfully by him in the Princeton controversies; yet he could not forget how often he had urged his students to accept the chance for public service when it came to them. Individually and as a group Wilson's supporters affirmed his absolute freedom to accept the New Jersey nomination, if offered.

There remained the neophyte's introduction to New Jersey's political leaders. This was accomplished at an afternoon conference at the Lawyers' Club in Newark on July 12. Present, in addition to Harvey and Wilson, were the bosses of the county machine—James Richard Nugent representing Essex County; Robert S. Hudspeth, Hudson County; and Millard F. Ross, Middlesex County. Richard V. Lindabury, a well-known Wall Street lawyer, attended on behalf of New Jersey corporate interests. This was a gathering of conservatives and old-line clubhouse chieftains, unleavened by any of the younger reformers who were to play so conspicuous a part in Wilson's subsequent campaign. After preliminaries the discussion got down to the two questions that really interested the local politicians: Wilson's attitude toward the machine, and his stand on the liquor issue. On the former Wilson repeated the assurances he had already given Smith; on the latter he expressed himself as in favor of local option. This was contrary to what the Democratic Party in New Jersey had long stood for. "Well," Wilson replied, "that is my attitude and my conviction. I cannot change it."[56]

Three days later Wilson crossed the divide that separated his career as an academician from that of political leader. He was not a candidate for the governorship, he said in a public statement; he would not in any circumstances do anything to obtain the nomination. His duties at Princeton satisfied him and he did not wish to draw away from them. But if it indeed turned out to be the case (as he had been assured by many persons) that a majority of the "thoughtful Democrats" of the state wished him to be their candidate, he would deem it his duty, as well as an honor and a privilege, to accept.[57]

The phrase "thoughtful Democrats" galled the Irish, and in the words of William Allen White, "cost the Jim-Jim machine a pretty penny in good beer and free lunch."[58]

The early autumn of another college year was bringing its soft airs to Princeton when, on September 14, Wilson was nominated for the governorship of New Jersey. He immediately announced that, at the upcoming board meeting, he would offer his resignation as Princeton's president. On October 20 he submitted a brief letter, and then, picking up his hat and coat, left forever the room where he had passed through so many critical experiences.

Wilson's contribution to the university world consisted, as much as anything, of the very factors that had led to his defeat: the controversies he generated, the ideals he upheld, the visions he offered. As would be true of his later career, he was perhaps bound to fail, but in failing he left a legacy others could not ignore. His specific contribution to Princeton was well described by McGeorge Bundy in 1956: "Wilson was right in his conviction that Princeton must be more than a wonderfully pleasant and decent home for nice young men; it has been more ever since his time."[59]

But the price paid for the Wilson shake-up was high. Many years were to pass before the bitterness of it subsided in the little town of Princeton. A generation later men and women still took sides and raked over with passion the embers of long-dead issues. The graduate college was built on the golf course site, where it stands in lordly isolation, dominated by the bell tower erected in memory of West's old supporter, Grover Cleveland. Students find it a long walk from the college down to the main campus, and particularly to the school of international affairs that bears the name of the university's thirteenth president. As for undergraduates, they often pass through their four years without ever entering the graduate college. The quad plan was not realized at Princeton until Yale and Harvard, beneficiaries of the kind of large gifts Wilson had sought in vain, created systems of undergraduate colleges almost identical to what he had fought for. But by the 1980s the wheel had come full circle. The collegiate plan was established at Princeton with the first of the new colleges named for Woodrow Wilson.

West's power as dean of the graduate school was finally clipped by the board, under the impetus of the faithful Jacobus. Hibben was elected president, a bitter blow to Wilson, who neither attended his inaugural nor sent a message. Hibben turned out to be what Princeton needed, not a man noted for courage yet one who restored the fabric of the institution's torn life, keeping in its service many of Wilson's followers and adherents. Pyne, after thirty-six years on the board—it was said of him that he had done more for Princeton than any other man had ever done for any college—died in 1921, and his funeral cortege wound through the campus he had served well according to his lights, and had regarded with so much affection. His portrait hangs in the graduate college. In the main courtyard, clad in full academic robes, a life-size sculpture of Dean West surveys the Gothic buttresses and the windows of stained glass.

CHAPTER FOUR

Politician

———◆———

NEW JERSEY TRIUMPHS

At fifty-four Wilson entered a new world, throwing off like a light cloak the cares, labors, and frustrations that had gathered about him during the last years at Princeton, and dropping, too, the rewards and delights of his old job. The change was surrounded by the kind of ambiguity that marked almost every stage of his ongoing career. It would be easy to see the entrance into politics as a convenient escape from an intolerable situation he had created for himself at Princeton. Only inordinate ambition and the compulsion to get out of a hopeless dead end could have impelled him into so rash a leap, it could well be argued, as that into the maelstrom of local New Jersey politics. Only an ingrained capacity to mask defeat could have led him to see it in the light of morality and principle.

Such an interpretation overlooks the degree to which, from youth, Wilson had been committed to political action. He reconciled himself to deferments of this goal, or accepted as a substitute indirect roles of leadership, through scholarship, popular writings, and academic statesmanship. To casual observers he did not in his mature years appear as a man in any way thwarted or disappointed by the turn his life had taken. Even his close friends, and even his most intimate letters, suggest that he had adapted well to other roles. But all the while the fires lit in his boyhood still burned, however damped down by circumstance.

From the compact made as an undergraduate with the young Talcott he had been given no release; and when the chance for action on the public stage arose, he accepted it without apparent excitement, as a work that had long since been given him to do—as a man passing, so one journalist commented at the time, "from one room to another."[1] To messengers from the political bosses at Trenton arriving at Prospect to tell him that his nomination for governor seemed secure and that he should immediately leave to appear before the convention, Wilson declared, "Gentlemen, I am ready."[2] What else could he say, considering the years that moment had been in the making?

Nor do suggestions that Wilson left Princeton a defeated man and took up politics as a convenient escape conform to underlying facts. Wilson simply did not see his career at Princeton as ending in failure. In this attitude there was, no doubt, a certain amount of self-deception. He was not one who could easily admit being beaten in any circumstances; besides, in the Princeton situation were elements that justified his own optimistic view. He could be reasonably sure (as indeed the future would prove) that he had been right on the major issues. Moreover, the setbacks had come about through such elements of chance, such strange conjunctions of fortune, as to remove a sense of personal stigma. He had kept the unwavering support of a dominant portion of the board, and the rejection of Joline in the alumni vote of June 1910 showed his strength in that quarter.

The defeat, if defeat it was, revealed him as a man of outstanding qualities—and incidentally revealed Princeton as a university where intellectual values were taken seriously. Like his later, infinitely more grand and tragic defeat in the battle for the League of Nations, this one had elements of something very much like victory woven into its dark pattern. Of course the final judgment waited upon the future. Yet taking things as they appeared in the autumn of 1910, Wilson could well go forward with self-assurance into his new world, his mood bordering on a cavalier and contagious gaiety. "It will not be dull," he told one campaign audience of the plot waiting to unfold; "it will be interesting."[3] It was indeed.

Nevertheless there were difficulties with Wilson's candidacy, and at the beginning nothing seemed to go right. Far from being greeted with enthusiasm among New Jersey voters, his announcement was looked on with the suspicion a protégé of Harvey and Boss Smith was bound to arouse among the progressives in both political parties. New Jersey had been the state above all others to be under the domination not only of bosses but of big business; yet for many years a small band of reformers had fought, with some success, against corporate and railway interests. Republicans included the "New Idea" men, led by George L. Record, and Mark Matthew Fagan of Jersey City; and, among the Democrats, young assemblymen like Joseph Patrick Tumulty, also of Jersey City.

To such men the Wilson boom was dismaying. They saw reactionary Democrats making a bid for power, with Boss Smith riding on the professor's coattails to gain for himself a second term in the U.S. Senate.

Through the summer of 1910, in Old Lyme with his family, Wilson watched without comment a political scene largely obscure and often highly disconcerting. He had thought the Democratic bosses would have things sufficiently under control so as to secure the withdrawal of his chief rival for the nomination, Frank S. Katzenbach, Jr., of Trenton. Katzenbach had waged a strong fight for the governorship three years previously; he was highly regarded by Democrats, who felt he deserved a second chance. Now he remained in the race. "I do not understand this Katzenbach business at all,"[4] Wilson wrote to Colonel Harvey. Matters were made worse by the fact that Wilson was determined not to be forced into declaring his views on issues, and not to appear actively to seek the nomination. His silence was galling to progressives in both parties.

Opposition within organized labor was particularly strong. In earlier writings and public addresses Wilson had made statements on the labor situation scarcely capable of being interpreted in any other way than as hostile to unionization. On this issue, in response to a public letter from the editor of *The American Labor Standard* of Orange, New Jersey, he did speak out. Wilson claimed that he had always been "the warm friend of organized labor,"[5] only criticizing the unions when he thought they had been wrong on particular actions. It was not an altogether accurate defense, nor a convincing one to the state labor leaders who looked for a more thorough and undeviating support. Wilson continued to be bedeviled by the issue as the nominating convention approached.

More generally among the public, opposition to Wilson emerged because the voters did not know him, because they thought him too bookish or austere, or because they resented the intrusion of a newcomer into a field they had cultivated as their own. The Trenton *Evening Times*, edited by James Kerney, made a poll of party members in Mercer County, where Wilson had lived for twenty years. Of these, an overwhelming majority favored Katzenbach.[6]

This opposition in his home county particularly dismayed Wilson. He had been persuaded by Harvey that a vaguely defined goodwill was calling him to the governorship. He had supposed that the personal popularity that he enjoyed among the merchants and tradespeople of Princeton's Nassau Street was the expression of a countywide sentiment. During the Princeton battles he was sustained by the conviction that however particular enemies might attack him, the rank and file of the college constituency were solidly on his side. In this new world of politics the situation seemed uncomfortably reversed. Among the politicians whom he dealt with directly he found only deference, while the wider community indicated sullen or uncomprehending mistrust.

The nomination of Wilson did not, as a result, look certain by any means when on the night of September 14 the party leaders gathered at Trenton to prepare for the following day's convention. The democracy of the state was there, men accustomed to the more sordid aspects of local politics, powerbrokers in shirtsleeves smoking the proverbial large cigars, sweating out the deals and maneuvers of their trade. Smith was busy among them, but even he was not certain that he and his allies could hold the pro-Wilson forces in line.

When the gavel fell next day at noon in the Taylor Opera House, the delegates were anything but united, and those prepared to vote for Wilson were far from jubilant. To pay their debt to Katzenbach and to get on with the business of the campaign was probably the best hope of the majority. "In that convention," wrote Kerney in an admirable understatement, "there were no hearts aching for the salvation of the world."[7] The same mood was symbolized by a somber Colonel Harvey, gazing down on the delegates from his box in the opera house.

Convinced that he and his friends would be able to control their candidate once his nomination had been secured, Harvey had shrewdly permitted Wilson to write the platform. It was enthusiastically endorsed, especially by the progressives, and then these same progressives paraded to block Wilson's nomination. Judge John W. Wescott, who would twice nominate Wilson for the Presidency of the United States, made a nominating speech for Katzenbach, setting off a pandemonium of cheers. Speaking for Wilson, Smith admitted defensively that few of those present could have more than "a passing acquaintance" with his candidate.[8] As the convention seemed on the verge of getting out of control, as disorder and protest broke out on the floor and dissent showed itself even among the normally submissive county organizations, the balloting began. But the bosses held their lines. By four o'clock that afternoon it appeared that Wilson's nomination was assured.

In Old Lyme Madge Axson had been married on September 8 to Edward Graham Elliott, in the early 1900s a young assistant to Wilson and his choice for first dean of the college after he became president. "It is a novel sight," Wilson wrote, "to see Madge surrender, and show all the tender signs of sentiment."[9] Ellen and Woodrow invited the guests to the marriage of "our sister." The occasion was a last, bittersweet family reunion before the forces of political life took over. It is also one of the last glimpses we get of Madge, who moved to California, where her husband practiced law and where she (suffering the fate of so many of the Axsons) was subject to recurrent illnesses and depressions.

A few days after the marriage, Wilson left Old Lyme for Princeton. Late into the night of September 14, while the politicians milled about at Trenton, he worked in the silent spaces of Prospect upon the draft of an acceptance speech. The next morning he played golf, and after messengers arriving from Trenton assured him that affairs were progressing favorably, he motored the few miles that led into the turbulent heart of a new life. Wilson was hustled into the Trenton Hotel, prepared to be taken surreptitiously back to Princeton if, at the last moment, Boss Smith failed to get his man nominated. There he waited, calm while everyone else was agitated and tense, until the balloting was completed. Out of 1,403 votes, Wilson on the first ballot received forty more than necessary for the nomination—not a famous victory, but it was enough, as Harvey assured the candidate a little glumly. Afterwards the nomination was made unanimous, according to custom.

As the weary delegates prepared to leave the hall, the chairman announced dramatically that the candidate for governor—"and the next President of the United States"—was on his way to address the convention.[10]

The delegates saw that day, stepping out onto the platform of the Taylor Opera House, a man in his prime, vigorous and tall; his face was still ruddy with the aftereffects of his morning's exercise. Informally dressed amid that top-hatted crowd, he moved quickly, a figure lithe and slim, with the brisk authority of one accustomed to rule. Read over in the context of his collected works, Wilson's speech of acceptance does not appear remarkable.[11] But to the delegates in the fetid convention hall it came with striking freshness. From the first sentence, spoken in conversational tones yet reaching the farthest corner of the hall, Wilson had the audience under his spell. Even the most skeptical or the most hardened sensed that a new leader had appeared.

Only someone remembering how Adlai Stevenson's acceptance speech electrified the tired and contentious Democratic National Convention of 1952 can readily conceive the effect of Wilson's words, of his style and bearing, on the Trenton politicians of 1910. He spoke of his freedom from pledges or deals of any kind; he promised to serve the people of the state with singleness of purpose, on the basis of the party platform alone. Interrupted frequently by applause, he came to the end of his prepared remarks. Still the audience called for more. He resumed with an impromptu peroration, a poetic evocation of the meaning of the American flag, such as Wilson knew well how to frame and the audiences of that day rejoiced to hear.

Afterwards men wept as if they had been redeemed; they struck each other on the back in self-congratulation and tried to carry Wilson in triumph from the hall. Unfortunately Judge Wescott, leader of the anti-Wilson forces, had quit the convention in disgust and would only be converted on a later encounter. But a young man who was to play a large part in Wilson's future had paused after turning to leave and waited skeptically near the stage. Joe Tumulty, a knight of the progressive forces in New Jersey, as a fledgling lawyer had made his reputation among the Irish Americans of Jersey City's Fifth Ward and in 1906 had won an assembly seat. He had come to the 1910 convention as an onlooker, a disgruntled, despairing figure in the balcony, sure that the flame he had seen flicker out under Jersey City's liberal Mayor Fagan had been extinguished for good.[12] Yet something held him when it was announced that the candidate would appear in person; and what he heard in the next quarter-hour changed his life.

The Trenton nomination brought Wilson to the attention of a national audience. Editors across the country sensed that unexpected events were in the making for New Jersey and, perhaps, for the Democratic Party. With the 1912 Presidential race on the horizon, every political development was under scrutiny, and in the eyes of many an experienced candidate-watcher, a significant new figure had to be reckoned with.

A few days after the convention, while still answering a flood of congratulatory mail, the candidate met with the bosses responsible for his nomination. Smith, with his nephew, James Nugent of Newark, was accompanied to Princeton by the liberal editor James Kerney, and the three set about planning the forthcoming campaign. Shortly afterwards the leaders of Wilson's own Mercer County joined the group. The candidate asked apt questions, but he was obviously an innocent, and he had his own stubborn ideas about how he wanted to operate.[13]

He disliked the handshaking, baby-kissing type of campaign, Wilson informed the bosses. He did not wish to engage in day-long barnstorming trips; he hoped, indeed, to keep three days of the week free for Princeton business. As for finances, he expected to be able to pay for the campaign out of his own pocket, relying for transportation on automobiles borrowed from friends, and paying overnight hotel expenses and local train fares from the proceeds of three lectures after the campaign. Together, he said, these would bring in the needed sum of five hundred dollars.

The politicians must have smiled. Smith alone before the campaign was over would contribute as much as $50,000 for the expenses of organizing a statewide drive. But they liked their candidate despite his naïveté. Sitting in Prospect's handsome library, they marveled that a man should abandon such a place of quiet reflection for the tawdry hurly-burly of their world.

Wilson opened the college year as usual on September 22, speaking to the undergraduates on the ties between religion and sound learning. A few days later, before a crowded meeting of the university's religious organization, he chose for his text the fine biblical injunction "Thou therefore endure hardness as a good soldier."[14] Then he went forth himself to do battle.

His opening speeches of the campaign at Jersey City and Plainfield found him still too much the professor to please the rank and file— particularly to satisfy the liberal elements, independent Republicans as well as Democrats, who were now watching him with hopeful interest. They felt that he spoke appealingly, but in generalities. After one of these speeches Wilson accosted Tumulty, asking him how he judged the effort. The young Irishman hesitated; the older man urged him to be frank. "Well," said Tumulty, "your speech was most disappointing."[15] At about the same time a letter from a sympathetic stranger warned Wilson that he was seen as "too nice a man—a schoolmaster rather than a leader." He had made a favorable impression by his first speech, the letter went on, "but not a favorable one from a political standpoint."[16] The candidate got the point. In a major address September 30 in Newark, he hit his stride with a militant call for control of corporations and for a public service commission to regulate utilities.

The campaign, at best, was not going to be an easy one. Spurred by the example of the Democrats, the Republicans nominated a strong candidate, Vivian Murchison Lewis, a moderate progressive with wide experience in state politics.

Pushed by this circumstance, not less than by the advice of the progressive faction around him, Wilson gave way to his inclinations and assumed an increasingly bold posture. The activist strain in his nature began to affect his style. The habits of the classroom slipped away as he assumed the role of popular leader. Delivered from brief notes, the New Jersey campaign speeches, taken as a whole, form a remarkable chapter in the Wilson corpus—lucid appeals to the common sense and to the latent idealism of his growing audiences, solid expositions making the business of the state seem interesting and significant. As the heat of

the campaign mounted, Wilson's prose grew more spare, more colloquial. The politicians, Wilson sensed, were "strong for perorations." But
with concrete matters to debate, he laid about him with unadorned prose.

The determining event of the campaign occurred in the last week of
October and was subtly intertwined with Wilson's formal resignation
from Princeton at the board meeting of October 20. In the last chapter
it was noted only that he submitted a brief letter and then left the room.
The surrounding circumstances throw a sharp light upon Wilson's actions over the following, crucial days.

The Wilson stalwarts on the board had hoped that a final decision
might be deferred until the end of the gubernatorial campaign—it was,
after all, but two weeks away. Pyne, however, was adamant in wanting
to get rid of Wilson once and for all. Distrusting Wilson to the point
where he felt he might go back on his public statement that he would
offer his resignation, Pyne drafted and put into the hand of one of his
faction a resolution demanding the resignation if it should not be voluntarily offered.[17] On the night before the meeting Wilson's friends
agreed to go along with Pyne's insistence that the resignation be accepted
forthwith, partly on the grounds that anything else might be interpreted
as showing Wilson less than confident of winning the governorship.

So it was that on the morning of October 20 a grim group of men
went through with their business and a grim Wilson accepted it un-
questioningly. But after he left the room there were unpleasant exchanges
and niggling demands. Wilson on hearing of them reacted in bitterness
and anger. He had persuaded himself that old scores could be considered
settled and that his entering upon a political career would bring a general
relaxation of tension. Now he refused to accept a day's salary after the
official date of his resignation. A well-intentioned treasurer regularly
sent him checks. They were as regularly returned, and he resolved to
move out of Prospect at the earliest possible moment.

A Scotchman, always careful in regard to money, Wilson cannot have
found it easy to renounce these payments. For the first time since student
days he found himself without a regular salary. He undoubtedly had
some savings from the sale of the house in Library Place and from
earnings on his books, particularly the *History of the American People*.
But entering into politics, he was finding himself squeezed financially
and concerned for the future of his family. Only a deep personal affront
could have caused him to act so peremptorily toward the Princeton
treasurer.

Had he not been in the midst of a campaign that absolutely dominated his thoughts, he wrote a friend, he would have been shattered by "the mortification of what I discovered . . . to be the real feeling of the Pyne party towards me."[18] As for Pyne, he had opportunity to gloat over his coup. "The thing was done, I think, in a very satisfactory and diplomatic way," he wrote to his old friend Procter. "According to the newspapers he [Wilson] forced his resignation on a reluctant board, although actually he . . . had to be told pretty positively that it had to be done."[19]

The break with Princeton thus made final and irreparable, a crisis presented itself capable of wrecking his political hopes. In one of his campaign speeches Wilson had offhandedly challenged any politician who disagreed with him to public debate. The challenge was noted and taken up by George L. Record, then a Republican candidate for Congress and columnist for the *Jersey Journal*. A longtime battler for progressive ideas, he was a man as much admired for his integrity as he was feared for the consistency of his aggressive liberalism. Wilson's advisers, close to panic, urged him to ignore the challenger. For a brief time Wilson seems to have agreed with them. Then, in one of the master strokes that occurred at moments in his political career, he sallied out on his own with a promise that he would reply to any questions that Record might submit in writing.

Record agreed to this arrangement and in a letter shrewdly framed submitted on October 19 a list of questions covering every issue then on the progressive agenda in New Jersey. Over the days following his resignation from Princeton, Wilson pondered his reply in solitude. In so complex a man, interaction of the two crises was inevitable. "Endure hardness," he had told the Princeton undergraduates a short while before. Now he took with a show of impunity the trustees' blow to his self-esteem. At the same time he uncompromisingly and obdurately faced up to all that was implicit in the Record challenge.

To a long series of questions on his support of workmen's compensation, establishment of a public utilities commission with power to fix "reasonable" rates, extension of the primary laws to virtually all state officials, on the direct election of U. S. senators and passage of a stiff corrupt practices act—Wilson answered with an unequivocal and often breathtaking "Yes." When asked whether he admitted to the existence of the boss system as Record had specifically described it, Wilson replied: "Of course I admit it. Its existence is notorious." When asked, further, whether in referring to the Republican "Board of Guardians" he meant certain particular names, and how these differed from such bosses as Smith and Nugent, Wilson replied: "I refer to the men you name. They [the "Board of Guardians"] differ from the others in this, that they are in control of the government of the state while the others [the Democratic bosses] are not and cannot be if the present Democratic ticket is elected."

A final dramatic answer gives the tone of the exchange. Wilson was asked by Record: "Will you agree to publicly call upon the Republican and Democratic candidates for the legislature to pledge themselves in writing prior to election in favor of such of the foregoing reforms as you personally favor? If not, why not?" "I will not," Wilson replied. "Because I think it would be unbecoming in me to do so. That is the function of the voters in the several counties. Let them test and judge the men, and choose those who are sincere." Wilson closed with brief thanks to Record for the opportunity he had been given to "express with the greatest possible definiteness" his convictions upon the issues of the campaign.[20]

In his replies Wilson completed the change in his views and in his public persona begun when he first responded to the lure of the New Jersey race. If he had not reversed himself on positions previously held, he had certainly pushed them to a logical extreme, beyond the caution with which they had previously been framed. The break with Princeton had, in a way, liberated him. It had emboldened him to be a full-fledged progressive or nothing. Henceforth he would give quarter to no one, as among his Princeton enemies none had given quarter to him. He would make no compromises, even for the sake of those who had launched his political career and who were now vigorously promoting him. Wilson was compelled by the logic of events, one may almost say he was compelled by fate, to go forward, not one mile but two. He may have surprised himself; certainly he astonished Record by the inclusiveness, definiteness, and audacity of his position.

Well might Wilson thank Record for the forum provided by his letter; when the reply was published in all New Jersey newspapers on October 26, the outcome of the campaign suddenly seemed assured. Waverers among the progressives of both parties came back into the fold as the New Jersey press, and then the national press, hailed the ringing manifesto of liberalism. At the same time Wilson's platform appearances showed increasing fire. In the remaining weeks of the campaign he crossed and recrossed the state; he engaged in the barnstorming trips he had professed to abhor. New Jersey had never seen anything like the crowds that turned out to cheer him, and when he ended the campaign at Newark with one of the grand emotional passages he had previously avoided, the most hardened cynics succumbed to the spell. Smith sat in the balcony the night of November 5 as Wilson, closing the campaign, prophesied a time when men would look to the uplands with a great shout of joy: "What difference does it make if we ourselves do not reach the uplands? We have given our lives to the enterprise."[21] And Boss Smith wept. He would leave to another day the settling of accounts with this extraordinary figure, who declared so blithely his independence of boss rule, and yet who surely must be a "practical" man.

Wilson's victory on November 5 was astonishing in its sweep. Two years before, the Republicans, with Taft heading the national ticket, had carried New Jersey by over 82,000 votes. Now Wilson defeated a strong gubernatorial candidate to carry the state by a majority of 1,333,682 to Vivian Lewis's 684,126. An unusually large proportion of the electorate had voted, and the State Assembly went overwhelmingly to the Democrats. In the process, men and women had found politics to be significant once more, its issues relevant to their lives and hopes.

The Wilson household was flooded with congratulations from near and far. Even more enthusiastically than hitherto the editorial writers of the nation took up their pens to salute the new leader and predict great things for his future. But the battle, as it turned out, was not over. Wilson went directly from the gubernatorial victory into a struggle that tested him to the core.

It began with a conference at Princeton on November 13, with Boss Smith coming to present his respects to the victor and to discuss the question of the New Jersey senatorship. More basically, as the two men knew, the discussion turned upon who was to be the real leader of the Democratic Party in the state. Named once before by the legislature for an undistinguished Senate term, Smith had withdrawn from the national stage to exercise power locally. He was in poor health, and at the beginning of the Wilson candidacy had repeatedly given assurances to intimates that he would not run again. "Not once but a dozen times," James Kerney wrote in his memoir, "he declared that in no circumstances would he be a candidate for the U. S. Senate, should the campaign eventuate in a Democratic legislature."[22] Now, however, he was beginning to have a change of mind. He was feeling better, he told Wilson at the Princeton meeting. "The majority of the caucus would give me the nomination," he asserted soon afterwards, "and there would be no further question of the result."[23] Still, he had not yet come to a final decision. Wilson strongly dissented and the outlines of the coming confrontation became plain.

Wilson owed his nomination to Smith; he owed him much for his role in the campaign. Smith, moreover, was by no means the popular caricature of a boss. He was worldly wise and genial, moving comfortably in the journalistic and financial circles where Colonel George Harvey and Colonel Henry Watterson were at home. To let the legislature take its course might have seemed to Wilson and to others the natural repayment of a debt. Besides, what right did the governor have to intrude himself into such a situation? Yet Wilson was pledged to rid the state of bossism. During the campaign he had constantly reiterated his determination to be the leader of the party, the representative of the people, not merely the state's chief executive.

The issue was complicated by the fact that in a little-noted primary campaign the majority of a small Democratic vote had gone to James E. Martine. The primary was not binding on the legislature. Martine, moreover, was as unlikely a candidate for the Senate as could be imagined. Independently wealthy and known as "Farmer Jim," he had run for virtually every office in the state and never been elected to any. Yet he was a progressive, if a somewhat absurd one; and the party's choice, if by an inconsequential minority. Unless principles under the new administration were to mean nothing, Martine could not be treated as the joke he seemed to many.

Wilson admitted to Smith his low opinion of Martine, broached the possibility of a substitute candidate, and pointed out the personal advantage that would accrue to Smith if he should generously disclaim his ambitions. Smith's position only hardened. He declared soon afterwards to Harvey, "Well, by God, I guess I'll let him [Wilson] beat me."[24] Two days after the Princeton meeting, Wilson was writing to the same mentor. "Ridiculous though it undoubtedly is," he said, he would have to support Martine.[25] Meanwhile Smith was summoning up the support of James Nugent, chairman of the state's Democratic committee, and of Bob Davis, boss of the Hudson County machine.

Without even a brief vacation following the strenuous campaign, Wilson plunged into a new round of activity. At the end of that November month he journeyed to Chicago and Milwaukee, delivering the lectures he had promised earlier and which he had once supposed would pay for his campaign. In Frankfort, Kentucky, he made an important address at the national conference of governors, presenting a carefully argued case for the enlarged role in national politics and administration for state executives. It was not a plea for states' rights, such as Wilson might have made on earlier occasions, but for bold leadership widely decentralized. "In brief," he told the governors, "we are setting up, outside the sphere of the Federal Congress, a new instrument of political life."[26]

The speech did not go unnoticed in New Jersey. It was Wilson's way of bringing the senatorial controversy into line with large developments.

While progressives fretted over his delay in declaring himself publicly, Wilson set in motion a thoroughgoing campaign to sound out, and subtly to win over, the local politicians. His most striking initiative was a visit to the Jersey City bedside of Bob Davis, the old boss now in the terminal phase of a cancer. The two men canvassed the arguments on both sides of the question, but Davis had given his word to Smith and would not go back on it. Reports of the meeting between the stricken warrior and the seemingly invulnerable governor-elect touched the public imagination. Davis had been loved by Hudson County's poor; he was a boss of the old style, incorruptible according to his particular lights. In seeking him out in his modest home Wilson shed whatever appearance of aloofness still clung to him. Then, early in December, he went to another home, that of James Smith in Newark, making one final effort to persuade him to reconsider.

Wilson informed Smith frankly that he would oppose him if he persisted. Would the governor-elect draw the line at publicly expressing his opposition? Smith asked. No, Wilson replied. "I shall actively oppose you with every honorable means in my power."[27] He wrote personally that his determination meant war and perhaps another stumping tour of the state.[28] Having failed to get definite word from Smith by December 6, Wilson issued a public statement declaring it the duty of every Democratic legislator "who would keep faith with the law of the State and with the avowed principles of his party" to vote for Martine.[29] Smith countered with a bitter assault. The governor-elect, he said, "has given striking evidence of his aptitude in the art of foul play."[30]

As Christmas approached Wilson held nightly meetings at Prospect. The young Tumulty was in general charge of this campaign to oust the old guard; but the man who only a few months before had been the amateur in politics took a personal part and astonished the professionals by his sure-footed skill. Virtually every Democratic member of the assembly scheduled to meet in January had been consulted by the end of the third week in December. By then Wilson was confident he would win, and on December 23 issued a strong statement describing the progress of the battle.[31]

In the midst of all this he went up into the tower of Prospect, where as president of Princeton he had been accustomed to withdraw to do serious work. Now he had one scholarly task remaining, the presidential address

to the American Political Science Association at its annual meeting in
St. Louis. Returning to the field he had first made his own and in which
he had won his early reputation, Wilson set himself to speak with unusual
gravity of things that had meant much to him and were now rapidly
fading into the background of another existence. He was Prospero
"drowning" his book; but before the spell was broken he summoned
up a statement of what he believed and what had become the ruling
passion of his life.

Entitled "The Law and the Facts," the address was an appeal for a
view of politics transcending narrow legalisms and hampering precedents. There was a law which codifies facts; there was another law which
runs ahead of the facts and fixes the moral parameters of the living
generation. It was this second law which gives substance to politics and
political science. "Politics," he declared, "is of the very stuff of life. Its
motives are interlaced with the whole fibre of experience, private and
public. Its relations are intensely human, and generally intimately personal."[32] The man of letters and the statesman must be reconciled in the
new politics. "Your real statesman is first of all, and chief of all, a great
human being, with an eye for all the great field upon which men like
himself struggle, with unflagging pathetic hope, towards better things."
He is a man "big enough to think in the terms of what others than
himself are striving for and living for. . . . He is a guide, a comrade, a
mentor, a servant, a friend of mankind. May not the student of politics
be the same?"

"Know your people and you can lead them," Wilson concluded;
"study your people and you may know them." But the study was not
to be of "congeries of interests"; the scholar must work "not as you
would calculate forces, but as you would comprehend life."

In this farewell to the scholarly world Wilson came as close as ever
he would to declaring the humane basis of his liberalism. For a fleeting
moment he made the two large parts of his career merge into one.

That was the last time Wilson mounted to his tower. On January 17,
three days before the inauguration at Trenton, he and his family moved
out of Prospect. With the closing of the house (the trustees had as yet
named no one to be Wilson's successor), not merely a tenancy but a
whole way of life was being closed. Amid the turmoil Ellen took care
that Woodrow's study, with its books and its memories, be the last room
dismantled.[33] New Jersey provided no year-round home for its chief
executive, so that family possessions had to be packed and stored. The
Wilsons moved into four rooms at the Princeton Inn. Margaret, studying

voice, was living in an apartment of her own in New York; but Jessie, working at a settlement house in Philadelphia, and Eleanor, also in Philadelphia for art classes, would be returning home regularly.

"My heart aches at the break-up of the old life," Wilson wrote. He had not realized the anguish he would experience "until it touched our home and sent us into lodgings at an inn. I feel like a nomad!"[34] Not until the following autumn did the Wilsons, with the Smith sisters of New Orleans, rent a pleasant house at 25 Cleveland Lane in Princeton. Here they lived until they left for the White House in March 1913.

The governor-elect's speaking tour on behalf of Martine opened January 5 in Jersey City. The stage was grandly set, with St. Patrick's Hall filled to the last cranny with a tumultuous crowd of citizens, a thousand flags floating aloft, and the sounding of cymbals and trumpets as Wilson appeared. He had made sure of his defenses; he knew he was on solid ground. The politicians had been appeased or won over, and now he could go above their heads, above the heads of the county leaders and the special interests, to speak directly to the people.

It was the occasion to spur an orator to his best, and Wilson reached the top of his form, hitting home again and again as the great crowd roared its approval. Only that day had he jotted down brief notes guiding what he should say. He needed no more; he was speaking to a constituency he had come to know well. He could play upon their hopes by using homely phrases, and stir their resolution by touching familiar themes. They were combative, against compromise, and Wilson stood before them as the incarnation of the fighting spirit. "These are our terms," he concluded amid mounting storms of applause: "War if you are allied with the enemy. Peace if you are on the . . . side of justice."[35] On January 14, three days before his inauguration, he concluded his campaign at an equally boisterous and equally successful public meeting in Newark.

The inauguration itself was carried out with the traditional trappings. To compose his inaugural address Wilson had to ask for a temporary hideaway in the college library. On this occasion he read what he had to say—a sober, detailed account of the reforms to which he felt his party was committed. Afterwards he reviewed the joyful Democratic parades, returning to power after sixteen years of exile. He entertained the state's dignitaries, and at the State House held an open reception for New Jersey citizens. Wilson enjoyed this latter part best of all. "All sorts and conditions of people came," he wrote Mary Peck, "men, women, and children, and I felt very close to all of them, and very much touched by the thought that I was their representative and spokesman, and in a very real sense their help and hope."[36]

The first business of the legislature was the election of a senator. At a preliminary Democratic caucus on January 23 Martine received thirty-one votes to Smith's fourteen, with forty-one necessary for election. The outcome was by now almost certain, but in the immemorial fashion of campaign managers, Nugent announced that Martine had "peaked" and could not be elected. That day Smith and his entourage arrived to take rooms at the Sterling Hotel, followed by a delegation of the rank and file transported in special buses from Smith's hometown of Newark. Brass bands kept up a bold front. Meanwhile the governor and his close associates worked into the night, preparing against any miscarriage in the morrow's battle,

The first official ballot saw several of Smith's earlier supporters moving over to Martine. The old boss reluctantly released his delegates, and the next day, when the legislature voted a second time, Martine was safely over the top. Only three of the Democratic legislators, members of the Newark delegation, remained faithful to their chief. Wilson had done his work well. But at the end he pitied Smith. His friends deserted him as power fell away. He left the Trenton headquarters, so recently the scene of bustling adherents, attended only by his four sons.

Wilson's widely acclaimed victory gave him precisely the momentum he required to launch a successful reform program. He had consolidated his party, aroused public opinion, given proof of his own skill. Tumulty, an effective lieutenant in the fight, was appointed private secretary, a post he would keep during Wilson's two terms in the White House. Wilson was served faithfully by the young Irish Catholic, with his bouyant disposition, his feeling for the human factors in any situation, and his instinctive knowledge of practical politics. He would "act as my secretary," Wilson wrote the liberal journalist Oswald Garrison Villard, "in order that I may have a guide at my elbow in matters of which I know almost nothing."[37] Tumulty, besides his unwavering loyalty to his chief, became devoted to Ellen Wilson (as did James Kerney). We find Ellen at this period, recovered from her long depression and the misery of the last year at Prospect, once more her husband's confidante in daily crises, a steady balance to his impetuous idealism. She quickly learned the political game. Though she worried about Woodrow's physical endurance, she rejoiced in the new fields that had opened to him.

What Wilson lacked, and what no member of his personal or official

The governor, 1911

Wilson speaking at Sea Girt, summer 1911

Politicians: the Governor and
Champ Clark

Colonel House

Barnstorming, 1912

Leaving the house at Cleveland Lane,
with Ellen, March 3, 1913

household could supply, was detailed knowledge of legislative drafts-
manship. He had early decided to concentrate on four major reforms,
thus avoiding the error of traditional liberals, a determination to make
over the whole world at once. These four consisted of changes in the
election laws; a corrupt practices act; workmen's compensation; and
the establishment of a commission to regulate utilities. He could not
rely for the formulation of this program on the discredited party chieftains, nor upon any of the legislature's new recruits. In a bold move he
turned to George Record, the uncompromising Republican journalist.

The day before his inauguration, Wilson held a meeting with Record
and with legislative leaders and progressives of both parties. Great was
the wrath of the county bosses at finding themselves excluded. Their
journalistic spokesmen thundered for days against the coup. Not only
was the conference in their eyes unconstitutional, subversive, and conspiratorial, but it suffered from the fatal defect of having been held in
the alien city of New York. Whatever the complaints of the old leaders,
the reform program was made clearly comprehensible to those who
would have the chief responsibility for carrying it out.

Wilson's active role did not stop there. In a pregnant passage of his
inaugural address he had stated that he would "take the liberty from
time to time to make detailed recommendations . . . sometimes in the
form of bills if necessary."[38] Over the next months he made plain his
meaning. He played a role in drafting bills; he consulted constantly with
committees and with individual lawmakers; he issued statements and
made public appeals. Yet as governor Wilson refrained from the formal
messages to the legislature that later as President he employed with telling
effect. He preferred at this stage to play down the role of the state's
chief executive and seemed anxious to have his bills emerge strictly from
the lawmaking process. If he was in fact the prime minister he had long
ago seen essential to the working of popular government, he kept up
the appearance of being a mere "comrade" in the lawmaking task.

The first reform scheduled for introduction went to the heart of all
the others: a broad-scale revision of the electoral laws. It was designed,
in Wilson's words, "to put the whole management alike of parties and
elections, in the hands of the voters themselves."[39] By its terms primaries
were extended not only to the election of congressmen, senators, and
governors, but also to party leaders and to delegates to the national
nominating conventions. It carried the name of the Geran bill, being
introduced by Assemblyman Elmer H. Geran, a former student of Wilson's at Princeton, and was designed to put New Jersey at a single stroke
in the forefront of those states striving for a wide popular participation.

The bill was of crucial importance because it was aimed directly at the power of the bosses. With the people in control significant measures of social progress seemed attainable; with the bosses lodged in their old seats of power, the alliance between politics and big business would continue. Because of its essentially radical nature, the Geran bill was bound to provoke severe opposition. The party bosses had been publicly routed; Smith never reappeared at Trenton after his defeat; but the party chairman, James R. Nugent, Smith's nephew and ally, a rough, unpolished fighter, was constantly on the floor of the assembly, exercising the kind of informal pressure that had long been an acknowledged part of the political process. To the alarm of county leaders who saw themselves in danger of being cut off from the very roots of their power was added the intense bitterness they felt toward Wilson personally. Every maneuver known to them, every trick of their trade, was mustered against passage of the Geran bill.

The state senate was still ruled by a Republican majority. The governor set much store on establishing good relations with this opposition, going out of his way to win them by personal as much as by political tactics. Almost daily conferences were held with them. At Tumulty's suggestion a dinner was arranged for Republican and Democratic senators at the Trenton Country Club. It was an evening of easy fellowship, ending with a Virginia reel led by the governor himself. Wilson would sit late in his office, swapping stories with all comers. In his own party Nugent remained Wilson's chief stumbling block. One afternoon Nugent came to the governor's office, and a strong argument was concluded with Wilson rising from his chair and pointing to the door. "Good afternoon, Mr. Nugent," he said icily. Nugent stormed out, but not without a final exchange. "You're no gentleman!" he shouted. "You're no judge," responded the governor.[40] The story, no doubt spread by Tumulty, got into the New Jersey newspapers and was the happy sensation of a day.

The most dramatic and perhaps the single most effective move in the fight for the Geran bill was Wilson's announcement in March that he would attend a Democratic caucus. It was unprecedented that the governor should break what was taken by many to be the constitutional guarantee of separation of powers. Challenged on this point, Wilson produced a copy of the state constitution from his pocket and cited a passage giving the governor the right to communicate with the legislators by message at the opening of each session "and at such other times as he may deem necessary." That was sufficient for his purposes. The meeting lasted for three hours, with Wilson speaking with great earnestness for much of the time. His address may be compared to the speech he had delivered before the Princeton faculty at the height of the quad controversy in 1906. As then, he was speaking to intimate associates, for a cause he deeply believed in and of which he commanded the most detailed information. No newspapermen were present that day in Trenton, but versions of the address leaked out (again, no doubt, by the shrewd initiative of the governor's secretary); and among those who heard it were many who considered it the most wonderful speech of their lives. "You can turn aside from the measure, if you choose," Wilson was quoted as saying in a climactic passage. "You can decline to follow me; you can deprive me of office and turn away from me, but you cannot deprive me of power so long as I steadfastly stand for what I believe to be the interests and legitimate demands of the people themselves."[41]

The Geran bill passed in the assembly on March 21, by a margin narrow enough to justify all the efforts Wilson had spent in its behalf. He was speaking in the Midwest when news of the senate's final approval was announced by the chairman of the meeting, and that distant audience rose in applause. It was a nice conjunction, marking the effect of Wilson's home victories upon his national fortunes. He was himself in a mood of relative exuberance. "I cannot manage to think ill of my fellow men as a whole," he wrote in a private letter at almost this time, "though some of them are extraordinary scoundrels."[42]

Afterwards, success came more easily. The corrupt practices law and the workmen's compensation statute were passed quickly, and by April 21, a day before the legislature's adjournment, a public utilities law was on the books. The accomplishment was unprecedented and complete. "The present legislature," wrote George Record in his influential newspaper column, "ends its session with the most remarkable record of progressive legislation ever known in the political history of this or any State." Without Wilson, he added, "nothing of substantial importance would have been passed."[43]

The closing hours of the session found the lawmakers relaxed but unusually orderly. Until three in the morning business proceeded on the floor, while the men singly or in groups came to the governor's outer office to exchange stories with the newspapermen and friends who had gathered for the climactic scene. Afterwards most of the members dropped in to say good-bye to the governor, and by 4:00 A.M. the old statehouse was quiet.

The next day Wilson basked in his triumph, tired, as he wrote, but "quietly and deeply happy that I should have been of just the kind of service I wished to be to those who elected and trusted me." As for the success of his first political venture, he looked upon it, he wrote Mary

Peck, as "just a bit of natural history." He had come to office "in the fullness of time, when opinion was ripe on all these matters, when both parties were committed to these reforms, and by merely standing fast, and by never losing sight of the business for an hour, but keeping up all sorts of (legitimate) pressure *all the time*, kept the mighty forces from being diverted or blocked at any point."[44]

TOWARD THE PRESIDENCY

It is difficult to say at what point Wilson definitely decided to run for President. He was modest in contemplating such a race; in offering himself for what he viewed as an awesome responsibility, mere ambition seemed an inadequate guide. A man waited for a "call," and Wilson was not sure by mid-winter of 1911 that the call had come to him, either in the form of popular demand or of a deeper voice within his conscience. So far as practicable he was inclined to let matters take their course. With an impersonality characteristic of him in large matters, he was, he told a friend, observing a career that seemed not his own, "but a sort of inevitable, detached thing." In the early stage of the Presidential boom at the end of 1910, when people wrote to him asking what they could contribute, "not an idea comes into my head," he confessed privately. "I do not in the least know what to say; it all seems so silly, so premature."[1]

This attitude, however admirable in a private man, nearly cost him the prize. Through a critical period of fifteen months Wilson worked in large measure alone, without a circle of intimate advisers and without adequate support from professional politicians. He lacked the composure to think through the problems of establishing a national constituency, or of putting down roots into the subsoil of political power. In consequence his schedule became helter-skelter; he abandoned positions he had long held as a scholar and publicist, and adopted new ideas as the occasion or his own impulse suggested them. Along the way he was beset by unanticipated hazards. Even after he was committed to running, the fragile structure of his campaign seemed more than once on the point of collapse.

Yet in part because of this very lack of system, because of his creaking, amateurish organization and unfettered thinking, Wilson fashioned an image in some ways more important than conventional political assets. He appeared to the public as a new and disinterested leader, a figure with a certain degree of nobility of character and a mind of refreshing intelligence. He recalled lost ideals. He made men and women uncomfortable with their habitual assumptions, and their discomfort seemed to call them to something better for themselves and for their country. Wilson was canny enough to sense this unique basis of his appeal, and, fearing the image might become clouded, he resisted too much stress on efficiency and organization.

As he moved toward the nomination, events on the national stage overlapped and became entangled with the unfolding drama in New Jersey. From the time of his election as governor he began receiving letters urging him on to the Presidency, and victories over the state's bosses fortified a growing national support. Yet at the climax it was the bosses, beaten in the open field but entrenched and sullen in their urban strongholds, that might well have cost him the nomination. He was moving through an intricate web of circumstances, jostled by crowds and beset by conflicting advice, with little but his instincts and a few long-held principles to guide him.

While Wilson was beginning his term as governor, important changes took place in the forces backing him. Harvey and Watterson had been active in recruiting support for a Wilson candidacy among conservative Democrats and pro-business elements. But the successful campaign against Smith for senator, and Wilson's assumption of leadership of the progressives, caused these supporters to take a second look. In the pages of *Harper's Weekly*, Colonel George Harvey maintained fervent editorial support—"I should like to be the true original of such a portrait," wrote Wilson upon reading one of Harvey's encomiums—but the correspondence of the two men showed a loosening of their personal ties, and Harvey's political network disintegrated. While support was thus vanishing from among conservatives, a new and more popularly based movement was in the making.

This was composed of individuals across the country, many being former students of Wilson at Princeton or Johns Hopkins, and others who had heard his public lectures over the years. The first "Wilson for President" club was launched in Staunton, his birthplace; during 1911 it was followed by others in different parts of the country. At the core of the movement was now a small group of southerners, attempting to give direction to the formless but increasing national interest. These included Walter Hines Page, Wilson's friend of Atlanta days, a North Carolinian who by 1910 was editor of the influential *World's Work*; William F. McCombs, born in Arkansas, a former Wilson student and a New York lawyer; and Walter McCorkle, a Virginian by birth, also practicing law in New York. Despite pressure from these three, Wilson was reluctant to see established any kind of campaign organization. However, he did go along with plans for out-of-state addresses and, after the close of the New Jersey legislative session, for a speaking tour taking him to the Far West.

If there was a moment in his own mind when Wilson decided he should make a try for the Presidency, it was in early March 1911, when, somewhat grudgingly, he accepted an invitation to speak in Atlanta to a meeting of the Southern Commercial Congress. "I am not going because I want to go," he told Mary Peck, ". . . but, I am half ashamed to say, because I thought it wise (which, being translated means politic) to go. I hate the thing done for policy's sake!"[2]

A week later he wrote again, reporting his immensely enthusiastic welcome. "I was given a dinner, a breakfast, and a reception," he told her, "and on every possible occasion was nominated for the presidency!"[3] At the main event, in an auditorium crowded with eight thousand people, he had received (he was told) a warmer ovation than had been extended to Theodore Roosevelt on the previous evening. Wilson's speech was only a half hour in length, but it showed him at his best as a spokesman for emerging forces and new issues.

From Atlanta Wilson hurried back to Princeton for what was to be one of the significant encounters in his rise to party leadership. Ellen was responsible for this small coup. Staying at the Princeton Inn, relieved for the first time in years of domestic chores, she was observing the political situation closely; her letters to Woodrow show growing self-confidence in offering advice. Hearing that William Jennings Bryan was coming to Princeton to lecture at the theological seminary, she took matters into her own hands. Bryan had looked on Wilson as an unconverted conservative, her husband upon Bryan as an irresponsible radical. Now Ellen would try to promote an understanding between them.

Wilson arrived in haste from the South to attend the Great Commoner's lecture and afterwards, as a result of Ellen's invitation, the two men dined together. It was a family affair, with two of the Wilson daughters present, and was altogether successful in its purpose. Wilson wrote afterwards that he had found Bryan's religious address, on the subject of faith, to be most impressive. "He held the audience easily for an hour and a half. . . . I was exceedingly pleased." "I can say now that I know him," he added, "and have a very different impression of him from that I had before seeing him thus close at hand. . . . A truly captivating man, I must admit."[4] As for Bryan, he thought well of Wilson, too, and although in the months ahead he did not endorse him outright (his own ambition for the Presidency being still too much alive for that) he took to speaking kindly of him and to instructing him with something like fatherly concern. Wilson did not afterwards miss an occasion to praise Bryan's stalwart party leadership through dark years.

The Princeton meeting was crucial because Bryan, standard-bearer in three Presidential campaigns, was still the man Democrats had to reckon with. For Wilson to win Bryan's approval was essential; yet to appear to seek his place as the foremost progressive spokesman was to risk alienating him—as it was also to risk alienating the party's conservative wing. The two men were compelled to engage in a complicated political minuet, and in the dining room of the Princeton Inn, under Ellen's approving eye, they took their first halting but significant steps.

With the pressures in New Jersey relatively relaxed by early May, Wilson was prepared to set forth on his journey to win the West. But first he had one more mission to undertake in the South. The South was important to him; he recognized its support as essential to his political hopes, a base upon which his future success depended. He also felt toward his native region a bond of honor. At Atlanta he had (at least in his own mind) made the first step toward acknowledgment of his candidacy, and now, before he went forth openly in search of the nomination, he wanted to touch home soil. More important, he was to make sure that his people understood fully what he was about.

To Mary Peck, as he did frequently in this period, he divulged his innermost thoughts. "I wanted to say something at this particular time in the South," her wrote her, referring to an invitation to address the Pewter Platter Club in Norfolk, Virginia. The South was showing increasing interest in his candidacy; but the South was conservative—"and I am *not* conservative. I am a radical. I wanted a chance to tell my friends in the South just what I thought, just what my programme is, before they went further and committed themselves to me as a 'favorite son.' I do not want them to make a mistake and repent it too late. I hate false colours."[5]

Wilson's speech, before an audience that included outstanding bankers, railway managers, and lawyers, attempted very honestly to set the record straight. He came out unequivocally for the initiative, referendum, and recall—then the very symbols of radicalism in politics. As he continued with "a terrific arraignment" of secretive business methods and of stand-patters alike in the political and commercial world, he seemed to stun his audience. "The boldness, the directness, the incisiveness, the fearlessness and the force of the 'Virginian-Jerseyman's' words crashed at times through the throng like a series of thunderbolt jolts," the local newspaper reported. Yet it seemed impossible at that moment to quench the faith of his would-be supporters. "His frankness and eloquence aroused the crowd into a storm of enthusiasm."[6] They seemed to love him the more because of his heresies. It is the irony besetting great oratory that the very skill it uses to set forth the truth beguiles men and puts them under a spell of disbelief.

Wilson needed to worry no more about wearing "false colours" in the South. Whatever the fervor he provoked at Norfolk, his radicalism hurt him as the campaign developed. In the southern primaries he would lose essential support, and in the convention at Baltimore he would see the Virginia delegation in an opponent's camp.

His conscience satisfied, Wilson left Princeton on May 3. He was accompanied as his train moved westward toward Missouri by Frank Parker Stockbridge, a newspaperman who had been hired by the Page-McCombs-McCorkle group to make advance arrangements and to disseminate his speeches. A lone reporter, representing the Baltimore *Sun*, completed the party. Seldom in American politics has so frail a bark navigated such vast seas—or returned with its mission so effectively completed.

Wilson made his first major stop at Kansas City, with speeches following in Colorado, California, Oregon, and Washington, and then the little party moved back to Minneapolis, the Midwest, and finally into the South. Everywhere he was greeted by large audiences, was covered fully by the press, and praised by local editorial writers.

What Wilson had said of his entrance into New Jersey politics, that it came "at the fullness of time," was even more true of this sortie upon the national scene. He made his appeal at a time when the country was looking for new leadership to cope with widespread ills; his ideas, if not new in themselves, were expressed in novel forms. The industrial growth of the late nineteenth century had put power in the hands of businessmen unprepared for responsibilities wider than their own profit sheets. They had produced economic growth and prosperity, but they had failed to take account of the fact that whole classes of people, and whole regions of the country, had been left out and left behind. Workers, farmers, the dispossessed in the swarming cities were looking for reforms to put them within reach of political power and a more just distribution of the national wealth. They had found their hopes catered to by Republicans in their more progressive guise; by Democrats of the Bryan stripe; by powerful insurgents in both parties; and by individuals like Robert M.

La Follette ambitious for a third-party realignment. Now came a new leader, who seemed fresh when the others were beginning to look jaded; who trailed the scent of victories in far-off New Jersey, and spoke in calm and often hauntingly evocative words.

Wilson's first speech of the tour, at Kansas City before the Knife and Fork Club, had been carefully prepared to set forth the basics of his program. It was not different from what he had said often before, stressing the degree to which the common man had been dethroned by the "interests" and calling for a liberation alike from business and political bosses. Most noted at the time was the fact that Wilson came out squarely for the watchwords of western reform, the initiative, referendum, and recall, measures designed to give the individual voter a more direct influence over the political process. (Then, and afterwards, however, he expressed opposition to the recall of judges.)

As early as March Wilson had indicated in a private letter that, on the basis of evidence from Oregon, he was reconsidering his stand on these three fundamental measures; and he had announced his change publicly to his southern supporters at Norfolk. But it was not forgotten that he had long opposed them. In his lectures to Princeton students he had regularly assailed these forms of direct democracy as undermining the principle of representation, making of the legislators a rubber stamp for the views of their constituents rather than the interpreter of their true interests. In Kansas City Wilson explained that he saw the initiative, referendum, and recall not as means to revolutionize government, but as means of restoring it to the people whose power had been illegitimately usurped.

To western ears, accustomed to the heated rhetoric of insurgents in both parties, Wilson's speech sounded cool and moderate; it was reprinted many times and praised precisely because it was not demagogic. But back in the East the seeming change in his views (apparently nobody had read what he said in Virginia) roused up the conservatives, while even newspapers long favorable to Wilson questioned whether he was not putting the expediency of the office-seeker above principle.

The party proceeded to Denver where it arrived on a Sunday, a day of the week Wilson had specifically excluded from speechmaking. But he had seen no reason to refuse an invitation to address what he supposed was to be a modest religious service marking the three hundredth anniversary of the King James translation of the Bible. To his surprise he found when he got to Denver that the event had become formalized and enlarged so that, with almost no time for preparation, he faced an audience of twelve thousand people in the municipal auditorium. The orator in him rose to the challenge, and he had, as if physically at his side that night, the presence of forebears who had preached the word in season and out—of his eloquent old father; of his uncle James Woodrow, the valiant heretic. The great audience, he wrote afterwards, moved him deeply, and he had been delighted to find that his voice carried "to every corner of that vast space."[7]

The address, entitled "The Bible and Progress," was important because it brought Wilson's new political radicalism squarely within the sanction of Protestantism. The Bible, he affirmed, was "the book of the people," the direct revelation to individuals of God's will. It embodied a harsh lesson for the conservative or the special pleader: "the man whose faith is rooted in the Bible knows that reform can not be stayed, that the finger of God that moves upon the face of the nations is against every man that plots the nation's downfall or the people's deceit; that these men are simply groping and staggering in their ignorance to a fearful day of judgment."[8] The stenographic text reads awkwardly in places, and there must have been some conservative men and women in the audience that night who were surprised to hear of the doom that awaited them. But as oratory it was grand. It touched a vital nerve in the American public, and the speech was reprinted more often, in more different forms, than any except Wilson's major wartime addresses.

Arriving in Los Angeles, Wilson was thrust into the midst of new issues and personalities. He was pressed, in particular, for his views on woman suffrage. Despite two of his daughters being suffragettes, he was firmly opposed to it at this time, and took refuge in a bland insistence that since it was a matter for the states to decide any comment would be inappropriate. At San Francisco the organization of a Yale-Harvard dinner, which he was scheduled to address, had been taken over by the city's bankers and by the conservative wing of the local party. Hiram Johnson, the insurgent Republican governor, refused to attend and to make the scheduled introduction. But even from this unpromising situation Wilson emerged unscathed. Turning to the businessmen in the hall—"well-groomed men of affairs," the local press described them—the speaker declared they had done things which, though not dishonorable, were politically noxious. "You thought you were acting in self-defense, that you were defending property," he said. "As a matter of fact you were debauching business and injuring property."[9]

"These direct sentiments," reported the San Francisco *Examiner*, "were received with great cheering."

Moving up the coast, Wilson found the wave of favorable publicity gathering force. In Portland he renewed an acquaintance with Williams

U'ren, the pioneer advocate of electoral reforms, and pleased the citizens by declaring that he was in Oregon to learn at first hand how the new order was working. Turning eastward he gathered useful support in Minneapolis and ended the midwestern portion of his tour at Lincoln, Nebraska, Bryan's hometown. Bryan was away, but sent messages of regret and delegated to his brother the responsibility for a hearty welcome.

The tour was an exciting experience for Wilson. He was astonished to find himself known wherever he went, and looked to as one expected to reach the top. "It daunts me to see their admiration and trust," he wrote of the people who crowded the halls where he spoke and afterwards pressed to shake his hand and be close to him. Again, as he reached Oregon: "I am having a sort of triumph out here. Wherever I go they seem to like me—men of all kinds and classes." He was reminded of the big rallies of the New Jersey campaign—"they [the people] are so friendly, so intent, so easily moved and held." He was determined "not to be duped or made a fool of," he said in regard to their confident assurance that he would be the next Democratic candidate, yet it was "astounding to find how they have watched me here and how well they know me. They receive me as they would a familiar leader."[10]

In this state of exhilaration he turned once again to the South. Without resting, and in the mood of a man on native ground, he spoke to large assemblies at Chapel Hill and Raleigh, and in Columbia, his boyhood home. It was as if he sought validation for the success he had found elsewhere, a final impetus to going forward.

More or less to everyone's surprise, he turned up at the end of the tour in the nation's capital. Newspaper reporters, pleased at the chance of interviews, were given the impression he was just passing through, having been delayed between trains on his way to Trenton. Democratic leaders, shepherded to his hotel by the much-indebted and grateful Senator Martine, were delighted to wait on him. From New York, led by McCombs, Page, and Tumulty, came the little band of the faithful who for a month had been holding the fort while their chief traveled up and down the land. More eager than ever to organize a full-blown Presidential campaign, they found that Wilson still held back. He admitted in private that he would like to be President; there were so many things, he said, he wanted to see done. But he felt the movement ought to be allowed to take care of itself—that "the further we keep away from the usual methods, the better."[11] In this mood, jubilant and still a little vague about his ultimate course, Wilson returned on June 6 to resume the duties of governor.

﹡   ﹡   ﹡

The summer of 1911 saw the Wilson family installed at Sea Girt, the official summer residence of New Jersey governors. A large "cottage," built originally in Chicago on the grounds of the World's Columbian Exposition of 1893, it had been taken down and transported, piece by piece, to its incongruous seaside location in a small New Jersey resort. A railroad ran nearby and tourists arrived at unexpected hours; the New Jersey National Guard held its annual encampment upon the lawn. These distractions seemed rather to amuse than to dismay the family. Ellen got rugs and favorite pictures out of storage and managed to give the large rooms a homelike air; as for the National Guard, Wilson had a surprising weakness for military display, going back to his youthful fantasies and his dream navies. He found an imperfectly concealed pleasure in mounting a horse to review the troops, dressed in tail coat and high hat.

For a week in August he traveled about the state to inspect his domain. Ellen went with him, an unusual outing for her. Together the governor and his wife visited such publicly supported institutions as the Soldiers' Home, the Home for Feeble-Minded Women, the State Home for Delinquent Boys, the Tuberculosis Sanitarium, and the State Village for Epileptics. It did not sound like a very cheerful itinerary, fit for a holiday; but the two had been much separated, and Ellen, who had not often been motoring, experienced for the first time the pleasures of traveling in an open car.

Far from having lost interest in New Jersey affairs, Wilson on his return from the West plunged into state politics as if to prove he had nothing else on his mind. At the end of the 1911 session, the legislature had passed a law permitting as an option the commission form of government for New Jersey cities. Urban reform had long been a special interest of Wilson's, the substance of one of his regular courses at Johns Hopkins. In embarking on a statewide campaign to attain the required assent of individual cities, he was not, however, indulging in an academic hobby. The local bosses were solidly dug in behind the established political order, and he was determined to rout them out, singly and as a group.

He did not achieve his goal. At least he did not win the kind of victories that his vigorous campaigning and his fiery rhetoric seemed to call for. A majority of the cities opted for maintaining the existing system, while those that followed the governor's lead were not in general the most populous. A few weeks after the frustrating verdict, Wilson nevertheless had the satisfaction of seeing the most obdurate and the most personally offensive of the bosses defeated. Despite Wilson's new broom, James Nugent had remained, incongruously, the Democratic Party chairman, with the governor preferring to bide his time rather than to take him on in a frontal attack.

Soon enough, as was hoped, Nugent brought about his own downfall. One evening in Scotty's Cafe, in Neptune Heights near Sea Girt, he arose and, obviously in his cups, proposed a toast to the governor, "an ingrate and a liar." "I mean Woodrow Wilson," he added, looking into the faces of several off-duty members of the National Guard. "Do I drink alone?" Plainly he did.[12] The chairman's ousting was accomplished a few weeks later, not without scenes of violence as mobsters hired by the Nugent faction tried to forestall a vote. Nugent's official power was curbed, but he remained a major force in the Essex County machine.

With the autumn of 1911 came further strenuous efforts by Wilson, this time campaigning to support progressive democrats, in primaries newly established by the Geran law. In an early speech before an audience of fifteen thousand at a farmers' picnic he said, "I serve notice on all the constituencies of the state that I intend to stand by the men who stood by me. If there is to be a fight I want to help do the fighting."[13] In this, as in subsequent speeches, Wilson showed himself a master of down-to-earth politicking, omitting few words of abuse from his vocabulary. It was a fine Donnybrook, and when the primary votes were counted the progressive Democrats, those that had made the legislative session of 1911 memorable in state annals, were firmly in control of the party. The newcomer to politics had not only broken the old machine but had apparently forged one of his own.

Ahead, however, was still the hurdle of the November state election. Again Wilson was out on the campaign trail, fighting as hard, it seemed, as he had a year earlier for his own election. He made the contest a referendum on his leadership, a vindication of his policies—as later, with more fateful results, he would do on the national stage in the congressional elections of 1918. The returns, when they were counted on November 7, proved bitterly disappointing. The Republicans, dominated by the regulars of their party, were put back in control of both houses of the legislature.

The outcome seemed a clear repudiation of Wilson and the reform program. But analysis of the vote told a somewhat different story. In Essex County the Smith-Nugent machine had deliberately thrown its vote to the Republicans rather than to the support of Democratic candidates. In other, less dramatic ways, the extent of Wilson's influence manifested itself, as in the upsurge of Democratic voting in many normally Republican areas, and the election of an overwhelming majority of Democratic sheriffs throughout the state.

The legislative session of 1912 did not repeat the achievements of 1911. A strong spirit of partisanship prevailed, but, even so, Wilson might have gained cooperation in shaping reform measures. He made no serious attempts to reach or to persuade the Republicans. There were this time few consultations with legislative committees, few efforts to win over individual opponents, few public appeals or dramatic interventions in the legislative process. Wilson did all that was strictly required of him as governor; that he did not do more may be explained by the fact that he was busy with other things. Besides, he was now aiming at national leadership of the Democratic Party, with little incentive to make the Republicans of New Jersey look better than they were.

On July 20, 1911, the New York press announced the opening of Wilson headquarters at 42 Broadway. McCombs in an interview indicated that a nationwide drive would be organized, based on the support of Princeton alumni. Wilson was unhappy with the publicity and told a reporter that there was in effect "no campaign."[14] The office would merely take care of answering mail and disseminating information. But that summer and fall two figures entered the Wilson circle, far more serious in what they implied for his political fortunes than the establishment of any campaign headquarters.

The first was a tall, hatchet-faced Tennesseean who had come to New York to make his way as a businessman. William Gibbs McAdoo was no ordinary businessman, however. "The public be served" was his slogan when his marked organizational abilities led to his being put in charge of tunnelling under the Hudson River. He met Wilson at Princeton in 1909, and the two got on well from the start. Wilson counted on him for practical advice, and by the summer of 1911 he was rivaling McCombs for first place in the direction of the embryonic, undeclared campaign. McAdoo was cool while McCombs was subject to wide swings of mood; unshakable where McCombs was easily discouraged; discreet where McCombs was talkative. Above all, McAdoo was ambitious, both for Wilson and for himself. This strangely compounded man would play a leading role in the Wilson administration, dreaming of being his successor. More astonishing, given McAdoo's age (he was only seven years younger than Wilson), he became a Wilson son-in-law.

The second recruit was very different from McAdoo and even more important in the long run. In that autumn of 1911 a wealthy Texan was staying at the Gotham Hotel in New York, a pause in the trek that took him annually from his home in Austin to the watering places of Europe. Edward Mandell House had always been interested in politics, as a behind-the-scenes participant but not as a candidate. His health, he alleged, was frail—in fact, it was adequate for all practical purposes; and besides, as he noted in an unpublished autobiography, "my ambition has been so great that it has never seemed to me worth while to try to satisfy it."[15] A successful businessman, he kept an office which he rarely visited, preferring to have the important men of his day in Texas—the politicians, lawyers, editors, educators—come to talk with him on the shaded verandah of his spacious home. He had always been a liberal in Texas politics and was a supporter of the well-known liberal governor, James Stephen Hogg, who bestowed upon him, in return for his good counsel, the honorary title of colonel.

Colonel House had stood aloof from the Bryan movement, awaiting the day when when he could play a prominent part in nominating a Democratic candidate more to his liking. In 1910 he had taken a close look at New York's reform mayor, William J. Gaynor. But Gaynor proved disappointing, and he began to consider the rising star of Woodrow Wilson. A meeting of the two was arranged at his hotel in mid-November 1911. They talked for an hour. The Colonel decided Wilson was the man to serve.

"Never before have I found both the man and the opportunity," he noted shortly afterwards, and added, with what could only be described as a condescending air, "I think he is going to be a man we can advise with some degree of satisfaction." After a short conversation, the two, he said, "were exchanging confidences which men usually do not exchange except after years of friendship." "My dear Friend," Wilson replied, "we have known one another always."[16]

House immediately set himself to being both ingratiating and useful. His first objective was to approach Bryan with the idea of attaining a Wilson endorsement. "He knew exactly which of Wilson's qualities would attract Bryan and therefore deserved emphasis,"[17] says Charles Seymour, House's biographer. His amiable personality played a part in smoothing rough edges of the Bryan-Wilson relationship; but claims to a larger influence in building up the Wilson movement in his native Texas are exaggerated. House's important role came later, after the election.[18]

Wilson now stood high among Democratic contenders. But his advantage was built largely on journalistic acclaim and on popularity with the public. He was exposed to attrition during the long months before the next summer's nominating convention; to personal attacks fomented by old enemies and not viewed as displeasing by Democratic rivals in the field; and above all to the steady, underlying antagonism of political machines. On his western tour he had won the people, but political control in the states he passed through was left in the hands of unconverted bosses. In the South, where his personal appeal was indisputable, conservative forces harbored resentment at his support of radical election procedures.

Strong precisely where Wilson was weak, the men most likely to be his opponents in the spring primaries guarded their political base and waited their turn in the limelight. In the South Oscar Wilder Underwood, a leader for tariff reform, had political weight as chairman of the House Ways and Means Committee. James Beauchamp (Champ) Clark of Missouri, a Kentuckian by birth, had been a loyal Bryan supporter and wore the mantle of western agrarianism. When the 1910 elections put the Democratic Party in control of the House, Champ Clark was made Speaker. Finally Judson Harmon, newly elected governor of Ohio, seemed an alternative to Wilson as a rising star and a progressive. An Underwood-Clark-Harmon amalgamation to stop Wilson was one of the dangers to his movement; indeed, evidence of such tactics by his Democratic rivals became a lively campaign issue in the winter of 1912.

Apart from his failure to win support of local political machines, it was Wilson's misfortune to be perceived by the public as aloof and even cold. His strength, conversely, was in his disinterestedness and in a certain moral elevation. He was peculiarly vulnerable, therefore, to anything that seemed to show flaws in his armor of righteousness or to indicate indifference toward supporters and friends. In these respects he could fall before arrows that would scarcely prick a lesser man. This Achilles' heel was clear to Wilson's foes, who were fully prepared to exploit the weakness.

At a meeting in the Manhattan Club in December a trap was laid; or at the least an opening was provided into which Wilson fell improvidently. Relations between Harvey and Wilson had been cooling for some time, and at the meeting Harvey asked Wilson point-blank whether the support of the conservative *Harper's Weekly* was an embarrassment to him. Wilson hesitated; he was urged to be frank; reluctantly he admitted that this was indeed the case. Shortly afterwards Wilson wrote a longhand note apologizing for his "one-track mind" and regretting the failure to have given a clear expression of his indebtedness for all that Harvey had done.[19]

Gossip and innuendo embellished the incident. An endlessly talkative

Watterson, who had been present at the meeting, jumped to the support of his friend Harvey, while the latter, maintaining a chilly silence, removed Wilson's name from the masthead of *Harper's*, where it had been prominently displayed as the chosen candidate. The furor aroused by Wilson's alleged ingratitude fell more heavily than charges of a major felony against a figure of less obvious (and perhaps less galling) rectitude.

The break between Harvey and Wilson was, in any case, inevitable. Once the candidate had begun his warfare against political bosses and moneyed power, Harvey and Watterson found themselves in a very different situation from that which they had anticipated. Conservative Democrats joined them in attacking Wilson. The New York *World*, with some humor and justice, suggested that in such a case as Wilson and Harvey, ingratitude might not be a bad thing, and that more of it could be healthy in public life.

At the same time, from old enemies of the Princeton battles, came charges potentially of great damage to the candidate. The first indication of concerted attacks appeared in an article in the hostile New York *Sun* of December 5. It recounted that on leaving Princeton and entering politics Wilson had applied unsuccessfully to the Carnegie Endowment for the Advancement of Teaching for a pension provided for teachers of twenty-five years' service. The request was turned down, presumably on the ground that Wilson was a somewhat special case. Now it became the talk of the day. Some objected to the "tainted" money Wilson had solicited; others felt that his image as an idealist had been tarnished by the effort to provide a measure of security for himself and his family.[20]

Before the dust of this revelation had settled the rumor was spread, again undoubtedly from Princeton circles, that the deceased Grover Cleveland had left a letter impugning Wilson's personal integrity. It is doubtful that such a letter existed, but the rumors were in themselves harmful, and Wilson was sufficiently concerned to draft, for release if necessary, a statement of the issues that had been at stake in the Princeton controversies. The unpublished document remains a highly effective summary of complex and many-sided events.[21]

What could have been a far more serious blow to the candidate's cause—again revealed in the *Sun* and this time acknowledged as having a Princeton source—was the release in early March of a letter Wilson had written to Joline in 1906 expressing Wilson's hope that some way might be found, "at once dignified and effective," to knock William Jennings Bryan "once and for all into a cocked hat."[22] As with many of the phrases Wilson came to regret, its felicity, quite as much as its indiscretion, gave this one a wide and immediate currency. It had been written in a private letter, but the recipient, whose defeat for the Princeton board Wilson had engineered, was not inhibited from releasing it at the moment when its effect could be most devastating. The blow fell on the eve of the Jackson Day dinner in January 1912, the big Democratic powwow where all the party chieftains, including Bryan, would be present.

Before the event Wilson conferred in Washington with his staff and close advisers. A mood of discouragement and almost of panic had seized them. They urged Wilson to issue a statement "explaining" the offending remark. Fortunately, after composing a draft, Wilson desisted. Fortunately, too, Bryan had been visiting in North Carolina with Josephus Daniels, editor and publisher of the Raleigh *News and Observer*, a genial host and a friend to both men. Traveling north with Bryan to the scene of the dinner, Daniels smoothed his guest's ruffled feelings. On arrival the Great Commoner appeared calm, but his remarks to newspapermen left them guessing as to his real attitude.

An almost intolerable tension pervaded the audience as it gathered for the banquet at the New Willard on January 8. Besides Wilson and Bryan, all the major party figures were to speak. It was almost midnight when Wilson's turn came, with Bryan scheduled to conclude. Wilson's speech was short, compared with many of those delivered by the party stalwarts, and was couched in the graceful eloquence of which he was master. He began with a tribute to Bryan, reviewed the issues of the coming campaign, and closed with an appeal for party unity. "Let us apologize to each other that we ever suspected or antagonized one another," he said; "let us join hands once more all around the great circle of community of counsel and of interest which will show us at the last to have been indeed the friends of our country and the friends of mankind."[23]

The speech was a tremendous success, acknowledged even by newspapers unfriendly to Wilson as the best of the evening. The ovation he received excelled all the others. Bryan was observed to be wreathed in smiles; he put his hand upon Wilson's shoulder, declaring, "Splendid ... splendid." Bryan's own speech closing the program was almost in the nature of a farewell. "No friend of mine," he said, "need be told that I am much more interested in the things for which we are struggling than I am in office."[24]

The incident of the Joline letter did Wilson more good than harm. Besides turning the table on his foes, he gained the support of at least one of the important big-city bosses. "That was a great speech, Governor," said Roger Sullivan of Chicago as Wilson was leaving the next day. "I cannot say to you now what the Illinois delegation may do, but you may rely upon it, I will be there when you need me."[25] It was a promise fairly given and, in the heat of the Baltimore convention, fairly fulfilled.

Nevertheless, the fracases of the early winter left Wilson wounded, and the failure to accomplish during his second year as governor the same kind of miracles as in the first further clouded his image. With spring came the primary contests. Wilson was by now thoroughly committed to the race. He traveled repeatedly to the Middle West and South, always amid rousing receptions from the people, but always facing the question of whether he was leaving behind an organization capable of getting out the vote. When the test came, he was confronted by a series of disasters. Where he had seemed most secure, as in the southern states of Georgia and Virginia, he saw the conservative wing of the party carry the slate of delegates for Underwood. The Kansas delegation was instructed to vote for Wilson's other major rival, Champ Clark. Despite frantic last-minute efforts he suffered a defeat in Illinois devastating in its effects upon politicians across the country. With Underwood sweeping the conservative South, and the progressive Clark showing strength in the Midwest, Wilson appeared at an insuperable disadvantage.

Favorable outcomes in a few states (Oregon on April 20, Delaware on April 30) could not dispel the gloom settling over the Wilson headquarters. "To all intents and purposes," Arthur S. Link, later summed up the situation, "the Wilson movement had collapsed by the latter part of May 1912."[26] McCombs was in despair. Funds were running low. Wilson suffered at this time a spell of ill health, leading to rumors of a breakdown. The intensely loyal base of the Wilson movement had simply not translated itself into primary victories, and it looked as though Clark might enter the convention with a majority of the votes, two-thirds being necessary for the nomination.

A decisive test remained, the election of New Jersey's delegates. Failure in his home state would have removed all hopes for the nomination and probably ended Wilson's political career. Smith and Nugent launched a last-ditch anti-Wilson effort. The candidate himself felt it inappropriate to conduct an extended campaign in the state. He had appealed to the public again and again to take a stand against the bosses; he had called upon the reform elements to support particular legislative measures, to back commission government for the cities, to return a Democratic majority to the legislature. But he could not bring himself to ask them to support him personally in their choice of a delegation to the Baltimore convention. On the eve of the vote in late May, however, he issued a statement addressed to Democrats of the state, reminding them of struggles their party had gone through to throw off the domination of the old political crowd: "They care not a whit for principle," he said. "They love profit and power." "We are now to decide," he concluded, "whether the state shall go forward or return to the things which besmirched and debased her."[27]

Though he lost Essex County, Wilson won the rest of the state on May 28. On the same day, along with North Carolina, South Carolina, and Wisconsin, he carried Texas. These were victories desperately needed. Success at the coming convention in Baltimore now appeared possible, though still an outcome unlikely and remote.

Through this anxious and troubled period Wilson spent himself in enormous physical efforts, yet retaining his good spirits and (with the one exception noted) his good health. Ellen watched over him when she could. "Of course my own anxiety, though concealed from him, is constant,"[28] she wrote Judge Wescott, who had noted disturbing signs of fatigue. Wilson himself remained optimistic, as always. Although admitting to Mary Peck that he had been "knocked out" by his cold, and though left "with a little less than his usual vigour," he was "quite fit and in excellent spirits."[29] Others, remembering earlier incidents, feared that something more dangerous than a "slight cold" was hanging over him.

The house on Cleveland Lane provided a pleasant retreat for him. Half-timbered, it reminded Ellen and himself of the house they had built for themselves on nearby Library Place, in years that now seemed far in the past. A cramped office opened toward the garden, and down a few steps from the front living room was a large studio (the house had been built for Parker Mann, a local artist) where Ellen could paint. The Wilson daughters were frequently at home, aware of their parents' need for help in dealing with the mail and with streams of visitors. The family's two favorite "cousins," Lucy and Mary Smith of New Orleans, were living with them and sharing the rent, a not unimportant consideration at a time when Wilson found himself under financial strain.

The bitterness of the last Princeton years had not subsided. One October afternoon, walking around the campus, Wilson returned feeling unutterably sad. "I went about from familiar place to place," he wrote Mary Peck, "with a lump in my throat, and would have felt much better if I could have *cried*."[30] Hibben was living next door on Cleveland Lane. It was a black day for Wilson when in February he was elected president of the university. Wilson sent no word of congratulation and arranged to be out of town at the time of the inaugural ceremony. He would never recover from what he felt to have been the betrayal of his love and trust.

Princeton had its somber memories, but it had its lessons, too. Until his climactic struggle with Senator Lodge, he did not let his emotions become involved as they had in the contest with Pyne, or allow sorrow to take over as in his break with Hibben. He seemed afterwards a more measured man, more circumspect, perhaps less given to illusions about his fellow human beings. Politics afforded an infinitely wider stage than the small world of Princeton, shadowing events with a certain fatality and preventing one from looking too much within. And so Wilson went through the ups and downs of 1912 outwardly jaunty and self-possessed, an attractive, well-balanced human being.

The stakes were large, and lifetime ambitions were clearly on the line. Yet he kept an impersonal outlook on what was happening around him. Sometimes he saw it as part of a game, or found detachment in the recurring sense of being in a play of which he was not the author. More fundamentally, a religious faith sustained him. "I believe very profoundly in an over-ruling Providence," he wrote in a private letter as the campaign was getting under way, "and do not fear that any real plans can be thrown off the track." On the other hand it was quite possible that he was never intended to be President. "That would not break my heart—and I am content to await the event."[31]

THE BALTIMORE CONVENTION

The Baltimore convention of 1912 stands in American political history as an irresistible showpiece. It possessed extraordinary elements of suspense; it revealed human nature in its varied forms; it had a happy ending. Only the Republican gathering of 1940 that named Wendell Willkie, or the Democratic gathering of 1952 that named Adlai Stevenson, can be compared with it; and neither of those brought in their aftermath the kind of election-day victory which Baltimore prepared for its candidate. Every possibility of drama was wrung from the weeklong proceedings, with the Wilson forces being at one time ready to give up, and then seeing their cause gain, ballot by anguishing ballot, until a two-thirds majority was attained. Public opinion expressed itself through urgent editorials, telegrams, and messages from across the country; and at times the crowds in the galleries seemed to play a role almost as important as that of the delegates on the floor. Through the noisy, picturesque, and seemingly irrelevant rituals of this nominating convention, the best interests of the Democratic Party were ultimately served.

When the delegates along with the political experts and hangers-on descended upon Baltimore on Tuesday, June 25, Wilson's immediate work was done. He had put his case before the country; he had organized a small group, headed by McCombs and McAdoo (House had gone off to Europe a few days before), who installed themselves in the Emerson Hotel and prepared to take charge. A special telephone line provided a direct link between Sea Girt and these managers, but it was used infrequently. At one point pressure was put upon Wilson to go down to Baltimore and address the convention; the New Jersey Railroad held a special car ready to be dispatched on ten minutes' notice. But Wilson was not tempted to depart from his strict view that the convention was its own master and would work out its fate pretty much in its own way.

The newspapermen who covered him through the full week of suspense were alternately frustrated by his refusal to show emotion as the tides of hope rose or fell, and struck with admiration at his absolute calm. He motored, played golf, joked with the reporters and recited verses. "It was the universal view," wrote a reporter for *The New York Times*, "that there is no possibility of any crisis arriving within the next four years for which he will not have a limerick as handy as Lincoln['s] . . . stock of anecdotes." As for Tumulty, who remained close to Wilson during this time, the same reporter said that he "nearly collapsed" under the strain.[1]

The Wilson family left their house on Cleveland Lane a few days before the convention was to meet, settling themselves in Sea Girt to share the long vigil. Soon the people would come to cheer and dance upon the lawns stretching down to the sea, picking partners at random in a spontaneous burst of celebration. But for the moment all was quiet. From outward appearances Wilson, his wife, and three daughters might have been gathered for a week's vacation. The weather was cold at the start, as it is so often on seaside holidays, and fires were lit in the large chimneys, "to keep our spirits (and our temperature) up," Wilson wrote; "but here we are a home group with that within us that can defy the depressing influences of the weather."[2]

The depressing influence of the political scene was more difficult to combat. At Baltimore Champ Clark had close to a majority of the committed votes, and the big-city bosses were in command. Wilson himself was not at all sanguine about his chances. Nor could he be sure at that point that he really wanted to bear the responsibilities of an office he held genuinely in awe. One morning before the convention he said to the family, "Two weeks from today we will either have our sweet Sunday calm again, or an all-day reception with an army of reporters camped on the lawn." His daughter Eleanor asked him which he would prefer. "Need you ask?" was his reply.[3]

The stage had been set for Baltimore by the Republican convention held a week earlier. Amid tumultuous protests the incumbent President, William Howard Taft, was nominated by the regulars of the party. Theodore Roosevelt stalked out, prepared to launch an independent campaign. At Chicago the conservatives of the party had stood foursquare against the progressives—and the conservatives had won. Would the same story be true of the Democrats in Baltimore? Were Wilson's chances increased or diminished by these developments? With the Republican opposition divided and bitterly at odds, it seemed to some that the Democrats would take the easy course, confident of winning with a lackluster candidate. Others were impressed by the force of the progressive tide. To them, a Democratic candidate who was anything less than a confirmed progressive would fail either to detract from Roosevelt's vote or to offer a convincing alternative to Taft.

The basic question at Baltimore, the one on which Wilson's chances for the nomination hung, was whether a confrontation between progressivism and conservatism could be dramatically staged. If it could not, a candidate like Clark or Underwood would seem an inevitable choice. The issue was clarified in part by the cast of characters attending the convention. August Belmont, representing all that was held most ominous on Wall Street, arrived flamboyantly by special train, accompanied by conservative bosses. The financier Thomas Fortune Ryan, spokesman for southern reactionary elements, was a delegate from Virginia. But the man who most effectively pointed up the contrast between conservatives and progressives was William Jennings Bryan. His announcement on the fourteenth ballot that he would withhold his vote for Clark has often been taken as the critical factor in reversing the anti-Wilson tide. But this was only one, and not the most important, in a series of moves putting the delegates on notice that they must make a conclusive choice between the two wings of their party.

Bryan's first bold stroke, launched before he arrived in Baltimore, was to send a telegram to the chief contenders protesting the selection of a traditional conservative, Alton B. Parker, the Democratic Presidential candidate in 1904, for temporary chairman, and asking each candidate for his views. At the opening of the convention, Bryan took the floor to oppose Parker, loosing a pandemonium of mingled boos and cheers. The old leader, "his heavy black brows . . . contracted over his piercing eyes,"[4] sat down unperturbed to cool himself with a palm-leaf fan. The delegates voted for Parker, but the vote served its purpose. It gave evidence of the degree to which the delegates might find themselves unwilling captives of the machine politicians. A day later Bryan again stirred an uproar by introducing a resolution proposing the withdrawal from the convention of any delegates subservient to New York financial interests, or the naming of any candidate of that ilk. It was a preposterous resolution; but few seemed willing to align themselves openly with the city bosses, and after a minor change, and a vehement defense by Bryan from the floor, it passed overwhelmingly.

Eyes were now fixed upon the Wilson managers, and upon Wilson himself, to see their response to Bryan's initiatives. McCombs was at heart on the side of the political realists. He figured that his candidate had only 248 votes pledged to him at the start of the convention, compared with 436 pledged to Clark. An additional 400 were for Oscar Underwood, for favorite sons from various states, or were marked as uncertain. In McCombs's judgment, Wilson's only hope was to make alliances with major uncommitted groups, the most tempting of which was the ninety-member New York delegation dominated by the Tammany leader Charles F. Murphy. Having this in mind, he deplored any tactic drawing Wilson too closely into the Bryan camp.

To Bryan's telegram asking for Wilson's views on the selection of Parker as temporary chairman, McCombs drafted an evasive, noncommittal reply. Wilson came close to approving it. He had already told the Baltimore *Sun* that it was up to the delegates to organize their own convention. But fortunately Tumulty, abetted by Ellen Wilson, realized how crucial a test he confronted, and persuaded him to reconsider. He found the means to reconcile his earlier statement with a militant defense of Bryan's position and in pencil drafted a reply which opened unequivocally: *"You are quite right."*[5] From that time on the candidate at Sea Girt rejected all efforts to enlarge the base of his support by courting conservative votes. In Baltimore the balance of power between Wilson's advisers shifted rapidly from McCombs toward McAdoo.

On the sweltering night of Thursday, June 29, the nominating speeches began. The names of Underwood and Clark were presented along with several others, each setting off noisy and protracted demonstrations. It was past 2:00 A.M. when New Jersey's Judge John W. Wescott stepped forward to put in nomination Woodrow Wilson, "the seer and philosopher of Princeton."[6] Despite the exhaustion of the crowd, Wilson's supporters managed to cheer and parade for an hour and a quarter. When dawn came, the first ballot was taken. Clark had 440 votes to Wilson's 324. The showing was slightly better than the progressives at the convention had counted on, but not enough to inspire large hopes. The following ballots continued to show slight gains for Wilson, until at Sea Girt the candidate was able to tell the reporters a characteristic story.

It was about a man riding in a buggy who stopped to inquire how far it was to the next town. Twenty miles, he was told. The man traveled on, stopping three times more to ask the distance, and each time he received the same reply, "Twenty miles." "Well, John," said the man in the buggy to his companion, "I'm glad we're holding our own."[7]

The crisis came next day, Friday, when on the tenth ballot Charles Murphy rose to declare New York's entire delegation for Champ Clark. A vast upsurge of emotion swept the convention. The pro-Clark forces cheered and marched as their victory seemed assured. Clark now appeared to have a majority of the votes, and not since 1844 had the Democrats failed to give a majority candidate the two-thirds necessary for nomination. A stampede to Clark was imminent.

Fortunately for Wilson, the next state to be called was North Carolina, its delegation strongly in his camp. After Ohio, committed to Harmon, its favorite son, came Oklahoma. Faithful to Wilson, its delegates demanded that each member be polled. This gave the convention a saving moment of relative calm, and provided "Alfalfa Bill" Murray, a picturesque character with a voice like a bullhorn, a chance to declare that his state would not join Tammany in validating Clark's nomination. Another uproar ensued. The battle had again been defined as between the bosses and insurgents, and the lines held precariously. At the end of the tenth ballot Clark was eleven votes over the majority, but Wilson's strength had barely diminished.

Going home late at night in Sea Girt, Tumulty saw his chief in pajamas at an upper window. "Any news from Baltimore?" he called down.[8] The doughty Tumulty answered evasively, but his crestfallen appearance told the tale. The next morning Wilson faced up to the dire situation. McCombs advised that the situation was hopeless, and Wilson instructed him to feel free to release the pledged delegates. Ellen Wilson, usually so discreet in public, later revealed in a rare interview the discouragement of that hour. "Now we can see Rydal again"—the beloved Rydal of the English Lake District—her husband told her.[9] But in Baltimore McAdoo kept a more sanguine view. He shook up the weary and dejected

McCombs, and called Wilson to tell him the battle was far from over. No delegates were released.

Wilson's readiness to give up seems hard to explain in a fighter usually so unwilling to accept defeat. He was convinced, however, of the soundness of majority rule in the convention proceedings; he still had confidence in McCombs as his manager; and he was himself outside the play of those powerful, often irrational, forces that make of national political conventions an arena where almost anything can happen. Possibly, too, as he had written earlier, he considered it not altogether unlikely that in the dispensation of Providence he was not intended to be President. A Presbyterian would fight to the end against worldly powers; he did not fight against destiny itself.

What McAdoo and the hardier Wilsonians saw from the convention floor were the latent forces working on their chief's behalf. The major newspapers, led by the New York *World* and the Baltimore *Sun*, were strongly behind him and daily reiterated their endorsements. A wider public reflected support in thousands of letters and telegrams. Supporters on the convention floor and vociferous outbursts from the gallery manifested an enthusiasm for Wilson incomparably greater than that revealed for Clark. Underlying all this was the basic issue—acted out by Bryan, spelled out by Oklahoma's "Alfalfa Bill"—of progressivism versus the bosses. The switch of New York's Tammany leader nearly lost Wilson the nomination; but at the same time it gave pause to the average delegate seriously concerned with winning in November.

On the fourteenth ballot Bryan again dramatized the conflict. Demanding recognition when Nebraska was called, he characterized the New York vote as representing "the will of one man—Charles F. Murphy—and he represents the influences that dominated the Republican convention at Chicago and are trying to dominate this convention."[10] He announced that he was withholding his vote for Clark as long as New York's delegation was backing him. In the meantime and on this understanding he was voting for Wilson, Nebraska's second choice. The move was more subtle and effective than a mere switch in his vote from one candidate to another. Even Bryan's influence with the rank and file of the party could perhaps not have made that a decisive act, free of personal or quixotic overtones. By stressing the issue of bossism first and foremost, however, he gave an impetus to forces that would make Wilson's nomination inevitable.

Clark rushed from Washington, prepared to appear on the convention floor. The session had adjourned when he arrived. His moment had passed, and his strength had reached its peak. On the following ballots Wilson slowly climbed; he told newspaper reporters in a rueful calculation that at the going rate it would take 175 ballots for him to win. Bryan had been the great catalyst; now more and more he became the great obstacle and threat. So greatly was he feared and hated by the conservative elements of the party, that an accommodation with him seemed unthinkable. At the same time his breaking the deadlock by himself becoming the candidate could never be entirely discounted by the Wilsonians.

On the thirtieth ballot, on the sixth day of the convention, Wilson for the first time topped Clark, his vote standing at 460 to Clark's 455. For twelve more weary roll calls the deadlock held, and then Roger Sullivan, the Illinois boss, made good on his promise of the morning after the Jackson Day dinner. He switched fifty-eight votes to Wilson.[11] Virginia finally shook itself free of its commitment to Underwood and at the eleventh hour came out in support of its native son. After the forty-sixth roll call, the notorious New York boss who had fought tooth and nail against Wilson's nomination, John J. Fitzgerald, moved that the vote be made unanimous.

The business of a platform was quickly taken care of: it was a progressive declaration on which Wilson could stand comfortably. For Vice President, Wilson's preference was for his defeated rival, Oscar Underwood. But Underwood refused to serve in that capacity, and the choice of the convention veered toward the governor of Indiana, Thomas R. Marshall. Wilson thought him "a very small calibre man," but upon the recommendation of the Texas congressman, Albert S. Burleson, he accepted what was to prove a highly questionable choice.[12] He never learned that McCombs had traded the Marshall nomination for Indiana's votes in the balloting.

The first news of the nomination came to Wilson in an anonymous phone call from Baltimore, through a man whose voice he did not recognize. In the tense moments of the final balloting the family had dispersed to their separate rooms upstairs in the cottage, and now Wilson went alone to Ellen. They would not be going to Rydal after all, he told her. The family reunited, messages began to come in, but for an hour or more quiet hung over the house and its immediate grounds, a contrast to the bustle and confusion of recent days and to the celebrating that filled the auditorium in Baltimore. The spell was broken when a brass band, followed by virtually the entire population of the nearby village of Massaquam, arrived in front of the porch. By then cars and buggies decorated with little flags lined the beach road. The band played "Hail to the Chief" and Princeton's "Old Nassau," and Wilson came out to make his way slowly among his neighbors, speaking his thoughts in a low voice.

The next days saw leaders of the party descend on Sea Girt to express their homage, while secretaries struggled with a mountain of mail, within which the personal letters Wilson cared about—from his nephew George Howe, from James Sprunt of Wilmington, from Mary Peck—were constantly getting lost. Toward the end of the month he fled with Ellen for a six-day cruise on the large sailing yacht of his Princeton classmate Cleveland Dodge. As they moved in mild airs down Long Island Sound, Wilson wrote out in his clear shorthand the formal acceptance address which would be the candidate's first official utterance.

During the uphill struggle for the Democratic nomination, Wilson wrote regularly, often at length, to Mary Peck. As he felt himself losing the last vestiges of private life, he turned to her for assurance that confidence and friendship still existed in the world. Her letters are missing, but judging from his side of the correspondence they were not very bracing or cheerful. They were often not forthcoming when he wanted most to hear from her. After the legal separation beginning in 1909, she had wandered unhappily, usually in poor health and spirits, in New York, Pittsfield, and Bermuda; by 1912, with her decision for a divorce final and the "hateful" name of Peck soon to be discarded, she was trying to make a life for herself on Nantucket Island. Wilson's letters to her are invaluable for describing in his own words his emergence into a political leader—the more so because he and Ellen were not often enough apart to encourage letter writing. There is a poignancy about the correspondence, too, as seeing his own personal freedom ebb away he urged upon her the courage to make the most of the freedom that her liberation from a wretchedly unhappy marriage was finally giving her.

By the time of his nomination she was in Nantucket, among strangers, her mood depressed. "You do not belong in New England," he wrote her, thinking of the dismal Pittsfield years; but no longer need she feel caged. "You are like a splendid flower, native of rich woods or the breezy mountainside, transplanted to those sands, to dominate them with a new note of life and colour."[13] Did she recall a talk with him long ago, he asked, "when we had walked to the South Shore [in Bermuda] and were sitting together on the sand?" Had he not told her he would go into politics if he were called on, "but that the next President of the United States would have a task so difficult as to be heartbreaking and that I'd probably sacrifice my life to it if I were elected?"[14]

He was making ready to seek that election now. It was as if at the beginning he already knew the end.

THE GREAT CAMPAIGN

Wilson's nomination cast doubt upon Theodore Roosevelt's next move and, consequently, upon the whole political scene. A conservative victory in Baltimore would have left Roosevelt to command the center of the stage, the one figure to whom progressives of both parties could turn. But Wilson was now clearly a spokesman for the cause. Whatever uncertainties might persist as a result of his earlier views, whatever doubts about the capacity of the Democratic Party to escape domination by the urban bosses, Roosevelt was now only a competitor for the role of progressive leader. His army had to be recruited piecemeal from a host of puzzled and divided liberals. Nevertheless, he went ahead, his demonic energy overcoming innate doubts, and in August the Progressive Party was launched in Chicago at a convention combining aspects of a revival meeting and a Rough Rider reunion.

Public figures took their places, painfully and sometimes unpredictably, in the lineups. It was, in the words of historian Samuel Eliot Morison, the Old Testament against the New.[1] Roosevelt was the battle-scarred veteran whose rallying call had thrilled a generation. Wilson was a bright figure burst suddenly onto the stage, lucid, rational, calling men to a higher vision of themselves and their destiny. "His mastery of himself and of affairs" (as one admirer put it), "his imagination, his literary ability, his sense of humor"[2] summed up a democratic personality of fresh appeal. The choices to be made were not easy, neither for Republicans choosing between the support of the regular ticket and the insurgents, nor for the broader constituency making their choice between the two progressive candidates. In the end so stalwart a Wilson supporter as George Record took up Roosevelt's cause, standing incongruously with Wilson's first mentor, George Harvey. On Roosevelt's side were the young Walter Lippmann and the humanitarian Jane Addams. La Follette, who had at one time contended with Wilson in the hope of leading a progressive party of his own, remained unofficially neutral through the campaign, though privately favoring the New Jersey governor.

Wilson faced the difficult practical and psychological task of completing his change from an academic to a political leader. He had to create a new image of himself in the popular mind and come to terms with a world in which he was still essentially a stranger. The transformation was made easier for him by the fact that from the beginning he had conceived the organizing and directing of a university to be a political function. For the public to accept this unregenerate intellectual as one born to move effectively amid the dust and heat of national politics was more difficult. The change in Wilson, in his inner poise, his rhetoric, in the shadow he cast, was forged during the hard months of campaigning between September and late October 1912. He discarded, sometimes to the dismay of his admirers, long-cultivated restraints; he rose above a habitual and instinctive diffidence. At the time of his election to the Presidency Wilson was still far from being the shrewd politician of later years. But he was well on his way; he was close to fulfilling his own youthful prescription for a leader of men.

Wilson gave much of his time in the month after Baltimore to consolidating his control of the Democratic Party. Receiving at Sea Girt delegations of party chieftains, as well as individual visits from the men he had defeated for the nomination, he stressed the need of holding all wings of the party together. He then turned to the task of organizing the forthcoming campaign. McCombs, still party chairman, presented a formidable problem. He was plainly out of step with the increasingly progressive candidate. Besides, he was a sick man, moody, hypersensitive, and irritable, suffering from the effects of Baltimore's protracted exertions upon a constitution frail at best. Wilson was under much pressure to relieve McCombs of his post. He was resolved, however, not to be caught in the trap baited by his opponents and by some well-meaning friends. The Harvey incident nine months earlier had taught him the price of seeming ingratitude; he resolved to keep up appearances at all costs. Despite his distaste for McCombs, despite his deep mistrust, he swore eternal fidelity, content to see the actual management of party affairs drift irreversibly into McAdoo's hands.

The importance of the western vote was recognized in the membership of the new national committee and in the fact that campaign offices were established both in New York and in Chicago, with the battle plan calling for extensive western forays by the candidate. Henry Morgenthau, a wealthy New York realtor, was made chairman of the finance committee. He was instructed by Wilson not to accept contributions from corporations and to place heavy emphasis upon donations in small amounts from the widest possible public. Morgenthau succeeded admirably in raising adequate campaign funds, notwithstanding these restraints. When a corporate contribution slipped through, in the form of a gift from Wilson's Princeton classmate Cyrus McCormick, it was summarily returned.

To counter a chief argument of the Roosevelt forces, that whatever his personal predispositions Wilson would be checkmated by Democratic machines in the big cities, the candidate clarified unmistakably his relations with two of the most notorious bosses. The first was his inveterate enemy, James Smith, Jr., of New Jersey. Smith had surfaced again as a candidate for the U.S. Senate and was running under the reformed election laws in the state primaries. Returning to his old stamping grounds of Hoboken and Jersey City, Wilson took up the challenge in powerful appeals to the voters, ensuring a final defeat for the Essex County leader and the nomination of William Hughes, a labor congressman.

In New York a more delicate situation presented itself. Progressive forces of the state (led by a young state senator, Franklin D. Roosevelt) were strongly opposed to the renomination of the Democratic governor, John A. Dix. Behind Dix was the same Murphy whose Tammany connections had so agitated the Baltimore convention. Wilson was opposed to everything Murphy and Dix represented; but he had stated he would not enter local contests. If he followed his more militant advisers, moreover, he risked disrupting the state party and jeopardizing his chances of carrying New York in the November elections.

Wilson was served, in this case, by the gross obtuseness of the New York bosses. Visiting Syracuse, New York, to address the state fair early in September, he found that unbeknownst to him the state Democratic committee had arranged to meet in Syracuse on the same day. Murphy and Dix were prominent among the politicians on hand and did everything short of the outrightly comical to sidle up to Wilson, to lunch at his table, to slip into his car, and to be photographed with him. Wilson was not amused. His speech that afternoon to the assembled Democratic leaders was a virtuoso performance in which, without naming anyone, he made clear his disgust with the Murphy-Dix faction. The only chance for Theodore Roosevelt's new party to win, he said, was that both of the old parties should be discredited. "One of the old parties is discredited. Ours *shall* not be." He lashed out at political organizations sustained by the old type of politics, and made a declaration of faith he might well have framed at the somber apex of his later career: "I would

a great deal rather lose in a cause that I know someday will triumph,"
he told the politicians that afternoon in Syracuse, "than triumph in a
cause that I know some day will lose."[3]

When it was over a reporter asked if Governor Dix would be renom-
inated. Murphy replied, "It looks cloudy but I hope it doesn't rain."[4]
Rain, however, it did. In a dazzling victory for Wilson, Dix withdrew
at the state nominating convention early in October. Murphy lay low
and the handpicked candidate of the progressives, Representative William Sulzer, was named.

Wilson had one more task before making the electoral appeal that was
to lift the campaign of 1912 to the level of a great national debate: he
had to clarify in his mind and come to terms with the nature of the
economic problem confronting the United States. On August 28 he was
visited in Trenton by the progressive Boston lawyer Louis D. Brandeis,
long a champion of the small businessman and a foe of monopolistic
restrictions in all forms. The two men conferred for several hours. Brandeis was well impressed by Wilson. "It seems to me," he wrote a friend,
"that he has all the qualities for an ideal President—strong, simple, and
truthful, able, open-minded, eager to learn and deliberate."[5] As for Wilson, he had come in those few illuminating hours to revise his own
approach to the problem of the trusts.

Brandeis defined with sharp contrast the difference between the Democratic and Progressive parties in regard to monopoly. The Democrats
insisted that competition be maintained, and if necessary created and
enforced, in all branches of private industry. The Progressive Party, on
the other hand, accepted private monopoly as inevitable in some
branches of industry; it maintained that in such cases existing trusts
should not be broken up or dismembered, but should be regulated so
as to moralize them and prevent them from doing evil. "This difference
in the economic policy of the two parties," Brandeis wrote in a subsequent memorandum to Wilson, "is fundamental and irreconcilable."[6]
The approach of Roosevelt and his Progressive Party meant constant
regulation and control by big government; the approach of the Democrats meant a regime of liberty, once the conditions of a free market
had been established and enforced.

The idea of establishing a free market by deliberate government action
was far from new to Wilson. The classical economists had not denied
that some degree of human intervention was necessary before their "in-
visible hand" could bring about the benefits of unhampered competition.
Indeed, Wilson's economics professor during his undergraduate years,

the highly conservative Lyman H. Atwater, had recognized a free market to be a purposeful creation of law, needing to be constantly and subtly regulated.[7] Wilson was clear on the principle, now that Brandeis had argued it forcibly and applied it to the trusts. But he was still uncertain in regard to its application, and later in the campaign telegraphed Brandeis somewhat frantically asking him "please [to] set forth as explicitly as possible the actual measures by which competition can be effectively regulated."[8] Brandeis's reply seemed too detailed and technical for use in speeches. But Wilson did not really need details. He had gotten hold of a central idea which he could develop in his own way. The idea liberated him once and for all from thinking that the only alternative to concentrated economic power was resort to the power of big government.

His capacity to absorb advice, to grasp its implications, and to fit it into his own philosophy never was better proven than in the days following the encounter with Brandeis. Busy as he was with the practical details of the campaign, besieged by callers and driven by speaking engagements, he managed to recast overnight his approach to industrial problems, and in doing so to give his argument a new precision and depth. In Buffalo, four days after the talks at Trenton, he got his campaign under way with an effective Labor Day address in which for the first time he defined the existence of the trusts as the result of deficient competition within an unregulated market. Lack of competition, he asserted, "has permitted . . . men to do anything that they chose to do to squeeze their rivals out and to crush their rivals to the earth."[9] And he forcefully described the kind of massive and pervasive control that, under his rival's approach, would be necessary to keep the existing monopolies in line.

In later speeches Wilson's imagination was fired by these concepts; he saw the full establishment of a free market as underlying his belief in the capacities and the opportunities of the common man. He had felt increasingly during the Princeton battles that it was the "man on the make," the man fighting against the tide, the man rising by his skills and ardor from the mass, who gave democracy its special character. In Lincoln he had found his ideal. Basing his campaign upon the elimination of monopoly in all forms, he rose to the kind of popular eloquence first exemplified in the Pittsburgh speech of 1910. More than that, he came to see the major reforms of banking and the tariff as means to eliminate the privileges, the nooks of entrenched interest and advantage, which distorted the functioning of the free market. He was thus able to infuse with visionary zeal even the most workaday policies of the state.

*   *   *

The Buffalo speeches, followed by addresses in New York City, set the pattern of the campaign. Throughout, Wilson spoke extemporaneously. What purported to be advance texts were occasionally issued to the press, but Wilson followed these only in broad outline, if at all. His speeches, he said at the start, would be delivered as he liked to do them, "right out of my mind as it is working at the time."[10] They achieved in this way an immediacy, a high level of emotional persuasiveness, and often a surprising eloquence—though not without some cost in redundancy or inexactitude of phrasing. In their style as well as their substance, Wilson's speeches of the 1912 campaign rank with the greatest platform accomplishments of American political history.

Wilson hoped that he would be able to escape extended campaign tours; he was particularly set against "stump speeches" delivered from the rear platforms of trains. He wanted to talk sensibly to the American people, and he sought conditions in which, avoiding personalities, he could elucidate the issues rationally and in the simplest phrasing. "My dream of politics all my life," he said early in the campaign, "has been that it is the common business, that it is something we owe it to each other to understand, and . . . to discuss with absolute frankness."[11] As for rear platform appearances, he enlarged humorously on his objections at the start of the first western tour. "This is the kind of platform that I don't like to stand on," he advised a waiting crowd. "It moves around and shifts its ground too often. I like a platform that stays put."[12] In fact, the engineers of those days paid little attention to the candidate whose special car might be attached to the rear of one of their trains, and the text of Wilson's remarks show them often being cut off in the middle of an argument or even in the middle of a sentence.

He maintained toward his opponents, particularly toward Roosevelt—for Taft ceased to be an important factor after the first weeks—a tone of semihumorous detachment. The Progressive, or Bull Moose, Party he described as "the irregular Republicans, the variegated Republicans." Suppose the people chose for President the leader of the third party, he asked, "Don't you think he will be pretty lonely? Not that he'll mind it, because I believe he finds himself rather good company." Yet he needed, Wilson continued amid the cheers of his audience, "a medium of transmission for his energy."[13] Even he, as yet, had not claimed the right to pass the laws of Congress.

In his private letters of this time Roosevelt was showing, meanwhile, a rather unexpected and appealing diffidence. He probably should not be running; he would not have allowed himself to be pushed into the race, he told one correspondent, if Wilson's nomination had come before the Republican convention.[14] Wilson, he told another, was "a good man" (though showing no special fitness to be President); and again, "an able man" who would perform creditably if elected.[15] Looking forward to the campaign, Roosevelt thought it unlikely he would himself be able to win. In the heat of battle, however, his manner and his arguments became characteristically heated. He stormed and cavorted in the way his followers demanded of him. When Wilson in a speech of early September let slip the remark that the history of liberty "is a history of the limitation of governmental power, not the increase of it,"[16] Roosevelt felt he had found a basic issue. His suspicions in regard to Wilson's progressivism seemed to be confirmed, and he went on the warpath with true Rooseveltian fervor.

By such attacks Wilson was drawn out upon the campaign trail and was induced into making the specific charges and countercharges beloved of the crowds. As the weeks of the campaign advanced he found himself facing conditions that made it difficult, if not impossible, to discuss issues in the calm and undistracted way he had planned. His style of speaking caught on; huge crowds gathered to hear him, as many as thirty-five thousand in a single audience—at a fairground, at a baseball park or racetrack—until they defeated their very purpose in coming. They found it difficult to see, far less to hear, the speaker. Without any means of amplification even Wilson's trained voice was harshly tested. He was often foiled by the indiscriminate enthusiasm of his sympathizers, by the competition of brass bands, by unruly demonstrations, and by deplorable acoustics. Yet he would push on undeterred with his argument until the audience quieted itself and even at the edges of the crowd men began to listen. At Wilson's side throughout the campaign was a skilled stenotypist, Charles L. Swem, who took down the candidate's words. Many of his shorthand pages remained undeciphered until scholars a generation later applied themselves to reconstructing the historic speeches.

On September 15 Wilson embarked on his first journey into the West. The Democratic National Committee had provided an old wooden railway car, the *Magnet*, which swayed and bounced along the dusty route. For this trip, moreover, it had been attached to a local train, which was invariably late and provided precisely the kind of stops which compelled the candidate to appear on its mistrusted rear platform. In Iowa, South Dakota, Minnesota, Michigan, and Ohio, the days were crowded with receptions and with speeches. Arriving in Sioux City, Iowa, the candidate made an address to students at the local college (throughout the campaign the academic community would give him strong support), was initiated with appropriate remarks into the Sioux Indian tribe, and in the afternoon delivered a major address on social legislation. He boarded the *Magnet* again for the short trip to Sioux Falls, South Dakota, arriving two hours late for an evening speech in the crowded municipal auditorium, and for still one more in a nearby theater.

The next day at Minneapolis he was up early for an address in which he attacked the preconceptions of several hundred breakfasting businessmen, without noticeably diminishing the warmth of their applause. He went on to address a crowd of schoolchildren, then students of the University of Minnesota, and at noon made a major declaration on social justice. "I say, therefore," he declared, "that property as compared with humanity, as compared with the vital red blood in the American people, must take second place, not first place."[17] In the evening at St. Paul he spoke on the tariff before the largest crowd up to that point in the tour.

By now his campaign was receiving favorable comment from the local press and from the reporters who accompanied him. Curious crowds had gathered to weigh this new type of electoral appeal, an appeal understated, more witty than vitriolic, aimed more at the intelligence of audiences than at their emotions; and they were remaining to listen with an unusual degree of attention. The orator, in turn, warmed under the glow of the popular reception. The journey through Michigan and Ohio saw overflow audiences and sometimes wild demonstrations. At Columbus, Ohio, he brought the tour to a close in a fine blaze of eloquence, enjoining his now-hushed listeners to take up the torch and run a "race of freedom"—a race that would end only when "the torch is lifted high upon those uplands where no light is needed, but where shines the brilliancy of the justice of God."[18]

Tours of Pennsylvania and New England filled the last, crowded week of September, climaxed at a meeting in Tremont Temple, Boston, where the elite of Beacon Street joined with the Democratic Irish in a huge ovation. By now it seemed that Wilson would very probably win in November, and a new disposition to unbend before the crowds marked the candidate's manner as he returned through Bridgeport for a short rest in Princeton. Two days later, on October 2, he set out on a second western trip. The next weeks saw him passing through Indiana, Nebraska, Colorado, Kansas, Missouri, and Ohio.

On the first stop, in Indianapolis he threw out almost casually a phrase, "the new freedom," by which his whole domestic program would subsequently be known. The country, he maintained, was not interested in personalities but in issues. "I tell you frankly," he confided to a tumultuous crowd at the Indianapolis baseball park, "I am not interested even in the person who is the Democratic candidate for President. I am sorry for him. I am sorry for him because I believe he is going to be elected. . . . And there will be no greater burden in our generation than to organize the forces of liberty . . . and to make conquest of a new freedom for America."[19]

At Lincoln, Nebraska, Bryan's hometown, the two Democratic leaders met for the first time since the convention. The hall was filled, with hundreds standing, and a mighty ovation broke out when Bryan introduced the man on whose behalf he had been tirelessly campaigning. The next day was Sunday, with Wilson staying at Fairview, Bryan's nearby home. The two Presbyterian elders went to church together, entertained callers, and were photographed with Bryan's grandson standing between them. In the afternoon Wilson again climbed upon his special train (the wooden *Magnet* had been replaced by a modern steel car) and the party was off for Colorado.

Denver had been Wilson territory since the days of his earliest visit to the West as a college lecturer in 1897. Here lived his cousin and first love, Hattie Welles, whom he still managed to see whenever he passed through the city. On October 7 he spoke in the same auditorium where a year before he had made his memorable address on the Bible. This time the crowd lusted for political blood, and though his speech that night was one of the most eloquent of the campaign, it failed to satisfy his audience. Moving on through Kansas, Nebraska, and into Illinois, the campaign resumed a more sharply partisan tone. The crowds yelled and cheered, often interrupting the speaker with their remarks. The acoustics in the great halls were unfavorable, and the candidate's voice was growing hoarse. But from early October on, it was plain that victory was in the air. "Is it not true," Wilson declaimed, "that this solid phalanx [the Democratic party], with its banners now cast to the wind, is marching with a tread that shakes the earth?"[20]

On October 12 Wilson returned to Princeton, tired but confident. Two days later Theodore Roosevelt was shot by a fanatic in front of the Hotel Gilpatrick in Milwaukee. The bullet, passing through his metal eyeglass case and the bulky manuscript of the speech he was about to deliver, lodged just short of his right lung. After demanding that his assailant be left unharmed, Roosevelt proceeded to the Milwaukee Auditorium. "Friends," he began, "I shall have to ask you to be as quiet as possible. . . . I have been shot. . . . The bullet is in me now so that I cannot make a very long speech. But I will try my best."[21] The speech lasted for more than an hour, the audience more captivated by the spectacle of his survival than by any words he spoke. Then he was taken to the hospital. It was reported that because of its location the bullet could not be removed, but that he would recover.

The event, occurring in these dramatic circumstances, seemed capable of evoking so much sympathy for Roosevelt as to alter the whole nature of the political contest. Wilson announced that while Roosevelt was hospitalized he would restrict his campaigning to a few engagements already arranged along the eastern seaboard. Proceeding through Delaware, West Virginia, and Pennsylvania, he praised the stricken fighter, concentrating his attacks upon the regular Republicans; he was greeted by crowds making his passage a triumphant procession. It was evident by then that the Wilson movement could not be checked.

For the next week he remained at Princeton, out of the public eye, enjoying the delights of home and of familiar surroundings. Roosevelt was now on his way to full recovery, and on October 28 Wilson went to Philadelphia to address in the Academy of Music an audience composed almost entirely of Republicans. Rested, speaking in a hall where he could be clearly heard and appealing to men of independent mind, he made what is generally considered the most effective of his campaign speeches.

A traditional ceremony remained—the candidates' appearance in Madison Square Garden in New York. On October 30 Roosevelt made a dramatic reappearance and the auditorium was rocked by the cheers of the faithful. On the following night the Democrats were determined to outdo their opponents in vociferous dedication. Ellen Wilson and two of her daughters sat in one of the boxes; the ever-loyal friend of Princeton days, Cleveland Dodge, was among the speakers who endeavored to hold the restless audience. The candidate's appearance was the signal for all emotional restraint to be cast off. The demonstration ran for a full seventy minutes—twenty-three minutes longer than that accorded Roosevelt the night before. Wilson was obviously moved, and later admitted he forgot the speech he had prepared. But what he said that night was of less importance than that victory seemed assured for a party that had been out of power for sixteen years.

There followed two speeches in Rochester, several appeals to his fellow New Jerseyites, and then on November 5 the family gathered at the house on Cleveland Lane. Wilson voted early at the local fire station. In the afternoon he walked with a few friends across the Princeton countryside and through the campus. In the evening, after a leisurely dinner, the family listened as election returns came in over the wire.

They were clearly favorable and Wilson fell into a solemn mood. Near ten o'clock a special operator informed Ellen that victory was certain. It was she who brought the news to her husband, as he stood with his back to a blazing hearth.*

For a short while quietness cloaked the little village of Princeton, until at about eleven the bell in Nassau Hall rang out. The students and townspeople were astir, arriving presently by the hundreds before the Wilson house. An impromptu band was formed while a lone bagpipe player emitted his brazen notes. Wilson came out with his wife and daughters on the porch, and when silence at last prevailed he spoke movingly a few words expressing the idealism of the hour. Seeing the students in the torchlight, he said he was carried back to his own "happy and laborious" days. He had himself no feeling of triumph now: "I have a feeling of solemn responsibility. I know that a great task lies ahead of the men associated with me and ahead of myself. Therefore, I look upon you almost with the plea that you with your thoughts, your best purpose, your purest impulses, will stand behind me and support the generous men of the new administration. I feel as if I were standing among my younger comrades tonight."[22]

The crowd cheered, and it cheered again when it was announced that President Hibben had declared the following day to be a holiday.

---

*It was a strange, but nevertheless decisive political victory. Wilson won 435 electoral votes, with only eleven for Roosevelt and eight (Vermont and Utah) for Taft. The popular vote, however, told a different story. Wilson won 6,293,019, less than Taft and Roosevelt together (7,604,463). The Democrats thus remained a minority party, and Wilson actually polled fewer popular votes than had Bryan in 1908. Nevertheless the Democrats won control of both Houses of Congress. The situation was complicated by the fact that Eugene V. Debs, running as a Socialist and drawing many Progressives to his cause, polled almost a million votes, many of which would have gone to Wilson had Debs not been in the race. Not until 1916 would Wilson succeed in gaining a majority of the popular vote.

CHAPTER FIVE

Emerging Statesman

———◆———

PRESIDENT-ELECT

It was 1:00 A.M. when the triumphant candidate retired, and the next day he was awake early as well-wishers—Princeton faculty members, political enthusiasts, would-be advisers—began arriving in a stream. He once more escaped on a walk across the campus, stopping at the athletic field to spend some time watching football practice. Newspapermen were awaiting his return. "I am through with statements," he told them; "I am now going to do some hard thinking."[1] He planned to go off for a month of absolute quietness. "I find myself, after two years of continuous strain, rather completely fagged out," he confided to Bryan.[2]

Before he could get away, decisions had to be made and a number of rituals gone through. Wilson announced that he would not resign as governor until the new legislature met. Immediately after his inauguration the following March he would call a special session of the Congress to deal with tariff reform. For the time being there would be no discussion of cabinet appointments. Expressing sentiments characteristic of such a time, a delegation invited the President-elect for a birthday celebration late in December in his native Staunton. Another delegation came from Columbia, South Carolina—his cousin James Woodrow, son of the formidable uncle of the same name, among them—announcing that the new President's boyhood home would be restored for his use on winter visits. Once again there was a dinner of the Princeton Class of 1879 to celebrate a milestone in the career of their illustrious "Tommy."

Above all other places, Bermuda seemed to him made for the relaxation of body and mind he desperately needed. On November 16 he set sail with his family group, Ellen and two of his daughters. (Margaret remained in New York to pursue her singing lessons.) He had rented Glencove, the house in Paget Cove that had for him many past associations. What a return it was for him, no longer the college president fleeing a contentious board of trustees, haunted in the lonely hours by nightmares of their bickering; no longer the lonely fighter finding romantic refreshment in the company of Mary Peck—or romantic despair in her absence: but a dominant figure already on the path to world fame.

On shipboard, Wilson set the pace for the idle, carefree days he would follow throughout the coming month. He slept late, walked the decks, regaled his fellow passengers with stories. At the landfall he took his place by the rail to point out to an assembled company each rise and inlet of the familiar island. He was met by an official delegation and the streets were lined with applauding crowds; but a few hours later, like any tourist, he was to be seen shopping at Hamilton or rowing in a small boat.

The cottage was idyllic, set on a secluded point overlooking the sea, its white walls and tin roof typical of the island architecture. Meals were taken outdoors at the rear, under the shade of tropical foliage; across the front stretched a wide verandah furnished with rocking chairs and hammocks. Here the President-elect received the newspapermen on their daily visits, daily insisting he had nothing of interest to tell them—and then taking pains to make sure this should be so. Carriage rides, sailing, bicycling, picnics along the shore formed the texture of leisurely and unscheduled days that were of no concern, he insisted, to the public. Once, when a cameraman tried to photograph him on a bicycle within the grounds of his cottage, he threatened to thrash the intruder on the spot.[3]

It was impossible, nevertheless, to escape official duties and social obligations. He had letters to write—sometimes to old friends, as to Dean Fine, his fellow warrior in the Princeton battles; sometimes to new political associates, reassuring them they were not entirely forgotten. The journalist William Bayard Hale came down to go over with Wilson the rearranged and edited version of his speeches in 1911 and 1912, published afterwards as *The New Freedom*. Bermuda's governor-general, Sir George Bullock, entertained the Wilsons with a splendor usually reserved for royalty. Afterwards the family felt obliged to attend Lady Bullock's first "at home" of the season. The President-elect dined with a Princeton graduate, attended a session of the local parliament, and was guest of honor at a dinner of the Royal Yacht Club, given by the American consul. Despite such interruptions the days rested and restored Wilson. Like all good days they were soon over.

The trip north in mid-December was logged in record time, the *Bermudian* sighting the Ambrose lightship five hours earlier than on any previous passage. Wilson went directly to the Waldorf Hotel, where McCombs was waiting; then back to Princeton for the routine of daily trips to the statehouse at Trenton. On one of these trips, soon after his return, Wilson found himself motoring through snows unparalleled since the blizzard of 1888. As so often, rest had not made him passive or self-content; rather it had heightened his zeal for combat.

The day after his return, Wilson "electrified" a large gathering of the Southern Society at the Waldorf by the militancy with which he defended progressive principles, promising "a gibbet as high as Haman" to members of the financial community who might deliberately induce a panic.[4] On visiting Staunton for his fifty-sixth birthday—a homecoming which he might have let pass as a purely nostalgic occasion—Wilson again let loose with an unexpected affirmation of progressivism.

He had been suffering a bad case of grippe as a result of his exposure to the New Jersey blizzards, and was carefully watched over by doctors as, against their orders, he traveled toward his native South. The weather was cold and drizzling and his voice was reduced to a hoarse whisper. But the airs of Virginia seemed to benefit him. He slept in the room of the Presbyterian manse where he had been born; perhaps more important to him—for he had been an infant when his family left Staunton—were glimpses of the Mary Baldwin Seminary he had visited so often during law school days when courting Hattie Woodrow. Apart from the necessary bows to sentiment, however, Wilson's mind was now strictly on business. "This is not a rosewater affair," he said, contemplating the near future; he described the Presidency as an office "in which a man must put on his war paint."[5] He added that his own features were of a cast which would not suffer too adversely from the disguise.

At a birthday banquet that evening he revealed his bitterness over the stand of the Virginia delegation at the Baltimore convention. It had stood by Underwood almost to the end, and now Wilson drew a sharp contrast between himself and conservative Virginians. "The trouble with some gentlemen," he said, "was that they had ceased to believe in the Virginia Bill of Rights."[6] It was a strong challenge, and one member of the Baltimore delegation, Representative Henry D. Flood, cried out from the floor to challenge him.

In Chicago, soon afterwards, he created a stir even more far-reaching. Addressing the Commercial Club, its exclusive membership composed of the most powerful industrial and financial leaders of the Midwest, he emphasized again that he belonged to the progressive wing of the

Democratic Party. He called his audience to account for past malpractices and urged them so to conduct themselves as to merit public confidence.

Nothing Wilson said on this occasion was new; he had preached the same theme again and again during the campaign. But the audacity of carrying the message to those most directly affected shocked his hearers. "It is hard to give any idea of the dumbfounding effect that Wilson's speech had on these men," *The New York Times* reported; and the New York *World* asserted two days later that the spokesmen of big business were "overwhelming the governor with protest and rebuke."[7] As if to make sure he had not been misunderstood, Wilson immediately after his return to New Jersey declared in a speech to local politicians that his course would not be diverted from radical lines.

Particular circumstances accounted, in part, for the tone of these post-election speeches. Wilson was in an angry mood when he appeared before the Southern Society in New York, having suffered a defeat over jury reform by the New Jersey bosses. He was still under the effects of grippe when he fired his shots in Virginia. More significant was the fact that he had in truth done some "hard thinking" in Bermuda. These speeches, seemingly unpremeditated, all delivered without prepared texts, displayed an instinctive political skill and on the whole served him well. They made it clear that his words in the campaign precisely defined his thought—that after November 5 he sang the same tune as before. They gave radical warnings which perhaps made unnecessary some later radical acts. To the Democratic leadership they sent the clear message that it must organize the new Congress so as to be ready to carry out a reform program.

Meanwhile the task of cabinet-making went forward. "Well, I guess I am a politician again," Wilson remarked immediately after his return from Bermuda.[8] The politician worked slowly, in his own mysterious way. Leading members of the Democratic Party were summoned to Trenton, where they would arrive with expectations of definite offers. Wilson talked to them courteously and at length, the door of his state-house office open as usual so that casual visitors could see the conferences in progress; the aspirants were ushered out after a canvas of measures and men, without any word as to their own fates. Much to Wilson's annoyance, the press was unwearying in its quest for news. Colonel House in New York was meanwhile giving advice and supporting various aspirants without ever being quite sure that his influence was as decisive as he would have liked to believe.

Many years earlier, as a youthful professor, Wilson had written an article on Grover Cleveland's problems in forming his cabinet of 1892. As President-elect he now found himself with limited knowledge of men on the national stage—the politicians, the party leaders, the tested public servants from among whom he might choose his official family. But at least he had thought carefully about the problem. "What kind of government are we to have?" was the first question needing to be raised. In 1892 as in 1913 Wilson saw the answer to be one with authority centered on the President, the cabinet being chiefly administrative in character. Nevertheless, both as professor and politician, Wilson was tempted by the idea of responsible party government—in which case the cabinet, "a natural connecting link," would be composed of proven party leaders. Now, in his quest for such men, the President-elect found himself reluctant to cut into an already slim Democratic majority. He did seek out two leaders from the Congress. Most of the rest were unknown to the public; and that was inevitable, because (as Wilson had written in 1893) "we do not yet know the new Democratic party which is . . . in process of formation."⁹

Of the new men, McAdoo was an easy choice for Secretary of the Treasury. Far more complex was the choice of a Secretary of State. That Bryan should be given this post seemed not only a way to repay an immense political debt but also a return to the early practice of placing in this office a figure with a wide public constituency. Yet in Wilson's mind, and also in the minds of many who had followed him or feared him over a long political career, Bryan's name raised serious doubts. On December 19, in a phone conversation with House, Wilson asked whether he still held to his opinion that Bryan should be named. "This is the third or fourth time he has asked me this," House confided to his diary. "It shows how distrustful he is of having Mr. Bryan in his Cabinet."¹⁰ *The New York Times* commented editorially: "Certainly he [Wilson] cannot expect that Mr. Bryan will abjure Bryanism, nor can he find in the recent career of that gentleman any remote indication that his future will not be consistent with his past." The *Nation* still viewed him as "flighty and unstable" in nature. There was a question in the editor's mind whether he would give attention to detailed work. Yet as a frequent traveler he knew something of the world and its leaders. Besides, concluded the *Nation*, he was a man of peace.¹¹

At a meeting in Trenton on December 21 Wilson offered Bryan the office. Not to do so, his friends had advised him, would be political suicide. In spite of all, moreover, Wilson had personal respect for Bryan as well as the kind of affection that opposing chieftains sometimes develop for one another. Bryan accepted the offer promptly; yet he had the good sense to make no approaches to Wilson during the Bermuda holiday. On his return, Wilson was still reluctant to engage in conferences with the Great Commoner, not fully trusting his advice on policy or eager to have his recommendations on political appointments. In public he maintained that he had not yet come to a decision on the post. He indicated to newspapermen that several others were being considered, though under questioning he proved embarrassingly forgetful of their names.[12] It may not have seemed the most propitious way to begin a relationship, but when in February Wilson finally announced the appointment, Bryan could not conceal his pleasure, and the President-elect outrode serenely the expected criticism.

Almost as awkward for Wilson, though on a lesser scale, was the problem of McCombs. He was a sick man, fatally indecisive, yet by any test of loyalty Wilson seemed bound to offer him a position in his official family. McCombs wanted a post; but merely to have him around gave Wilson a headache; to be with him for an hour or more, Ellen told Colonel House, was to make her husband feel that he had been "sucked by a vampire and left weak and ill."[13] On grounds of his poor health Wilson excluded him from consideration for the cabinet, offering him instead the ambassadorship to France—a post he alternately accepted and refused over a period of several months.

Colonel House could have had any position he asked for. But that astute counselor knew that the source of his influence was precisely in being unattached to official responsibilities, while maintaining intimate access to the President himself. Wilson would have liked another of his personal friends, Walter Hines Page, in the cabinet. The politicians quashed the idea, though they approved with alacrity Wilson's choice for Secretary of the Navy, the southern Democratic journalist and national committeeman Josephus Daniels.

The choice of Daniels was noteworthy to a degree not foreseen at the time, because he in turn named as his Assistant Secretary Franklin D. Roosevelt, then a young reformist politician, veteran of legislative battles in New York. Roosevelt had made the pilgrimage to Trenton in 1911 to see Democracy's rising star, had fought enthusiastically for the Wilson cause in the 1912 convention, and had the merit of being a confirmed sea-lover—unlike Daniels himself, who at that time could not have told one end of a ship from another. On Wilson's first day in the White House Daniels proposed the nomination; "Capital," said the new President, and the matter was settled.[14] Daniels had been warned that a Roosevelt would try to run anything in view, and such proved true of

Theodore's young cousin; but Daniels was a big enough man to overlook occasional condescensions and even insubordinations, and the two men worked in harness up to and through the First World War.

Wilson was strongly inclined to name Brandeis as Attorney General. From Boston, at the first rumor of such an appointment, came noisy protests. The very mention of Brandeis's name, commented the Boston *Journal*, was enough to cause "a general collapse" in banking and trust offices.[15] Wilson personally reviewed the charges being circulated against the controversial lawyer. He was convinced they were groundless, yet to avoid a party split he gave in and nominated James C. McReynolds for the post. The retreat, however, was no more than tactical. A few years later Wilson would take a stand on Brandeis's behalf; and this time, despite even more severe opposition, he would win.

For other posts he turned to men he did not know personally, or knew only in the most casual way. From Texas he summoned as Secretary of Agriculture David F. Houston, a man intellectually congenial to Wilson, a university president who would remain in the cabinet to the end of the administration. William B. Wilson (no relation of the President) was named Secretary of Labor. A Scot who had come to the United States at the age of eight, he had been active in labor affairs, a major force in organizing the United Mine Workers of America, before running successfully for Congress. Albert S. Burleson, an experienced politician and highly conservative Texan, became Postmaster General. He had served seven terms in the House and had the confidence of his fellow legislators.

Given the propensity of Democrats to adhere to a states'-rights philosophy, the choice of a Secretary of the Interior was especially delicate. Wilson wanted to stand by his party's commitment to conservation yet he knew the danger of outraging traditional Democratic concepts. On House's suggestion he named a westerner, Franklin K. Lane, who had a progressive record and had been appointed by Theodore Roosevelt to the Interstate Commerce Commission. Wilson was at a loss, too, for a Secretary of War. Tumulty recalled Lindley M. Garrison, an outstanding judge of New Jersey's highest court. An interview was arranged; Wilson was favorably impressed and persuaded him to take the post. A final decision was made a few days before inauguration when Wilson, influenced by a recommendation of the liberal editor Oswald Garrison Villard, named for his Secretary of Commerce William Cox Redfield of New York, a liberal businessman and member of Congress.

When the cabinet was finally announced on March 3, observers were as much surprised as some of them, at least, were pleased. Had Wilson set out to confound the political gossip-mongers he could hardly have done better. Of his final choices, at least three had been on no list of prospects; others were unknown outside their own states. Even his political confidants, remarked the New York *World*, marveled at the new President's ability to keep a secret—"though they did not endorse his doing so."[16]

The process of cabinet-making had become helter-skelter in its later phases. The final result matched neither Wilson's criteria for a group of neutral administrators nor for strong party representatives. It was as if he had come to realize that he alone, after all, would determine the form and nature of the new administration. What the public saw was a group of variously gifted men marked by progressivism, with the South plainly overrepresented. It was a Wilsonian cabinet, and Wilson would have to forge it into a working whole or deal with its disharmonies as events unfolded.

The last session of the Trenton legislature was not one of Wilson's successes. While he was still on vacation in Bermuda the Smith-Nugent amalgamation reasserted its power. Tumulty led the fight for a speaker congenial to his chief; for his pains, he was threatened by the bosses' candidate with having his head knocked off. Wilson returned in fighting form. "Some gentlemen in New Jersey . . . ," he asserted in his Southern Society speech, "now count the day[s] when they get rid of me."[17] He was determined that those days should tell. A carefully written annual message to the legislature itemized an ambitious reform program: control of the trusts; jury reform; ratification of the income tax amendment, and of the amendment calling for direct election of U.S. senators. An act providing for a state constitutional convention was also urged.

Control of the legislature, however, was now in the hands of Republicans. Wilson succeeded in putting through the so-called Seven Sisters Acts, a medley of hastily conceived measures aimed at the trusts. Other planks in the reform program were emasculated, and on February 25, before most of the measures could be acted upon, Wilson wrote out in his own hand his letter of resignation as governor. "The pack is gathering for the kill," wrote the Newark *Evening News* in its requiem. "Word has gone out that with the departure of Woodrow Wilson there will be a return to the old order." So in fact it proved to be.

The days of living at Princeton, too, were drawing to a close. "We are not as light-hearted as we might be,"[18] Wilson wrote to Mary Peck at this time. On the night of March 1, fifteen hundred townspeople and students gathered in Cleveland Lane for a last farewell. A loving cup was presented to the President-elect, amid signs of what a correspondent described as unusual personal affection. "The real trials of life," Wilson said in response to a toast by the head of the local bank, "are the connections you break."[19] He was addressing neighbors, and thinking ahead to the long journey before him. But he must have thought, as well, of connections broken over the harsh years of struggle and combat at Princeton—of Hibben, whom he had once loved as a brother; of West, who had been an early supporter of university reform. He would never return to Princeton without pain, as if old wounds were being physically reopened.

On Sunday the Wilson family went for the last time to the First Presbyterian Church on Nassau Street; they spent the rest of the day packing up papers and personal belongings. The next morning the President-elect and Ellen—she looking unexpectedly small beside her tall and buoyant husband—walked from Cleveland Lane, past the house on Library Place they had built together years before, to board the train for Washington.

At the Union Station the Wilsons were met by an automobile sent by President Taft; they went almost unnoticed to the Shoreham Hotel while Washingtonians, and all the gathering crowds of sightseers and political hangers-on, were massed to watch a suffragette parade on Pennsylvania Avenue.[20] The Wilsons made a brief, formal call on the President and Mrs. Taft at the White House. That night there was a dinner of five hundred Princeton alumni, old men from as far back as the Class of 1859 and young men from the class graduated only the previous spring.

Inauguration day, March 4, dawned overcast but mild for the season. As Wilson left the hotel, the Princeton students, now joined by several hundred from the University of Virginia, followed the carriage, and on reaching the White House grounds broke into the familiar strains of "Old Nassau." Wilson paused and listened, then turned to the rituals of the day and to the tasks of the next four years.

Shortly afterwards he and Taft emerged arm in arm from the White House, the outgoing President seeming thoroughly to enjoy the occasion, smiling broadly; the incoming, grave in his high hat and formal dress. A few bills remained to be signed at the Capitol; in the Senate chamber Vice President Marshall took the oath of office. Accompanied by his family and his cabinet Wilson stepped to the outdoor platform where the people waited. There were cheers; but it was noted that the President-elect seemed a stranger to these crowds. Of the two, Bryan was the more quickly noticed and the more vociferously greeted. The oath was administered; Wilson stepped forward, and in a level, unstrained voice read his inaugural address from small sheets of notepaper. In seventeen minutes it was over.

The address was charged with subdued emotion. "This is not a day of triumph," it concluded, "it is a day of dedication. Here muster, not the forces of party, but the forces of humanity. Men's hearts wait upon us, men's lives hang in the balance; men's hopes call upon us to say what we will do. Who shall live up to the great trust? Who dares fail to try?"[21] It was "a profoundly religious appeal by a man of a profoundly religious nature," observed the *Outlook*.[22] But it was far more than that; as often with Wilson, its generalities, its ideals, were intended to be taken seriously; they were meant to be interpreted concretely and not abstractly. In addition to pledging his party to economic measures that were to form the first phase of the New Freedom—tariff and banking reform, trust and labor legislation—Wilson enlarged his vision to sketch a wide field of humanitarian and social needs.

The change in party, he said, meant that the nation as a whole had come to a sober second thought: it had seen the evils that the industrial system had brought in its wake. It had become aware of the cost of material progress: "the human cost, the cost of lives snuffed out, of energies overtaxed and broken, the fearful physical and spiritual cost to the men and women and children upon whom the dead weight and burden of it all has fallen pitilessly the years through." With riches had come inexcusable waste: "We have squandered a great part of what we might have used," he said, ". . . scorning to be careful, shamefully prodigal as well as admirably efficient."

For a time Wilson would seem to turn away from the measures of social justice implicit in such a judgment. He would himself declare the New Freedom to have been fulfilled with the passage of economic legislation transforming the organization of business. But that renunciation came in a season of personal depression and grief. As the record shows, Wilson never wholly lost the vision that gave to the First Inaugural a special eloquence. Its grave music was to echo down his administration and rise to a crescendo during the campaign of 1916.

After the ceremony, smiling and genial to the last, Taft boarded the train taking him back to private life. Wilson stood in the reviewing stand of the inaugural parade. The day by now was fair and brisk, and all Washington was in a festive mood. Westerners and southerners were out in force to take over the town. As evening came on, fireworks lit up the streets and monuments. Wilson had decided against a state ball (Ellen disliked the social ostentation accompanying such an event). The new President sat down at the end of the day to his first family gathering in the White House, the familiar circle enlarged by relatives who had come from far and near for the inauguration.

THE WILSON WHITE HOUSE

Much of a man's lifetime is spent in forming his character. He is made what he is as external forces interact with inherited qualities and accumulating experience. At some turning point the balance shifts: the individual, now come into his own, brings his character to bear upon the external world. When a man assumes high public office this changeover can be dramatic. In writing of a President of the United States, a biographer comes a little uneasily to the moment where the preeminence of private life gives way to the public role. The inner man does not stop living and changing; but biography, which is primarily the portrait of this inner man, yields subtly to history.

In writing of Wilson the shift of emphasis is inescapable. From the time of his entering the White House he was at the center of a stage where he acted, and where his actions were all-important. More than most men in the office Wilson continued to live a vital and sometimes tormented private existence. The eight years of his administration brought bereavement; saw him pass through deep depression and then courtship and remarriage. They saw a diminution of his physical, and even his mental, capacities—beyond that which ageing would normally bring. How Wilson passed through these experiences, adjusting himself to them, revealing changing facets of his personality and character, needs to be traced out by the biographer. Nevertheless the substance of the story henceforth is less the tale of what the world did to him than of what he did to the world.

When on March 5, 1912, Wilson awoke for the first time in the White House, a primary concern was to assure that the man he was would not be submerged by the new circumstances of his life. He was intent on remaining himself, on keeping what was within alive. A first move is highly suggestive. He announced that office-seekers would not be welcome at the White House unless specifically invited. To many it seemed that their worst suspicions had been confirmed and that Wilson's arrogance, as well as his political inexperience, had been proved. Disgruntled, a great horde of the hungry shifted their venue to the doors of the new cabinet members, or lay in wait at a distance outside the

Executive Offices. But the new President had in mind a purpose deeper than they knew. By this gesture he was affirming his determination to have freedom to see and to think, sometimes to be alone; to keep a cool space between the person who was Woodrow Wilson and the annihilating pressures of the public scene.

This first step was as much symbolic as it was practical, but the need for reflection was real. Throughout his Presidency, and especially in moments of crisis, Wilson would disappear into his study and remain isolated. Once his mind had been cleared and basic truths had been clarified he would consult with others and accept open-mindedly advice on the timing or the details of a given course. In these periods of withdrawal he did not feel the need to be told what other people were saying; but he deeply cared to know what was being thought by people who said nothing, and yet whose judgment, he believed, would prove valid in the end. "He sought above everything," wrote a contemporary, "to catch the trend of inarticulate rather than vociferous opinion." For this he needed composure, and he needed to be completely himself.[1]

Wilson's method of leadership depended heavily on being able to interpret the national will. In his early description of the leader he had made allowance for the historic moments when "a *Cause*" arises, when a man becomes the champion of "a political or moral principle."[2] Such a moment came for Wilson when he was defending the League of Nations; then his own judgment superseded a nice adjustment to the popular mind. But for most occasions he saw leadership as being actions taken in conformity to opinions which, though they might not be expressed, were nevertheless widely held. To ascertain these opinions was a prime gift of statesmanship. Lacking modern polling techniques, he felt compelled to rely on political instinct and an almost mystical identification with the people. When it appeared that a true public opinion had not been formed on an issue he would procrastinate, avoiding action even when his personal views and preferences were clear.

In a revealing speech to the national press early in his administration Wilson confessed to a "passionate sense of being connected with my fellow men in a peculiar relationship of responsibility." It made him tremble, he said, not only with a feeling of his own inadequacy and weakness, "but as if I were shaken by the very things that have shaken them."[3] This self-image was very different from the impression held at the time by most observers, who had judged the President to be cold and to be governed entirely by intellectual processes. A feeling of identity with the people could mislead Wilson, but at its best it could give him a Lincolnesque quality, often noted at the time. In any case it was a feeling he valued and guarded. It caused him to organize his life as President in such a way as to preserve a central calm and to create a White House that was more of a sanctuary than a sounding board.

Arrangements within the Executive Office were by modern standards extraordinarily spare. On the shoulders of a single secretary rested the burden—in later administrations to be shared by hundreds—of giving political advice, helping to draft speeches and messages, and overseeing relations with the press, the Congress, and the government departments. Wilson's first choice for this post of secretary was the young mayor of Cleveland, Newton D. Baker, an ardent progressive with a brilliant and lucid mind. But Baker felt that his task as urban reformer was not yet completed, and after some hesitation Wilson turned to the man who had been his political guide through the New Jersey years. Tumulty was unquestioning in his loyalty to the President, but he talked too much in House's judgment, and Wilson thought him parochial: "He cannot see beyond Hudson County," he complained.[4] Others opposed to the nomination feared that as a Catholic Tumulty would reveal secrets to the hierarchy. But Wilson's lack of sectarian bias was unqualified, whether in regard to Catholics or to Jews. Despite Wilson's continuing misgivings about his sophistication in national affairs, Tumulty got the appointment. He served Wilson for the next eight years, particularly valuable as a political buffer and as an intermediary with the press. His irrepressible Irish sentiment acted as a saving counterpart to the President's often dour Scotch disposition.

Below Tumulty was Wilson's stenographer, Charles Lee Swem, an early example of a tape recorder in human form, who not only took the President's dictation but recorded all his publicly spoken words. A mail clerk on the civil service list with the appropriately anonymous name of Smith routinely opened the mail and gave it to Tumulty, who decided which letters should be seen by the President. When critical troubles with Mexico arose, Wilson directed that every letter be opened by himself. Swem has left a picture of Wilson arriving at his office precisely at 9:00 A.M. to sit down with his stenographer and open letters one by one, dictating replies in order.[5] The whole task was normally accomplished within an hour.

Two additional staff members should be mentioned. Rudolph Forster saw to it that the President's instructions and inquiries were efficiently followed up. Irwin Hood (Ike) Hoover, whose career in the White House would stretch from Theodore to Franklin Roosevelt, was particularly fond of Wilson and was at pains to see that everything was running smoothly, with the President's comfort always uppermost in his mind. He left a diary and informal recollections invaluable in reconstructing the life of the White House during his long service.

This minimal staffing would not have sufficed had Wilson not continued his practice of drafting and writing an immense number of official papers. In an upstairs study he worked alone, often late into the night, setting down in meticulous shorthand the first version of speeches and important letters. In foreign policy matters, Wilson wrote all the significant diplomatic correspondence on his own typewriter. As a skilled publicist, he simply felt that he could best achieve the sought-for tone and style by writing notes directly, in his own way. During his periods of greatest productivity as a professor he had been able to impress his colleagues by an ability to keep leisure time for afternoon visits and chats; so now, in the early White House days, he appeared not to be working under stress.

The dictating sessions with Swem completed, the President gave the rest of the morning to receiving callers. As it had first been decreed for office-seekers, none of the great or powerful were admitted without an appointment, and every visitor was assigned an exact period from two to twenty minutes. A senator, a few minutes late, would find that he had missed his chance! But Tumulty was always available, and some waited in the outer office where the President would emerge to hold brief informal conferences.[6]

After lunch in the private quarters, almost invariably restricted to close family members, Wilson resumed appointments. On days when press conferences and cabinet meetings were not scheduled for the afternoons, he went out for a game of golf or an automobile ride. Golf was important to him, not only because of the physical exercise it provided but because, as he explained, the thought of hitting the small white ball drove all other thoughts from mind. Automobile riding was then a generally recognized form of recreation, smogless and relatively traffic-free, and for the President it was an indispensable form of escape from the smothering atmosphere of the White House. By an assortment of routes, each familiar and rigidly adhered to, the black limousine carried him through the city and out into the countryside as in silence he pursued his own thoughts, or, more rarely, conversed with a friend or staff member.

Overseeing the President's regimen of work and leisure was a young naval medical officer, Cary T. Grayson. Taft had warmly recommended Grayson to the President: "I regret to say," he added with Taftian humor, "that he is a Democrat and a Virginian, but that is a matter that cannot be helped."[7] On Inauguration Day Wilson's sister Annie injured herself falling on the marble stairs of the White House, and Grayson's solicitous attention sealed a bond between him and Wilson which lasted until the latter's death.

The young doctor was handsome, affable, agreeably nontalkative. He was "one part of the Navy," Wilson wrote Secretary Daniels, that he coveted for himself.[8] Daniels obliged, and Grayson quickly became a favorite companion at the White House table, on motor rides, and on the golf links. In later years he was inseparable from the President, and by a coincidence he became a bridge leading Wilson to the woman he married after Ellen's death. Departing from the strict principle that barred personal favoritism in making appointments, Wilson in 1917 jumped Grayson over several longer-tenured naval officers to make him a rear admiral. The action caused a minor scandal at the time, but it revealed a human side of Wilson sometimes thought to be nonexistent.

For his part, Grayson conceived preservation of the President's health to be a full-time, absorbing duty. On arriving at the White House his patient was frequently troubled by stomach upsets—what he called "disturbances in the equatorial regions." A first task was to put him on a regular diet, one that included a breakfast consisting of two eggs drunk raw in orange juice. A more agreeable aspect of the new dispensation was the open-air activity already referred to.

The patient whom Grayson took under his care was in apparent good health. At fifty-six his figure was trim, he moved quickly, his neck was round and firm, and his hair showed only slight streaks of grey. Yet frequent colds and recurrent digestive problems, as well as lingering blindness in the left eye resulting from the stroke of 1906, spoke of dangers below the surface.

Early in his association with the President, Grayson confronted a situation that put his diagnostic skills to the test—and, incidentally, revealed the President's characteristic approach to his own illnesses. In April 1913, he suffered from a severe cold and a recurrence of the old "neuritis." Writing to Mrs. Hulbert (formerly Mrs. Peck), he was almost lighthearted in regard to it. The neuritis, he said, was "as nasty a beast as ever attacked poor human flesh"; but it was a "slight ailment," and anyway, it was Sunday when he could afford to stay in bed.[9]

The recurrence of pains in Wilson's right arm was an ominous sign, and those around him in the White House were worried. Two weeks after the first attack he was still "tired and haggard," Cousin Helen

Bones wrote to her sister. He was still "having neuritis quite badly, which frightens everybody."[10] The President, meanwhile, carried on his work as usual.

Dr. Grayson was familiar with earlier incidents in Wilson's medical history and he undoubtedly suspected a circulatory problem. Yet he was not anxious to alarm the President and his family. He tended to attribute to the illness the same degree of seriousness as the President himself did, neither more nor less. Together, through this and later similar attacks, the two made their way—the President invariably cheerful and hopeful, the physician wary and discreet. In the great crisis to come, when Wilson suffered a major stroke, Grayson faced fearful dilemmas in deciding what to reveal or not to reveal—to the patient, to his family, and to the public.

We know that, a year after this first White House illness, Grayson was told by the Philadelphia oculist who had been seeing Wilson for a decade, Dr. George E. Schweinitz, that there were definite signs of the hardening of Wilson's arteries. Grayson kept to himself this confirmation of his fears. With the skill of a good doctor, and with a naturally sanguine disposition, he dedicated himself to helping make it possible for the President to fulfill his tasks.

Close family members formed the core of the President's private existence, as they had in previous stages of his career. The Wilson daughters were now in the national limelight, their every move watched closely, the comings and goings of their suitors becoming matters of general speculation. However abhorrent this publicity, the daughters found compensations in the glamour of their position. For the first time in their lives they knew the luxury of fashionable clothes and even of modest jewelry. Jessie and Eleanor lived in the White House, while Margaret, as had become her habit, pursued an independent way.

Ellen presided over the White House scene with characteristically unobtrusive efficiency and with her gift for making any place she lived in seem quickly a home. The White House, she told one visitor, was only "a larger Prospect, a Sea Girt with no servant problems."[11] As at Prospect she took delight in redesigning the garden. She engaged herself busily in social work. The back alleys of Washington became her special concern. Here thousands of Negro families were living in primitive destitution, some of them within a few blocks of the Capitol, largely concealed from the more prosperous population surrounding them. Ellen alerted congressmen to their plight, brought officials to visit the scene, and was gratified in February 1914 to see remedial legislation introduced.

At the same time she instructed herself in the conditions of female government employees, visiting unannounced the ill-lit and airless workplace of such an agency as the Government Printing Office.[12]

Official White House entertaining was dutifully carried out—cabinet luncheons, diplomatic receptions, teas, dinners; and soon, evidently encouraged by Margaret, a program of White House concerts was begun. Until her health began to decline, Ellen pursued the role of an active, involved First Lady. Yet she shunned personal publicity, made no public statements, gave no interviews, and allowed herself to be photographed by newspapermen only in the company of her husband.

In the early days of the Wilson Presidency, before the family had been split up by the marriage of two of the daughters and the scene rendered desolate by Ellen's death, the White House presented an agreeable version of a middle-class, intellectually and artistically inclined family. George McLean Harper, who had known the Wilsons in their previous career, remarked on how much an evening in the White House resembled earlier occasions at Princeton, with singing and readings aloud from familiar books. He recalled the President seated on the floor rocking back and forth before the fire as he recited the poetry of Wordsworth or Browning.[13]

The public rooms of the White House had been renovated under the Theodore Roosevelts, and long-needed quarters for the Presidential office had been provided by the construction of a west wing. This left the second floor of the mansion free for family use. A long corridor ran the length of the space, two Palladian windows providing the only light for the living areas at the east and west ends. Off the corridor were the family bedrooms, on the south side those of the President and his wife as well as the President's study, the latter the old cabinet room, now lined with books and with a large globe standing in one corner. Two guest rooms and accommodations for the Wilson daughters were also on this floor. With their ingrained habits of southern hospitality the Wilsons needed more space, and Ellen, besides redecorating the second floor to make it lighter and more cheerful, renovated the third floor to provide further bedrooms.[14]

In this extended domain the Wilson family made themselves quickly at home. Close family relatives arrived for short stays, as well as cousins young and old and occasional friends from Princeton. A frequent visitor, somewhere between a close friend and a member of the family, was Colonel House. He would come down from New York for a few days, stay in one of the small guest rooms, and share the family meals. As a semiofficial adviser he made the rounds of government departments and of foreign embassies, and after dinner held long conversations with the President in his study. So late would these sessions last that Ellen on one occasion inquired whether they were going to stay up all night. She was as usual concerned for the President's rest; besides, in her practical way, she wanted to discuss family finances with the Colonel.[15]

The President showed himself full of solicitude and affection for his special guest. House describes Wilson going with him to his room to see that everything was properly arranged and to exchange a last few words before the two bade each other good night. Often on these occasions, when matters of state had been laid aside, Wilson's mind would go back to Princeton days and he would ruminate on old victories and defeats.

Within the family circle, he was still capable of clowning and mimicry, playing the kind of fantastic roles that had delighted the daughters since they were children. In these displays he had Eleanor for a favorite accomplice. As Helen Bones reported, he divided the family up into groups—the truly refined comprised of Ellen and Jessie, and the vulgar consisting of himself and Eleanor. Margaret and Helen Bones formed a middle contingent.[16]

Despite such attractive glimpses, and even in the first, happy phase, the atmosphere of the White House seems to have been shielded to a surprising degree from novel currents of thought. With the whole world to command at his pleasure, Wilson guarded his privacy and conserved essential energies. He shied away from new personal or intellectual contacts. When the table was set for lunch or dinner, it was family or old friends who gathered around, and familiar themes that formed the substance of their talk.

The White House was marked by two principal, regularly scheduled events: cabinet meetings and press conferences. The cabinet gathered on Tuesdays and Fridays (its meetings were later restricted to Tuesdays). The President, as is usually the case in incoming administrations, revealed the best of intentions in regard to it: he would make it a participant in all important decisions; he would give heed to its members on matters others than those affecting their departments. In the beginning it seemed easy to seek advice from a group so largely composed of southerners like himself, and Wilson presided with a natural courtesy. He usually opened the meeting with a few anecdotes, and then placed before the group whatever policy matters were preoccupying him. Important messages and texts were read aloud. The President appeared open-minded and ready to take suggestions, while cabinet members shared in the exhilaration of men working together at the highest level.

Wilson had known few of the cabinet members well. One he met for the first time when they convened for the opening session, and most were unknown to each other. But they soon fell into recognized roles. Bryan, sitting at the President's right, was in every sense *primus inter pares*, deferred to as much on matters of domestic as of foreign policy. He obviously enjoyed his place, as pleased, said House, "as a child with a new toy," yet he did not speak sententiously or at length. McAdoo and Garrison early established themselves as "strong men," clear in their convictions and belligerent in military matters. Burleson, commented one of his colleagues, did everything "just as if he were killing snakes"; he could make a speech to an audience of one with undiminished enthusiasm.[17] But in his own field of party politics he was supreme. Houston was a wise counselor, in background and intellectual qualities more closely resembling the President than any of the others. Daniels was emotional, charming, every inch a southerner, the last man one would have guessed to be in charge of the navy. Lane created his own kind of image, a large man, full of talk; it was because he talked as much outside the cabinet room as in, becoming responsible for numerous "leaks," that the President soon decided that one cabinet meeting a week was enough.

Changes in the cabinet would occur over the next few years. First Bryan and then Garrison resigned on questions of principle. The President attached decreasing importance to cabinet deliberations and took its members less and less into his confidence. This was especially true in the field of foreign policy, which Wilson considered in large measure his own. The most important address of his eight years in office, his message calling for a declaration of war by the Congress, he did not even present to his cabinet in advance. But this decline in the role of the cabinet was far off from the sunny first days of the New Freedom. Further off still, and beyond the range of the most macabre imagination, was a meeting called by the Secretary of State when the President was hopelessly incapacitated; or that other cabinet meeting when the President first reappeared among them, an aged and broken man.

Wilson pioneered in establishing regular press conferences, at first held twice a week, some hundred newspapermen coming into the East Room to put their questions to him freely. It was a form of communication that never quite worked. Correspondents were forbidden to quote the

President, and the President, even so, was evasive to the point of occasional deception. He rarely volunteered anything on his own, seemed reluctant to acknowledge that his auditors had names or particular personalities, and acted as if he never had been a teacher famed for the ability to elucidate complex matters. He "gave the impression that he was matching his wits against ours," recalled one of the early participants, "with the object of being able to make responses which seemed to answer the questions, but which imparted little or nothing in the way of information."[18]

The difficulties and bewilderment of newspapermen under the rules laid down by the White House are illustrated in one of the later press conferences. By then complex international negotiations were in train and misinterpretation of the President's intentions could be fatal to their success. Nevertheless, the President's narrow interpretation of what could be alluded to was baffling.

In January 1917, a reporter wanted to get straight precisely what was forbidden and what was allowed under the rules. He knew the President could not be directly quoted. But which was preferable, to say "The President told correspondents" or "The President's opinion is such and such." Wilson replied that he regarded these as equivalent to quotation and unjustified. What then was the use of having the President state his views? "It is," replied Wilson, "for the guidance of your own minds in making up your stories."[19] That was meager satisfaction for journalists looking, sometimes desperately, for "hard news."

Yet there were obvious rewards in these meetings with the President, at least for the rare journalist who could appreciate the play of professorial wit and was willing to be reminded of the nice use of words. When asked during the controversy on Panama Canal tolls whether he was binding himself to any particular course, "I am not binding myself on anything," the President replied. "I am ready to break loose at any minute." When the State Department counselor resigned, he was asked whether he had found a successor. "It is not difficult to find one; it is difficult to select one. We haven't selected one yet." On being asked whether it had been suggested that he send a message to Congress on a particular subject: "It has been suggested that I send a message on everything under heaven; but I am not in the message business as a profession."[20]

Examples like these, which could be multiplied indefinitely, explain the newspapermen's frustration. They show a President aware of the almost overwhelming influence of the press. But more deeply they show one resolved not to become too closely involved in the making of news, anxious instead to learn through his own arcane and sometimes faulty powers of divination what he considered the real news, the trend of the average man's thinking.

APPOINTMENTS AND PATRONAGE

As he had promised immediately after the fall elections, Wilson summoned for April 7 a special session of Congress to deal with tariff reform. The Sixty-third Congress would run almost without break until the late summer of 1914. Before it expired, it had passed the major laws on which rest Wilson's claim to stand among the top few national reformers. Never before had measures of such far-reaching consequence been framed and adopted in such quick succession. Never had a party ruled with such discipline and clear sense of purpose. Tariff reform and the Federal Reserve Act would by themselves have made any President's first term notable. To these were added in the administration's first two years legislation concerning monopolies and labor. Throughout, Wilson's leadership was as clear as it was in the end beyond challenge.

In the months when the program was being prepared and when preliminary skirmishes were being fought, a number of subsidiary problems occupied the new administration. These included not only those of appointment and patronage—more difficult than in usual transition periods because the Democrats had been so long out of power and because they were entangled with the race issue—but also unexpected tests of foreign policy in Latin America and the Caribbean. There was even a potentially explosive crisis with Japan. In these areas Wilson often appeared fumbling, contrasting with the sureness of touch he exhibited in legislative leadership, where he had prepared himself by years of study and by the rough-and-tumble experiences of the governorship. As party leader he acted as one born to command. But in related fields he was like most new Presidents a novice, having to master—sometimes painfully—the office of Chief Executive. In his case the process could be complicated by his adherence to ideals, in a situation where the obduracies of a real world were often madly frustrating.

Many of the early perplexities extended, unresolved, into the congressional session, shading the clear victories of reform. Others (like patronage) became critically entwined with events in Congress. The two aspects of Wilson's early Presidency—one finding him fully prepared and one tentative and inexperienced—are parts of the same story, though they must be viewed separately and judged on their own.

*   *   *

The new administration's first task was to staff the government. Many thousands of posts waited to be filled. Besides candidates for administrative, judicial, and diplomatic offices, crowds of applicants clamored for such jobs as customs collectors, postmasters, revenue agents, marshals, and appraisers. All of them were hungry after years in the wilderness. Wilson had been a consistent advocate and exponent of the civil service system and like others before him he came to power with good intentions to make appointments strictly on merit. He soon found the task to be less simple than he had supposed.

The administration, first of all, had to weigh claims of merit *per se* against adherence to Wilsonian doctrines. That a prospective office-holder be honest and reasonably qualified was important; but it was also important that wherever possible he (and his sponsor) be followers of the progressive wing of the party. Wilson put much emphasis on this point. He told the canny and experienced Burleson, Postmaster General and one of his chief advisers on patronage, that he wanted to appoint only progressives and to consult none of the "old stand-patters."

"When I heard that," Burleson recalled years later, "it paralyzed me. I never felt more depressed in my life."[1] Burleson knew the "stand-patters" to be often the most loyal workhorses of the party, obeying commands rather than following notions of their own. He told the President, "If you pursue this policy it means that your administration is going to be a failure." In fact Burleson, along with other cabinet members, was given considerable freedom of action. Burleson recalled that a year later Wilson seemed pleased by the way principle had been adjusted to reality. "What you told me about the old stand-patters is true," Burleson quoted him as saying. "They at least will stand by the party and the administration. I can rely on them better than I can on some of my own [i.e., progressive] people."

In addition, Wilson had to learn the importance of patronage as a political weapon. The prospective appointee might lack many of the ideal qualities, but he assumed qualities of his own if his sponsor held the key to advancing or thwarting important legislation. In the struggle over tariff and banking reform Wilson kept long lists of posts unfilled. He spent whole days in the President's room at the Capitol discussing appointees with individual senators and congressmen, his eye fixed on their impending votes. In the end his Scotch rigidity gave way, without evident loss of face or loss of integrity, to a healthy Irish pragmatism.

A third consideration in the dispensation of patronage was giving support to progressives in the state Democratic parties. The administration was a scarce eight months old when the scattered elections of November 1913 provided a test of its standing with the public. To build up the forces of progressivism loyal to Wilson was important not only in itself but as a measure of strength in the ongoing legislative struggles. Careful use of the appointive power in fact paid off. In November, with the exception of New York, where Tammany still held sway, the results in the various states showed Wilson victories. Particularly gratifying was the defeat of the Smith-Nugent forces in New Jersey. The sum of it all, said *The New York Times*, was proof of "continuing confidence in the Democratic party."[2] It was also proof that Burleson and his fellow political strategists had done their work well.

Wilson personally gave an enormous amount of time to matters of appointment and patronage. He deplored the fact; he said, looking back, that no part of being President was as disagreeable as these tasks.[3] Besides supervising the general process, he gave personal attention to a considerable number of cases. He declared, for example, that the postmistress in Murfreesboro, Tennessee, should not be replaced. (She was the mother of Edward Elliott, Wilson's former dean and now husband of Madge.) The same was true in Gainesville, Georgia, where the postmistress was the widow of a famous Civil War general. "General Longstreet was a gallant soldier," Wilson wrote—notwithstanding the fact that after the war he had shown deplorable judgment in joining the Republican Party.[4] It happened also that his widow had run the hotel in Gainesville where Woodrow and Ellen had gone for the birth of their second daughter.

In one case Wilson agonized over such a personal decision and came down on the negative side. His brother, Joseph Wilson, wanted very much to be postmaster in Nashville, Tennessee, and friends had organized on his behalf. In a letter beginning "My dear, dear Brother," the President wrote that he was unable to accede to a request where personal factors were so deeply involved.[5] Poor Josie! (One always wants to say "Poor Josie.") If only Wilson could have overlooked his principles in this particular case—or if only he had not felt obliged to record his refusal formally in a letter.

Consular and ministerial appointments raised problems of their own. Candidates for these posts were particularly numerous and insistent, and most were politically connected. Often, too, they were quite unqualified. Matters were made worse by the fact that Bryan as Secretary of State was determined to use his office to reward what he called "deserving

Democrats." "Mr. Bryan is a spoilsman," House recorded in his diary; he was quite simply in favor "of turning Republicans out and putting in Democrats." Bryan argued "strongly and eloquently" for his position, while House noted characteristically that he himself "remained silent."[6]

The kind of arguments used by Bryan are suggested in a letter to his chief. While Republicans were being introduced impressively by their titles, "as Ambassador so-and-so and Minister so-and-so," Democrats in Washington had to go under such plain appellations as "Mister" or "Honorable." "We have been quite short of prefixes," he concluded sadly.[7] Wilson was determined to provide "prefixes" only for those who merited them or had passed the requisite examinations. By the autumn of 1913 he could reassure his old friend and worried critic, Charles W. Eliot of Harvard, that he was standing by civil service standards and that the record of his administration was not below the standard set by the two previous administrations. But Bryan had already done much harm to the service. Even Wilson had not shown himself averse to naming a consular official from Maine in the hope of favorably influencing a by-election in that state.

Within his own domain of the State Department, Bryan was determined upon a clean sweep. He welcomed the staff on the administration's first day with a warning of replacements to come. Morale among the department's top officers, as well as within the lower ranks, was shaken. The department's counsel, the learned and influential John Bassett Moore (a classmate of Wilson's at the University of Virginia), resigned. Wilson's efforts to have him reconsider his decision were unsuccessful, though Moore agreed to stay on for another year. His place was to be taken by Robert Lansing, who in 1915 would take Bryan's place as Secretary of State. The changes were not calculated to increase Wilson's confidence in his State Department, nor to lighten his load as unprecedented issues of foreign policy confronted the administration.

The filling of top diplomatic posts fell to Wilson himself. His goal was to procure the service of men of the highest caliber, but he suffered disappointments as he was turned down by one after another of those he approached. Charles W. Eliot and then John R. Mott, the well-known evangelist, rejected his appeals to take the U.S. Embassy in China. Wilson tried Eliot, again without success, for the post of ambassador to Great Britain; he also tried former Secretary of State Richard Olney of Boston. When he, too, refused, Wilson turned to his old friend, Walter Hines Page. Page was a cultivated and perceptive man, as vivid a writer as ever served in the post. He appeared one who would move easily among the British aristocracy, and indeed gave every promise of being an effective emissary. Unfortunately, as will be seen, his mission was to be clouded by an excess of well-intentioned zeal.

Far more unfortunate was to prove his choice for ambassador to Germany. For this, Wilson sought the services of Dean Fine, his able colleague of Princeton days. Fine refused, prompting a bitter letter from Ellen, who felt he had sold out to the usurpers of the new university regime. Wilson himself, though greatly disappointed, replied more generously that in the turmoil of politics he could not help "sighing" that he could not himself turn, as Fine was turning, "to study again and to the work that seems somehow to be part of the unbroken thinking of the world."[8] Wilson was coming regretfully to the conclusion that only men of "large means and leisure"[9] could face the financial sacrifice an embassy post entailed. He had vowed he would never appoint one of the "merely rich"; yet to Berlin he sent the Tammany judge, James Watson Gerard, who had made major contributions to the campaign and was the favorite of one of New York's Democratic senators. Gerard's naïveté, his ignorance of the intricacies of diplomacy, fell disastrously short of the demands that the world crisis was soon to impose on him.

Wilson named Henry M. Pidell, editor from Peoria, Kansas, as ambassador to Russia. The circumstances of his appointment were revealed to be so manifestly political, and his qualifications so negligible, that the court of the Czars formally objected. The nomination was withdrawn, and the post remained empty for a year. To appease Virginia senators a minor novelist of conservative opinions, Thomas Nelson Page, was sent to Italy. Wilson was even prepared to use the post in Paris to rid himself of the troublesome McCombs. But the chairman of the Democratic Party, after breathing hot and cold and after many embarrassing delays, decided in the negative. In a letter of beautifully honed irony Wilson wrote him that now at least, to his great satisfaction, he could count on McCombs remaining at the head of the party organization.[10] For the record he spoke of his "admiration for [McCombs's] abilities . . . my confidence in his tact and resourcefulness, as well as my affection for him."[11] In his place a former congressman from Ohio, William G. Sharp, was appointed.

No one could have foreseen in the spring of 1913 the importance that the major diplomatic appointments would assume with the coming of war and its accompanying strains. Wilson did no worse than other Presidents before and after him; but his case is the more striking because he had aimed so high and had been compelled so often to content himself with second-rate men. Ideals, once again, were being harshly accommodated to circumstances.

*   *   *

Related to the problems of patronage, but going beyond them in its implications, was the treatment of blacks in government. During the 1912 campaign, while Progressives under Theodore Roosevelt were pursuing an erratic and generally restrictive policy in regard to them, Wilson actively courted their support. He promised them justice, and he received a larger share of their vote than any previous Democratic candidate. Black leaders were convinced that Wilson would fulfill their hopes of an increased share of government offices. At the very least they hoped that black Republican jobholders would be replaced by Democrats of their race. Not even these modest expectations were fulfilled.

Republican blacks were swept from office in the South to be replaced by white Democrats. In the few cases where Wilson acted to appoint blacks to federal offices, he was confronted by threats of rejection by the Senate or of reprisals against his legislative program. In initiating such attempts he expressed himself apologetically to members of his party. "I feel bound to nominate for the recordership of deeds a man of the negro race," he began a letter to Senator Champ Clark.[12] "I hope with all my heart," he wrote another southern senator on nominating a black for a Washington, D.C., judgeship, "that my course will be understood and supported. . . . I know the dangers involved and deplore them just as much as you do."[13] But such tentative moves were received with scant sympathy from members of his party. "I do not care what is done in Yankeedom," a rabid Democrat wrote to him. "If they want negroes let them have them, but the people of this district do not want them and we . . . Southerners do not want them." The correspondent added that to approve the appointment of a black to any position where he might be the superior of "white girls" would "spell absolutely the political death of any Southerner."[14]

The atmosphere in Washington was not conducive to the fair treatment Wilson had promised the blacks. The national capital had always been basically a southern town, following the southern practice of separation between whites and blacks in all private facilities, and in social life condemning the minority to a level of permanent inferiority. Washington's role as the seat of government had served over the years to cover with a thin veneer of tolerance this deeply rooted social structure; but with a southerner residing in the White House for the first time since the Civil War, and with leadership in both houses of the Congress in southern hands, the city's population looked for a reinforcement of their way of life. Nor were the native southerners alone guilty of the prevailing prejudice. "As for the Northerners here," wrote one fair-minded journalist, "it takes but a little while for them to become infinitely more anti-negro than any Southerner."[15]

At the same time that opinion in Washington was hardening on the race issue, liberal opinion in the North was clamoring for reform. Church leaders and civil rights advocates (no less than the blacks themselves) were prepared for a new atmosphere and new policies; and they were bitterly disappointed in the reactionary approach of the administration and the equivocation of the President. Wilson himself was torn between losing the support of the progressive forces that had elected him, and losing the support of southern senators and congressmen essential to putting over the New Freedom program. "I think the [racial] question," wrote the observer quoted above, "by far the most difficult in all the circumstances, the most delicate, and perhaps the most perilous, confronting the President at this time."[16]

Wilson's own reaction was one of puzzlement, showing itself in contradictory and indecisive moves. He was a reasonable and enlightened man who had largely transcended his southern upbringing. He had long held toward the blacks an attitude of beneficent concern. As early as 1881, writing as a southerner when the South was still convulsed by racial fears and prejudices, he proposed "liberal aid and systematic encouragement" for them; he urged removal of impediments to their "highest worldly success" and (what was then an extremely radical idea) compulsory education to bring them fully into the political community.[17] The idea of a black's enrolling at Princeton had, when he was its president, found him unresponsive;* but on entering politics he assumed the position of one sympathetic by every instinct of justice and liberality to the betterment of race relations.

As President-elect he had met at Trenton with Oswald Garrison Villard, liberal editor of the *Post* and grandson of the famous abolitionist. Villard was anxious to see the establishment, with private funding, of a national commission on racial problems. Wilson agreed to support this, but early in his term changed his mind, pleading instead for the "slow pressure of argument and persuasion." "I never realized before

---

* "I would say that, while there is nothing in the law of the University to prevent a negro's entering, the whole temper and tradition of the place are such that no negro has ever applied for admission," Wilson wrote in a private letter (Dec. 2, 1904, PWW, 15:262), "and it seems extremely unlikely that the question will ever assume a practical form." The first black to receive an undergraduate degree from Princeton was Arthur Jewell Wilson, Jr., of the Class of 1948.

the complexity and difficulty of this matter in respect of every step taken here," he wrote. "What I would do if I could act alone, you already know."[18]

Most unforgivable in the eyes of the President's northern critics was the spread of segregation within the government departments. Such segregation had begun under Roosevelt and Taft, but two members of Wilson's cabinet took steps, or at least countenanced steps, tending to advance it. In the Post Office Department under Burleson, in the Treasury under McAdoo—two departments having significant numbers of black employees—the two races were separated in their work stations, eating facilities, and rest rooms. Discriminatory signs appeared, apparently on nobody's order but placed by subordinates thinking they had gotten a message, or who were themselves only too pleased to enforce a new standard. Wilson's response was equivocal. In the words of Frank Cobb, editor of the New York *World*, he might have "set his heel upon this presumptuous Jim-Crow government the moment it was established."[19] Instead he told his cabinet that the situation within the departments was to be handled "in a way to make the least friction."[20] Any impulse toward militancy on this issue was undermined by his privately held conviction that the blacks would advance more rapidly if they worked with members of their own race. Nevertheless, under a wave of protest, segregation in the Executive departments was checked and partially reversed by the end of 1914.

Two factors complicated Wilson's attempts to deal effectively with the racial problem through appointments and within the federal household. The first was the absolute priority he gave to economic reform, causing him to subordinate whatever might threaten or delay legislation. The second was his determination to accomplish this reform through the agency of the Democratic Party. The need for party responsibility had been a major theme throughout his years of teaching and writing; on coming into power he was resolved to act upon it. "From the day of his nomination," commented an astute observer, "his unwavering purpose, his absorbing preoccupation, has been the resurrection of the Democratic Party as a capable organ of government. . . . Never for one moment has he allowed this major purpose to be neglected or obscured."[21] During the legislative struggles of the first term, he was, as a result, compelled to work in close association with men whose views on the racial question he disapproved of, yet without whose support his legislative program would have been defeated.

That he indeed resurrected his party, and imposed an unprecedented degree of discipline on its normally disparate and contentious members, was proof of statesmanship of a high order. But to those concerned passionately with civil rights, he appeared to pay a dismayingly high price for the achievement. He paid a high price, too, in mental and spiritual anguish. To a visiting delegation of blacks he cried out in existential despair against his all but "intolerable burden"; he spoke of things he had to do which were "as much as a human spirit [could] carry."[22] He was a civilized man, and he was caught in a fearful dilemma. It was not that his intentions in regard to the blacks were odious, but that circumstances forced him to do what (at least in retrospect) must often seem odious things. He acted according to his lights, and the lights of his time; but, even so, he is to be faulted for not having more forcibly adhered to his professed objective of dealing generously with racial problems.

FIRST TESTS IN FOREIGN POLICY

Foreign policy issues provided from the start a severe challenge to the new President. In his inaugural address Wilson had not even mentioned foreign policy, and his mind—what he often called his "one track mind"—remained rigorously fixed on measures of domestic reform. In the early spring of 1913 it seemed that these were indeed to be paramount, and he remarked that it would be a supreme irony if his administration were to become heavily involved in foreign policy decisions.[1] Yet he was not as unprepared for these as has often been supposed. Twice his plans to spend prolonged periods of travel and study in Europe had been thwarted. Nevertheless he had given much thought to European cultures and forms of government. Through the 1890s he had watched closely the American march toward imperialism, pondering its consequences for policy and policy-making. The most closely reasoned chapter in his history of the United States dealt with Madison's administration and the growing entanglements with Britain. As President, he did not forget that he shared with Madison the distinction of being one of the two Princetonians elected to the country's highest office; and he was resolved that, unlike his predecessor, he would avoid being drawn into war.

Wilson was convinced that his administration had as much opportunity to transform the country's foreign as its domestic policy—to make it genuinely democratic, pacific, antiimperialistic, free of the manipulations of big financial interests. In this he had the enthusiastic support of his Secretary of State. He had also the fertile advice of Colonel House.

Wilson had long argued that the office of the Presidency attains its full scope, and the President his maximum power, when international issues dominate. He was not unambitious for fame, and House nursed his own latent dreams of glory. If Wilson could find ways to occupy the world stage, a place in history would be assured for him; and the Colonel would occupy a niche at his side.

The first steps in foreign policy were nevertheless inauspicious. In this field, far more than in national reform, the ideal came into conflict with prevailing conditions. From the start of his political career Wilson possessed an instinctive sense of the complexity of national life, a feeling for its rooted interests and obdurate and diverse conditions. The force of economic pressures was evident to him. But other societies, particularly those most distant or least developed, appeared in his mind to possess a simplicity of form and homogeneity of substance that led him into naïve judgments. He was strongly influenced, moreover, by a moralistic conception of America's mission. His Presbyterian background, combined with the natural predisposition of his mind, caused him to see America as a nation spared by history the struggles and corruptions that had debased older societies. Coming late into existence, it stood as man's hope and as an enduring example of political wisdom. Its destiny was to serve the civilized world, while guiding, liberalizing, and instructing the uncivilized.[2] Translated into policy, such beliefs came up against the entrenched conviction of other countries that they, too, knew something about good government and the good life.

Even when he was most free of these disquieting presuppositions, Wilson was served by a Secretary of State who held them unwaveringly and in their purest form. Bryan had, for example, a simple, long-held solution to the problem of war. His solution was to keep nations that might be at the point of conflict talking for a calendar year, while mediation proceeded. Treaties embodying this principle were (with Wilson's support) negotiated by the new administration—with the Netherlands, France, Britain, and half a dozen Latin American countries. The idea was not without merit. But events were to show how far more complex and stubborn was the life of nations than the Bryan treaties allowed for. Wilson learned this, but Bryan himself could never be persuaded that the causes of war were too deep to be dispelled by mere talk.

Unfortunately for the cause of international peace and progress, Bryan began to appear a slightly foolish figure. At the beginning he proved himself to be more industrious than his detractors had expected. He conferred constantly with the President and the two agreed on all major matters. Yet his appealing candor and his good impulses could not dissipate the impression of incurable innocence. Watching from the sidelines, Taft expressed the sentiments of many when he wrote privately that Bryan was showing "a greater sublimity as an ass"[3] than he had thought possible.

A first and not uncharacteristic gesture of the Secretary of State was the serving of grape juice and icewater instead of the traditional wine at a dinner welcoming Lord Bryce as the new British ambassador. Strong feelings of indignation were expressed in diplomatic circles, which would perhaps have done no permanent harm except that they were mixed with patronizing ridicule. One English newspaper bemoaned the fact that the Secretary "not only suffers for his principles and mortifies the flesh, but insists that others should suffer and be mortified." Had he really the moral right, it was inquired with mock gravity, "to condemn his enforced guests to ice-water?"[4] *The New York Times,* noting that Bryan had "employed the powers of office to complete the overthrow of the pagan god Bacchus," concluded that "diplomacy has not had such a shock in many years."[5]

The incident would have been but the topic of a day had not Bryan prolonged it by verbose explanatory statements. As with other controversies he fell into, he could not bring himself to suffer the taunts of the press in silence, and so by self-inflicted degrees passed from the vulnerable to the absurd. This decline was demonstrated a few months after the grape juice imbroglio when he announced that to supplement his salary as Secretary of State he had signed a contract to appear on the Chautauqua lecture circuit.

For years Bryan had been a star of this forum, a mixture of uplift, education, and popular entertainment. He might have gotten away with his return engagement had he not gone into endless detail on the subject, pleading poverty, and exposing the background of his private and political life. The New York *World* was moved to offer him the equivalent of the lecture fees in order to maintain the dignity of his office. Bryan's cause was not helped when an overzealous agent of the Chautauqua institution announced that the Secretary of State would share the platform with a different set of attractions at each appearance—with companies of magicians and jugglers on some nights, or that on others he would draw crowds to hear Alpine yodlers.

Wilson bore these diversions with admirable patience. He was yoked to Bryan, for better or worse; moreover, he was touched by Bryan's loyalty, and he counted heavily on his aid in political battles. In public he praised Bryan, his "character, his courage, his sincerity, his Christian principles."[6] But toward the end of his second year in office, with the European war in progress, Wilson realized that, whatever his virtues, the man was unsuited to the office. With Bryan's resignation, some of the naïveté, and some of the reliance on moralistic principles, disappeared from the administration.

Basic to Wilson's difficulty in formulating foreign policy was an inability to distinguish with any certainty between what he called "a profound revolution," an historical phenomenon to be meticulously respected, and a mere military or political coup. In one of his first cabinet meetings he attempted to deal with the problem. A statement read to his colleagues and then given out to the press declared that the United States would cooperate only with countries "supported at every turn by the orderly processes of just government." The administration would have no sympathy with those who attempted "to seize the power of government to advance their own personal interests or ambitions."[7] The statement was assumed to be aimed at Nicaragua, where popular forces were challenging the regime of Adolfo Diaz, an unqualified dictator supported by the United States. It was also supposed to be inspired by the administration's concern lest it be thought too tolerant of military coups. In fact it was a step in Wilson's tortuous efforts to draw the line between legitimate and illegitimate revolutions.

At the same time that the President was announcing his support for regimes established by strictly constitutional means, he was showing himself remarkably sympathetic to the inchoate forces striving to come to the surface in China. Withdrawing abruptly from American participation in a consortium designed to finance China's development, Wilson declared the administration to be on the side of the people's revolution. "The awakening of the people of China to a consciousness of their possibilities under free government," he asserted in March 1913, "is the most significant, if not the most momentous, event of our generation."[8] He wished to extend immediate recognition to the new government. But his cabinet questioned whether there really was a government in China. It was pointed out that the new president had assumed power without any popular vote, that indeed he was probably a dictator and not a president at all. This unruly situation might have been thought to be anathema to Wilson; but some other instinct than his instinct for constitutional order was at work, and he was willing to accept the fact that there had been "perfect acquiescence" by the people in the choice of a republic.[9]

Open-mindedness toward people in their struggle for self-determination was one of the more appealing aspects of Wilsonian foreign policy. It was to determine the President's attitude toward later phases of the Mexican revolution, and, more significantly, toward Russia, even under the Bolsheviks. To the degree that it penetrated his diplomacy it imparted a liberal and far-seeing quality. His own judgments could achieve a prophetic quality, for instead of seeing only recurrent lawlessness and disorder, he could at his best see the longer trends of history. When applied to specific situations, however, especially to events in Latin America, this deep sympathy for revolutionary forces resulted too often in ambiguities.

The difference between legitimate and illegitimate revolutions required a moral judgment—such a judgment as often only Wilson himself could account for. Was a particular uprising based on "personal interests and ambitions"? Or did it represent the profound aspirations of a people? On such a nice point of distinction the formation of policy rested. Not surprisingly, policy was often obscure and difficult to explain. "There are in my judgment," Wilson wrote in the midst of his agony over the long Mexican imbroglio, "no conceivable circumstances which would make it right for us to direct by force or by threat of force the internal processes of what is a profound revolution, a revolution as profound as that which occurred in France."[10] He believed this in a sophisticated way, his conclusion based on contemplation and study; Bryan believed it naïvely, as an article of faith. Yet both could be wrong, and between them they involved the United States in more military interventions than under any administration before or since.

The geographic area with which Wilson and Bryan found themselves compelled to deal at the start was particularly resistant to the kind of moral force they sought to apply. The countries of the Caribbean, bankrupt and torn by civil strife, with assassination and usurpation endemic to the political process, would at best have provided stony ground for the seeds of democracy. But even these conditions were made worse by rivalries among European powers seeking economic advantages, by the inexperience (and often the corruption) of American agents, and by the strategic necessity of guarding United States sealanes. In Nicaragua, and then in the Dominican Republic and in Haiti, Wilson and his Secretary of State sought vainly for a viable course. Here could be found neither a basis of stability and order nor a legitimate revolutionary force. In the midst of the Dominican crisis even the President confessed that he could not think out a satisfactory solution.

That there was no satisfactory solution both he and Bryan were loath to admit. From the first days of the administration to August 1914, they corresponded endlessly over the minutiae of Caribbean developments. When Bryan had resigned, and Wilson and Bryan's successor, Robert Lansing, had turned their attention to the far greater problems of World War I, the Dominican caldron still seethed, and bloody counterrevolts in Haiti confronted the administration with the specter of military occupation. This finally occurred in the summer of 1916, when Admiral William B. Caperton led a full-scale invasion, driving the guerrillas into the mountains and taking control of Haiti's customhouse and indeed of its whole economic life.

Wilson's justification for the use of military force was then, as in similar situations, the safeguarding of democratic processes; or, when these were lacking, the establishment of conditions that would permit peaceful civil life to continue. Yet in the Caribbean he was not acting with unmixed motives. As later in dealing with European powers, a strong element of realpolitik was at work. Within his idealistic wartime diplomacy the idea of a balance of power was never wholly absent; in the Caribbean he set out to check the inroads of foreign economic interests, while the necessity of keeping under U. S. control the sea routes to the Panama Canal was never far from his mind.

Despite mistakes in execution and a number of false moves Wilson set forth an ideal of Pan-Americanism that was to animate his later world policies. In October 1913, at Mobile, Alabama, he called for a new approach to problems of the hemisphere—for a future that would be very different from the past. "We must prove ourselves their friends and champions," he said of the Latin American states, "upon terms of equality and honor."[11] The seeds thus sown he sought to develop by giving new form to the Monroe Doctrine, converting it from a unilateral policy to a system of mutual security. His hopes for a Pan-American alliance failed, in large part because of suspicions aroused in the Latin American states by the record of military interventions which he had himself done so much to augment. But the idea of collective action against internal or external aggression remained vital in Wilson's mind. It was at the heart of the system for world security which, under Article X, he wrote into the Covenant of the League of Nations.

Mexican problems revealed the contradictions and paradoxes of Wilsonian foreign policy in circumstances particularly striking and often highly dramatic. A few months before Wilson assumed office, control of the Mexican government was seized by Victoriano Huerta, a soldier and despot, responsible for the murder of his predecessor, Francisco Madero, spokesman for the country's democratizing forces. European powers were quick to recognize Huerta, in part because they were accustomed to extend recognition without examining too closely the credentials of any claimant to office. To Wilson it seemed that they were, besides, anxious to protect their oil and commercial interests. In the last phase of his administration President Taft had deferred taking action on the matter. By neither granting nor withholding recognition to Huerta he thought he was behaving considerately toward his successor. In fact he was bequeathing an overwhelming amount of trouble.

From within Wilson's State Department persuasive advice in favor of recognition was offered by the counselor, John Bassett Moore. In a memorandum to Bryan, Moore deplored the "extraordinary stress" being placed on the issue and the undue importance attached to its effects. The U.S. government, he pointed out, once recognized five Mexican governments in the span of a few months, without suffering injury to its national interests. The argument that Huerta was an undesirable ruler he considered to be without relevance. "It might be possible," he remarked dryly, "to cite recent instances of much denounced despotisms with which we have been and possibly still are on very pleasant terms."

"Our deprecation of [Huerta's] political methods," Moore concluded, "can not relieve us of dealing with him."[12] Despite his respect for the counselor's experience (and no doubt also for his concise and elegant style) Wilson disregarded this advice out of hand. At this stage, and in regard to Mexico in particular, Wilson believed that the United States was, if not the censor, at least the judge of how self-government was to be created and fostered. Besides he had a suspicion, at least as lively and penetrating as Moore's, of the economic games being played in Mexico and elsewhere by Britain, Germany, and France.

Relations with Mexico were complicated by feelings of intense personal animosity mutually shared by the American President and the Mexican dictator. Wilson hated Huerta with a fervor once reserved for so relatively benign a personage as Dean West. As for Huerta, he declared he would not resign his office until he and Wilson were both in hell. In writing to Mrs. Hulbert, Wilson could affect a sort of chivalrous disdain for the dictator. "A diverting brute," he described him, "so false, so sly, so full of bravado . . . and yet so courageous, too." One moment you longed for his blood, Wilson continued, "and the next you find yourself entertaining a sneaking admiration for his nerve."[13] The two men saw themselves locked in combat to the bitter end, and Wilson so informed the European powers.

The situation was made worse by the fact that the American representative in Mexico City, a leftover from the previous administration, was a figure Wilson disliked hardly less than Huerta. Henry Lane Wilson was a passionate supporter of the dictator and was, in Wilson's view, altogether too intimate with the ambassadors of the European powers. Of the latter, the British representative, Sir Lionel Carden, was particularly offensive in administration eyes. Wilson hesitated for several months before recalling the ambassador he had been saddled with, bypassing him while dispatching the journalist William Bayard Hale with instructions to send him confidential reports. Hale's comments, brilliantly presented, largely supported Wilson's own views of Mexican events: the scurrilousness of Huerta, the cynicism of the European powers, and the hope for a truly representative movement.

This hope centered on Venustiano Carranza, a political leader based in the north, heir to the cause of the murdered Madero. Wilson felt for him the kind of idealistic sympathy that he had felt for the revolutionary party in China. Other observers doubted whether Carranza had the capacity to achieve power and to unify the country. For the moment, however, events worked in Wilson's favor. In the autumn of 1913 Huerta dissolved the Mexican congress and arrested the deputies. Wilson's estimate of Huerta seemed confirmed. His confidence in Carranza rising in proportion to his sense of outrage against Huerta, he hoped to see the Mexican situation presently stabilized under a new constitutional order. In this he was to be disappointed. The problem of Mexico would cast its shadow over much of his administration, lingering even when the European war absorbed all of his energies.

A crisis with Japan also arose early in the President's first term. Combining domestic and foreign policy, it evoked in unexpected ways many of the problems he would face at a later stage: threats of war, differences of opinion within his cabinet, complicated issues of human rights. To these was added a problem in regard to which the Democratic Party was particularly vulnerable and subject to division: the constitutional separation between the powers of the states and those of the federal government.

It began when early in April Japan issued a formal protest against legislation then being debated in California, the intent of which was to deprive the state's large Japanese population of the right to hold land. They were already denied citizenship, and to the majority of Californians the proposed law seemed consistent, for better or worse, with existing treaty provisions. They were not prepared for the strong protest by Japan, which saw the proposed restrictions as intolerable.

Wilson attempted to persuade the state of California to frame its legislation on landholding in less offensive language, avoiding mention of the Japanese by name. Yet he was reluctant to interfere in the actions of a state; he was careful, as the struggle for tariff reform got under way, to avoid affronting the states' rights wing of his party. The political situation was further complicated by the fact that the governor of California, Hiram W. Johnson, was a noted progressive, the representative of forces Wilson could ill afford to alienate.

Relations with Japan deteriorated to a point where war actually threatened. Discussion in the cabinet meeting of May 16 focused on that grim possibility. The immediate issue before Wilson's advisers was the disposition of three U.S. ships anchored in the Yangtze River. The Secretary of War, supported by McAdoo and McReynolds, favored moving them to the Philippines for greater safety. The Secretary of the Navy declared that although they were not very large ships, any action in regard to them might be regarded by the Japanese as provocative. The Secretary of State agreed. The President sided with the latter two. At a garden party the following afternoon, he remarked to Daniels: "At one time I think we had a majority . . . against me."[14] These were men still inexperienced in dealing with a foreign policy crisis; they were feeling their way, and preparing for greater crises to come.

Although the peace party prevailed in the cabinet, preparations for an emergency were set on foot. Orders to be on the alert and to be prepared to concentrate their forces at various given points went out by secret code to ships on the Atlantic and Pacific coasts and to garrison commanders in the United States and its island possessions. "People in the United States believe war is impossible," Daniels was told in a cogent report from Admiral Bradley A. Fiske, his chief of staff: "Russia believed the same thing in 1904." The United States had hit the Japanese "in their tenderest spot—their national pride"; and in a sentence Daniels's young Assistant Secretary, Franklin Roosevelt, might well have taken to heart, Fiske warned that the "Japanese make war without warning."[15] Meanwhile, jingoistic elements stirred the pot, with demands for war being hysterically cheered at mass meetings.

Still hesitant to interfere in a state's internal affairs, Wilson preferred having the courts determine whether the proposed California law was a treaty violation. Governor Johnson was adamant in his own views. "Much has been said about the dignity of Japan," he declared. "But what about the dignity of California?" In the Senate, devotees of states' rights were prepared to make the issue an excuse for opposing tariff reform. As a last resort it was decided to send as a special emissary to California no less a figure than the Secretary of State.

Bryan's mission was carefully prepared. The sensibilities of no foreign country could have been more delicately regarded, nor protocol more strictly observed, than in this approach to the "rather bumptious state" of California. Assent to the visit was obtained from the governor, the president of the state senate, and the speaker of the house; and Bryan, on his arrival, sent back to Wilson reports that would have been worthy of a major initiative among foreign potentates. Already chafing at being tied to his State Department desk, the ebullient Bryan viewed the journey as a fine mix of politics and diplomacy—something more of the former than of the latter. At one point Wilson felt compelled to send him a sharp warning that he was not to tell the Californians how to behave, but merely to negotiate less offensive phrasing in the proposed legislation. Bryan held press conferences, met in secret sessions with members of the legislature, addressed them publicly in his best oratorical style, and upon his departure offered an appropriate farewell statement. To Taft, watching from the sidelines, it was a source of considerable amusement that Bryan, "of all people," should be sent to stop "the fool performance of that arch-demagogue and fool Johnson."[16]

Wilson, meanwhile, was dealing with the larger issues of the controversy. Notes were exchanged with Japan and the groundwork laid for a new treaty, ensuring for the Japanese the same personal rights and privileges as other citizens of foreign countries. So the crisis passed. By the end of January 1914, with compromises having been made on all sides, he could tell the Senate that the matter was at an end.

In the handling of this potentially explosive issue, Wilson may be faulted for his timidity in asserting the supremacy of federal over state law (in a somewhat similar circumstance, Theodore Roosevelt had threatened to dispatch federal troops); and for his unwillingness to launch a more militant attack on a national policy shamefully discriminatory toward the citizens of Japan. Yet he had looked coolly into the face of war; he had stood his ground firmly against Garrison and others in the cabinet threatening to overreact. With the outraged Japanese he had dealt courteously and responsibly. The California brouhaha may be judged less as a failure in foreign policy than as part of the learning process that any new President must undergo.

CHAPTER SIX

National Leader

———◆———

THE NEW FREEDOM ENACTED

First on the agenda of domestic reform was a downward revision of tariff rates. To succeed in this was for Wilson an absolutely crucial test of leadership. If he succeeded, everything else would be easier, and much that would otherwise appear impossible might be achieved. If he failed—and precedents suggested the likelihood of failure—he would begin his term as an apparently foolhardy victim of political circumstances. The battle would go hard, and not until the end would the outcome be assured.

The democratic process had long seemed poorly suited for dealing with the tariff. However widespread might be the support for a lowering of rates as a general principle, political alignments fell into disarray when specific revisions were proposed. Not since before the Civil War had any substantial reform been attained. Cleveland's first effort had ended disastrously when a tariff bill passed by the House was defeated in the Senate. A renewed assault in his second term saw his bill so mutilated by the Senate that he refused to sign it. Wilson was well aware of these precedents and had written extensively about them.

As president of Princeton his first spectacular victory had come with reform of the curriculum, and on a larger stage he was facing a problem in many ways similar. In both an overall objective, appealing to men of principle and good sense, was under threat of subversion by the deeply held interests of individuals. College professors protecting their own portion of the curriculum were not essentially different from politicians holding inviolate some traditional economic preference. Long accustomed as a party to favor lower tariffs, Democratic politicians quailed when, as northeasterners, the rates on shoes came under discussion or, as westerners, they were confronted with the prospect of free importation of wool. Such negative factors could be counteracted by the force of leadership alone. The only path to successful reform, whether in the case of the curriculum at Princeton or the tariff in Washington, was to keep the main goal so steadily to the front that special pleading lost some of its effect.

Wilson achieved remarkable victories in both cases, and both came at the start of a new phase of his career. His resilience was then at its height. His resourcefulness, courage, skill in maneuvering, his capacity to see and to understand the case of the adversary, showed him at his best as a leader and as a human being. "The whole art of statesmanship," he had written in his Columbia lectures of 1907, "is the art of bringing the several parts of government into effective cooperation for the accomplishment of particular common objects."[1] Never was he to prove more clearly the statesman than in holding disparate elements to a single goal as he drove through the tariff reforms of 1913.

Why the tariff was first and foremost on the agenda of the New Freedom is understood only by seeing it in the context of the Wilsonian, or the progressive, philosophy. With its intricate, built-in preferential rates, with its complex shelters and entrenchments, the tariff was believed to be a principal means by which the trusts gained a firm footage in the economic system. The result was monopoly; it was also a heavy drain upon consumers. To reduce tariff rates all along the line would not by itself put an end to the trusts; that would require further changes in the fields of banking and business organization. But insofar as the tariff could become benign and general, applying with a rough justice to all, bringing in revenues without driving up the prices paid for the necessities of life, it would be a precondition to other essential reforms.

Wilson had come early to the conclusion that he must make the battle a party issue, and that he must, for better or worse, put his reliance on the imperfect instrument represented by the Democratic Party. He was to experience the southern wing's special attitude on the racial question and states' rights. He was to confront in the North the party's domination by the political bosses of the big cities—by Tammany in New York, by the machines of Sullivan in Chicago, and of Smith and Nugent in Newark. The whole was a coalition of groups under separate chieftains which, exiled for long years from power, had developed a formidable record of opposition while maintaining little capacity for constructive action.

The party had endured, moreover, the long schism of Bryanism. The

Great Commoner had performed the invaluable service of bringing it out upon the seas of progressivism, but many of its individual members had been left sullenly behind, stranded in the shallows of their parochialism. He had created among the rest much bitterness and division, and had fostered the image of an organization ill-fitted for national leadership or practical reform. Now Wilson was prepared to stake his fortunes on molding this quarrelsome and fractured entity into the servant of the whole people.

He discovered, happily, that some of the most contentious party figures were sufficiently realistic to accommodate themselves to the new order. In distributing patronage Wilson had learned that reliable support came more often from party stalwarts than from embattled ideologues; now he found allies in unexpected quarters. No one could have appeared a less likely champion of the New Freedom, for example, than the new head of the Senate Finance Committee, Senator Furnifold M. Simmons of North Carolina, long active in the party's conservative wing. Yet as a party man, Simmons was ready to acknowledge the party's leader. His loyalty to Wilson did not waver, and he played an important part in carrying the legislation through the protracted Senate battle. In the House, Underwood, a chief rival before the nominating convention, was a true stalwart of tariff reform.

Shortly after the inauguration the Ways and Means Committee of the House, with Underwood in charge, began holding daily meetings. The situation could hardly be called promising. "A majority of the Democrats in both Houses," reported the New York *World* on March 12, "are of cautious frame of mind regarding the scope of the proposed reductions." Bryan, taking the promises of the Democratic platform literally and favoring free wool, alarmed western members of the party. They hoped that the President would show a more sensible attitude. But the President, having his own ideas, considered free wool and free sugar minimum requirements of an effective tariff bill. He so informed Underwood, who redrafted the legislation to meet these difficult specifications.

The case would certainly have been hopeless had Wilson not seized the initiative and held it throughout the coming months. In an unprecedented move he let it be known at the start that he would address a special session of the Congress, speaking in person rather than having a clerk read his message. Consternation among the lawmakers was great as they conjured up nightmares of Executive usurpation. The Democrats had been in the habit of protesting against Presidential initiatives under Theodore Roosevelt. Now they found themselves in a particularly painful quandary. So considerable was the hubbub in the Senate that instead of a resolution calling the Congress into joint session to hear the President, the Vice President declared the occasion to be one of "special privilege," thereby eliminating the need for unanimity.

On April 8, 1913, the public and diplomatic galleries were crowded and every seat on the floor was taken as the President entered and took his seat below the Speaker. The atmosphere was tense with excitement and with a subdued uneasiness on the part of the lawmakers. Wilson began very quietly, saying he was glad to verify for himself the fact that the Executive was not a remote and isolated power, speaking through messages and not with his own voice.[2] His message was short (about eleven minutes); it avoided details; it set forth the main arguments for tariff reform with unadorned eloquence. The occasion was a complete success and set the stage for other interventions of this kind in domestic and foreign matters.

The next day Wilson broke another precedent, standing since Lincoln's day, by going to the President's room at the Capitol to consult directly with members of Congress.

Debate on the tariff opened April 23. On May 8 the bill was passed in the House by an overwhelming majority, 274 to 5. "The Democratic leaders are jubilant tonight," reported *The New York Times*. Yet other such bills had miscarried in the Senate, and now with a majority of only six, the Democrats faced a united opposition. The month that the bill had required to pass through the House would be multiplied many times before it was approved by the Senate.

A first alarm was sounded early in May when defections in the Democratic ranks made it appear likely that time-consuming public hearings would be voted. Party leaders adjourned the Senate for several days in order to regroup their forces. Was it possible Wilson would soften his position on free sugar and free wool? "No compromise!" was the word that went out from the White House. Boldness again paid off, and in mid-May the administration won a decisive victory when a Senate vote, almost strictly along party lines, removed the threat of public hearings. The Democrats had proved that under effective leadership they could act as a united party. Prospects for the Underwood bill brightened; but dangers of another kind lurked ahead.

In the course of the fight an army of special pleaders had descended on Washington, spokesmen for the varied interests of sugar, textiles, gloves—and of almost everything else, including protesters against the free importation of Bibles. An organized campaign flooded the mail of congressmen, while letters and telegrams piled up on the doorstep of the White House. At one of his regular press conferences in late May Wilson expressed his concern. A correspondent suggested that he issue a public statement on the subject. Wilson immediately took up the suggestion. Washington, he wrote, had seldom seen "so numerous, so industrious, or so insidious a lobby."[3] Meanwhile the people had no lobby, he continued, and were voiceless in matters vitally effecting their interests.

The statement caused a sensation in the press and was received in a critical spirit by both parties. Republicans eagerly made capital out of what seemed the President's first mistake, an attack on his opponents too broad and general to be substantiated, one that failed to make a distinction between illegal acts and legitimate, time-honored practices. As for the Democrats, they resented the implication that they were susceptible to false persuaders. Hoping to show up the hollowness of the President's accusations, the opposition called for an immediate investigation of the lobbyists.

Wilson might well have drawn back; instead, he gave a hearty welcome to the idea of an investigation. The public prepared itself to witness a good fight and to enjoy unsavory revelations. Individual senators indeed squirmed as they were called on by the subcommittee to reveal their financial involvement with industries affected by the tariff. It became plain that major lobbies, like the one representing the sugar interests, had spent millions of dollars over past years in creating an atmosphere favorable to protection. The press entered into the fray, with the New York *World* publishing a series of widely read articles by an ex-lobbyist revealing the secrets of his trade.

Practices turned up by the investigation were not for the most part illegal, but many of them constituted action on a new scale, seriously putting into question the capacity of Congress to act as the people's representatives. Wilson had won his point, and the army of special pleaders became at least less visible and less vocal during the remainder of the tariff fight.

The Senate debate beginning on June 20 promised to be protracted. Republican leaders were determined to keep pressure on the administration; they hoped, besides, that by delaying a resolution of the tariff issue, they could prevent the introduction of currency reform at the special session. The hot Washington summer was at hand, and as the Senate speeches rumbled on, the President at the White House kept an undeviating vigil. "Congress is quite certain to sit all summer," he wrote to Mrs. Hulbert, "and here I will sit also."[4] Virtually every other matter of public business, every private pleasure, was postponed. Yet the outcome remained discouragingly uncertain. Senator Thomas James Walsh, a Democrat from Montana, began making ominous noises, admitting afterwards he was only trying to placate his constituency and perhaps to bluff the President into a compromise on wool. He would ultimately stand with his party; but no one could be sure about him, or about a handful of other waverers, whose votes were all necessary in the final accounting.

For the summer White House the Wilsons rented a place in Cornish, New Hampshire, at the center of a small colony of artists, musicians, and writers. The sculptor Augustus Saint-Gaudens had come to Cornish in 1885, and had drawn about him as talented and eccentric a company of rusticators as ever gathered in a countryside of green hills and distant mountains. Among the later arrivals was the famed American novelist Winston Churchill, who commissioned the New York architect Charles Platt to design him a Georgian mansion approached, unlike the modest houses of the neighboring artists, by a long drive. The views across rolling meadows to the Connecticut River were superb. Here the Wilson family found an ideal refuge, particularly Ellen, who felt the press of White House affairs and the burden of its tropical summer climate.

She and Woodrow hoped to go up together in June, but the tariff controversy prevented his leaving Washington. Then he hoped to join her for the long weekend of the Fourth of July. Again, he had to change his plan. "I can hardly keep back the tears as I write this morning," he told her at the end of June. "It is a bitter, bitter thing that I cannot come." A celebration was being held at Gettysburg to mark the fiftieth anniversary of the turning point of the Civil War, and the President had been persuaded at the last moment that he must attend and speak. He did not forget that, since the 1860s, he was the first southerner in the White House; his absence would be misconstrued and resented. "I cannot choose as an individual what I shall do," he wrote disconsolately; "I must choose always as President."[5]

This first of many absences from the Cornish vacation home opened a correspondence between Woodrow and Ellen particularly sensitive and revealing. The excitement of politics, the taste of power and of coming victories, did not obscure the intimate side of Wilson's nature; it seemed, on the contrary, to sharpen it, as if he were living the more intensely at all levels. It may seem incongruous that the implacable warrior of the Executive Mansion should confess to being "almost in tears" when kept from his wife's side. But this was not unlike Wilson, who in the last phase at Princeton had merged public combat with a private romantic involvement.

Now he visited Gettysburg briefly—as indeed Lincoln had made only a fleeting stop when he delivered his address on the same spot half a century before. The last remnants of the Blue and the Gray, old men who had once been enemies, established a joint encampment at the battlefield, signaling what was hoped to be the end of sectional strife and the final healing of the nation. Wilson read his remarks, as he seldom did, from a typed manuscript. The tent flapped noisily in the hot wind, and the veterans seemed only imperfectly to grasp the import of his words.

It was not, despite the occasion, one of Wilson's more memorable addresses. The fifty years that had passed he praised for having meant "peace and union and vigour, and the maturity and might of a great nation." But he could not bring himself to envisage (as perhaps no orator could have done in that setting) the uncompleted task of giving blacks liberated by the Civil War their due place within American society. Besides, he was too immersed in immediate responsibilities to weigh the past imaginatively. "War fitted us for action," he said, revealing his mood, "and action never ceases." Again, in his peroration: "The day of our country's life has but broadened into morning. Do not put uniforms by. Put the harness of the present on."[6]

At that moment he was himself harnessed to the task of bringing the tariff reforms to fruition; his personal burden was the separation from his family at Cornish. "I shall thrive," he told Ellen, *if only I surrender my will to the inevitable.*" Through the long mid-summer holiday of the Fourth of July, with Washington deserted and the continent lying under a heavy blanket of heat, he stayed on at his post—alone, he wrote Mary Hulbert (for he was still writing her every Sunday), "in my majesty and discontent." "I feel more than ever like a prisoner, like a sort of special slave . . . in durance vile and splendid."[7]

In Cornish Ellen was finding in the cooler airs and amid congenial company the release that came to her at seasons all too rare in her life. She had shown before that she flourished when on her own, free from domestic and official duties. Devoted as she was to Woodrow—"Dear, *dear* heart," she wrote from Cornish, "I love, I adore you, in fact I am mad about you. When, oh *when* am I to see you again?"[8]—she managed to get on very well without him. Indeed she prospered being out from under his shadow. She had returned seriously to painting, a group of New Hampshire landscapes proving to be her best work to date. In her "great splendid car" she took long drives through the mountains with her family, entertained at small teas, and was herself entertained in the colony's most beautiful houses and gardens. It was almost as if Ellen had been once more the student in New York, or the young mother enthusiastically received by friends and relatives in her native South.

The three Wilson daughters came to Cornish, along with an appealing young man, Francis Bowes Sayre, then engaged to Jessie. Mary and Lucy Smith arrived from New Orleans; Stockton Axson appeared, cheerful and relatively robust. The summer residents at Cornish included Maxfield Parrish, the Saint-Gaudens family, Witter Bynner, Percy Mac-Kaye—artists, sculptors, poets. Among them was the ornithologist Ernest Harold Baynes. To support Baynes in his project of establishing a bird sanctuary, MacKaye composed a *Bird Masque* in which Eleanor played "the Bird Spirit" and Margaret sang the opening verses. The evening was considered a great success. Among other recreational and cultural events were weekly meetings of a literary club and "little dances" for the young.

Woodrow lingered in Washington, getting up to Cornish only four times that summer, and only once for a full week's stay. Besides the continuing debate on the tariff, preparations were afoot for a new currency bill, and crises developed with Mexico and Japan. He felt his presence to be important as an example, hardly less than for the constant oversight it provided him. In the White House he established the solitary regime he would resume later in tragic circumstances, with Tumulty and Grayson moving in for company, sharing his meals, his afternoon drives, his golf games. A few outside guests provided unexpected diversions. The Lord Provost of Glasgow came by one day for lunch. He was, as Wilson described him, "a very juicy and interesting and most unusual man," slim, scrawny, with an exterior that "did not in the least give intimation of what was inside him."[9] But mostly he kept a lonely vigil. He was feeling "perfectly well," he assured Ellen. But he missed his wife dreadfully, and he suffered, while rather enjoying his suffering, from the confusion into which ongoing renovations had plunged the mansion.

Upstairs, bedrooms were in the hands of paperers; the East Room was "dismantled, bescaffolded and possessed." Everywhere the furniture was in ghostly summer attire. "I feel like a ghost myself," he wrote, "as I move about echoing rooms and corridors."[10] On Sunday he went to church and then sat down to pour his heart out to Ellen. He also wrote his long weekly letters to Mary Hulbert, rather forced and dutiful letters, trying to comfort her in what seems to have been a continuing depression, while he vainly begged for more news.

In the White Office, with Joseph P. Tumulty

The Wilson family leaving church (Ellen Wilson, Margaret, the President, Jessie, Eleanor

White House romances
(Francis Sayre, Jessie; Eleanor,
William Gibbs McAdoo)

Indomitable golfer

At Cornish, New Hampshire, 1913: Ellen's last summer

Woodrow, relaxing

The months of separation, like other enforced separations through the years, gave Woodrow and Ellen a chance to feel out anew in their correspondence the depth and complexities of their feelings for one another. It was if they knew—although no one could possibly have known the fearful truth—that this was Ellen's last summer. Woodrow was genuinely proud of his wife's success at Cornish and bore with a minimum of self-pity the sacrifice he was making by insisting that she stay on in New Hampshire through mid-October. He saw clearly, at this pinnacle of their lives together, the independent woman she might have been, the accomplished artist it had been in her power to become. The sacrifice he recognized and accepted, but not ungratefully. "It is very wonderful how you have loved me," he wrote to her. "The soul of me is very selfish. I have gone my way after a fashion that made me the centre of the plan. And you who are so individual, who are so independent in spirit and in judgment, whose soul is also a kingdom, have been so loyal, so forgiving, so self-sacrificing in your willingness to live *my* life. Nothing but love could have accomplished so wonderful a thing."[11]

It was indeed a sacrifice freely given, but Ellen, as was her way, made light of it. Looking wistfully back, she commented with characteristic pride in him, with characteristic humor and adoration, that hers had been "the most remarkable life history that I ever even *read* about,— and to think *I* have *lived* it with you. I wonder if I am dreaming, and will wake up to find myself married to—a bank clerk,—say! I love you, my dear in every way you would wish to be loved,—deeply, tenderly, devotedly, passionately."[12]

His coming to Cornish for an eight-day stay provided a second honeymoon for them both. Ellen rejoiced to see her husband so happy. "What a wonderful warm feeling about the heart that blessed week has left me," she wrote after his return to Washington. And her husband replied, "It seems to me that I never loved you as I do now."[13] Yet even after so many years, there could be the kind of misunderstanding that darkens less profound relationships. Wilson recalled some carelessly spoken word, some slight that had hurt Ellen. "How often I make myself seem exactly what I am not, and carry grief and consternation to the heart of the one person in all the world to whom I try to show myself completely and truly" he wrote. "When I try hardest I fail most ignominiously. I pray God you will understand, and will see truly all the strange disguises I weave about myself."[14]

Ellen had always been less inclined than he to see things in a tragic light, and in her forgiveness she relieved him of his sense of guilt. "I should not let a mere word hurt me and so, by reaction, hurt you," she told him. "I will try hard to be more sensible."[15]

As autumn came on—an exceptionally beautiful autumn, with Ellen's New Hampshire trees turning to "rich, coppery red," the separation became particularly hard for her husband. He did not begrudge her the extended stay; he had steeled himself to it, knowing she was in the place where he would most have wanted her to be. But now, as the day of reunion drew near, he was at the same time jubilant and in despair because of its slow approach. "I am your lover, my sweet one," he wrote, "more deeply and truly than ever I was when I was a boy." Finally there was a *last* Sunday to bear alone. "Ah! my darling, my darling! I am beside myself with the joy of it all! My exile is over. I am about to come out of the gray country of duty . . . into the sweet gardens where you are!"[16]

With the galleries crowded and applauding, the tariff bill was handsomely approved by the Senate on September 10. Three weeks later it was signed at the White House. For Wilson it was a moment of supreme triumph. He had had the accomplishment of something like this at heart since his youth, he said in brief, moving remarks at a public ceremony. Yet he was ready to push on immediately to the next stage of reform. He hoped it would not be asking too much of those who had borne the brunt of the first battle if he now reminded them that their task was only partly done. "I feel tonight," he concluded, "like a man who is lodging happily in an inn which is half way along the journey."[17]

The other half of the journey would be reached, in Wilson's mind, only when banking and currency reform had been completed. In June, when the battle over the tariff was shaping up and when its outcome was far from certain, the President had taken the audacious step of putting banking legislation on the agenda and calling for its passage before the end of the special session. "There is nothing that succeeds in life like boldness," he told his classmates at a Princeton reunion in 1914, "provided you believe you are on the right side."[18]

What Wilson believed was that tariff and banking reforms were closely linked and formed together the core of the New Freedom's first phase. The tariff would free business from long-established shackles; a new banking and currency law would make available to business the credit essential to its expansion. In its sheer simplicity the idea caught the imagination of the country. If the two bills could be completed during the special session it would constitute an achievement, the *Nation* declared, "without parallel in the history of American politics."[19] It was a great wonder that along with the tariff—"by itself enough to fill the mind and exhaust the strength of the average executive"—Wilson should have "the resource and boldness to address a measure of still more far-reaching importance."

Appearing on June 23 for a second time before a joint session of Congress, the President had expressed reluctance to ask the legislators to extend their labors through an unbroken Washington summer. "Every consideration of personal convenience and personal comfort . . . dictate an early conclusion of the deliberations of the session,"[20] he told the lawmakers. But there were occasions of public duty "when these things which touch us privately seem very small; when the work to be done is so pressing and so fraught with big consequence that we know we are not at liberty to weigh against it any point of personal advantage." Such an occasion was, in his view, reform of the banking system.

The fight for the tariff had already proven Wilson's mettle. On this second issue, he faced opposition not only from the Republicans but from a considerable portion of his own party. Yet he fought on with unexpected success. "Who will tell us the secret of his influence?" asked the *Nation* editorialist. "Outwardly he has been the least assertive and ostentatious of executives. . . . Yet somehow, from this business President sitting at his desk, there has come an impulse and a sustained force which have made the legislation which looked impossible two months ago seem today almost within sight."

Banking and currency reform was difficult, in some ways even more difficult than tariff reform. On the tariff issue there could be clear agreement and clear dissent; on the question of new financial institutions a hundred men expressed a hundred varying views. Wilson had his own strong convictions about the role of banks and bankers in a democratic society; he had several times spoken on the theme. But the details were technical and complex. The struggle would prove subject to strong popular passions, and it provided a field where progressives would again be locked in battle with conservatives of both parties.

For chief lieutenant in the currency fight Wilson had in Carter Glass, chairman of the House subcommittee on banking, a legislator ready to follow his lead. The two men met in Princeton immediately after the return of the President-elect from Bermuda. Wilson had a bad cold and received the congressman in bed. Canvassing the field of banking and credit reform, the two formed a bond that was not to weaken through trying tests to come.

Wilson chose in this battle to assume the role of detached but powerful party chief—less the inflexible proponent than the leader accommodating himself to different views, making compromises where necessary and then choosing the ground on which to fight. The decentralization of credit was an essential principle from which he did not waver, and one which the progressives held as an article of faith. Where differences arose was on the degree of supervision over credit that should be established, and whether this should be under private or public control. As a conservative, Glass would have preferred the former, but at the Princeton conference Wilson suggested a federal "capstone," and with this the congressman, though reluctantly, went along.

The bill establishing the Federal Reserve System changed in the course of its passage from one under which the banking community exercised control over the nation's credit to one that put large powers in government. The change was not achieved without struggle. Arrangements worked out at the Princeton conference provided for the representation of the private sector on the Federal Reserve Board. When this became known progressives were up in arms, and the dissent penetrated even the President's cabinet. Bryan told Wilson he could not support the bill as drawn by Glass, and McAdoo framed an alternative scheme putting the government in direct and exclusive control of the money supply.

At this juncture Brandeis again proved an indispensable adviser. Visiting the White House on June 11, he was instrumental in persuading Wilson that attempts to appease the financial community could not succeed and that his crucial support must come from the progressive forces in the country. Following this discussion, Wilson rethought his position. In the following days he convinced Glass and the bill's Senate sponsor, Robert Latham Owen, that revisions were essential.

In an address to Congress on June 23, Wilson explicitly declared that control of the banking system must be "public, not private, must be vested in the Government itself, so that the banks must be the instruments, not the masters, of business."[21] Wilson had made his choice and he was now prepared to face the combined opposition of the financial interests and the conservative Republicans. Through the summer, when the family was enjoying their vacation in Cornish, he conferred repeatedly with the heads of leading banks. The wider business community slowly came to support the controversial legislation and began to put its own pressure on the bankers.

Conservative Republicans were more difficult to deal with. Besides their ingrained dislike of government control, they were already massed in strong partisan opposition to Wilson and his administration. A letter from Henry Cabot Lodge to the Boston financier Henry Lee Higginson, written in the wake of the legislation's enactment, expresses the general view of this group. "I know but one way to put a stop to these dreadful assaults on business," Lodge wrote, "and that is to turn out the present crowd."[22] Fortunately for Wilson and his program, the Democrats were in firm control of Congress.

It was not in the nature of Democrats, however, to remain united for long, especially on an issue touching so deeply upon sectional interests. Spokesmen for the agrarian wing of the party pressed for a series of amendments providing, among other things, for the reserve board to issue short-term rural credit. Wilson was at this time strongly opposed to what he considered class legislation. Not until 1916 were the purely economic reforms of the first New Freedom to be supplemented by rural credit and other measures of social justice. Through most of the hot month of August 1913, the Democratic Party, racked by deep political and ideological interests, met in a prolonged caucus. Largely as a result of the President's patience and strong leadership, a revised Glass bill was eventually accepted by a clear majority and was passed by the House.

The struggle in the Senate was enlivened by the opposition of three Democrats on the Banking Committee—Reed of Missouri, O'Gorman of New York, Hitchcock of Nebraska—whose defection raised them high in Wilson's contempt. It appeared that for reasons not based on principle, but on political or purely personal considerations, the bill would not get out of the committee for a vote in the full Senate. Reed felt he had been slighted in the choice for a postmaster of St. Louis; Hitchcock claimed that most of the Nebraska patronage had gone to Bryan. As for O'Gorman, he gave no reasons and issued no statements, but let it be known he wished to teach the "dictator" Wilson a lesson.

Wilson fumed in private, but he kept his temper and avoided personal recriminations. When the Washington *Post* quoted him as characterizing the dissidents as "rebels"—an opprobrious epithet in a country where memories of the Civil War were still green—he went out of his way to deny that he had ever used the word. He was content to engage in a quiet struggle that he knew must be fought through to the end. "A man of my temperament and my limitations," he wrote Mrs. Hulbert "will certainly wear himself out in it, but that is a small matter; the danger is that he may lose his patience and suffer the weakness of exasperation."[23] Exasperated he certainly was, and had good cause to be; but he had not passed through the indignities of the Princeton battles without learning important lessons.

Though reluctant to stake the outcome on his personal influence, Wilson nevertheless invited Reed and Hitchcock, separately, to the White House. "Why *should* public men, Senators of the United States, have to be led and stimulated," he asked privately, "to what all the country knows to be their duty?"[24] If his personal appeals failed, Wilson was prepared to ask the Senate leaders to discharge the committee of further consideration of the bill, letting it be taken up forthwith in a party caucus. The President could then use all his powers of public persuasion, going directly to the people if necessary.

During the week of October 8 Wilson conferred at length with various senators, endeavoring, as the New York *World* put it, "to save the situation by pacific means."[25] The House was restless, having no work to do. Wilson permitted it a month's recess; he allowed the Senate three-day adjournments provided the committees continued uninterrupted hearings. The bankers, finding their hopes of defeating the bill revived, brought fresh pressures on the administration. The President conferred, cajoled, refused to budge. Only his "dogged determination," as one journalist put it, was keeping alive the possibility of passing the bill at the special session. On October 16, O'Gorman, Hitchcock, and Reed were received together at the White House in a dramatic effort to alter their stand.

Then slowly, and in some ways inexplicably, the force of the opposition slackened. On November 8, Reed and O'Gorman fell in line— the latter, it was said, having been sensibly impressed by the size of the anti-Tammany vote in the New York election of a reform coalition mayor, John Puroy Mitchel. The bill could now be voted out of committee, as was done on November 22 when public hearings were terminated. The full Senate began its debate, and less than a month later, on December 19, passed the bill by a vote of fifty-four to thirty-five. With unprecedented speed the conference of the two houses completed its work.

At six o'clock on the evening of December 23 the President affixed his signature to the legislation establishing the Federal Reserve System, the most lasting monument of the New Freedom phase of the Wilson administration. The spirit of Christmas was in the air. In the East Room, Ellen stood at the President's right—"Happiness," said *The New York Times*, "was most apparent on [her] face"[26]—while Margaret and Eleanor stood nearby. Around the family group were gathered the cabinet, members of the two congressional committees on banking, and other official guests. The President was tired, and his brief address was spoken with slight signs of hesitation. But his words were without a touch of bitterness. He praised Republicans for their help; he even held out the olive branch to Democratic dissenters.

The country as a whole recognized that an extraordinary work had been accomplished. In letters and editorials a chorus of praise poured into the White House. A journalist writing for the *Saturday Evening Post* summed up in pungent words a judgment which not even Wilson's opponents could have wanted to contravert. "[T]his administration is Woodrow Wilson's, and none other's. He is the top, the middle, and the bottom of it. There is not an atom of divided responsibility. . . . The Democratic party revolves about him. He is the center of it, the biggest Democrat in the country—the leader and the chief." The writer went on to comment upon the mastery that permitted Wilson to cope effectively with congressional leaders. "He is always prepared. He has thought out his premises and his conclusions. He makes those premises and draws those conclusions with pitiless regularity and cumulative force."[27] To this rather cold estimate of Wilson's intellectuality, the *Post* added praise for his "persistency and unfailing tact" in dealing with recalcitrant members of his own party.

In a previous moment of triumph Wilson had remarked that he felt no sense of elation. Now he was not only tired but was also acutely aware of the pitfalls lying before any man who aspires to be a leader. On the day the currency bill was completed, in a conversation extraordinarily prescient, he told Colonel House that the Princeton experience hung over him sometimes like a nightmare. "He had wonderful success there," House records him as saying, "and all at once conditions changed. . . . He seemed to fear that such a denouement might come again."[28]

COMPLEXITIES AND TRAGEDY

Just before Christmas 1913 the President and his family left for a vacation in Pass Christian, Mississippi, a resort town on the Gulf of Mexico. There he found desperately needed rest and what in retrospect appeared to have been one of the happiest interludes of the Presidential years. The strain of legislative activities culminating in the signing of the Federal Reserve bill was evident. A bad cold in December left Wilson shaken and weak. "The trouble never went below my bronchial tubes," he assured a correspondent, but when he believed he was getting well the cold returned, "and the second edition of the wretched disease was worse, much worse, than the first."[1] Rumors spread about the President's health, leading the British ambassador to offer the Foreign Office a gloomy assessment of the capacities of the Vice President. But Wilson was capable of swift recuperation, and the journey south, with the train cheered as it passed through his native region, helped put him in the mood for three weeks of relative relaxation in the open air and in close companionship with Ellen and two of his daughters.

It was intensely cold when they first arrived, but the sun, Wilson wrote, was soon "softening the air wonderfully."[2] His mind was freer from strain that it had been since he was elected governor of New Jersey. Their big comfortable house looked out across the water and a golf course was nearby. For a while he could escape crowds and live the life of a normal human being.

One afternoon when he was returning from a golf game the Secret Service men noticed a fire in the attic of a house they were passing. With Grayson and the chauffeurs the Secret Service rushed to help put it out, while the President entered the front parlor to comfort Mrs. Susan Hart Neville, the owner.

"Oh, Mr. President, it is so good of you to call on me," said the astonished lady. "Won't you please walk into the parlor and sit down?" "I haven't time to sit down," the President replied. "Your house is on fire."[3] For his pains the President was made an honorary member of the Pass Christian Fire Department and received from the Nevilles a cake for his birthday. "I shall never cease to be gratified," he wrote in a note of thanks, "that our machine passed so opportunely."[4] It was just the kind of incident to provide family conversation for the vacationers, and to endear the President to the local population.

The Wilsons arrived back in Washington much refreshed and in seemingly good health. Busy days were ahead for Ellen as well as for her husband. On the evening of their return they entertained the diplomatic corps and on three other evenings of that week either gave or attended dinners. The Washington "season" was on. "None of us relishes these things in the least," Wilson wrote a friend, "but for the next two months we must make believe that we delight in them."[5] In addition, family events had both their poignant and their joyous sides. In the last week of November Jessie and Frank Sayre had been married at the White House. After a trip abroad they returned to Washington briefly. "I feel bereaved," Wilson wrote after they left to settle in their new home in Williamstown, Massachusetts, where he was at the start of an academic career. "I know from my own feelings how [Ellen] is suffering, and that adds to my own misery."[6]

Ahead lay a second parting. The Wilsons' youngest daughter, Eleanor, had become engaged to William McAdoo, Secretary of the Treasury. He seemed an unlikely suitor, twenty six years older than she, with sons already grown. But Eleanor had an adventuresome streak in her nature, drawing her toward this worldly figure around whom romantic rumors were easily woven. In falling in love with a man more than twice her age, she was perhaps unconsciously expressing, also, the extreme closeness she felt with her father.

Wilson had come to dislike McAdoo. Useful and able as he was, and loyal despite differences in opinion, he seemed a steamroller of a man, brash, insistent, overbearing. Like many such people, he was also a bore. His memoranda and letters were wordy to the point of suffocation, and his presence must often have been worse. McAdoo "stayed too long and talked too much,"[7] a comment by a member of the White House staff, very probably reflected Wilson's judgment, on that and on other occasions. Now that he was to become a member of the family, the prospective father-in-law put the best possible face on the matter, referring to him as a "noble" man. But it was not easy for either Woodrow or Ellen to see another daughter depart from the closely knit household. In the midst of what was to be a sudden decline in Ellen's heath, it meant, moreover, the strain of a second wedding.

Little in the public sphere seemed to go exactly right after the return from Pass Christian. Wilson was confronted by legislative problems more complex, and in the end leading to less satisfactory results, than in the early phases of the New Freedom. At the same time he faced crises in Mexico, and a bloody coal strike in Colorado, severely testing his leadership. These were to become entangled with personal tragedy, and to be capped by the entirely new situation created by the start of the Great War in Europe.

Wilson's first objective on returning was the development of an antitrust program. During the 1912 campaign it had been relatively easy to define a position distinct from his adversary's and in keeping with the New Freedom's emphasis on deregulation. Where Roosevelt called for a commission to manage the trusts, Wilson proclaimed that the establishment of a genuinely competitive market would eliminate the offenses of bigness. Facing the actual conditions of 1913, matters seemed a good deal more complicated; and Wilson, urged on by progressive elements in the Congress and the country, accepted ultimately a Rooseveltian solution.

While at Pass Christian he had studied the problem and had drafted a message to Congress. He was at this time impressed by what seemed the need to pacify and reconcile business interests, shaken by fears of what the Democratic administration might next undertake. An economic recession, worldwide in scope, had begun toward the end of 1913. Many individuals, including Tumulty in the White House and Burleson, McReynolds, and Garrison in the cabinet, were urging that antitrust measures be postponed and that business be given a a breathing space. Wilson, however, hoped that he might push for action on the trusts while at the same time comforting and reassuring business leaders.

"The antagonism between business and government is over," he wrote in his impeccable shorthand, under the benign airs of the Mississippi sun.[8] But the message, when delivered before the Congress on January 20, neither assuaged frightened spokesmen for the financial world nor reconciled differences among legislators. It did not, as a matter of fact, represent Wilson's own final opinion. Framed under the impetus of New Freedom dogma, the Clayton bill sought to define and prohibit specific practices deemed to be in violation of the old Sherman Antitrust Act. Labor spokesmen thereupon demanded exclusion of the unions from the Sherman Act. To admit a special status to any group was antithetical to all the New Freedom stood for. But Wilson approached the matter pragmatically, and labor professed itself highly satisfied with the liberal but unenforceable provisions finally reached.

Struggles over the Clayton bill consumed legislative interest through the spring of 1914. "There are, in this complicated structure here," Wilson wrote privately, "so many threads to be kept together and woven into a consistent pattern, and the pattern has to be studied so carefully and shaded so nicely."[9] Meanwhile, a second strategy was afoot, backed by progressives in the Congress, with Brandeis and the influential New York lawyer George Rublee directly influencing the President. It was becoming evident that the approach embodied in the Clayton bill could only match imperfectly the constantly shifting life of business; moreover, its severe penalties for specific offenses alarmed small businessmen scarcely less than the moguls against whom its provisions were directed. The new approach involved the setting up of a government commission, later to be known as the Federal Trade Commission, charged with overseeing day-to-day activities of big business so as to assure fair competition and prevent monopoly.

As soon as the Clayton bill passed the House, in June 1914, Wilson vigorously assumed leadership of the procommission forces. It was not the first time he had changed course in the midst of a battle, nor would it be the last. At its best his statesmanship contained, along with the fiber of principle, an adaptability to evolving forces and changing situations. By September 26, when the President signed the Trade Commission Act (a much-weakened Clayton Act would be signed without ceremony three weeks later), the New Freedom was to all appearances complete. Action on credit, tariffs, and the trusts was indeed a remarkable record to have been achieved within a mere eighteen months. The trouble was, such action confined itself to broad economic policy, leaving untouched the social and humanitarian issues that had been an underlying part of the New Freedom's agenda. By the time Wilson came to deal with these, he had changed, and the world had changed also.

In this same season Wilson put before Congress a measure of a quite different sort, no doubt convinced that his control over the Democrats was sufficiently assured to command a victory, even though obvious perils lay in the path. In a message abrupt, eloquent, and unpredicted, he requested repeal of the exemption from tolls granted to American ships in passing through the Panama Canal. The exemption was discriminatory against foreign commerce, and to the British, especially, was of a large practical importance. All political parties supported the exemption in the campaign of 1912, but Wilson had come to believe that it was a breach of the Hay-Pauncefote Treaty and that it suited poorly a nation claiming to act upon ethical principles.

It is not usual for a sovereign state to forgo self-assumed material advantages. Wilson ran into the kind of political opposition to be expected where the issue of patriotism is raised. In the House the two principal Democratic leaders, Clark and Underwood, defected on the ostensible grounds that repeal of the exemption would contradict the party's platform. More ominously—because it foretold the kind of opposition to come from pro-Irish, anti-British factions in the war— O'Gorman of Tammany Hall masterminded a last-ditch revolt. Yet Wilson found his allies, too. From England came words that must indeed have cheered him. The message to Congress, wrote his old friend James Bryce, was put "as John Bright would have put any similar question here, and he was of all our statesmen the one in whom the sense of moral obligation always found expression in the simplest and noblest words." (The British orator John Bright had been one of the young Wilson's heroes.) And there was in the Senate an unexpected ally in the form of Henry Cabot Lodge. "I have always held very strongly to the opinion that in the matter of foreign policy it is our duty always to stand by the President of the United States just so far as it is possible to do so," Lodge declared at a crucial turn in the debate. "I think it becomes the duty of all men who think as I do not to try to block his path."[10]

When Wilson won repeal of the Panama Canal tolls exemption, he stood the higher in public estimation, and in Europe he emerged as a leader who upheld what he believed was right, even when it was to the apparent disadvantage of his own country. Wilson's foes argued that he had taken up the issue of repeal to secure Britain's compliance with his Mexican policy. Both he and the British Foreign Secretary vehemently denied this. Yet with Wilson one could never be sure. His most idealistic acts often contained elements of shrewd politics. The President's relative success in holding British leaders at bay while dealing with Huerta, and his gaining of their tolerance (if not their approval) of some of the more quixotic moves next to be related, were perhaps not unrelated to his action on the tolls.

Dramatic events in Mexico, overlapping these legislative struggles and at intervals totally preoccupying the President, brought little in the way of satisfaction. Wilson's stubborn refusal to recognize Huerta will be recalled. In October 1913, when Huerta summarily dissolved the Mexican congress, this course of nonrecognition seemed to be justified, at least on principle. Thereafter the Mexican chief stood forth as the dictator Wilson had long said he was. To European powers, this made little difference. Huerta still appeared the one man who could keep order and ensure the safety of their financial investments. Persuaded that Huerta's days in power were numbered, Wilson did his best to encourage the opposition to Huerta and to isolate him diplomatically: in short, to pursue what he called a policy of "watchful waiting."

What Wilson waited for was the ascendancy of the so-called Constitutionalists led by Carranza in the north. But Carranza, whatever his ideological qualifications, was difficult to deal with. A proud and taciturn man, he proved impervious to advice from his northern neighbor and militantly opposed to any kind of foreign intervention. Wilson swallowed his rebuffs, convinced that despite his limitations and his annoying stubbornness, Carranza embodied the forces of renewal and change in Mexico. In Pancho Villa, his lieutenant, moreover, Wilson saw a rough-and-ready reformer, the sword of the revolution if not its responsible leader.

A bandit since youth, a man accustomed to living the dangerous life of an outlaw, direct, violent, brutal, Villa had certain redeeming virtues, including a more conciliatory attitude than his chief toward the advances of Wilson's emissaries. Besides, he had something of the born robber's largesse. During his Robin Hood existence he was said to have kept a butcher shop where he dispensed freely to the poor the gains of his nightly cattle raids.

This was strange company for the American President to be keeping, and the British, in particular, were highly alarmed. From London, Page wrote of the "universal fear of anarchy & murder & plunder" that would ensue if Huerta was replaced."[11] Was the United States prepared, officials were asking, to intervene to protect British citizens if the worst should occur? In the troubled condition of European politics, however (and after the settlement of the Panama Canal issue), the British had little inclination to forfeit American friendship. The Foreign Office sent over a trusted confidant, Sir William Tyrrell, not to complain but to assure the President that his country would support American policy. The Germans, too, professed themselves ready to withdraw support from Huerta if the Constitutionalists succeeded in establishing a government.

Wilson became convinced that Huerta's doom was sealed. "Little by little he has been completely isolated," he told the Congress. "By a little every day his power and prestige are crumbling and the collapse is not far away."[12] As a prediction this was to prove premature. Indeed Wilson's active encouragement of Carranza—particularly his removal of the embargo on the shipment of American arms to the Constitutionalists—seemed only to make Huerta the stronger. The landed aristocracy and the Catholic Church were thoroughly frightened, and, along with the business and banking elements, put their full support behind the existing government.

Although Wilson's antipathy to Huerta had overtones of personal enmity, neither that nor antidictatorial principles alone ruled his conduct. In constitutionalism, as represented by Carranza, he saw a force shaping a new Mexican social order. "We are the friends of constitutional government in America," he told the Congress; "we are more than its friends, we are its champions." He added significantly that America favored constitutionalism "because in no other way can our neighbors . . . work out their own development in peace and liberty."[13]

The crucial word in this statement was *development*. The British ambassador, Sir Cecil Spring Rice, discerned this when he had a talk with Wilson early in 1914. He reported to his Foreign Secretary that he had finally come to understand what lay at the bottom of the President's mind: it was not primarily the political but the economic organization of Mexico that concerned him. Only when a fair distribution of land had been achieved could one expect political stability.[14]

Spring Rice was shocked at his discovery. Not since the Congress of Vienna, he remarked, had one country endeavored to affect the social reform of another. But Spring Rice, a diplomat, missed the depth of Wilson's historical judgment. In refusing to support, then or later, plans for a Mexican government composed of reshuffled elements of the

Huerta faction, he was not attempting to impose his social or moral ideas on Mexico; he was taking his stand for revolution—the kind of revolution that would bring a radical reshaping of Mexican life. It was Wilson's shortcoming that he did not feel free to explain himself clearly to the Congress or to the press, but veiled his policy in deliberate ambiguity, to the point of being mocked and widely misunderstood.

On April 9 occurred an incident providing the administration with an irresistible opportunity to chastise Huerta. The American gunboat *Dolphin*, lying off Tampico, sent a launch ashore to purchase supplies. On debarking, the small crew was arrested and jailed. The incident seemed quickly to have been set right when the local Mexican commander freed the Americans and apologized to the commander of the naval squadron, Admiral Henry T. Mayo. On hearing of the incident, Huerta was astonished, and then conciliatory. There the story might well have ended had not Admiral Mayo, without consulting Washington, demanded a twenty-one-gun salute to the American flag.

Wilson was at this time at Hot Springs, Virginia, where his wife was suffering the early stages of the illness that was soon to prove mortal. The intense personal preoccupation may well have contributed to Wilson's ill-advised decision to support Admiral Mayo's demand. There followed an exchange between the two governments having aspects of *opéra bouffe*, as Washington and Mexico City argued over the precise form and timing of the salute. Huerta was ready enough to fire off his guns, as requested, but asked that the United States fire in return, simultaneously—a gesture Washington took as implying recognition of the outlaw regime. With these arguments in process, Wilson announced from Hot Springs that he would go before Congress on the issue. On April 22, after reviewing the Tampico affair, he asked for authority to use such military force as might be necessary to secure compliance with American demands. The Congress (as it is likely to do in such cases) backed the President overwhelmingly. The vote was 337 to 37.

Events were hastened by the chance arrival off Vera Cruz of a German ship bearing arms to Huerta. Informed by the local commander that his troops would not resist, Wilson ordered occupation of the port. But the landings were, in fact, stoutly opposed, and were not achieved without loss of life on both sides. The fatalities numbered 126 Mexicans and 19 Americans.

These actions by the administration confused, startled, and mystified the public both in this country and abroad. As a punitive measure, the occupation of Vera Cruz seemed grossly disproportionate to whatever offense the Huertists had committed, a move compounded of bravado and pride, and the possibility of being drawn into a long and costly war loomed ominously. Wilson justified the occupation of Mexican territory, not as a strategy to "punish" Huerta, but as a means of averting such further insults and abuses as would make a major conflict inevitable. The arrest of the crew of the *Dolphin* he described as being not an isolated incident, but as one in a series of affronts to the United States that must be halted decisively to prevent even graver crises.[15] The use of force, which others saw as reckless, he viewed as having been limited to a narrow purpose.

Whatever the justification in his own mind (and he later came to see the operation as a mistake, stumbled into because of his absence from Washington), his reputation as a statesman suffered severely. Despite congressional support, cooler heads saw the administration as having bungled the situation badly. Abroad, the response was harsh. Echoing other comments, official and unofficial, the *Economist* saw in the President's actions a return to "mediaeval conditions." "If war is to be made on points of punctilio raised by admirals and generals, it will," it added, "be a bad day for civilization."[16]

Wilson's emotional equilibrium suffered also. The loss of American lives at Vera Cruz, coming in the midst of growing concern for his wife's health, weighed heavily on him. To these were added the widespread public criticism, beyond even his stoical equanimity to discount. "I fancy that it is just as hard to do your duty when men are sneering at you as when they are shooting at you," he said in an indiscreetly personal reference during his memorial address for the fallen soldiers. And he added, in words that could better have been spoken at a later crisis of his career, "We are expected to put the utmost energy of every power that we have into the service of our fellow men, never sparing ourselves, not condescending to think of what is going to happen to ourselves, but ready, if need be, to go to the utter length of complete self-sacrifice."[17]

The American forces, meanwhile, had somehow or other to be got out of Vera Cruz. Carranza was objecting no less strongly than Huerta to their presence, and every day brought dangers of a wider conflict. In these circumstances Wilson accepted gladly the offer of the so-called ABC powers—Argentina, Brazil, and Chile—to mediate the dispute. They met at Niagara Falls, quickly disposing of the flag incident (by ignoring it) and forgoing, at American insistence, attempts to form a new government from the ranks of Huerta's followers. At the same time Carranza refused to allow Wilson to impose from the outside any plans for agrarian or social reform in Mexico. The proceedings dragged on, as indeed the administration intended they should, and in July, under mounting pressures, Huerta fled to Spain. A month later Carranza entered Mexico City in triumph.

In a striking but devious way, Wilson's policy had paid off. With Carranza's victory he enjoyed a brief moment of satisfaction and even of general approbation. This was not, however, to be the end of the matter. Carranza's authority was steadily undermined by Villa, his chief lieutenant. The administration in Washington swung its support to the latter. Though Villa was hardly less a usurper than Huerta had been, Wilson happily discerned no ideological stakes; indeed he expressed forcibly the doctrine of nonintervention in Mexican affairs. His political instincts, as well as sound scriptural authority, told him, "Judge not"; but he found the injunction difficult to follow consistently. He let things take their course for the time being, but in 1916 Villa presented a challenge to American interests more threatening than Huerta's; and another military incursion, more prolonged and costly than that at Vera Cruz, was undertaken.

Within a week of the time the President sent troops to occupy Vera Cruz, he sent federal forces to occupy a large portion of the state of Colorado. The labor situation among Colorado miners had been troubled for more than a decade, with workers tangled with mine owners in an unrelenting struggle. The principal employer involved, the Colorado Fuel and Iron Company owned by John D. Rockefeller and his family, was adamant throughout in its resistance to proposals for recognition of the miners' union, or for state or federal mediation. A strike in the autumn of 1913 led to the governor's calling out the National Guard. Workers were driven from company-owned housing, and in April 1914, in an incident unprecedented for its brutality in the country's industrial warfare, the Guard fired indiscriminately on one of the tent camps where the strikers had taken refuge. What came to be known as the Ludlow Massacre resulted in the deaths of eight strikers as well as eleven children and two mothers.[18]

The last thing Wilson wanted at this juncture was a military occupation in his own country. Moreover, the forces available to him were stretched thin by reinforcements that had been placed at the Mexican border. Yet the constitutional injunction to provide the states with protection against "domestic violence" was being reinforced by heartrending appeals for help from miners and their families, supported by the outcry of enlightened citizens throughout the country. Wilson, who had been urging federal mediation even before the strike began, made a final, personal appeal to John D. Rockefeller, Jr., young spokesman for the family. When mediation was again summarily rejected, Wilson decided he had no recourse but to send U. S. troops to Colorado.

The action brought order to the strike zone, but nothing could induce the company to alter its basic stand. Even when the United Mine Workers yielded its claim to recognition, the managers refused to meet with representatives of the workers. In December the embattled and exhausted miners abandoned their strike and the company imposed its terms of unconditional surrender. Federal troops were withdrawn.

The outcome was a defeat for Wilson (as it was a major disaster for the workers); but the administration's role had been creditable. The federal troops, under close surveillance by the Secretary of War, acted with exemplary discipline and self-control. The Secretary of Labor pursued every possibility of getting a hearing for the miners. Wilson made it a point throughout that recognition of the union and collective bargaining were essential preconditions of any mediation efforts. The show of force had not (as in previous federal interventions) been for the purpose of suppressing unionization, but of protecting labor's basic rights at the same time that order was being restored.

The complicated pattern of public events woven in the first months of 1914 was reflected in moods and emotions that the White House press corps followed observantly. Accustomed in press conferences to dry or evasive answers, they began to see flashes of the kind of wit that had once been the delight of crowded classrooms. Unforgettably, on one occasion, they witnessed the overflow of the President's anger. Wilson opened the regular press conference of March 19 by excoriating newspapers that spread gossip and breached the privacy of his wife and daughters. "I am a public character for the time being," he said, "but the ladies of my household are not servants of the government and they are not public characters. I deeply resent the treatment they are receiving."[19] It was the pure vehemence of the Woodrow strain exploding on that occasion; but in a humorous speech before the National Press Club the following evening he showed, in contrast, what Spring Rice called "the expansive Celtishness" of his nature. He told the newspapermen of the difficulties he found in being President—the constraints on normal freedoms, the deference beyond anything a mere mortal should receive. He sometimes felt that he ought to stand before a mirror and see "if [he] could not look like a Monument." At least being a monument might be better "than being shaken hands with by the whole of the United States." Or he considered going to a "theatrical costumer" and disguising himself, so that meeting with some newspapermen he might tell them what he really thought. Contrary to custom, the speech was made public, and it helped dispel the image of a president austere and governed wholly by the intellect.[20]

In his mind the past seemed to mix with the present. The Princeton struggles rose up in nightmares, casting over his days an apprehension of the future; and when he returned that spring for a thirty-fifth reunion, the bitterness became apparent. He made elaborate stipulations that he receive no attention from the university, whose president, he felt, had betrayed him. At the class dinner his address was dark with allusions to unforgiven enemies.

Yet happier sentiments bubbled to the surface. He was in that condition, he told his classmates, where one is "privileged to lay aside the wisdom of the world and come down to the simplicity of the heart"; he was in that "unquestioning frame of mind we enjoyed when we were undergraduates, when one man was like another to us."[21] For a day he walked amid familiar scenes; he dined with his classmates in the building they had donated to the university and sat in the room they had specified should be his study. He paraded amid cheers to the university athletic field where he witnessed "the only disappointment of the day," Yale's victory over the Princeton baseball team.

It is surprising that in this crowded spring he should have accepted, as well, the invitation to make an address at the Washington dinner of Princeton alumni. In describing to them what every alumnus wants his college to be, he rose to pleasing oratorical heights. "We want our mother, who is immortal," he said, "to be as young as the age in which she lives, as fresh as the year of grace in which we visit her, as new as all the forces that are blowing across the face of the world—younger and fresher and fuller of initiative than all her sisters."[22] No bitter reference marred the talk, spun extemporaneously from a mind that, amid the darkening scene of his personal life, seemed intent on recapturing past joys.

About this time Wilson dismayed his liberal constituency by appointing to the newly established Federal Reserve Board the conservative industrialist Thomas D. Jones of Chicago. The move was judged harshly, and has since seemed to historians a desertion of the liberal cause. But the fact that Jones had been one of the Princeton trustees who stood by him loyally to the end was a chief reason for the choice—as it was for Wilson's unrestrained anger when the appointment was rejected. This was one of the rare occasions when Wilson allowed personal affection and gratitude to overrule his normal detachment. In human terms, if not in terms of political consistency, it seems forgivable.

His wife's failing health, becoming increasingly evident through the spring of 1914, seemed to make the President more vulnerable and more sensitive to past ties. In March Ellen slipped on the polished floor of her White House bedroom. Two weeks later she was still confined to her bed by what appeared to be the aftereffects of the accident. In fact Ellen was showing symptoms of Bright's disease, a kidney ailment that would prove fatal. Grayson was circumspect; and in letters her husband maintained almost to the last that either Ellen's fall or a nervous breakdown was at the root of her trouble.

Accustomed to making light of his own illnesses, fighting them off as if exorcising the devil by prayer and faith, he could scarcely have been expected to recognize, in a case so near to him and so terrifying in its implications, the meaning of his wife's mysterious decline. Wilson's outburst at the press conference of March 19 was ostensibly directed against rumors spread by newspapermen in regard to his daughters' beaux; but a careful reading suggests that it was rumors about the severity of his wife's illness that chiefly unnerved him. Fighting to maintain a precarious illusion, he found the doubts of others to be devastating.

In mid-April Ellen was thought to be somewhat better. Leaving her in the care of nurses at Hot Springs, Wilson returned briefly to Washington to deal with the Mexican crisis. He could still fancy that she was "rapidly getting back her colour and her strength."[23] Staying with the family late in April, House found Ellen coming downstairs both for lunch and dinner; she motored with him out to the golf course where Woodrow was to play his afternoon round. When on April 20 the President addressed Congress on the Mexican situation, Ellen was watching as usual from the gallery.

In the uncertain White House atmosphere plans for Eleanor's wedding were kept indefinite. With only the immediate members of the family present, the ceremony finally took place at the start of May. Ellen steeled herself to attend and to greet the guests. Woodrow was torn between anxiety over his wife and dismay at seeing his daughter go off. Eleanor had always been his special favorite, as Jessie was Ellen's. Eleanor was his "chum"; together they played the clown in family charades and relaxed in mutual laughter. Now she was marrying a man about whom he had some doubt, and leaving him when he might need her most.

"I must rejoice in her happiness and be quiet," Wilson wrote Mrs. Hulbert. It was true that Eleanor would be living in Washington and that he would see her often. But "she will not be at my side . . . every day in my life, and I am desolate."[24] The desolation was but a shadow of what was to come.

By June, still convinced that Ellen was suffering from a temporary breakdown, Wilson wrote that "my dear one . . . grows weaker and weaker, with a pathetic patience and sweetness."[25] From then on there were few hopeful or cheering words. He would spend long hours of each day and night at her bedside, often writing as she slept. At the start of August the change in her condition was unmistakable: Ellen was "struggling through deep waters" with symptoms that changed from day to day.[26] Still, as late as July 28, he was convinced that despite the lack of favorable signs there was no organic disease; he was "hoping and believing" it was "only the weather that holds her back."[27]

By then Dr. Grayson had moved into the room next to Ellen's. On August 4 he advised that the family be called. The three daughters gathered; Stockton Axson set out from Oregon where he was teaching summer school. On the morning of August 6 Ellen told Woodrow of a last wish, that Congress might pass the slum-clearance bill she had long worked for. The same day Wilson's classmate, Dr. Edward P. Davis of Philadelphia, arrived at the White House. He examined Ellen, and taking Wilson aside told him that his wife could live but a few hours longer.

The family kept vigil at Ellen's bedside through the day. News was brought that Congress had acted favorably on Ellen's bill. She smiled; she drew Dr. Grayson near and asked that if she was to go away he would take good care of Woodrow. At five o'clock, with her daughters around her and Woodrow holding her hand, she died.

A scrawled note in Wilson's handwriting survives. "Of course you know what has happened to me . . . ," he wrote Mary Hulbert; "God has stricken me almost beyond what I can bear."[28]

Ellen's funeral was held in the East Room of the White House on August 10. The hearse was accompanied by Wilson and his immediate family to the Union Station where the coffin was placed in a special train waiting to leave for Rome, Georgia. Rain was falling over a grey Washington and all its flags were at half mast. Wilson sat beside the coffin during most of the journey, as he had kept a silent watch in the White House through the nights following Ellen's death. The train moved slowly through southern towns and villages where bells tolled and bareheaded crowds came out in a last gesture of respect to one they felt to be their own.

In the small city where Ellen was born and grew up all business ceased on the day of her last homecoming. Stores were closed; schools were dismissed. The church her father served, where the young Woodrow Wilson first glimpsed his bride-to-be, was the scene of a brief service. Again the rains fell, as the cortege moved past drenched and silent crowds up the hill to the cemetery. The strain upon Wilson had been almost intolerable. For long nights, despite the pleas of his physician, he had refused sleep. The Rome scene revived unbearably painful memories. In a neighboring street stood the parsonage where he had called on Ellen's father and come to know the veiled girl of the nearby pew; close by, on the banks of the Etowah River, was the sacred place where he had declared his love. He had maintained his composure through the ordeal, but as the coffin was lowered into Georgia soil the barriers gave way and the bereaved President sobbed uncontrollably.

His wife's death shattered Woodrow Wilson's private world. At the same time, almost on the same day, the First World War broke out in Europe. The full dimension of the catastrophe—for Wilson's generation and for the remainder of the twentieth century—was mercifully still veiled. But the President knew that the public universe with which he was familiar, the stage on which hitherto his part was played, had been shattered, too. Henceforth every aspect of politics would be different. Actions would be of a new complexity, often without precedents to guide them, and the scale of their impact would be magnified. Returning from Georgia, he faced this new situation bereft of the major force that had sustained and steadied him in the past.

When Dr. Grayson had indicated to the family gathered around Ellen's bed that all was over, the President walked to the window of her room, and looking out over the White House grounds murmured, "Oh, my God, what am I to do?"[29] Months of anguish would pass before he found the answer.

THROUGH THE SHADOWS

To Europeans war came with a sense of inevitable doom, and yet with the shock of almost complete surprise. In the summer of 1914 they were going about their tasks as they had long been accustomed, not more apprehensive than usual, not more understanding of the half-hidden moves of statesmen and soldiers: a little weary after long tensions, a little bored amid conditions of unsatisfying peace. When at Sarajevo on June 28 the Archduke Franz Ferdinand of Austria-Hungary and his wife were murdered by a Bosnian nationalist, no one foresaw the swift series of measures and countermeasures that by August 6 had managed to get the armies of all the great European powers marshaled and on the move.

The Archduke, heir to the Austrian and Hungarian thrones, was not a figure who seemed likely to tip the scales of destiny. In almost his last hour he revealed quite charmingly the happy-go-lucky indolence of his nature, along with what proved an untimely wit. Having been shot at in the morning during his official visit, he proceeded calmly in the afternoon to fulfill an engagement: he knew the Bosnians well enough, he declared, to be convinced that they rarely attempted two assassinations on the same day.[1] It was part of the irony of history that everyone was in a holiday mood when the fatal shots rang out. Ironical, too, was the fact that the fallen Archduke was the man above all other highly placed Austrians who was a friend to the discontented Bosnians, dreaming of a reconstructed empire where separate nationalities could be brought into a voluntary federation.

European powers reacted swiftly to the Archduke's murder. Austria issued an ultimatum to Serbia, making manifestly unacceptable demands. The German Kaiser, terming it reasonable and moderate, backed this ultimatum. Russia mobilized in support of Serbia, its ally; France, in support of its ally Russia; and when the German armies, following prearranged strategic plans, wheeled through Belgium on August 4, Britain came to the help of the small country whose integrity she was committed to defend. All the powers moved according to what were deemed military necessities. The doctrines of war were in control and statesmen yielded to a logic they could neither alter nor transcend.

Beneath the explosive events of these few August days lay a half century of history. The flaming enmities, the nationalistic rivalries and popular passions, had their roots in events as far back as 1870–71, when France's defeat by Germany was followed by the latter's rapid commercial, military, and naval growth. They had their roots in Bismarck's system of alliances designed to afford the new German empire time for consolidation; and in the Franco-Russian response—an alliance of its own. German-British naval rivalry, and Russia's aim to dominate the Balkans, were further aggravating factors. Despite continuous strains, the structure remained in a precarious balance until mounting forces of military destruction in all countries, combined with the statesmen's incapacity to control them, fanned the spark lit at Sarajevo.

For Woodrow Wilson, sitting at the bedside of his dying wife, the war came not entirely as a bolt from the blue. From his London post, Ambassador Walter Hines Page had perceptively analyzed the European scene. The Anglo-German rivalry made war seem inevitable, he wrote the President, except in those moments when he "shared the feelings of most men that perhaps the terrible modern engines of destruction would, at the last moment, cause every nation to desist."[2] Colonel House had been abroad that spring of 1914 on his first fact-finding mission for the President. In Europe he found "jingoism run stark mad." There was bound to be an "awful cataclysm," he wrote: "whenever England consents, France and Russia will close in on Germany."[3] House kept the hope that someone—he liked to think it might be his friend in the White House—could bring about an Anglo-German understanding on naval armaments. Diplomatic intervention might be feasible because the British, he remarked shrewdly, did not want an impotent Germany, leaving them to face Russia alone. Through the spring and early summer, Wilson pondered these reports; and when war came he saw it, much as did his advisers, as emerging from imperialistic rivalries and fears that had long contaminated the European mind.

Ellen Wilson never learned that war had been declared. Even in full health, the news would have been something she could scarcely have borne. Writing at her bedside the President drafted an offer of mediation. It seemed a necessary act, yet even he did not expect it to stay the mobilized armies. He was not prepared, moreover, either psychologically or by experience, to take a leading initiative in European affairs. His main task, as he saw it, was to calm public opinion in the United States. At a press conference on August 3 he sounded for the first time the note of America's aloofness from the conflict, not alone for its own sake but because only in this way might it ultimately serve the cause of peace. "I want," he said, "to have the pride of feeling that America, if nobody else, has her self-possession and stands ready with calmness of thought and steadiness of purpose to help the rest of the world."[4] In the months and years that followed he would constantly revert to that theme—laboring to seem detached, to subdue his own feelings of indignation or pity, until it almost appeared that he had none.

The war's outbreak brought many problems that Wilson, under the burden of his bereavement, could leave to the initiative of his aides. The Secretary of State dealt with the situation of American citizens stranded in Europe; the Secretary of the Treasury, with the mood of panic in the financial markets. But on the great issue, the defining and establishing of America's political and moral position, he acted alone. That strict neutrality was essential he never for a moment doubted. It was essential if the United States was not to be torn apart by minority conflicts, if it was not to become prey to opposing propaganda, and if it was to play a role in a settlement of the war. What sort of role it might play he could not foresee, any more than he could pretend to weigh justly all the factors that had gone into the war's making. But tentatively from the beginning, and then with increasing conviction, he believed that the United States would be a force in the outcome.

The concept of neutrality Wilson took hold of and enlarged, as all through his career he had enlarged any issue deeply engaging his mind. At Princeton he had made the fight for the quads a touchstone of liberal education; tariff reform and banking laws he saw as the emancipation of the common man. So now in the concept of neutrality, a course essentially negative and expedient, he perceived ideal implications for his own country and for a world at war. In Wilson's thought such a policy rested on high qualities of personal and national disinterestedness; moreover, it provided the best hope for civilization. As war grew in scope, as new forms of weaponry blurred the distinctions between combatants and noncombatants, and as total victory came to seem the one acceptable goal, the maintenance of neutral rights took on a new meaning. To keep (in his phrase) "all possible spaces cool"[5] was the means of preserving some limits to warfare and of ensuring an entering wedge for reason.

From the beginning Wilson was under pressure to take a position for one side or the other; he steered a course requiring him to subdue natural sympathies and even to transcend, under the overriding compulsion to be neutral, his weighing of the country's other interests. When the French ambassador was received on August 27, he reported to his foreign office that the President had spoken of the European conflict "with an emotion that he did not attempt to hide." "If things are as they seemed," he added cautiously, "the President's expressions were stamped with a real sympathy for France." Calling at the White House in September, Spring Rice received a similar impression in regard to Britain. He had been asked that his "most sincere sympathy" be conveyed to Sir Edward Grey, the Foreign Secretary, and he quoted the President as remarking that "everything that I love most in the world is at stake." Actually, the two ambassadors, hungry for crumbs of comfort, were probably overstating the President's sympathy for their cause.[6]

Wilson was not being duplicitous, but he had a long way to go before he felt free to express his feelings publicly—or even to avow them to himself under his rule of neutrality. In a talk with Spring Rice (as he had done previously in talks with House) he indicated that a German victory would force the United States into a posture of militarism inconsistent with its form of government; yet at this stage he felt the need to be at least as reserved, even to be as courteous, toward Germany as toward Britain and France. David Lloyd George was later to put the matter of Wilson's sympathies in a characteristically astringent phrase. His deportment, Lloyd George wrote, was "so studiously unpleasant to both sides that each suspected [him] of being antipathetic to their own."[7] But Lloyd George was summing things up after violations of American rights had been freely committed by both sides. In August 1914, Wilson still believed that he could be friendly toward both.

He embodied his concept of neutrality in an appeal issued to his countrymen on August 18. He asked them to do the difficult—and for some the almost impossible—thing of showing the "true spirit of neutrality, which is the spirit of impartiality and fairness and friendliness to all concerned." For the citizens (as for himself) it was not enough that they be impartial in action; they must also be impartial in thought. He asked that the United States act as a nation "that neither sits in judgment upon others nor is disturbed in her own counsels and which keeps herself fit and free to do what is necessary and disinterested and truly serviceable for the peace of the world."[8]

To the President and his colleagues it became quickly apparent that neutrality was not merely a posture or a state of mind, but a policy to be defined, a series of measures to be worked out. Was it, for example, within the law and spirit of neutrality to permit private bankers to make loans to belligerent powers? Bryan, convinced that it was not, argued his case so forcibly that for a brief while Wilson went along with him. Under pressure from McAdoo and Houston he then reversed himself. To sell submarines to Britain was plainly unneutral; but did that apply to submarine parts, or to submarines manufactured in sections? After consideration, the President's decision was in the negative.

Particularly difficult for Wilson was the question of whether or not he should formally protest acts of an allegedly barbarous or inhumane nature. Germany's invasion of Belgium was indisputably an act contrary to international law and morality. It was followed by reports of atrocities committed by the invading armies, and then by the burning of the world-famous library at the university in Louvain. Wilson was deeply shocked, as any civilized and sensitive man would be; but for him to assume the role of judge contravened standards of thought and conduct he had urged upon the whole citizenry. Despite his own feelings of growing outrage, he strove to subdue his emotions and to appear impartial.

In most of the cases of atrocities alleged by one side or the other, the facts were simply not known. Accurate evidence could not be gathered, and Wilson was loath to be swept up in the winds of popular clamor on both sides of the Atlantic. When in September a Belgian delegation headed by Minister of Justice Henry Carton de Wiart visited him in the White House, bearing written evidence of atrocities committed in their country, he responded with subdued emotion, thanking them for their presentation and promising to give it his full consideration. "You will, I am sure," he continued, "not expect me to say more. Presently, I pray God very soon, this war will be over. The day of accounting will then come when I take it for granted the nations of Europe will assemble to determine a settlement. What wrongs have been committed, their consequences and the relative responsibility involved will be assessed. . . . It would be unwise, it would be premature, for a single government, however fortunately separated from the present struggle . . . to form or express a final judgment." In a similar vein he addressed himself to the German Kaiser. On this position he stood fast, often being accused of heartlessness or lack of conviction, until in 1916 he felt compelled to speak out against Germany's deporting Belgian citizens for forced labor.[9]

The President was facing the difficult questions imposed by the war while in deep mourning for his wife's death. He passed through the phases of grief, from the first mood of spiritual exaltation to the combativeness that often signifies recovery and reconcilement. Along the way he experienced severe depression. Stockton Axson recorded that on his return from Georgia he appeared a prophet looking out upon a tortured humanity. As in an instant of revelation he saw four achievements necessary to its survival: an association of nations, the guarantee of equal rights for all, absolute sanctions against aggression, and the manufacture of munitions removed from profit-making corporations and restricted to governments.[10] But the visionary mood passed. He withdrew to the level of simple duties fulfilled and daily tasks accomplished. He did his work; he met the newspapermen, often jaunty and witty in his remarks; he pushed essential legislation; but at the center was an immense void. Grayson, going into his room one morning in August when he had been ordered to rest because of some minor indisposition, found him with tears streaming down his face. "A sadder picture, no one could imagine," Grayson wrote. "A great man with his heart torn out."[11]

On long motor rides he appeared drowsy and silent. Helen Bones— "dear little Helen"—would go with him on these afternoon excursions, a perfect companion, Wilson described her, because she was not anxious to talk and have her own way. "But I hate to think how dull it must be for her," he added, "and chide myself for accepting such sacrifices."[12] In the melancholy evenings he read familiar verses, from Wordsworth, from Gray's "Elegy in a Country Churchyard"; he recited limericks. He longed, he said, for "some far-away improbable tale that does not seem to be of this world at all. . . . In short I want to run away. . . . It is selfish; it is puerile; it is, I trust, short-lived; but [the wish] is often my master these barren days."[13]

Remembering Ellen and the artist she had always aimed to be, he visited Washington's Corcoran Gallery, where he purchased (for the then-considerable sum of $500) a portrait of a young woman in a blue mandarin coat, a charming figure that must have reminded him of his wife in early youth. It was the work of a woman artist, Mary Brandish Titcomb.[14] The painting remained a treasured possession and would hang through his own last days in the room where he slept.

The big house at Cornish, rented once more, had stood empty through the summer. But in September Wilson made the journey to New Hampshire, to settle his sister Annie and her children for a visit. A few weeks later he returned, bringing his "cousins," Lucy and Mary Smith. House came up to stay with him, touched by the fact that he was given the room that had been Ellen's the summer before. The two men talked of the past, the widower finding himself almost for the first time able to speak of the lost one; and they let their minds wander freely over the landscape of the present. But for Wilson it was a heartbreaking return to the place where but a summer ago Ellen had found so much to delight her. He found what comfort he could in the thought that his bereavement caused him to be the more thoughtful of others. "It pays to be wiped out oneself, if only to be forced into another world of sympathy," he wrote in a sad mood. And again: "I do not see the light yet; but it is not necessary for me to see it: I know that it shines, and I know *where* it shines. . . . All that I need do now is to go straight ahead with the near duty, and lean on that to be steadied: for it comes from where the light does."[15]

In November he told House that he was broken in spirit; he was not fit to be President because "he did not think straight any longer and had no heart for the things he was doing." Ten days after this diary entry, House described a strange scene of the President and himself walking through the streets of New York at night, moving across Seventh Avenue to Broadway, going down to Herald Square and over to Fifth Avenue. There the two men, being recognized and followed by a growing crowd, ducked into the Waldorf-Astoria Hotel. By a subterfuge they escaped through a rear door. Finally they boarded a bus and rode back to House's apartment.

In the late hours of that night the President said that as they went about the city he had wished someone would kill him. He no longer wanted to live, but he knew perfectly well that unless somebody killed him he would go on to the end, "doing the best he could."[16]

As autumn passed, life in the White House became increasingly dreary, its only diversions being the interminable automobile rides, with the President sitting silent, wrapped in his own thoughts, and visits to the golf course where he played almost mechanically. Outside visitors, rare even in the best of times, were no longer invited to lunch or dinner. In vain members of the family—daughters, cousins, his sister Annie and her "Little A"—sought to divert him. Courteous and punctilious as always, he bore nevertheless a pall of grief. Helen Bones, staying on as mistress of the White House, was in despair and fell ill. Indeed in the winter of 1914–15 everyone, including Grayson, came down with severe colds; but to the President even this numbing of his deeper feelings was denied. "Why he doesn't succumb, I don't see," wrote Helen Bones. "No matter how he suffers," she added in the same letter, "he does not make others suffer with him"—a fact, however, not diminishing the gloom: "for he can't help their grieving with him."[17]

He poured out his feelings frequently at this time to Nancy Saunders Toy, a longtime friend, wife of a Harvard professor; and his correspondence with Mary Hulbert took a pathetic turn. Divorced, now living in Boston, she was in poor health and in the midst of financial difficulties. Wilson wanted to be the friend she desperately needed, while in her mind Ellen's death had opened the prospect not only of the continuance of close ties but undoubtedly of a future marriage. Her letters of this period do not survive, but from Wilson's side of the correspondence we catch the tone of her wretchedness and of her forlorn hopes.

Mrs. Hulbert's unstable son Allen, a constant preoccupation and an increasing burden, had fallen into some sort of grave illness, and a short while later had lost much of what remained of her small fortune in speculative financial schemes. Wilson turned from his own misery to be sympathetic and solicitous. He asked Mrs. Toy, who was living in nearby Cambridge, to invite her for tea, extolling her "extraordinary taste and knowledge" in matters of furnishings and interior decoration. "You see what I am driving at," he added.[18] In the same vein he wrote to his acquaintance of Princeton days, the architect Ralph Adams Cram, asking whether he could not put her talents to use. No suggestions of employment developing, Wilson encouraged her to write an article drawing on her culinary skills. A manuscript of hers was typed in the White House, edited by Wilson, and sent with his endorsement to the editor of the *Ladies' Home Journal*.

These efforts must have provided cold comfort to Mrs. Hulbert, who looked for more than testimonials and letters of recommendation. Wilson's own feelings toward her are indicated, with unusual candor, in a letter to Mrs. Toy. "She has had a hard life," he wrote of her, which "compelled her to be (or to play at being until she all but became) a woman of the world, so that her surface hardened and became artificial."[19] This was a far cry from the child of nature, beautiful and bountiful, by whom Wilson had been enchanted in Bermuda. The end of Mary Hulbert's troubles and humiliations was still far from having been reached, however.

Thanksgiving, 1914, Wilson spent with Jessie and Francis Sayre at their home in Williamstown, and as the sad year drew to a close the family gathered for Christmas at the White House. The President hung his stocking by the chimney, and the wife of the Secretary of the Navy baked a cake for him. When Mrs. Toy visited the mansion a few days later she found him looking better physically than she had ever seen him, but "the old buoyancy" was gone. Margaret was acting as official hostess (a role suiting neither her tastes nor her talents); the Sayres were staying over until the expected birth of their first child. On January 17 the baby arrived—a boy, following a long succession of Wilson girls, the "young prince" of whom Dr. Joseph Wilson had dreamed long before. The President experienced a rare moment of joy. "None of us can think straight," he confided to Mrs. Hulbert. "I forget where the keys of the typewriter are as I absent-mindedly try to write this."[20]

Autumn 1914 had brought the midterm elections. Wilson had no heart for campaigning, and he felt, besides, that the war compelled him to remain in Washington. His major act was a long letter addressed to Underwood, chairman of the Ways and Means Committee of the House, setting forth, for campaign purposes, a record of the administration's achievements. His argument went over familiar ground, stressing tariff reform, banking and antitrust laws, and arguing that the effect of these measures had been to set business free.[21] The President revealed himself as one who considered his reform program completed. In the letter to Underwood and in a similar communication to McAdoo he wrote almost like a defeated man—a man defeated by his own success.

These manifestos followed similar Presidential efforts to appease the business and banking community. The nagging economic recession beginning in 1913 had deepened with the outbreak of war. The disruption of trade and shipping brought serious unemployment. Through the summer of 1914 leading bankers became regular visitors to the White House. The most conspicuous sign of Wilson's determination to calm business fears, even at the risk of alienating his liberal constituency, was his putting representatives of financial interests in control of the newly established Federal Reserve Board.

Wilson's apparent belief that progressivism had been fulfilled by enactment of the New Freedom legislation shocked many of his supporters, and was at odds with his deeper convictions. To establish conditions for full and fair competition was part of the Wilsonian program; but another dimension, an underlying theme in the 1912 campaign speeches and in the First Inaugural, consisted of the promise of social justice. Had the President forgotten his assurance that human rights were above property rights, that in the rush to be great America had neglected the poor and downtrodden? "How can a man of [Wilson's] shrewd and masculine intelligence," asked Herbert Croly of the New Republic, "possibly delude himself into making the extravagant claims which he makes on behalf of the Democratic legislative achievement?"[22] It is probable that Wilson would not have written his letter to Underwood had he not been in a time of depression. The Wilson of 1916 would be a different man, and a whole new series of reforms, affecting labor, farmers, and other deprived groups, would constitute a second New Freedom.

The 1914 elections were a setback and a disappointment, sharply reducing the Democratic majority in the House. The economic recession was seen as having been a major cause, along with the fact that, with the dissolution of the Progressive party, most Republicans had returned to their own fold. Yet Wilson took the defeat as another straw upon his load of sorrow. It hardly seemed worthwhile, he told Colonel House, to have worked so hard over the past two hears when the citizens seemed to care so little.[23]

The coming of the New year saw a different mood beginning to assert itself. The negativism of Wilson's autumnal broodings was not transformed at a stroke to new and vigorous policies, but at least it gave way to a rising spirit of combativeness. On January 7 he set out for the Midwest to make an address marking the traditional Democratic celebration of Andrew Jackson's victory at New Orleans. Along the way he made several of the rear-platform appearances he professed so heartily to dislike. He had not made a speech for so long, he told one of the crowds, that he feared he had forgotten how. He had been confined for a couple of years at hard labor but was out on parole for a day or two. It was plain the President was enjoying his freedom, and when he delivered his principal address at Indianapolis he spoke extemporaneously, in his best campaign form, letting the blows fall with the skill of a practiced politician.

"The trouble with the Republican party," he said, "is that it has not had a new idea for thirty years. . . . The Republican party is still a covert and a refuge for those who are afraid, for those who want to consult their grandfathers about everything." The indictment was hardly fair to Theodore Roosevelt and his administration, many of whose ideas Wilson had appropriated, but the crowd liked it and cheered lustily. Nor did Wilson's own party escape unscathed.

The Democrats, said the President, were still on trial. "The only party that is serviceable to a nation is a party that can hold absolutely together and march with the discipline and with the zest of a conquering host." Wilson, having at that time troubles with the Democrats in Congress over the so-called ship-purchase bill, threw down the gauntlet to the dissidents: "If any group of men should dare to break the solidarity of the Democratic team for any purpose or from any motive, theirs will be a most unenviable notoriety."[24]

The speech caused a good deal of head-shaking, among Democrats as well as Republicans. Mrs. Toy was shocked that he had so far fallen from his usual dignity as to refer to himself in public as "Woodie." Others were struck by the vehement departure from levels of wartime statesmanship. But anyone knowing the dark days through which the President had passed could take heart from this unexpected outburst. An aggressive stance is often a stage in recuperating from grief, and Wilson was emerging, painfully, from the shadows.

In this way, too, must be explained Wilson's extreme bellicosity, extending beyond his Indianapolis challenge, in pushing the ship-purchase bill. German ships, caught in American ports at the outbreak of war, had been fearful of risking capture on the high seas. The ship-purchase bill set up a government-financed corporation to purchase these vessels and make them available for American trade. The President had been acutely aware of the deterioration of the U. S. Merchant Marine, pointing out, even before the start of hostilities, that of all merchant ships upon the seas, only six sailed under the American flag. By 1915, with the loss of belligerent ships to submarine attacks, with others refuged in U. S. ports, and with neutral shipping declining sharply, the situation was felt by Wilson to have become critical. Tonnage was not adequate to carry American export goods; supplies were piling up, wasting or rotting on the wharves. A means of rendering impartial service to the belligerents (as well as of gaining legitimate profits) had been virtually cut off.

A shipbuilding program was one answer to the problem. Wilson, always involved and active where ships and the sea were concerned, supported an emergency program for the construction of wooden, rather than steel, hulls; he proposed a return to vessels powered by sail— perhaps the same kind of sails he had drawn so meticulously as a teen-ager. Meanwhile the ship-purchase bill seemed to him a practicable, interim measure. The program, however, was anathema to conservatives in the Congress, to the lords of the shipbuilding industry, and to the wider business community which decried this proposed government in-trusion into the private sector. To such interests were added the fears of many impartial observers, seeing the use of ships formerly owned by belligerent powers as leading to incidents on the high seas, possibly dragging the United States into the war.

The British were hardly less vigorous in opposition to the bill than Wilson's domestic opponents. They had first feared that German ships sold to private individuals would make available to the enemy such noncontraband goods as cotton. Somewhat relieved by the fact that the ships would be under the control of the U. S. government, they never-theless were acutely disquieted by possible consequences. Would Wilson use the ships only for Latin American commerce, or would they enter European ports? Would not the enemy receive disproportionate financial rewards? Wilson brushed aside these questions (along with Bryan's pleas that he accept a clarifying amendment) and headed toward a major crisis with Britain.

Whatever the merits of the ship-purchase bill, the President invested on its behalf the full force of his prestige, as well as a degree of irra-tionality and anger against his opponents that had not been evident since Princeton days. "There is a real fight on," he wrote on January 31 to Mrs. Toy. "The Republicans are every day employing the most unscru-pulous methods . . . to destroy this administration." The fight, he con-tinued, was "to save the country from some of the worst influences that ever debauched it." And a week later: "The influences that have so long dominated legislation and administration here are making their last and most desperate stand to regain their control." They would give no quarter and, he wrote, "so far as I am concerned, they will receive none."[25]

On successive days and nights the President went down to the Capitol to exert the pressure of his office. The ship-purchase bill was made a party measure binding on all Democrats. Senator Lodge led the Republican opposition in a personal contest that in its bitterness on both sides prefigured the League fight, and seven Democrats joined the opposition. The "unenviable notoriety" that in his Indianapolis speech the President had promised for members of his own party who defected he was now ready to spell out. His words were as brutally harsh as he had ever penned. "Irremediable damage," he said in a statement prepared on March 4, had been done by the "unnatural and unprecedented alliance" formed in opposition to the ship-purchase bill. Yet he would call no extra session to attempt a remedy: "Their opportunity to rectify their grievous disloyalty has passed."[26]

Wilson's disposition to see a conspiracy in the forces opposing him; his insistence upon uncompromising adherence to his views; his readiness to push ahead at the risk of dividing his party, of provoking a violent controversy with the British government, even of jeopardizing the upcoming Presidential elections: such postures were uncharacteristic of his middle years. The Princeton community had had a taste of these qualities; the world would see them displayed in the last fight over the League. But in the time of his strength, of his maturity as a national leader, it was a very different Wilson that made his way with prudence and almost always with magnanimity across the political scene. Even now he would draw back before the final outrage. The statement he had drafted on March 4 was, fortunately, never made public. Instead, closing the congressional session, he used conciliatory words, even praising it as a "great Congress." Coming down on the last day to the President's room in the Capitol he greeted all Democrats in a cordial spirit.[27]

"Spring should be here presently," Wilson wrote on March 7 to Mary Hulbert and Mrs. Toy, in letters rare for being almost identical: spring "with its kind and healing airs. . . . One waits for he does not know what."[28] It was evident that light was being renewed in the man who had passed through the abyss of sorrow and despair. On March 14 he wrote his daughter Jessie that he still could not talk much about Ellen, even in writing: "My heart has somehow been stricken dumb."[29] But the ice floes were breaking up, as his conduct both in public and private would soon reveal. Even after such a winter, a spring would come.

ENTER EDITH BOLLING GALT

On an afternoon in February when the President and Dr. Grayson were on one of their daily motor rides, Grayson waved to an acquaintance as they drove down Connecticut Avenue. "Who is that beautiful lady?"

Grayson recalled the President's asking him. A few weeks later the "beautiful woman," then in walking clothes and wearing muddy shoes, emerged from the White House elevator to find herself face-to-face with the President.[1] She had been assured by her companion, Helen Bones, that no one was at home and her embarrassment was evident. Wilson, on being introduced, asked her to stay for tea, along with Helen Bones and Grayson.

The guest that day was Edith Bolling Galt, a Washington widow who, since the death of her husband, had been living quietly in a red-brick house near Dupont Circle. At forty-two years of age tall and shapely— "somewhat plump by modern American standards,"[2] commented one of the Secret Service detail in his memoir—Mrs. Galt had grey eyes and an abundance of dark hair. She talked in a soft, musical voice, and laughed easily. With an undeniable flair in all she did, she would become the first American First Lady whose stylishness and manners would be widely admired by the public. Her favorite flowers were orchids. Her hats and dresses were in the latest French mode. She drove her own car, a small electric model, proud that she was the first Washington woman to perform such a feat.

Member of a Virginia family tracing its lineage to Pocahontas, the fabled Indian princess who in the seventeenth century had married the Englishman John Rolfe, Mrs. Galt was a southerner through and through, yet rejoiced in being a sophisticated woman of the world. Her father, like so many other southerners of his generation, had found his plantation in ruins and his fortune destroyed at the close of the Civil War. Moving to a family homestead in Wytheville, Virginia, William Bolling became a respected judge. His daughter was reared in straightened circumstances, with scant education, but surrounded by a cultivated and affectionate circle of relatives. In 1896 she married Norman Galt, who with his family owned Washington's most celebrated jewelry and fine silver store.

Through a succession of deaths in the Galt family, and the death in 1908 of her husband, the establishment came into Edith's sole ownership. She kept experienced managers in place, although herself remaining remote from day-to-day decisions. Under her proprietorship the store became the source of a comfortable living for herself and for other surviving members of the Galt family.

It happened that in 1914–15 Dr. Grayson was courting a younger friend of Mrs. Galt's, Alice Gertrude Gordon. Altrude, as the latter was generally known, was also a Virginian. She and Edith had traveled to

Europe together the previous winter and they saw each other often in Washington. Grayson, who had known Mrs. Galt for some years, found her not only pleasant company but a sympathetic supporter in his pursuit of Altrude. It was natural, when he became concerned about Helen Bones's loneliness and isolation in the White House, that he should have thought of Mrs. Galt as a possible companion, particularly because the latter enjoyed taking long walks and because Helen, according to his professional judgment, needed exercise and fresh air. By March Mrs. Galt and Helen were going regularly on afternoon excursions, and it was on returning from one of these that the two of them confronted Woodrow Wilson.*

From the first meeting around the tea table Wilson found himself entranced by Edith Galt's spirited liveliness and her humor; nor would he have failed to note her being a handsome woman. She shared with the President memories of the South, together with a code of behavior derived from tradition and a strong sense of honor.

Helen Bones was encouraged to pursue her friendship with Mrs. Galt, who on March 23 dined at the White House in the company of the President and Grayson. Afterwards Wilson read aloud to the little group. During the next days he found himself joining Helen Bones as she went out for drives with Mrs. Galt (he would sit in the front seat, leaving the two women to chat together in the back), or being with them at teas or at the evening meal in the White House. A mid-April photograph showed Mrs. Galt in the President's box as he threw out the first ball in a game pitting the Washington Senators against the New York Yankees, but newspapermen were not yet ready to catch the significance of her presence.

April 28 stands as a significant date in what was now a blossoming friendship. On that day Wilson wrote a letter to Mrs. Galt, the first in a series he would write daily—and sometimes even more frequently—over the seven months that passed before their marriage the following December. "If it rains this evening," he asked of Mrs. Galt, "would it be any fun for you to come around and have a little reading,—and, if it does *not* rain, are you game for another ride?" In much the same spirit, thirty-two years before, Wilson had penned his first shy note to Ellen Axson, asking whether she would go on a drive with him. Now

---

* It was not, apparently, the first time Mrs. Galt saw the President. She told her biographer, Alden Hatch, that she had met him at a White House reception and had heard him address the Congress.

Mrs. Galt pleaded that she had an appointment with her mother which she could not break. "My dear Mrs. Galt," he had opened his letter to her, and her reply bore the salutation, "My dear Mr. President."[3]

Less than a week later, after dinner on May 4, Wilson took Mrs. Galt onto the south portico of the White House. The moon was bright and the spring airs seasonably warm. Family members drifted discreetly away, and the President, drawing his chair close to Mrs. Galt's, told her that he loved her and wished to marry her. Mrs. Galt was not one to be swept away by the fact that a man even of Wilson's eminence had proposed to her. In her autobiography she tells how she was shocked by what seemed a breach of normal decorum in the President's suggesting marriage after so brief an acquaintance. Nevertheless, on returning home that night, she wrote him proudly: "I am a woman—and the thought that you have *need* of me—is sweet!" Standing by the declination she had made when he declared his love, she wrote, "You have been honest with me, and, perhaps, I was too frank with you."[4]

Wilson was undeterred by Edith's quiet rebuff. "God has indeed been good to me to bring such a creature as you into my life," he wrote her the following day. "Here stands your friend, a longing man, in the midst of a world's affairs—a world that knows nothing of the heart he has shown you and which would as lief break it as not. . . . Will you come to him some time, without reserve and make his strength complete?"[5]

In that hope Wilson carried on a courtship that could not be hidden from the White House staff. Helen Bones acted as chief intermediary in the intrigue. Every day the President sent flowers to the house on Dupont Circle. Letters, sometimes several a day, were posted by Helen in public mailboxes, and the chief usher, "Ike" Hoover, made sure that messages in Mrs. Galt's firm hand were carried directly to the President. On her side, Mrs. Galt found an unexpected ally in her lawyer and business adviser, a white-haired, avuncular figure who also had the name of Wilson. "Child, I don't know why," he told Edith as early as May 11, "but I feel you are destined to hold in this woman's hand a great power—perhaps the weal or woe of a country."[6]

In mid-May Wilson sailed on the Presidential yacht *Mayflower* to New York. If among Presidential perquisites there was one he particularly enjoyed, it was the use of this yacht. He had always loved ships and the sea, and now his pleasure was increased by having Edith on board among the official party. It was the first time the two had an opportunity to be together for more than evening hours or the length of an automobile ride, and the occasion seemed made for their enjoyment. As they sailed northward a severe storm sent everyone scurrying below—even Dr. Grayson, that experienced tar. But the President and Mrs. Galt seemed impervious to the disturbance.

For two days Wilson basked in popular acclaim, as he reviewed a parade standing in front of the New York Public Library, or, with Josephus Daniels and the young Franklin D. Roosevelt at his side, received an eight-hundred-gun salute as the U. S. fleet sailed down the Hudson and then out to sea for maneuvers. On the way home the *Mayflower* stopped at Washington's birthplace and at Lee's former home, both along the Potomac. If Woodrow Wilson ever counted up the truly happy days in his life, these few must certainly have been among them.

It is not possible fully to understand Wilson without taking account of the letters he wrote to Mrs. Galt during this period. The passion, the imagination, the overwhelming aspiration they reveal were part of the statesman as well as part of the man, though in the public figure emotional displays were rigorously masked. The profound feelings released by Ellen Wilson's still-recent death merged with the coming of a new love, and all was colored by the suppressed but powerful apprehension of the tragedy of war. At Princeton his season of most pervasive inner turmoil and outward change had come about through the combination of rising political ambitions and the affair with Mary Hulbert Peck. In much the same way, but on a larger stage, Wilson was again giving his private emotions a free rein, while reaching toward the mantle of world leadership he would presently assume. His praise of the beloved was in part drawn from the southern heritage they both shared, but it was part, too, of the romantic tradition of the Celt, seeing the world veiled in mysterious and sun-pierced mists.

"You are so vivid. . . . You are so beautiful!" Wilson wrote to her. "I have learned what you are and my heart is wholly enthralled. You are my ideal companion. . . . You are my perfect *playmate*, with whom everything that is gay and mirthful and imaginative in me is at its best." Again: "How deep I have drunk of the sweet fountains of love that are in you . . . how full of life and every sweet perfection! . . . The old shadows are gone, the old loneliness banished, the new joy let in like a great healing light. I feel, when I think of the wonderful happiness that your love has brought me, a new faith in everything that is fine and full of hope."[7]

The course of their love had its ups and its occasional downs. There were days of unaccountable silence on the part of Mrs. Galt, driving the

President to distraction. Helen Bones—"that sweet ally of ours"—was called upon to speed messages of conciliation after Wilson and Mrs. Galt on one occasion came to some sharp disagreement sitting alone in the curtained backseat of their automobile. It would be easy to deduce that the President made advances which she repulsed. A careful reading of the letters seems to suggest something far more serious, that she attempted to lay down conditions as to the nature of their future relationship. Edith Galt's first marriage had not been a happy one and as a widow she had obviously been sexually repressed. The drift of Wilson's letters to her is a delicate and sensitive effort to free her from her constraints and to make her capable of the fullness of love. In much the same way, as a young man, he had wooed Ellen Axson, not only to win her for himself but to liberate her from a professed coldness toward the opposite sex.

So on the morning following the episode in the car, Wilson wrote, after "an almost sleepless night of agonizing doubts and fears," "For God's sake try to find out whether you really love me or not."[8] Edith, in a note crossing his, wrote: "I know . . . that I am asking something that is childish and impossible. But, try as hard as I can, *now* it seems the only way. If this can be changed it will be because you are master of my heart and life . . . but *you* must conquer!"[9] The incident closes with Wilson's writing to her: "*I* have been blind as well as you. I have *said* that love was supreme and have feared that it was not!"[10] It seems clear that Edith Galt, whatever her views at this time about marriage, had views about the sexual relationship—what she called "this *more* than painful subject"[11]—at odds with Wilson's passionate nature. That he should indeed have conquered her, that he should have led her to a full realization of her womanhood, gives depth to their romance and justifies what must otherwise seem the excessively ardent tone of his correspondence.

In the midst of all this Mary Hulbert turned up for a visit. The President had urged that she come, goaded by the same imprudent but chivalrous spirit that had once urged West to remain at Princeton. It could hardly have been a less opportune time, but Mrs. Hulbert had her own reasons: she wanted to press upon the President her need for a loan. Helen Bones met Mary Hulbert at the railway station in the early morning and then went riding with her. After hearing the President make a Memorial Day address at Arlington she was hustled off on the four o'clock train to New York.

There had been time, nevertheless, for the housekeeper, Mrs. Jaffray, to escort Mrs. Hulbert through the White House, on a private tour marked by embarrassing allusions by Mrs. Jaffray to the fact that she might become mistress of what she surveyed.[12] There must have been time, also, for Mrs. Hulbert to speak of her need for financial help. She was then preparing to leave for California to join her son Allen, whose business affairs were, as usual, in a highly precarious state.

Mary Hulbert, recalling the hectic White House visit, had the good grace to refer to the "tonic of that one day of happiness."[13] Others must have viewed it in a different light.

As the friend of Helen Bones and of Margaret Wilson, Mrs. Galt was invited that summer to the Presidential retreat in Cornish. On the way north she stopped off to be shown about Princeton. Wilson, following a few days later, stopped to have a long talk with House, then visiting his son-in-law, Gordon Auchincloss, on Long Island. House had certainly caught the drift of what was going on, but he feigned surprise on hearing news of Mrs. Galt from the President himself. Asked for his advice on a possible marriage, he urged gently that it be postponed.

At Cornish the days were long and blessedly quiet. The family went on walks and picnics, or in rainy weather read aloud; the President and Mrs. Galt sat alone on the porch as the President disposed of affairs of state, or in the evenings, when the others had retired, remained with her before the fire. After one such evening the President received a note in her familiar hand. "I promise," Edith wrote, "with all my heart absolutely to trust and accept my loved Lord, and unite my life with his without doubts or misgiving."[14] The depths in Edith had, as Wilson foresaw, been stirred. She found herself capable of receiving love. The two were now secretly engaged.

The President returned to Washington in mid-August, earlier than he had planned. Recalling that he had been in White Sulphur Springs when the Tampico affair exploded, he felt the need to be on the bridge as difficult decisions waited to be made with respect to German actions at sea. Now, along with the daily letters, there were sent to Edith packets of state papers, on which he had usually written marginal notes and which he expected her to read and comment on. Their marriage, when it came, was to be one that found them working together; and she was being prepared for responsibilities that neither of them could foresee in that fortunate and happy summer.

Edith left Cornish a week later to motor at a leisurely pace through the Finger Lakes region of New York, visiting friends, and then shopped in New York City. When she arrived in Washington in September everyone seemed to suspect that a wedding was at hand.

*   *   *

One dramatic and near-fatal incident still waited to be played out. House had hinted his concern over Wilson's remarriage when the two men met on Long Island that June. Others in the White House entourage also feared that the public would look less than sympathetically on a man who had fallen in love less than a year after his wife's death. The Presidential elections of 1916 were approaching and the affair's adverse political consequences weighed heavily on those who had their own fortunes, no less than those of the President, at heart.

Josephus Daniels, the President's oldest friend within the cabinet, was delegated to raise the issue and to urge a postponement of any marriage plans until after the elections. But Daniels had no taste for the assignment. To perform as "Minister Plenipotentiary and Envoy Extraordinary to the Court of Cupid," upon an errand in which neither his head nor his heart was enlisted, and in the course of which he might well suffer official decapitation, tempted him not at all.[15] The task then fell to McAdoo, who as an aspirant to the Presidency in some later election had a particular interest in not seeing Wilson and the Democratic Party go down to defeat.

The problem was complicated by what Grayson, in a highly confidential message to House, referred to as "that California situation." It was by then known among Wilson's intimates that he had sent to Mrs. Hulbert just before her move to California a check for $7,500 as a loan against two mortgages. The money was to enable her to purchase property near Los Angeles where her son was to embark on one last business venture, an avocado ranch. Apparently in a panic, McAdoo took it upon himself to cause a complete break between the President and Mrs. Hulbert. He concocted a story to the effect that information had been received indicating that Mrs. Hulbert was planning to sell some incriminating letters of the President's, revealing a past affair between them. Callously, McAdoo related this to his father-in-law.[16]

Confronted by the cruel hoax, Wilson sat down and in handwriting showing a highly agitated state, told Edith Galt on September 18 that there was a personal matter about which he wanted to see her at once. He asked that he be permitted to come to her house instead of her coming, as had been the case up to then, to the Executive Mansion. "I love you with the full, pure passion of my whole heart," he concluded, "and *because* I love you beg this supreme favour."

"Of course you can come to me," Edith answered, "but what is the matter?" She asked of her fiancé that Grayson accompany him, trusting him to withdraw discreetly so that they could talk.[17] In these circumstances Wilson for the first time crossed the threshold of the house where so much of his thought had centered over past months.

What happened afterwards is indicated by a letter Wilson wrote early the next morning. Evidently he told Edith the whole story of his relationship with Mrs. Hulbert, as well as of the threat of a scandal. In dismay, and after some hesitation, she agreed to continue the engagement. He had come to her, he wrote, under the burden of "a folly long ago loathed and repented of"; he had stood before her "stained and unworthy." Edith, in a letter that crossed his, repeated her assurance of the night before: "I will stand by you—not for duty, not for pity . . . but for love."[18] The incident shows the two at their best, and puts Wilson—abject, humbled, but not willing to surrender to blackmail— in a touchingly human light.

Mary Hulbert had no intention of blackmail, but she was a woman who felt she had been grievously let down. Two days before the formal announcement of his engagement to Edith, Wilson wrote Mary: "I want you to [be] one of the first to know of the good fortune that has come to me." "The cold peace of utter renunciation is about me," Mary replied. She complained of his not having informed her sooner, but added "I need not tell you again that you have been the greatest, most ennobling influence in my life. You helped me to keep my soul alive."[19]

A check of undetermined amount was sent to her in Helen Bones's name, apparently a sort of consolation gift. But that was not the end of the matter. Six weeks afterwards a highly disturbing letter arrived, showing Mary Hulbert at the end of her tether. The avocado ranch on which she and her son's hopes had been pinned was being put up for sale. "We have $1800.00 left to live on," she wrote. "If we fail [to sell the land], it is the end. And I am going out in *some way* if it does."[20]

The salutation on the letter was "Dear Woodrow." "I want to call you that hereafter," she stated. "And I wish that you would address me as Mary." Never in all their known correspondence had they used their actual names; it had always been "Dear," or "Dearest," or "Friend"— the vagueness and ambiguity suiting the changing status of their relationship. Now they were a man and a woman face to face, unmasked; and Mary could state baldly that she was asking Woodrow to give the help necessary to her survival—and to give it without delay. At the White House Wilson received a business representative of Mary's, Horace H. Clark; and a secretary of McAdoo's, at the President's expense, was sent out to California to check on the Hulbert affairs.

*   *   *

At summer's end the President's immediate family was made privy to the engagement. By then surprise could no longer be feigned, and even those who had been closest to Ellen accepted the situation stoically, with pleasure in Woodrow's obvious joy. Colonel Edward Thomas Brown and his wife—he Ellen's first cousin, the son of the straight-backed Aunt Louisa—had been spending much time at the White House since Ellen's death. Their reaction seems to have been mainly one of relief that the long period of mourning and depression was over. Ellen's brother, "dear old Stock," took the news just as they supposed he would: "sensibly and understandingly." "Isn't she a *vivid* person?" Axson wrote. "He *might* have chosen wrong. Thank God the choice is what it is."[21]

With the engagement publicly announced on October 8, the two months before the wedding found the President engaged with the writing of an unusually long annual message to Congress and an important speech on preparedness; yet he was absorbed throughout in a newfound happiness. He charmed Mrs. Galt's mother, Sallie White Bolling, and members of her family; he filled the long-silent White House with his own friends and relatives as he introduced the bride-to-be. He was free at last to visit at will the house on Twentieth Street where she lived. Edmund Starling of the Secret Service accompanied him regularly as he went there, usually on foot, and would await the President's return to the Executive Mansion.

A pleasant passage in Starling's memoir pictures Wilson's high spirits as he made his way late at night through the darkened and all-but-deserted town. "We walked briskly," Starling recalled, "and the President danced off the curbs and up them when we crossed streets. If we had to wait for traffic—delivery trucks were about all we found abroad at that hour—he jigged a few steps, whistling." The tune he most often whistled was one he had heard at the vaudeville: "Oh, you beautiful doll! You great big beautiful doll!"[22]

A few days after the announcement the President took Mrs. Galt and her mother to New York, the main purpose being to introduce the future bride to Colonel House. Wilson stayed at House's apartment on Fifty-third Street, the two women at the St. Regis Hotel. Before dinner with the Colonel, Mrs. Galt selected a diamond engagement ring from among thirteen—Wilson always considered thirteen his lucky number—that a leading New York jeweler had submitted; and then the party went to a Broadway comedy with the not very promising title of *Grumpy*. The next day the couple traveled to Philadelphia to open the World Series, and on to Baltimore where a stop was made to see the President's brother.

Throughout the journey Wilson and Mrs. Galt were cheered by crowds that let their delight at seeing the engaged couple—and seeing a bride-to-be so handsome as Mrs. Galt—overcome whatever doubts the President's advisers had feared.

The wedding, on December 18, was held at Edith's house, in the parlor fronting on Twentieth Street. "Ike" Hoover had arranged the floral decorations, as well as the buffet served after the ceremony for the three-score guests made up almost wholly of members of the Wilson and Galt families. House had been invited but found himself too busy in New York to attend (or was it that he found it too painful?); Madge was again absent because of illness.

Afterwards the Wilsons escaped reporters, shunning the Union Station and motoring incognito to board the train at Alexandria. At Hot Springs they enjoyed a rare two weeks of privacy. The White House saw the Wilson families gathered for the traditional ceremonies at Christmas, bereft of their chief; Wilson's fifty-ninth birthday passed; the new year came quietly in. The honeymooners, as Wilson wrote, did not do "anything that needs to be described." There was little to do at Hot Springs anyway, he added, "but walk and ride and play golf and loaf and spice it all with a little work."[23] Affectionate and grateful letters to family and friends carried postscripts in Edith's hand.

House was then making preparations for getting off on his third mission to Europe, hoping to turn up possibilities for peace, and Wilson sent messages of farewell and the assurance that his friend needed no specific instructions, so closely did their minds work in harmony. The Secretary of State transmitted his usual portion of diplomatic business. At sea the Germans continued their attacks on merchant shipping. When the British steamship *Persia* was torpedoed, with two American lives lost, Wilson cut short his stay in Hot Springs and returned to Washington on January 4.

CHAPTER SEVEN

Diplomatist

———◆———

DIPLOMACY OF NEUTRALITY

The year and a half that saw Wilson facing changes in his private life —the death of his wife, his courtship and remarriage—also found him coping with new problems posed by the European conflict. The private man met private crises; but through this same period, though often absorbed and distracted, he was still the President. It is difficult to realize that Wilson's courtship of Mrs. Galt was intertwined with so major an international predicament as that caused by the sinking of the *Lusitania*, or the domestic storm raised by Bryan's resignation. But in fact these and several other far-reaching events were unfolding simultaneously.

The paramount task of the United States was, as Wilson saw it, to preserve its full neutrality—which meant preserving the rights long accorded to neutrals by international law. The upholding of these rights Wilson sometimes stated in vague and emotional terms; but the essential purpose of neutrality was clear, and was founded on a close study of Jefferson's policy and of Madison's unsuccessful effort to avoid war in 1812.

From the beginning Wilson recognized that the struggle for neutral rights, besides being difficult to make meaningful to a broad public, was bound to be of an uncertain outcome. Yet for several reasons he persisted in this priority. He knew the importance of international law, even while knowing it to be a frail growth; he believed that only to the extent that it was successfully defended could a durable peace be achieved after the fighting. Moreover he never lost hope of himself playing a role as mediator among the warring powers. For this it was essential that some great nation remain genuinely apart, one of the "cool spaces" where peacetime standards were sustained.

The nature of the Great War brought the threat to neutrality almost equally from both groups of belligerents. Despite the general perception that Germany had caused the outbreak, and despite its many reported atrocities, the danger to American interests was not by any means so one-sided as in World War II. Indeed of the two principal belligerents, Britain as a sea power was the more likely to infringe upon the country's rights. Britain not only claimed a wide freedom of action but, as it fought with increasing desperation, bitterly resented any interference, even when international standards of maritime warfare were being demonstrably breached. Germany was, by contrast, a land power. Its offenses against the rules of land warfare, however shocking on moral grounds, left direct U. S. interests unimpaired, besides leaving Washington powerless to oppose them.

The basic nature of the war—the underlying contrast between navalism and militarism—was clear at the start; but it was radically altered by Germany's growing use of the submarine to hunt down and destroy merchant shipping. As a result of this development the United States increasingly found itself in direct confrontation with German policy, not as something to be merely denounced or protested against, but to be restricted by every peaceful means at the President's disposal. Caught between the two warring camps, Wilson directed his diplomatic offenses now against one, now against the other, trying prudently not to take on both at the same time, and in neither case pushing the U. S. case to its extremes. Much of the time he took account of Britain's plight as a sea power fighting all out against tremendous odds; and most of the time he accepted the submarine as an irreversible factor in modern war. Within these limits he negotiated patiently; he wrote his endless notes; and in certain pivotal cases, at least, he won his point.

In the grim Anglo-German minuet two major moves, occurring early in 1915, made difficult demands on Wilson. The German imperial government declared that, after February 18, waters around Great Britain would be considered a war zone, with all enemy ships found in the area subject to being destroyed on sight without regard for crews or passengers. As a riposte, the British declared a total blockade of the enemy, prohibiting trade with Germany and, as it soon developed, with such neighboring nonbelligerents as Belgium and Holland. Thus in an early phase of the conflict the stage was set for the great maritime drama of the war. Germany was on the way to unrestricted submarine warfare; Britain was on the way to indiscriminate measures against the whole

German population. Both policies were, in the exact sense of the word, frightful. And both deeply involved American rights.

To take the German initiative first: The demarcation of waters adjacent to Great Britain as a war zone not only cut athwart Britain's lifeline but put in jeopardy citizens of neutral countries traveling or working on British ships. Indirectly it imperiled neutral ships as well. Under existing practice it was considered a legitimate *ruse de guerre* for the ships of belligerents to raise the flags of neutral nations when being attacked. A miscalculation by one of the German captains could thus at any time mean the loss of a nonbelligerent ship. A note of protest was immediately dispatched from Washington, with Wilson warning that Germany would be held to "strict accountability" for the results of her policy.[1]

The phrase "strict accountability," though uttered at an early stage in the German-American confrontation, was of potentially momentous implications. No one could precisely appraise its meaning (least of all the President himself); but how it was to be interpreted and applied in particular cases formed the substance of diplomacy over the next two years, and largely determined the ultimate military involvement of the United States. For the moment, however, the effects of Wilson's protest were clouded. The imperial government was slow in putting its new policy into action. In February the days were short, the weather unsuited to aggressive submarine tactics. Also at that time Germany had few U-boats in service, and their captains remained under orders to respect neutral shipping.

Late in March 1915, a test case occurred. The British steamship *Falaba* was sunk off the coast of Africa with the loss of 111 lives. On board was a lone American, Leon Chester Thrasher. His death touched the fundamental issues at stake. The sinking itself demonstrated the incipient horror of Germany's submarine warfare, it being of "a wickedness," stated one U. S. weekly, "such as the history of war will find it difficult to match."[2] In dramatic form the issue of total war appeared in contrast to older conceptions of war between fighting men at sea and in the field. More urgent was the question of an American's right, hitherto deemed inviolate, to travel or work on merchant ships of any nation, belligerent or nonbelligerent.

A debate on this issue opened among Wilson's advisers. The State Department counselor, Robert Lansing, argued in his plain, categorical way that a fork had been reached: the United States had either to challenge Germany's basic policy of submarine warfare or resign itself to accepting the consequences. In effect, it had to hold Germany to "strict accountability" in the case of the *Falaba*—or retreat and do nothing. Bryan spoke for a different point of view. A convinced pacifist, he saw peace at almost any price as the goal. His argument, which was not without the support of reasonable men in the cabinet and elsewhere, was that American citizens traveled on belligerent ships at their own risk. They had no more "right" to be passengers or crew members in a war zone than to move about with impunity where war was being waged on land.

For Wilson, neither of these opposing positions was tenable. He was aware of the fatefully ambiguous position in which he was placed as President. To maintain the rules and restraints of civilized nations was an objective worth pursuing by every means of diplomacy—and in the end, if absolutely necessary, by fighting for the nation's rights. Yet fighting under modern conditions meant abandoning virtually all restraints, and suffering the loss of almost all rights. War as it was being carried out (and had been first exemplified in the American Civil War) omitted the niceties of reason and justice, and obliterated the idea of international law, except as some strong power remained neutral to uphold it. These subtle paradoxes Wilson intuitively apprehended, in a way that Lansing and Bryan did not, with the result that he often stood alone, and that his policies in regard to submarine warfare appeared (and indeed were) often confused.

His response to the sinking of the *Falaba* and to Thrasher's death was cautious. The incident was starkly suggestive, but it did not seem in itself sufficiently grave to invite a stand on fundamental principle. At first he considered a note pointing out calmly the unsuitability of the submarine as a weapon against enemy commerce; but he withdrew even from this position, and, siding for the moment with Bryan, bided his time.

As the days lengthened in the spring of 1915 a number of neutral ships were sunk in the war zone, by chance none of them being American. But in late April a German aerial bomb hit the American merchant ship *Cushing*, and on May 1 the tanker *Gulflight* was torpedoed. These incidents sharpened the issue. Loss of life in both was confined to the death of a captain by heart attack and of two sailors by drowning when they jumped into the sea; but Lansing characterized the events as representing a German naval policy "of wanton and indiscriminate destruction."[3] Wilson waited on the full facts. He took the view, for which there was some good evidence, that the attacks could have been accidental and that, in any case, a settlement of claims could be postponed

DIPLOMACY OF NEUTRALITY   363

to the end of the war. It would take a far more tragic and destructive act to force him to face ultimate principles.

Before Wilson was called to deal with that major crisis, he confronted the British declaration of a blockade of Germany. By many it was considered an act as arbitrary, as contrary to international law, and in the long run as inhumane as Germany's use of the submarine. The declaration of a blockade was legal only if it was capable of enforcement and was total in its effects—conditions which did not prevail at the start of 1915. Britain's order, a major weekly declared, meant merely "the revival of a wholly unregulated right of capture at sea"; it furnished the British with "a plausible excuse for dispensing with an inconvenient group of international regulations."[4] Britain appeared in the worse light when she refused to negotiate on a German offer to retract its war-zone declaration in return for a British concession on the blockade. Under the blockade order, American shipping was subjected to vexatious harassments and the right of United States citizens to trade in noncontrabrand articles was totally denied.

Wilson was inclined to accept the British blockade, as he was inclined not to push principles to their logical extreme. Yet he was coming to a point where he wanted to balance his objections to Germany's course with a protest at least as vigorous to Britain—"for the sake of diplomatic consistency," he told House, as well as to satisfy public clamor.[5] The British, however, were to be spared the dubious pleasure of receiving a Presidential communication, at least until early spring had turned to autumn. For while Wilson was contemplating such a note, the nation's full attention was turned to an unprecedented German outrage.

At 12:30 P.M. on May 2, 1915, the British passenger liner *Lusitania* set sail from New York with 1,257 passengers on board. The previous day the German Embassy had given warning that in going into the war zone the passengers ran grave risks. Only one cancellation occurred. The New York *World* reported that most Americans appeared to treat the warning "as a joke," and the general manager of the Cunard Line declared the ship to be the safest afloat, "since she could easily outrun any submarine."[6]

Five days later, off the Irish coast, in the early afternoon and in beautiful weather, Captain Otto Schwieger of the German submarine U-20 observed (as he reported in his log) a great passenger ship with four smokestacks and two masts. The ship at that moment turned to starboard; the submarine proceeded at high speed to attain a forward position. From a distance of seven hundred meters a torpedo was fired. "An extraordinarily great detonation occurred," the captain noted; "there comes into existence great confusion." On the forward part of the vessel, as she rolled slowly over, the name *Lusitania* appeared in gold letters.

Two hours later the same submarine rose to a depth of eleven meters and the captain took a look around through his periscope. "In the distance there moves about aimlessly a number of lifeboats. Nothing is to be seen any more of the *Lusitania*," he recorded. A second large steamer now appeared and the captain maneuvered into a "very favorable" position for a shot. "The torpedo does not hit," the log concluded dryly, and so that day's work was done.[7]

In Washington that Friday Woodrow Wilson was finishing his lunch when news of the sinking reached him. First reports indicated no loss of life. But at evening from the American consul at Queenstown came a message stating that at least a thousand persons, many of them Americans, had perished. In an uncharacteristically impulsive gesture the President left the White House alone, without even the usual Secret Service guard. Heedless of the light rain that was falling, ignoring the newsboys already scampering through the streets with their "extras" carrying the latest news of the sinking, he walked down Pennsylvania Avenue cloaked in his own thoughts, turned to make a swing through the side streets, and returned to the White House.[8] He closeted himself in his study without having talked to anyone.

Over the weekend Wilson evidently determined to set an example of calm amid the mounting public excitement. He carried out his regular Saturday and Sunday routine of golf, motor rides, and attendance at church. He called no special cabinet session, did not even confer with his Secretary of State. Through Tumulty he issued his one statement: that the President was considering "very earnestly, but very calmly, the right course of action to pursue."[9] On Sunday evening he sat down at his typewriter to compose a note to Germany protesting against the outrage. He also prepared the outline of a speech to be delivered the following day in Philadelphia.

The sinking of the *Lusitania* raised in brutal and inescapable form the question of peace or war. Nations had taken up the sword for offenses far less heinous than this massive drowning of American citizens. In England, Page reported, the freely expressed unofficial opinion was that the United States must declare war or forfeit all European respect. "So far as I know," he added, "this feeling is universal."[10] In America general opinion was highly inflamed. Ex-President Taft wrote Wilson that without doubt he would be heartily supported if he called Congress into special session and declared war.[11] Yet below the surface a different mood still prevailed. Two of his close congressional advisers informed Wilson that the legislature would not support him in such a course.

It was now the President's task to interpret the long-range interest of the United States. Through his period of withdrawal he sought the formula that would enable him to confront Germany with its crime and yet not to alienate fatally a nation still capable, he was convinced, of rational policies.

What was not known at the time was that the very days of the *Lusitania* crisis coincided with a profound period of turbulence in the President's private life. It was only three days before the sinking that he had declared his love to Mrs. Galt and been confronted by her refusal to commit herself. She called on him to prove that love was not dead within her; if he could, she would bid love welcome. Wilson was aroused to his depths. As the international crisis developed, he rose almost recklessly to her challenge. She was with him on a drive Saturday evening; twice on Sunday he wrote her; on Monday before he left for Philadelphia she came to the White House. "I do not know just what I said in Philadelphia . . . because my heart was in such a whirl," he wrote her the next day.[12]

What the President had in fact said startled the world and constituted one of the major errors of his career. The greater part of his speech, delivered before an audience of fifteen thousand of whom nearly a third were newly naturalized, was in praise of the diversity of America. It was by nature a peaceful nation, he went on; and its example to the world must be of a special kind. Then, carried along by powerful rhythms, he fell into one of those traps that await the popular orator. "The example of America must be the example not merely of peace because it will not fight, but of peace because it is the healing and elevating influence of the world, and strife is not. There is such a thing as a man being too proud to fight. There is such a thing as a nation being so right that it does not need to convince others by force that it is right."[13]

Though the speech as a whole was much praised at home—the repetition of the word "peace" in the above sentences echoed the mood of the country—it was greeted abroad, and by many in the United States, with contemptuous sneers. "Too proud to fight"—when a generation was spending its lifeblood in what it deemed a holy cause fought on behalf of humanity!

The next day at a press conference Wilson explained rather lamely that by these words he had not been making reference to any particular policy the country might adopt. "I was expressing a personal attitude, that was all. . . . I did not regard that as a proper occasion to give any intimation of policy on any special matter."[14] Wilson regretted the use of the phrase and afterwards sought to have it removed from a printed version of the speech. Unhappy and misleading though they were, the offending words had been often anticipated in his comments on the war and were close to the heart of his faith. The curious use of the word "proud" sprang from Wilson's southern background and from a southern conception of conduct. Long before, when he was a freshman at Princeton, "Tommy's" mother had warned him in words close to these against becoming hotheadedly involved in a fight.[15] Whatever the extenuations or explanations might be, there was little tendency in the heat of war to search for them, and Wilson's credit with the Allied nations, and among many American citizens, suffered severely by the slip.

On Tuesday, May 11, the cabinet met in its regular weekly session and Wilson read to them his draft of the *Lusitania* note. The document was a calm and even generous appeal to the German government and its people, expressing disbelief that a nation which had hitherto shown concern for justice and humanity could have sanctioned such an act. The German authorities had never explicitly denied the right of civilians to travel in safety on unarmed passenger ships or freighters; the use of the submarine against such ships was incompatible with this right, and none of the "warnings" that had come from Berlin could justify or excuse the inhumane and unlawful act. Washington, therefore, counted on the German government to disavow the action of the submarine commander, and, making all possible reparation, to prevent such deeds in the future. Despite the restrained tone of the note, its basic position was clear: Germany must do nothing less than abandon its submarine war on commerce.[16]

For three hours the cabinet considered the document. Bryan was unhappy. Garrison wanted to face up squarely to the fact that the note could lead to war if Germany did not change its course. But all were in agreement that Wilson was right in not confronting Germany with an ultimatum or with a direct threat of war. Following a State Department review the document underwent some verbal changes and was dispatched to the American ambassador in Berlin for delivery to the German foreign office on May 14.

The clarity of its underlying doctrine, combined with its courteous and conciliatory tone, showed the President at his best. He had reflected the sane heart of the country and his words received almost universal commendation. In his withdrawal, and amid the perturbations of his private life, he had sensed currents below the excited expressions of public opinion; he had managed to express not only policy fit for the occasion but a mood and spirit at work within the large body of the people. His role had not been so much one of leadership, at least as popularly understood, as one of even graver responsibility: that of interpreter of the national will. Wilson in the later phases of his career has been described as a prophet, one who foresees events, often dark and menacing events, that are to come. But his gift in this resilient prime was the kind of prophecy that sees into the depths of the present, discerning the thing that is actually there when others see only bubbles on the surface.

In Germany the note was received with consternation. Its condemnation of submarine attacks on any except vessels of war struck at the heart of German strategy and was publicly deplored, alike by civilian and military leaders of the empire. Yet a profound debate, unknown to American leaders at the time, was stirred by Wilson's words. Naval chiefs refused to brook any curtailment of their rights. Civilians led by Chancellor Theobold von Bethmann-Hollweg were apprehensive of America's entrance into the war; some of them perhaps even sensed how untenable by any previous standards were submarine tactics then in force. The Chancellor expressed himself as ready to exempt large passenger ships from attack and to offer reassurances to vessels proven to be from neutral countries. In these circumstances the reply to the first *Lusitania* note could not be anything but evasive. It was phrased, undoubtedly to mask the underlying disagreements on principle, in highly contentious and abrasive language.[17]

The receipt of the German reply on May 30 caused disappointment in government circles and heated indignation in the press. Wilson consulted his cabinet on an appropriate second note and then sat down to indite on his own typewriter a reply somewhat more severe in tone than the first note, yet in its underlying argument making important concessions to the German position. The draft set off within the Wilson administration an explosion which, unlike the disagreements in Berlin, could not be masked from the world.

The Secretary of State had watched with mounting unease the President's determination to confront Germany on the basic issue of submarine warfare. Bryan argued in favor of restrictions on the right of Americans to travel in the war zone and to sail on enemy ships. He considered the cause of peace to be far more weighty than the assertion of what he perceived as shadowy and unenforceable rights. In advancing his view he was loyal to the President and moderate and discreet in tone. But his unhappiness could not be assuaged. In addition, he felt himself increasingly ignored, even humiliated, as Wilson turned to others in the administration for advice—and especially to the ubiquitous outsider, Colonel House. A break could not in the long run be avoided, and as discussions on the second *Lusitania* note went forward Bryan's determination to resign became firm.

For the Great Commoner it was not an easy step. He had found in high office rewards that his long years of Presidential aspirations had not brought him. He enjoyed its tasks and was far more serious in carrying them out than his detractors had anticipated. He had been loyal to his chief; his services in helping to achieve tariff reform could not be underestimated. Yet he remained wedded to his essential pacifism. Though he could not accuse Wilson of being belligerent or aggressive, he felt steps were being taken that, however innocuous in themselves, would in the end risk war. And so on June 5 in an emotional interview with the President he made his final purpose known.

Wilson braced himself for the public storm which was certain to greet the news. Foreign countries would be tempted to put his policies in question and to discount his prestige. At home he was to suffer almost as much from the contempt for Bryan expressed by those who had long hated and ridiculed him as he did from the peace lobby claiming that its hero had been betrayed. Yet on the whole Wilson knew he was better off for the change forced upon him. Bryan's usefulness as Secretary had been outlived, and the administration was on the verge of establishing new positions vis-à-vis the war.

Wilson approached warily the choice of a successor. It was evident that he was, and in the future would become increasingly, his own Secretary of State. He considered names outside the administration, but he settled without too much difficulty on the State Department counselor, Robert Lansing. An unimpressive man on the surface, a lawyer with a lawyer's mind, Lansing was skilled in the minutiae of diplomacy. No one could write a memorandum more effectively or cite precedents with greater authority. He was unfeeling and he was cold. "A mere routine clerk," Page had described him when he was State Department counselor. "O God, what a crime and what a shame to have this mannikin in that place now! . . . If England were blotted out, the world would be the same to him."[18] But House reassured Wilson that Lansing would "not be troublesome by obtruding or injecting his own views"[19]—an argument that helped turn the scales.

Wilson needed someone like Lansing, objective and unemotional, to counter his own ardors and to correct his occasional factual slips. But Lansing provided more than this. He had a realistic view of international affairs matching one aspect of Wilson's mind—not that which seemed predominant and was expressed in his speeches, but which lay below the rhetoric and made him a more stubborn and tough-minded negotiator than he was often judged. Lansing was convinced that nations would limit force, and would respect humanitarian rights, only insofar as it was in their interest to do so. He saw the world in terms of a precarious equipoise, and in holding steadily to this view he strengthened what was an important subordinate strain within the philosophy of his chief.

Through momentous years of service Lansing would find himself often in basic disagreement with Wilson. He poured forth his self-justifications in private memoranda and diaries, and on at least one occasion he was manifestly insubordinate. Yet in the main, as Wilson put up with his legalisms, Lansing put up with what seemed to him an excessive moralism in U. S. diplomacy. He valued the job, and he was a discreet public servant. Whatever the later phases of their relationship, the two men were in reasonably close accord on the issues immediately before them.

Before the *Lusitania* issue could be settled another critical event occurred at sea. On August 19 the White Star liner *Arabic*, sailing from Liverpool, was torpedoed, with two American citizens among the casualties. The United States threatened a diplomatic break unless Germany repudiated the action. Amid popular clamor in the United States and divisions within the imperial government, Count Johann von Bernstorff, the German ambassador in Washington, saved the situation. In a communication to Lansing on September 1, he quoted a decisive sentence from Germany's second *Lusitania* note, not yet received by U. S. authorities. "Liners will not be sunk by our submarines," it read, "without warning and without safety of the lives of noncombatants, provided that the liners do not try to escape or offer resistance." This settled the case of the *Arabic* with what was considered a triumph for Wilson and his administration.

Negotiations over the *Lusitania* continued. Wilson did not get what his first note had demanded—abandonment of the submarine campaign; a third note settled, inconclusively, for its being carried out under accepted rules of cruiser warfare. (That is, unarmed merchant ships would not be sunk without warning.) Meanwhile, if Germany's position was judged by its deeds rather than by its declarations, the fact had to be recognized that after the *Arabic* no attacks on passenger ships were made through the remainder of 1915. Ultimate issues had not been settled, but the President's firmness, his patience, and his civilized tone seemed to have brought rewards.

While these diplomatic initiatives were being pursued, Wilson felt the need for a more direct peace effort. The only sure way to preserve neutral rights was to bring the war itself to a close. Besides, he was being prodded to new forms of action by a strong peace movement within the country. Liberated from the constraints of office, Bryan was industriously playing upon popular emotions, especially in the Midwest, and was threatening to go to Europe on a mission of his own. Jane Addams, the influential social reformer and exponent of women's rights, did go to Europe, to accumulate (in House's words) "a wonderful lot of misinformation."[20] In December of that year, just as the President was preparing to remarry, Henry Ford embarked upon his "peace ship," a pathetically doomed adventure promising to get "the boys" out of the trenches by Christmas.

As a result of such unauthorized and ill-informed initiatives the United States was in danger of appearing an ignorant meddler in European affairs. The very idea of peace was at the point of being discredited. If anyone was to act in this field it must be the President. But how was he to act? Where was he to find an opening into the maze of passionate convictions and tenaciously held policies of the two camps at war? Wilson meditated on this question and on several occasions talked about it with House, who was beginning to shape a plan of his own.

In the autumn of 1915 House had received two letters from Lord Grey, the British Foreign Secretary, which impressed both him and the President. Grey seemed to indicate that U. S. involvement in plans to establish permanent peace would be welcome. Encouraged and stimulated, House formed a scheme of calling upon the warring powers to open secret discussions for an immediate peace. The fundamentals of a settlement, as he saw them, were clear and simple: a restoration of Belgium, assurance of French security, and establishment of a system for preventing future wars. Should either side refuse these general terms, the United States, according to House's plan, would align itself against the defectors.

Considering the lust of the warring powers for revenge and booty, and the absolute determination of both sides to avoid negotiation while there was hope of victory, House's approach was naïve; and Wilson was incautious, to say the least, in giving it his general approval. House thought he could keep the first stages of the negotiations secret from Germany, and so weight the proposals as to make Germany the side more likely to reject them. Wilson, meanwhile, far from wanting to side actively with the Allies, was determined on enforcing neutrality. His State Department was engaged at that very time in framing a strong reprimand to Britain because of its infringements of maritime law.

It appeared that only by direct conversations in Europe could House advance his proposals. Late in December, while the President was on his honeymoon in Hot Springs, the Texan prepared his departure. Elaborate secrecy surrounded the mission that was to include visits to Britain, France, and Germany. The press was told only that House was to consult with American ambassadors in those countries. Unfortunately the secrecy of the enterprise was only equaled by its vagueness. "I feel that you do not need any [instructions]," the President wrote House. "You exactly echo my own views and purposes."[21] To this broad grant of confidence were added many affectionate good wishes and farewells as the Colonel set sail.

The President's trust in House was more complete than should be expected in any human relationship. As with Hibben at Princeton, Wilson assumed an almost supernatural degree of mutual understanding, when at best two men would be moving in their own way, sometimes for their separate purposes, toward roughly similar ends. As House embarked, numerous points remained unclarified. It was never specified, for example, whether the "force" the United States was to apply on behalf of those who accepted the proposals meant military or moral force, or something between the two. It was not agreed whether to "side" with the Allies meant to enter the war or merely to adopt supportive policies. These were dangerous gaps in understanding. Undoubtedly they would not have been allowed to persist had the President not been so involved in his remarriage.

Matters were made worse by House's inclination to think and to speak as a committed supporter of Britain and France. Like Page (though without Page's unsophisticated enthusiasm) he informed Allied leaders that the United States would not let them go down to defeat. House was less moved by emotion than by his firm grasp of the strategic effects of a German victory. If Germany were to triumph, the United States would stand alone and vulnerable without British sea power as its shield. Wilson shared these views, but he was far from ready at this stage to invite war, or to risk the kind of fierce civil dissension that belligerency would provoke at home. He felt he had no choice but to pursue neutrality, while his spokesman increasingly gave assurances of commitment.

House was busy seeing everyone of influence in London, journalists, diplomats, almost all the members of the Cabinet. He saw the king, and met on several occasions with the dynamic Lloyd George, then Minister of Munitions and within a year to be prime minister. He was on particularly friendly terms with the foreign minister, Lord Grey. In all his talks he pressed his plans for mediation of the conflict by President Wilson. In the hope of softening Wilson's opposition to the blockade, the wily Britons were willing to lead him on. In an expansive mood at at a private dinner on January 14, Lloyd George expressed dreams of a day when the American President would step in to end the conflict, set the terms of peace, and banish militarism forever. It was heady wine, and despite some cautionary remarks by Grey, House left for the continent with high hopes.

He stopped in Paris, where he found the mood of the government hostile to any idea of mediation, and then moved on to Germany. To Chancellor Bethmann-Hollweg and Foreign Minister Gottlieb von Jagow, House presented an unrealistic view of Britain's readiness to accept a settlement making major concessions to the Germans. He did not reveal the substance of his negotiations with the British leaders—the offer of American support in return for mediation on his proposed terms; instead he developed with them a concept of freedom of the seas which the United States and Germany could, for their own separate reasons, unite in upholding. Germany would be rid of fear of strangulation by blockade; the United States would find neutral rights assured. Only the British, dependent for survival on their ability to control international commerce, would be seriously hurt. But this did not seem to disturb House, who was now seeking whatever he could get in the way of good marks from the Germans.

Returning, he stopped for a second time in Paris where he cheered the French leaders with unsupported assurances. "I again told them," he recorded, "that the lower the fortunes of the Allies ebbed, the closer the United States would stand by them."[22] At a final stop in London he brought his negotiations to a head.

A document to be known as the House-Grey Memorandum, signed on February 22, 1916, embodied the understanding of the two men. President Wilson, as the document was originally drawn, "was ready, on hearing from France and England that the moment was opportune, to propose that a conference should be summoned to put an end to the war. Should the Allies accept this proposal, and should Germany refuse it, the United States would enter the war against Germany."[23] Before it was signed Wilson had the word "probably" inserted as a limitation on the American promise to go to war. Even so, the memorandum embodied a dangerous commitment. Worse, as Wilson was to discover later, it was a vague gesture on the part of the Allies, without any real support from the governments in either Paris or London.

House was welcomed by the President on his return to Washington with the document in hand. Both shared the idea that mediation might prove feasible within a short time. It was, of course, a delusion. Anxious to provide a grand opening for Wilsonian diplomacy, House had interpreted British and French conversations in his own way, and had left the President with erroneous impressions of the Allied mood. Over the next months Wilson would proceed on premises largely false. Only gradually and after sharp rebuffs were the illusions redressed by Wilson's own more realistic sense of the international situation.

German questions being temporarily quiescent following the *Lusitania* notes, Wilson took up outstanding issues with Great Britain. During the spring and summer of 1915, Britain's course upon the sea was hardly less disturbing than Germany's. Her tactics were not as wanton and they did not pose the same immediate threat to human life as did submarine warfare. But they were not to be endured without protest by a commercial nation like the United States, jealous of its rights and standing to lose large profits in trade. In the month of May alone four hundred cargoes were seized in British waters. Ships bound for neutral countries along the Atlantic coast, no less than those bound for Germany itself, were subject to seizure.

In addition to these restraints on trade—generally considered illegal because the blockade was unenforceable—mail and parcels were being taken from American ships. On humanitarian grounds the whole policy of trying to "strangle the Hun," which involved the interdiction of food and even hospital supplies destined for the German civilian population, seemed offensive.

Wilson's personal attitude toward the British was complex. It was at least as harsh, and sometimes seemed more harsh, than his attitude toward the Germans. His early admiration for British statesmen, the memory of walking tours in a land from which his grandparents had set forth to a new world, remained to temper these feelings. As an historian he recognized that through crucial decades Britain had been a natural U.S. ally, its fleet providing the protection that allowed the young America to turn safely westward. Yet as an historian, too, he attached to the War of 1812, fought against Britain, a significance second only to that of the Civil War.

Fortuitous circumstances played a part in creating an ambiguous attitude toward Britain. The British ambassador in Washington when Wilson came to office had been Lord Bryce, an old friend whom the President greatly admired. Bryce was replaced by Cecil Spring Rice, a high-strung, nervous man, often in ill health. On an earlier mission Spring Rice had become a firm friend of Roosevelt and Lodge. He now called on them regularly and shared with them the frustrations of his habitually gloomy nature.

Bernstorff was by contrast a genial character, liked by the Washington press corps whom he greeted individually as he walked the streets or drove himself about the city in his big Packard, providing a source of news when almost everyone else in Washington was close-mouthed. Wilson felt he could talk man-to-man with Bernstorff. Just prior to dispatching the first *Lusitania* note he received the ambassador in what the latter reported to Berlin as "an extraordinarily friendly exchange of views."[24] Unlike some other German leaders, Bernstorff was strongly of the conviction that America's entry into the war on the side of the Allies would be catastrophic for his country. On the whole he labored in good faith to keep relations on an even keel.

By a perverse fate, the American ambassador in London contributed to a certain hardening of Wilson's attitude toward the British. Walter Hines Page was nothing if not pro-British. Indeed he was so crassly of this mind, and so often waspish toward the more neutral policies of the administration, that his views were discounted by the State Department and ignored by his old friend in the White House. The traditions of Western culture, and indeed the hope for civilization itself, Page saw bound up with a British victory. He sympathized with the people in their deprivations, grieved for their losses, sided with them in their disappointments. When he died after returning to the United States shortly before the end of the war, the British placed a memorial plaque in Westminister Abbey. It was unveiled by the then-former Foreign Secretary, now Viscount Grey. "To the friend of Britain in her direst need," it read. It was the kind of thing, an historian has written acidly, which "ought not to happen to an ambassador."[25] By 1916 Wilson had reduced his correspondence with Page to expressions of concern for his health, and was often heard to remark that the ambassador should come home and get a good bath in American public opinion.

It was not surprising, all things considered, that when the long-delayed note of protest to Britain was dispatched in October 1915 it should have been couched in terms not likely to warm the British heart. Wilson had left its composition to Lansing, only going over it at the end to make some verbal changes. The Foreign Office found itself to be the recipient of a communication seven thousand words in length, together with a number of additional memoranda and appendices, all written in the cold legalese on which the new Secretary of State prided himself. It did not go unobserved in London that the communication lacked the diplomatic courtesies, to say nothing of the "rather exaggerated compliments," which had flavored notes to Germany tapped out by Wilson on his own typewriter. That the United States could not "with complacence suffer further subordination of its rights and interests,"[26] was the theme and burden of the long document.

The British Foreign Office sensibly delayed its answer—as indeed it delayed during this period all its answers to American protests; Wilson, for his part, was wise enough not to push matters to extremes. Whatever the legal arguments and complaints, it was not conceivable that the United States should go to war with Britain—nor for that matter, that it should become Britain's close and unquestioning ally, an accomplice of its naval policy and, as a minor partner, committed to her dubious war aims.

And so Wilson temporized. The legal questions raised by Lansing he would leave unresolved, and he would reenter the diplomatic field with initiatives more mature and timely than those contrived by House. Meanwhile, he risked wide public misunderstanding. Defense of the country's legal rights was at best a case difficult to make vivid; neutrality remained a negative and unexciting policy in the popular mind. Wilson made no concerted effort to enlighten the people, perhaps fearing the kind of emotion that would draw the country closer to war. The agony suffered by the belligerents he sensed as a deeply humane man, and as a statesman he knew the constraints under which they all labored. And so he chose to protest piecemeal the constant infractions of international law, without being uncompromising in demands for full compliance.

Even more difficult for Wilson to explain to the people were efforts to shorten or mediate the conflict. The extreme sensitivity of the belligerents, their hidden ambitions and their covert fears of peace, compelled an almost conspiratorial secrecy on his part.

The outcome, as the year 1915 drew to a close, was a general sense of letdown and confusion. The country was at peace—but at what price? It seemed condemned to play on the sidelines an ignoble role of self-enrichment and, because of the official policy of neutrality, not even capable of expressing moral fervor. The New York *Herald Tribune* complained of a "bitter consciousness that in a time of world crisis . . . their own country and their own countrymen [had] fled duty, avoided obligations, shrunk from honor." They had chosen "the easy path of prosperity and monetary self-interest." The President, another journal asserted, had accomplished much for the material welfare of the people but had also done "a serious disservice to their national spirit and . . . to the vigorous ideals of democracy."[27]

To find these words spoken of a leader so idealistic as Wilson is unexpected; but he had in fact gotten into a corner from which he would be able to extricate himself only by daring leadership and by actions in the international field more sophisticated than anything yet conceived.

1916: DIPLOMACY PURSUED

Cutting below other public preoccupations as the war progressed was a constant drumbeat of opinion favoring a higher level of military and naval preparedness. On the Eastern Seaboard pressures on the President were particularly heavy, coming both from the press and from congressional spokesmen. Wilson had refused to be stampeded into what he considered warlike measures. "We shall not alter our attitude," he said coolly in his annual message to the Congress in December 1914, "because some amongst us are nervous and excited."[1] But by the summer of 1915 he found himself giving much thought to questions of defense.

During July he sought advice from his Secretaries of War and of the Navy. Along with the Mexican situation, defense was a chief topic of study during the summer weeks in New Hampshire. As Republican criticism mounted, the President was not immune to political considerations; and to these were added his own desire to see the United States sufficiently strong to be taken seriously in the continuing diplomatic negotiations.

By the end of 1915 he was sufficiently sure of his position to open a full-dress discussion of preparedness in an address to the Manhattan Club in New York. The beginning of 1916 saw him carrying his case directly to the people in a series of speeches delivered on a western tour. After stopping in Pittsburgh and Cleveland, he moved on through Illinois into Iowa, Kansas, and Missouri—states that might be thought the least receptive to talk of increased military expenditures.

The decision to go to the people on the issue was unexpected, and was not characteristic of Wilson's Presidency up to that point. He had succeeded in making contact with the mass audience in the 1912 campaign; but once in office he restricted himself to formal addresses to Congress and occasional speeches on ceremonial occasions. At Princeton he had gone out to the alumni on all important issues; as governor, he was in constant touch with his constituency. But as President he remained so aloof as to make himself an enigma. The administration seemed at least as taciturn as Cleveland's; and in the years since that last previous Democrat, Theodore Roosevelt had accustomed the people to a wholly new level of intimacy with their President. Wilson, declared the *New Republic*, was making himself "scrupulously inaccessible." His strength, it said, "consists in his concentration. He is dealing with the Presidency as a self-centered artist deals with an arduous and exhausting piece of work."[2] The results were often commendable, but the price of this isolation was high. In regard to preparedness, and more generally to the attitude of the United States toward the belligerents, it was causing widespread confusion.

Wilson was sensitive to this kind of criticism, extending into *The New York Times* and even to the normally supportive *World*. Moreover he was beginning to feel cut off from the kind of intuitive knowledge of the popular mood on which he relied for guidance. The fact that Edith Wilson would be accompanying him on the tour, hearing the plaudits of the crowds and herself the focus of admiring attention, may have played some part in his decision.

The case for increased defense expenditures was not, for Wilson, an easy one to make. He was far from being a military enthusiast. He had long opposed defense measures and had to explain away his previous position. The danger of fanning volatile popular emotions was on his mind, as was the fact that a stand for preparedness was bound to alienate liberal and progressive opinion. He could admit that times were changing and that as a statesman he must change with them; but even so, troubling questions persisted.

The country must arm—but arm for what? It must be ready to defend itself—but against whom? No threat to U.S. territory was glimpsed, and its national interests, at best poorly understood, did not appear to be directly challenged. Nor could the public be made aware of the large plans for diplomatic intervention forming and reforming in the President's restless mind, plans that would be more likely to be realized if America possessed at least some degree of military strength.

Wilson justified his appeal for arms partly on the grounds that in the disturbed state of the world no one could predict what actions harmful to America one country or another might take; and partly on the need to be in a position to defend the nation's "honor." The word "honor" by itself raised questions. It was a vague concept, not necessarily identical with the basic interests of the people. For Wilson "honor" meant more than chivalrous sentiments or ideals. It was closely tied up with the preservation of historically sanctioned rights. These rights were the rock on which rested the stability of the international order and the integrity of the nation itself. Wilson put his argument in simple terms before the public. "We are relying upon you, Mr. President," he imagined one of his audiences as saying, "to keep us out of this war, but we are relying upon you, Mr. President, to keep the honor of the nation unstained."[3] He seemed to indicate that he could succeed in doing both, but there was the underlying premise that at some point the two objectives might prove incompatible.

The military program was for a reserve, or Continental Army, consisting of half a million men trained in the use of arms and combat techniques, supplementing the National Guard and under direct control of the federal government. Goals for the navy, embodied in the naval appropriations bill of 1916, included a five-year plan of major construction of battle ships, cruisers, destroyers, and submarines. The plan as adopted by the President represented a cutback in Daniels's more ambitious requests; but it bore the mark of Wilson's dedication to a big navy, and, as he fought for it effectively and drove it through the Congress, caused considerable alarm in British governmental circles.

Toward the end of his preparedness tour, indeed, Wilson was so carried away by enthusiasm for the cause as to announce that he favored "incomparably the greatest navy in the world."[4] The remark was plainly a gaffe and it acerbated British suspicions of an Anglo-American naval rivalry. Yet in calmer moments Wilson knew that the naval forces of the United States had been, and in all foreseeable circumstances would continue to be, closely related to the size and mission of the British navy. In a talk that autumn with House he had agreed that the most effective naval policy would be worked out jointly with Britain—"our interests and Britain's [being] so closely allied"[5]—and House had been empowered to pursue the point with the First Lord of the British Admiralty, Arthur James Balfour. The two powers had a common interest in defending the New World, Britain's role in Canada and South America being together hardly less than that of the United States. More broadly there existed in Wilson's mind the possibility that at some future time the two countries acting together might be able to establish a general pacification of the seas. All this was sharply different from the bristling jingoism of his remark about "the greatest navy in the world." Wilson tried rather awkwardly to undo the damage of his oratorical excess, and later insisted that what he had really meant was "incomparably the most adequate navy in the world." In this form the remark went into the official record.

As the President moved westward on his tour the crowds increased; enthusiasm for him and for the cause of preparedness rose perceptibly. By the time he reached Kansas, considered the seedbed of antiwar sentiment, his appearances took on the aspects of a triumphal campaign. He spoke with fervor, directly to the understanding of the plainest citizen. The tour was important not only because it helped establish in the national mind a balance between peace and preparedness, but also because it demonstrated to Democratic politicians what might be expected in the coming Presidential elections of their seemingly reserved and inaccessible leader.

For Wilson personally the tour was a tonic, reestablishing his direct contact with the people and confirming his long-held beliefs about the nature of popular leadership. It foreshadowed the western tour of 1919 when Wilson tried in a last supreme effort to reach the people and to confirm support of the League of Nations.

On his return to Washington Wilson found himself immediately embroiled in fights over preparedness in the Congress, and within his cabinet and party. Garrison, the Secretary of War, was adamant in demanding the Continental Army and was strongly opposed to reliance on the National Guard, subject as it was to control by the separate states. In this he was undeniably correct, as shown by the experience of the United States in all its previous wars. Wilson did not so much differ with his Secretary on substance as on the degree of conciliation which ought to be shown to states' rights devotees in the Congress. The head of the Military Affairs Committee in the House, James Hay, was a Virginian, opposed to federal control, and, incidentally, to such inclusion of blacks as would occur in the Continental Army. Convinced that he could conciliate Hay, Wilson lavished on him what seemed, indeed, an extraordinary amount of deference and consideration.

The Secretary of War was, by contrast, a northerner, and abrupt and impolitic to boot. His manner, hardly less than his views, provoked strong congressional antagonism. To his insistence that he disregard Hay, the President replied: "This is a time when it seems to me patience on the part of all of us is the essence of bringing about a consummation of the purpose we all have in mind."[6] Garrison, however, was in a fighting mood. When Wilson jettisoned the Continental Army plan (at the same time strengthening federal control over an enlarged National

Guard), Garrison abruptly resigned, along with his Assistant Secretary
of War, Henry S. Breckinridge.

This second major defection from his cabinet hurt Wilson and seemed
to many to cast doubt on his leadership. But he knew he was dealing
from a position of strength. He had returned from the West reinforced
by popular acclaim and with his own views clarified. He was prepared
to negotiate with confidence on military preparedness, seeking to create
as wide a consensus as possible in support of a compromise.

Uncertainty about the administration's policy on defense nevertheless
continued. It was not allayed when the President chose for Garrison's
successor Newton D. Baker, small in physical stature, mild in manner,
and given to stating pacifist views. At forty-one, Baker had completed
a highly successful term as mayor of Cleveland; he had given Wilson
effective support at the Baltimore convention of 1912 and was widely
known as a spokesman for progressive causes. An orator comparable
to Wilson in his capacity to sway audiences by the force of convictions
quietly spoken, by the lucidity of arguments shaped extemporaneously,
he was, like Wilson, a southerner (coming from Martinsburg, West
Virginia), and at Johns Hopkins he had passed through the same historical seminar, under the same Herbert Baxter Adams who had once
tried the patience of the man now urging him to join his administration.
Indeed, he had been among those crowding the classroom of Professor
Wilson on his annual visits to the university. To the end of his life Baker
remained a scholar in politics, an omnivorous reader and a classicist,
haunting the Democratic Party with a promise of leadership never quite
fulfilled.

Baker was highly skeptical of his capacity to run the war office (being
skeptical about his abilities was part of his charm, along with a singular
serenity of disposition and purity of character), and only Wilson's determination persuaded him to make a try of it. He would prove himself
an able administrator and would become a major figure in the cabinet.
But the immediate effect of his appointment was a political outcry—
against Baker because he appeared ineffectual, and against the President
because he seemed less than serious about preparedness. Even impartial
observers, in the winter of 1916, could well question whether the country
was ready to undertake strong measures, with Baker in charge of the
army, and with the affable Josephus Daniels in charge of the navy.

Garrison was not the only member of the cabinet to cause trouble at
this juncture. While the preparedness debate was unfolding, Lansing was
pondering on his own a scheme to reduce the chances of America's being

drawn into the war. He saw the submarine as the dominant new element in the conflict; it was causing major military and diplomatic problems, and yet the rules governing its use were vague and unsettled. That legally minded and logical man set himself to devising a formula capable of defining the proper conduct of belligerents in regard to it, while at the same time protecting the rights of neutrals. He found the quest more thorny than he had suspected.

The difficulty with the submarine, in Lansing's mind, was that it was still being viewed as an outlaw on the high seas, dealt with under laws traditionally applied to pirate ships. It was a frail vessel, and under international law it could be sunk by armed merchantmen on sight. The submarine captains were understandably reluctant to risk being fired on while giving warning to merchant ships or permitting the crews to escape.

The likelihood of their being fired on was not an illusion. Merchant ships had long been in the habit of carrying on their sterns small guns capable of warding off illegal marauders. These guns were enlarged in caliber as the war progressed. Increasingly they were manned by trained gunners not averse to opening fire upon any submarine coming into view. These gun crews were perfectly willing, moreover, to destroy by ruse an underwater craft that had given fair warning of intent to search and seize. The situation was hard on the submarine commanders. It was equally hard on the captains of merchant ships, liable to be sunk without warning by a submarine torpedo.

Lansing brooded on these facts and devised what he considered a compromise fair to both belligerents and at the same time likely to save American lives. By the terms of this compromise the British would agree not to arm merchantmen, and the Germans would agree not to sink such unarmed ships without warning. Merchant ships continuing to bear arms would be considered fair game; moreover, being regarded as warships they would not be able to call at neutral ports except briefly for coaling in emergencies. Citizens of neutral countries would travel on them at their own risk.

However reasonable this approach may have appeared to Lansing, he should have known that reason had become a casualty of war. The British saw the proposal as one changing the rules in the middle of the game—and changing them to their disadvantage. They particularly objected to the fact that under the indicated procedures their merchant ships if armed would be considered warships, and therefore prohibited from stopping in neutral ports. The Germans, on the other hand, were delighted: the proposal permitted them to attack armed merchantmen without fear of American protests or reprisals.

Lansing conceived the scheme as one to be adopted voluntarily by both sides, a gentleman's agreement between the belligerents, a *modus vivendi* eliminating for the duration of the war further controversies over submarine tactics. He put it before the President, who accepted it rather hastily in the midst of controversies over national defense. Wilson had been warned a few months earlier that Britain would look with extreme disfavor upon any effort to restrict the arming of merchantmen. But he believed the British had much to gain from the Lansing proposal and was surprised by the bitterness of their reaction.

In Washington Spring Rice interpreted Lansing's scheme as part of a massive anti-British campaign, in keeping with November's harsh diplomatic note. Grey told Page in London that he saw a concerted effort to appease Germany in the hope of getting a favorable settlement of the *Lusitania* claims before the 1916 election. The proposal, he said, was "wholly in favor of the Germans theoretically and practically and wholly against the allies." "He spoke," added Page, "as one speaks of a great calamity."[7] At the same time Grey cabled to the British ambassador his sense of "most painful surprise"; Spring Rice delivered the message to the State Department in a stormy mood. How, he asked the Secretary, would the United States respond if the Germans sank an unarmed merchant ship? It would be a *casus belli*, Lansing replied. The British ambassador sneered in disbelief.[8]

Countering the unexpectedly fierce British reaction was the German government's rather embarrassing enthusiasm for the *modus vivendi*. A *New York Times* editorial, not alone in its disgust, accused the President of "knuckling under to Teutonic demands,"[9] surrendering all that had been gained in the *Lusitania* negotiations. Coming to realize the error he had assented to, Wilson resolved to take charge himself. The controversy was aired at a cabinet meeting on February 15, and that afternoon Lansing announced important concessions to the British point of view. Armed merchantmen would not be treated as ships of war while in American ports; and, when armed solely for defense, American citizens would not be warned against traveling on them. In adopting these concessions, the administration was in effect returning to a previously established position.

The *modus vivendi* fiasco had consequences at home no less unfortunate than abroad. Wilson had lost credit with the Allies; he also put in jeopardy his control of foreign policy. The subtlety of administration policies seems genuinely to have confused congressional leaders. For the sake of affirming nuances, of upholding nice distinctions the essence of which was difficult to grasp, the country seemed constantly on the threshold of war. Outside Congress factional revolts were developing against the general drift of Wilson's foreign policy. Irish and German minorities were making themselves heard. Bryan was working on the sensibilities of the peace party in Congress. A movement to make Champ Clark the Democratic candidate in the 1916 Presidential race was taking shape. Spurred by the administration's muddle on the *modus vivendi*, these various forces coalesced. Wilson met at length with congressional leaders on February 21, but he failed to quell the rising fear that controversies over submarine tactics were putting the country on a course leading dangerously toward war. When it was reported that the President would ask the country to fight to defend the right of Americans to travel on armed merchant ships, something like a panic ensued.

Democrats in Congress mounted as grave an attack on the President's authority to shape foreign policy as an American Chief Executive had ever faced. Resolutions forbidding citizens to travel on armed merchantmen were introduced in the House and Senate; then an immediate audience was demanded. Clearly, Wilson must play his cards very carefully or suffer irreparable damage to his prestige abroad and his capacity to govern effectively at home. "The President has need of all his firmness," said *The New York Times*, "all his power, all his great authority, to circumscribe the men who are plotting against him in and out of the Congress."[10] It was such a crisis as called forth Wilson's qualities as a leader, the dark side of his political genius no less than his innate power to command assent. Refusing to answer at once the Democrats' urgent call for a conference, he bided his time; he waited for an opening to allow him to shape the issue in his own terms. A critical letter from Senator William J. Stone, chairman of the Senate Foreign Relations Committee, gave him his opportunity.

Wilson replied to Stone in a militant letter, and only after it had been dispatched did he consent to meet with the congressional delegation. "You are right," Wilson wrote the senator, "in assuming that I shall do everything in my power to keep the United States out of war." But, he continued, "I cannot assent to any abridgment of the rights of American citizens in any respect. . . . We covet peace, and shall preserve it at any cost but the loss of honour. To forbid our people to exercise their rights . . . would be an implicit, all but an explicit, acquiescence in the violation of the rights of mankind everywhere."[11]

The letter was not that of a diplomatist; it was a blazing manifesto in a national debate, the bold maneuver of a man driven into a corner. Not Lansing but the politically oriented and highly emotional Tumulty had provided the draft on which the President worked with haste. In maintaining his absolute adherence to neutral rights Wilson did less than credit to the flexibility and resourcefulness of his diplomacy; he went beyond the literal facts of the record. But the ploy worked. The congressmen he summoned to a parley on the morning of February 25, so early that the epithet "Sunrise Conference" was coined to describe it, were in a subdued and cautious mood. In the early edition of the papers they had read the Wilson-Stone exchange and they were not ready to be caught in a trap.

Wilson had defined the issue in terms of patriotism; and lack of patriotism, as he well knew, was the one thing with which congressmen did not wish to be charged. As on other occasions where his leadership was challenged, Wilson moved in for the kill. He demanded of Congress a vote on the offending resolutions, and had the satisfaction of seeing them tabled by a large majority in both houses.

This complex imbroglio was, at one level, merely the fallout from a mistake of Lansing's, consented to by the President. It did, nevertheless, settle some things. It made the public face up to the submarine as an irreversible fact of war. It affirmed the right of the President to conduct diplomacy without interference by Congress. But the substance of policy had not been notably clarified. That would await subsequent events and a further testing of the President's will.

The events were not long in coming. On March 25 Americans learned of the torpedoing in the English Channel of the *Sussex*, an unarmed ferry sailing under the French flag. The ship, still afloat, was towed into port, but the killed and wounded numbered eighty. Four Americans were among them.

The act was a flagrant indication that U-boats were operating outside of all limitations. It undid at a stroke the understandings in force since the exchange of the *Lusitania* notes. Indeed, the American public reacted with emotions almost as strong as in the former case, their anger the more implacable because of growing disillusionment with German promises and assurances.

The results of an official French investigation, confirming beyond question that the *Sussex* had been sunk by a torpedo (not by a mine as Germany at first insisted), were received in Washington on April 5. Lansing and House both urged the President to threaten a breach in relations if Germany did not fully abandon use of the submarine. Soon afterwards a note from Germany—in Bernstorff's phrase "probably the most unfortunate document ever sent from Berlin to Washington"[12]—

treated the incident with what seemed a maddening duplicity. In effect it denied that any of its torpedoes had sunk the *Sussex*, though admitting that some other ship had been torpedoed at the same time and in the same place. "It is remarkable," Ray Stannard Baker states, "that the President did not break with Germany then and there."[13]

The President, however, moved in his own way, showing a different aspect of his character, and a different method of leadership, from that which had marked him in recent controversies on the home front. No longer was he the fighter challenged and at bay, but the patient explorer amid what seemed insuperable dangers. As in the *Lusitania* crisis he took great pains to avoid giving an impression of alarm. It was Saturday when news of the *Sussex* broke, and he again followed his normal weekend routine, playing golf in the morning, motoring with Mrs. Wilson in the afternoon. On Sunday he went to church and motored again.

As in the earlier crisis, too, he withdrew even from intimates and trusted advisers. "His immediate entourage, from the Secretary of State down," House confided to his diary, "are having an unhappy time just now. He is consulting none of them and they are as ignorant of his intentions as the man in the street."[14] The isolation was emphasized by his boarding the *Mayflower* for a brief cruise with Edith. But he took with him at this week's end Lansing's draft of a note to Germany. It was a bristling document, threatening a break in relations. Wilson reviewed it in solitude and came to his own, very different, conclusion.

At some point while he was considering the situation Wilson evidently perceived that a new approach was possible. Returning to the White House he barricaded himself in his study; Monday he canceled all appointments and spent most of the day at his desk. Late that night the first version of the note was completed.

In those long hours conflicting ideas were sorted out, chosen, rejected. A disciplined and normally facile writer, Wilson was searching for more than the exact words and means of expression. As he would say later in an address on Lincoln, he was engaged in "that lonely search of the spirit for the right [which] perhaps no man can assist."[15] To state the American case in a way that would permit no further cavil or debate; to face up resolutely to Germany and yet not close the door to acceptance of his terms; to carry on the quest for peace and yet make war, if it came, a rational course enlisting the full support of his countrymen: such were the President's objectives. He embodied them in a note setting forth the irreducible minimum of American claims, involving Germany's immediate rejection of submarine tactics she had been pursuing. The text, reviewed by Lansing and House, Wilson again worked on the following weekend, and it was on its way to Germany when he called in congressional leaders. On the same day he appeared before a special session of the Congress. No advance copy of the President's address was given out (it was in substance an elaboration of the note he had dispatched to Germany); and he read from the version he had himself typed. Without emphasis except that given by the drama of the occasion, he completed the delivery in sixteen minutes—the simple laying before Congress, in the words of *The New York Times*, "of a memorable state paper."

Wilson had taken a daring step. Whether the break in relations came or was averted—whether it was to come now or later—was up to the leaders of imperial Germany to determine. In London and Paris, America was seen as being practically at war already. Congress was prepared for the worst. Bryan arrived on the scene, hoping he could make one more plea for peace, but on finding he could accomplish nothing in the prevailing atmosphere, slipped quietly away. Daniels was instructed on preliminary steps for putting the navy in readiness; Ambassador J. W. Gerard, on what course he should take in the event of a break. In the days following the dispatch of the note Wilson showed himself, as Bernstorff reported to Berlin, in no mood for concessions. For the first time Germany found itself facing Wilson's relentless implacability.

In Berlin the issue was seen in stark terms. Could Germany achieve victory through total, unrestricted submarine war even if the United States were to enter the conflict on the Allied side? Could it win before the military forces of the United States were organized and brought to bear? Chancellor Bethmann-Hollweg and Foreign Minister Jagow held to the absolute necessity of preventing a break; the military, and especially the naval, authorities felt that American intervention would not, if it came, be in sufficient strength to offset advantages they were prepared to gain by intensified U-boat attacks. Decision fell ultimately to the Kaiser. He fretted at Wilson's "impertinence"; he heard out his military advisers. But when the reply to Wilson's note went out on May 4, it contained the essential kernel that could make possible American acceptance.[16]

It was an ambiguous document nevertheless. Editors saw it as arrogant and aggressive and calls for a diplomatic break were renewed. "The more I study the reply," Lansing wrote to the President, "the less I like it."[17] Wilson pondered it by himself and then slowly typed out his answer. In a brilliant diplomatic stroke (similar to that followed by a later President, John F. Kennedy, in the Cuban missile crisis of 1962) Wilson disregarded the hedges, the restrictions, the peripheral issues raised by

Germany; he cut through the rhetoric and took as the heart and essence of its position the statement that it would henceforth constrain U-boat warfare to the rules of cruiser warfare. This was a clear departure from existing practices and a concession from which Germany would withdraw at its peril.

The wringing of this pledge from Germany was a solid victory for the United States and for all neutral nations. Wilson had achieved it by patience, by undeviating firmness, by skillful diplomacy. The plaudits he received from all sides testified to his first spectacular success in foreign affairs and raised him to a position he would later exploit effectively.

Accompanying events in Europe, often surpassing them in popular interest, were developments occurring during the first months of 1916 in Mexico. They were picturesque and colorful, and if they had not held so many potential dangers for the United States they might have provided a pleasant diversion from the somber drama unfolding overseas. For Wilson, Mexican problems occasioned constant labor, endless frustration, and added immeasurably to the workload he was carrying through this crowded period. They left him with little by way of success to console him.

At least in this phase of the Mexican embroilment Wilson was not struggling to impose personal preferences on a hopelessly confused political situation, or pursuing an elusive ideal of freedom. He had a simpler task: to track down and overtake a gang of border thieves. It happened because Pancho Villa, upon whom he had previously pinned his hopes, was out to make as much trouble as possible for his Mexican rival, Carranza, and for the United States.

Marauders crossing northward over the Rio Grande seemed at first obscure in their origin and loyalty and were not identified with any political faction. But by the autumn of 1915 the connection with Villa was becoming plain. The governor of Texas, James E. Ferguson, asserted that his state was being attacked by what he considered well-organized groups. They appeared unexpectedly, robbed and terrified the local population, and quickly retreated across the border. "Your army and our rangers," the governor asserted, "find great difficulty in apprehending these invading bands."[18] As head of the *de facto* government Carranza either would not or could not do much to halt the raids. Limited recognition by the United States provided Carranza an incentive to cooperate, but at the same time it inflamed Villa's anger and desire for revenge.

In a battle late in December Villa's troops were dislodged from their stronghold at Nogales by Carranza forces under General Alváro Obregon. Three hundred were captured; the rest disappeared into the mountains. At the year's end peace seemed at last to have descended on the troubled land.

As so often in Mexican affairs, the calm was illusory. Three weeks after Villa's defeat at Nogales, on January 11, 1916, Mexican bandits held up a train in the northern part of the country, removed seventeen American citizens and, lining them up beside the cars, shot them. The uproar in the United States matched the excitement caused by the worst offenses of German sea warfare. Despite inflammatory resolutions introduced into the two houses of Congress, Wilson stood firmly against military intervention. He wanted to give Carranza, who attributed the outrage to Villa, a chance to restore order and to bring the murderers to justice. Before this could be accomplished a second, equally grave incident occurred. On March 10, Villa invaded before daylight the town of Columbus, New Mexico, with a force of fifteen hundred men. Nineteen Americans were killed and many buildings set on fire before the U.S. garrison drove the Mexicans back across the border.

This time there could be no delay in retaliating. Wilson ordered U.S. armed forces "to proceed promptly across the border." It was explicitly stated (as was to prove important in later events) that the mission of these troops "should be considered finished as soon as Villa's band or bands are known to be broken up."[19] Carranza, unfortunately, was not notified in advance. He took a jaundiced view of this intrusion into his territory and demanded, in exchange for consenting to the President's orders, the reciprocal right to pursue Villa's bands on American soil. This questionable privilege being granted, four thousand U.S. troops under General John J. Pershing joined with Carranza's troops on March 15 to enter Mexico in an impressive show of unity. Apart from such vindication of international rights as may have spurred that rough adventurer, Carranza had the satisfaction of believing his chief rival would be eliminated once and for all.

At first everything seemed to go well for the U.S. forces and their comrades-in-arms. Though Villa had a head start of a hundred miles, the pursuers moved with speed along his trail. At Casas Grandes they turned southward, moving by night marches under the brilliant Mexican moon toward the mountainous slopes where it was known Villa had fled. Five days after the start of the expedition, the New York Times correspondent reported that Villa was "hemmed in" at Babicora between the advancing American cavalry and Carranza's forces to the south. But two days later the same source reported that Villa had escaped. The punitive force was now 230 miles south of the border, and fear was expressed that Villa would retreat into the high mountains still farther to the south.

Hopes were again aroused on April 1. After a march of fifty-four miles without rest, the Americans came upon Villa's forces rising at dawn from the night's encampment. Villa himself, either wounded or sick, was believed to have been seen lifted into a carriage and then "driven at break-neck speed ahead of the fugitive band." His pursuers followed the carriage tracks in the snow, but the trail soon ran out. Aviators, playing a pioneer role in warfare, were supposed to provide information for the columns, but without result they surveyed each gorge, canyon, and watering place. At about the same time, an ominous silence had begun to fall over Mexicans in the villages where Americans passed.[20]

From the start, the attitude of the native population had been uncertain. Americans were warned to avoid passing through the larger cities, but even in villages a few shots had been fired. As the forces moved south, supplies were more difficult to raise, information grew scarcer, and local guides no longer volunteered their services. Yet the Americans advanced until, as Carranza not illogically complained, it was "hard to convince the population that a force of thousands of men of the three branches of service do not have the semblance of invasion."[21]

While the public followed the pursuit with mounting excitement, doubts arose in official quarters. "It does not seem dignified," said the army chief of staff, Hugh L. Scott, "for all the United States to be hunting for one man in a foreign country." The Mexicans themselves, he added, "do not know half the time which side they are on."[22] Early April would have seemed a good time to declare that Pershing's mission had been successfully concluded, with Villa's "band or bands" known to have been broken up. But the momentum of a military expedition is not easily checked. And Wilson, it should be noted, was at this time deeply involved in the *Sussex* crisis.

Spurred by repeated rumors that Villa was dead, that his body had been found and identified, the American forces pushed on to an area five hundred miles south of the Rio Grande. At this point Carranza demanded their withdrawal, claiming that the original incursion had been "without warrant." It was next reported that Carranza's troops were gathering to oppose further American advances. Wilson set terms for negotiation, and a border conference between Generals Scott and Obregon seemed at the point of bringing the punitive expedition to an end. But at the last minute the Mexican leader refused to sign. The American forces remained, while an angry Carranza vowed to compel their complete and unconditional withdrawal.

A crisis was reached on April 12 when approximately a hundred cavalry troops, seeking to buy food and forage, entered the town of Parral, on the border between the Mexican states of Durango and Chihuahua. Facing opposition, they attempted to withdraw, but a crowd followed them to the outskirts of the town, joined by troops from the local garrison. Through a hail of stones and bullets the Americans fought their way out, but not without two dead and two wounded. The Mexicans suffered as many as a hundred casualties.

With Carranza resolved to block the American advance, and indeed to force an immediate retreat, General Pershing urged such strong measures as occupation of the country through which the expedition was passing and seizure of the railroads necessary to safeguard its supply lines. These actions, if pursued, would have meant war. Wilson and his Secretary of War were shocked by Pershing's demands and sent the more moderate General Scott to intervene. A compromise resulted in Pershing's being ordered to withdraw to northern Mexico. In this uneasy posture matters remained through the months of late spring.

Through the vexed winter of 1916 Wilson had not given up his determination to make a major effort to shorten the European war. His prestige enhanced by his successful handling of the *Sussex* affair, and with German relations relatively quiet, he thought the time ripe to explore the possibilities of mediation in the context of the House-Grey memorandum.

The German advance at Verdun had by then been repulsed; yet the Allies were unable to make a dent in the enemy's lines. In these conditions of stalemate it seemed that words of reason might be heard. On April 7, at Wilson's request, House sent a message to Grey asking for discussions to carry forward the commitments of their joint memorandum. He was given no encouragement. The fact that German forces were at a standstill seemed to the British a good reason for avoiding talk of mediation. "War must yet continue," Grey cabled House, "to have any chance of securing satisfactory terms from Germany."[23] Put differently, peace could only be mentioned when Germany had been beaten to her knees.

Wilson was already impatient with British tactics at sea and the violent repression of the Easter Rebellion in Dublin; he intimated to House that he possessed the means to bring the British leaders to their senses. "We must either make some move toward peace," he wrote House, "or must insist to the limits on our rights of trade."[24]

The French, even more than the British, were disturbed by talk of peace. Their ambassador, Jean Jules Jusserand, was a quiet professional who had been at his Washington post since 1902, a diplomat of scholarly mind with neither the eccentricities of Spring Rice nor the busy camaraderie of Bernstorff. He spoke, when he did speak, for a nation that knew precisely what it wanted and refused to be diverted by a hair's breadth from its somber purposes. Seeking an interview at the State Department in mid-May, he revealed himself to be in a suspicious and hostile frame of mind. In a speech the President had delivered the previous week in Charlotte, North Carolina, Jusserand caught a hint of mediation, and he had undoubtedly heard rumors of the pressure being exerted on Britain.

Lansing was ill, but meeting with the acting Secretary, Frank L. Polk, Jusserand warned strongly against mediation or "any other steps to bringing about peace." France wanted a real peace, he said, "and not a breathing-spell for Germany"; the result of the war must be "decisive, not a draw." In closing he made the ominous remark that anyone talking of peace at that juncture would be considered by his people "a friend of Germany."[25]

Wilson was puzzled by so strong a stand by the leaders of countries that were paying an agonizing price in men and national wealth for each day's continuance of the conflict. Inevitably the ugly question arose of what the Allies were really fighting for, beyond the restoration of Belgium and arrangements to assure the future safety of France. What unspoken war aims justified the slaughter of trench warfare, the mowing down of a whole generation of the nations' youth? That the French wanted more than Alsace and Lorraine, Grey wrote to house, "is true, but they cannot be said . . . to be so far prolonging the war for more than this."[26] It was an obscure and not reassuring answer. For the time being Wilson forbore to raise publicly the question of Allied war aims. But in view of allied opposition, he considered it wise to abandon ideas of mediation.

He decided instead to emphasize America's participation in schemes to prevent future wars, seeing this as setting the stage for implementation of the House-Grey memorandum. An address scheduled for May 27 before the League to Enforce Peace, a citizens' group headed by ex-President Taft, provided the opportunity. He began preparing the speech with much care, and on the eve of its delivery visited the home of the ailing Lansing to read him the text. He had already carefully solicited House's views. "It may be," he wrote House, "the most important [speech] I shall ever be called upon to make." He wanted it to be "as nearly what you deem Grey and his colleagues to have agreed upon in principle as it is possible to make it."[27]

Unfortunately for Wilson's purposes, the House-Grey memorandum had been framed in terms excessively vague, and Grey's colleagues had been only perfunctorily consulted. The French had not been brought into the discussion at all. Wilson did not realize how greatly House had inflated the memorandum's significance and he stepped, unwittingly, into a void.

The address was relatively brief, an impassioned plea for a postwar union of peoples standing for justice and against aggression. Wilson outlined the "fundamental things" for which America stood and for the sake of which they would join in guaranteeing a peace settlement: the right of every nation to choose the sovereignty under which it lived; of small nations to be assured the same territorial integrity as great ones; and that of all alike to be free of threats of aggression. "So sincerely do we believe these things," Wilson concluded in a momentous declaration, "that I am sure that I speak the mind and wish of the people of America when I say that the United States is willing to become a partner in any feasible association of nations formed in order to realize these objectives."[28]

At home the importance of the speech, taken on its own and without any reference to the forces it was intended to trigger, was widely recognized. Its significance was reflected in the cheers of the immediate audience and in subsequent newspaper comment. It was widely seen as a turning point in American policy, a statement in some ways comparable to the promulgation of the Monroe Doctrine. The *New Republic*, in an editorial showing clearly the style of the young Walter Lippmann, hailed it as a decisive event. "For us in America it literally marks the beginning of a new period in American history and the ending of our deepest tradition. . . . It will be said of Mr. Wilson that he lived in a time of supreme opportunity, that he had the vision to grasp it and the courage to declare it; that on the central issue of modern life he chose the noble part."[29]

On the other side of the Atlantic, where the speech was supposed to have its chief impact, Wilson's words fell amid a chilling official silence. Neither British nor French sources commented; no indication was given of the actions which, according to the House-Grey memorandum, were to follow in the wake of America's commitment to an international order. On the contrary, at the State Department on June 3 Jusserand expressed himself as being "very upset" by current peace talk. At the same time violent criticism of the speech was being voiced in the Allied press because of peripheral comments made by the President in an opening passage.

Speaking of the war "that broke so suddenly upon the world," he declared that "with its causes and its objects we are not concerned. The obscure fountains from which its stupendous flood has burst forth we are not interested to search for or explore." Lord Bryce suggested charitably that the President had merely said that for the present and for the purposes of his argument, he was not examining how the war began. But most others saw in the remark an indifference to the humane causes which inspired the Allies and a tendency to equate the moral position of the two sides.

Wilson's harsher critics among the Allies were undoubtedly right in their interpretation. Even after the United States was thoroughly engaged Wilson would keep a brooding conviction that the war had emerged from the power politics of a corrupt European system; that Belgium was not the cause—certainly not the sole cause—of Britain's intervention, while Britain's desire to dominate the seas was not basically different from the Germans' desire to dominate on the land. Wilson's hope was to transcend these origins, to transform a war born of old evils into one fought for a new evangel. When he talked of the "obscure fountains" from which the flood had burst forth, he used words carefully; when he said he was not interested in exploring the past, he was speaking his precise conviction.

Like Lincoln, Wilson believed in an ultimate reconciliation of the warring factions and in atonement for an ancient human evil. Such beliefs, needless to say, were not congenial to the Allied leaders, who were carrying on a supreme struggle and who were convinced that right was on their side. They would make Wilson pay for what they conceived to be his heresy.

TOWARD A SECOND TERM

The year 1916, one of frustrations on the diplomatic front, was dominated in domestic affairs by the upcoming Presidential elections. Congress and the press weighed the political consequences of Wilson's every move, and he was himself not inclined to ignore the partisan implications of his words and acts. He was by this time too seasoned a politician, as he was by nature too unyielding a fighter, to let opportunities slip needlessly by.

That he would run for a second term seemed probable by the start of the year. If he had serious doubts after Ellen Wilson's death, they were dissipated in the renewed strength brought by his second marriage.

Edith Wilson was a woman of the world, anxious not only to see her husband fulfill his destiny but to be part of it herself. She enjoyed, as Ellen never had, the crowds, the excitement, the sense of power. She was at her husband's side on every public occasion and was his close collaborator during the working day. Wilson had educated her, expecting her to read and comment on state papers. He could foresee a second term with Edith as participant and coworker in every sense.

His purpose was sharpened by the challenge of events abroad, as well as by the ambitions of potential rivals. A campaign committee for Champ Clark was opened in January, and although the Speaker disclaimed knowledge of its formation, he was certainly ready to step into the fight if Wilson should withdraw. Disaffected by the President's stand on defense, Bryan was becoming another potential threat. An open break between him and Wilson was a matter of concern within the White House. But in mid-February Wilson registered for the Ohio primary. With that quiet move his role as a candidate for a second term became official, and rivalry for the nomination vanished.

Wilson stood at this time as an effective President, a commanding personality, but without the aura that was to surround him as World War I progressed. He had experienced since 1912 startling successes, but he had also had his share of disappointments and his times of uncertainty. Passage of the New Freedom reforms was an achievement of historic proportion. Yet the crucial measures dealing with the tariff, banking, and trusts met only a portion of the expectations and hopes Wilson had first inspired. Their predominant emphasis on encouraging competition and private enterprise left unanswered the need for social reform. His determination to unite the Democrats had cast him in the role of party leader, a great party leader by every test, but had left him hostage to the dogmas of segregation and states' rights. He had yet to establish his claim to being a great President.

In foreign policy the foundation of virtually all the later Wilsonian positions had been laid: preservation of neutral rights; self-determination and acceptance of the legitimacy of revolution; readiness to mediate and to participate in a postwar league. Yet these positions had been achieved as part of a process of learning, and costly mistakes were made along the way. In Mexican affairs, while affirming the right of a people to choose its own government, he let personal and moralistic impulses intrude. His larger purposes in dealing with Mexico were obscured by the awkward imbroglio at Vera Cruz and by failure to cut short Pershing's punitive expedition. Efforts at mediation in European affairs and offers to participate in a league to prevent future wars were based on misconceptions embodied in the House-Grey memorandum. Above all, the policy of neutrality was essentially negative. Perhaps no leader could have made it seem otherwise.

Whatever the flaws in their execution, the policies of the first term set a new pattern in both domestic and foreign fields. Wilson himself, during the same period, emerged as a new type of President. He was a man of subtle intellect and at the same time a man of strong will; an idealist and yet a practical, even an opportunistic, politician. Sensing with almost mystical penetration the trend of public opinion, he remained as an individual relatively unknown. He did not possess Roosevelt's ability to project a single, vibrant image. His more attractive qualities—modesty and humor, courtesy under stress—were not fully conveyed to the people; and before this human side of the man could become familiar, he changed. It was as if the Woodrow strain in his nature was bound ultimately to surface. What remained in the last years, after illness and defeat had overcome him, was but the ghost of the sprightly, many-sided personality that in his heyday of office changed the politics of the United States.

One deficiency of the first term Wilson addressed before setting out to achieve a second. The New Freedom had been left with the establishment of an order in which economic competition could flourish; it stopped short of doing more than touch the surface of social reforms which liberals expected of him. Now, in an abrupt change of course, he put his personal prestige and the force of his administration behind an agenda of progressive legislation. He supported rural credits, workmen's compensation, a child labor bill, with the singlemindedness formerly reserved for promoting economic equality; and to these the eight-hour day was soon to be added in dramatic circumstances. By September, with the campaign ready to begin, a second New Freedom had come into being.

The accomplishment was startling in its sweep and boldness. Nowhere did Wilson proclaim the start of a new direction in domestic affairs. Even confidential letters and conversations reveal little of a changed purpose. He simply acted, building on a consensus of progressive opinion within the country and the Congress. The shift was almost as complete as that which had turned him at the outset of his political career from being a protégé of the New Jersey bosses to a champion of radical reform. In both cases electoral calculations played their part. He took over, in 1916 as in 1910, a liberal program cultivated by others. Indeed, as he now adopted the chief measures of the defunct Progressive Party, its adherents had nowhere to find shelter but among the Democrats. As for the Democrats, Wilson by this time had no need for elaborate concessions to hold his party together. Fear of the ticket's defeat was enough to bring even the most conservative into line.

With Wilson the simple explanation, or the assumption of a single cause, rarely is adequate. In addition to pure political considerations, ideas long simmering just below the surface of his political philosophy were at work. Notes struck repeatedly during the 1912 campaign, the grave appeal for social justice in his First Inaugural, were as an undertone that now swelled into a major theme. The circumstances of 1916 conspired, moreover, to release within Wilson a fresh burst of energy. His health was good; his second marriage confirmed an ambition which had been nearly snuffed out by Ellen's death. He was enjoying the scent of approaching battle. Liberated to embrace the new program of legislative reform, he acted in the threatened railway strike, shortly to be related, as a man who feared nothing and was daring to the point of recklessness.

An opening in the Supreme Court provided him with an opportunity to rally the forces of liberalism. To the seat vacated by the death of his childhood friend, Joseph R. Lamar, he nominated Brandeis, and then fought for him in a rousing battle. Brandeis's name, as it was a touchstone to Progressives, was anathema in industrial and financial circles. Fearing the costs of political strife, Wilson had withheld a cabinet appointment for Brandeis in 1912. Now, as the mounting opposition assumed bitter and often scurrilous forms, Wilson saw the nomination not only as a test of loyalty to a man he greatly respected and who had enlightened him at crucial moments, but as a test of principle. The fact that Brandeis was the first Jew ever to have been nominated for the Supreme Court poisoned the controversy;* almost as abhorrent in certain circles was his well-known sympathy to labor. Wilson was totally without religious prejudice, and he had long held the conviction that law must speak not merely for a body of precedent but for the values of a living and changing society.

He watched the campaign of hate rise in intensity, and in early May addressed to the chairman of the Senate Judiciary Committee a public letter backing Brandeis. "The propaganda in this matter has been very extraordinary," Wilson wrote, "and very distressing to those who love fairness and value the dignity of the great professions." After countering the main charges of radicalism against Brandeis, he summed up his

---

* As governor Wilson had appointed Samuel I. Kalisch to New Jersey's supreme court, the first Jew to be seated on that bench.

support in words that stand proudly in any collection of his writings: "He is a friend of all just men and a lover of the right; and he knows more than how to talk about the right,—he knows how to set it forward in the face of its enemies."[1] Brandeis was approved by the committee, and by a full vote of the Senate on June 1. The victory bore testimony to Wilson's standing as a leader, and was a fitting prelude to his appeal to progressivism in the coming campaign.

A more mundane matter of business had to be settled before that campaign got under way, the question of the party chairmanship. McCombs had remained in the post, ineffectual, ill in body and mind; and it was the nightmare of Wilson's supporters that he should resist efforts to replace him. Wilson had no doubts about his lack of fitness, but still hesitated to break with a man who had been one of his first political sponsors. A young Wilson supporter and admirer, a debonair financier who had recently come to Washington and was beginning to make his mark as a Democratic loyalist and a man of princely entertainments, Bernard M. Baruch, was assigned the task of managing McCombs's withdrawal. Baruch passed this first test well. In late April McCombs assured the President that he would quietly give way to a successor. He had been got rid of, House remarked jubilantly, "for all time."[2]

To follow McCombs, Wilson wanted a real political warhorse, "not an alien or a highbrow," to inspire the political workers.[3] He did not altogether succeed in his quest. More or less by default, the choice fell upon Vance C. McCormick, a newspaper publisher and leader of the progressive forces in Pennsylvania. With Morgenthau recalled from his post as ambassador to Turkey to take charge of campaign finances, the main preliminaries of the campaign were in place.

Meanwhile the Republican Party was selecting a candidate to oppose Wilson. By spring, the obvious choice appeared to be Charles Evans Hughes, twice governor of New York and then a Justice of the Supreme Court. Hughes had impeccable credentials, including a record of fighting the insurance companies during a governorship almost as spectacular as Wilson's in New Jersey. On issues of social policy he was acceptable to the liberal wing of the party, while on such matters as defense and America's attitude toward the European war he had the advantage, having just descended from the bench, of having given no expression of his views. His candidacy would have appeared certain except for the complicating factor of Theodore Roosevelt.

The tattered remnants of Roosevelt's Progressive Party met in Chicago in early June, at the same time that the Republicans were convening there. The old leader kept the hope that through his diminished but faithful followers he might exert enough pressure on the Republicans to win their nomination; or at the very least that he might enforce the adoption of a platform strong in regard to defense and to "Americanism." In neither respect did he succeed. The Republicans were mindful of the pacifist attitude extending through much of the country, particularly the Midwest, and adopted a highly evasive platform. On the third ballot, Hughes was made the party's candidate.

Roosevelt had the galling satisfaction of being nominated by the Progressives. He declined it as an empty honor, being convinced that the goal superior to all others, including fidelity to the party he had himself formed and led, was the defeat of Wilson. "I did not desert the Progressives," he wrote later. "The Progressives deserted me." Coming out in support of Hughes, he kept no illusions to assuage his bitterness. The candidate himself was, in his phrase, "a bearded iceberg"; and as for the convention that nominated him: "a more sordid set of creatures . . . could not be imagined." In his furious zeal to defeat Wilson the Progressive Party came in itself to seem a thing of evil. "Small divided parties," Roosevelt wrote, "are a natural prey of cranks with a moral twist." As for his own fortunes, he added with prescience, the cup had been drained and only the dregs were left.[4]

The Democratic convention, opening in St. Louis on June 14, 1916, was expected, in comparison to the scenes of anger and frustration in Chicago, to be a mild and even boring affair. It was projected by Wilson and the party leaders as a demonstration of patriotism, a ritual of Americanism. On its eve the administration staged in Washington a huge parade in honor of Flag Day, with the President and members of his cabinet leading a five-hour-long march. All government offices and most businesses in the Capital were closed for the event. Wilson's speech, unassailably patriotic, was marred by intensely bitter attacks on pro-German groups. "There is disloyalty active in the United States," he said menacingly, "and it must be absolutely crushed."[5] More on this theme was expected to be heard in St. Louis, and no one doubted that it would be popular with the delegates and with the crowds.

Wilson wrote most of the planks in the platform and dispatched Newton D. Baker as his special emissary to make sure that all changes were cleared with him. An early move to substitute for the ineffectual Marshall another candidate for the Vice Presidency proved abortive. Baker would have been the choice of many for Vice President; Agriculture Secretary David Houston had been proposed, and almost anyone would have seemed better than the inconspicuous man from Indiana who was out of sympathy with almost all Wilsonian positions, alike in the domestic and international fields. *Harper's Weekly* railed against "the wickedness of having the vice presidency filled casually, wearily, or as a political compromise." But the gathering in St. Louis was denied a good fight even on this issue; Marshall was routinely chosen for the second term. With its slogan of "Peace, Prosperity, Preparedness" the convention was assured of being, in the words of *The New York Times*, "one of the quietest and smoothest . . . in political history."[6]

As often with predictions concerning Democratic Party conclaves, this one proved to be false. St. Louis turned out to be one of the noisiest of conventions, and one that unfolded in ways quite different from what its managers had foreseen.

Not that these managers were anything less than meticulous in their planning. With the overarching theme of Americanism in place, they intended to recapture the flag from the Republicans. As the opening hour approached, the only serious question before them was the length of the various projected demonstrations. How was the cheering to be set off by the playing of the national anthem—the first expression of patriotism—to compare with that planned for the nominating speech; and how were these two to be related to the duration of the uproar that would ensue upon the naming of the candidate? These arcane considerations were thrown to the winds when the temporary chairman of the convention, ex-Governor Martin H. Glynn of Ohio, embarked on the keynote address.

Glynn had prepared, according to instructions, a fervid appeal to patriotism and to the flag, along with rousing remarks upon such familiar topics as tariff and banking reform. His words were greeted with perfunctory applause. Then he began on a part of his speech which he offered with some diffidence, fearing he would lose his audience among its intricacies. He listed occasions in the past when Americans had suffered provocations and yet had refrained from going to war. Suddenly the great audience became alive. Cheering and applause rose to a frenzy as it called upon the orator to repeat sentences or whole paragraphs of his argument. It discouraged his skipping over or condensing any of its details. When he came to one particular precedent, the so-called *Chesapeake-Leopard* Affair of 1807, he appeared to hesitate. The unavenged killing by the British of three American sailors had long been treated in American history books as a moment of national weakness and humiliation. Yet now, on its being recalled by Glynn, the huge gathering only cheered the louder.

"The impression created," wrote a reporter on the scene, "was that the delegates had been strongly in favor of peace under provocation, but that they were not sure this was an heroic attitude. When Glynn told them that it was ... true Americanism to bear with provocation and to settle disputes without war ... the effect was simply electric. He identified in their own minds the cause of pacifism with that of Americanism, and made the two identical."[7]

Nothing like this had ever happened before in a national convention. On other occasions leaders had suddenly emerged and rival candidacies had provoked unexpected results. But here was a vast boisterous crowd, whom the managers had thought fit to be brainwashed, discovering for itself, at the very height of passion, its true convictions. By its response to the sallies of an astonished orator it created a new mood and defined issues in a novel form.

Next day the permanent chairman, Senator Ollie James of Kentucky, rekindled the fires. He was forewarned and prepared. An immense man, with a voice matching his size yet full of subtle tones and modulations, he far exceeded the expectations of the convention managers, bringing his audience spontaneously to its feet. "Without orphaning a single American child," he intoned, in a panegyric of Wilson, "without widowing a single American mother, without firing a single gun, without the shedding of a single drop of blood, he wrung from the most militant spirit that ever brooded above a battlefield an acknowledgment of American rights and an agreement to American demands."[8] The crowd interrupted him with its roar, silenced itself to hear the last syllables, and then broke out in cries of "Repeat! Repeat!" James stepped to the edge of the platform. He pronounced again the measured words. In the silence, and then in the twenty-minute whirlwind of cheers that followed, the Democratic Party seemed to have found its soul.

Among newspapermen covering the convention was William Jennings Bryan. Hailed on entering the hall, he was invited after Senator James's speech to address the gathering. Previous demonstrations had put the vast audience in a mood to acclaim the very apostle of peace, the man who had sacrificed his career for the cause. Again pandemonium broke loose. For a moment the intensity of the ovation was disquieting. "My friends," said Bryan, his marvelously resonant voice by itself stirring memories of old victories and defeats, "I have differed with our President on some of the methods employed, but I join with the American people in thanking God that we have a President who does not want this nation plunged into this war."[9] Party unity had been maintained, and from then on the delegates could give the Great Commoner the kind of tribute that rose unrestrained from their collective heart. The "Cross of Gold" speech at the convention of 1896 had opened Bryan's controversial career; this one closed it in honorable triumph.

To Wilson, following the convention closely over the telegraph wire at the White House, these unpredicted events were revealing and impressive. He knew by how narrow a margin war with Mexico had been averted; and how drastically the country's course would be changed if Germany resumed unrestricted submarine warfare. But he knew also what the people desired. He himself soon picked up the antiwar theme of the convention, and used it with devastating effectiveness.

VICTORY AT THE POLLS

After the turmoil and excitement of the conventions the party chiefs withdrew to prepare themselves for autumn's campaigns. The usual calm settled over Washington. The hot days returned. For Wilson, however, there was no rest. Giving up the agreeable house at Cornish, he and his wife rented Shadow Lawn, an ungainly mansion on the New Jersey shore. Here a stream of official visitors descended, while national and international problems piled up mercilessly. Private grief intruded on these public duties. Wilson's sister Annie Howe, to whom he had so often given a home, whom he had supported financially for many years and whose children he had watched over almost as a father, was dying of peritonitis in New London, Connecticut. In September, while she was still able to recognize him, he paid her a last visit.

Relations with Great Britain continued to cause concern. Wilson was angry and bitter after the icy reception accorded his commitment to a postwar league. For the immediate future he was determined to act as he saw best, isolated if need be, without such mutual arrangements as House had tried to effect. "It will be up to us to judge for ourselves when the time has arrived for us to make an imperative suggestion"— imperative, he explained to House, "because the opinion of the non-official world and the desire of all peoples will be behind it."[1] The consequences of Wilson's anger were visible in his dealing with a broad range of problems affecting Britain.

Judging themselves under the compulsion to intercept foreign intelligence, the British had for some time been seizing mail from neutral ships. In the summer of 1916 this provocation was compounded by the issuing of a "black list"—the names of firms in neutral countries that had been trading with Britain's enemies. Although not contrary to international law—Britain had the right to tell its own citizens with whom to deal—it was nevertheless a painful intrusion into American business affairs. It was, Wilson wrote, "inevitably and essentially inconsistent with the rights of the citizens of all nations not involved in the war."[2] Besides, to many observers it seemed that under the guise of interrupting enemy commerce, Britain was building up its own postwar trade.

To make matters worse, the British were engaged in violent suppression of a rebellion in northern Ireland. The execution of prisoners in Dublin, and particularly of the Irish patriot Roger Casement, shocked American opinion, not alone the Irish-American element which had been irreconcilably hostile throughout. With war aims of the Allies coming under suspicion, the current acts of the British cast doubt upon their sincerity in claiming to defend the rights of other subjugated peoples.

While the Senate passed (in vain) a resolution asking clemency for Casement, Wilson stormed privately against the British. Her show of inhumanity, along with her position on the mails and the blacklist, fueled a degree of Presidential ire seriously threatening the underlying bonds between the United States and the Allies. Through most of the period of neutrality Wilson kept a sense, based partly on strategic concepts and partly on cultural affinities, of the way in which the United States was ultimately bound up with Allied interests. But now, as he wrote House, he was "about at the end of [his] patience" with the British; the black list was "the last straw. . . . Can we any longer endure their intolerable course?" A week after this outburst, he showed his disillusionment in a speech at the White House, in which he described the war as being "just a fight," one in which the United States had "nothing to gain and nothing to lose."[3]

In irate notes Wilson protested Britain's policies. Bristling with incivilities, these notes made demands in terms almost as strong as had been used against Germany in regard to submarine tactics. More than that, he took the lead in getting Congress to enact legislation permitting retaliatory measures. British restrictions on U. S. trade could be countered, under terms incorporated in the revenue act of 1916, by having the President prohibit all British imports. Further amendments empowered the President to deny use of American ports, by armed force if necessary, to nations engaged in abnormal trade restrictions. Throughout this tense period, Wilson was not unaware of the favorable political implications of a strong stand *vis-à-vis* the British. But because of reluctance to seem to be playing politics with foreign policy, he refrained from using the retaliatory measures permitted him under the legislation. His restraint was based, also, on the historian's recollection that in the

War of 1812 the United States had been more hurt than benefited by attempts to retaliate against Britain.

Watching these developments from London, Page was gravely disaffected. Assistant Secretary of State Frank Polk reported to the President in July that a communication had recently been received from the ambassador which "showed extraordinary ignorance of our point of view, and it was quite querulous in its tone." In regard to the State Department's official complaints to Britain, he "seemed to feel that we are imposing on the good nature of the British government."⁴ Beginning to wish that he might put Page in some such post as Secretary of Agriculture, trusting that a vacation might bring him back "a little way at least to the American point of view,"⁵ the President called him to Washington for consultations with himself and with the State Department. Page set out with high hopes, fortified by his deep-rooted convictions, and armed with facts after conversations with Lord Bryce, the Foreign Secretary, and the Prime Minister.

From the beginning the mission was ill-starred. On his arrival Page found his twenty-four-year-old daughter-in-law severely ill with polio. He rushed to her bedside in Garden City, Long Island, where she died the next day. In Washington, five days later, he lunched with the President, but during the conversation foreign affairs were scarcely mentioned. He found Lansing "lacking the smallest touch of human nature"; he talked of "vague nothings" and invited the ambassador to see a movie. Polk and Spring Rice were afraid of polio infection. "They called me at home and then—skedaddled," Page wrote with mounting disillusionment.⁶

A second lunch at the White House, with the President and the ambassador to France, William G. Sharp, took place on August 29. The President was preoccupied with an address to Congress he would deliver that afternoon on a subject unrelated to foreign policy, and again Page could not unburden himself. When a serious conference did take place in Washington a few days later, Wilson was away for the funeral of his sister Annie.

"No one ever takes me seriously about anything," Page complained to his wife. "The Cabinet are jocular. No member of Congress has a serious word."⁷ Meanwhile, back in New York things were no better. He failed even to see House, who was then vacationing near Boston. On September 27 at Shadow Lawn the President again received Page and this time there was at least talk of foreign policy. Wilson shocked his ambassador (as was no doubt his aim) by speaking once again of the war's having many causes, some of distant origin. In general he tried to give a tougher and more complex view of foreign affairs than Page had been willing to entertain. The latter left with Wilson the folders of material he had laboriously amassed, and the two men parted, never to see each other again. Page returned to England a bitter man. His advice was heeded even less than before. Yet he continued to write the official letters, witty, perceptive, informative, which were to make a best-selling book after his death.

The friendship in its day had been one doing honor to both men and it ended without the pain Wilson felt, or inflicted, in other cases. The President had learned how to avoid the ultimate hurt, but at the cost of not facing frankly the divisive issues. The failure of Page's mission was in large part Wilson's failure, too. It left British-American relations to unfold according to their obscure destiny, the differences between the two countries finally resolved by events beyond the power of either man to control. Page resigned in 1918 and died soon afterwards at home in North Carolina. A last letter written from his hospital bed gives pathetic thanks to Wilson for a gift of flowers.

Mexican problems continued to fester. In his pursuit of Villa, Pershing had seen the scent grow cold, and Carranza was increasingly determined to get the Americans out, even at the risk of war. For Wilson and Baker complete withdrawal was unacceptable until Carranza had established his authority over the northern provinces and secured the U. S. border against incursions.

During the St. Louis convention Wilson toiled with the implications of the stalemate. The War College was by then making plans for an invasion. Additional forces were dispatched to the border and the National Guard was called to service to free regular troops if needed. A week later occurred an incident so grave as to make full-scaled conflict seem inevitable. Following the incident at Parral, American troops were ordered to advance in search of information. They failed to take seriously threats of armed opposition, and at Carrizal Carranza's troops killed fourteen Americans and took twenty-five captive.

Pershing considered this to be a general attack on his command. "The break seems to have come,"[8] Wilson observed resignedly. With Baker he waited through the night of June 22 to learn whether Pershing had begun offensive operations; and after conferring with legislative leaders he prepared a message to Congress requesting authority to make full use of American forces to occupy northern Mexico. The message, fortunately, was never delivered. Mexico released the captives and the

With Edith Bolling Galt at a World Series game, October 9, 1915

Accepting the nomination, at Shadow Lawn, September 2, 1916 (Franklin D. Roosevelt at le
just below the railing)

The President and Mrs. Wilson, returning from the Second Inaugural

Secretary of State Bryan

Secretary of State Lansing

Delivering the war message, April 2, 1917

General Pershing
and Newton D. Baker,
in France, 1918

situation eased. Wilson took advantage of the lessening tension to evoke the country's strong peace sentiments in an impromptu address in Philadelphia. The next day in New York he sounded his basic message: "The easiest thing is to strike. The brutal thing is the impulsive thing."[9] He had touched a chord to which public opinion eagerly responded.

The Mexican situation still hung uncomfortably over the precampaign season. Wilson knew he must dispose of it to avoid giving the Republicans strong debating points. The Mexican government offered a way out when in July it proposed a joint high commission representing the interests of Mexico and the United States. This commission met in September in Atlantic City and during the next months the issue was quiescent. In February 1917, General Pershing's troops were finally withdrawn. After successful elections Carranza was accorded full *de jure* recognition. This represented a victory for the man who had as often exasperated Wilson as he had aroused his hopes; and for Wilson it was better than victory in that it left the United States at peace with its troublesome neighbor.

In August the President found himself confronted by a major domestic crisis, an imminent nationwide strike by railway workers. It was a situation to which he reacted with assurance, as a man liberated and in his element. In contrast to diplomacy, where the power to act seemed rigidly circumscribed, he found the threat of economic and social chaos at home a challenge calling forth his innate qualities as a leader. The response showed his political skills at their best.

The gravity of a railway strike was universally recognized. Such a strike, said *The New York Times* of August 15, "threatens to be the greatest industrial battle in the history of the country." Had it occurred, wrote a leading senator, it would have been "the greatest catastrophe that ever befell our country . . . it would have almost culminated into a civil war."[10] Such judgments were not exaggerated at the time. The country was dependent on the railroads for all internal transportation as well as for the supplying of coastwise shipping. Without them the economy would quite literally come to a halt. The underlying bitterness of the industrial struggle, made vivid two years before in the Colorado coal miners' strike, was, moreover, unabated.

When in early summer the railway brotherhoods presented their demands, the company presidents dug in with unyielding determination. Through July the sides faced each other in sullen claims and equally sullen rejections. The workers by an overwhelming majority voted for a strike and subsequent efforts at mediation proved barren. Then, on

August 17, the President stepped into the controversy, summoning the contestants to the White House.

Two days of conference, marked by presentations from the opposing sides and fervent appeals for compromise by the President, brought no results. In a dramatic move the President thereupon offered his own terms. What he proposed was startling: the eight-hour day, which had been at the heart of the union's demands, he accepted as the *sine qua non* of a settlement, with ancillary issues to be determined by arbitration. As compensating measures, the unions were not granted the overtime pay they deemed essential; and Wilson promised the employers an investigation to determine the economic effects of the shorter work day. Revision of railway rates was assured if the economic burden required it. Thus in one breathtaking move Wilson sought not only to avert immediate catastrophe but to shape the framework of a new industrial order.

In seizing on the eight-hour day as the basis of a settlement, making it fundamental and nonnegotiable, Wilson acted with extraordinary boldness and the kind of vision he had long before characterized as the essence of leadership. He asked for no protracted inquiry, no prior study by a committee. The eight-hour day, he asserted with supreme confidence, had the sanction of "the judgment of society in its favor."[11] Everything else could be argued but this radical gain was to stand firmly at the center, the minimum to which labor would accede and to which justice entitled it.

Telegrams poured into the White House when these terms were made public. Industrial leaders attacked the eight-hour day with ferocity, and the unions were hardly less extreme in their opposition to submitting the overtime provisions to arbitration. "Since the abolition of slavery," cried one of labor's excited advocates, "no more effectual means has been devised for enslaving the working-man."

On Tuesday, August 29, a strike was ordered, to begin on the following Monday. Immediately Wilson went before Congress to ask legislation embodying the settlement as he had proposed it. The heat had been sweltering throughout this period, and abandoning the black tailcoat he had always worn on these occasions, he appeared dressed in a blue jacket and white flannel trousers. The jacket, noted *The New York Times*, "fitted him well"; he looked "especially strong and vigorous and quite youthful."[12] For the next several days the President and Congress worked in close and strenuous harmony, the President going down to the Capitol even at night to confer with the leaders and appealing to them with all the arts of pressure and persuasion.

The outcome remained in doubt. As the week progressed Wilson admitted privately to being in the midst of "deep anxieties and perplexities."[13] But on Friday, when the House passed the bill embodying the revolutionary eight-hour day—known thereafter as the Adamson law—he relaxed his vigil. Leaving Washington for Shadow Lawn, he delivered before thousands of cheering Democrats the formal acceptance of his candidacy for a second term.

On the strength of Wilson's assurance that he would sign the Adamson bill when passed by the Senate, the brotherhoods called off their strike and disbanded the temporary union office which for the past three weeks had been a visible and active force on the Washington scene. The Senate's work completed, the President on Sunday signed the bill in his private railway car in Union Station, and then with Mrs. Wilson departed for Hodgenville, Kentucky. In one of the most eloquent and self-revealing of his addresses he accepted on behalf of the nation the log cabin in which Abraham Lincoln had been born, now newly enshrined in a marble pavilion.

It had been a tremendous week, for the country and for Woodrow Wilson. Presidential power had rarely been exercised with such daring or finesse, and, as at all such moments, the life of the nation had been deeply stirred. Though economic disaster had, by common consent, been averted, Wilson by no means received unanimous acclaim. The conservative press was loud in denouncing a sellout to the unions, and a surrender by Congress to an imperious President. At Democratic headquarters, where preparations for the autumn campaign were going forward, financial contributions ceased abruptly. Yet Wilson had acted not only vigorously but with an enlightened capacity to take the demands and interests of opposing factions and to shape them into an innovative long-range solution.

"Mr. Wilson has done what high statesmanship in a democracy must do," said the often querulous New Republic. ". . . In a very real and accurate sense the President has made himself the spokesman of a whole people."[14] Wilson was well aware, nevertheless, that Congress in its haste had left unprovided for that part of his program calling for a commission to study the eight-hour day in operation. "There is a great deal more to do," he wrote a little wearily,[15] as the nation turned to its routine affairs and he prepared to embark on the campaign trail.

The acceptance speech on September 22 at Shadow Lawn had been in the tradition of that time, which still called for the candidate to act as if news of his nomination were being brought by horse and rider. Receiving a delegation on the front porch of his home, weeks after the convention had closed, he would explain in carefully prepared words why he would accept their call. Wilson observed these proprieties, and his hour-long speech provoked the faithful to repeated laughter and cheers. Subsequent occasions saw the scene repeated. On September 23 he addressed a group composed predominantly of businessmen, defending the Adamson law and boldly declaring it should be extended throughout industry. His fervor mounting, Wilson hit his stride as a campaigner in an address a week later to a crowd composed mostly of youthful Democrats. It was as if he were again amid the Princeton students he knew so well. "The President," remarked *The New York Times*, "has been renowned for the intellectual quality of his speeches. Yesterday he took his place beside the other great leaders of his party who have won fame for their ability to play on the emotion of their hearers."

The emotion he appealed to was in large part his audience's progressive sympathies. But there were also passages which showed Wilson not averse to the demagoguery of peace. "A great, fundamental, final choice with regard to our foreign relationships is to be made on the seventh of November," he asserted. "Some young men ought to be interested in that." The candidate was striking the same chords that had so passionately aroused the convention in St. Louis. "The certain prospect of the Republican party is that we shall be drawn, in one form or another, into the embroilment of the European war." Through most of his campaign Wilson stressed themes of progressivism rather than of peace. The Democratic Party, he said at the beginning, had "opened its heart to comprehend the demands of social justice"; in four years it had "come very near to carrying out the platform of the Progressive party."[16] But the theme of peace echoed and reechoed. It was taken up enthusiastically by party orators, particularly in the Midwest; and wherever Wilson spoke, banners overhead proclaimed that he had kept the country out of war.

Wilson's cause was buoyed at the campaign's start by an effective blow struck against extreme pro-Germans. A telegram received on September 29 from the Irish-American leader Jeremiah A. O'Leary denounced the President's allegedly pro-British policies. Couched in words of extreme vituperation, it gave Wilson the opportunity he needed to strike the combined notes of patriotism and neutrality. "Your telegram received," was the candidate's reply: "I would feel deeply mortified to have you or anybody like you vote for me. Since you have access to many disloyal Americans and I have not I will ask you to convey this message to them."[17] The rebuke resounded through the country, the more so because Hughes had been truckling to the pro-German vote.

"The American people," said the *Nation*, "have a great fondness for strong words that are said at exactly the right time and have exactly the right ring."[18] Wilson in his estimate of the situation was more modest. "It is one of the fine points of Providence," he told newspaper reporters in a long and jovial press conference, "that Providence so often makes damn fools of crooks; they haven't got sense enough to be successful."[19]

The tide was running in Wilson's favor. Hughes's campaign speeches had been a disappointment to even his most ardent followers. He had been narrowly partisan, often offensively bitter, and had concentrated upon small technical details. "It is as if one of our most assured national assets had melted away under our very eyes," declared the *Nation*.[20] The political insensitivity Hughes displayed throughout the campaign was climaxed by his snubbing the progressive champion, Governor Hiram Johnson, when both were staying at the same San Francisco hotel. There, as elsewhere, Hughes was under the sway of the conservative Republican faction.

Meanwhile Wilson was picking up support from prominent progressives. By early fall he had been endorsed by such outstanding figures as Lincoln Steffens, Jane Addams, and John Dewey. Walter Lippmann visited the candidate's headquarters in late September and went away entranced. "I have come around completely to Wilson," he wrote privately. In the last months Wilson had "developed a power of decision unlike anything he has shown before." It would be "a sheer calamity to throw him out."[21]

On the broader scene the President found himself in an unusually favorable posture. The Mexican situation was under control. Relations with Germany were calm, while the nagging difficulties with Britain failed to stir the deeper currents of American opinion. On the legislative front, planks appealing to progressive sentiment were being put firmly into place—some of them belatedly, with the kind of expediency which purists may deplore but which is not unfamiliar in American Presidential campaigns. Child welfare laws and workers' compensation had been put on the President's "must" list and backed with the full force of his prestige. Woman suffrage was now a cause to be fought for. Rural credits, highway construction, and a tariff commission were as much a part of the Democratic achievement as they were of the progressives' promises.

The sense that Wilson was personally cold persisted, and leading journalistic supporters enlisted in a concerted effort to correct the image. Articles by Ray Stannard Baker and Ida Tarbell pictured the President as he had long been known to his intimates, a man of strong family affections, humorous, open-minded, courteous. More difficult than the issue of "coldness" were the rumors of scandal perpetrated anonymously, bringing up old suspicions about Mary Hulbert Peck and insinuating that the President was a womanizer. Partly as an answer to such rumors Stockton Axson was induced to write a widely circulated article on the President's home life and his devoted relations with Ellen Axson.

The various elements of a successful campaign were in place; but still Wilson hesitated to leave the pillared sanctuary at Shadow Lawn and go forth to make his case to the people directly. "I think it is a sort of impropriety for the President to campaign," Wilson told the newspapermen late in September. "The record is there, and he can't change it. And he doesn't want to stand up and commend it." There was no method of campaigning by an incumbent that didn't "more or less offend good taste."[22] Nevertheless the candidate overcame his scruples. By the first week in October he was passing through Ohio and Indiana on his way to Omaha—refusing to make rear-platform speeches but responding to large crowds. In Omaha on October 5 he received what was probably the greatest reception of his career up to that time. Late in the month at Cincinnati and Chicago he was cheered by other big crowds, and returning by way of Buffalo he was met by overwhelmingly friendly demonstrations. Wilson had made his appeal where he was strongest, in the states of the Middle West where the joint attraction of progressivism and peace was irresistible.

The campaign wound up in traditional ceremonies at Madison Square Garden in New York. Huge crowds jammed the hall and filled the streets outside; Colonel House, dropping by, felt assured that all was going as he had planned. But the crowd was unruly and noisy. Wilson was scarcely heard above the interruptions of his partisans. Later that night he spoke in more congenial surroundings to a gathering made up largely of young people in the hall at Cooper Union where Lincoln had made one of his most famous addresses. A final campaign speech was delivered at Shadow Lawn, with Princeton undergraduates conspicuous among the representatives of New Jersey's various counties.

In closing Wilson returned to the large theme which amid the exigencies of campaigning had almost been lost from view. "In the days to come," he said, "men will no longer wonder how America is going to work out her destiny, for she will have proclaimed to them that her destiny is not divided from the destiny of the world, that her purpose is justice and love of mankind."[23]

Thus he prophesied, and then he awaited the event.

The outcome was far from being immediately apparent. It was not until November 22, more than two weeks after the election, that Hughes sent a telegram conceding his defeat. "It was a little moth-eaten when it got here," Wilson remarked wryly in private.[24] By then the count in the crucial state of California was almost complete, and it was evident beyond any possible doubt that the President had won a second term.

In the last days of the campaign Wilson had taken the extraordinary step of preparing for his resignation if the election should go against him. Writing to the Secretary of State he explained that the delicate situation in foreign affairs made essential the President's having the full authority of popular backing. For the country to be ruled by a lame duck for four months between November and March (then the constitutional date of a President's inauguration) would subject it, he felt, to dangerous uncertainties.

The plan called for the resignation of the President and Vice President and the appointment of the President-elect as Secretary of State. The latter would then serve with full powers as the next-in-line for the Presidential office. The Vice President's consent to this plan was never sought, and Wilson's letter to Lansing, delivered in the deepest secrecy, was not published at the time. It remains, nevertheless, an important document, a culminating expression of Wilson's lifelong dedication to the principle of responsible government.

That the plan might indeed be put into effect must have crossed Wilson's mind many times during the anxious hours after the polls closed on November 7. As the evening advanced, the family at Shadow Lawn was apprised of early returns showing Hughes piling up majorities in all the eastern states. The seemingly essential state of New York was clearly being lost by the Democrats. Wilson retired at ten o'clock, as the lights in New York's Times Square proclaimed his defeat. The next morning, in banner headlines, The New York Times announced that "Charles E. Hughes Has Apparently Been Elected President."

Wilson appeared reconciled to defeat. "It did not seem in the least to disturb him," Edith later recalled.[25] The Times reporter at Shadow Lawn commented that "outwardly he was . . . as calm and unruffled as if he had nothing personal at stake."[26] Tumulty, however, refused to give up hope. While Illinois (but not Ohio) and the East (with the exception of New Hampshire) were plainly though by modest pluralities going to

Hughes, Tumulty made up seemingly fantastic combinations of states where the vote remained undecided. These, he maintained, could still give his boss the victory.

Then gradually the tide turned. Normally Republican states like Utah and Kansas swung into the Democratic column. By afternoon, California, Minnesota, North Dakota, and New Mexico were in doubt, and then (with the exception of Minnesota) were slipping over to the Wilson column. In the decisive state of California an early Hughes lead in the south was overcome as the Wilson vote piled up in northern districts.

In the end Wilson won by 277 electoral votes as opposed to Hughes's 254; and by a popular majority of 691,385. It was, as these figures indicate, an exceedingly close election. Wilson's lead in New Hampshire was 56 votes; in California, a slim 3,806. He lost Minnesota by 392 votes. Elsewhere changes in a few thousand votes could have altered the result. Yet it was, in its way, a remarkable victory. Wilson had won against a united Republican Party (at a time when the Republican Party was numerically the larger); he had won despite the crisscrossing interests created by the war in Europe. Most important, he had won because he had forged anew the political amalgamation of South and West. He had recreated the Democratic Party—the party of farmers and small businessmen—which had brought Jefferson and Jackson to power.

It was no less a personal victory for Wilson. In comparison with 1912 he had enlarged his popular vote in many states, and overall had polled 2,830,000 more votes than in his previous election. In almost every contest he had outstripped the local Democratic candidate. The man's capacity as a national leader had been tested, and his image emerged as one whom the people trusted.

The results of the election were becoming clear—though still lacking official confirmation—when, on November 10, Wilson, his wife, and several members of his family embarked on a journey to Williamstown, Massachusetts, for the christening of the President's granddaughter, Eleanor Axson Sayre. A telegram from Tumulty, received as the train drew toward its destination, hailed the President's victory, based upon evidence that now seemed incontrovertible. The christening took place that afternoon at St. John's Episcopal Church, with the President acting as godfather. Afterwards the president of Williams College, Harry A. Garfield, one of the bright stars whom Wilson had once brought to the Princeton faculty, came by to greet his old friend. By now the politicians were up and stirring. Political clubs from the neighboring towns staged an old-fashioned political rally with torches, a band, and a fife-and-drum corps.

A wild demonstration greeted Wilson when he appeared on the porch of the Sayre house. He had carried himself through the day with what one reporter described as "the bearing of a boy on a holiday"; but when the cheers subsided he showed a different mood. "Let us remember," he said very quietly, "now that the campaign is over, to get together for the common good of all."[27] It was such a scene, under the torchlights, in that small New England town, as the dramatist might have contrived or the philosopher conjured up, as an ideal expression of democracy.

The President lingered for a day with his daughter and son-in-law, and then returned to Washington, boarding the Presidential yacht at Rhinebeck, New York, and sailing down the Hudson to pick up the night train to the capital. The next morning crowds were on hand to greet him at the station and to cheer him as he made his way down Pennsylvania Avenue. He had been out of Washington since the last week of August, and his homecoming was in the nature of a triumph.

He settled down to thanking the many who had helped seal the victory; and then he looked toward the work ahead. Major problems he found virtually in the same state as when he had embarked on the campaign trail. The Mexican-American commission was grinding away in meetings that had as yet brought no tangible results. Relations with Germany— despite some menacing clouds on the horizon—had remained remarkably stable since the *Sussex* pledge. As for the Anglo-American situation, the strains appeared unsurmountable. "The truth of it, I fear," wrote Assistant Secretary of State Polk, "is that nothing we do will please the English and we have to make up our minds to face and endure their unfriendliness."[28]

In December, Ambassador J. W. Gerard was recalled for consultations. This time there would not be the lack of communication that had marred Page's visit a few months earlier. House took pains to ensure that there would be an early meeting, and the President was prepared for a full exchange of views. In Germany, the ambassador's return started rumors of a critical deterioration in relations. Wilson did not see it that way, but he was not at all averse to giving the German imperial government some cause for puzzlement and concern.

Before entering on a new stage of diplomatic initiatives, Wilson had some domestic matters to settle. Making his annual address on the state of the Union in December, he called on Congress to complete the program for settling disputes in the railway industry. During the following weeks, on repeated trips to the President's room in the Capitol, he put his prestige and power at stake in pushing the necessary legislation.

Closer to home, indeed within his own political household and in large part behind his back, a different sort of business was afoot.

Colonel House and Edith Wilson had come to the conclusion that the way the President could best be served was by ridding the administration of Tumulty and "good Josephus Daniels." House was assigned the elimination of Daniels; Mrs. Wilson was prepared to take on Tumulty. She had disliked Tumulty from the start; she considered him "common"; and at a deeper level she was resentful of his closeness to her husband. A week after the elections, House found the President inclined to keep on all his cabinet—"even Daniels," provided they were willing to stay. "What about Tumulty?" Edith inquired. Wilson replied that he was planning to offer him the post of appraiser of the Customs House, in order to better his financial situation. "Mrs. Wilson," House records, "wanted the President to compel Tumulty to take this."[29]

But Tumulty refused to play the game. He was not interested in money; he was, in spite of House's and Grayson's persuasions, "making a terrific fight" in order to stay with his chief. Wilson relented; Tumulty stayed on, while Edith waited and licked her wounds. As for Daniels, he stayed, too. He survived to the administration's last day, one of the President's most faithful and articulate friends and advisers.

With Grayson in some disfavor because of the insistence with which he had pushed his promotion to a vice-admiralty, and with Tumulty under siege, House had his particular reasons to feel satisfied. "The little circle close to the President," he would write in January 1920, "seems to have dwindled down to the two of us, Mrs. Wilson and myself."[30] In due course the conspirators themselves were to fall out. By the end of the peace conference Mrs. Wilson (who disliked the Colonel at least as much as she disliked Tumulty) saw that he was relegated to the outer dark.

Before the event-filled year ran out, Wilson held one of his increasingly rare press conferences. He was not exactly in a communicative mood and he disappointed newspapermen by ruling out all questions about peace moves then secretly in progress. But he gave them the impression of a man firmly in control—in control of himself, of the government, of his relations with the press corps. The *New York Times* reporter was left with the "very distinct impression that he was in better health than he had been at any time since he entered the White House." Wilson was then ten days short of his sixtieth birthday, and he did not look his age, the reporter continued. There was, indeed, "a striking youthfulness about the entire appearance of the President . . . his figure looked trim . . . almost boyish."[31]

WHEN THERE IS NO PEACE

While Wilson was campaigning, and in the months following his election and the beginning of his second term, European countries were feeling the deepening stress of prolonged conflict. The 1916 offensives had failed to gain a decisive victory, leaving the countries at war in a fearful quandary: whether to cast all into preparations for a renewed slaughter the following spring and summer, or to explore a final chance of peace. If the peoples on both sides were hungry for peace, the military still pressed for a solution by force.

To shore up their determination for victory, warring governments made sure that the most militant leaders were in control. In December 1916 the liberal Asquith coalition was replaced by one headed by the more aggressive and more brilliant David Lloyd George. In Germany the moderate foreign minister, Jagow, was replaced by Arthur Zimmerman. Everywhere the brutalities of war were acted out as if to prove the depths of man's unreason. Turks engaged in the massacre of Armenians; Germans dropped bombs from zeppelins on the civilian populations of London and Paris while deporting large numbers of Belgians for forced labor; Poles were caught up in devastating marches across their territory by German, Russian, and Austrian armies. The relatively sane British, whose role as a sea power had traditionally preserved them from the worst degradations of war, found themselves by the summer of 1916 fully engaged in land warfare, exposed to all the catastrophic effects of the slaughter in Flanders.

The prime task for Wilson, as he saw it in the postelection period, was to keep the United States outside the maelstrom in the hope that it might persevere as a detached and cooling presence. He was more impressed than ever by the need to have in the immediate postwar period one voice speaking some other counsel than that of hatred and revenge. All he had known of war as a child and of its aftermath during his teenage years in the South warned him of its terrors and corruptions. He was by nature untuned to violence. If a romantic southern strain had sometimes led him to dream of chivalrous exploits, especially in battles at sea, he had been thoroughly disabused of it by war's modern techniques. War, he wrote in an unpublished paper at this time, "used to be a sort of national excursion . . . with brilliant battles lost and won. . . . But can this vast, gruesome contest of systematized destruction . . . be pictured in that light?"[1] With foreboding he saw the cost not only in death and physical destruction but in reforms abandoned and freedoms jeopardized. He perceived instinctively—what later as a man going to his own doom he would act out step by step—the surrender to war's emotions of basic standards of fairness and civility.

That armed conflict was a possibility for the United States, though one to be skirted by every means, Wilson acknowledged in steps taken to increase military preparedness. The National Defense Act, passed in the spring of 1916, enlarged the army and made provisions for a more effective navy. Insignificant in comparison to the national mobilization a year later, these actions were important in making the United States face war as a perhaps inescapable contingency. Portents of involvement could be seen also in establishment of the Council of National Defense and the Shipping Board, agencies that were to prove invaluable in America's later contribution to the Allied cause.

Partisans of the Allies, led by Roosevelt in the press and Lodge in the Senate, gained support as Germany exceeded former outrages. One German maneuver, of an insolent rather than a particularly brutal nature, especially roused public opinion. The giant German submarine U-53, one of the new class of vessels increasingly becoming the terror of the seas, surfaced in October 1916 before the eyes of astonished citizens in the harbor of Newport, Rhode Island. Its captain went ashore to deliver a letter to the German ambassador and to pick up local newspapers. Putting to sea, the submarine sank nine enemy vessels in the next twenty-four hours. Alarming as they were, these actions violated neither the *Sussex* pledge nor the rules of international law. In the midst of autumn campaigning Wilson summoned Bernstorff to Shadow Lawn to read him a stiff lecture, and more than ever it was plain how war could graze American shores.

Spurred by the various forces in play, Wilson at some point in the days following his reelection came doggedly to the conclusion that the only certain way to keep America out of the war was to end it. For him to jump into the role of peacemaker was a course abhorrent to his chief foreign policy advisers, House and Lansing, and in Page it created a mood close to hysteria. Such a step involved major risks and at the least was bound to cost the President personal revilement. Peacemakers have always been a hated breed, condemned as meddlers, suspected of hidden motives. Christian teaching—though acknowledging them to be among the sons of God—places peacemakers in the category of the meek, the persecuted, and the poor in spirit. Wilson was fully aware of the dangers of injecting himself into the headlong passions and rooted interests of the combatants. Yet he was resolved to take this course.

The task was the more formidable because it was Germany, not the

Allies, that in the post-election period first proposed a conference to end the war. England and France rejected the idea out of hand, being determined to achieve unconditional victory by force of arms. They had reason to be suspicious of any truce. German armies stood athwart Belgium and most of northeast France, and would remain—whatever their promises of withdrawal—in physical possession of vast conquered territories. France acknowledged only one overriding aim: expulsion of Germans from her soil. Under Lloyd George, Britain was being roused to primitive lust for victory and revenge. To enter into this vortex of force was for the American President a perilous course indeed.

Nevertheless he proceeded as soon as his own mandate was assured. On his typewriter he tapped out successive versions of a peace note to be sent to the Entente—Britain and France—and to the Central Powers. His strategy was to avoid the dreaded word "mediation" and to concentrate on securing from the warring nations a plain and detailed statement of the terms on which they would make peace. As a minimum he hoped the information thus gained would provide some unexpected basis for discussion. His larger goal was to ensure that, a just peace having been negotiated, the United States would be in a position to help guarantee its permanence.

Most audacious in this move was Wilson's supposition that the belligerents could be induced to state more magnanimous terms than those which they had generally affirmed. Aims of expansion or revenge, deals and concessions embodied in private arrangements, he dared think might be laid aside; he believed that the growing threat to civilization might induce the leaders to see their respective causes in a different light from that which shone murkily across the battlefields. But the belligerents on both sides were hardened and cynical after three years of savage war and they had no idea of departing from declared and undeclared objectives.

Wilson toiled at the peace note through late November and early December. He made elaborate provisions for having it delivered in secrecy to the governments concerned. Two factors, however, caused him to delay its dispatch. The furor aroused in Allied and neutral countries by Germany's forced deportation of Belgian citizens made talk of peace untimely. The submission of Germany's own peace note of December 12, couched in truculent terms, declaring the invincibility of the Central Powers and hinting at renewed horrors if negotiations were rejected, was an acute embarrassment. Coming shortly after such a move, Wilson's note was in danger of seeming part of the German ploy. He waited; in a revised text he explicitly disassociated the United States from any possible allegations of complicity, and on December 18 dispatched his inquiry to all the nations at war.

On being released to the public a few days later, the note was accompanied by a statement of Lansing's so subversive of the President's purpose as to make it nothing less than an act of betrayal. Lansing, it has been noted, was not interested in promoting peace so much as siding with the Allies in war. Gratuitously seeking to elucidate the President's words, "the situation," he told the press, "is becoming increasingly critical. I mean by that we are drawing nearer the verge of war ourselves. . . . The sending of this note will indicate the possibility of our being forced into the war. . . . Neither the President nor myself regard this note as a peace note."[2] It would have been difficult to find words more directly falsifying the President's intention. Furious, Wilson called Lansing to the White House, and a second statement, in effect withdrawing the first, was issued by the Secretary of State. Wilson must have been sorely tempted to request Lansing's resignation on the spot.

The governments of Britain and France received the note as if it were deliberately hostile. Page did not overstate the Allied reaction when he described it as one of "surprise and sorrowful consternation." The British, he added, felt the war to be "holy and defensive"; an inquiry into their aims cast doubt upon all their sacrifices.[3] A little later he cabled Wilson an account of his conversation with the Minister of Blockade, Lord Robert Cecil, its argument precisely that which, gripping statesmen in the advanced stages of a great conflict, may well doom civilization to a final holocaust. Failure to carry the war to complete victory, Cecil was quoted as saying, "would leave the world at the mercy of the most arrogant and the bloodiest tyranny that had ever been organized." European civilization had been "murderously assaulted," and there was nothing to do but to "defeat its desperate enemy or *to perish in the effort.*"[4] Despite Wilson's disavowal, the Allies took the substance of his note to be supportive of the German peace proposal.

Matters were made worse by the fact that Wilson had chosen to make explicit the premise underlying his hopes for peace. This premise was that the war was, in essence, a civil war within the European community and that it was susceptible to mediation because the two sides professed allegiance to the same ultimate goals. The President, declared the note, "takes the liberty of calling attention to the fact that the objects which the statesmen of the belligerents on both sides have in mind in this war are virtually the same, as stated in general terms to their own people and to the world."[5] Even granting Wilson's shrewd understanding that the propaganda of the warring powers only approximated their true aims, the sentence cut at the heart of the Allied cause. For the President to put the two sides on an equal moral basis seemed not neutral but actually malicious.

Yet Wilson was not writing heedlessly. Never had he been more deliberate in his choice of words. He saw the need to jar the Western world out of the fixed preoccupations of a deepening morass: by an act of the will and the imagination to set the problem of peace in the light of an unconditioned justice. Lincoln had done much the same thing in his Second Inaugural when he declared of the two warring camps, "Both read the same Bible, and pray to the same God; and each invokes His aid against the other. . . . The prayers of both could not be answered."

Wilson was prepared for the kind of misunderstanding his peace note inevitably invoked, trusting that with a little time the peoples of the warring powers would begin to see the futility of a longer war. His fateful note having been dispatched, he faced Christmastime 1916 in a relaxed, reflective mood. He wrote informally to friends and political supporters thanking them for various favors of the past year. Lucy and Mary Smith received an account of a "very happy" Christmas in the White House. The three Wilson daughters were there, along with Stockton Axson and several members of Edith's family—"in all twenty-two very jolly people." A tree was lit and traditional charades took place. Stockton played the "tough" characters with ability, and the Wilson girls, their father reported, "showed alarmingly finished histrionic gifts."[6] A few days later he marked his sixtieth birthday. Cleveland Dodge recalled another birthday, at Princeton, just ten years before. "How big the lively scrapes of those days seemed at the time," he wrote, "and how small they seem now."

The afterglow of victory still colored this brief interlude of calm. Ahead were inner struggles and grave decisions. "We thank God for all you mean to the world," Dodge concluded, "and trust that your life and strength may be spared for many years."[7]

The first reply to Wilson's peace note was handed to Gerard on December 26 by the German Foreign Secretary. It consisted of a brief avowal of Germany's willingness to meet with its enemies on neutral ground for direct exchange of views on terms for ending the conflict, and promised to cooperate with the United States in devising means to prevent future wars. The Allied reply, received two weeks later in Washington, was more lengthy if not more helpfully explicit. It reviewed the long train of German abuses, declared the uncontested cause of the war to be the aggression of Germany and Austria-Hungary, and protested strongly against the President's appearing to equate the moral positions of the two warring camps. The objects of the war, it declared in a sentence ominous for the future, "will not be made known in detail with all the equitable compensations and indemnities suffered for damages until the hour of negotiations."[8] Meanwhile, minimal requirements were the evacuation of all occupied territories with adequate reparations and guarantees for lasting European peace.

Wilson got little new information from these replies. But as a result of the exchange he saw opening before him a dramatic challenge. If the belligerent governments would not respond constructively to his inquiry, he would go over the heads of the contestants (as he had done recently in the railway dispute) and himself propose the terms of settlement. Speaking for the most powerful of the neutral countries, on behalf of the peoples of the world, he would set forth the outlines of a just peace.

The preparation of a major address was immediately begun. "The thing is in course," he wrote House on January 11. Lansing reviewed the text, as did the chairman of the Foreign Relations Committee, Senator Stone. Neither was "very expressive," said the President, but they had acquiesced—"Stone, I thought, a little wonderingly, as if the idea stunned him a bit."[9] The State Department code clerk worked day and night through the weekend getting the speech ready to send to U.S. embassies and legations, with instructions that they were to get the full text into the newspapers of their respective countries.

Still maintaining closest secrecy, the President on January 22 requested permission of the Senate to address it, and when he appeared a few hours later the mood was one of high expectancy. He opened by recalling his peace note of the previous month; putting the best interpretation possible on the replies he had received, he stated that "we are that much nearer a definite discussion of the peace which shall end the present war." When that time came, the United States, he continued, would render the service of adding "their authority and power to the authority and force of other nations to guarantee peace and justice throughout the world." It made a great deal of difference to the United States on what terms the war ended, and it was right that the United States should "frankly formulate the conditions," which would justify to its people this long-range commitment.

A just peace, he declared, must be "a peace without victory." This phrase he let fall with deliberation and went on to explain precisely what he meant by it. "Victory would mean peace forced upon the loser, a victor's terms imposed upon the vanquished. It would be accepted in humiliation, under duress, at an intolerable sacrifice, and would leave a sting, a resentment, a bitter memory upon which terms of peace would rest, not permanently, but only as upon quicksand." A peace among equals alone could last, and a peace accepting the principle that all just governments derive their authority from the consent of the governed. "The world can be at peace only if its life is stable, and there can be no stability where the will is in rebellion, where there is not tranquillity of spirit and a sense of justice, of freedom, and of right."

To the idea of peace among equals, and government based on consent, Wilson added general disarmament and freedom of the seas. He concluded with a double appeal—to his own people and to a worldwide constituency. "I feel confident," he declared, "that I have said what the people of the United States would wish me to say." But he went further: "I hope and believe that I am in effect speaking for liberals and friends of humanity in every nation. . . . I would fain believe that I am speaking for the silent mass of mankind everywhere."[10]

The audacity of this January 22 speech, the elevation of its style and tone, won for it a reception of immense fervor. The common people were given a glimpse of another kind of world from that in which they had been living. To men and women bitter after years of inconclusive conflict, bereft of loved ones, deprived of the simplest comforts and living under known and unknown threats of terror, the President offered a healing vision. At a time when militarism was becoming the prevailing mood, he had spoken in the noblest tradition of Western liberalism.

Allied statesmen firmly rejected any negotiation before a final conquest. Yet from their point of view the timing of Wilson's appeal was particularly dangerous. Not only were their peoples sick of war, but their resources were running low. Britain's financial credit was severely strained; France's manpower was exhausted to the point where more than one additional offensive was considered by the military to be unfeasible. As for the Prussians, they also pressed for unconditional surrender. But their militarists were not in unchallenged command of policy, and civil authorities were beginning to weigh a negotiated settlement in the west against the possibility of consolidating a vast empire in the east, the old dream of a rule stretching from Berlin to Baghdad. The British blockade, meanwhile, was beginning to exert its toll. No more than the Allied leaders were the Germans certain they could induce their population to accept another summer offensive, with its heedless slaughter and its quite possibly indecisive results.

The situation into which Wilson had stepped with his peace note and his January 22 address was, in short, more fluid than it appeared on the surface or in official statements of the war leaders. Determined to take advantage of every opening, Wilson was carrying on through House, at the same time he was preparing his address, a highly secret diplomatic dialogue with the governments of Britain and Germany. The possibility of preliminary talks leading toward a peace conference was at one moment so encouraging that Wilson allowed a gleam of hope to penetrate his habitually somber and wary mood. As the year 1917 dawned, a further opening on the diplomatic front, an opportunity to neutralize Austria, presented itself. The newly appointed Austrian Foreign Minister, Count Ottokar Czernin, sent an indirect message to the President that could be interpreted as a readiness to enter into secret discussions of peace, provided its terms permitted the empire to remain intact.[11] This was a positive response to the Wilson peace note and the first time he had been recognized as the sole figure capable of breaking the international deadlock.

Again, he experienced a gleam of hope. Through Page he informed the British Prime Minister that the allies should encourage negotiations with Austria on the condition indicated by Czernin. The view that Wilson was determined at all costs to break up the Austro-Hungarian empire, to sacrifice it to the dogma of self-determination, is countered by his eagerness to respond affirmatively to the Austrian Foreign Minister. Indeed he was convinced that the monolithic sway of the Habsburgs had already been undermined and that within a federation the older parts of the empire, including Hungary and Bohemia, could be accommodated. The British, however, were not interested in the idea of a separate peace with Austria. Lloyd George replied coolly to Page's inquiries that he preferred to keep Austria-Hungary in the war to act as a drain upon Germany's economic resources.[12]

The fragile and tentative advances toward peace in early 1917 were abruptly shattered by two events. The first was the Germans' decision to renew unrestricted submarine warfare, a decision based on the belief that they could achieve victory before the United States mobilized its forces. The second event was the interception and decoding by the British of a highly secret message from the new German Foreign Secretary, Arthur Zimmerman, to the German ambassador in Mexico. The latter was instructed, in the almost certain case that renewed German submarine warfare brought the United States into the war, to propose to the Mexican government an alliance with Germany. Mexico was to be assured, moreover, that at the peace table following a German victory, she was to be given back lost territories, including the states of Texas,

New Mexico, and Arizona. Known to history as the Zimmerman telegram, this act of astonishing bravado was for a few days kept from the press, but it signaled the end of any hope for peace negotiations.[13] There was to be no sparing the world of the bloodbath of the 1917 offensives; no possibility of saving from final dissolution an Austro-Hungarian empire, shorn of its oppressive centralization to act as a stabilizing factor in a new Europe.

On the last day of January 1917, Bernstorff called formally on Lansing to announce the decision taken two weeks previously by his government in Berlin that it would resume unrestricted submarine warfare. Both men knew that a decisive point in their countries' relationship had been reached. The ambassador's eyes, Lansing noted, filled with tears as he took his leave. In his memoirs the normally unfeeling Secretary of State went so far as to express compassion for Bernstorff. However devoted to the German cause—in fact because he was devoted to it—he had been sincere in believing that his country's interests would best be served by keeping on good terms with the United States and above all by avoiding an open military break.

For Wilson this revelation of German policy was a profound shock. His distrust of the German government was made complete when he discovered that Bernstorff had continued discussion of a peace conference when already privy to his government's decision for a new submarine offensive. All he had worked for had come to nought. The *Sussex* pledge was now a nullity; the period of relative calm upon the seas was to be broken by fresh terrors. In the circumstances a diplomatic breach with Germany was inevitable. Beyond that loomed the prospect of America at war, the twilight of reason, and probably the end of hope for a just peace. He felt as if the sun had suddenly reversed itself, he told House the next day; "that after going from east to west, it had begun to go from west to east and that he could not get his balance."[14] He reacted to the first news as had been characteristic of him in other crises, withdrawing to think his own thoughts.

"There is a terrible isolation," he had said of Lincoln a few months earlier, "for the conscience of every man who seeks to read the destiny in affairs for others as well as himself, for a nation as well as for individuals. That privacy no man can intrude upon." Such isolation was his for a few hours; then in the evening he called in his Secretary of State. For almost two hours the two men talked.[15] Lansing urged an immediate break in diplomatic relations. Wilson knew well it would probably come to that, and before the discussion ended he instructed Lansing to prepare the formal papers for a break, to be held on a standby basis. Yet Wilson still sought for a way out.

He argued the importance of husbanding resources so that the United States could help rebuild a ravaged continent after the war. He predicted destruction of the historic community of Europe; he expressed the fear, as he had put it earlier, that "an injury be done to civilization itself which can never be atoned for or repaired." If it were possible for the United States to stay out of the war, he would be willing to bear any amount of abuse and accusations of weakness. Contempt, he said, was nothing to him personally.

Before the evening's discussion was through, Wilson saw his course clearly. He would hold out for peace as long as he could; would play for time; would endeavor by every means to find an entering wedge for negotiation. Yet he would face war as perhaps inevitable. Germany's resumption of unrestricted submarine tactics made the rights of neutrals impossible to maintain; the Allies, very probably, could not survive in the circumstances without direct military aid. His mood the next day, when House came down from New York, was that of a man who had faced last things and come to terms with them. He "nervously arranged his books and walked up and down the floor," House recorded after his visit. "We had finished the discussion within a half hour and there was nothing further to say." The President suggested that the two men play a game of pool.[16]

At the cabinet meeting the next day opinions ranged from pleas for further patience to a demand for a declaration of war. Wilson, who had feared dissensions and even resignation within his official family, managed to keep the more ardent of his advisers in line. He was himself still convinced that it would be best if the conflict ended in a draw, and the cabinet as a whole was ready to avoid an irreversible act of war. A break in diplomatic relations with Germany was the middle course—the minimal response that seemed tolerable, and the maximum required by the immediate situation.

From the cabinet meeting Wilson went directly to the Capitol to confer with Stone and other leading legislators. Again there was agreement that the United States could not accept with impunity the abrogation of American rights implied by the German order; and again reluctance to see the order as a *casus belli*. Thus fortified, the President worked late into the night on a message to Congress, and the next day at noon appeared before the houses announcing that he had instructed the Secretary of State to inform the German ambassador that diplomatic relations between the two countries had been severed. Bernstorff was to be given his passports forthwith and Gerard to be immediately recalled from Berlin.

What was striking in the President's address, though scarcely noted by his applauding audience, were the limits and restraints it expressed. It was still incredible, Wilson declared, that the Germans would indiscriminately destroy American and other neutral ships. Only "actual overt acts on their part" could make him accept the fact. Meanwhile he kept the option of returning to Congress for authority to arm American merchant ships defensively. The President thus staked out a middle course, and he still refused to turn his back on the Germans. "We are the sincere friends of the German people," he concluded, "and earnestly desire to remain at peace with the Government which speaks for them. We shall not believe that they are hostile to us unless and until we are obliged to believe it."[17]

The diplomatic break with Germany released a fierce debate within the United States, setting off massive antiwar demonstrations while mobilizing those with an instinctive sympathy for the European democracies. Yet the American people as a whole were certainly not ready to go to war at this time. As in earlier crises Wilson was striking a note remarkably close to the attitude of the great body of the population. Severance of relations with Germany, combined with readiness to defend the country's rights if the submarine decrees were pushed to their extreme, was a popular stance, and at the same time one permitting Wilson to prolong a search for peace. Notwithstanding the break, indeed, indications persisted that the German government was prepared, at least for the time being, to avoid sinking neutral ships.

Following his reelection Wilson had dealt vigorously and astutely with foreign policy. But during the same period his relations with Congress deteriorated sharply. Here he made errors of judgment, acted intolerantly toward the opposition and, when thwarted, exercised unmasked the powers inherent in his office. At times he was genuinely puzzled by what appeared to be the unreasoning hostility of the opposition; the national interest, questions of war and peace, seemed so largely to transcend routine politics as to rule out partisanship or thoughts of personal advantage. But at other times he was simply angry, prepared by any means available to override those who stood in his way. Between his first peace note and the close of the congressional session he fostered the kind of bitterness that was to be his undoing in later, climactic fights.

Congress found no objection to the general idea of his peace note of December; but specific references to a future league of nations ignited the passions of a small group. Roosevelt led the pack from the outside. In the Senate, Lodge showed his remorseless hostility to the President, along with a politician's capacity blandly to repudiate what he had formerly stood for. These were joined by Senator William E. Borah, arch-spokesman of midwestern isolationism. Before framing his "peace without victory" speech Wilson was aware that a cabal in the Senate, echoed by vociferous outside opinion, would block a proposed resolution implying support for an international organization of which America would be a part.

Considerable as were these provocations, Wilson could have done better than to match them in bitterness. Invited to attend a church function where Lodge would be present, he let it be known that he would not associate with the senator. A little later the ban was extended to the whole cabinet. Far more serious, Wilson loosed his wrath against a handful of hostile senators who delayed by filibuster what he considered an essential war measure.

He had submitted quite suddenly, in the closing days of the session, a request for standby powers to arm American merchantmen. He had previously alluded to such a possibility; but in fact he already possessed the necessary constitutional authority, and in any case he could have timed his appeal so as to have it fall prior to the hectic closing days of the session. To senators fearful of being drawn into the war it appeared that the President was deliberately putting them on the spot, leaving them with the uncomfortable choice of abandoning their principles or publicly dissenting from a popular and patriotic move.

At the same time an unlikely coalition was formed favoring a special session of Congress. Senators like Borah were convinced that the President's course required surveillance; Lodge and his associates, that he needed to be prodded into a more militantly pro-Allied stance. To both these factions, and to the general idea of a special session, Wilson was adamantly opposed. He threw the full weight of his prestige, together with resort to some dubious political maneuvers, into thwarting the special session while wringing from the reluctant legislators explicit approval for arming merchant ships.

On February 28, in the midst of the battle, he made public the Zimmerman Telegram. Violent expressions of outrage against Germany arose as was to be expected, and overrode every other consideration. In the surge of patriotic emotion the armed ship bill passed overwhelmingly in the House. To the already embittered senators it appeared that Wilson had deliberately timed the telegram's release so as to force their hands.

As if this were not enough, the administration made political use of the sinking of the *Laconia*, a British liner lost with American citizens on board. Spokesmen for the President suggested this was such a clear, overt act as required more militant steps against Germany. Yet in fact the sinking of belligerent ships, even with American casualties, had not been defined by Wilson as an act sharply challenging American rights. The apparent change in position seemed aimed at recalcitrant legislators.

Although the House had capitulated, the situation in the Senate continued uncertain. On the eve of the session's end and of the inaugural ceremonies beginning the President's second term, bitter controversy still prevailed. Senator Stone, previously the administration's strong supporter, turned against the bill on the grounds that arming merchantmen would lead to war. Four midwestern senators started a filibuster. Through the night of March 3 Wilson kept watch at the White House, his anger and frustration mounting. The next morning, a Sunday, he went down to the President's room in the Capitol to sign last-minute bills. At noon he rose from his desk chair to take the oath of office and then immediately sat down to continue with his work. It was, said *The New York Times*, "the strangest inauguration in history."

Meanwhile the filibuster continued. The President that afternoon composed a statement bitterly denouncing the eleven dissident senators. It was a situation, he wrote, unparalleled in the history of the country. Then came the stinging words that in the next morning's press echoed through the country. "A little group of willful men, representing no opinion but their own, have rendered the great Government of the United States helpless and contemptible."[18] Again Wilson had coined an unforgettable phrase, and, as in the case of his earlier rebuke to lobbyists in the tariff fight, public wrath fell upon the offenders. This time, however, the statement in retrospect appeared harmful and ungenerous, and Wilson came to regret having impugned the patriotism of the protesting senators.

Formal inaugural ceremonies, following the private oath-taking, were held on Monday. Wilson drove to the Capitol under heavy guard while armed men scanned the scene from rooftops along the way. Not since the Civil War had such precautions been manifest. Rain had been falling for forty-eight hours and with high winds it continued as the President stepped forth to read his inaugural address. The winds carried his voice away so that only those closest to him could hear.

The address, in any case, was not one of his most notable. He had composed it hastily, amid other preoccupations. Besides, his denunciation of the Senate's "willful men" upstaged whatever he now said. Recalling briefly domestic accomplishments of the last four years, he reviewed America's critical posture on the international stage. The country must continue to be neutral; yet he warned that it must be prepared to be drawn into "a more immediate association with the great struggle itself." The conclusion was an affecting and personal plea, which in other circumstances might have minimized the effects of hard blows taken and bestowed. "I pray God I may be given the wisdom and the prudence to do my duty. . . . I beg your tolerance, your countenance and your united aid. The shadows that now lie dark upon our path will soon be dispelled and we shall walk with the light all about us if we be but true to ourselves."[19]

That evening, after a quiet dinner, the family went upstairs to watch the fireworks illuminating Washington. The President and Mrs. Wilson sat apart, holding hands, and called House over to be with them. It was a happy moment, and it was good, House confided to his diary, that "we three" rather than the Hughes family should be sharing the triumph of the day.[20]

CHAPTER EIGHT

War Leader

DECISION FOR WAR

Wilson was now the central figure at a turning point of the twentieth century. Whether the United States should go to war—with all the consequences for itself and for the rest of the world—depended to an extraordinary degree on his decision alone. During the month of March external events did, it is true, push the United States closer to belligerency. A number of American ships were sunk. Economic frustrations were intensified by the reluctance of American shipowners to breast the dangers of the high seas. At the same time the international atmosphere was cleared as by a lightning stroke by revolution in Russia. But these, neither singly or together, made U. S. entry into the war automatic or inevitable. The country had borne worse provocations and observed more far-reaching possibilities, and under the President's prudent leadership had remained at peace. The dramatic shift in U. S. posture occurred in large part because Woodrow Wilson willed it. The change from his determination to remain outside the conflict, expressed as late as the Second Inaugural, to his call for war on April 2 was caused by outside circumstances playing upon his own slowly congealing purpose.

The fact that Wilson defined America's interest in terms of rights to be maintained against belligerent actions, both those of the Entente and those of the Central Powers, meant that he had faced the possibility of going to war at some point. He had recognized since the start of the European conflict—and he painstakingly led the people to recognize as well—that the country might be called to vindicate what had been guaranteed to neutral nations by historic precedent and international law. Patience, national discipline, a strict regard for the facts of each incident

433

upon the high seas were not incompatible in his mind with the possibility of an ultimate resolution by force of arms.

Yet Wilson did not conceive America's interest in terms of rights alone. He saw its wider concern: the establishment of a regime of liberty in the world, within which the United States could prosper and develop. The long-range advantage of an Allied rather than a German victory was plain to him. Despite his almost constant annoyance at British policymakers, he knew how closely American values were linked to the preservation of Anglo-Saxon civilization. And not moral or cultural values only. America's security from attack, and its freedom from a heavy burden of armaments, depended on the shield provided by British sea power. The shield was threatened by increasing military peril, and that fact, hardly less than the erosion of neutral rights, caused Wilson to incline toward war.

The devastation of the European conflict, similar to that of the American Civil War but going beyond it in scope and horror, caused Wilson to think not only of the need for peace but the larger need to guarantee the world against future catastrophes. Direct American intervention, both to end the war and to assure a lasting peace, loomed as an alternative to neutrality. Countering this, and countering the strategic considerations, was Wilson's dread of ordering young men into battle, the pain of Vera Cruz multiplied a million-fold. He dreaded, too, the sacrifices of freedom on the home front, the coarsening of national sentiment and perception, that war fever would all too certainly induce.

The precise balancing of Wilson's inner thoughts against the changing exterior scene is impossible to determine. Much in the weeks between March 4 and April 2 remains obscure. That he went through a period of agony and self-doubt is plain—the agony of a man clear in his objectives and values but tormented by the necessity of reconciling things that appeared increasingly irreconcilable. His travail had the mysterious quality of a man coming face-to-face with his own fate. Because Wilson at his best interpreted the nation's deepest convictions and its true interests, he seemed to be bringing the American people face-to-face with their fate, too. That they accepted his decision for war with so little dissent indicated a rare moment of union between a leader and those whom he leads.

The winds and the cold of inauguration day left the President, as it did many others who participated, with a cold. On March 7 Grayson put him to bed and during the next week kept him in his room, canceling almost all official appointments. His wife acted as a transmitter of messages while she kept watch to preserve his seclusion. It is impossible to know all that passed through Wilson's mind during this period. It may well be that the illness was a reflection of inner turmoil. It may be that during this confinement he came to the conclusion that the United States had to enter the war. His actions immediately subsequent to this illness give no clear indication, one way or the other. He maintained up to March 21 an impenetrable façade.

The effects of Germany's unleashing of her submarines did not have the immediate consequences foreseen by many. In part this was because American ships waited in their home ports, fearful to venture forth. One steamer was sunk without warning by shellfire on March 12. "If he does not go to war," Roosevelt wrote privately of the President, "I shall skin him alive."[1] The public, however, let the incident pass without excitement. The reaction was different when a week later three ships were sunk, two after warnings and without casualties, but a third unwarned, causing the deaths of fifteen Americans. War fever flamed anew, and Wilson examined with his Secretary of State the whole maritime situation.

By then the President and his official advisers had concluded that even without specific Senate approval U.S. ships could be armed for defense. Orders were issued and naval officers put in command of the guns. Wilson reviewed carefully the orders under which they operated. He visited Daniels at the Navy Department to check on progress and to make suggestions for action against the German marauders. On one of his walking trips in England, he advised the Secretary of the Navy, he had noted three dogs being used to round up sheep. The sheep managed to avoid two of the dogs but always seemed surprised by the third. Might not fast motorboats be launched from American merchant ships, similarly in groups of three?

Despite the careful preparations, no encounters occurred upon the seas. The Germans did not get themselves into a position where their ships could be fired on by American vessels, an action tantamount to a declaration of war. The piling up on wharves in American ports of supplies vital to the Allies (and hardly less so to the prosperity of U.S. traders) remained, however, a cause for concern.

On March 17 news reached Washington of a momentous change in the European scene. Revolution had taken place in Petrograd and the Russian Duma had deposed the czar. A wave of relief and exhilaration swept through the Allied world. The cause of the democracies had been heavily shadowed by having on its side the cumbrous tyranny of the czarist regime, an incongruous ally, an uncertain and vacillating military force. The freedom won by the Russian people in one breathtaking night was a tonic to all professing to fight for freedom, an added incentive to make certain that Prussian militarism, which would surely extinguish it, did not triumph.

Wilson shared in the spirit of hope. He told the cabinet enthusiastically that the new Russian government must be a good one—it was headed by a professor. The next day he regaled his Secretary of the Navy with a detailed account of President Pavel Nikolaevich Miliukov's relations with the University of Chicago.[2] On being invited to lecture there, he had resolved to learn English in a year. The Russians jailed him, but obligingly arranged for his release so that he could pursue his studies in English.

Wilson was anxious to proceed immediately with recognition of the new government. The old order of things was passing away everywhere, he told the French ambassador; therefore the new should be acknowledged at once. Russian democracy might well be a frail structure; therefore it needed support the more from the American people. Indeed the United States became the first country to establish diplomatic relations with the fledgling regime.

The cabinet meeting of March 20 was remarkable in the depth and candor of its discussion of the war issue. No one present ever forgot it. We are fortunate in having Lansing's detailed if somewhat lumbering account of the proceedings.[3] The meeting took place in the midst of rising public indignation over the sinking (previously noted) of three American ships; the press gathered in force outside the cabinet room to await news of the momentous decisions it sensed to be in the making. Wilson entered, Lansing noted, "smiling as genially and composedly as if nothing of importance was to be considered." Composure, the Secretary continued, was a marked characteristic of the President. "Nothing ruffles the calmness of his manner or address," and this had "a sobering effect" on all who sat with him in council.

After some preliminaries the President put two questions to his official family. Should he summon the Congress in extraordinary session? If so, what precisely should he put before it? McAdoo and Houston were in favor of a declaration of war at the earliest possible moment. Redfield had always been strongly pro-Ally and was now for immediate engagement. Baker "with wonderful clearness" argued for a declaration of war accompanied by rapid buildup of the armed forces. Lansing recorded his own comments, solemnly and at length; no one was surprised that he believed the United States should range itself on the Allied side.

So it proceeded, Burleson and Gregory echoing opinions already expressed. "Well, Daniels?" the President inquired at last. Pacifist by disposition, a friend of Bryan's, no one believed Daniels could bring himself to agree with the majority. He "hesitated a moment," Lansing records, "then spoke with a voice which was low and trembled with emotion. His eyes were suffused with tears." He saw no other course, Daniels declared, than to enter the war. Did he speak with conviction or from lack of strength of mind? Lansing wondered in an aside. "I prefer to believe the former reason, though I am not sure." (It is a rather typical Lansing remark, exhibiting his own virtue while casting subtle doubt upon that of another.) In his record of these events Daniels admits the challenge to have been "a supreme moment" in his life. He had hoped and prayed "this cup would pass"—"But there was no other course opened."

"Everybody has spoken but you, Lane," the President continued, as calmly as if here conducting a Socratic dialogue. Lane favored war, expressing great indignation against the Germans. Thus the opinion of the cabinet was unanimous both in regard to calling an extraordinary session of the Congress and declaring war. "Well, gentlemen," said the President in a cool, unemotional way, "I think that there is no doubt as to what your advice is. I thank you." The meeting was over. The cabinet members passed silent and expressionless through the phalanx of waiting reporters. As to what was the President's decision, no one of his advisers knew.

Early the next morning Wilson dictated a statement that he was calling the Congress into extraordinary session on April 2 for the purpose of receiving "a communication concerning grave matters of national policy." Then he and Grayson left the White House for a game of golf. The weather was bad and they did not play, but a long motor ride provided a substitute form of relaxation. The days that followed had an air of suspended reality. The President's desk, noted Thomas W. Brahany of the White House staff, was piled high with letters and papers. "Apparently he is not in a working mood these days. He spends nearly all his time with Mrs. Wilson, reading, playing pool or visiting."[4] Brahany's description fits a man who is coming to a grave decision or who, having made one, invites his soul while the details of life take care of themselves.

One Saturday during this period the President and Edith Wilson took a walk together and on the way home stopped for calls upon the Secretary of War and the Secretary of the Navy. "I think this is the first time in American history," Brahany remarked, "that a President's wife has accompanied the President in a purely business call on a Cabinet Officer."[5] Edith admired a sword that had belonged to John Paul Jones and, according to Daniels, she hung on the President's stories and comments "with enthusiasm."[6]

Through these days the press was in despair over the lack of news, or even of any faint intimation of the President's thoughts. Lansing was so disturbed he drafted a statement explaining that the President was in fact not "undecided" but that his "course of silence" was due to the constitutional provision giving Congress the right to declare war. Lansing's lack of sensitivity was thus once again manifested; but the incident is more interesting because of Wilson's response. After telling his Secretary of State it would be a mistake to issue such a statement he added that it had been consistently shown that the way to face criticism was "not by words, but by some action which has met with the approval of the major part of the country."[7] The capacity to be silent, to withdraw and bear mounting criticism, and then to act boldly is an important element of leadership. Now, on the noblest scale, Wilson showed that he possessed it.

By March 28 he had made an outline of the topics he intended to cover in his forthcoming address; two days later, refusing to see the Secretary of the Treasury and the Postmaster General in a joint interview they had requested, he told Brahany to inform them that "he had locked himself in his study to work on his address to the Congress, and did not wish to be disturbed by anyone."

The following day, a Saturday, he was still toiling away. Some noise occurring downstairs in the White House, an usher was dispatched to shut the door of the President's study. "Who told you to shut that door?" the President, normally so courteous with his staff, inquired sharply. On being given the name of the offender, "Tell Hoover that I don't want [the door] closed—all I want is quiet."[8]

"He is certainly getting all the quiet he wants now," Brahany noted; "all of us are walking tiptoe and speaking in whispers."

At the last cabinet meeting prior to the extraordinary session the President spoke of the message he had been working on, but he did not read it to his official family nor give them much enlightenment on its substance. He told a few anecdotes, complained that he was stiff from sitting at his writing table all morning, and stood up to perform calisthenics at his end of the table. In the discussion that followed, the

President remarked that he wanted his message to be free of argument and emotion and to keep to a plain recital of facts. McAdoo, who was always saying the wrong thing, expressed the hope that in the message the worst crimes of the Germans would be set forth to stir up the people. The President must have sent his son-in-law a devastating glance. He proceeded to comment on the absurd stories being told about the Germans in the United States. The mansion's housekeeper had objected to there being "a German in the cellar"—an innocent old man tending the fires.

"I'd rather the blamed place should be blown up," Wilson exploded, "than to persecute inoffensive people."[9]

When the extraordinary session of the sixty-fifth Congress assembled on April 2, it took the members most of the day to get organized. Wilson watched the hours pass, outwardly calm but to his intimates showing signs of nervousness. Colonel House had come down from New York, and he was the only man to see in advance the text of the speech Wilson was to deliver that evening. Dinner was at six-thirty, with House and a few members of the family present; they talked of everything except the momentous event that was to take place. A little before eight-thirty, the President entered an automobile surrounded by armed cavalry, and through streets filled with crowds, many of them carrying flags or placards, made his way to the Capitol.

The scene within was not essentially different from what it had been on other occasions since the President renewed the custom of speaking directly to the Congress. Every place was filled, with members of the cabinet, the Supreme Court, the diplomatic corps, and important visitors crowding the floor and reaching to the remotest seats of the gallery. Having mounted the rostrum, with one arm resting upon it, Wilson began to read without ostensible emotion, but as he progressed the vibrancy of his voice increased and the marshaled sentences sounded out across the expectant hall, beautifully cadenced, complex, and subtly rounded.

He was a trained orator, one of the most accomplished of his generation, and this was the oration for which, in one way or another, he had been preparing all his life. Reaching successive climaxes—"each sentence was a pennant," one observer wrote of it, "and every word a blazoning"—he moved to an unforgettable conclusion. "Only a statesman who will be called great," Walter Lippmann wrote of the speech at the time, "could have made America's intervention mean so much to the generous forces of the world, could have lifted the inevitable horror of war into a deed so full of meaning."[10]

In the address Wilson went back to Germany's declaration of unlimited submarine war: for a while he had been unwilling to believe that the German government would in fact do the things it had declared itself ready to do. Armed neutrality had proven but a temporary posture, for the Germans were prepared to treat the armed guards upon merchant ships as "beyond the pale of law and subject to be dealt with as pirates would be."[11] Then came the first climax. "With a profound sense of the solemn and even tragical character of the step I am taking . . . I advise that the Congress declare the recent course of the Imperial German Government to be in fact nothing less than war against the government and people of the United States." Men arose from their seats and cheered, and the cheers echoed again as the President outlined the vigorous steps that would be taken to prosecute the armed struggle.

Yet the cheers were not permitted to sound for long. In even tones Wilson immediately proceeded. "While we do these things, these deeply momentous things," he said, "let us be very clear, and make very clear to all the world what our motives and our objects are." They were the same objects as he had declared in his address of January 22, the much misunderstood "peace without victory" speech. "We have no quarrel with the German people. We have no feeling towards them but one of sympathy and friendship." Then the second climax: "We are glad . . . to fight thus for the ultimate peace of the world and for the liberation of its peoples, the German people included: for the rights of nations great and small and for the privilege of men everywhere to choose their way of life and obedience. The world must be made safe for democracy."

A recent scholar, remarking on the "somber beauty" of the address, adds that it lays major stress on "uncertainty, limitation, and inescapability."[12] Wilson used the word "tragical" in describing the step he was taking, and it expresses the underlying theme. By tragical Wilson was not referring to the loss of life the struggle would entail, though that was never far from his mind; he was using the word in a much deeper sense, to imply that at the last, when everything else had failed, the fate of America was to achieve its predestined end by means that were dubious and perhaps evil. War was a tremendous risk, the risk not being defeat, but corruption of the goals for which it was fought.

Then Wilson advanced into his peroration, a passage that lives in the anthology of American political prose along with a few of the great utterances of Lincoln, engaged in an earlier war and in an earlier fateful contradiction of ends and means:

There are, it may be, many months of fiery trial and sacrifice ahead of us. It is a fearful thing to lead this great peaceful people into war, into the most terrible and disastrous of all wars, civilization itself seeming to be in the balance. But the right is more precious than peace, and we shall fight for the things which we have always carried nearest our hearts,— for democracy, for the right of those who submit to authority to have a voice in their own governments, for the rights and liberties of small nations, for a universal dominion of right by such a concert of free peoples as shall bring peace and safety to all nations and make the world itself at last free. To such a task we can dedicate our lives and our fortunes, everything that we are and everything that we have, with the pride of those who know that the day has come when America is privileged to spend her blood and her might for the principles that gave her birth and happiness and the peace which she has treasured. God helping her, she can do no other.

The President was back at the White House by nine-thirty. He sat with Edith, his daughter Margaret, and Colonel House in the Oval Room, discussing the evening "as families are prone to do after some eventful occasion." Through the night of April 4 the Senate debated and then acted upon the war resolution; on April 6, Good Friday, the House approved. The House vote was by a majority of 373 to 50, a remarkable tribute to the unity Wilson had forged through long months of patient seeking and waiting. A messenger brought the document to the White House and the President, leaving the luncheon table, perched at the chief usher's desk and signed it immediately.[13]

Lieutenant Byron McCandless, aide to the Secretary of the Navy, went to the Executive Avenue entrance to the White House grounds and in a prearranged signal waved to an officer in the Navy Department. By wireless and cable the message went out to ships at sea. The United States was at war.

AT THE SIDE OF THE ALLIES

The country woke up on the morning of April 8, 1917, to find itself at war; but when the rhetoric had cooled and the first emotion had subsided, war seemed to most people a far-off and nebulous condition. No danger of sudden attack confronted them, as no immediate opportunity for getting at the enemy was apparent. For the administration in Washington the long process of reaching a decision gave way to days without

drama and often without visible results. Wilson's first impulse was to
believe that the American contribution to the war would be largely
confined to logistical support. The Allies required ships, arms, foods,
credits. The manpower of the country needed to be allocated so as to
create maximum efficiency in the production of goods; transportation
needed to be rationalized and industrial peace ensured. Despite the contemplated increase in military forces, their intervention on a large scale
was not in the beginning a top priority.

Wilson foresaw a period of carefully managed adjustment during which
the country would move by orderly degrees into a full military posture.
The Allied powers were not prepared to be so logical. Anxious to test
out immediately the depth of the American commitment, they were also
eager to appraise the leader who had hitherto appeared remote and
incalculable. Echoes of Wilson's war message had scarcely died away
before the British let it be known that they would like to be invited to
send the Foreign Secretary, Arthur James Balfour, at the head of a
mission of experts to align the war effort of the two countries. The
French, not to be outdone, were prepared to send René Viviani, a former
Premier and now Minister of Justice, together with a miliary mission
headed by Marshal Joseph Jacques Joffre, until recently commander-in-
chief of the French armies.

Wilson was reluctant to receive these missions at so early a stage in
America's belligerency. He felt he had other tasks than those that seemed
likely to prove distracting and largely ceremonial. Suspicious of the war
aims of the Allies, he did not want to be pushed into supporting the full
spectrum of their objectives. He would have preferred to await such
consultations until his standing as a war leader had been demonstrated,
and the country's growing military and economic might was manifest.
It was difficult, nevertheless, to do anything but respond affirmatively
to the expressed desires of the British and the French.

His concern was allayed when the Europeans agreed that the question
of an alliance with the United States would not be raised. While committing itself to every kind of aid and support for the common war
effort, America, as an associate, not a full-fledged ally, would retain its
independence of political and diplomatic action. This posture avoided
many troublesome problems at the start of the new relationship, and,
at the end of the war, it revealed its full significance. The fact that the
United States was free in principle to make a separate peace became
Wilson's trump card in a last-ditch effort to secure from the Allied leaders

acceptance of his peace program. The French and British, in their relief at being able to draw fully on American strength, were meanwhile quite willing to yield Wilson this nice, but in the end highly important, distinction.

On April 22, after stopping in New York to see House, Balfour arrived with his group in Washington. The capital was decorated with British flags and a large street crowd "cheered, clapped, honked, tooted" as the mission proceeded with cavalry escort.[1] The next day, when the Foreign Secretary arrived at the White House, all available military and naval aides were on duty. A formal dinner in his honor nevertheless fell rather flat. The President forgot to toast the British king. "No music," reported a disappointed Tumulty, "no speeches, and not enough soup."[2]

The first business meeting between the President and the British statesman left Wilson similarly dissatisfied. He had hoped to prepare grounds of mutual understanding with a man whose cultivation and wide knowledge he admired. But Lansing was present, and Lansing, complained the President, "has a wooden mind and continually blocked what I was trying to convey."[3]

Sensing that things were not going well, House proposed a subsequent small family dinner at the White House where he, the President, and the Foreign Secretary could withdraw into private conversation. The agenda of the discussion was carefully worked out by House, but he overdid (as often he could) the complimentary epithets and introductions he felt called upon to make. The result was that Wilson seemed anxious to live up to the picture of literary brilliance House had painted. During dinner he talked at length, ranging widely over historical subjects, maintaining (as he had done many years before in an essay while at Wesleyan) that the "untruths," or myths, of history were sometimes as important as what actually occurred. After dinner Wilson continued to dominate the conversation. The two statesmen went over the map of Europe, from east to west, discussing its points of tension, its uneasy boundary lines. House, who had heard it before in a preliminary run-through, sat quietly and said nothing.

The French delegation under Viviani and Joffre arrived meanwhile with due ceremony, disembarking at Hampton Roads and sailing up the Potomac on the *Mayflower*. Assistant Secretary of State Breckinridge Long, delegated as official host, was eager to preside over an appropriately celebratory banquet. He was dismayed to find that no liquor could be served aboard the yacht, it being under the temperance rules of Josephus Daniels's navy. A hasty *démarche* seeking an exemption in favor of the illustrious guests proved unsuccessful. The French delegation would have no wine with dinner. "It will be a novel experience for them, I dare say,"[4] commented a member of the White House staff.

Receptions for both the British and the French were held by the Congress. Balfour, who remained in the United States for five weeks, made an address to the legislators. Meanwhile, Joffre went off on a cross-country tour, extolling ancient French-American ties. Ceremonies apart, the visit of the two missions had a tonic effect on the administration. Not only was the American relation to the Allies defined, but the realities of war were brought close. Arrangements were set on foot which, a year later, found the military and economic affairs of the powers intricately meshed.

The need for joint planning was evident. Far from solving the problems of the Allies, America's entrance into the war had in some ways made them worse. The British, for example, had put American dockyards under contract for the building of desperately needed ships; they had signed up virtually all available labor and materials. But the United States was about to begin its own intensified program of shipbuilding, setting the two powers in a competitive position bound to create shortages and to drive up prices. Similarly, the Americans were competing with Britain for the raw materials of the empire—rubber, wood, jute, tin. What was required was some form of rationing among the Allies, with prices fixed so as to avoid any of them benefiting from the inevitable shortages. Before the conflict was through American and British experts would be working side by side on boards and missions the creation of which dated from Balfour's extended Washington visit.

The manufacture of munitions for the European Allies had been proceeding apace in American plants. Now, unless efforts were coordinated, hastily stepped-up plans for equipping American troops would curtail supplies to troops already in the field. Airplanes provided a special challenge. The war opened with America having virtually no air force. The President and Secretary of War, determined to make a major contribution in this field, found themselves frustrated by difficulties in manufacturing the delicate planes then in use, with their wooden frames and stretched cotton or linen covering. More by trial and error than by joint planning, a division with the Allies was worked out—the Europeans supplying the frames, and the Americans, who were thoroughly familiar with the intricacies of internal combustion, supplying the excellent Liberty engines.

Difficulties in meshing the activities of the United States and its associates extended to every aspect of the war effort. The assigning of priorities to transportation in this country as well as abroad, of getting clearance for debarkation in the overloaded European ports, taxed officials dealing with totally unprecedented problems. The final success of these efforts is difficult to judge, for the war ended before the American contribution could come to a crest. Yet the degree of cooperation should not be underestimated, achieved in harsh circumstances from men with their normal share of pride and national jealousy.

Both French and British delegations used the occasion of their first wartime mission to get Wilson's measure. Their verdict was in general favorable—a fact somewhat surprising, considering the degree to which the long period of neutrality had tested their patience and sometimes outraged their opinions. Now they were reassured in regard to his absolute determination to see the war through, to cooperate fully in the economic and military spheres, and to take charge himself of all major policy decisions. They also sensed qualities of the man previously veiled, finding him more human, more businesslike and accessible, than had been conveyed to them by secondhand reports.

On the eve of Balfour's departure he met with the French ambassador in Washington. The latter reported him much pleased with the results of his visit. He was convinced that the President would continue the war "until the security of the liberal nations is assured." He was entirely confident that victory was near. "You will no doubt come then to Europe," he told his colleague, "and we shall celebrate together." Wilson had paid Balfour a great deal of attention, "drawn to the reflective side of his character," Jusserand added; and their mutual respect had certainly strengthened Britain's cause.[5]

The official French view, nevertheless, remained more reserved than that of the British. The language barrier, and the desperate French desire for unconditional victory, created a measure of aloofness not to be overcome by recollections of historic ties. But Joffre was not unpleasantly surprised when in a long interview he was closely catechized by the President on details of military organization and training, and on the deployment of future American contingents. Joffre's interpreter, Emil Hovelaque, summed up impressions of the President in a style that the old soldier was not accustomed to employ. Hovelaque wrote of "the sudden intensity of life" that revealed itself when Wilson spoke, a warmth that was unexpected coming from so impassive a mask; as were the supple inflections of his musical voice emanating from the stern mouth. The overall impression was that of a mystic combined with a man of action: "This lay Pope, separated from everyone by an icy solitude, is attentive to the least movements of the crowd and obedient to its wishes as he perceives them."

"I watched this austere, wise face of a Scottish dialectician," Hovelaque concluded, and "the Celt appeared to me in the rapid flash of a smile, in the sudden humanity of its clear eyes."[6]

Underlying discussions with the French and British, as it underlay discussions with the administration itself, was the question of when and in what circumstances a United States expeditionary force would be sent across the Atlantic. Wilson's first emphasis being on aid to the belligerents in the form of food, military supplies, and ships—both transport ships and destroyers to deal with the acute submarine menace—the foreign missions gave the impression of going along with him. At least they began by suggesting that no more than a symbolic American presence was necessary to raise morale at the front.

As the talks proceeded, however, the emphasis on manpower became more grimly insistent. A relative abundance of ammunition was available, it was pointed out; but this was because casualties had decimated troops which would otherwise have been on the firing line. It was revealed that the British were nearing the end of their reserves and that French reserves were exhausted. The front could not again be manned as at the start of previous offensives—at least not without massive American reinforcements.[7]

These revelations were ominous, but neither Wilson nor Baker had ever seriously doubted that sooner or later, if the war continued, a major force would be needed. To underline their conviction a small detachment of Americans was sent to France in the late spring of 1917, vanguard of the army that a year later would total more than two million men. At their head was General John J. Pershing, recently returned from the punitive expedition to Mexico. Stiff, sharp-eyed, independent-minded, Pershing was no enthusiast for Wilson's policies, and his appointment as commander-in-chief signaled that the war was to be run by professional soldiers, with a minimum of political interference.

The unresolved question in Wilson's mind in the spring of 1917 was not *per se* the sending of troops to Europe, but the timing, the scale, and the proportion of industrial and military aid. An entire nation was to be mobilized, not merely an army raised. Selective Service, which was at the top of Wilson's priorities and was quickly passed by Congress, was only in part a way of getting men into uniform; more significantly, it was a way of allocating manpower throughout the industrial system, putting groups and individuals in the place where they could contribute most effectively to the war effort.[8] To avoid diverting men from farming and essential industries was as important as putting into military training those who were best fitted and could most easily be spared for such duties. Selective Service was an essential part of mobilization—of the organizing and restructuring of the nation's total force; but it was not in itself a commitment to a particular military strategy.

"The business now in hand," Wilson asserted, "is undramatic, practical, and of scientific definiteness and precision."[9] Such standards applied to military as well as to industrial operations, even to the point of thwarting what appeared to the public as a highly appealing and chivalrous intervention. Soon after the country's entrance into the war, amid much publicity, Theodore Roosevelt arrived at the White House, proposing the immediate organization of a division to be dispatched under his command to the western front.

At the meeting between Wilson and Roosevelt in the Oval Office, the President was stiff and formal at first, but unbent as the old warrior talked on. He treated the ex-President with deferential courtesy, while the White House staff, lining the corridors, warmly greeted the man whom they had come to love for his personal zest and kindness.[10] But a few weeks later, when Roosevelt's offer was formalized, Wilson had a negative response in readiness. The war, he insisted, was not going to be won by heroic gestures made at the expense of serious military planning. In turning Roosevelt down, Wilson suffered the wrath of the Colonel's myriad admirers, but he had the full support of his military advisers.

The necessity of getting Americans into battle became more evident with each passing day, as casualties mounted among the Allies and morale declined. The winter of 1917 had been bitterly cold in Europe. Adequate fuel for the civilian population was lacking; inflation and taxes added their burden to the universal mourning. When Pershing arrived in Paris in June he was solemnly received by Marshal Philippe Pétain, just made commander-in-chief of the French armies, who presented him with a gloomy view of the French situation. Pétain described the riots and mutinies that had threatened to spread through the French troops; he spoke with something close to contempt for the politicians in control.[11] The young Felix Frankfurter, on an official fact-finding mission, reported to Lansing a scarcely less somber view, adding to Pétain's characteristic pessimism his opinion that the French were losing even their fervor for the recovery of Alsace and Lorraine, while being virtually oblivious to Wilson's ideals of a just peace.[12]

Wilson was aware of the deteriorating morale and wanted to give support to the Allies where it was most needed. But it was difficult to have enthusiasm for the French leaders' thinly masked view that what was wanted above all was a supply of human bodies trained or untrained, to be fed into the remorseless machine that traded casualties by the hundreds of thousands for gains measured sometimes in hundreds of yards. Morever, the idea of having America's young manhood supplied anonymously in piecemeal reinforcements, without the identity of an American army, was abhorrent to him, as it was to Pershing. Nevertheless, through the spring and early summer of 1917 preparations for a massive contribution of troops went forward, with no one knowing when or in what precise circumstances they would be deployed.

Naval forces might have been expected to reinforce Allied sea power upon the declaration of war. But in fact the navy was still far from being in a state of combat readiness, and Daniels was criticized for a reluctance to move it from a defensive posture. His chief of operations, Admiral William S. Benson, hated the English, and seemed more anxious to guard the Atlantic coast and the Caribbean than to move aggressively into the European theater. But Daniels was spurred on by his assistant secretary, Franklin D. Roosevelt; and with Henry T. Mayo in command of the Atlantic, he had a man who has been judged "one of the best fleet commanders in our history."[13]

It was Wilson himself, however, who acted as chief goad in naval affairs. He recognized the situation on the sea as critical, with the U-boats sinking ships faster than they could be built (875,000 tons in April 1917), and faster than the British would admit in public. Studying the figures he became convinced that at the rate of current losses the war might well be lost before it could be won. He had been interested in naval warfare since his youth, and now he saw the British as making inefficient use of their immense naval superiority. They were not effective in hunting down submarines at sea, nor were they seeking out and destroying bases where the U-boats harbored.

Shortly before the declaration of war Admiral William S. Sims, known for his independent and original mind, was sent to London, where he was prodded by Wilson not only to secure full information but to urge bolder measures upon the British. In particular, Wilson wanted to know whether the British were using convoys. If so, were they convoying merchantmen singly or in groups? Was it not possible to establish sea-lanes guarded by small craft in an unbroken line across the Atlantic?

Sims was well thought of in British naval circles—too well thought of, it appeared to the President, who constantly prodded him to assume a more independent and aggressive stance. Nevertheless the probings had an effect. Convoys were now used for the first time, without the confusions and collisions predicted, and with an immediate improvement in the rate of sinkings. All American destroyers that could be mustered were dispatched to the waters off Britain and France and put in convoy duty under British command. This was the beginning of the end of the most desperate phase of the submarine menace. By November the tonnage sunk had been reduced by two-thirds. With ten thousand American troops leaving the United States each day in midsummer 1918, the losses in life at sea had been virtually eliminated. By then there was no longer any doubt that the Americans would arrive in numbers sufficient to alter the balance on the western front.

The President's idea of guarded sealanes was, however, judged to be impracticable except across such a short stretch of sea as the English Channel. On the Atlantic seaways the periscopes of submarines could be detected only at a distance of a thousand yards, less in bad weather; with the result that the number of vessels on guard would have been self-defeating. Besides, ships from America were being dispatched to different European ports, and were following different routes across the sea.

A stubborn man, Wilson was not persuaded by such arguments. He continued to press Sims on the point. He insisted that American shipyards concentrate largely on the construction of destroyer-type vessels with armaments no heavier than required to outmatch the U-boats. Another concern of his was the relative inactivity of large capital ships. That the mighty British dreadnoughts should be so ineffectual in war struck Wilson as bordering on the absurd. Their impotence he attributed to British caution and reliance on traditional naval tactics. They should be used, he maintained, to strike at the U-boats in their home ports, rather than to pursue them singly across the seas, and he was undeterred by rejoinders that the ports in question were heavily mined. So convinced was he of the need for destroyers and light naval vessels, he was prepared to forgo construction by the United States of large battleships, the traditional measure of naval strength, and to rely in any postwar crisis upon cooperation between British and American navies.

In an off-the-record talk to the officers of the Atlantic fleet, in August 1917, Wilson gave vent to his insistence on new ways of fighting the war at sea, and incidentally to his frustrations with British naval policy. "We have got to throw tradition to the wind," he told the men. The war was a different war from any that had been previously fought, and only the inventive qualities of the "amateur" could formulate tactics necessary to win it. He was himself the "amateur," daring to ask questions; and "every time we have suggested anything to the British Admiralty, the reply has come back . . . that it had never been done that way." "We are hunting hornets all over the farm and letting the nest alone," he declared. In searching out the nests of the U-boats he was ready to see done "the thing that is audacious to the utmost point of risk and daring. . . . You will win by the audacity of method when you cannot win by circumspection and prudence."[14]

The address, had it been known of at the time, would not have pleased the British, but to those present it gave a striking glimpse of Wilson the war leader, prepared to goad traditionalists of the sea as well as of the land.

THE HOME FRONT

The President had succeeded in leading a united nation into war, but beneath the surface political and social dissent burned fiercely. In an interview with Frank Cobb, editor of the New York *World*, Wilson predicted, while in the midst of making his fateful decision, that war would loose uncontrollable passions and prejudices. War, Wilson told Cobb, "would mean that we should lose our heads along with the rest and stop weighing right and wrong. . . . Once lead this people into war and they'll forget there ever was such a thing as tolerance. To fight you must be brutal and ruthless, and the spirit of ruthless brutality will enter into the very fibre of our national life, infecting Congress, the courts, the policeman on the beat, the man in the street."[1] When he faced the ultimate choice, Wilson knew well what the costs of war would be in civil rights and human decency at home.

He was fated to see the fulfillment of his grim prophecies, and being a sensitive and humane man he experienced particular agonies. His private correspondence of the time gives much evidence of his dismay at the effects of war hysteria. When a correspondent wrote suggesting that Thomas Edison be put to work inventing a faggot-bearing bomb to set fire to German wheat fields, the President responded to the proposal with some fire of his own. "I have received your letter," he wrote, "and take the liberty of saying that I have been greatly shocked. . . . [To] act upon such a suggestion would be to emulate the spirit which we have so condemned in the Germans themselves."[2] Proposals to prohibit the teaching of the German language he characterized as "ridiculous and childish";[3] and when a German teacher at Goucher College (which two of his daughters had attended) was dismissed by the trustees for being insufficiently enthusiastic about the war, Wilson responded with a touching letter expressing confidence in the man and professing readiness to see him serve the government.[4]

"I have a very great passion for the principle that we must respect opinion even when it is hostile, and I should feel . . . that we ought to be very careful to vindicate that principle": so he counseled a well-meaning member of a school board who sought his advice on means of sorting out and disciplining youthful dissenters.[5]

Wilson's reaction to serious breaches of civil rights was more complex. Upheavals brought about by the war included a large migration of blacks toward industrial centers. Racial tensions were inflamed, and in East St. Louis on July 2, 1917, during a particularly vicious race riot, a mob set upon the black community. Thirty deaths resulted. Long-standing grievances within the labor movement came to a head in this same period. The crisis was especially acute among copper miners in western states. Seeing swollen profits going to the owners while their own situation deteriorated, the miners sought recognition through their union, the IWW (Industrial Workers of the World), a radical organization accused of being a tool of the Germans. In Butte, Montana, a mob dragged one of the union's top officials from his home, and shot and hanged him.

Two weeks after the East St. Louis race riots a major crisis was precipitated in Bisbee, Arizona, when vigilantes, led by the local sheriff, raided the homes of striking copper workers, putting a thousand of them forcibly in cattle cars and sending them into New Mexico. There they were deposited on the desert, without shelter or food. In private Wilson deplored these "disgraceful outrages" and publicly he warned against the dangerous precedent of having the community take law into its hands.[6] He dispatched army officers to report on the situation, provided federal aid for the deported workers, and set up a high-level mediation board headed by his Secretary of Labor.

Waging war abroad, the President dared not divide the nation at home. Besides, with the National Guard mobilized into the army, he was deprived of effective means of giving support to local authorities. More generally, he looked upon himself and the nation as living through a time of madness. "God only can deliver us from this tragedy," he wrote House, thinking of the growing distempers and their effect on individual men.[7] Moreover, a further reason explains his reluctance to speak out against moral offenses as strongly as some were demanding: as President, he was loath to express indignation in a void. More than most men he believed in the efficacy of words; he did not intend to debase words by employing them where they could not be joined with the legitimate exercise of power. His attitude often caused misunderstanding. Europeans were as dismayed by his refusal to denounce the burning of the library at Louvain by the Germans as were some of his countrymen by his refusal to comment more vigorously on outrages at home.

Not until July 1918, when his role as the leader of world liberal forces made denunciation of lynchings and mob actions virtually inescapable, did Wilson express himself fully in public. In a moving appeal to the American people he gave vent to smoldering indignation, showing himself once more the master of telling invective. Every man who had engaged in the outrages—most acting under the cloak of super-patriotism—had "adopted the standards of the enemies of his country, whom he affects to despise."[8] Such words spoken earlier would have greatly strengthened liberals fighting a lonely battle to maintain sanity under the rule of force.

The hysteria of the public was largely beyond the President's control; it is doubtful whether any Chief Executive could have done much to moderate the excesses of feeling and prejudice generated by the war. But Wilson does bear responsibility for having failed, then and at the war's end, to hold some of his officials in check. Under the Espionage Act, the passage of which Wilson supported in 1917, the Postmaster General was authorized to bar from the mails material deemed subversive of the war effort. It was, at best, a broad and dangerous grant of power. Burleson was diligent, narrowly and stubbornly diligent, in carrying out what he conceived to be his duties. The President questioned him closely on certain of his decisions under the act; he expressed disagreement with interpretations having the effect of barring criticisms made on ideological grounds. But in the end, on the basis of what seemed irrefutable legal arguments, he accepted his subordinate's judgment on the intent and purpose of the act.

Much of the foreign-language press fell under Burleson's peremptory ban. The *New Masses* was denied mailing privileges, in effect putting out of business a journal whose criticisms of the administration, admittedly harsh and exaggerated, seemed to many to fall short of sedition. In vain such intellectuals and Wilson admirers as Herbert Croly, Walter Lippmann, Upton Sinclair, and Max Eastman pleaded with the President for a more tolerant approach even to extreme dissent. To say that the draft law ought to be resisted, to argue that the war was being fought for capitalistic privileges, was to advance views that even in wartime a democracy ought to be capable of tolerating. To deny them circulation came dangerously close to protecting government from essential criticism and legitimate attack.

Wilson was not insensitive to such arguments, and he could be disarmingly frank in dealing with his critics. All too well he knew the dangers of abuse in the application of emergency powers. Yet in wartime, he wrote Max Eastman, a line had to be drawn somewhere—"and I cannot say that I have any confidence that I know how to draw it. I can only say that . . . we are trying, it may be clumsily but genuinely, to draw it without fear or favor or prejudice."[9] The fact that editors of the *New Masses* had appealed to the courts further reduced Wilson to inaction in this case.

In Thomas Gregory, the Attorney General, Wilson had a cabinet member far more sophisticated and liberal than Burleson, one who had played an important part in securing Brandeis's nomination to the Supreme Court. But in actions against elements considered subversive, as against the controversial IWW, Gregory was not above showing the zeal of a small-town prosecutor. With the President consenting, he ordered raids on the labor union's offices in thirty-three cities, arresting labor organizers and even those employed as their secretaries.

In dealing with strikes and labor unrest the President was guided by William B. Wilson, who had himself participated in the struggles for labor's rights; and here the administration's record was highly creditable. The problem of strikes in wartime was a particularly vexing one; for under total mobilization, with each man serving in the place where presumably he was contributing his due to the war effort, work stoppages smacked of subversion. Yet labor had legitimate grievances. As a result of inflation and wartime dislocations it had been robbed of many of its prewar gains, while business was not hesitant about taking advantage of constraints imposed upon the unions.

The administration came out strongly in favor of labor's right to organize and bargain collectively and enforced this policy wherever possible. Where strikes threatened output in major industries, negotiating panels were appointed by the federal government. Peaceful settlements were achieved in areas vital to the war effort, a cause of much satisfaction to the President and his Secretary of Labor.

The administration's support of labor's rights won an invaluable ally in Samuel Gompers, president of the American Federation of Labor. He purged labor's antiwar wing and constantly stressed loyalty to the administration. Wilson responded by carefully reciprocating Gompers' goodwill. At the latter's invitation he agreed to address the annual convention of the AFL, the first President to make such an appearance. Journeying to Buffalo in the autumn of 1917, at a particularly crowded and difficult moment, he departed from his rule of not leaving Washington in wartime. Faced by an enthusiastic audience of workmen, he showed himself in his best speaking form. Following his speech, the unions passed resolutions pledging full cooperation and support.

During this period the administration was being subjected to a stream of criticism and to constant attacks from the press and from Congress. It was said that mobilization was moving slowly; that expectations of the Allies were not being met; that confusion prevailed in the war agencies. The approach to dissenters was assailed as being either too harsh or not harsh enough.

In fact there was some cause for the criticism. Within the administration agency heads were often at odds. Particularly embarrassing to the President, and illustrative of the kind of problems he faced, was a widely publicized quarrel between two members of the shipping board, General George W. Goethals and William C. Denman, a civilian. Their difference was, in essence, over the type of ships to be built for service in coastal waters. The need for ships to relieve inland transportation was pressing, and Wilson believed that if these were constructed of wood they could be produced rapidly, without putting further strain on scarce supplies of iron and steel. Moreover the program would put to use a class of skills not being fully exploited. From these views Goethals strongly dissented; Denman backed the President. It was the kind of row the press loved to seize upon and which partisan critics in the Congress could inflate.

Wilson acted speedily and even brusquely. He secured the resignations of both Goethals and Denman and put a business man, Edward N. Hurley, in command. Hurley proved an able administrator and through the vicissitudes of war and peacemaking remained a firm supporter of the President. Both Goethals and Denman accepted the solution without public complaints. This was a very different Wilson from the one who at Princeton had hesitated fatally over letting West depart. As a seasoned administrator he had learned to deal resolutely with a human problem without letting the quarrel become personal.

Congress took the Goethals-Denman dispute as one more reason for attacking the President. As the congressional session ended a plan was introduced to have a watchdog committee exercise surveillance over the President, the first of several attempts to curb his authority. Basing himself on Lincoln's experience in the Civil War, Wilson peremptorily dismissed all such proposals.

Unknown to the President, criticism was even growing within his inner circle. In July McAdoo went to House, complaining that he had not been accorded proper authority and threatening to resign unless interference from the President ceased. In the same month Hoover was telling House that "matters are getting into a jam in Washington."[10] The President talked to no one except Tumulty, it seemed, and he did not know that the mobilization was running far from smoothly. As for House, his chief complaint was that the President failed to take up his offer to reorganize the war effort for him.

Between the initiation of a great enterprise and its fulfillment, when hopes are deferred and doubts take over, crises are bound to erupt. Wilson was rarely free of attacks on his conduct of the war; and by the early winter of 1918, with all the pieces in place but without results being fully visible, a single misstep could cause an explosion. The spark was lit when Harry A. Garfield, in charge of fuel supplies, issued an order closing down all manufacturing plants and businesses for a single period of five days and on Mondays thereafter. Garfield was liked and trusted by Wilson, who had conferred with him before issuance of the controversial order.

The purpose of the plant closings was less to save fuel than to free the transportation system for carrying vital supplies to ports of embarkation for Europe. Abruptly imposed, without adequate explanation or consideration of other possible options, the order was met by a thunderous outcry of opposition. The editor most friendly to Wilson, Frank Cobb of the World, saw it as "a terrible calamity";[11] the head of the National Association of Manufacturers characterized it as an "appalling disaster."[12] From New York, on the day the order was announced, House wrote that he had never heard such a storm of protest.[13] In his diary he carried out the metaphor, writing that it was indeed like a storm at sea, coming when all seemed relatively calm, and in an hour transforming the waters into a turbulent and dangerous element.

Workers objected because they were deprived of a day's wages. Business not only saw its profits threatened by the plant closings but fumed at Wilson's suggestion that it make up for labor's lost hours of work. Even relatively objective observers began to wonder whether anything less than a breakdown in mobilization could lie behind so drastic an interference with normal economic life. Congress, in these circumstances, was not slow to react. George F. Chamberlain, Democratic chairman of the Senate Committee on Military Affairs, led the band with a speech declaring that the military establishment had "fallen down," and that inefficiency reigned in every "Bureau and every Department of government."[14] Again bills were introduced, this time calling for the establishment of a war council, and for a director of munitions to take management of the war effort largely out of the President's hands. Theodore Roosevelt, the most extreme critic, rushed down to Washington to spend four days conferring with Chamberlain and other hostile members of Congress.

Wilson responded as he had when faced by other threats to his leadership. He stood squarely back of Garfield. He denounced Chamberlain's charges as "an astonishing and absolutely unjustifiable distortion of the truth."[15] On the bills aimed at curtailing his powers, he refused unequivocally to compromise, calling for their withdrawal and telling the senators that such legislation would not be passed "until he was dead."[16]

Amid the raging controversy, the Secretary of War was put under hostile questioning by Chamberlain's committee. In five hours of testimony Baker went far toward reversing the common estimate that he was a poor administrator. Demonstrating under fire his qualities of firmness, lucidity, and intelligence, he not only made an effective defense of his own contribution but made a compelling case for the whole of the administration's program. His performance reinforced Wilson's credibility at a time of desperate need.

In the end the President came unharmed through this crisis in his leadership, yet not without having gained the realization that substantial changes were required in the personnel and organization of the wartime services. As will be seen, the winter of 1918 brought about an important realignment. Yet the strain told on him. A visitor to the White House in January remarked of the President that "he looked tired, and his voice was decidedly weak."[17] As often when the tide went against him he developed a cold and was kept from his office for several days.

If the war loosed passions of political and social intolerance on the domestic front, it also fueled the zeal of reformers. For the most part Wilson went along with the reformers. He believed strongly that labor's economic gains, especially those won as a result of his leadership, should not be abandoned because the nation was at war. Moreover he sensed that a just peace would ultimately depend upon America's capacity to ally itself with the progressive forces of Europe. With this in mind he overcame earlier hesitations in regard to woman suffrage. Women's right to vote he saw as a dynamic force in keeping with the widespread social and political liberation he expected the war to bring. He opposed the Prohibitionists, however; in demanding a ban on alcoholic beverages they appeared to him to be using the war as a means of imposing their particular nostrum.

Pressing for a woman suffrage amendment, Wilson moved against a wall of political apathy, as well as against what seemed often an excessive ardor on the part of the women themselves. In July 1917 a large group of the Women's Party picketed the White House. A number were seized by the police and transported to the district workhouse. Wilson was even more enraged by this overreaction of the police than he had been discomfited by the tactics of the protesters. In immediately issuing a mass pardon, however, he failed to take account of the fury of the marchers, who not only continued to denounce the administration but refused to be pardoned. Legal authorities testified to the fact that a pardon was invalid unless freely accepted, and an ugly stalemate threatened. Happily, the women changed their minds. Meanwhile, Wilson was quietly continuing his pressure on Congress.

Tied down though he was by day-to-day problems, he had moments when he let his mind range to the domestic situation in the postwar era. A meeting of political leaders in New Jersey, attempting to bring together the ever-warring Nugent and reformist factions, provided the occasion to sketch the concepts he believed essential to a period of reconstruction. It would be a time, he wrote, when all prevailing social concepts would have been changed by the war; when the ruling test in regard to any political action must be "Is it just, is it for the benefit of the average man, without influence or privilege; does it embody in real fact the highest conception of social justice?" The leaders of the new epoch would be required to possess "genuine sympathy with the mass of men and real insight into their needs and opportunities."[18] Here was the hint, as there had been in the First Inaugural, of a future revolution in values and political ideals.

The New Jersey politicians may not have gotten the point; but the sensitive antennae of the *New Republic* were alert to the message's significance. For the first time, said the editors, the President had indicated the direction in which his mind was working—"had suggested the burden of radicalism which in his opinion a responsible political leader can afford to carry." Already there appeared to be shaping up, in the obstinate if smoldering antagonisms in Congress and in attacks of the conservative press, some premonition of a postwar battle of "enormous proportions." Among U.S. leaders Wilson stood alone, concluded the

New Republic, "in anticipating radical changes in domestic political issues and in adjusting his mind to deal with them."[19] These were words not lost on the liberal forces of Europe, disillusioned with war and with its iron rule.

One evening shortly afterwards House sat with his friend, conjuring up a program of reform as sweeping as that of the New Freedom in its 1912 and 1916 phases. It could be Wilson's great opportunity, House said, to lead the liberal world movement. "That is a big program for a tired man," the President responded.[20]

While full-scale mobilization was beginning at home, an event of significance occurred in the foreign field, giving Wilson an opportunity not only to evoke fresh energies from his fellow citizens but to enhance his role as spokesman for the warring powers. In mid-August 1917, Pope Benedict XV issued an appeal to the belligerents proposing terms of peace. Asserting that all Europe was tending toward suicide and was engaged in a "more or less useless massacre," the Pope called for the immediate cessation of hostilities, the substitution of arbitration for the force of arms, and the settlement of outstanding claims in a spirit of equity and justice. It was a potentially explosive document. Lansing saw it as emanating from Austria-Hungary and most probably sanctioned by Germany. Britain and France decided to ignore it on the ground that it was a propaganda document. For Wilson, identified as he was with the cause of peace, the problem was more difficult.

Could he restate his own attitude toward the war without seeming to rebuff a figure of moral preeminence? Could he dare take upon himself the responsibility of speaking not only for the United States but for the Allied powers? He was for a time doubtful that he should make any reply. He showed House a possible draft and finally framed a text with the care given only to his major state papers. When made public it turned out to be a widely popular statement, not only in the United States but abroad, and did much to reinforce Wilson's position as a negotiator of final peace terms.

The message was popular in large part because it restated forcefully the President's determination to have no parley with the military autocracy ruling Germany. Wilson was still thought in some quarters to attach more weight to peace for its own sake than to defeating the Hun. He was looked on by certain American and European politicians as a man likely to be seduced by precisely such a moral appeal as the Pope's. These estimates were rudely overturned. Though respectful of the Church's spokesman, Wilson in his reply left no doubt that it was the

Pope who was either being fooled or was seeking terms favorable to the Austro-Hungarian Empire.

The message was striking in other ways. Wilson placed squarely on Germany the responsibility for the outbreak of the war—a position he had been loath to come to and that would deeply influence his role in the settlement at Paris. Nevertheless he still held doggedly to his conviction that neither the United States nor other powers should seek selfish gains from the war. "Punitive damages, the dismemberment of empires . . . we deem childish and in the end worse than futile," he wrote in his first draft.[21] At House's urging Wilson omitted the word "childish," but the thought of renouncing economic and territorial gains remained abhorrent to the Allies. Shortly after the note had been delivered, the President got wind of Jusserand's having criticized him for making the suggestion. Indeed, the ambassador appears to have been in a heated frame of mind, and in private Wilson condemned him for his "excitable impertinence."[22] Jusserand was certainly representing accurately the Allies' point of view; but the President of the United States was speaking out boldly, if not for the Allied governments, then certainly for their peoples. He was leading them down paths which, however much their leaders might protest among themselves, they did not at the time dare to repudiate.

As for his own people, Wilson had stated clearly where they stood and had challenged them to forge the tools of victory.

THE FOURTEEN POINTS

Wilson's conviction that the United States should maintain an independent position within the Western alliance was strengthened by continued doubts about war aims. During Balfour's visit there had been talk of secret treaties by which Italy and Romania had been enticed into the war on the Allied side. These involved the kind of territorial barter Wilson abhorred and which he believed incompatible with a stable peace. He ignored the texts of the treaties when they were sent to him by the British Foreign Office, stuffing them away, apparently unread, in his personal files; but it is clear that from 1917 on he realized that several of the lesser Allies (and in some respects the major Allies, too) were fighting for objectives with which he did not wish America to be identified.

Nevertheless, amid the exigencies of war, he found himself moving toward the closest possible working arrangements with the British. The intimate cooperation was facilitated by improved communication at the highest level. When the United States declared war, ambassadorial contacts on both sides of the Atlantic were, for different reasons, unsatisfactory. In London Page was regarded more as a former friend of the President's than as an adviser on current developments or a participant in decision-making. Spring Rice in Washington was looked down on as a sick man who consorted with such enemies of the administration as Lodge and Roosevelt. In these circumstances Colonel House became more than ever Wilson's chief channel of communication with the British.

When the coalition government of Lloyd George replaced Asquith's government at the end of 1916, House found himself cut off from some of his most valuable sources of information. The departure of Sir Edward Grey as Foreign Secretary was a particular loss for him. But by a coincidence House was visited a few days after the cabinet change by William Wiseman, then substituting for the British naval attaché. The slight figure, appearing younger than his thirty-two years, impressed House by his knowledge and good sense, and the two men formed an instant liking for each other. Wiseman confided in due course that he had direct access to the British Foreign Office, bypassing the ambassador. Thus House was assured of precisely the link he required, and by the summer of 1917 an arrangement of remarkable efficiency had been worked out.

The maturing of plans between two governments not always on the best of terms—with Wilson suspicious of British aims and often scornful of its conservative tactics, and with the British not wholly convinced of Wilson's commitment to victory—was greatly advanced by the connivance of these two subtle, sophisticated men. Wiseman kept House informed of British developments, at one stage moving into House's apartment building so as to be in easy touch at all hours of the day and night. House, meanwhile, was journeying regularly to Washington, taking advantage of the White House welcome invariably accorded him.

A crucial issue was a sharing of the financial burden of the war. Britain with its vast resources had assumed the debt of the Allied countries for the costs of arms and men, and now Britain was dangerously drained. McAdoo as Secretary of the Treasury was too much a businessman to be easily moved by Britain's plight. But if Wilson was Scotch, he was a canny Scot, and he foresaw that at the end of the war a chief leverage over the Allies would be through credits extended by the United States in their time of need. House helped nudge the government toward the rapid extension of such credit. The delicate problem of assigning shipping—principally British shipping—for the transport of American troops was also eased by Wiseman working through House. The role of American manpower and the possibility of intervention in Russia were discussed by the two men in terms of coalition diplomacy, a field where the paucity of existing precedents was matched by the ever-present danger of conflict. The unorthodox collaboration of House and Wiseman served Wilson well in the period when understandings with the British were essential to winning the war.

Direct American participation in Allied war councils had become at this time a major preoccupation of the British. Their insistence on the point was, to Wilson's suspicious mind, reason enough for standing aside. But in a long personal letter to the President in the autumn of 1917 Lloyd George put the case in terms difficult to resist. The Prime Minister pictured grimly and frankly the Allied military position. After three years of war the Germans held more, not less, territory than at the outset. The renewable resources of Allied manpower were becoming increasingly limited. Lloyd George attributed the military impasse to the lack of a unified leadership. The Germans did not suffer from such a handicap; having put their whole empire under "rigid, unified control," they could be flexible and imaginative in the use of power. The Allies, by contrast, seemed condemned to pursue a single remorseless strategy, that of pounding at the western front. The war had taken on the form of a siege. It perhaps required, Lloyd George suggested, a resort to siege tactics: that is to say, an attack at the enemy's weakest point, not at its strongest—in short at whatever second front could be established.[1]

Wilson had given little thought to the strategy of land warfare, but he knew that the attrition of the trenches could not go on indefinitely, and he, too, was searching for new ways to fight the war. He was flattered by the Prime Minister's suggestion that the kind of large-scale planning necessary for averting defeat could be carried on only with the full participation of the Americans. On the other hand, Lloyd George's suggestion that the military might of Turkey be "smashed" seemed not unrelated in Wilson's mind to Britain's postwar territorial aims. Nor was it difficult to surmise that the Prime Minister, having been rebuffed by his own military authorities, wanted the Americans to take responsibility for a new approach.

Through such a welter of crosscurrents the President moved slowly toward his own position. Urged on by House (and, behind House, by Wiseman) he accepted the idea of a closely integrated U.S. and Allied planning effort, with America represented on the major Allied war councils—on those dealing with supplies and with neutral nations, and, at the highest level, on the Supreme War Council, formed by the Allies in November 1917, as Italy was being defeated at Caporetto. The President, Wiseman reported in October 1917, had "changed his mind" about membership in various planning bodies.[2] More significantly, he had gained in confidence as a war leader, and he was convinced that U.S. spokesmen had much to give as well as much to learn.

The question of who should represent the United States on the Supreme War Council narrowed quickly (and not surprisingly) to House. Wilson quite unrealistically hoped that his emissary might go as a delegation of one and that most of its members would return after a brief stay abroad. But Wiseman was again quietly at work, and with House he elaborated a broad representation of experts to accompany House and mesh with British personnel. These included delegates for the army and navy, for munitions, food, finance, shipping, and embargoes. As the head of this enlarged mission the Colonel was bid an affectionate farewell at the White House on October 24. The group set sail on two cruisers accompanied by a destroyer, and was met by four additional destroyers as it approached the war zone. The welcome accorded the delegation by British officials on land, and the solicitude shown to House as its head, matched the naval resources that had been expended in getting them all safely to shore.

The delegation started its work at a time when the need for Allied-American cooperation was painfully evident. A double crisis posed crucial strategic problems. Defeat of the Italian armies at Caporetto put into serious question Italy's capacity to continue as an ally on the southern front. The almost simultaneous taking over of Russia by the Bolsheviks threatened a vacuum of military force to the east. In the circumstances the American emissaries brought moral encouragement, as well as fresh ideas and the promise of an increasing military contribution.

Events in Russia were to provide both the greatest incentive for Allied-American cooperation and also to produce some of the most severe strains. At two crucial junctures Russian developments had already affected America's relation to the war. The overthrow of the czar in March 1917 had removed an almost insurmountable barrier to America's joining the conflict; and in the following summer the disintegration of the pro-Allied Kerensky government had relieved the Germans of a major threat to their eastern lines. The subsequent transfer of troops to the western and Italian fronts rendered the Germans capable of outnumbering whatever armies the European Allies might put into the field, making a large-scale American expeditionary force essential for the battles of 1918.

As the House mission settled in London an even more dramatic event shook Russia. During the night of November 6, the revolutionary Bolsheviks quickly took over power from the liberal successors to the czar. Wilson had extended a warm hand to the Kerensky government, sending a commission under former Secretary of State Elihu Root to make recommendations for support. The United States had been the first to accord recognition and had been generous in providing credit for war supplies. But as a partner in the military coalition Russia remained a weak reed. The new Bolshevik rule created even more uncertainty.

Wilson's response to the revolution had two sides. In a speech immediately after the coup he characterized as "fatuous dreamers" those who supposed it possible to deal with the new Russian government.[3] At the same time, with a longer historical perspective, he wrote Congressman Frank Clark: "I have not lost faith in the Russian outcome by any means. Russia, like France in a past century, will no doubt have to go through deep waters but she will come out upon firm land on the other side and her great people, for they are a great people, will in my opinion take their proper place in the world."[4] Thus Wilson endeavored to balance in his mind the historic Russia against what seemed the surface froth of Bolshevism.

What he perhaps failed to grasp fully was the contempt of the Bolshevik leaders, Lenin and Trotsky, for all capitalist powers, whether democratic or militaristic. An intense band of radicals shared Wilson's hope of bringing the war to an early close, but they felt no concern for the kind of liberal settlement that inspired the American President. Lenin saw peace as a means of validating and augmenting his own power. He turned a deaf ear to Wilsonism. And so the two great polar figures were left to stand in fateful opposition, at the fork in the road where the destiny of the twentieth century was being decided.

The hard-pressed British and French had as little interest in a reborn, democratic Russia as the Bolsheviks had in Wilsonian ideals. They saw in the political turn experienced by the eastern giant, now stricken and divided, a heresy to be mortally feared; and they saw also a means to establish a second front. Allied forces in Russia could now be expected to play a double role: as a knife thrust into the German rear, and as a way of dealing a blow to Communism in its early stages.

Following the Bolshevik takeover, Allied pressure on the United States for participation in a military intervention in Russia was intense and unremitting. The French ambassador kept the path to the White House worn smooth as he argued relentlessly the case of his government; Lord Reading, who had been sent over to supplant the ailing Spring Rice, was pressed by Lloyd George into equally importunate appeals. Two possibilities appeared open to the Allies: an operation in the northern ports of Archangel and Murmansk, or an invasion of eastern Siberia by the Japanese. To both of these Wilson was stubbornly opposed.

He was convinced on military grounds that the Allies did not have the resources to intervene effectively. They would be tempted to divert vitally needed forces to the east, while the troops employed would be insufficient to cause appreciable German withdrawals from the western front. On grounds of statesmanship and diplomacy he objected as strongly. He had little confidence that the Japanese, were they to enter Siberia, would act as a disinterested power. More deeply, he could not bring himself to despair of the revolution of the Russian people. Although not prepared to grant the Bolsheviks formal recognition, he viewed them as an expression of the national will. He was determined, moreover, to let the Russian people work out their destiny in their own way.

Military activity on Russian soil, without full consent of the Bolshevik government, was abhorrent to Wilson and was opposed to all he had been saying about America's nature and its war aims. Wanting the United States to be known by the Russians as their friend, he realized that such trust as existed after the Bolshevik takeover was held "by a very slender thread."[5] He had no wish to jeopardize it by military adventures. Besides, he had learned from the Mexican experience the endless embarrassments of seeming to impose democratic forms of government on another nation. To the extent that he had been seduced into trying to dictate how Mexico should be governed, he had traveled a road he did not wish to enter upon again.

As the pleas of the Allied ambassadors proved unavailing—as Lord Reading, indeed, sought more interviews than the President was willing to grant—other forms of persuasion were tried. The French sent over Henri Bergson, the noted philosopher and man of letters, to establish a special contact with the President. Bergson prudently stopped off in New York to inquire of House the best way to pursue his mission. House advised him not to press upon Wilson facts and arguments with which he was already thoroughly familiar. For himself, House remarked acidly, he had heard the arguments for intervention in Russia so interminably recited that he could repeat them in his sleep. From abroad at the same time came a flow of urgent messages—from the Prime Ministers of France and Britain separately, and from them jointly with the name of the Italian Prime Minister added. The Supreme War Council proffered its own earnest recommendation. In addition, Wiseman was urged to make use of his special powers of persuasion.

Wiseman had the gift not only of stimulating Wilson by his questions but of reporting the replies with their flavor intact. After raising all the arguments for Allied intervention, and having them countered by the President one by one, Wiseman remarked that in any case it was not possible to make the situation worse than it already was. Wilson answered that on that point he strongly disagreed. "Then," Wiseman queried, "are we to do nothing at all?"

"No," the President retorted, "we must watch the situation carefully and sympathetically, and be ready to move whenever the right time arrive[s]."[6] It was not uncharacteristic of Wilson, nor was it the least significant element in his statesmanship, that he would not be rushed into a decision, and that he considered deliberate and perceptive "watching" to be in itself a form of policy.

As the structure of inter-Allied cooperation was being successfully established, Wilson moved to reorganize the war effort at home. He had learned something from the ongoing congressional attacks and was determined to put new men at the head of the agencies principally concerned with mobilizing the economy. A moribund Council of National Defense became the crisis-oriented War Industries Board, first headed by Frank A. Scott and then, in a dramatic maneuver, put under the direction of Bernard M. Baruch. Overruling doubts about the administrative capacities of the flamboyant and wealthy speculator, Wilson was rewarded by the services of a man intensely loyal and energetic, capable of swift decision and not afraid of responsibility. Baruch's War Industries Board was in overall charge of purchases by the government and the Allies; its business was to see that manufacturers focused on goods essential to the war effort, and, indirectly, to see that goods destined for civilian use were made in ways least wasteful of labor and of scarce raw materials.

McAdoo, in charge of war financing, was most visible in his management of successive war bond drives. Garfield was in charge of conserving fuel. He introduced daylight saving time, gasless Sundays (the President rode to church in a carriage drawn by two horses), and in general saw that unnecessary consumption of fuel was curtailed.

To conserve food and augment its production Wilson named Herbert Hoover, the mining engineer whose work for Belgian relief had brought him wide acclaim. Hoover was a dour man, then as later; his accomplishments were the fruit of hard work and superior administrative talents, not of personality. Yet he had the kind of imagination plodders sometimes possess, seeing in small steps rigorously pursued the way to astonishing results. Beyond his powers to organize the supply and purchase of major farm products, fix prices, and halt profiteering and hoarding, he exercised a broad influence over the daily fare of millions of consumers. On certain days meat could not be eaten; on others, wheat; on all days candy without sugar was the people's lot. The high degree of voluntary compliance he gained for his edicts ensured vital supplies for military forces and civilians abroad. Hoover admired Wilson and amid his own later troubles wrote of the wartime President with marked generosity.

No aspect of the people's lives remained untouched by these administration chiefs; but they were touched most pervasively by the propaganda activities of the Committee on Public Information, headed by George Creel. Within the first week of the war a cabinet committee, with Daniels the most convinced and active member, recommended to the President the need for censorship of military secrets and for centralized clearance of the news. Wilson responded favorably. To guide the new committee he chose a colorful and temperamental newspaperman, an activist, a confirmed western progressive. Creel immediately made it plain that the work of the committee would exceed its original scope. Though censorship was not neglected by the committee, and though even Tumulty acceded to giving it clearance of White House releases, its main operations were in selling the war to the American people.

What Creel conceived as "the world's greatest adventure in advertising" was carried out through every available channel and by all communications media.[7] No artist, orator, writer, or musician could avoid being drawn into its service. Newspapers, pamphlets, posters, the speaker's platform, the moving picture screen—all were mobilized in a vast effort to bring the war home to the average citizen, to overcome lethargy, and to mold suitable attitudes. The committee created an incongruous background for Wilson's sober appeals; it often stirred up the kind of emotion he was at pains to suppress, both within himself and among the public. Wilson was aware of Creel's defects yet defended him through thick and thin against almost constant attacks by Congress and the press. His task was not made the easier by Creel's frequent outbursts—as when, asked if he knew what was going on in the mind of Congress, he replied that he had not been slumming lately.[8]

The man's outspokenness appealed to Wilson, and he probably admired in secret the tough way he handled the press. But more deeply,

Creel gave form to the side of Wilson that was at home in the rough and tumble of practical politics. As one knowing that truth must often wear strange guises, a leader who was himself withdrawn and uncommunicative for long periods, he saw no contradiction in Creel's cacaphony. His own silences, indeed, were complemented by the crude drumbeat of that propaganda machine.

The chiefs of the war agencies—notably McAdoo, Hurley, Baruch, Garfield, Hoover, and Vance McCormick, head of the War Trade Board—now met regularly on Wednesdays at the White House, in what came to be known as the "war cabinet." The President, as one of the participants recollected,[9] waited regularly at the door of his upstairs private study, greeting each member by name on his entering. The room contained Wilson's flat-top desk as well as a few comfortable chairs, but never enough places for the whole group. Extra chairs had to be brought in, and the President was invariably concerned with the comfort of those consigned to them. He removed the flowers that regularly graced his desk, passed out cigars, and often told a brief story. From then on the meeting was all business. The technical aspects of the war effort were discussed and settled, politics playing no role; all participants, including the President, were as brisk and competent as corporation heads.

To the efficiency of this group was due much of the success of the culminating phases of the war effort. The meetings of the regular cabinet inevitably declined in importance. They were frequently canceled under the press of competing business. When held, the matters brought before them seemed of secondary importance. "Nothing talked of . . . that would interest a nation, a family, or a child. No talk of the war. No talk of Russia or Japan."[10] So Lane, Secretary of the Interior, complained in a letter to his brother. Lane did not perceive that in addition to the dominance of the war cabinet a major reason for the President's reticence in the regular meetings was Lane's own incurable tendency to feed Washington gossip.

In a way this was a happy period for Wilson. Despite immense burdens and an overriding sense of war's horrors, he was uplifted by the urgency of the job. Distracting elements fell away, and the famous "one-track" mind—the sort of mind he had once described as "stripped and athletic" in the exercise of power—he could now concentrate completely.

In Congress the Overman bill moved toward passage, providing the President with wide authority to reorganize the Executive Branch of the government. "Senator after Senator has appealed to me most earnestly to 'cut the red tape.' I am now asking for the scissors,"[11] he wrote the bill's sponsor as it was reported out of Senate committee. But Wilson resisted suggestions coming from Baruch and others that he set up special processes to check on how well the various departments and agencies were meeting their schedules. As a wise administrator he saw beyond such mechanical routines, putting his emphasis upon shared confidence and high morale. "I deal with sensibilities every day," he wrote; "I know how much . . . they play in efficiency itself."[12]

Everything except war was pushed into the background. "Just now there doesn't seem to be any private life left for any of us," Wilson wrote in one of the rare personal letters of the period. "We must fight our way out of this jungle and then be normal human beings again."[13] House would come down regularly from New York to occupy the Yellow Room of the mansion. In April he fell ill and was touched to find the President canceling an evening at the theater so that the two friends might be together. Jessie Sayre came for what she remembered as "a perfect little visit." She was surprised to find how well her father appeared. "One gets in the way of thinking that all these burdens *must* be crushing you physically," she told him; but she had found him fit in health "as well as so marvellously fit every other way."[14] A British journalist, after the President had addressed informally a group of foreign newspapermen, described him in a cable to his editor as "a lightly built . . . alert man evidently in buoyant health . . . with a rare gift of charm."[15] His mind seemed open and resilient. He would read the latest volume of the British socialist Sidney Webb, he promised a correspondent: "Webb gives me thoughts," he added, "even when I do not accept his own."[16] Wilson was evidently enlarging the diet of Browning and Wordsworth to which his reading had been restricted in other seasons.

Mobilization on the domestic front and joint planning with the British and other Allies formed the secure base from which Wilson felt able to launch a diplomatic offensive aimed at ending the war and avoiding sacrificial spring offensives. By early 1918 the situation seemed to him ripe for a bold move. Stirrings of discontent in the French armies, defections among the Germans, and demoralization of the Italians after the defeat at Caporetto joined themselves with the chaos in Russia to suggest that a final supreme effort could result in peace. It might still be a peace achieved without the dismemberment of empires and without humiliation imposed on either side.

At the start of 1918 the diplomatic front was active. The long-frozen positions of European belligerents were giving way, half in hope and half in despair, to a tentative and sometimes bewildering thaw. In November the Bolsheviks' first move had been to call upon the Entente for negotiations leading to a settlement based on the principle of no annexations and no indemnities. The same general approach was urged by Count von Hertling, who during the fall of 1917 had become German chancellor, and was echoed on Christmas Day by Count Czernin of Austria-Hungary. Signing a preliminary peace with Germany on December 15, the Bolsheviks appealed for a conference of all the belligerent powers to be summoned at once.

That Wilson should step forth and speak for America at this juncture was in keeping with the moral and political position he had been preparing by successive and consistent acts. He could move from strength, unlike the leaders of the beleaguered Central Powers, and with the disinterestedness of a country that had joined the war seeking no territorial or economic gains. Above all, he could move upon the basis of America's democratic faith, a vast countervailing power placed in opposition to German autocracy, as to the emerging Communism of the Russians. The problem was to find the method, the point of entry into the growing international debate. It had to be a method that would not demoralize the British and the French or distract the United States from the urgency of its mobilization.

In his annual message to Congress in December 1917, he had raised the question at the heart of all others: "When shall we consider the war won?"[17] That it must be won was plain; but American soldiers, once engaged, did not intend to go on fighting forever. To talk of peace in the midst of battle was dangerous, but it was the only course for a nation that professed ideal aims. The one acceptable victory was that which would free the victors to do "an unprecedented thing"—to base peace on generosity and justice. Wilson went on to say that "we do not wish in any way to impair or to rearrange" the Austro-Hungarian Empire. "We only desire to see that their affairs are left in their own hands." As for Germany, the wrongs wrought by her military rulers would have of course to be righted: "But they can not and must not be righted by the commission of similar wrongs against Germany and her allies."

It remained for Wilson to set forth in a further message, on behalf of the United States and the Allied Powers, the nature of a just peace. This he prepared to do in a declaration that would sound across the world under the name of the Fourteen Points. Essentially he returned to the idea of "peace without victory." First formulated when America still stood aside from the conflict, those words had been relatively easy to state and had an inevitable aura of lofty righteousness. To propound the same idea when engaged in battle, when demanding deprivation and sacrifice from one's people, called for a higher degree of civic virtue and statesmanship. Not deterred by the challenge, Wilson persisted in his approach; and for a few breathless weeks in the winter of 1917–18 the realization of his hope seemed almost possible.

In formulating his peace terms Wilson was guided by studies carried out by a group set up under his direction by Colonel House. Operating in utmost secrecy, not in Washington but in New York, its purpose masked by its innocuous name of "The Inquiry," it gathered geographers, historians, political scientists, and other specialists to amass and analyze a vast body of material on the European situation. Early in January 1918, Wilson called House to Washington. House sensed what was up and arrived with such a volume of maps and documents that a geologist member of The Inquiry was delegated to help carry the load.

The shape of the world was going to be remade, but that did not prevent the train traveling south from behaving as trains often do, in peace as in war. It drew into Washington three hours late. House went directly to the Executive Mansion where he and the President settled down to work. It was midnight when they completed the first outline of what was to be Wilson's Fourteen Points address.

The Inquiry had done its work well. A memorandum written by Sidney Mezes, its chief, with David H. Miller and Walter Lippmann, set forth a detailed description of the existing diplomatic and military situation with a list of peace aims. The President, in consultation with House, wrote shorthand notes on the face of the document and rearranged the order of the points. All Saturday the two men worked and reworked the details. With the message entirely retyped on Wilson's machine, they read the text to each other several times.

Wilson was under the urgent pressure of time. Events were moving at a speed beyond anyone's expectation or control. Apart from other eventualities, it seemed possible that Lloyd George would take the initiative. Aiming to quiet the mounting peace fever among liberals and laborites in his own country, the Prime Minister had indeed hastily scheduled an address for Saturday, January 5—the same day on which Wilson and House toiled together. Wilson was apprehensive lest the unpredictable Lloyd George reveal the extent of Britain's intransigence to the Russians and to the neutral world. Quite the contrary, he followed so closely Wilsonian ideas that the President, in a mood of despondency, supposed the impact of his forthcoming message to have been irreparably blunted.

Reassured by House, he spent Monday rethinking issues that still troubled him. That afternoon Lansing was called in to hear the message read; his few suggestions for word changes were accepted. The work was now completed and the President was in a restless and wakeful mood. House found him refusing to go to bed and wanting only to read poetry.

The preparation of the message had gone forward in complete secrecy. With the exception of Lansing, no member of the cabinet was informed that the President was about to address the Congress on a matter of great importance. Even Tumulty was kept in the dark. Wilson's typescript, unseen by any secretary or clerk, was sent to the public printer. House had urged that the Tuesday morning papers be allowed to carry a story stating in general terms that in his address the President would set forth America's war aims. Wilson would not consider such a proposal. As a consequence much of the diplomatic corps was absent when he spoke, and some of the cabinet failed to be in their accustomed seats. But Wilson was not looking for an immediate effect on his hearers. He wanted to address a world audience. That audience, by every art and skill that he possessed, he was determined to reach.

His reasons for secrecy and surprise tell much of Wilson's methods. "The newspapers," House quoted him as remarking, "invariably commented and speculated as to what he would say and . . . these forecasts were often taken for what was really said."[18] What he wanted was, on the contrary, a sort of public stillness. The word itself was what counted, the simple word as it was spoken without interpretation or gloss. Wilson's most successful acts were prepared in isolation; they were performed by irreversible moves. His major oratorical efforts, having themselves the impact of deeds, were delivered out of silence, the kind of silence from which all definitive works, and all great works of art, derive.

The address of January 8, although foreshadowed by other spokesmen and by Wilson himself in previous utterances, came as a climactic event in the war. It stood as if alone, having power to shape future events: to create and to destroy. The speech was written in the style of Wilson's best state papers, revealing the particular qualities of eloquence he had mastered, the lucid exposition, the alternations of mood, the subtle and unanticipated appeals to emotion. It contained passages uniquely his, as when he referred to the "new voice" of the Russian people, "more thrilling and more compelling than any of the moving voices with which the troubled air of the world is filled"; or spoke of the German people, the distinction of their learning and pacific enterprise, he said, being "such as have made her record very bright and very enviable." It was not the rhetoric, however, but the substance that gave the address its power.

The famous points were nothing less than the terms of peace as Wilson defined them—not only a peace between America and the Central Powers, but among all the belligerents.[19] True, he had not directly consulted any of them, certainly not the British and the French; but "the programme" seemed to him "the only possible programme," and on the basis of it he committed the United States to stand with the Entente, "together until the end."

Later the Fourteen Points will be seen with reference to their application and enforcement at the peace table; here it is enough to characterize them briefly. The first six dealt with such general principles of diplomacy as no secret engagements, freedom of the seas, and fair settlement of colonial claims. Then Wilson embarked on the more delicate ground of defining for the United States (and for the other belligerents) specific territorial issues. These included the evacuation of all Russian territory, restoration of Belgium, adjustment of Italian frontiers on lines of nationality, and (in addition to the evacuation of all French territories occupied by the Germans) righting of the wrong done to France by Prussia in 1871. The final point was the establishment of a general association of nations to guarantee the independence and territorial integrity of all states—the future League of Nations. Wilson realized that in entering into the details of specific European and Middle Eastern issues he risked going beyond what the American people considered their direct concerns. But there was no drawing back now. The United States was a world power and he was convinced it must assume world responsibilities.

Under Creel's supervision the words were translated into all languages and were carried to the people by every means of dissemination then available. They lifted to the realm of reason a dialogue in danger of being reduced to partisan or nationalistic advantage. Whatever reservations the Allied leaders were later to express, whatever annoyance they felt at having peace terms declared without their being consulted, they kept silent for the time being. For a brief moment it did indeed appear that an armistice, accompanied by an agreement to summon a general peace conference, was attainable. On January 24 both Hertling for Germany and Czernin for Austria spoke in terms that seemed constructive; and on February 11 Wilson once more addressed Congress, this time in moderately optimistic words. But the dialogue was to end abruptly. The fighting forces on both sides were to be condemned to another summer of intolerable slaughter before peace could be again talked of—and then it would be with the voices of unreason in the ascendant.

The fatal, hope-shattering event was the announcement on March 3 of the final terms imposed by Germany upon the Russians at Brest-Litovsk. These constituted the peace of a conqueror, perhaps not more severe than what in the past had been suffered by a defeated nation; but in the atmosphere created by Wilson's ideals they seemed to be particularly brutal, condemning the Russians to total military and economic subordination. As in the resumption of U-boat warfare, the German militarists had wagered they could defeat the Allies before the United States threw its weight into the balance. Their decision was to wage all-out warfare on the western front, transferring some forty divisions from the east and abandoning the fragile hope of a peace negotiated among equals.

Wilson was profoundly and bitterly disappointed. From then on his contempt for the German political-military system was complete. His confidence in Britain and France was insufficient to let him believe that they would insist on anything other than Draconian peace terms. He possessed a trump card in the allied dependence on continued American credits, and he knew he would be supported by the liberal and socialist forces in the two democracies. Yet neither of these factors gave much assurance of achieving a just peace, a peace between foes who, having suffered absolute defeat on neither side, would compromise for the sake of avoiding future wars. From this time on Wilson knew that his chances of success were slim.

Yet for the present it seemed that Wilson had come through the critical period with his credentials as an international spokesman confirmed. His self-confidence was high and his reputation both at home and abroad enhanced. He had spoken for the democratic cause with an authority and gravity which even those who had reservations found it inexpedient to challenge openly. He kept alight the latent idealism of his own people, to be fanned when armistice negotiations opened in a later season. Through it all he diverted neither his nor his people's attention from the immediate task of forging an efficient war machine. Indeed in the midst of the diplomatic moves related above, Wilson took the unprecedented step of nationalizing all the railroads of the United States.

After the disillusionment of Brest-Litovsk, Wilson's tone and his central preoccupation changed subtly. From the day of entering the war he had been committed to winning it; but now he saw that there were no shortcuts to victory. The Prussian militarists would have to be defeated on sea and land, whatever the cost and however long it took. "They exploit everything to their own use and aggrandizement," he said in an address on the first anniversary of America's entering the conflict; and he envisioned an empire under their domination ultimately extending to Persia, India, and the peoples of the Far East. He had proposed the terms of a fair peace; now they had responded, "and I cannot mistake the meaning of their answer."[20]

"There is therefore but one answer possible for us," Wilson declared: "Force, Force to the utmost, Force without stint or limit." To help supply that force would be his sole objective until the Germans came to him seeking an armistice.

THE WAR'S END

The promise of "force to the utmost" was what the Allied Powers wanted desperately to hear. On March 21 the Germans opened what their field marshals hoped would be the war's decisive offensive. Shrouded in early morning mists the vanguard of an army heavily reinforced by transfers from the east assaulted the British lines at Arras. In a week the Germans had made advances of as much as forty miles. April and May saw further attacks, driving a wedge briefly between the British and French forces. In Washington Jusserand pointed out to the President that the enemy, its forces converging along two valleys, was as close to Paris as Washington was to Baltimore. Driven by the crisis the Allies at last unified the supreme command, with Field Marshal Ferdinand Foch placed at the head of their combined forces. An appeal went out immediately for more American troops, at any cost, trained or untrained.

The April crisis put the governments of the United States and of the Allied Powers under severe criticism from their respective publics. In the United States attacks on the Wilson administration were particularly harsh. The pieces of America's vast war machine were in place, but by the spring of 1918 the outpouring of men, soon to revolutionize conditions on the western front, had not begun. In the interval it was easy for the press and for Congress to jump to the conclusion that the war effort had been a fiasco. The British Prime Minister complained privately that the Americans had fallen down on their promises of manpower; but (fortunately for Wilson) he was persuaded by Reading and Wiseman to say publicly that the United States had done everything possible to aid the Allies.

At this juncture fresh strains appeared within the Wilson administration. Creel, always a target of the press, was under particularly vicious attacks on the issue of censorship. McAdoo, exhausted by his many jobs, fell ill with a severe throat infection and was confined in silence to his bed for weeks. This did not prevent him from engaging in bitter quarrels with Garfield nor from repeatedly threatening to resign. Wilson remained outwardly imperturbable. He had laid the basis for action and with an aplomb that surprised his associates he indicated no doubts about the ultimate result.

The President's overriding preoccupation was how to get as many troops as possible, as quickly as possible, in action on the western front. To this end he drove himself and his colleagues mercilessly. By the late spring, with the British putting all available shipping at the disposal of the United States, and with sealanes largely cleared of submarines, the tide of men grew into a flood. In June Baker announced that a total of one million American men had reached France. Wilson was prepared to continue troop shipments unabatedly, even beyond limits foreseen by the French or the British; and he was determined to get the new troops into action on a large scale at the earliest possible time.

He "stood on no ceremony," he told Wiseman in regard to the use of these troops: they were to be deployed in whatever way was necessary, "regardless if need be of national sentiment."[1] If Pershing should by any chance demur from putting them into action before an American army was created, Wilson would reluctantly have to overrule his top general.

Actually, both the President and Pershing were strongly against the idea of "brigading" United States forces into French and British units. In the spring emergency they assented to placing these troops under Foch to be used at the latter's discretion; but this was a temporary expedient. By August 1918, the goal of an independent U.S. army was achieved, in time to play a decisive role in the war's final battles.

Determined as he was to avoid diverting military forces, Wilson continued to search for ways of adjusting American policies to the Allied pressure for a second front in the east. On June 19 he received Thomas Masaryk, spokesman for the cause of the Czechoslovakians. Masaryk described how at Vladivostok, threatened by attacks of Austrian and German prisoners of war, seventy thousand Czech soldiers waited to fight their way out. Wilson was impressed by Masaryk and began to see the shadow of a plan for a Russian policy consonant with his ideas of not intervening in Russian affairs and of not employing major Allied resources. To come to the aid of the beleaguered Czech legion, helping it to move safely to join compatriots in Siberia and thence to make its way to the western front, seemed to him a valid objective. On July 6, at a high-level meeting held late at night in the White House, a scheme was hammered out that met, in part at least, the urgent British and French requests.

In coming to this decision Wilson arrived at an important turning point in his European policy. Disappointed by failure to obtain a separate peace with Austria, and also impressed by the hopes of the Czechs, Poles, and Yugoslavs, he told Lansing in June that the Habsburg Empire was "artificial."[2] Thereafter the independence of struggling peoples of Central Europe became a major element in his view of a just postwar order.

His immediate plan, to help the Czechs and at the same time indirectly to support the Allied determination to place troops in Russia, called for the deployment of seven thousand U.S. soldiers and marines, together with an equal number of Japanese. The sole objective of these joint forces was to guard the rear of the Czechs moving toward Vladivostok. The plan called for a detachment of Americans to join Allied troops at Murmansk to protect military supplies from being captured by the Germans. The President was considering also the dispatch of a mission composed of outstanding civilians to look into economic aid for Russia, and was prepared to provide a small armed contingent for its protection.

The Allies accepted without enthusiasm the President's decisions, which fell far short of establishing a second front. They suspected, nevertheless, that having gained the dispatch of limited American forces to Russia, further United States actions would follow. In this they were shrewdly right. As will be seen, Wilson found it difficult to withdraw American troops before having stretched his commitment and obscured his original goals. By late 1918 the Secretary of War was warning him that, despite his clearly defined purposes and despite the exemplary conduct of his commanding general in the field, American troops were being used for "purposes for which we would not have sent them in the first instance": in effect to give indirect support to Allied intervention in the Russian civil war. Besides, they served, rather than thwarted, the buildup of Japanese strength in Siberia. It was being argued, Baker continued, that with the increase of Japanese troops from seven thousand to seventy thousand men, the United States could not withdraw; but in fact, "the longer we stay, the more Japanese there are."[3]

It was a classic dilemma, which later American Presidents were to face in other theaters of war.

*   *   *

In May a trip to New York to make a speech on behalf of the Red Cross gave the President a welcome relief from Washington. For a few days it also made him accessible to the citizenry as he had not been since the start of the war. During this period his day-to-day activities were carried on largely out of public view. Holding no press conferences and making few addresses except in formal appearances before Congress, the image of the popular leader was becoming dim.

New York was not the place Wilson would have preferred for a long-deferred outing. He always considered it hostile territory. It had been such when as president of Princeton he faced his most hardened opposition among the city's alumni. He had not carried the state in 1916 and thought of it as a seat of reactionary financial powers. With some misgivings he and Edith set forth upon their journey.

House met them at the Pennsylvania Station and for two hours they motored together at a leisurely pace along the parks and drives of the city's West Side. The men fell into the kind of intimate conversation that was a boon to them both—to House because it gave him the drift of the President's mind and provided him with morsels, often spicy and self-serving, to be inscribed in his diary; to the President because he could relax completely. On this occasion Wilson was apparently in a combative mood. He expressed his contempt for U.S. senators in general, including the newly appointed chairman of the Senate Foreign Relations Committee, Gilbert M. Hitchcock, a man who was, however, to serve him faithfully in his time of need.

The Wilsons dined with Colonel and Mrs. House at their apartment and afterwards went to see the noted comedian Fred Stone in a current play. The audience cheered enthusiastically as Wilson entered. They were mistaken, he told them in response, in believing that they saw the President of the United States; they merely saw a very tired man trying to enjoy himself.[4]

The next day he called at the Scribners office of his old friend Robert Bridges (it was a Saturday, and Bridges was not there);* he motored up to Riverdale in the Bronx for a long talk in the spacious library of another Princetonian, Cleveland Dodge. Then he surprised almost everyone by marching two miles on Fifth Avenue at the head of a huge parade in

---

* "Bobby" was, however, in the audience when Wilson spoke that night at the Metropolitan Opera House. "It was a great day's work," he wrote afterwards, "and I step higher for having witnessed the triumph." (R. Bridges to WW, May 21, 1918, PWW, 48:112.)

honor of the Red Cross. In the evening, at the Metropolitan Opera House, a major address was scheduled. For ten minutes after dinner he retired, as was his custom, to look over the brief notes he had drafted. Sitting that evening in House's study, topics and even phrases formed themselves whole in his mind; afterwards when he faced the audience his words appeared entirely extemporaneous, drawn from a bottomless reserve and falling with an almost infallible exactitude. Nevertheless, he had told House on a recent occasion that he was always nervous before speaking in public. Walking across a crowded stage he "wondered whether he would drop before he reached the speaker's stand."[5] On such occasions House would be nervous, too, fearing the President might make a serious slip.

Wilson went out of his way at the start of this speech to challenge those New Yorkers whom, as in years past, he considered his foes. No man, he said, would be permitted to make a fortune out of the war. More significantly, he remarked that the United States would "stand by Russia as well as France."[6] The audience rose to its feet and cheered. They did not know what the President intended; and given the chaos of Russia's internal affairs and the disturbing excesses of the Bolsheviks, the President was evidently not quite sure either. Yet it was a rare moment in public life, with hitherto unexpressed sympathies finding a spontaneous voice. The remainder of the speech was not notable, but the kind of appeal to duty and service Wilson could deliver with the eloquence of unforced emotion. Its impact extended to each individual in the large hall, and it was climaxed by a generous ovation.

The affection and praise of friends during these days was a tonic for the President. Equally so was the demonstration of public support. The image of the man came into focus as crowds saw a human being instead of imagining a remote power. With the mass media still in their infancy, the personality of any President was hard to make out; and this was especially true of Wilson, an immensely private individual, except as his presence flashed intermittently across the public consciousness.

From the panic of March and April the Allies rose to efforts that not only repulsed the enemy but established a new mood of confidence. This would not have been possible without the heroism of French and British troops hardened by more than three years of battle; but neither would it have been possible without the arrival of the Americans in an ever-increasing stream. They were largely untrained; they relied upon European veterans for initiation into the hell of trench warfare. But once in battle, they competed effectively with their tested comrades-in-arms.

On May 28 the First Army Division helped French soldiers scale the heights at Cantigny. Members of the First Marine Division held up the German advance at Château-Thierry, and on June 6 the marines went on the offensive at Belleau Wood. Their losses were heavy, but they captured a salient held by crack German troops, a victory having repercussions not only on the Allies but on the enemy. Most important, the Americans closed the gap between the French and British lines. Thereafter the German High Command saw how risky had been their gamble to win outright before the Americans could be forged into a fighting force.

The Allied offensives of early summer culminated in a concerted attack upon the Somme area. Benefiting from surprise, moving across lands devastated in earlier battles, Allied forces overran forward German positions and at a relatively light cost in casualties took twenty-one thousand prisoners of war. By August 8 the Germans had once and for all lost the military initiative. That date General Erich von Ludendorff later wrote, was the "black day of the German army in the history of this war. . . . [It] put the decline of that fighting power beyond all doubt."[7]

As the end of the war approached, the President found himself amid particularly complex military and diplomatic choices, without precedents to guide him and with a Secretary of State in whom he had little confidence. In these circumstances Colonel House reached the apex of his influence. He stood closer to the center of events than anyone except Wilson himself. Whatever the future was to hold for their relationship, there was in midsummer 1918 little to mar Wilson's trust or House's record of usefulness. A natural inclination led Wilson, after the New York visit, to spend his few days of vacation a short walk away from House's summer residence at Magnolia Point, Massachusetts.

The President's retreat was clearly visible from the sea. An increased force of Secret Service men and a detail of marines from Boston patrolled the grounds, while destroyers offshore and a group of hydroplanes searched the adjoining waters for submarines. By modern standards it was little enough protection for a President in the midst of war; but for a few days Wilson was able to relax in body and mind.

Arriving with Mrs. Wilson August 15, he immediately walked over from his cottage to the Colonel's residence, and on the seaside verandah began the kind of wide-ranging discussions he could hold with no other man. As the war in Europe turned clearly toward victory, the two let their minds dwell upon postwar settlements. Wilson had brought with him a draft of a league of nations composed by a British cabinet committee. It was the first time he had been prepared to give serious thought to such actual arrangements; indeed in private he had frequently expressed impatience with those whose emphasis on the details of a postwar organization seemed too specific and premature. Now he could begin to think seriously about his own plans for a league.

In regard to the postwar situation as a whole, Wilson's public rhetoric had undergone a hardening since the United States became an active belligerent. No longer did he prescribe a "peace without victory": in mobilizing his people, all-out victory had come to seem an essential goal. But in moments of deeper reflection, as in the talks at Magnolia with House, he believed that victory at best should still be limited, leaving Germany intact and capable of playing a role in the European community. He expected it to be a member of the new league from the start. Indeed, despite the change in outward circumstances, Wilson's basic ideas had remained remarkably unchanged. He stood by the Fourteen Points, and he wanted justice—in a phrase he inserted in a speech and then was persuaded on tactical grounds to eliminate—"which does not discriminate between friend and foe."[8]

Wilson and House were both well aware of how tenuous and probably short-lived was the President's ability to enforce these views upon the Allies. In some moods Wilson seemed to believe that the socialist and liberal forces in England and France would hold their rulers to his conception of a just peace; at other times he relied more realistically on the postwar economic strength of the United States. Fundamentally he sensed that some approximate balance of power was necessary on the European continent if negotiation and compromise were to be possible. So with victory seeming to draw near and cries of revenge arising in Europe and America, he held stubbornly to his idea that Germany, though it must be defeated, must not be humiliated or totally destroyed.

A fundamental need was to exploit the President's momentarily strong position. Prodded by House, Wilson determined once more to set forth his minimal expectations in the strongest possible terms. Returning to New York a month after the Magnolia talks, he delivered an address prepared with more than usual care, ostensibly to open the Fourth Liberty Loan drive. Explicit, stark and urgent in tone, the words passed over the heads of the immediate hearers, gathered to cheer a patriotic harangue. But an infinitely larger audience, on both sides of the firing line, was made to understand that Wilson was prepared to push a diplomatic offensive in its way as powerfully concerted as the military offensive then unfolding.

Something of the resonance of the last, burning Princeton addresses came back into the President's words. The conflict, he said, was started as a statesman's war but had become a people's war—"and peoples of all sorts and races, of every degree of power and variety of fortune, are involved in its sweeping processes of change and settlement." The issues had grown clearer and clearer, "and it is now plain that they are issues which no man can pervert unless it be wilfully. I am bound to fight for them, and happy to fight for them."[9]

For the first time Wilson defined as an absolute priority the incorporation of the institution of a league of nations in the general peace treaty, an integral part of it and not a separate provision to be delayed or compromised. And he set forth a newly hardened attitude toward Germany. The existing German rulers had revealed themselves to be utterly untrustworthy, he proclaimed, and could not be dealt with through any process of adjustment or bargaining. They were free to intimate terms acceptable to them, but the world was not looking for "terms." It was insisting on such universal standards of decency as these rulers did not comprehend or honor. Upon the victors, and upon the victors alone, would rest the responsibility of treating Germany fairly. Yet that responsibility was in itself inviolable: the impartial justice he saw underlying a durable settlement forbade discrimination "between those to whom we wish to be just and those to whom we do not wish to be just."

Thus Wilson came close to the positions he would maintain in ending the war and at the peace table in Paris—supremacy of the league, exclusion of the Germans from the bargaining process, and adoption by the victors of standards of justice. His own views had been sharpened by the speech; the Central Powers and the Entente had been given a clear message. Sooner than anyone could have foreseen, in circumstances totally unexpected, Wilson was given the charge of applying these principles in a supreme test of statesmanship.

On October 6 a message signed by Prince Max of Baden, the new German chancellor, was directed personally to President Wilson. The chancellor had come to power two days earlier, a respected figure in touch with Germany's liberal and socialist elements. "The German government," read the message, "requests the President of the United States of America to take steps for the restoration of peace. . . . The German government accepts, as a basis for the peace negotiations, the program laid down by the President of the United States." The brief note ended with an expression of Germany's desire to terminate the bloodshed by concluding a general armistice.[10]

Events lying behind this sudden appeal were complex, played out on the western and eastern fronts and in discussions between the military and civilian authorities in Germany. The situation on the battlefield had deteriorated steadily since the repulse of the spring's major offensive. Foch's counteroffensive broke the Hindenburg Line on October 1, and the massed Allies were approaching the Belgian and German borders. In the east, Bulgaria had surrendered. The military situation was not, however, in itself decisive. The Germans could still have withdrawn their forces and waged a long defensive war. But the government saw the situation in a more comprehensive and a gloomier light. The inexorable British blockade had taken its toll; the introduction of tanks as a new weapon of war, and the waves of American reinforcements, shattered the basic German calculations. As a result of these and other factors—not least the hope of a fair peace held out in Wilson's speeches—the morale of the German fighting forces and civilians was sagging.

For Wilson the German appeal for an armistice, and for a peace based on the Fourteen Points, was a triumph; it produced also the most severe challenge he had confronted. Awesome pitfalls opened before him as he took up with advisers the nature of his reply. Compared to the choices now before him the decision to enter the war had been, as House noted, relatively easy. Wilson considered the existing German government demonstrably untrustworthy; yet if his long search for peace meant anything, it meant that their appeal could not be ignored. In whatever he did, he must balance the interests of the United States on the same scale with those of the Allies; he must keep in view the public opinion in his own country, now whipped up to a pitch of war fever. Above all he must avoid falling into the trap of having Germany use the proposed armistice as a means of regrouping its forces and prolonging the war.

He moved warily and with skill. The response to the German government was a brief series of testing questions. Did their note mean they accepted the Fourteen Points as the basis of the peace, or only as a starting point for negotiations? Were they prepared as a preliminary to evacuate all occupied territories? Also, from what constituted authorities did the plea for an armistice derive? Within a matter of days the reply came back, on the whole meeting Wilson's criteria of a valid commitment.[11] Now he faced the heart of the problem, acting amid the most delicate of considerations both at home and abroad.

Allied leaders were alarmed, even incensed, that the American President had taken it upon himself to deal with the enemy. In the United States, a highly vocal part of the public was calling for a drive into Germany. Senate and House elections were but two weeks away, and the widespread perception that Wilson was "soft" on Germany played into the hands of the Republicans. Many nonpartisan observers feared he would be seduced by his desire for peace into a premature and prejudicial military settlement. Taking all such factors into account, and consulting fully with his cabinet and with other advisers, Wilson framed a further communication.

The second note, dispatched October 23, struck a sterner tone than the first and was received with consternation in Berlin. From it the European Allies could draw reassurance and even the fire-eaters at home were offered a measure of appeasement. Along with the public at large Wilson had been outraged by the recent acts of needless brutality committed by the German army as it retreated across northern France. Devastation on land and the sinking of still another passenger ship at sea called forth words of withering rebuke and gave the President cause to question the legitimacy of the existing German government. He made it clear that with the nations at war with Germany rested the sole determination of the terms of an armistice, terms that would absolutely guarantee continued military supremacy.

Wilson had judged well the enemy's basic need and desire for peace, for although his note provoked heated debate between the German Foreign Office and the military authorities, in effect they capitulated to his terms. Ludendorff and General Paul von Hindenburg, recovered from the panic that had provoked the call for an armistice, were now ready to fight to the bitter end. But the civilian leaders knew how difficult it was to put down the idea of peace, once it had been raised. In their reply to the President they only asked that the terms of the armistice reflect the power of the opposing camps in the field. Though recognizing their subordination to the demands of Allied military chiefs, they stated their hope that "the American President will approve of no demand which will be irreconcilable with the honor of the German people."

Wilson was close to ending the war, single-handedly and on his own terms. He realized the tremendous risks inherent in his next step. One false move could alienate the Allies and launch them on their own course, in pursuit of nationalistic interests rather than of his peace program. With his own people whipped up to a vengeful fever, he faced the further risk not only of seeing the Democratic party defeated in the approaching elections but of being deprived of power to lead effectively. Moreover, in the midst of his diplomatic triumph he was possessed of a characteristically Wilsonian doubt. He was not absolutely convinced, he told Jusserand, that an immediate armistice was desirable.[12]

At a special White House meeting of the Cabinet on October 23 the situation was thoroughly aired. The coming elections were inevitably brought up. Wilson at first objected to their being discussed. "I am dealing in human lives," he said, "not in politics."[13] But it was pressed on him that the maintenance of his authority was essential to fulfilling his peace program; and indeed the harshness of the third note, as finally framed, took the domestic political situation into account.

On the basis of the latest German response, Wilson declared, he was willing to submit the enemy's request for an armistice to the Allied governments, but he was adamant that the final determination of its terms lay within the hands of the United States and its associates alone, and that these terms must be framed in such a way as to make the renewal of war impossible. What he asked was as close to total surrender as words could come. Moreover in a concluding passage he all but demanded the Kaiser's abdication.

Two days after dispatching this note, with an armistice virtually assured, Wilson released an appeal to the voters of the United States for the return of a Democratic Congress. He was at this juncture high in public favor. The country knew he had traversed with success the most perilous of diplomatic precipices. Although grievances had piled up with the sacrifices and dislocations of war, he seemed relatively secure against the assaults of the opposition. But in his partisan appeal to the voters, and in the phrases at once bitter and egotistical in which it was phrased, he made a mistake that was to cost him heavily in prestige and power, hardly less abroad than in his own country.

That a President should ask for the support of the voters, that he should urge the retention of a majority of his own party in the legislature, was not without ample precedent. Examples could be adduced from Lincoln to the recent occupant of the office, Theodore Roosevelt. As governor, Wilson had himself given urgent expression to the argument that a hostile legislature would imperil his reform program. The 1918 appeal had not, moreover, been issued without careful review by Wilson's staff. Why it unleashed such denunciations and led to such catastrophic results tells much about the nature of the latent but growing opposition to Wilson's policies.

Through the autumn of 1918 the White House was keenly aware of the approaching elections, and various means were discussed of bringing the President's influence to bear on them. Tumulty urged the President to make a tour on behalf of the Fourth Liberty Loan, suggesting that this would create a favorable atmosphere for a subsequent appeal for political support. The President rejected the proposal as too transparently partisan, but a stream of requests from individual candidates persuaded him to consider a general endorsement. The draft of such an appeal was read to Edith Wilson and was submitted to Tumulty and to Democratic leaders Vance McCormick and Homer S. Cummings. Virtually all their suggestions were included in the final text.[14]

Wilson and his advisers were completely unprepared for the violent reaction not only from Republicans but from the press. They had seriously underestimated the intractability of the President's opponents, especially in the Senate. They had failed to take account of the degree to which the administration, despite its apparent successes, was losing touch with grass roots public opinion. Events of the next year were to validate the signals raised in the fracas over Wilson's appeal. In the Senate Republican leaders headed by Lodge showed themselves far more powerful and effective than Wilson had judged them, while a slow erosion of popular support, a distancing of the President from the public whose deeper purposes he had hitherto so successfully interpreted, became disastrously evident. All this, veiled from Wilson's eyes, was in the making at the very moment of his greatest triumph of statesmanship and diplomacy.

The wording of the controversial appeal suggests Wilson's growing tendency to draw power to himself and to characterize all government actions as his own. Twice (despite elaborate protestations of modesty) it spoke of "*my* leadership"; it asked that the voters "sustain *me* with undivided minds." It revealed a rising spirit of partisanship, coming dangerously close to identifying successful prosecution of the war with the Democratic Party and to questioning the patriotic support of the Republicans. Most unwisely, instead of minimizing the effect of possible Republican gains, it predicted that return of Republican control to either House of the Congress would be interpreted abroad as a repudiation of the whole Wilson program. In an earlier wartime election Lincoln had advised against "swapping horses in midstream." If Wilson had been able to deal with the forthcoming elections in a phrase so homely and impersonal, the elections—and much else besides—might have come out differently.

As it was, Republicans won a a majority in both Houses of Congress. For the first time in his Presidency Wilson faced a legislature organized and dominated by the opposition, when his flexibility and his sense of political accommodation were at an unusually low ebb. Isolationists hailed the defeat as indicating (what Wilson himself had predicted) that his ideas and ideals were discredited. What might have been brushed off as a characteristic swing in American politics, brought on by discontents with high taxes and wartime restrictions, was interpreted in Europe as Wilson had rashly and unnecessarily foretold that it would be.

Yet, as he invariably did when an election was over, Wilson took the results with apparent good grace. He believed in the people, and he believed in Providence. "We are all well," he wrote to his daughter Jessie in mid-November. "I am very tired, but not too tired, and not at all dismayed or disheartened by the recent elections." The Democratic campaign manager, Homer Cummings, after an interview with the President on November 8, gives a surprising picture of a man at peace with himself and reconciled to events.[15] "He was very much saddened by the result," Cummings wrote. "He told me frankly that it made his difficulties enormously greater." Nevertheless, "he was very kind and generous in his attitude toward me. . . . He felt that I had done everything that was humanly possible and that it was simply one of those things that had to be. He was not bitter toward anyone." Wilson could not foresee at that juncture the absolutely disastrous results that would follow on his loss of a Democratic majority in Congress.

During October, while the President was carrying on the exchange of notes with Germany, he was aware that he had some matters to settle with the Allies, too. The enemy might have accepted his Fourteen Points as the basis of peace; but it was essential that the victors be similarly committed. The peace program had been drafted with sensitive concern for Allied interests but without their consultation; officially they had taken no position on its substance. Now it was Wilson's need to secure their binding assent. It was also his supreme opportunity. Had he haggled with Allied leaders at the time the Fourteen Points were framed they might never have come to agreement. But with the German government signed up, France and Britain were on the spot.

For the task of securing Allied compliance the President chose House as his agent, requesting him to leave immediately for Europe. The French and British were relieved, for they greatly needed to be reassured that in setting the final terms of the armistice the President was acting in their interests as well as the interests of the United States. Wilson saw his emissary depart with complete confidence in the rapport between them.

Arriving in London on October 26, House was made immediately aware of the suspicion in high Allied circles of the President and of his peace program. Knowing well that the terms of the armistice would largely predetermine a later peace settlement, the Allied leaders were set to assert their control. And they had one intention, to give Germany no quarter. The Fourteen Points they were inclined to consider more effective as war propaganda than as the terms of a settlement.

Through four stormy sessions at the end of October House confronted the Allied leaders in what was his finest hour. He fought for his chief rather than cultivating the goodwill of his opponents, and on October 30 he played his trump card with courage. If the Allies persisted in their views, he said, the logical consequence was for the President to consider afresh whether it was worthwhile for the Americans to go on fighting. "My statement," reported House, "had a very exciting effect upon those present."[16] The threat of a separate peace left France and Britain with no choice but to accept the Fourteen Points in principle. It was a major diplomatic victory for which the foundations had been laid by Wilson's consistent refusal to become a formal ally of the European powers.

The British and French still asked for clarification on certain points of the Wilsonian program. A memorandum from The Inquiry, framed under great pressure of time by Lippmann and Cobb and cabled to London, contained significant interpretations of Wilson's original words.[17] "Open diplomacy," it was explained, meant that treaties should be public but not necessarily the negotiations leading up to them. More fundamental was the difference of principle on two issues raised by the British: reparations, and freedom of the seas. Wilson fumed at what he considered British intransigence, especially in regard to the latter. He cabled House that he took his stand unequivocally in favor of freedom of the seas—in effect a ban on the control of neutral commerce in wartime. "I hope," he added, "I shall not be obliged to make this decision public."[18] In a calmer moment he recognized, nevertheless, that as an island Britain had special problems, and he was inclined to admit a blockade if sanctioned by the projected league of nations. He was ready to admit that the issue was open to "the freest discussion and the most liberal interchange of views." He also acceded to the British in agreeing that the Germans should make reparation for all damages they had done to civilians by their aggression on land and sea and in the air.[19]

The problem of the Fourteen Points having been disposed of, for the time being, House was free to devote his full attention to the terms of the armistice. "My deliberate judgment," Wilson cabled him on October 28, "is that our whole weight should be thrown for an armistice which will prevent a renewal of hostilities by Germany but which will be as moderate and reasonable as possible within those limits, because it is certain that too much success or security on the part of the Allies will make a genuine peace settlement exceedingly difficult if not impossible."[20] The line was a difficult one to hew, the more so because the terms were shaped by the Supreme War Council. In this situation Pershing was not supportive of the President, submitting a long statement which called for the continuance of the war until the enemy surrendered unconditionally.

The Colonel was pleased with his work. "I consider that we have won a great diplomatic victory," he cabled the President on November 5, "in getting the Allies to accept the principles [you] have laid down. . . . This has been done on the face of . . . the thoroughly unsympathetic personnel constituting the Entente governments."[21] Although in negotiating the armistice he had gone beyond the President's instructions, Wilson did not specifically object to House's having followed the Supreme War Council in reducing Germany to military impotency. Indeed he had himself said that Germany must accept such terms as would make it impossible for her to resume hostilities. In adopting this position he abandoned, before the peace talks began, an important element in his bargaining position *vis-à-vis* the Allies—the threat that Germany would resist if she considered the peace too harsh.

The German reply to Wilson's third note again split the military and civilian authorities in Berlin. But when on October 26 Austria requested separate peace negotiations, the case for further military resistance was seriously weakened. Constitutional reforms were hastily enacted. A formal reply to Wilson amounted to virtual capitulation, although it expressed the hope that the armistice would be "the first step toward a peace of justice." It remained for Germany to accept the final armistice terms as drawn up by the victorious powers. On November 11 at Compiègne, near Paris, the document was signed, silencing the guns on all the battlefields.

In Washington Wilson issued a brief statement: "A supreme moment of history has come . . . the hand of God is laid upon the nations."[22] The same afternoon he addressed Congress. In spite of the occasion the applause was subdued. He read the clauses of the armistice one by one. The remainder of his address was a solemn warning of dangers still to come. He expressed no pride in victory nor allowed himself a touch of drama. Revolution in Germany and the deposition of the Kaiser raised the specter of Bolshevism in Germany and Central Europe, and Wilson feared the disorganization of society more than he feared a revival of militarism. To help counter the threat he announced forthcoming shipments of food to Germany (an act of prudence and generosity to be repeatedly thwarted by Allied and congressional intransigence). In praising "the humane temper and intention of the victorious governments" he spoke for a mood that was all too quickly to pass.[23]

Nevertheless, for the President it was a supreme moment of triumph. He had slowly been climbing to an eminence that placed him, not only among the three or four top men of the world, but as first among them. He had been heeded by foreign governments as no President before him; he had reached out, beyond the people of his own country, to masses of men across the globe. Shadows on his path—opposition in the Senate, ill-concealed resentment among Allied leaders, a bargaining position weakened by the terms of the armistice and by the recent elections— seemed capable of dissolving under his leadership. Wilson's inflexibility on many issues, his prejudiced judgment of many men, were defects of personality that would grow worse under stress and increasing illness; but in that hour he seemed invulnerable, armored with a clear idealism and a sure faith.

From far and near came words of congratulation mixed with hope. "You have done this great thing. May God's blessing rest on it and you," wrote the ever-faithful Secretary of War. From Wilson's old friend Cleveland Dodge: "You must be a happy man today when you realize what you have wrought. May God who has so far led you all the way continue to guide you." From George V of England: "I thank you and the people of the United States for the high and noble part which you have played in this glorious chapter of history."[24] Brandeis caught the armistice mood in lines which he sent the President, quoted from Euripides: "To stand from fear set free, to breathe and wait, / To hold a hand uplifted over Hate. . . ."

Wilson had indeed played a major role in defeating the heresy of militarism and had single-handedly laid the foundation for a peace that could save the world—or at least save the West—from future internecine wars. He was entitled to a sense of satisfaction more profound than his restless, driving spirit ever quite allowed him.

The decision to go to Europe and to play a part in the peacemaking was almost inevitable, given Wilson's feeling of responsibility for the outcome. At the cabinet meeting the day after the signing of the armistice he indicated that he would probably leave after the opening of the lame-duck session of Congress early in December. Lansing thought the plan a mistake and immediately saw the President privately to tell him so. The President was not pleased (he rarely was by Lansing's interventions): "He said nothing," the Secretary wrote in a personal memorandum, "but looked volumes."[25] Others had their serious doubts, best summed up by the President's longtime supporter, the journalist Frank Cobb, in a letter from Paris. "The moment the President sits at the [council] table with these Prime Ministers and Foreign Secretaries," Cobb wrote, "he has lost all the power that comes from distance and detachment. Instead of remaining the great arbiter of human freedom he becomes merely a negotiator dealing with other negotiators."[26] Outvoted, he would either have to accept the will of the majority or disrupt the proceedings in what appeared to be the complaint of a thwarted and disappointed individual.

Allied leaders, already resentful of his power and jealous of his popularity, would miss no opportunity to harass him and wear him down. They would seek to play him off one against the other, a game in which they were marvelously adroit. Wilson's "extraordinary facility of statement," Cobb continued, would be lost in secret harangues and would be blurred in translation. All this the journalist put in opposition to the commanding position as a judge of last resort Wilson would hold if he remained in Washington.

There was no question, however, of Wilson's not going; and it is doubtful whether, had he escaped the perils and degradations of Paris, he would have been able to preserve at a distance any control over events. The European peacemakers were too determined to have their way; the liberal forces of Europe, too weak and disorganized to affect their conduct; and the peoples of the victorious powers, too prone to relapse into a mood of bitter vengeance. As to the role Wilson would play abroad, a good deal of uncertainty remained. For a while he thought it would be enough if he participated only in the preliminary conference where "the greater outlines of the final treaty" would be settled.[27] But in the details, as events were to prove, lay the power to sustain or to betray his ideals; and once engaged he had little choice but to proceed to the end. If the European prime ministers ground him down, as Cobb had predicted, if they "harassed him and played him off one against the other," it was not because he was weak or ineffective, but because the grim outcome was written into the nature of things. As martyrs before him had gone to their martyrdom Wilson went half-knowingly, not entirely cheerless, and ready to put up a good fight.

The immediate task before the President was to choose the members of the American peace delegation and to settle the list of those who would accompany him abroad. For one who disliked personal confrontations as much as Wilson did, and whose limited strength warned against long sessions of elucidation or persuasion, the obvious solution was to choose for his peace commissioners men whom he knew well and who understood and agreed with him. From the beginning a delegation representative of different parties, factions, or interests was ruled out. Besides, he was narrowly limited in numbers. Neither Georges Clemenceau, the French Premier, nor Lloyd George was prepared to determine at once the size of their delegations. Lloyd George had embarked immediately after the armistice upon an election designed to reinforce his authority, notwithstanding the likelihood (which proved all too real) that he would thereby fan the flames of a bitter nationalism. Clemenceau simply wanted a rest. He was not averse, besides, to delaying the business of peace-making so as to let the immediate wave of postwar idealism subside. It was clear to all, nevertheless, that relatively small delegations, of from three to five members each, were alone practicable; a total of five was settled upon.

The British and French Foreign Secretaries were to be included without question and Wilson had no choice but to appoint Lansing. He could hardly have had a man with whom he was personally or intellectually less in sympathy. He considered Lansing a pettifogger; he mistrusted his arid professionalism and obtuse sense of practicality. At Paris Lansing would be continually shunted aside, driven to confide his growing doubts about the treaty and his dislike of the league of nations to self-justifying memoranda and diary entries. Equally inevitable as a choice, but far more warmly welcome, was House. As a confidential adviser House had become indispensable to Wilson, and whatever doubts Wilson may have had about House's handling of the armistice negotiations, he thought of him as a sound negotiator. Yet it proved a mistake, for House as well as for Wilson, to have the conciliatory and impressionable Texan in an official post, where his gifts for frank counsel were blunted and a hitherto concealed personal ambition made itself apparent.

For an adviser on military matters Wilson would have preferred his Secretary of War, but McAdoo having announced his determination to resign immediately after the armistice, Baker felt he could be most useful at home. He was needed in the cabinet, the wisest head among its members and the most trusted by Wilson. With characteristic selflessness he advised that General Tasker H. Bliss be appointed in his stead. Bliss was a student of military history and had a rare instinct for the political elements in strategy; he also had a genuine hatred of war. Wilson would come to feel that he had the most "statesmanlike mind" in the delegation. His being chosen left one place open, and the need for a Republican was obvious.

The President would not consider Lodge, for what seemed to him the good reason that he would be totally out of sympathy with everything the peacemakers were trying to accomplish. Elihu Root seemed to him too conservative to deal with a world in revolution. He finally settled on a veteran diplomat, Henry White, former ambassador to France, participant in the Algeciras Conference of 1906, a friend of Roosevelt and his circle. He was a figure of urbane charm, prominent in Washington society where he and his wife entertained lavishly. White was taken completely by surprise by Wilson's offer, but accepted—perhaps like many older men eager for one more adventure. He would appear out of place among the younger Americans in Paris, the representative of a bygone day. But his knowledge of diplomacy made him a helpful addition to the group of peacemakers. The trouble was, he lacked entirely a political base. He held no place within the hierarchy of the Republican Party; his friendships, with Lodge and others, were purely social.

Finally, and most important, Wilson himself would go as head of the American commission.

When these names were announced on November 29, they were greeted with derision by Republicans in Congress. White's appointment they saw as a totally ineffectual gesture of appeasement. By others the group was considered unnoteworthy—no woman delegate, no labor representative, the choices entirely predictable considering the President's clear intent to be his own chief policymaker and negotiator. What ultimately happened in Paris would be neither helped nor seriously marred by the four aides who, with good intentions and variable gifts, sought to play their small part in history.

It remained to choose the President's personal entourage. There was never any doubt about Mrs. Wilson's going. Grayson was indispensable, not only as physician but as daily companion and confidant. The same might have been thought true of Tumulty, but an unexpected letter to the President stated that although there was nothing in the world he would rather do than go to Paris, he felt his duty was to remain at his desk in Washington. One wonders whether it had been conveyed in some way to Tumulty that his Irish ways would be out of keeping with the polished diplomatic style in Paris, and whether the letter had not been written to bolster his self-respect. In any case remain he did. His chief service during the peace conference was to comment on newspaper clippings and by occasional cables to offer advice that was mostly disregarded. To meet his office needs in Paris the President brought only Charles L. Swem and Gilbert F. Close, his chief stenographers. Along with him went seven Secret Service men; the White House major domo,

Irwin (Ike) Hoover; and Mrs. Wilson's social secretary, Edith Benham, together with her maid and the President's valet.

A last remaining task was the delivery on December 2 of the President's annual message on the state of the Union. On this occasion Wilson allowed himself the brief satisfaction of basking in the "great days of completed achievement."[28] He dwelt on the recent victory, praising the sacrifices and heroism of those who had made it possible. But when it came to setting forth a legislative program for the immediate future, he was strangely uninspired.

During the war he had envisioned a new society emerging from the maelstrom; now he saw demobilization and reconstruction taking place by the traditional methods of private enterprise, and a normal economy presently being regained. There were a few exceptions. The railroads presented a special problem and could not immediately be returned to their former owners. Soldiers back from France would require help in finding employment, and a program of public works, mostly land reclamation, was suggested. But principally, in Wilson's view, it was a matter of getting back to business as usual. His mind was absorbed in questions of foreign policy, and he failed to provide leadership at home.

The close of Wilson's address was a plea for conciliation, which, had it been heeded on both sides, would have left a happier tale for history to tell. He was, he said, going on a long journey, and he hoped for the support of Congress, for its "countenance and encouragement." He would be away no longer than was essential and would not be inaccessible when needed. It was his prayer to return in due course "with the happy assurance" that it had been possible "to translate into action the great ideals for which America has striven."

CHAPTER NINE

World Spokesman

―――――◆―――――

ODYSSEY

The European mission upon which Wilson embarked at midnight, December 3, 1918, a few hours after the conclusion of his address to Congress, was without precedent in American history and formed the supreme adventure of his career. No earlier Chief Executive had, while in office, traveled outside the United States; none would have dared conceive making of European publics a vast constituency to be appealed to in person, or of sitting with the world's leaders to consult and negotiate over a period of many months. Moreover, the reception Wilson received, in numbers and in the fervor of its adulation, perhaps exceeded any previously accorded to any mortal. First in France, and then in Great Britain and Italy, he became the focus of all the pent-up emotions generated at the war's end. To the common people, longing for permanent peace, he alone appeared to have the key.

Scenes and images from that time linger as a vital part of twentieth-century legend: the frenzied ranks of humanity where he passed, the chorus of faith poured out as if by one exultant voice; flowers in his path, hands stretched out to touch the charismatic figure, the pictures of the lean Calvinist visage lighted by candles in the homes of laborer and peasant. The great personages of the time, the kings and heads of state, responding to this tumult—indeed not daring to fail to respond to it—yielded him extraordinary honors. Whatever reserves they harbored, or whatever conflicting emotions ran below the surface of the crowd, there streamed for a few brief weeks the light of a pure, an almost holy dedication; and Wilson was placed by destiny at its center.

He had often seen himself playing a part in some historic drama; but he was an essentially modest man, and the scale and intensity of the

European reception took him by surprise as much as everyone else. He lived up to the all but overwhelming challenge. He walked with simplicity and grace in the path prepared for him, and his quietly spoken words had the eloquence of a shared idealism. Yet there was always a second side to Wilson, something hard and canny. Now he was not quite taken in by a mood he knew must pass.

Unimpressed by the deference of rulers, he kept a distance born of long-nourished suspicions of their aims and methods. The plain people with their passionately expressed faith were another matter. He truly wanted to serve them, yet he felt burdened and almost afraid, knowing that in the nature of things he could only partially fulfill their expectations. An experienced leader, he was prepared for their sake to take advantage of any opportunity to benefit his cause, and their own. He would make use of their hopes, and even of their illusions, in battles against apostles of the old order. And so he courted the people, often against the predilections of his official hosts; he went out of his way to reach allies among Europe's liberal and leftist forces. Indeed through the first phase of his journey he moved with an almost unfaltering political skill.

The last days before the trip had been spent amid a different sort of politics in Washington. The cold reception Wilson received from the Republicans in Congress during the delivery of his final address—an "ice bath," Daniels described it, "sullen and quiet"[1]—capped days of hostile oratory on the Senate floor. Determined to discredit the President before his departure, the Senate Republicans formally protested his decision to go abroad; they passed a resolution calling for the Vice President, Thomas R. Marshall, to be in charge of the country during the President's absence. (The resolution had no legal effect, but Wilson did ask Marshall to preside at cabinet meetings.) From the New York hospital where he lay dying, Theodore Roosevelt issued a statement repudiating the Fourteen Points, and calling upon Britain, as victor in the war, to claim whatever spoils it felt entitled to. To make matters worse, Jusserand, the French ambassador, brought to the White House a last-minute memorandum, outlining his government's conception of how the coming peace conference should be organized. It was an entirely sensible document, but to Wilson anything harping back to the old diplomacy was anathema.*

---

*The document also indicated that the French were ready to support a "suspension of all previous special agreements arrived at by some of the allies only" (en-

No ceremonies of farewell marked the start of the President's momentous journey. Taking the midnight train from Washington, he arrived early the next morning in Hoboken, New Jersey, where a disconsolate Tumulty said good-bye to him. Newton D. Baker had accompanied him this far, but he, too, returned wistfully to Washington. Men and women on their way to work paused to watch the President's train, moving in reverse through Hoboken's crowded streets to the army wharf where the *George Washington* was waiting. After breakfasting in his private car, Wilson boarded and went directly to the seagoing office assigned to him.

The *George Washington* had been built as a great German liner, and named so as to appeal to American tourists. Impounded at the start of the war and converted to a transport carrying as many as five thousand troops, it had been only partially restored to serve the President's mission. Four times he was to cross the Atlantic on board, always refreshed and rested by the voyage, and coming to think of the ship as almost a second home.

On subsequent crossings it carried returning soldiers along with the Presidential party, but now its cavernous spaces were mostly empty. The main smoking room, converted to a hospital capable of caring for as many as four hundred cases of influenza, harbored a few crew members. The refrigeration plant below, recently a morgue for not less than eighty men lost to the dread disease on a single voyage, was again in use only for preserving food. A luxurious main dining room was the crew's recreation and entertainment area. Several officers' cabins, repainted and freshened up, were given to the President and members of his official party. The latter included the French and Italian ambassadors, Jean Jules Jusserand and Count Macchi di Cellere; John W. Davis, Page's successor on his way to the Court of St. James's; and two of the American peace commissioners, Lansing and White. Younger advisers, mostly from The Inquiry, together with representatives of the three national news agencies, were installed in more modest quarters.

The President was exhausted when he boarded the *George Washington*. He had a cold and his voice was raspy and muffled. Yet he gave the newsmen a background conference before sailing, venting harsh feelings toward the European powers. He spoke particularly of Britain,

---

closure in F. L. Polk to WW, Dec. 2, 1918, PWW, 53:298)—that is to say, of the secret treaties. That this should have been passed over without further discussion by Wilson and the State Department suggests how little importance was attached to the secret treaties, or how little was known about them at the time.

whose naval dominance he had long considered almost as great a danger as Germany's armed might. Implying that his voice would by then have fully recovered, he "would have to do some plain talking when we get on the other side,"[2] he said. Grayson put him to bed, and Miss Denham was soon confiding to her diary that Wilson at least disproved the idea that great men need little sleep.[3]

As the *George Washington* sailed down the bay hundreds of vessels in the harbor tooted their whistles in an impromptu salute. Out past the Statue of Liberty, approaching the Ambrose Lightship, several destroyers formed an escort. Planes and a dirigible flew briefly overhead.

For a day the seas were rough and the airs harsh, but as the armada entered the Gulf Stream the temperature rose and Wilson's health, along with his spirits, improved. At meals he told stories and talked amusingly of men and events. With Mrs. Wilson he walked the decks, on Grayson's orders often two miles at a stretch, wearing a golfing cap and followed by four Secret Service men and a marine officer. A small boy on board, son of the Italian ambassador, jumped up from his chair, saluting and spilling his toys onto the deck, each time the President passed. The President paused on one of his rounds to assure the lad that to rise and salute once was enough. Sunday he went down into the hold to attend religious services with the crew of a thousand men. "A poor little Navy Chaplain," so scared he could hardly speak, preached "a poor little sermon," according to one of the President's aides.[4] But the President had no complaints. Indeed he seemed to enjoy himself increasingly as the ship moved toward Europe, and the comments of those who watched him closely and recorded their impressions in letters and diaries give us a rare, almost a last, look at Wilson the private man.

Hardly less important, they give us a glimpse of Edith Wilson before she became, less than a year later, the mysterious figure behind drawn shades at the White House. That she was devoted to her husband, and that the two were deeply in love, was plain. "The more I am with the Wilsons," noted Edith Denham, "the more I am struck with their unrivalled home life. I have never dreamed such sweetness and love could be."[5] Raymond Blaine Fosdick, a former student of Wilson's at Princeton and now traveling to survey morale in the American army camps, observed how when walking the deck Wilson took small, swift steps, attuned to his wife's. "He seems to listen interestedly to her conversation," he added in an evident understatement.[6] Indeed she was never far from him, and was no stranger to the business of state. Twice during Wilson's conversation with advisers Mrs. Wilson entered the cabin, in search of official papers she had misplaced. She appeared completely unaffected;

she made a pleasant, but not a striking impression.[7] That along with her stylish ways and soft southern appeal she had a will of her own was apparent to those serving the President.

With the news representatives on board Wilson held two extended talks, frank to the point of indiscretion and clairvoyant in awareness of difficulties to come. The Italian ambassador, eager to press his country's claims, was politely turned aside by the President; Jusserand, more tactful, was rewarded with a long private conference. The two peace commissioners were not much in evidence during the voyage. Busier, more curious, and more prompt to record their impressions in letters and diaries were the experts, most of them young and connected with The Inquiry, who had come on board with tons of documents and maps stored in the hold. The *George Washington*, wrote Harold Nicolson in his later account of the peace conference, "creaked and groaned across the Atlantic under the weight of their erudition."[8]

Not knowing the President's mind, feeling left out, a few of these younger experts did not conceal their doubts and misgivings. As the ship passed the Azores on December 7, Wilson called them together and in a well-documented session laid bare his basic presuppositions about the peace conference. He made it clear that he would rely heavily on the advice of the scholars and social scientists; more than that, he revealed the human and appealing side of his nature. He was "genial and charming," wrote the economic historian Clive Day, "with a fund of humor and of happy literary allusions."[9] Others present were totally enlisted in the fight he promised to wage on the basis of the right as they would reveal it to him. Most of them never forgot the Wilson who had won their affection that day. During the remainder of the voyage several of the young men—Raymond Fosdick, Charles Seymour, William Bullitt—established easy personal relations with the President, being able to speak to him with surprising frankness and finding that he frequently accepted their suggestions.

With the officers and crew of the ship Wilson was at his best. At the end of the voyage Fosdick could report "the strongest feeling of admiration and love" for him. One night after a moving picture show he asked whether he might shake hands with all the enlisted men; on another occasion, when they put on a musical comedy, he was observed to "laugh his head off."[10] Usually reluctant to be photographed, he acceded to any request of the men, in whatever part of the ship they asked him to pose. The last night on board, December 12, the choir of the *George Washington*, concealed during a film in which Geraldine Farrar was starring, broke forth with the support of the ship's orchestra into the hymn "God Be with You Till We Meet Again." The President, visibly moved, joined heartily in a final rendition of "Auld Lang Syne."

From the moment the *George Washington* swung into her anchorage at Brest the nature of Wilson's reception was established. A tender drew up alongside and officials, French and American, admirals and generals of the Allied forces, debarked to welcome him. Decorated with flags and garlands, the craft took the President ashore where he exchanged brief speeches with the mayor of the city. Automobiles, dispatched from Paris, carried him and his party to the railway station. The whole population was in the streets. The women wore (when they did not wear black) colorful native costumes and showered blossoms in the path of the President. Crowds hailed the passage of the special train moving through the Brittany countryside. Looking from the window of his drawing room at 3:00 A.M., Grayson saw men and women and little children standing with uncovered heads as the train sped by.

Arrival in Paris was set for mid-morning. At a station platform ordinarily reserved for reigning monarchs the President stepped down to a brilliant scene of flags and flowers. Raymond Poincaré, President of the French Republic, and Clemenceau, the Prime Minister, were both on hand to greet him. On a day of sunshine all Paris was on holiday, with immense crowds lining the route to the Hotel Murat, the palace set aside for the President's use.

From a balcony of the Hotel Crillon Ray Stannard Baker looked down on a hundred thousand people packed into the place de la Concorde. Henry White, who claimed to have witnessed in the French capital every historical street demonstration since the reception for Napoleon III in 1867, asserted there had never been anything like this one. At evening the celebrations continued. It was like armistice day at home, Fosdick wrote in his diary, "without quite so much rough-house and with a little more lovemaking." And then he added with prescience, "Poor Wilson!" A man with his responsibilities was to be pitied—"the French think that with almost a magic touch he will bring about the day of political and industrial justice. Will he? Can he?"[11]

On December 15 Wilson held an extended conversation with Clemenceau. Having been given an enthusiastic appraisal by House, Wilson was prepared to get on well with the indomitable French leader. Often in the political wilderness, a former physician, his brilliantly erratic mind as much at home in literary and journalistic circles as in the parliament, Clemenceau had emerged in the last years of the war as one purified by fire, a politician stripped of all ambition except the fierce determination, first, to save France, and then to see that she was not placed again in the same peril. Like many clever older men, he was by turns charming and intractable.

The two men were different in their approach to European problems. Clemenceau saw the Bolsheviks as an evil force with which there could be no parley. He saw the Germans as a people that could not be trusted, who yielded only to naked power. The two men were equally different in their mental attitudes. Clemenceau believed that the shape of the world was determined by historical experience, impervious to ideals or abstract formulas. That Wilson and Clemenceau formed a sincere friendship for each other shows something important about both men.

Wilson perceived the French leader as one whose motives could be understood and whose constancy was assured. More than that, he penetrated to the essence of his colleague's great passion. It was not so much that Clemenceau was consumed by the idea of revenge against Germany—he was too sophisticated a statesman for that; he was consumed, rather, by a determination to prevent the Germans from ever again invading France. In this he could count on Wilson's understanding, and also on his sympathy. For Wilson, as his course in the peace conference revealed, was acutely sensitive to the needs of the various countries (and of France particularly) for safety from attack. Safety was to be promised by the League of Nations; but defensible boundaries were the foundation stone on which the League was to rest.

During their intimate association Wilson was sometimes driven to despair by the French leader's obstinacy. On one occasion he charged House with having presented a misleading impression of the old man's virtues. But in the beginning (and indeed at the end) Wilson and Clemenceau kept respect for each other, deepening into affection, and sealed with the realization that they were linked by a common fate.

Wilson hoped to start immediately on the work of the peace conference, but he had not counted on the French penchant for ceremony. Within the first days he was given a formal lunch by Poincaré; he was received at the Hôtel de Ville with a reception which House declared to be "beyond anything in the history of Paris";[12] he was presented an honorary degree at the Sorbonne. At ease amid the pomp of these grand occasions, Wilson responded to the official oratory in words of quiet eloquence, spoken without notes.

The French pressed him, meanwhile, to visit the battlefields and war-devastated regions. To this he was strangely (and yet not uncharacteristically) resistant. He felt he did not need to observe at first hand the effects of the war. He had weighed and measured them in his mind. He understood the French concern for security against future invasions. "I am sure that I shall look upon the ruin wrought by the armies of the Central Empires with the same repulsion and deep indignation that it stirs in the hearts of the men of France and Belgium," he had stated in the first formal remarks he made on French soil.[13] Was that not enough? He had recognized the necessity for action that would "not only rebuke such acts" but provide "the certainty of just punishment." In his own time and his own way he would visit the battlefields; but to be pushed and manipulated, he complained in private, made him "see red."[14]

From Washington Tumulty urged frantically that the press be given opportunities for filing "human interest" stories. But when the President went out to visit American soldiers at the hospital in Neuilly he made the rounds with Mrs. Wilson in private, pausing at the bedsides of hundreds of wounded men. Christmas Day he spent at General Pershing's headquarters at Chaumont. Having reviewed the troops on the muddy field, he was chagrined and angered when he found he was not to eat with them outdoors as he had requested, but in the officers' mess. Later he went through the cold barns and houses where the men were billeted, a sad army anxious only to get home. From the experience the President drew his own lessons. But Tumulty got little of the human touches his Irish heart was set on.

Still there was no sign of the peace conference getting started. Clemenceau was not yet ready. Lloyd George was in the midst of a political campaign, the "khaki election" called hastily after the armistice to reinforce his position. Fretting in ignorance of what the leaders intended, the American commissioners found no other delegations joining them in Paris. A corps of five hundred American newsmen milled about, strangers to Europe and frustrated by the lack of hard news. At the Hôtel Murat delegations and individuals came and went, pouring into the President's ear the woes and the hopes of half the world, but providing little except gossip to indicate what had been discussed.

Meanwhile Europe was in turmoil. In a vain effort to establish their authority, the Bolsheviks in Russia waged civil war. Germany, still under the incubus of the blockade, was starving, its economy at a standstill and its demobilizing armies in a disorderly rout. Smaller states, new and old, were prepared to use armed force if necessary as they jockeyed to win favorable frontiers. If peace was not established promptly by the Great Powers it was plain there might be no peace for a generation. And yet the Great Powers, as 1918 ran out, seemed loath to come to grips with their task.

Wilson on the *George Washington*

Crowds in the rue Madeleine, December 14, 1918

With President Raymond Poincaré
of France

The Big Four, June 28, 1919

Wilson presenting the League of Nations, at a plenary session of the peace conference, February 14, 1919 (from a painting by George Sheridan Knowles)

Speaking at Suresnes, Memorial Day, 1919

*   *   *

In this interval Wilson undertook two official visits, to Great Britain and to Italy. He had a message to preach, followers to sustain, and recalcitrants in official circles whom he could hope to impress. His prestige was at its height and he risked seeing it worn away if he remained immobilized in Paris.

On December 25, returning from his day with the troops at Chaumont, he went by train directly to Calais where the British hospital ship *Brighton*, escorted by a British cruiser, took him on board. Overhead, in battle formation, flew a squadron of British airplanes. The group awaiting them at Dover included Lord Reading and the new U.S. ambassador— Page had died just three days earlier; and when the king's special train, sent down to meet them, drew in that afternoon to Charing Cross Station, King George and Queen Mary were themselves on hand to welcome the President, and to whisk him and Mrs. Wilson to Buckingham Palace where they were to be guests.

The London crowds were large and enthusiastic, if not quite so demonstrative as those in Paris, but the official welcome was unsurpassed. A dinner at the palace saw gathered all the luminaries of Britain's official as well as literary life, with such stars as Rudyard Kipling and Conan Doyle among the guests. For the first time since the start of the war wines and liquors were served. The next day, Wilson's sixty-second birthday, in a splendid ceremony at the Guildhall, he was made a citizen of the capital.

That night Lloyd George entertained him at a stag dinner before he was escorted to the royal train that was to serve him and Mrs. Wilson on their continuing journey. His remarks at the dinner, recently come to light,* are a surprise in view of Wilson's often stormy relationships with the British. In that relaxed atmosphere, amid congenial company, he forgot how he had railed against the Allies in controversies over wartime shipping; he spoke in ignorance of the derogatory counsels voiced during his visit by British and imperial statesmen. Reminding his audience how in two wars the Americans and British had fought each other, "at last," he said, "on land and sea, English and American forces have fought so close together, that the colours of their flags were made into one banner of the free."

---

*The text of these remarks, published neither in the press nor in the collection of Wilson's official speeches while abroad, was found among papers of Cary T. Grayson made available to Professor A. S. Link by Cary T. Grayson, Jr., and James Gordon Grayson, the former's sons, in June 1990. It is now in PWW, 64:491.

"I am one of those," he asserted, "who believe that the greatest good that has come out of this war is the bond of deathless friendship, born in a common cause, and dipped in fraternal blood, which shall ever unite the British Empire and the American commonwealth."[15]

It was unfortunate that these remarks were not given out to a public that felt Wilson lacked warmth in his tributes to Britain's participation in the war. What the public heard in other toasts and speeches were outlines of his approach to the peace. He discerned in the cheers of the populace, Wilson said at the Guildhall, "the voice of one people speaking to another people"; and what they were expressing was the determination of the victorious powers: the determination "to do away with an old order and to establish a new one." The words were a warning to the old guard, and their meaning was not lost on Lloyd George, with whom, during the days of this visit, Wilson established what appeared to be a cordial relationship.

The two men met for the first time at the railway station on Wilson's arrival, and the Prime Minister later recorded his impression: "The frankness of his countenance, the affability and almost warmth of his manner, won my good will. . . . He had the charm which emanates from a fine intelligence." The favorable impression, he added, deepened on subsequent meetings. (In these memoirs Lloyd George also dwelt on what he saw as the less amiable side of Wilson's nature—vindictiveness, and bitterness toward individuals he did not like.)[16] Wilson's first impressions of the British leader were not recorded. But when he sat down next day for a prolonged and serious talk, he went over the major issues with the frankness of one who was dealing with a friend or, if such was to be the case, with an able adversary.

Wilson's side of the discussion is revealed in a report which Lloyd George unveiled a few days later at a meeting of the Imperial War Cabinet. The majority of those present were in an assertive, excitedly anti-German frame of mind. Wilson's London visit had coincided with the final count of the British election, the results showing an overwhelming victory for British conservative and imperial opinion. At the top of the national coalition Lloyd George sat uncomfortably, and rather incongruously. He was, if he was anything consistently and on principle, a liberal. From among his many changes and reversals there shone forth generous impulses and humane insights; he was often right on the big questions, and when he was not, energy and fertility of mind masked his errors or defections. In the election just concluded he had responded to the national mood by demanding a Draconian peace with Germany. Though it was not he who invented the often-repeated phrase about squeezing the lemon "till the pips squeak," he professed himself quite ready to hang the Kaiser, and made promises of exacting reparations that were to haunt him in subsequent, more statesmanlike moods. Later he admitted to being embarrassed by the campaign and thankful that it had not gone on any longer.

In reporting to his colleagues on the talk with Wilson, Lloyd George stressed the President's determination to give the League of Nations first priority.[17] Indeed he deduced that Wilson would be ready to go home after such a league had been established, leaving particulars of the peace to be determined or modified by the international organization. Wilson had not previously spoken of the League as a continuing body, capable of administrative acts. Evidently he had gotten the message of the British elections, as he had of the official atmosphere in Paris, and was looking for some way to have major decisions deferred to a calmer time. Indeed he had begun to grasp that the enthusiasm with which he was acclaimed did not reflect fully the realities of the situation—the intransigence of Allied chiefs and the fickleness of the peoples they led. "The key to the peace," he had said in his Guildhall address, was "the guarantee of the peace [i.e., the machinery created to administer it], not the items of it." This was no doubt what he had expressed to Lloyd George—though the latter woefully underestimated the fight Wilson would put up when such "items" as colonies and reparations came under discussion.

The President, Lloyd George continued in his report, was not "pro-Bolshevik" but was "very much opposed to armed intervention." He was set against major claims of Italy and Japan. On German indemnities he was "stiffer than on any other question," and he would not countenance France's claim to the Saar or the left bank of the Rhine. Quixotic as several of these points may have appeared to the Imperial War Cabinet, it was when Lloyd George set forth Wilson's views on the prewar German colonies that the temper of the gathering exploded.

Present were the Prime Ministers of the dominions, not precisely spokesmen for the old diplomacy, but among them rough-hewn leaders believing in raw power and on what a later age would call "body counts." The idea that the former German colonies would not be turned over to the dominions that had conquered them, but placed under mandates responsible to a league, struck the more belligerent of these as nonsense. Up spoke William Morris (Billie) Hughes, old and deaf Australian Prime Minister, demanding by virtue of what contribution to the war the United States had earned the right to lay down rules for the rest of the world. What monetary sacrifices had they made? How many of their men had been killed? So far as Hughes was concerned, Lloyd George and Clemenceau could settle things as they willed. Lord Curzon gave his opinion that many in the war cabinet agreed with Hughes. Perhaps on major issues, he suggested, the British and French should act together, ignoring the Americans and their visionary leader. Wilson may well have suspected the mood among the British and dominion leaders. Yet leaving London the crowds were still cheering wildly, and he continued as he journeyed northward to preach in calm tones the evangel of a new age of peace.

In Paris, during that same week, a political drama unfolded, similar in its implications to the discussions within the Imperial War Cabinet. For five days a debate in the French Parliament had proceeded without intervention from Clemenceau. Goaded by the opposition to reveal his plans for a European settlement, the Premier remained hunched in his seat, derisively silent. At last, near midnight on December 27, he rose and in a witty and wide-ranging speech indicated that he was not exactly taken by the socialist (or the Wilsonian) vision of a new world. "There is," said he, "an old system which appears to be discredited today, but to which I am not afraid of saying I am still faithful."[18] To Wilson he paid an elegant brief tribute, praising him for his "noble candor." The sharp reaction that followed indicated that both sides of the chamber appreciated Clemenceau's ambiguity, the word "candor" in French carrying the implication of innocence as well as of openness. The Premier thereupon received an overwhelming vote of confidence, 396 to 60.

The French socialists had been routed as decisively as had the Liberals in Britain. Lloyd George and Clemenceau emerged from their political tests apparently victorious, as Wilson emerged apparently defeated. But all three were in thrall to forces greater than themselves, a wave of nationalist sentiment that in the end would have more to do with shaping the peace than any of their individual convictions.

On the way to Manchester, the home of British Liberalism, Wilson stopped at Carlisle, where his mother was born and where his grandfather had been minister before emigrating to America. It was Sunday, and the President attended services at his grandfather's church. Requested at the last moment to speak, he rose in his pew, and his brief words formed an unforgettable moment in the Wilson odyssey.[19] He recalled his grandfather: "I remember how much he required. I remember the stern lessons of duty he spoke to me." And his mother: "Her quiet character, her sense of duty and dislike of ostentation, have come back to me with increasing force." What the world was seeking was a return to the paths of duty, a turning away "from the savagery of interest to the dignity of the performance of right." It was from quiet places all over the world, he concluded, that forces were rising which would overbear any attempt to accomplish evil on a large scale. "Like the rivulets gathering into the river and the river into the seas, there come from communities like this streams that fertilize the consciences of men, and it is the conscience of the world that we are trying to place upon the throne which others would usurp."

He was finished in less than three minutes. The words, read over and often reprinted, lingered among all that Wilson said and did, a kind of Gettysburg Address in the simplicity of their style and purity of their conception. There would be later triumphs, but he never reached beyond the spiritual summit of that Sunday morning in Carlisle.

On his return to London the President was again met at Charing Cross by the king and queen, and when next day he left for France they were at the railway station to bid him more than a formal farewell. On this English journey Wilson had not been able to forget his mistrust of Britain's naval supremacy nor entirely to transcend his wartime exasperations. British tactics inimical to American shipping and to the principle of freedom of the seas still rankled in him. His failure to pay the expected fulsome tribute to Britain's wartime sacrifices was noted and resented. Yet from the English people he evoked the tribute of a common idealism; they instinctively respected the honor and decency of his approach to world affairs. The king's farewell spoke the sentiments of his subjects as well as the warmth of his own feelings.

Reaching Paris on December 31, Wilson set out the following day for Italy, a complex and difficult mission. He was aware of Italy's postwar claims, ignoring the Fourteen Points and embodied in treaties with Britain and France. At the same time, Italy was bound to America by long-standing ties of sentiment. Wilson would be called upon to maintain a delicate balance between the excessive, quasi-religious emotionalism of the popular reception, and the heavy-handed efforts of officials to limit and circumscribe his contacts. He would be subjected to both the government's nationalistic demands and the resolve of the masses never to fight another war.

The government's pressure was first exposed in its absolute insistence that Wilson and his party ride the Italian royal train from Paris to Rome—an insistence going beyond hospitality and seeming to curb the President's independent stance. The popular pressure was manifested in the frenzied demonstrations wherever he appeared. Addressing the Parliament, Wilson attempted to moderate the leaders' demands by calling for a new concept of the future. "Our task is no less colossal than this," he told the political leaders: "to set up a new international psychology, to have a new atmosphere."[20] But when he tried to bring this message to the people massed in the Victor Emmanuel Square, he found the route of his motorcade diverted by official order.

Wilson did insist successfully on a meeting with the Italian socialist Leonida Bissolati, who had resigned from the government in protest against excessive territorial demands. After the day in Rome, at once frustrating and triumphant, he overruled his hosts to journey northward to the industrial cities of Milan and Turin. Again he was greeted by vast crowds, closer to him in thought and feeling than Rome's worshipful demonstrators. "I want to reecho the hope," he said at the Palazzo in Milan, "that we may all work together for a great peace as distinguished from a mean peace." In that dazzling moment it seemed that such a peace was possible. "The light that shined upon the summit now seems almost to shine at our feet," he said.[21] Perhaps the old treaties, with the grandiose concessions Italy had exacted as her price for entering the war, would indeed vanish like mist.

Wilson was buoyed, on his return to Paris, by reports from advisers that American opinion was altering in his favor. His European tour was judged a success; the eloquence and dignity with which he had represented the United States made his unprecedented absence seem worthwhile. On the train as he journeyed back to France he received the news of Theodore Roosevelt's death at sixty. The event removed from the field a man who in his last years had grown unreliable and bitter, but who had been a towering presence and Wilson's most formidable adversary. In private Wilson did not conceal his harsh feelings, but he wrote a generous tribute. He could afford to be generous toward one who, almost symbolically, had departed the scene just as he rose to the shining peak of his own career.

It was important, Tumulty cabled, that he proceed rapidly to the conference table. His popular triumphs would prove evanescent unless he struck promptly to enact his program. To get down to work with his European colleagues Wilson found, however, extremely difficult. He fretted at continued postponements. Lloyd George had not arrived in Paris. Clemenceau was insisting upon ten days of rest before the deliberations started. Whatever the justification for the delays, it was evident that French and British positions were strengthened as the tide of Wilsonian fervor began to subside. In what seems an accurate assessment, the journalist Ray Stannard Baker wrote that at the time of the armistice

Wilson was the majority leader of world opinion favoring a just and liberal peace; by the time the conference opened, he was the leader of the opposition—"a powerful opposition, but undoubtedly a minority."[22] From this posture—isolated, often deadly tired, and at stages ill—Wilson had now to carry out the fight for his ideals.

PEACE CONFERENCE: FIRST PHASE

On January 12, after long delays, the men who were to be responsible for the peace came together for the first time at the Quai d'Orsay.

They took their places, these peacemakers, around a table in the handsomely paneled and tapestried conference room of the Foreign Ministry. At one end was a fireplace; two windows looked out into a garden, bare under the mists of winter. Although others would come and go, the company in that first meeting consisted of the political heads of the chief wartime powers and their foreign ministers: Clemenceau and Stéphen Pichon, Wilson and Lansing, Lloyd George and Balfour; along with Premier Vittorio Emanuele Orlando and Baron Sidney Sonnino of Italy, Premier Saionji Kimmochi and Baron Shinken Makino of Japan. Together they formed what came to be known as the Council of Ten. They carried on the chief business of the peace conference until, in March 1919, Clemenceau, Wilson, Lloyd George, and Orlando met alone for the rest of the conference as the Council of Four.

The atmosphere in the room was stifling. Grayson, solicitous of his chief's welfare, opened a window onto the garden. It was, muttered Lloyd George, probably the first fresh air to be admitted since the days of Louis XIV. But Clemenceau waved his arms in protest and the window was quickly closed.

Ironically, the meeting began as a session of the Supreme War Council. While the new order waited to be established, Foch and other generals entered and held center stage. It was Marshal Foch, commander of the Allied troops, who opened the discussion.

This beginning was symbolic of the way the peace conference would proceed through the months to come. Peace was the theme, but war, and the fear of new wars, was the underlying obsession. Again and again as the statesmen grappled with an issue of world settlement, something like the rattling of sabers, the march of booted feet, would be heard in the wings; Foch and his generals would make their entrance—now to report some incipient new defiance by Germany, now some uprising in the states of Central Europe, or again (and most frequently) some fresh danger posed by Bolshevism. Peace, in that atmosphere, would appear a frail contender in the arena of men's hopes.

On this first day, Foch wanted to talk about the German armistice. It was subject to renewal month by month, and the commanding general saw the need for including additional security measures. Wilson took the opportunity to state a characteristic view. The armistice, he said, had been accepted by all concerned, and new conditions should not be imposed with Germany lying demoralized and helpless. Poland was the next subject Foch took up, proposing that transportation be provided the Polish army, now in France and Italy, so that it might help stem the Bolshevist tide. Again, Wilson responded in character. It was questionable, he said, whether Bolshevism could be stopped by force of arms; in any case, such large matters ought to be dealt with by the peace conference, not by military men.[1]

Foch departed. At four o'clock servants and footmen cleared the tables for afternoon tea—"an old ladies' tea-party," Wilson described it later. He was disturbed by this witness to the leisureliness of the proceedings. But "it was a foreign custom," he declared; "he was among foreigners so he gracefully accepted it."[2] After tea, when discussions were renewed, the statesmen were meeting in a first preliminary session of the peace conference.

The Ten operated informally, more like a faculty meeting, a young member of The Inquiry observed,[3] than like a council of state. Clemenceau, in the chair, rarely intervened to direct the course of the discussions. He sat hunched, his back to the fire, grey gloves covering his hands, shaggy eyebrows concealing his eyes, and a heavy mustache shading a frequently sardonic smile. Seated at Clemenceau's right, Wilson was thoroughly at home amid the debates, brisk and genial, informal in utterance. Lloyd George was like an energetic little bird, hopping from one subject to the next with more zest than knowledge—except that when his interests or passions were aroused, he could pour forth streams of eloquence or engage in startling intellectual maneuvers. Orlando (in contrast to the somber Sonnino) was the image of Old World charm and polish. Makino, mostly silent, was impassive except when the raw claims of Japanese diplomacy became engaged.

That first day, and for many wearisome days to come, the statesmen discussed the methods and the organization of the conference. Nothing had been worked out in advance. They arrived at the summit with virtually no agreements on procedure or on the agenda. Each participant knew what he wanted for his country, but each had different ideas on how to arrive at his objectives. The makeup of the conference, its structure, its rules of publicity, its priorities, the language that should be considered official, and the role of experts and of committees—these and other issues were left open to debate.

Wilson approached these procedural questions with patience and with the enjoyment of a skilled debater. His purpose was clear. He intended to inject his concepts of a new diplomacy, a new world order, into all issues affecting the conference. He intended to establish an atmosphere and method of procedure making it possible to arrive at decisions based not on national jealousies and paranoid fears but on evenhanded justice. He was himself in these early stages of the conference a model of open-minded, if determined, rationalism. He lost on some points, made effective compromises on others; but to a surprising extent, despite latent opposition from his colleagues, he succeeded from the start in injecting into the proceedings the standards and approach of his liberal program.

A first procedural question confronting the Council of Ten was attendance at the conference. Wilson had originally argued that Germany must be fully a part of the peacemaking process. But this view had been altered during the last period of American belligerency, and the concept of total victory, embodied in the armistice, put the enemy's presence in a different light. Besides, the victorious powers had questions to settle between themselves before there could be any question of dealing face to face with the Germans.

Russia's place in the Paris conference was more difficult to determine. That huge country was still at war, outside and inside its borders. The Bolshevik regime was far from having attained legitimacy at home and was, moreover, judged in sharply different ways by Wilson and by Clemenceau. Wilson's view went back to his first enthusiastic reaction to the Russian Revolution of April 1917, and beyond that to his long-held belief in the validity of change, even violent change, if made by the people in their own interest.

The coming to power of the Bolsheviks shook, but did not alter, his basic conviction that the people of Russia should be allowed to work out their own fate without interference. By 1919 Bolshevism had come to seem, to him as to others, an insidious poison, threatening to reduce eastern Europe to chaos and even to infect the United States. Still, he did not favor a military solution. Bolshevism, he told members of The Inquiry, was "a protest against the way in which the world has worked."[4] The basic remedy was to make the world work better. As Bolshevism began to affect Hungary and Germany, he remained convinced that it was endemic in starving populations and could be alleviated by economic countermeasures.

Clemenceau had a very different view. At the first meeting of the peace conference he declared roundly that no Bolshevik was to set foot on French soil. The question of how Russia might be represented in the peace talks was left in the air, but on January 20 the conference suspended other business to hear a long report on Russia by the French expert, Joseph Noulens. His thesis was, quite simply, that Russia was out to conquer the world. Should the Western powers be weak enough to negotiate with such a government they would, on the very next day, find themselves infested with "propagandists, money and explosives."[5] Their one goal was the spread of revolution by any means. This appraisal was evidently close to Clemenceau's views, while Lloyd George, not atypically, took a middle ground between Wilson and the French premier.

Lloyd George had no taste for military adventuring, being under pressure at home to get the British troops demobilized at the earliest possible moment. Moreover his instinctive liberalism made him suspicious of doctrinaire views. He wanted to see Russia represented in some way at the peace conference, and, with Wilson's support, he concocted a far-fetched plan.

An appeal would be made to all Russian groups, émigrés as well as those on home soil, to declare a truce and to meet for the purpose of choosing representatives to the peace conference. Clemenceau's interdiction against any Bolshevik setting foot on French soil caused Wilson and Lloyd George to suggest a remote spot for the conference, the island of Prinkipo in the Sea of Marmara in Asia Minor. Wilson was asked to draft the invitation to all Russian groups including the Bolsheviks. He wrote in his strongest, most lucid style an appeal declaring it the solemn intent of the conferees in Paris to interfere in no way with the internal life of Russia, but to secure, in the most appropriate form, the country's participation in making peace.[6] Wilson's draft was accepted and the invitation dispatched. For better or worse (as was probably expected) it did not achieve the desired results. Except as a ghost at the feast, a problem underlying virtually all other problems, Russia was not to be present in Paris.

Also to be determined was the role of small states at the peace table. As their recognized champion, Wilson did not want to have them excluded while the Great Powers ran the conference. (The Great Powers "ran the war," growled Lloyd George *sotto voce*.[7]) It was necessary, Wilson admitted, that the Council of Ten meet regularly for discussion, a sort of world supercabinet. But substantive negotiations should be carried out in plenary sessions where small and great nations participated.

The proposal was quickly challenged. Recalling that he had just been through a popular election, Lloyd George warned against peace terms being settled by "general clamor." Insofar as the Great Powers came to prior agreement among themselves, he continued, the plenary sessions would be mere window dressing; and if they did not agree there would be chaos. Wilson acceded to the force of these arguments. A compromise permitted the smaller countries to join with the Council of Ten, but only where their direct interests were involved.

The question of publicity for the proceedings of the conference, occupying much time, had been made the more complicated by Wilson's original promise of covenants "openly arrived at." He had raised public expectations, and particularly expectations of the newspaper reporters, not easily to be put down. Obviously some practical rule was necessary. In the prolonged debate on this issue, subtle distinctions, worthy of medieval dialecticians, were worked out. Much, in the end, seemed to depend on the word used to describe a particular meeting—whether it was a "conversation" (secret) or a "conference" (public); or upon the room in which the meetings were convoked. Those held in the large salon of the Quai d'Orsay would be, by definition, plenary sessions, and would be open to the press. Everything taking place in the conference room would be off-limits, and reporters would not have access to the principals involved in the discussions.

The press, especially the American press, became highly agitated when these arrangements were announced. With the plenary sessions reduced to a showcase, reporters saw themselves effectively barred from all significant negotiations. Wilson received a formal protest from the five hundred U.S. newsmen. He admitted that he did not see precisely how to handle the problem.[8] Privacy, he insisted, was absolutely necessary to the negotiating process; only harm would result if every dispute or difference among the principals was aired before a world audience.

The President was facing a larger problem than placating the newsmen. He knew well where his strength lay—with the common people who had placed their trust in him, and with the liberal forces in European politics that were not represented at the peace table. Unless he could keep this constituency informed, unless he could appeal to it as a last resort, he would go into the negotiations with hands tied. In the crises to come he would indeed suffer heavily from the early decision to restrict publicity. He was criticized for not upholding positions for which, in point of fact, he had fought strenuously. Matters were made worse by the fact that the Paris newspapers, largely under control of the government, were provided with "leaks" of a strongly anti-Wilson bias, and were given clear indication of what Clemenceau wanted, or did not want, to see in print. These handicaps Wilson endured silently in public, having in good conscience agreed to stage the conference in a closed arena.

A last preliminary issue was not without humorous aspects, as the statesmen debated, for most of two sessions, what should be the official language of the conference. Clemenceau had been relatively silent up to this point, letting Lloyd George tangle with the American President. But when the glory of the French language was at stake, he had to rouse himself to its defense. For centuries, he averred, French had been the first language of diplomacy; besides, added Pichon irrelevantly, France had borne unprecedented privations in the war. Was she now to be stripped of her ancient prerogatives? Wilson's retort was characteristic of him in its courtesy and deference; but it also showed his resolve to impress upon the conference, as each issue arose, his underlying point of view. It was a new day, he asserted, and perhaps things should be done in a new way. In its sardonic wisdom, Clemenceau's reply was also characteristic. He, too, "wished to make a new world and to do new things, but . . . the future was attached to the past."[9] A compromise provided for two official languages, with French the source for final interpretation of treaties. Clemenceau thereupon subsided, awaiting more crucial tests of strength.

The leaders were now ready to begin—but where were they to begin, and in what order were they to take up substantive issues? Holding that a formal agenda smacked too much of the old diplomacy, Wilson resisted French pressure to establish one. He wanted to keep discussion open and fluid, capable of dealing with new situations as they arose. Nevertheless he was determined that the League of Nations receive first priority. Lloyd George, under the thumb of the Dominions, was more interested in first dividing up the former German colonies; Clemenceau, in getting at territorial claims; and both insisted on giving high place to reparation. At Wilson's urging, they came to agreement on a rough list of topics to be taken up in the following order: the League, reparations, new states, boundaries, and colonies.

The priorities were never strictly observed. Items came up more or less haphazardly in the discussions, and Lloyd George did not fail to get the disposition of colonies promoted from the last to near the first of questions considered. But giving the League primacy was a clear victory for Wilson; and giving reparations second place was an indication of the strong tides running against Germany.

With their preliminary work accomplished, the statesmen proceeded to call the first plenary session of the conference. It took place on January 18, nearly five weeks after Wilson's arrival in Europe. This grand display was what the world had been waiting for—a solemn convocation of states and peoples, a panoply of power marshaled to create a new international order. For his own good reasons Clemenceau had chosen the date, the anniversary of the peace of 1871, when France had suffered crushing humiliations at the hands of Germany.

Crowds watched the great men of the world arrive at the Quai d'Orsay. The scene, unfortunately, was soaked by torrential rains. Five hundred American newspapermen jostled each other outside the conference to catch a glimpse through the curtained arches. There was Wilson at Clemenceau's right; Lloyd George at his left. President Poincaré welcomed the delegates. In a graceful speech Wilson nominated Clemenceau for permanent chairman. Clemenceau responded: "Success is only possible if we all remain firmly united. . . . We have come here as friends; we must leave this room as brothers."[10] It was a fine sight, even if nothing much happened.

The door having been thus briefly opened, it was closed again, and the press continued to fret as the Ten submerged themselves in secret deliberations. Through the following weeks major substantive issues overlapped and were intertwined, entering and disappearing from the discussions. Except for the military and naval terms, none ever seemed to reach a final solution. Lloyd George made sure that the colonial question was not postponed. In vain Wilson argued that the war had its roots in Europe, not in Africa or the Pacific, and that European settlements came before the disposition of colonies. Europe, living under a precarious truce, was, in his words, "a seething body of an uncertain and fearful people who did not know what fate awaited them."[11] He did at least get the Ten to issue a warning against territorial grabs by national groups and states ready to confront the peace conference with a *fait accompli.*[12]

Wilson had a further reason for wanting to defer the colonial issue. That Germany should be stripped of all its overseas possessions neither he, nor anyone else at the peace table, questioned. But he foresaw their being placed as mandates under the League of Nations, and it was difficult to argue the point until the League had at least been discussed. Lloyd George, on the other hand, wanted the colonies to be transferred rapidly to the dominions that had conquered them. Meanwhile Japan was claiming under wartime treaties the possession of all Pacific islands situated north of the Equator.

Lloyd George saw his chance when, on January 26, an opening occurred in the conference agenda. He proposed that the afternoon session be devoted to preliminary presentations by the dominion chiefs, a suggestion seeming to imply nothing more than a formal and perhaps tedious exposition. Certainly no one was prepared for the carefully staged event Lloyd George now masterminded. The Prime Ministers of the dominions, well primed and set to put forward their case in aggressive detail, marched in as a group. The British Prime Minister opened with an urgent statement, followed by Hughes of Australia, laying claim to New Guinea; Massey of New Zealand, to Samoa; Jan Smuts of South Africa, to German Southwest Africa. Their plea was for direct annexation, an undisguised division of the spoils of war. Not to be outdone, France set forth its demand for "annexation pure and simple" of Togoland and the Cameroons.[13]

Over the following week, the discussion thus launched raged within the Council of Ten. Wilson fought alone, articulate and persistent in the debate, but condemned to public silence. In the session of January 28 his anger became evident. He asked his colleagues to consider how the peace treaty would look if the Great Powers "just portioned out the helpless powers of the world," and thereafter formed a league to perpetuate the arrangement. When Massey indicated that this was not different from the way things had been done at a previous peace conference, Wilson exploded: he hoped, he said, that "even by reference the odor of Vienna would not again be brought into the proceedings." When he asked whether Australia and New Zealand were in effect presenting an ultimatum to the conference, "That's about it, Mr. President,"[14] retorted the Australian Prime Minister.

It was not possible, said Lloyd George, to wait for the League to be established. He added his own, more subtle ultimatum, stating that until the question of the colonies was settled everything else would remain unsettled. Clemenceau was no less uncompromising, but for a different reason. His conception of the League was that of a defensive alliance, formed to undergird the peace arrangements; he did not intend it to be an administrative body charged with responsibilities, such as governance of the former colonies, that it could not effectively carry out. "Furthermore," said Clemenceau, with all the biting irony at his command, "if this new constitution for the whole world was to be produced in eight days he was bound to feel some anxiety."[15]

At this time stories highly critical of Wilson began to appear in the French press. Attacks from conservative British quarters also circulated. Lord Curzon, British ambassador in Paris, reported that delays in the peace conference were entirely Wilson's fault. The business of the conference was to deal with Germany, not with a league; profound annoyance was felt against the American President because of his insistence on matters that seemed to have nothing to do with ending the war or making peace.

Nevertheless, on the important issue of the colonies, and against the overwhelming opposition, Wilson won. A resolution introduced by Lloyd George on January 30 established the mandatory system under the still-to-be-constituted League. The arguments on that final day were particularly intense and bitter, yet even Australia and New Zealand went along with the reluctant British and French Prime Ministers. The President's case was simply too powerful, and had been argued with too much cogency, to be overtly resisted at that point. Even countries greediest for territory were reluctant to be held responsible for the "cold bath of disappointment," which Wilson, at the start of the conference, had predicted in the event that the principle of self-determination or the ban on annexations were to be flouted.[16] Besides, not without reason, they counted on being able to water down or to evade the full effects of the mandatory system.

Wilson had stood boldly by his guns, had effectively employed his skill at persuasion, and on the whole had kept his good temper. From that day on there was no doubt within the Council of Ten that the League would be established as an integral part of the peace settlement. Yet public opinion was poorly informed of the President's victory. He paid for it, moreover, in the lingering effects of the hostile press campaign unleashed by the French.

Amid controversies over the colonial issue, Russia continued to preoccupy the peacemakers. Even when ignored it remained a decisive factor, shadowing almost all specific problems. The majority of those at the peace table saw Russia as a force to be defeated, or at least contained. Wilson, as has been noted, believed that Bolshevism could not be dealt with by military means. Indeed he flirted for a time with extending recognition to the Bolshevik government, causing an alarmed Tumulty to cable that "consternation" reigned in the American press.[17] But the President, if ever he considered the move seriously, did not pursue it.

In February, when the idea of the Prinkipo conference had gotten nowhere, Colonel House and Lloyd George hatched a scheme to send emissaries to make contact with the Soviet authorities. William C. Bullitt was chosen to head the mission, accompanied by the journalist Lincoln Steffens. The President, understanding it to be a fact-finding mission, gave his assent. He had failed, however, to take into account the youthful Bullitt's zeal. Making contact with Lenin and Trotsky, Bullitt went beyond his instructions, entered into negotiations, and returned with terms of peace allegedly acceptable to the Soviets.[18] On arriving in Paris, Bullitt saw Lloyd George (who later denied the meeting); he failed, however, to see Wilson. Despite pleas by House, Wilson was wary of the ambitious emissary, and besides, he was at the time totally absorbed in French security demands. As a result of what Bullitt considered a snub (as well as of his subsequent dissatisfaction with the terms of the peace treaty) he turned ferociously against the President, aiding the isolationists in their fight against the League and later coauthoring with Sigmund Freud a bitter and highly tendentious psychological study of Wilson.

Largely outside the peace conference, in sessions of the Supreme War Council, Germany's fate was meanwhile being decided. The periodic armistice negotiations became an arena in which Clemenceau and Foch on one side, and Wilson (occasionally abetted by Lloyd George) on the other, fought out opposing views. Implacably, meeting after meeting, Foch reported on German violations of the armistice terms and made demands for more rigid and more exacting provisions. With equal insistence Wilson continued to stand upon the original terms. The victorious powers had been in a position to make Germany incapable of renewing the war, and Wilson saw no reason why the burdens on its shattered military and economic system should be repeatedly augmented. If the terms were not being adhered to, he argued, then it was up to the military to enforce them. If new terms were required, they should be adopted with the enemy's consent. Wilson was being logical; he was also insisting on the kind of justice with which he still believed Germany should be treated.

In the Supreme War Council meeting of January 24 Foch urged keeping an army of 450,000 men in Europe as a counterweight to German might. If Germany was so strong, Wilson asked acidly, why had not full German demobilization been written into the armistice agreement? Foch replied it would be a condition difficult to execute. Yet sooner or later, Wilson continued, Europe would have to learn to trust Germany's promises. The Foch argument was too much even for Lloyd George, who wanted to know whether the armies of occupation in Germany could *ever* be reduced. A memorandum from General Pershing reinforced the more moderate view. Germany, Pershing stated, was simply not in a position to resume offensive operations. It had but a million men in service, and these were scattered and demoralized. Her ports were open to the British navy; the Allies controlled the Rhine; ships and arms had been surrendered.

In answer to continuing fears of the French that Germany might renew hostilities, Wilson proposed negotiations: if the Germans would cut back their forces, the army of occupation would be similarly reduced, while a relaxation of the blockade would allow raw materials, including food-stuffs, to be imported. At this Clemenceau flared up. He knew the Germans, he declared. Despite the armistice they were still at war; their goodwill could not be purchased, and any concession or sign of weakness would be taken as a signal for renewed aggression. Above all, Clemenceau insisted that the blockade be continued.

Supported by Lloyd George, Wilson gained at least a part of his objective. It was agreed to add civilian experts to the military commission. The idea of using food as part of a larger strategy, however, was rejected by the Allies. It was also rejected by actions of the American Congress.

In November 1919, Wilson collaborated with Herbert Hoover on plans to include Germany in the list of countries to receive shipments of foodstuffs in the immediate postwar period. Hoover, arriving shortly afterwards in London, found the British intractably opposed. (Only Winston Churchill, with one eye fixed steadily on building a bastion against Communism, supported such a course.) Meanwhile Wilson was running up against the same opposition in his own country. Although foodstuffs were piled up in American warehouses, Republican leaders rebuffed Wilson's plea for funds to send them abroad, unless Germany were struck from the list of recipients. As a result, the blockade of Germany was maintained throughout the winter of 1919, adding immeasurably to the people's misery and bitterness.

Formation of the League of Nations was a further continuing preoccupation through the first phase of the peace conference. The proposed institution, vital in all Wilson's thinking, was viewed by his colleagues with varying degrees of enthusiasm and was conceived as having different functions and serving different purposes. The issue was deflected to a special committee, where Wilson pursued it energetically. Before taking up that narrative, let us look at Wilson's personal situation during these Paris days—his living conditions, his methods of work, his entourage.

WHITE HOUSE IN THE RUE MONCEAU

The palace where the President and Mrs. Wilson lived had been put at their disposal by Joachim Napoleon, fifth Prince of Murat. In scale, in architectural grandeur, it was fit for royalty, standing in spacious grounds beyond the Boulevard Haussmann and looking out on one of Paris's most elegant parks. The Wilsons first saw it on the memorable December 19 when crowds filled the nearby streets and the whole city was out to acclaim them. The Garde Républicaine, mounted on jet-black horses and wearing gold helmets, had escorted them past the heavy iron gates to the inner courtyard, where Prince Murat was on hand to welcome them and show them about.

The prince was of a family closely connected with the First Empire. Throughout the palace were portraits of Napoleon I. One of the prince's ancestors (as he no doubt informed the President and the First Lady) had fled to the New World after the emperor's fall, and there married a young Washingtonian.[1] It was a series of magnificent spaces through which he now showed his American guests. On the ground floor of the palace were living rooms, a ballroom, and a dining room easily seating thirty-five people. Upstairs was a smaller dining room, suites for the President and Mrs. Wilson, and two libraries—the larger one, decorated with carvings of Cupid and Psyche and adorned with a fine painting by Jacques-Louis David, was to serve as Wilson's study and office. The rooms contained exceptionally fine furniture of the period, heavily decorated with brass, and were hung with tapestries and works of art.

The President's bed, unfortunately, was too short, but Mrs. Wilson was delighted with her own quarters. "There are closets & Armrues [armoires] & Cabinets galore," she wrote her family, "each lined with blue satin in which to put everything you ever owned. All the servants [there were seventeen of them]—are in Livery—knee breetches, crimson coats, etc. & we have delicious food."[2] Unfortunately, at least one of the servants who waited in the dining room was suspected by the Wilsons of speaking English and to be spying for the French government.

With the formal receptions and dinners completed and the peace conference under way, Wilson settled into an exhausting routine. Sessions of the Council of Ten and of the Supreme War Council were held most mornings and afternoons, with recesses for lunch; and when the Commission on the League of Nations began its work, he felt it necessary as its chairman to attend almost all its meetings. These usually occurred at night.

In his study, heavily guarded by Secret Service men and by the military, he passed the first working hours of his day. Out of deference to the absent Tumulty he refused to name a secretary, and had only his stenographers to keep his papers in order and his schedule straight. Here, at least, he could maintain his privacy and his isolation. Something of the aura which a young observer had attributed to him before his arrival in Europe—"a figure of almost mystical proportions," it had been written then, "of really incredible power but altogether out of reach"—clung to him in this new setting.[3] Besides his regular advisers and colleagues he occasionally received newspapermen for interviews. He met with representatives of those gathered in Paris from all quarters of the world, spokesmen for humanity's faint hopes and submerged minorities.

The President's evenings were reserved so far as possible for family meals. As the conference lengthened he would confine himself afterwards to silent games of solitaire while Edith crocheted nearby; but at the start he enjoyed sessions of reading aloud. Margaret, in Europe to give concerts for the troops, spent several days with the family, invariably late when her presence was expected, while the President was almost obsessively punctual. Jessie Bones Brower of the Sand Hill adventures in Augusta days, in Paris for war work, came by. Along with Grayson, Edith Benham—tall and dark, the daughter of an admiral—was treated as a family member and favored as a discreet conversationalist.

Grayson soon began to concern himself with the President's lack of diversion and physical exercise. Sundays were, at least, a break in the routine, spent much as they had been at home, with attendance at church services at the American Presbyterian church in the rue de Berri and with long automobile rides in the afternoon. Presently the rides began to punctuate weekday afternoons as well, an escape from papers piled high on the President's desk, from visitors, and from his own increasingly somber thoughts. Occasional games of golf, played on the links at Saint-Cloud, became another essential form of recreation. Wilson did not entirely forgo the visits to the theater which had been so regular a feature of Washington life. After one performance at the opera, he remarked of the soprano that "only her very high notes caused pain." The Paris revues presented more difficult problems than did Keith's Vaudeville at home. "I feared for the worst," wrote Edith Benham in her diary, "when the girls began slipping off their garments."[4]

Occasionally there were diversions of a less formal kind. One afternoon, accompanied by Grayson, Wilson sauntered out along the Parisian boulevards, the two of them unrecognized in that pretelevision age. They seated themselves to watch the crowds go by, the President commenting on their deportment and dress. Another day, while on such an expedition, they noticed a small stream and the President insisted on following it to its source in an adjacent park. He lingered afterwards to watch the children at their play.[5] Getting the President to walk in the mornings to the Quai d'Orsay proved more difficult. The exercise might be beneficial, but he complained that it took too much time. And so he would proceed in his large black Packard, Edith almost invariably accompanying him and then going off on her own errands of shopping or sightseeing.

The President's official family assumed a new form in Paris. Colonel House, who on Washington visits saw the President at all hours, had now a more formal relationship. As a peace commissioner he led the other commissioners in influence and prestige and yet had lost, without quite realizing it, the mystery and power accruing from unique access to the President. He was still consulted frequently; a direct wire between his bedroom and the President's was often in use. But he no longer confined himself to appearing the selfless shadow of his chief. He had his own staff, his own work to do, and he plainly enjoyed the new status, both social and official.

House had not come over with the President on the *George Washington*, having been in London to negotiate the armistice, and he accompanied him on neither the British nor the Italian visits. He was often ill during this period, suffering from a form of the current influenza; besides, he would not have appreciated the purely ceremonial aspects of the journeys. Mrs. Wilson, whose underlying coolness toward House never declined, kept him aside as her own services to the President became constantly more indispensable. The later break was made the easier, and the less painful, because the personal intimacy had already dissolved when the Wilsons were established in the rue Monceau.

Of the other U.S. peace commissioners Wilson saw little except in their official capacity. He would go more or less frequently to the Hôtel Crillon, taken over as the American headquarters, a sort of State Department in exile, to review the progress of the negotiations. He treated the delegation, Henry White reported back to Washington, with "nothing but courtesy." "In my own case," White added, "he has always been ready to listen, and in several cases to accept suggestions."[6]

Wilson liked Henry White, and the old diplomat built up a real friendship with Edith. He was her type; and he was, indeed, an endearing figure. Sixty-eight at the opening of the peace conference, he struck the young Charles Seymour as "certainly doddering."[7] But as no other American he knew his way through the precedents of European diplomacy and protocol; the only Republican member of the delegation, he was nevertheless unimpeachably loyal to Wilson. His stream of letters to Lodge advising him of events in Paris did not, however, dampen the senator's partisanship. Indeed White may have unwittingly fanned the flames when he wrote of "the dignity and distinction which have characterized everything which he [Wilson] has done in Europe."[8] It was like Henry White to be generous, and to expect that others might respond in the same vein.

Lansing was another matter. In less close daily association with the President in Paris than in Washington, the Secretary of State more constantly provoked his annoyance. With his lawyer's mind and his ill-concealed hostility to the League, exchanges between them were reduced, until Lansing confined such advice as he had to disgruntled entries in his private diary. During Council sessions he doodled ceaselessly—caricatures of strange beasts and stranger humans, done with considerable artistic skill. On the trip over Seymour had found him "expressionless and mute,"[9] an on being called for the first time into a meeting of the Ten, he remarked of the Secretary of State that he moved slowly and appeared an ill man.

In contrast, General Tasker Bliss aroused the President's admiration. Although a soldier he possessed, said Wilson, "the mind of a statesman."[10] With forceful memoranda Bliss backed the President on major issues, particularly on nonintervention in Russia and on measures toward Germany short of bankrupting and humiliating it. When he did differ with the President, as on the Shantung agreement, he offered his advice in strong words and it was accepted without reproach.

In addition to the peace commissioners Wilson had his corps of "experts," mostly members of The Inquiry. Upon these he counted heavily. He had won their confidence on the trip over them when he told them, "Show me the right and I will fight for it." Most of these younger men appreciated his efforts to be guided by their professional judgments. (A few of the more naïve would be embittered when he failed to do so.) Wilson also had at Paris a group of seasoned economic counselors, including Vance McCormick, Thomas W. Lamont, Norman H. Davis, and Baruch. These played their major role when the question of reparations came up.

Not quite a Wilson intimate, and playing a less important role than Tumulty in a similar position at home, was Ray Stannard Baker. Wilson made Baker his liaison with the press, and after the secret conferences met with him to shape the daily communiqué. Baker was an essayist, well known under his *nom de plume* of David Grayson, and a staunch political liberal who had spent months in Europe before the peace conference establishing contact with liberal leaders. Upon these, he was firmly convinced, rested Wilson's chance of making his ideals prevail. The President sympathized with Baker's views and knew the importance of reaching out to the constituency Baker had defined. But he could never satisfy his press attaché's hunger for information. As the latter confided to his diary, there was no man who in general and in principle could so thoroughly favor publicity as Wilson—publicity about ideas, about ultimate ends and objectives—and yet could so closely guard the privacy of negotiations.[11] Again and again Baker would grieve at what seemed to him missed opportunities to correct misunderstandings or to win support for the President's cause.

Sitting behind his desk in the rue Monceau, Wilson was still the Chief Executive of a vast republic. Yet all the energies of his "one-track mind" were concentrated on peacemaking; no one advised him regularly on domestic problems. McCormick's political knowledge was called on irregularly. In brief cables, often garbled in transmission, Tumulty did his best to inform the President of opinion at home. He covered the American press; he alerted Wilson to growing opposition in the Senate. The exchanges, however, covered mostly a small range of problems. Tumulty urged the President to put additional pressure to get the woman suffrage amendment out of Congress. (It lost, despite Wilson's pleas, by one vote.) He urged that the President throw his full support behind an appropriation of $100 million for distribution of food in European countries. (It won, but only after being amended so as to exclude Germany.)

The wires carried fervent messages from Tumulty in regard to the appointment of a new Attorney General. To Gregory, who was resigning, Wilson wrote: "I cannot tell you with what grief I think of your leaving the Cabinet. I have never been associated with a man whose gifts and character I have admired more. . . . I shall feel robbed of one of my chief supports when you are gone."[12]* Tumulty and the Democratic Party leaders were backing A. Mitchell Palmer, a Pennsylvania politician, who was considered able, energetic, progressive, and able to put new life into party forces dispirited after the disastrous congressional elections. Wil-

---

*Gregory, in submitting his resignation (JPT to WW, Jan. 9, 1919, PWW, 53:705), wrote: "No man ever served a leader who was more uniformly considerate, more kindly[,] helpful, and more generously appreciative. No subordinate was ever more deeply grateful for the numberless friendly words and acts of his superior." Such testimony may be weighed against frequent accusations of Wilson's being cold toward those who served him.

son dragged his feet. He did not want Palmer; he did not trust him, yet he came up with no name except a routine subordinate in the Justice Department. McCormick, Newton D. Baker, and others whose judgment Wilson valued (but not House, it must be said to his credit) supported Palmer's appointment. Had Wilson been in Washington, and able to give more than passing attention to the choice, one of the blackest marks against his administration—the 1920 raids on radicals and aliens— would have never taken place.

As the President began to think about returning for a brief visit at the close of the congressional session, urgent problems of demobilization and reconstruction pressed for solution. With the return of the armies from France, men by the hundreds of thousands waited to be reabsorbed into farms and factories. Industries diverted to the needs of a nation at war had to be converted to peacetime production. With the war agencies disbanded, free markets had to be restored and economic discrepancies adjusted. Seizing his opportunity, Tumulty overflowed with advice. The problems, he wrote the President, should be tackled on Wilson's visit "with the same vigor and enterprise" he had shown in organizing for war. "You should have prepared and considered plans so that you can begin issuing orders as soon as you land."[13] Tumulty listed an assortment of moves and measures. But Wilson was not interested. He seemed far removed from all that was going on in domestic affairs.

More gently and tactfully Newton D. Baker made the same point about lack of leadership on the home front.[14] Looking out from his War Department office across the White House lawns, he watched the grazing sheep, brought in during wartime to provide wool to be auctioned by the Red Cross. They were not the only ones, Baker wrote the President, that lacked a shepherd.

THE LEAGUE OF NATIONS

The League of Nations sprang from various streams of thought. It became inseparably connected with the name of Woodrow Wilson less because of his original conception than because of the tragic battle he later fought on its behalf. In his mind it began as a measure of statesmanship; only later did it become, in words he had first used as a teacher at Wesleyan, "one of those great Influences which we call a *Cause*."[1] Back in the United States he was to engage in controversy "more cruel than the collision of arms"; he came to see the League as a "political and moral principle." But in Paris, though he fought for its inclusion in the peace treaty with all his energy and with a high commitment, he was still the statesman rather than the seer. The League was not then a visionary grail, but a practical and essential element in his design for a world settlement.

Wilson made this clear in his speech at the second plenary session of the peace conference, called for January 25 to vote on a resolution of the Council of Ten. That resolution mandated the creation of the League of Nations and the setting up of a commission to determine its form. Clemenceau, presiding, called on the President to introduce the motion. Wilson had already gained his major point when he had succeeded, ten days before, in getting Clemenceau and Lloyd George to accept the idea of a league as an integral part of the treaty; now he was less concerned with persuading his larger audience (a favorable vote was a foregone conclusion) than he was in indicating the nature and the overarching role of such a league.

The peace conference, he began, had assembled for two purposes: to make the settlements necessitated by the war, and also to secure the future peace of the world. For the fulfillment of both these major purposes a league was crucial.[2]

The required settlements could not, in Wilson's view, all be reached within a period of a few weeks or months at the conference table. Many would need to be postponed; others would need to be flexible and subject to later revision. As early as his arrival in England, sobered by the power of conservative and imperial forces, Wilson had been moving toward the concept of a league that would put over to the future, and to a more favorable atmosphere, the determination of many difficult issues. "I am not hopeful," he had said publicly after his first talks with Lloyd George, "that the individual items of the settlements . . . will be altogether satisfactory."[3] What did give him hope was a league that could later correct the deficiencies of the present.

This idea was repeated in the plenary session. He could easily imagine, he said, that many complicated questions could not be worked out successfully at the peace conference. "Many of the decisions we make will need subsequent alteration in some degree, for . . . they are not susceptible of confident judgments at present." "We may not be able to set up permanent decisions," he summed up; but it was possible to set up "permanent processes."

Wilson urged a League of Nations that was "a vital thing—not merely a formal thing, not an occasional thing," but one that was "always functioning in watchful attendance upon the interests of the nations." He was drawing the line between his concept of the League and that of others who saw it as an organization restricted to maintaining and enforcing decisions reached at the peace table. Clemenceau, in particular, was opposed to a body with general administrative powers. He thought it would be unwieldy; he also thought it might act to weaken French security.

Wilson's second role for the League, that of avoiding future wars, had from the start been the essential justification in his mind for bringing the United States out of its isolation into the responsibilities of a world power. So he had announced in his address of May 1916, before the League to Enforce Peace. Later, the Fourteen Points were climaxed by a declaration in favor of a permanent international organization. "We regard it," he said now, speaking for the United States at the plenary session, "as the keystone of the whole programme which expressed our purpose and our ideal in this war." He was by this time keenly aware of the fragility of the world political system. Increasingly, with the formation of the new states of central and eastern Europe—the Baltic countries, Poland, a truncated Austria, Czechoslovakia, Yugoslavia, Romania—he perceived that an overarching body was essential to resolve their disputes and assure some kind of viable economic life.

A league had come to seem to him, moreover, the only way out of the impasse of decolonization. Former German colonies had either to be handed over to their conquerors as spoils of war—an intolerable solution; or else they had to become mandates under a league, administered not in the interests of the governing powers but of the developing peoples. Finally, a league provided the instrument for introducing into the new world order such standards of social justice as had been implicit in the revolutionary ferment of the Great War. Fair treatment for labor, protection of nationalities and of religious minorities, elimination of racial and gender discrimination—all were to be enshrined in a league and brought toward fruition.

The various aspects of the proposed League—its role in managing and modifying the peace settlements, in outlawing future wars, in providing mandates for liberated colonies, and in promoting social justice —were not to be more than partially glimpsed by world opinion. They were not equally acceptable to the powers that finally ratified it. Wilson may have erred in seeking too much, too soon; but his overall conviction of the need for the League was certainly correct. Setting forth this conviction in the plenary session of January 25, he was moving on the highest levels of world statesmanship.

With the establishment of the League of Nations Commission having been duly approved, Wilson the very next day made a long-deferred journey to French battlefields and war-devastated zones. In heavy snow he visited Château-Thierry and Belleau Wood—scenes, he described them, "of desolation and ruin."[4] The mayor and the archbishop of Rheims showed him about their prostrate city, the target of epic German bombardments, where a prewar population of 250,000 was reduced to 3,000, most of them living in cellars to escape the cold. The ruined cathedral, lacking its world-famous stained-glass windows, stood mournfully at the center.

More even than most Americans, Wilson was affected by such scenes. A vivid imagination was fired by conscious and unconscious memories of the post–Civil War South. Significantly, he had postponed the ordeal of immersing himself in these war scenes until approval of the concept of a league at least gave hope that such wars would not be repeated. His resistance to French pressures for immediate inspection of the battlefields was not good politics or good diplomacy. The Allies continued to attribute to him a lack of sympathy for their sufferings. But it was Wilson's way—to skirt emotional confrontations and to focus his gaze on rational, long-range solutions.

When Clemenceau assented to a commission to draft a charter for the League of Nations, he assumed it would be dominated by the smaller countries forming the majority of its membership. He expected that it would be sidetracked in interminable debates. But when Wilson boldly assumed the chairmanship, he assured for its meetings as much interest as for those of the Council of Ten. Colonel House served with him in representing the United States; Lord Robert Cecil and Smuts gave to the British representation the full weight of their prestige. Orlando and Baron Makino speaking for the Italians and the Japanese, respectively, were a further indication of the importance attached to these deliberations. The French followed a strategy of their own, naming two men outside the close circle of the peace conference, Léon Bourgeois, a senator and former prime minister; and Fernand Larnaude, dean of the law school at the Sorbonne. They both were given to long, technical arguments, clothing the French cause in legalisms that drove Wilson to distraction.

Wilson was not an impartial or silent chairman, but intervened constantly in the debates. Outside the meetings, in negotiations with Cecil (neither man liked the other but they worked harmoniously) he settled many of the details. He had come slowly and rather late to his version of what the League charter should contain. What he had said as a young professor contemplating the future was true in regard to his present role:

he did not so much originate ideas as take those that were current, filter them through a lively mind, and adapt them to the needs of the time.[5] Although he kept in view the big picture of the League and its functions, he had been anxious until now to avoid committing himself to specific clauses. Ex-President Taft and the League to Enforce Peace had been busy drawing up drafts, but Wilson considered the work premature and in private was scornful of their efforts.

Wilson's first preference was for a loosely defined structure, one that would evolve over the years, bringing the states together for mutual protection. In Britain, over the same period, the idea of a league of nations was being much discussed in private and governmental circles. In March 1918, Balfour (then Foreign Secretary) appointed a high-level committee which issued a report submitted to the War Cabinet and made available in Washington. Known as the Phillimore Report, its recommendations were similar in essential points to the program of the League to Enforce Peace. It envisaged a continuing conference of member states, meeting anywhere, unarmed, and without formal organization. It was this report that House brought to the attention of Wilson during his visit to Magnolia in the summer of 1918.

House added significant recommendations of his own. He urged several forms of guarantees of the peace, including compulsory arbitration of international disputes and a declaration against territorial invasions. (Designed to placate the French, this proposed declaration was the original form of the controversial Article X of the League.) Wilson assented to these changes and arrived in Paris with the Phillimore Report, amended by House, as his basic text.

Here he first gave serious and concentrated thought to the form of the League, stimulated by two new drafts, one from Lord Cecil and one from Smuts. The latter, a hero of the Boer War, was a statesman of fertile imagination and large ideas whom Wilson came to respect deeply. He borrowed from the Smuts draft the concept of a permanent secretariat for the League, of a small executive council and a larger deliberative body, and, not least in importance, a system of mandates. To Smuts, too, he owed the formulation of provisions affecting labor and minority rights.

In his study in the Hôtel Murat the President now typed out his version of the League and prepared to fight for it as his own. A lifelong love of constitution-making inspired him; he must have called up memories of shaping rules for the baseball club in Augusta, of the Liberal Debating Club in Princeton, of the Jefferson Society at the University of Virginia. Even so idiosyncratic a trait as his seeing good luck in the cipher thirteen found expression in the document. Major articles were limited to that number, with material that did not fit consigned to "Supplementary Agreements." He then gave to the whole the name of Covenant, a reminder of his own forebears and of their fighting faith. With some changes introduced by American and British experts, this draft was submitted to the commission at its first meeting on February 3.

The ensuing meetings found the Americans and British supportive of each other. Other nations, which included Belgium, Brazil, China, Portugal, and Serbia, raised technicalities which did not affect the basic structure. The French were more difficult. They wanted the League document to contain a clause branding the Germans as having initiated the war; they wanted something in the form of an international force that would guarantee their own security. In a morning session on February 11, Bourgeois and Larnaude launched a full attack, arguing that the League, unless it could give to the French public the feeling of safety it demanded, would "simply arouse general distrust."[6] Basically they saw the League as a defensive alliance, with its own army and general staff, capable of enforcing over the long future the terms they wanted to impose on Germany.

Wilson was shocked, and in strong rebuttals insisted that it would be clearly unconstitutional for him to subject the armed forces of the United States to international control. Such an army as was being proposed, he said, would make it appear that the nations were "substituting international militarism for national militarism." He sympathized with the French desire for security, but the only way the League could function was through a spirit of trust among its members. "When danger comes, we too will come," he asserted, "and we will help you, but you must trust us. We must all depend on our mutual good faith."

Cecil warned the French in private that they would lose everything if they insisted to the point of wrecking the League. In the end they yielded, but they would come back to make the same demands for security at other junctures, with more justification, and Wilson would accept many of them. They were not altogether mistaken in their insistence. History was to show the remarkable capacity of the Germans to recuperate even after crushing defeat; it would show the difficulty of marshaling the overwhelming force necessary to counter aggression. The "mutual good faith" Wilson had invoked would be made effective only at the eleventh hour, and where clear national interest was evident.

The commission's work was completed by unanimous vote ten days after its first session, and on February 14 a third plenary session was convoked. It was Wilson's hour, and the day itself was to be one of the high points of his life.

At noon, meeting for the first time since his arrival in Paris with the American newspaper corps, he talked with them and answered questions for more than an hour.[7] Frankly, but not for publication, he described the difficulties encountered in the League of Nations Commission. The French situation was delicate, he indicated, but he understood France's fears after the horrors from which she had emerged. He explained in detail how the League would work. Yet what the newspaper correspondents carried away with them, more vividly than their awareness of the difficulties of peacemaking, was a characteristically Wilsonian picture of a world threatened by hunger and economic difficulties. He insisted that lifting the blockade was essential if Germany were not to become another Russia.

In the afternoon, at the plenary session called to receive the report of the League commission, Wilson read out the full text of the charter. Summing it up in a brief address, he characterized it as a simple structure—a Body of Delegates, an Executive Council, and a Permanent Secretariat. Within the Body of Delegates discussion was virtually unlimited, but the Executive Council, dominated by the Great Powers, kept the right of committing the League on specific matters. Many details of the organization, he said, were purposely left for later determination: what had been created was "not a straitjacket, but a vehicle of life."[8]

On the issue of using force, he maintained (as he had in the debates of the commission) that the organization was to be "not a league of war"; it would be chiefly dependent on "the moral force of the public opinion of the world." Yet armed force—resorted to following the processes of discussion, arbitration, and economic boycott—remained always in the background. "A living thing is born," Wilson concluded, with the pride of a father, if not with the prescience of a true prophet.

Early that evening Wilson attended briefly a meeting of the Supreme War Council. Winston S. Churchill, then Secretary of State for War, had just arrived from England, brimming with ardor to launch an Allied crusade against the Soviets. Without such an intervention, he declaimed urgently, the Russian people faced "an interminable vista of violence and misery."[9] Wilson listened to the exposition, standing, with arms akimbo, and when Clemenceau interrupted, he urged Churchill to proceed. Then with cool logic he broke in to say that existing forces in Russia could obviously not stop Bolshevism; moreover none of the Allies was disposed to reinforce its troops. Churchill persisted, saying that volunteers could be sent. Whom would these volunteers be supporting? Wilson asked. He gave his own answer: reactionaries that nobody knew.

The historic day was not yet finished. The *George Washington* was waiting in the harbor at Brest to take Wilson home. Clemenceau, Poincaré, and other French officials saw him off from Paris at 9:00 P.M. He looked happy, House noted in his diary.[10] It was indeed a moment of triumph for the American President.

The first four weeks of the peace conference had found him playing with force and discretion a commanding role among his associates. Every circumstance that was to darken the next months had already manifested itself: the decline in public idealism, connivance between the British and the French, Clemenceau's obstinacy, Lloyd George's changefulness. But Wilson had held at bay his adversaries, seen and unseen. He had established his priorities, secured accommodation on major issues. Above all, he had won preliminary acceptance of the League of Nations. Planning to be away briefly to take care of business at the end of the congressional session, he was entitled to a rare moment of hopefulness and satisfaction.

CHAPTER TEN

Peacemaker

———◆———

POLITICS AT HOME

Wilson's departure, on February 14, 1919, created a break in the progress of the conference; at the same time his presence in Washington provided opportunity for political foes to consolidate their forces. When he returned to Paris three weeks later, he found a different atmosphere among his colleagues and a mood of growing disillusionment in the public. The successes of the first phase of the peace conference were not to be repeated, nor was Wilson to regain the prestige he had enjoyed in the immediate postarmistice period.

The journey marking this turning point seemed ill-starred from the beginning. Four days out of Brest, extraordinarily heavy seas developed. Wilson was almost the only one of the official party to be unaffected by the ship's motion, taking his regular walk on deck as prescribed by Dr. Grayson. A column of destroyers assigned to escort the *George Washington* wallowed in the mounting waves, while the battleship *New Mexico*, on its maiden voyage, was unable to keep up. Among those returning with the President was the Assistant Secretary of the Navy, Franklin D. Roosevelt, who ordered the destroyers to abandon course and make for the Azores.

In the midst of these storms a cable from Lansing announced that Clemenceau had been shot by an anarchist. Five bullets had been fired, one of which pierced the old leader's neck. He was seriously wounded; but he survived, and even regained his health. Yet those watching him closely during the later phases of the peace conference concluded he had lost some part of his physical stamina and mental resilience.

The approach to U.S. shores was marred, as had been the start of the journey, by adverse weather conditions, abetted in this case by what appear deplorable human failings. In a heavy fog off the New England coast the *George Washington* lost its bearings. One of four destroyers dispatched from Boston as escorts, seeing the inbound ship headed for a sandbar, swerved across its bow to head it off. A collision was only averted by the *George Washington*'s putting its engines full speed in reverse. Soundings were taken; a search was made for familiar landmarks; and it was discovered that the President's ship was seventeen miles off course.[1]

The landfall had been set for Boston after several cable exchanges between Wilson and Tumulty. Wilson owed a visit to New England, where he had not made a public appearance for three years; moreover, as was sure to be noted by all concerned, Boston was the political base of Senator Lodge. To court a welcome in the home city of the League's arch-opponent was to throw down the gauntlet in what Wilson recognized as the greatest battle of his life. Struggles with European statesmen fell into the background as even more formidable enemies readied their weapons at home.

Wilson rose to the encounter with all the instincts of a fighter. It might have been better had he risen to it as a politician, placating his Senate opponents, delaying the confrontation while dealing with adversaries overseas. But he was still the Scotch-Irishman who at Princeton "simply could not be conquered," the lonely figure fighting on "without a knack for hoping confidently." In his first public utterance in America he challenged all who had doubts about the League; and in a climactic Metropolitan Opera House speech, delivered just before he returned to Europe, he invoked for his opponents such a doom as only his most perfervid rhetoric could conjure up. The image of Wilson as a grim figure, unsmiling, unforgiving, dates from this visit home.

He was unquestionably right in his estimate of Lodge's entrenched hostility and, hardly less disturbing, that of a small group of Republican leaders. The 1918 congressional victories had given them the taste of blood. Looming on the political horizon was the Presidential election of 1920. Wilson refused to remove himself from the race, and the thought of his running for a third term was hardly more abhorrent to his foes than the thought of some lesser Democratic candidate winning on his party's record in war and peacemaking. To defeat the League, and to discredit Wilson once and for all, was the monstrous—if politically comprehensible—objective of the Republican cabal. A growing coolness toward Wilson was reinforced in other quarters by legitimate reservations about the League, by a mounting national desire to get back to business as usual, and by accumulated economic grievances left in the wake of the war.

The general public at this time was clearly for the League, if in an unsophisticated and poorly informed sort of way. Outstanding public figures like Taft and Eliot, the nation's editorial writers, the churches, and peace groups led by the League to Enforce Peace were behind it. But Wilson tended to ignore these reserves of goodwill, or to take them for granted. He measured with an experienced and practiced eye the political obstacle posed by the Senate leaders, and he responded with an uncompromising aggressiveness altogether in character. Thus his return to the United States, instead of creating an impression of reassurance and reconciliation, brought a deepening division within the country.

At ten-thirty on the morning of February 24 the President said goodbye to the troops that had come home with him on the *George Washington*. His own return was fittingly marked. A delegation headed by Boston's mayor and by the governor of Massachusetts—the latter was Calvin Coolidge, himself to be President within a few years—boarded the ship to greet him. Every steamboat in the harbor held down its whistle. A procession of thirty cars passed through large crowds on its way to Mechanics Hall where the famous tenor John McCormack led the audience in singing the national anthem. After extraordinary adventures on foreign soil, the first President ever to have left the United States while in office, Woodrow Wilson was home again and in his own element.

The speech he made on this occasion was rambling in form, delivered from a page of notes he had jotted down that morning. He had come back, he said, to report progress; but he did not chart the progress in peacemaking in any detail, nor was there any hint in his speech of the struggle of wills between himself and his European associates. As for those who differed with him at home, it was evident he would give no quarter. "Any man who resists the present tides that run in the world," he said, "will find himself thrown upon a shore so high and barren that it will seem as if he had been separated from his human kind forever."[2]

Without delay the President proceeded to the train waiting to carry him to Washington. At New Haven and New London crowds waited to see him pass through, and late that night, as if to prove his determination to tackle pent-up business at once, he signed in his train compartment a revenue bill providing a large increase in taxes. His arrival next morning in the national capital was, according to his request, unmarked by public ceremony.

Ignoring the advice Tumulty had cabled to him in Paris, Wilson was in no mood to take the capital by storm or by dramatic steps to assert his national leadership. His actions were deliberately underplayed and within the routine of his office. He met with the cabinet to give them an account of events abroad; he led a parade of soldiers from the District of Columbia; he went down to the Capitol to confer informally with members of Congress. Ominously, no Republicans turned up among the two-score individuals who came by to greet him. Appearing before a gathering of state officials, convoked at Tumulty's suggestion, he showed himself clearly unprepared to give serious consideration to postwar domestic problems. His attendance was brief and his speech was confined to generalities.*

One piece of domestic business he could not postpone was appointment of a new Attorney General. In his mind he had reluctantly narrowed the choice to Palmer, and now Daniels's strong support confirmed the choice. To replace the able and balanced Gregory he named a politician who might well invigorate the demoralized Democrats but who lacked essential qualities for the job.

To end wartime restrictions on civil rights and to terminate excessive punishments was one of Wilson's continuing concerns. An ugly strain of intolerance was at the time running just below the surface of public opinion and was reflected in high government circles. In a hasty note to Burleson on February 28, Wilson told his Postmaster General: "I cannot believe that it would be wise to do any more suppressing. We must meet these poisons [of radical acts and opinions] in some other way."[3] At the bottom of the letter Burleson scribbled: "Continued to suppress and Courts sustained me every time." Indeed it was only a few days after this exchange that the Supreme Court, with Justice Oliver Wendell Holmes writing the unanimous opinion, defined the limits imposed on free speech in wartime.[4] The First Amendment, the Court held, did not apply when speech created "a clear and present danger" of bringing about evils that Congress had the right to prevent.

In this atmosphere the new Attorney General was entirely comfortable. Wilson's first letter to Palmer asked that he reconsider sentences ap-

---

* An act not strictly domestic but having far-reaching implications for American politics was accomplished during the trip to Washington. Wilson met with a delegation of Zionists headed by Rabbi Stephen S. Wise. After the meeting he issued a statement reaffirming his support of the Balfour Declaration, giving formal approval to the idea that "in Palestine shall be laid the foundations of a Jewish Commonwealth." (A news report, Mar. 2, 1919, PWW, 55:386. See also earlier letter to Wise, Aug. 31, 1918, PWW, 49:403.)

pearing "clearly excessive."[5] No reply has been preserved, but Palmer's whole record shows how far he was out of sympathy with the President's liberal approach.

Before leaving Europe Wilson was considering how, when he got home, he could best "render an accounting to the people and to Congress." He evidently had in mind an address to Congress, but he wanted to "wait and see how things looked when he reached Washington."[6] They did not look good, it seems. He relied for his "accounting" on a closed dinner meeting with the members of the Senate and House foreign affairs committees, originally suggested by House, for which the invitations were sent out before he left Paris.

It is strange that Wilson, who had formed the habit of addressing Congress regularly on policy developments, should have failed to take advantage of this occasion. To have reviewed the Paris negotiations, indicating the forces in play and the obstacles to an easy agreement, would have seemed the natural course. Such an address, framed with a worldwide audience in mind, could have done much to set matters in perspective and to redefine Wilson's position as international leader.

Twice during the peace conference Lloyd George returned to London to address Parliament, each time resuming the discussions in Paris with fresh political strength. That Wilson did not follow such a course suggests that he was already feeling toward Congress the disdain that was to mark his attitude when the Republican majority took over in March. Perhaps it suggests, also, that he did not quite trust himself to treat candidly the strategies of his European colleagues without doing harm to the negotiations. In any case he found himself, as in the Paris meetings, confined to off-the-record remarks, when his voice might have guided and enlightened opinion in his own and other countries. The great argument over the League began, not within the context of a shattered and suffering civilization, but with its articles scrutinized, one by one, as in a lawyer's convention or a high school debating society.

In his invitation to senators and congressmen Wilson had sought to constrain them from beginning discussion of the League until he should have had a chance to interpret it to them. This shocked the members of the honorable bodies. Besides, the dinner got off to a bad start when the arch-isolationist Senator William Borah of Idaho refused to attend on the grounds that nothing the President might say could alter their opposition to him and to the League.

After that setback, things seemed to go better. On the appointed evening, two days after the President's return, Senator Lodge escorted

Mrs. Wilson to the White House dining room where he sat at her right. The forty guests, withdrawing afterwards to the East Room, sat in a large oval with the President at their head. It must have been by a supreme effort that Wilson remained mild and in good humor that evening, among a company several of whose members he recognized as mortal enemies and for whom he had already, both in public and private, expressed disdain. Yet until nearly midnight he answered their questions patiently.[7]

Two days after the White House dinner, on February 28, Lodge opened a full-scale attack on the League. In a powerful Senate speech he demanded of the President that he prove it compatible with the sovereignty of the United States, with the Monroe Doctrine, and with the country's hitherto basic posture of nonentanglement. On that same day, speaking off the record before the Democratic National Committee, Wilson branded those who were opposing the League as "of all the blind and little provincial people . . . the littlest and most contemptible."[8]

Lodge did not confine his attack to oratory. With the close of the sixty-fifth congressional session approaching, he and his colleagues framed an anti-League resolution which, had it come to the floor, would have been overwhelmingly voted down. By a parliamentary maneuver, however, its sponsors were able to present it to the public as a statement signed by all those Republicans (including voteless senators-elect) who would have chosen to cast their ballots in its favor. The result showed a putative Republican opposition capable of defeating the League in its existing form.

Two days later the offensive was widened to aim at the heart of the administration itself. By the device of a filibuster, as the clock moved inexorably toward the session's end, urgent pending legislation was killed. Going to the Capitol in the session's last hours the President found himself with few bills to sign, and the country deprived of essential fiscal appropriations. It was for the ostensible purpose of signing such bills that he had made his long trip to Washington, and now he saw himself humiliated and betrayed. Canceling a projected statement laudatory of the session's work, he issued an angry attack on the Republican leadership. Then he immediately left for New York on the first stage of his return journey.

On the train he retired for an hour to compose in his mind the speech he was to deliver at the Metropolitan Opera House that evening. At Philadelphia he got off to visit Mercy Hospital where he saw his new grandson, Woodrow Wilson Sayre, born February 22 to Jessie. Vast crowds along the New York streets were awaiting the Presidential party. The sense of an impending battle stirred the populace, eager for a glimpse of a leader acknowledged by all to be an unyielding fighter. Going directly to the opera house, Wilson emerged on the stage arm in arm with ex-President Taft. It was a show of bipartisanship not lost on the great audience. But the speech that followed was highly belligerent in tone and concealed nothing of Wilson's bitterness toward the offending senators. It contained no hint of a possible compromise on League issues, no suggestion that amendments might be considered. Wilson was sure, as he had been in every crisis of his career, that the people were on his side and that the opposition would be defeated.

His challenge to Lodge was unequivical. The senator was mistaken if he thought the treaty of peace and the League charter could be separated. "When the treaty comes back," he said, "gentlemen on this side will find the covenant not only in it, but so many threads of the treaty tied to the covenant, that you cannot dissect the covenant from the treaty. . . . The structure of the peace will not be vital without the League of Nations, and no man is going to bring back a cadaver."[9] In rousing terms he returned to the image of an onrushing tide which he had used on his arrival in the United States: "The forces of the world do not threaten, they operate. The great tides of the world do not give notice that they are going to rise and run; they rise in their majesty and . . . might, and those who stand in their way are overwhelmed."

After the meeting Wilson had a stormy encounter with a delegation of Irish-Americans. Why, they wanted to know, did the League not provide for Ireland's independence from England? Wilson replied firmly that this was not a matter for the League but one to be settled directly between the two parties involved. Then he crossed the Hudson River to Hoboken where the *George Washington* once more awaited him.

On the return journey to France Wilson suffered an illness that marked the beginning of a decline in his health. His temperature rose to 102 degrees under the impact of what Grayson diagnosed as a severe cold. But once again the President showed his remarkable powers of recovery. After two days of confinement he resumed the familiar shipboard routine, appearing to all who stopped to talk with him as he walked the decks, or who watched him in the evening at concerts or film showings, as a tired but sturdy man. Ray Stannard Baker, who saw the President frequently, reported his impressions of the voyage. "It has been very quiet & simple," he wrote in his diary, "a small group and friendly. Coming out of strenuous days, controversies & great meetings, the President has rested. He looked worn and gray when he came aboard: I have never seen him looking wearier than at the Metropolitan speech, but he soon recuperated . . . so that now he looks as well as ever."[10]

Baker added that he wished the American people, many of whom thought him a "cold, unamiable man," could see him in the informal relationships of shipboard life.

PEACE CONFERENCE: SECOND PHASE

The arrival at Brest repeated the earlier scene: the welcome by high French officials and military leaders when the ship dropped anchor outside the seawall, further greetings on the dock and a waiting assemblage of townspeople. But there were changes in detail and atmosphere. Colonel House now waited at the landing place full of troubling business. A parade of automobiles through Brest was canceled, and the French authorities, for what were said to be reasons of security, failed to make public the schedule of the President's train.

When it arrived in Paris eleven minutes late (considered unusual for the French railroads) the President greeted Clemenceau with a warm handshake; referring to the attempt on his life, he said he hoped the French premier was not feeling any ill effects. "On the contrary," answered the old tiger of France, "I think it did me good."[1] Whereupon the President and his party were whisked off to the new Paris White House at 11, place des États-Unis. It was less grand than the Hôtel Murat, but it suited the President just as well, or better; and it had the convenience of being situated across the street from Lloyd George's residence. The President's and Mrs. Wilson's rooms were on the ground floor, connecting through a concealed passage to the library where the most significant meetings of the peace conference would take place.

From the moment of the President's return he knew that things had not gone well in his absence. Perhaps he sensed also the troubles that lay ahead. The next three months were to see a decline in his health, in his worldwide prestige, and in the expectations evoked at the war's end. That "we may all work together for a great peace as distinguished from a mean peace" had been his hope in the days of idealism before the peace conference began.[2] Now it would seem to many that "a mean peace" was exactly what was being shaped. The treaty in its final form would be assailed by liberals who saw in it less a long-range guarantee of peace than an invitation to future wars. The achievements of the first phase of the peace conference were followed by setbacks for Wilson, by compromises in which he bartered away or saw subtly eroded many of the Fourteen Points. The fact that something, indeed much, was saved of the original ideal, and that Wilson fought gamely and not always unsuccessfully for his stated principles, did not mask the discrepancy between what was promised and what was ultimately delivered at Versailles.

On the train leaving Brest Colonel House briefed the President on what had taken place during his absence. House complained in his diary that he was not able to tell the President much, for Jusserand saw fit to "entertain" him; but it was evidently enough to cause a profound shock.[3] In her memoir Edith Wilson describes how her husband emerged from his talk with House seeming to have aged ten years; "his jaw was set in that way it had when he was making [a] superhuman effort to control himself."[4] He smiled bitterly, saying, "House has given away everything I had won before we left Paris." Edith Wilson's recollections are often inaccurate; yet if not that evening on the train, then certainly the next morning, when House relates he had "ample opportunity" to enlighten the President, the true situation was revealed.

Violating Wilson's instructions to deal only with the military and naval clauses of the treaty with Germany, House had approved compromises, tentative but nevertheless damaging, on basic issues of the peace and the Covenant of the League. From the *George Washington* en route to the United States Wilson had cabled that he was "immovably" against French plans to occupy the left bank of the Rhine; that above all "we should not think of being hurried into a solution arrived at solely from the French point of view."[5] Nevertheless, in Vance McCormick's diary for March 2 appears the ominous notation that Colonel House and French military adviser André Tardieu had come for tea and had "agreed on plan for Rhenish Republic."[6] They also agreed on "Saar Coal Basin" and discussed ways of getting Lloyd George's approval. The Rhenish Republic and the Saar valley were both questions on which the President was determined not to yield. As if this were not in itself a betrayal, House cabled the President on March 4: "Everything has been speeded up. . . . By the time of your arrival all questions will be ready for your approval."[7]

Assuming that on the train House spoke candidly of these things, it is not surprising that the President was shocked. Even worse from his immediate point of view was House's agreement to the idea of a preliminary German treaty, leaving the League to be taken up separately. This played directly into the hands of the opposition and was contrary to what Wilson had been saying in his speeches back home. House himself (whatever the intentions of others) had no desire to jeopardize the League by allowing it to be deferred or whittled away. Yet in his characteristic role of amiable conciliator, in his subservience to the French, and undoubtedly, too, in his desire to prove himself a more able diplomat than his chief, he had led the American delegation down a dangerous and unauthorized path.

The break between Wilson and House, which was to be so portentous a development of the President's last years, was often set (as it was by Edith Wilson) at the moment of House's revelations on the Paris-bound train. Certainly the relationship was never quite the same after that interview. Yet the final distancing of the two men took place slowly, over a longer period, and had more than a single cause. They needed each other too much—House for his own self-esteem, Wilson for a thousand practical services—to have their bond cut at one stroke. Through the next months Wilson continued to lean on House for advice; the private telephone line between the President's bedside and the Colonel's would be often in use. The role Baker assigned House as a sort of "supersecretary" of the peace conference was too important to be abruptly eliminated. "A busy, useful, kindly, liberal little man" was the way Baker described him,[8] in words the President would probably have agreed with at this time.

Yet the Colonel's vanity and conviction of his own importance were certainly growing. He was increasingly persuaded that he could manage things more efficiently than the President. Within a week, he told one friend, he could settle all outstanding issues of the peace.[9] He regretted, even to the point of resenting, the downgrading of his position once the President had returned. "I have no authority to [decide] questions on my on initiative," he complained to his diary, "as I did while the President was away."[10] On one occasion, having arranged a conference between the President and Lloyd George in his own rooms, he confided with incredible presumption: "The reason . . . was to keep my hand on the situation. . . . My main drive now is to get peace with Germany at the earliest possible moment, and I am determined that it shall come soon if it is within my power to force action."[11]

Wilson did not experience this arrogance directly (House was too clever to let personal confessions influence his outward manner); but he must have sensed it and been put off by it. Besides, he was undoubtedly influenced by Mrs. Wilson's deep-rooted dislike and growing jealousy. Wilson's changing attitude is indicated by a remark he made to House shortly after his second landing in France. "Your dinner to the Senate Foreign Relations Committee was a failure," he said—undoubtedly with an emphasis on the word "your."[12] Presently he was indicating his extreme displeasure at the idea of having House's son-in-law, Gordon

Auchincloss, placed in a confidential position where he could insinuate the Colonel's point of view. For all his usefulness, House had gradually become an adviser excluded from the full trust and confidence of his chief.

For Wilson the immediate task was to undo the harm to the League perpetrated during his absence. On the first day after his return he skipped a meeting of the Supreme War Council to appear before the American delegation. He was, according to House, in a "very militant" mood, leaving no doubt in the minds of the commissioners as to the absolute priority of the League. Two days later he broke the silence he normally observed on matters under negotiation. Since his departure, he declared in a public statement, nothing had changed in regard to the League; whatever might be supposed to the contrary was baseless.[13]

The effect of the statement was electrifying and conclusive. It revealed the power over public opinion possessed by Wilson, yet utilized so rarely during the peace conference. It cut short talk of anything but a single treaty, with the League at its core. Thereafter, European opponents of Wilson's League were left with a choice of opposing it outright or bending it to their own purposes.

The next weeks, from March 15 to the President's illness of early April, appeared to those who passed through them as the "dark days" of the conference. Later would come the shock of compromises accepted and ideals surrendered, but even that period would seem to those closest to the President less agonizing than the fierce stalemate of March. For it was then that the French launched, fully developed and seemingly unassailable, their case against Germany.

During the first stages of the conference Clemenceau had presided in relative silence. Meanwhile Lloyd George had been getting satisfaction for Britain's major concerns: elimination of Germany as a naval and continental power, together with the redistribution of former German colonies. Only on the issue of reparations was he forced to bide his time. Now it was France's turn.

Clemenceau had prepared his ground well. The case for a Rhenish republic, a puppet state separating French soil from that of her historic enemy, had been broached while the President was away. Demands for sovereignty over the coal-rich Saar valley, for a strong Poland constructed at the cost of a dismembered Germany, for economic terms that could bankrupt Germany for a generation were now set forth. Behind Clemenceau in this carefully planned diplomatic offensive stood the military, the French economic experts, the foreign ministry; at the same time the Paris press, controlled and orchestrated by the government, loosed daily its chorus of demands, usually combined with ridicule of the American President.

The "dark days" precipitated by the French were the darker because the public was left in ignorance of what actually was passing at the conference. Alarmed by the depth of divisions between the chief Allies, frustrated by the diversions within the Council of Ten (often crowded by several-score observers and participants), Wilson suggested private meetings between the so-called Big Four—France, Britain, Italy, and the United States. The first of these meetings, held over the next two months in Wilson's private study, took place on March 23.

Some of these conversations were not even recorded in formal minutes, but history was well served when a young French scholar and diplomat, Paul Mantoux, added to his duties as interpreter that of making each evening unofficial, but complete and lively, accounts of the day's talks. The public, however, continued largely in ignorance, with rumor and gossip taking the place of news. The President, having missed the opportunity to set the issues in perspective during his American journey, was now further immobilized. Calling in the late afternoon at the place des États-Unis, Baker would plead for at least a summary of the issues discussed and for a general view of the American position. Even this was often denied. Cocooned within his self-imposed public silence, Wilson was defenseless against the French propaganda barrage.

Outside the conference room, across the face of Europe, continuing disturbances added to the general gloom. "At this moment," Wilson told his colleagues in March, "there is a veritable race between peace and anarchy."[14] He did not overstate the crisis. While the leaders appeared to dawdle in Paris, armies at almost all the disputed borders jostled to establish rights of possession. The Russian colossus threatened to enlarge its sway. When the liberal Károlyi government in Hungary was overthrown by the Communist Béla Kun on March 23, something like panic overtook the military. Foch urged the creation of a *cordon sanitaire*, an armed line manned by Allied troops extending across much of eastern Europe. It would be as useless, Wilson remarked dryly, as trying to sweep back a spring tide. And he stressed again the urgency of sending food.

Meanwhile Germany lay under the continuing blockade, its people deprived and demoralized if not actually starving, its southern provinces tempted by Communism, and its capacity and will to sign any peace treaty in doubt. In mid-February a moderate government under Friedrich Ebert set up what was to be known as the Weimar Republic. At best a frail reed, it received no support from the victorious powers. History was dwarfing men's best (or worst) efforts to give meaning to the tragedy that had so recently engulfed the civilized world.

Two consuming preoccupations, fought out in two different and exhausting series of meetings, drove Wilson through these winter weeks. To moderate the extremism of the French claims was one. The other was to achieve revisions of the provisional League charter. Twice a day in his own library the Four met in contentious and frequently stormy sessions, where Wilson found himself sometimes allied with Lloyd George, and where more often—with Lloyd George letting him carry the burden of resisting Clemenceau—he fought alone. At the same time he was presiding in the evening over the commission on the League, reconvened to consider amendments to the original draft. The schedule was one to drain the strength of any man, and was made the more onerous by Wilson's mounting sense of anger and frustration.

To make matters worse, Wilson became gradually aware of a dismaying connection between the two meetings. His European colleagues were prepared to use his commitment to the League to exact concessions on unrelated matters. Lloyd George opposed a crucial amendment, one excluding the Monroe Doctrine from the League's provisions, until his fears of American naval superiority were allayed. The French were prepared to debate interminably if their security program made no progress.

Naval issues apart, it may be asked what fundamental differences divided the Americans from the British; or more precisely, why Wilson could not have formed with Lloyd George an unbreakable amalgamation against French claims. The British Prime Minister was a liberal; by background and instinct he sympathized with almost everything Wilson was fighting for. But he was also a supreme politician, and following the 1918 elections he faced a Parliament as insular and reactionary as any in modern British history. Within his delegation at Paris were men stubbornly determined on revenge against Germany; while at his heels the arch-nationalist Northcliffe press yapped daily against any manifestations of compromise.

The British Prime Minister was adept at keeping his balance amid such forces. He could be defiant; he could be placating; he could even toy, as he did at one meeting of the four, with ideas of valor and self-sacrifice. There was nothing, Wilson interjected, that seemed to him more glorious than to go down fighting for one's convictions. The Prime Minister appeared to be impressed. But in the last analysis victory—or at least survival—was too sweet to be sacrificed to heroic acts. Besides, the game involved too much sheer enjoyment to be brought prematurely to a conclusion. When all was over he could declare that the peace conference—Wilson's Golgotha—had been for him "a wonderful time."[15]

One weekend in March, when relations between Wilson and the French were particularly tense, Lloyd George and a group of his younger advisers retired to Fontainebleau to take a look at where the peace negotiations were heading. They talked long and candidly, letting the preoccupations of the conference give way to a larger perspective. A paper was drawn up by Philip Henry Kerr, the Prime Minister's private secretary. Afterwards known as the Fontainebleau Memorandum, it breathed the spirit of Wilsonism, calling upon the statesmen to make a fair peace that would give Germany no excuse for withholding its signature or harboring resentment.[16] It was easy, the memorandum argued, to make a peace for only thirty years; but Germany would find means of retribution if she felt she had been unjustly treated. The victors could be severe, stern, even ruthless. "But injustice, arrogance displayed in the hour of triumph will never be forgotten or forgiven." The memorandum called for a League of Nations that would be "the effective guardian of international right and international liberty throughout the world."

If only Wilson himself could have withdrawn from the day-to-day conflict to restate the truths he had made seem so irresistible! But he was mute, and Lloyd George's flirtation with ideals was to be short-lived. Copies of the Fontainebleau Memorandum were sent to Wilson and Clemenceau, and it was discussed in the Council of Four on March 27. Wilson was in full accord. "We must avoid," he said, "giving our enemies even the impression of injustice." Clemenceau, while promising to consider specific points in the document, warned against compromising the fruits of victory. "To wish to spare the conquered is a good thing," he declared caustically, "but we must not lose sight of the victors."[17] As for Lloyd George himself, within a few days he was taking positions in direct contrast to the spirit of his memorandum.

When news of the Fontainebleau Memorandum leaked out, the Prime Minister faced a renewed outcry from Parliament. For a brief moment he considered standing on his liberal ideals, admitting that he had overstated the case for punitive reparations, and facing the wrath of the obscurantists. But when he returned to England to address Parliament in mid-April, the central portion of his speech, far from being a *mea culpa*, was a resounding declaration, hailed with shouts of approval, to the effect that he stood four-square behind his most extreme demands. To his colleagues at the conference he complained that his experts were stubborn and that he could not change their minds about reparations; with his eye characteristically upon the political factor he indicated that what was important, after all, was not the amount Germany ultimately paid, but the amount the public of the day might be led to think she might pay. And so it was that on this issue he remained intransigent—Clemenceau's ally, not Wilson's.

The week spent back home had raised troubling questions about the need for changes in the League charter. At first Wilson was inclined to disregard all suggestions, seeing the agitation as being based less on valid doubts than on the hard-core opposition of partisans like Lodge and unconvertible isolationists like Borah. He feared that no matter what he did, the attacks would continue. House, in a diary entry a few days after the President's return to Paris, commented on the latter's "usual stubbornness."[18]

In fact, however, Wilson was beginning to reconsider. Cecil pointed out to him that Europeans, too—by no means all of them unenlightened—were anxious to see some modifications. Voices from home were suggesting the same conclusion. On March 21 Taft cabled a list of suggestions for amendments, adding that, if they were adopted, he was "confident that all but a few who oppose any League at all would be driven . . . to stand for the League."[19] Before a large audience in Boston's Symphony Hall a week later Senator Lodge and Abbot Lawrence Lowell, President of Harvard, conducted a widely heralded debate, with Lodge claiming not to be opposed to a league *per se*, and with Lowell conceding that the charter as it stood required changes.

Wilson now took Taft's suggestions almost word for word and made them the text of a proposal to the reconvened League of Nations commission. Three principal amendments were indicated, concerning the right of withdrawal from the League, the exemption of domestic issues from the League's jurisdiction, and the inviolability of the Monroe Doctrine. Wilson did not have much difficulty reconciling himself to the first of these. He had written (notwithstanding the fact that he was himself a southerner) against the right of the South to secede from the union; nevertheless he did not see how a sovereign nation could be prohibited against its will, and after due notice, from withdrawing from the League. Moreover, withdrawal seemed to him a remote and unlikely issue. A time would come, he said in a strong speech supporting the amendment, "when men would be just as eager partisans of the sovereignty of mankind as they were now of their own national sovereignty."[20]

Both the other proposed amendments he accepted with difficulty, fearing they would prove not only superfluous but hazardous in their implications. Insistence coming from the Republicans on the limits of League jurisdiction in domestic affairs was largely aimed, Wilson perceived, at U.S. immigration policies. Prejudice against Orientals was, in some quarters, as strong as he had found it in the first days of his administration, and he did not want to offend Japan by bringing it to the surface. Even more vexing from his point of view was widespread concern in the United States for asserting specifically that the Monroe Doctrine was exempt from the League's operations. Wilson felt this to be invidious, inviting similar exemptions for other regional arrangements. To support it also meant denial of his basic concept of the Monroe Doctrine. In his long-cherished but abortive plans for a Pan-American pact, he had urged an internationalist view of the doctrine, with countries of the New World pledged to support one another against aggression from within, as from without, the region. Later, in his address to the Senate of January 22, 1917, he had described his highest ideal as being nothing less than adoption of "the doctrine of President Monroe as the doctrine of the world."[21]

The third amendment proposed also seemed to put in question the delicate security arrangements being worked out with France. In any specific reference to the pledges of mutual support implied by the Monroe Doctrine, the highly sensitive French claimed to see a weakening of American commitment to mutual support in Europe. Fighting extreme militaristic demands, Wilson wanted to make sure that no legitimate aspect of her defense was watered down.

Against his preferences, but with the advice of American moderates in mind, Wilson decided to accept the three amendments. To secure their passage he launched himself on a campaign as taxing as any he was to face in Paris. The League commission met for long sessions, often extending past midnight, while the French (and with less excuse the British) put every obstacle in the path of adoption. The French used the new debates to reinforce their earlier efforts to turn the League into an armed alliance against Germany with its own military forces and general staff; while the British held out for assurances on the shipbuilding program. With world opinion turning against the peacemakers, and against the American President in particular, it was widely reported that the treaty was being held up by useless debates over the League. Wilson was forced to issue a statement denying this. Unfortunately he could not reveal the true reason for the delays—France's uncompromising insistence on its full program of security.

Wilson's honorable and successful struggle to secure these amendments should be placed in the context of the later fight for ratification of the League. When the Senate insisted on reservations, he could feel with some justification that he had already faced up to that issue. He had given all that reasonable men asked of him; he had tested the Allies to what seemed their limit. To bow to further demands appeared to invite an indefinite nibbling away of the League's provisions, and to cast doubt on America's good faith. An embattled Wilson certainly made his mistakes in his fight with the Senate; but those mistakes are in part explained by the changes he had already accepted, amid so intense a struggle, while in Paris.

In meetings of the Ten, and then of the Four, the interconnected issues of reparations, occupation of the Rhine's left bank, and the making of Poland into a buffer state were being discussed throughout this period. French economic experts Louis Loucheur and Louis Lucien Klotz repeated *ad nauseam* arguments totally unacceptable to Wilson; the military advisers, Tardieu and Foch, insisted without deviation on the narrowest conception of French security. Clemenceau orchestrated the drive, by turns grave and wheedling, capable of flights of eloquence or touching moments of self-deprecation. In vain Wilson tried to reassure the French, demonstrating his concern for their problems and fears. But mostly, where they were demanding hard military and economic guarantees, he could offer only what Clemenceau derided as "abstract justice" and the promise of the League's moral sanctions.

The French offensive came to a head on March 28, in the afternoon session of the Four which the French interpreter Paul Mantoux recorded, doing full justice to the significance of the occasion. Indeed, in his account the very words and voices of the antagonists seem to be heard in a confrontation worthy of being transposed without change to the staging of a classic drama.[22] The Saar, long in the background as a nagging issue, was now brought to the fore. This coal-rich region, in the possession of Germany since 1814, had been mentioned neither in the Fourteen Points nor in the armistice agreements; yet Clemenceau was prepared to make it a *sine qua non* of his signing the peace. Tardieu and Loucheur set forth in their characteristically dogmatic styles the historical and economic reasons why France should be allowed to take it over. Wilson immediately protested. He was prepared, he said, to make sure that France was compensated for mines willfully destroyed during the war; also he saw the necessity of maintaining the Saar region as an economic and industrial whole. But these objectives, he asserted, had to be reached without annexation.

"If we do not wish to place ourselves in the wrong and break our word," he said at the climax of the ensuing debate, "we must not interpret our own principles too generously to our benefit. I say this solemnly: let us avoid acting in a manner which would risk creating sympathies for Germany; neither let us interpret our promises with a lawyer's finesse."

"I will keep in mind," replied Clemenceau, "the words and excellent intentions of President Wilson. He eliminates sentiment and memory: it is there that I have a reservation about what has just been said. The President of the United States disregards the depths of human nature."

"You seek to do justice to the Germans," he said, turning directly to Wilson. "Do not believe that they will ever forgive us; they only seek the opportunity for revenge."

"I wish to do nothing," Wilson answered, "which would allow it to be said of us: 'They profess great principles, but they admitted exceptions everywhere, wherever sentiment or national interest made them wish to deviate from the rule.' "

Mantoux's notes discreetly omit the climax of this great argument, but it is reported in the diaries of House and Lansing, as well as of others close to the conference. Clemenceau infuriated the President by accusing him of being pro-German. "In that event," Wilson inquired, "do you wish me to return home?"

"I do not wish you to go home," said Clemenceau, "but I intend to do so myself." With that he left the room.[23]

Clemenceau would return without apologies at the next conversation, but the tensions that had been slowly building up became almost more than the President could bear. Week after week was passing with nothing accomplished. He was standing fast while the world around him was going to pieces. On his regular afternoon call on April 2, Baker found him deeply discouraged. "He said that it could not go on many days longer," Baker wrote in his diary, "that if some decision could not be reached by the middle of next week he might have to make some positive break."[24]

Baker etched a touching portrait at this time, contrasting Colonel House and his profoundly frustrated chief. At evening he found the Colonel seated in his long lounge chair with a figured blanket drawn over his chilly legs. He was the picture of the dilettante: "he stands in the midst of great events, to lose nothing. He gains experiences to put in his diary, makes great acquaintances, plays at getting important men together for the sheer joy of making them agree." He was "quite cheerful, quite optimistic."

Meanwhile, Baker added, "the great serious man of the conference—grey, grim, lonely there on the hill—fights a losing battle against heavy odds. He can escape no responsibility & he must go to his punishment not only for his own mistakes and weaknesses of temperament, but for the greed & selfishness of the world. . . . *He is real.* He is the only great man here."[25]

The break came, not as a result of events in the conference chamber, but in a grave though brief illness that took Wilson temporarily out of the battle. It struck him in the full tide of the day's work. On the morning of April 3, the King of the Belgians came to pay a personal call at the President's house. It was "more like the talk of two old friends," noted Grayson, "than of two men who had met now for the first time."[26] In the conference of the Four that afternoon, as the Yugoslavs were presenting their case against Italy, Wilson suddenly became (in Grayson's words) "violently ill."[27] The meeting was adjourned and the President withdrew to his room nearby. He complained of intense pains in his stomach, back, and head. He suffered racking coughing spells, and in the night Grayson tried every possible remedy "to end the paroxysms which were seriously weakening him." His fever rose to 103 degrees. Grayson adds in his diary that "the President's condition was distinctly serious." To the press, after first saying that his patient had "a severe cold," he announced he had come "very near having a serious attack of influenza, but . . . he has apparently escaped it."

Wilson again evidenced his powers of rapid recuperation. Following the night of danger and vigil he showed distinct improvement. In the study adjoining his bedroom, meetings of the Four continued, with messages from House (who was serving as his representative in the discussions) passing through the secret passage that connected the two rooms. At evening, hearing that Baruch was in the building, he called him in for a conversation. The next day, summoning the American commissioners to his bedside, he talked with them at some length. Monday he sat up, lunching with Grayson and Mrs. Wilson at a table before the open fire. That afternoon Baker saw him for the first time since the onset of the illness. He found him "still thin & pale," with a slight hollowness around the eyes, but fully dressed and alert.[28] On Thursday he resumed his accustomed place in the conversations of the Big Four.

The precise nature of this sudden illness was to be much debated by scholars and medical authorities, seeking to find in it clues to Wilson's subsequent behavior. It was interpreted as some form of the deadly influenza that swept the world in the autumn of 1918 but had largely subsided by the following April; as a stroke; and, most convincingly, as "an acute respiratory illness."[29] Some of those around the President were persuaded that his personality and his behavior had been altered by the illness. Looking back, the White House usher, Ike Hoover, wrote that Wilson "was never the same after this little spell of illness." In his memoirs Herbert Hoover remarked on what he observed as a decline in the President's mental acuity coinciding with the attack. It is certain that weariness and disillusion, accompanied by increasing irascibility, weighed on him henceforth.

Members of the Paris household complained that they suffered re-proofs for offenses that earlier had been genially tolerated. Use of the official cars was questioned; brief absences were noted critically. All this was unlike the chief who was normally the soul of courtesy toward his staff. Grayson records a bizarre scene in which, one day after lunch, the President personally rearranged the furniture in the large room where the meetings of the Four took place. "I don't like the way the colors of this furniture fight each other," he said. "The greens and the reds are all mixed up and there is no harmony. . . . This will never do. Let's put the greens all together and the reds together."[30] The doctor, after con-niving in this weird activity, noted "a marked improvement in the ap-pearance of the room."

The President seemed intent on piloting a tight ship—enforcing on the people and on the objects around him an even more strict order, regularity, and promptitude than had already made the place reminiscent of a Presbyterian manse.

When he first returned to the peace negotiations his colleagues found him in an altered mood. He was a man in haste, insisting on getting things done, often without regard for the niceties of principle and logic that had earlier characterized his approach. Had he not fallen ill, Wilson would undoubtedly have brought matters to a head by some drastic and dramatic move. But it was now as if he saw everything in a terrifying perspective. Sickness had sharpened his resolve, giving him a sense of passing time and of his own mortality. His reaction was indeed similar to that after the Princeton stroke of 1906. Then, too, he had acted as a man in a hurry, bringing forth the quad plan with an urge for immediate results leaving little time or energy for consultation. In the far greater crisis in Europe he moved as under an inescapable fate; and to all who looked back, the long night of fever and paroxysms seemed to form a watershed in the conference.

*   *   *

While on his sickbed, he told Grayson, he did "a lot of thinking." On being called in for a solitary conversation, Baruch found him going over the state of the negotiations. "When you get ready to act," Baruch advised him, "I would suggest that you do as you always do—not threaten, but perform." "That's exactly what I have in mind of doing," the President is reported to have replied.[31] On the following day, a Sunday, he told Grayson to inquire of Admiral Benson the whereabouts of the *George Washington*. He wanted the ship ordered to Brest immediately. The message to her captain leaked out even before Baker was able to announce it and caused a sensation among the Allies and in the United States.

Nothing Wilson did while in Europe was deemed so inexplicable or was so variously interpreted as this call for the *George Washington*. Those close to the President saw it as heralding a last, climactic stand on the Fourteen Points. The U.S. press judged it in two opposing lights: as an indication that the President was preparing to quit the conference, and also as a sign that negotiations were proceeding rapidly toward a close. Tumulty, who had urged upon the President some bold stroke "to save Europe and the world," now responded in a panic. The ordering of the *George Washington* to Europe was being looked on, he cabled, as "an act of impatience and petulance"; it was not "accepted here in good grace either by friends or foes,"[32] all of whom saw withdrawal in the circumstances as a desertion. As for the French diplomats, they were thrown off balance and alarmed.

Much of this confusion was probably what Wilson intended when he ordered the controversial telegram. He had long kept in his arsenal of leadership the weapons of ambiguity, secrecy, and surprise. He knew when to speak, and also how to let the blow fall without words. Despite indications to the contrary that he had let slip to his confidants, Wilson had probably never seriously considered breaking up the conference. But he did not mind throwing a scare into the French, or giving encouragement to the smaller nations. Above all, he wanted his colleagues at the peace table to know that he was resuming with a fresh resolve.

His course was now characterized by a sort of large expediency, the expediency he had once admired in Burke. It was the expediency of a statesman (in Burke's phrase) "who, not losing sight of principles, is guided by circumstances." He would cease, so far as possible, to play the role of moralist and lonely fighter. "I am obliged to remain faithful to my Fourteen Points," he told his colleagues at one of the first sessions after his illness, "but without inflexibility, and going as far as possible to meet your legitimate wishes."[33] If that was not exactly a "new" Wilson—he had consistently shown deference and even courtliness in his discussions with the European leaders—it was a Wilson subtly redefined by his brush with death.

He was laboring, during this time, under a double charge. He was Woodrow Wilson, spokesman for the hopes of the world; he was also President of the United States, committed as a responsible leader to getting a peace settlement he could lay before the Senate and the American people. The politician in Wilson was not, in truth, ever entirely subordinated to the moralist. Throughout his career there were evidences of a more wily, a more ruthless Wilson, than was the common image. Now, with his leadership at home and abroad in jeopardy, he chose the way of the practical statesman. The highest priority, as he saw it, was to reach an understanding with Clemenceau.

The President's return to the conference table witnessed the first agreement formally signed by the representatives of the victorious powers. The agreement approved putting the Kaiser on trial. Wilson had adamantly opposed holding the German leader responsible for ordinary war crimes. But he declared himself willing to accept a trial for gross crimes against civilization and international law, including the breaking of treaties and the invasion of Belgium. Lloyd George and Clemenceau were both agreeable to this treatment of the Kaiser—provided they could hope to hang him for one reason or another. As if to emphasize this gesture of compromise—this first insidious and dangerous draught—he himself passed the paper around the room to secure the required signatures.

After that the basically insoluble problems of the Saar and the occupation of the left bank of the Rhine were upon the table. On April 14 a settlement was reached. Wilson recognized the need to compensate France for the output of northern coal mines deliberately flooded and wrecked by the Germans. He consented, therefore, to see placed under French ownership the actual mines within the Saar territory. The French, still not content, wanted political control of the Saar. Supported by Lloyd George, Wilson effectively resisted this demand, and then he offered a compromise calling for a civilian government of the disputed region, under control of the League, and with provision for a plebiscite after fifteen years. These arrangements were widely criticized at the time by those who felt the American President had given away too much. Yet, in the aftermath, German sovereignty was never abrogated; and when the plebiscite took place in 1935, the vote of the Saarlanders was nine to one in favor of a full restoration to Germany.*

Clemenceau was convinced, nevertheless, that he had won his point. On hearing of Wilson's final acquiescence to the Saar settlement, he embraced House in a mood of exhilaration. Journalistic attacks on the American President were muted, and French filibusters in the League of Nations commission ended. From this point begins the relation of mutual understanding, deepening to a kind of rough affection, between the President and French Premier. With progress on two thorny problems the atmosphere in the council chamber, as well as among the public at large, cleared noticeably.

Still remaining to be settled was the disposition of territories on the left bank of the Rhine. Foch and others had pursued efforts to establish a Rhenish state, independent of Germany. But Clemenceau could not argue wholeheartedly for such a naked transfer of sovereignty. Various schemes were proposed to maintain a permanent French occupation as security against a new invasion, all coming up against Wilson's and, less consistently, Lloyd George's objections. In this new phase of the conference a compromise on this point became possible. Wilson accepted the idea of a French occupation, without an abridgment of sovereignty, provided that the arrangements were limited to fifteen years. The rationale was understood to be a guarantee of Germany's fulfilling its obligations under the peace treaty.

Wilson paid a price for this compromise. To allay French fears he and Lloyd George each agreed to make a treaty with France, promising to come to its assistance in case of a new German aggression. The treaty was supposed to last only until the League was fully operative; but for Wilson it became a major embarrassment, giving fresh ammunition to his Senate foes. That he should have proposed it, and that it should have been accepted by the French as a valid offer, suggests how self-confident he was at this juncture, and also how undiminished was his prestige among his peers at the peace table.

Reparations formed a third matter crying out to be settled. The imposition of harsh economic terms seemed essential to the French, to make possible their own recovery and reconstruction, quite apart from

---

*After World War II the French occupied the Saar. In 1954 an agreement for a referendum was worked out by the French and German authorities; this again showed the majority of Saarlanders in favor of staying within Germany and the disputed territory was turned over to the German Federal Republic.

satisfying their latent desire to see Germany remain subjugated. Despite occasional moments of good sense, the British were equally adamant. Lloyd George had made election promises; he was in thrall to a reactionary parliament and press. He had a mind, moreover, made for calculating costs to the last penny. When he wavered he was called to task by the "heavenly twins," his economic advisers, the Lords Cunliffe and Sumner. As often, he used them as an excuse for not wavering.

Wilson, backed by his own experts, saw the matter as reasonable men might have been expected to do. They were prepared to make Germany pay for the damage it had inflicted, but they argued that unrealistic demands would jeopardize the country's capacity to pay anything at all. German factories were being dismantled, former territories annexed, colonies that had supplied vital raw materials cut off. To impose unlimited payments on top of these deprivations was to expect a third-rate industrial power to deliver as if it were still a first-rate one.

During Wilson's illness the reparations issue was thrashed out. On his recovery he found positions hardened and the Allied spokesmen intractable. They were demanding reparation not only for damages inflicted by the enemy but for the total costs of waging the war. The latter concept seemed unrealistic and unjust to Wilson. He fought to get agreement upon a definite sum—payments of $35 billion were considered by his experts to be reasonably within Germany's capacity to pay. He fought for a limited time period—thirty years—within which the transactions could be completed. The French and British preferred to keep the Germans in uncertainty as to the total sum that would finally be exacted, claiming that their own publics would consider any stated figure, no matter how unjust or how unrealistic, to be inadequate.

One particularly controversial aspect of the costs of war was the pension demanded for wounded Allied soldiers. Wilson was strongly opposed to this extension of Allied claims. He stood alone, under intolerable pressures. Lloyd George delegated Smuts, whom he knew Wilson admired, to make a fervent, personal appeal. Wilson yielded—a concession deemed by some later historians to be the culminating proof of his pliancy. Wilson, however, was convinced that agreement on a total figure for reparations would be reached. His concession, therefore, did not add to Germany's liability; its practical consequence was to enlarge that part designated for Britain and to decrease France's share. With a matter of unreasonableness rather than of principle involved, and acting within the shifting environment of give-and-take, Wilson's decision was neither foolish nor weak.

Through this period the Commission on Polish Affairs was meeting to determine Germany's eastern borders and the shape of the new Poland. Headed by the French diplomat Jules Cambon, the commission was, from the French point of view, provided with a double opportunity: to weaken Germany and also to create a strong buffer between Russia and the rest of Europe. The French were assiduous in the pursuit of both aims. It was difficult at best to shape from territories long populated by both Poles and Germans a nation that was strategically and economically viable. To do this without violating the principle of self-determination seemed almost impossible. When the commission reported to the Council of Ten on March 19, Lloyd George expressed understandable concern on finding that more than two million Germans were included within the proposed borders of the future Polish state.

Backed by his American experts, Wilson contended that economic and strategic factors, including secure access to the sea, counted for more in the case of Poland than boundaries drawn strictly along ethnic lines. Supporting Cambon and Tardieu, he seemed once more to be making unfortunate compromises. But in fact he saw himself facing an inexorable dilemma. If boundaries were drawn on ethnic lines, Poland would be incapable of defending itself. On the other hand, the inclusion of German minorities would give Germany an incentive to move in, both from the east and the west. It was a question, Wilson said, of "balancing antagonistic considerations."[34] Later critics, disillusioned with the treaty as a whole, denounced the Polish settlement as a betrayal of principle and as an unwarranted retaliation against Germany.

By April 13, with the exception of the still unresolved questions of reparations and of the Polish boundaries, France had received satisfaction of its major demands. On this same date a communication was addressed to Germany, inviting a delegation to come to Versailles for the final phase of peacemaking.

Through the eight days extending from his recovery to this turning point, the Four had been meeting morning and afternoon for many hours, while separate conversations among themselves and with their advisers prolonged the day. By mid-April Wilson was tired, dangerously so. The observant Edith Benham found it increasingly difficult to find items to record in her diary, as the President sat mute at the dinner table, retiring immediately afterwards in lonely silence. At the end of a difficult day he would ask his wife to place essential telephone calls; and Baker, coming by at evening for an account of the day's meetings, found him relying on Grayson to recall details that had escaped his mind. On April 28 he suffered what was evidently another small cerebral incident.[35] The hypertension with which he had been afflicted so long now plagued him not only in the form of lapses of memory, but in a slowly narrowing sphere of interest and pleasure.

The sessions of the Four, as Mantoux recorded them, show Wilson to have been effective in debate throughout this period, notwithstanding the physical and mental handicaps from which he suffered. He was not making decisions out of weakness; he was fully aware of the implications of the major compromises he was proposing and carrying through. His posture was that of a man ready to accept criticism and even obloquy (both of which he received in full measure) for what he considered necessary concessions, not only to hold the peace conference together, but to meet legitimate concerns for French security.

When twenty years had passed and Germany was again on the path of aggression, Clemenceau's insistence on security for France did not appear to have been unreasonably obsessive. Wilson's response to it could then be judged more fairly than by liberal critics of his own day. Yet the compromises—on the Saar, on the left bank of the Rhine, on Germany's eastern border, together with the failure to get a satisfactory settlement on reparations—did hurt Wilson greatly at the time. They dimmed the image of a man dedicated to absolute principles. No longer the voice of pure idealism, he began to appear as one bargaining from a weak hand—alone and presumably outwitted at the conference table—while his political support was crumbling at home.

Not least, the concessions made to the French disarmed him for the next contests he was to enter, the settling of Italian and Japanese claims in an atmosphere even more clouded than that which had surrounded his dealings with the French.

A JUST PEACE?

When it was announced on April 14 that the German plenipotentiaries had been invited to come to Versailles, the public statement drafted by Wilson emphasized that other items in the peacemaking process would go forward without interruption. "It is hoped," the statement said, "that the questions most directly affecting Italy, especially the Adriatic question, can now be brought to a speedy agreement."[1] In this, Wilson and his colleagues were to be proven highly unrealistic. The Italian settlement, far from being speedy, was to drag on until near the end of 1920.

With the French satisfied, Orlando was determined that ample attention be paid to his country's case. Feeling that Italy had been too long ignored, he objected strongly to having the Germans invited prior to a full hearing of its claims. Not that Orlando's position was unknown to the peace conference. More than once, in private interviews, Wilson had heard him out in detail. For weeks, advisers to the conference had been considering how Italy's claims might be reconciled with Wilsonian standards. The American experts were convinced that the major part of the Italian case was unacceptable, and their advice to the President was that he stand by the Fourteen Points in all particulars.

The Italian territorial claims, set forth formally by Orlando and Sonnino in the April 19 meeting of the Council of Four, were as extensive as they were tenaciously held. Sovereignty over areas of mixed nationality reaching north to the Swiss border, over the port of Trieste on the Adriatic as well as over the Dalmatian islands and the littoral of Yugoslavia, had been promised Italy by the secret Treaty of London in 1915. On the basis of this treaty Italy had joined the Allied side in the war. Not content with these acquisitions, Italian demands now included the Adriatic port of Fiume.

In what he afterwards attributed to an error based on insufficient knowledge, Wilson had approved the interpretation of the Fourteen Points allowing Italy to take over the Austrian Tyrol to the Brenner Pass. But Dalmatia and the offshore islands, also granted by the secret treaty, he was resolutely opposed to ceding; and on the subject of Fiume he was adamant. The British and French stood by their obligations under the treaty. Was not the sanctity of treaties, they asked, one of the ends for which the war was fought? But they were not willing to go further, and they supported Wilson in his unremitting fight against Italian claims to Fiume.

The grand opening discussion among the Four found Orlando maintaining that, even if the Treaty of London did not exist, Italy was entitled by history, as by strategic and economic needs, to hold the lands which had been granted under it. By the same reasoning they were entitled to Fiume. The Italian statesman set forth his case with clarity and controlled eloquence, in a way that could only win Wilson's respect. The arguments were taken up by Foreign Minister Sonnino in a very different spirit. An unyielding infighter, tough and plainspoken, he echoed in harsh terms what his chief expressed with civility and often touching personal solicitude.

A skilled debater, Wilson in his reply embraced Orlando's suggestion that the secret treaty not be considered the ruling factor. That treaty ought not to have been entered into; he would not recognize it, and he would argue the case upon grounds of justice and of conformity to the

Fourteen Points. The whole point, he said, was that the victorious powers were "trying to make peace on an entirely new basis and to establish a new order of international relations."[2] Within that order legitimate needs of defense had their place, and Italy could be reassured by its control of the northern mountain passes. But with the Austro-Hungarian Empire dissolved, and democratic states established in eastern Europe, how could Italy think it needed Dalmatia and the islands for its security? How could it argue as if a single autocratic power confronted it across the Adriatic, when in fact the situation was completely different.

On the question of Fiume Wilson felt even more strongly; for it involved not only an unjust claim by Italy, but one that, if acknowledged, would undermine the new order the peacemakers were seeking to establish. The regeneration of central Europe, he argued, depended on its attaining a viable economic life. Fiume served the commerce of Czechoslovakia, Hungary, and Romania, as well as Yugoslavia. Its free use as an international port was essential.

Having set forth his case, having made his appeal on grounds of principle and honor, Wilson on the same day showed a side of his diplomacy not always recognized. A directive to the financial counselor Norman Davis ordered the withholding of a credit of $50 million to Italy "until the air clears—if it does."[3]

In this first great debate, part of a continuing argument that would be carried on for months, Clemenceau admitted himself "shocked" that Italy should bring up Fiume at the eleventh hour. With Lloyd George he stood on the Treaty of London, however contrary to the Fourteen Points, including the granting of the Dalmatian coast to Italy. But he would not recognize further claims.

While backing the President on Fiume, Clemenceau could not refrain from expressing characteristic skepticism. Listening to President Wilson, he said, he felt that the peacemakers "were embarking on a most hazardous enterprise." They were "seeking to detach Europe and the whole world from the old order which had led in the past to conflicts and finally to the recent War." It was "a very noble purpose," but it was not possible "to change the whole policy of the world at one stroke."[4] Amid later discouragements at the peace conference Wilson would tend to agree with this view.

The next day was Sunday, Easter besides, but in his eagerness to reach a settlement Wilson consented to further meetings of the Four. The tall windows of the President's living room opened on a garden in early spring bloom as the statesmen went over once more the whole Italian agenda. They searched in vain for an accord. The emotion in the room was almost palpable. When Wilson restated his basic objectives, Orlando arose and was seen to sob despairingly.

Through the two following days the efforts to reach agreement continued, with Orlando threatening to withdraw and to refuse to sign the peace. The Four met in almost constant sessions; Wilson met individually with his colleagues; the three representing the signatories of the Treaty of London met alone. On the sidelines House met with almost everyone. The American ambassador in Rome sent emotional reports of the rising anger of the Italian people.

When personal appeals had failed, when logic and the cajolery of minor concessions had been rejected, Wilson played the one card that seemed left to him. He issued a public statement, an appeal to the conscience of the Italian people, which in other circumstances might have succeeded. But by then public opinion in Italy was too hysterically aroused to heed counsels of reason or moderation, and the government had organized a diplomatic offensive of overwhelming intensity.

Wilson suffered storms of abuse on the grounds that, in his attempt to reach the Italian people, he had gone over the heads of their government. In Paris, newspapers subsidized by the Italians added to the outcry. Supporters of the President, many of whom had been urging such a tactic in regard to other nationalistic demands at the peace conference, at first saw their highest hopes fulfilled; but they were then stunned by the popular reaction. Clemenceau and Lloyd George stood aside. They had promised to follow Wilson's statement with a similar one of their own. In the hubbub they chose silence as the more prudent course.

Two days after the appeal was issued the Italian delegates carried out their threat of leaving the peace conference. They would return, slipping in surreptitiously, as if nothing had happened, to the President's living room when the final terms of the German treaty were under discussion. But that could not be foreseen at the time, and the crisis appeared acute.

The fact that storm signals had been raised in another quarter made it worse. While France's and Italy's claims were being discussed, the Japanese had sat in ominous silence. Now they put forward their own program of expansion, framed in unyielding terms and including demands that Wilson considered totally unacceptable. The program involved the taking over of large areas of Chinese territory and the establishment in China of a long-premeditated hegemony. The Italian defection, grave as it was, had not been perceived as being in itself capable of wrecking the conference; but a peace signed without them, and also without the Japanese, would make a mockery of the idea of a world settlement. The absence of the two powers from the League of Nations would reduce it to ineffectiveness from the start.

Wilson's attitude toward the Japanese had long been one of suspicion bordering on hostility. He had expressed faith in the Chinese people during the first days of his administration; he believed they must shape their own destiny, free alike of force imposed by Western powers and by their formidable island neighbor. With the opening of the European war, however, the expansive tendencies of Japan became clear. Joining the Allies, it overran the German concession on the Shantung peninsula, and in return for pledging significant assistance to the Allies, gained from them secret assurances that its conquest would be confirmed at the peace table. In addition, Japan was to receive ownership of former German-owned islands north of the Equator.

After the United States joined the war, a Japanese mission headed by Kikujiro Ishii arrived in Washington with the purpose of confirming these claims. The Lansing-Ishii agreements, negotiated in October 1917, recognized Japan's special interests in China, in return for vague assurance of respect for the Open Door policy and for China's territorial integrity. Wilson was not entirely reassured. His reluctance to have large forces enter Siberia was based on continuing apprehension as to Japan's strategy and motives.

Now at the peace conference, at the height of the Italian crisis, the Japanese representatives demanded full payment, under terms of its secret treaty with Britain and France. To complicate the latter issue, China in its weakness had succumbed to Japanese pressure, acknowledging the same rights of domination over Shantung as had been exercised by its German conquerors. The Chinese case, set forth in the Council of Four by the young V. K. Wellington Koo, was fatally flawed by this submission. Wilson, moreover, came up against the same British and French insistence on the sanctity of treaties—whether secret or open, whether in accord with the principles of the Fourteen Points or diametrically opposed to them—as he had in the case of Italy. For the cause of justice to China he fought on almost alone, coming close to the point of exhaustion and despair.

From his own counselors he received little help. According to Grayson, House told Lloyd George and Clemenceau that he could persuade Wilson to compromise. Bliss wrote Wilson a long letter deploring a proposed settlement; when the settlement was reached, he told his wife that the whole American delegation was "mortified and angry."[5] In vain Wilson himself sought a way out of the impasse. "My experts," he said, "seem only to give me one answer and that is to stand by the principles; but they do not seem to realize what the results might be at this crucial time in the world's history."[6] To Baker, on one of his evening calls, the President remarked in a rare admission that "he could not see clearly just where [in the case of Japan] his principles applied."

"They [the Japanese] will go home," he added bitterly, "unless we give them what they should not have."[7]

Single-handedly in days of tense negotiation Wilson extracted assurances from the Japanese that their rights in China would at least not exceed those exacted by the Germans. Moreover, Shantung would be given back to China "in full sovereignty," notwithstanding the continuance of economic privileges. These included the operation of the railroad, together with maintenance of a police force adequate to safeguard it. Such fine points were defined as the makeup of this force—wholly Chinese; and the makeup of the group of instructors—Japanese, but appointed by the Chinese government. Wilson, moreover, received personal assurance from the Japanese that they would evacuate the area within a reasonable time.

In the end, worn, and after sleepless nights, he accepted what he considered the best to be extracted from a bad situation. As if to profess his own deep sense of responsibility, he himself drafted the memorandum formalizing the agreement. He had "never seen the President more fatigued," Grayson noted when the Japanese case was settled and while the Italian claims were still rankling.[8]

The German peace delegation, meanwhile, had arrived at Versailles. Quartered in a hotel, barred from any contact with the French people, they waited out the days until the treaty should be put in form suitable for presentation.

The long-anticipated encounter between the victors and the vanquished took place at Versailles on May 7. It was held in a relatively small room in the Petit Trianon with only a handful of newspapermen to observe it, along with secretaries, interpreters, and the delegates of the victorious powers. As at all plenary sessions, Clemenceau sat at the head of a long table, with Wilson on his right. At the prearranged moment the chief usher of the French foreign service, clad in black knee breeches with a heavy gold chain around his neck, escorted the German plenipotentiaries to their seats at the far end of the table. The Allied delegates rose in an unpremeditated show of respect.

The tension in the chamber was electric. No one knew how the Germans would conduct themselves, or what was the character and temper of their chief delegate, Count Ulrich von Brockdorff-Rantzau. Wilson complained privately that he would rather meet with the "old crew" of Prussian militarists than with these "nondescripts" of the new Germany.[9] In the person of Brockdorff-Rantzau, the President and his colleagues now faced a spokesman who might as well have come out of the old Germany as the new, a thin, bald, bespectacled logician with shrewd eyes and a harsh, metallic voice. Over the whole gathering, winners and losers alike, hung the realization that the peace, embodied in a plain book of two hundred pages, had been framed in a harsh and unyielding mood.

In the silence Clemenceau arose. It was neither the time nor the place, he said, for superfluous words. In a few staccato sentences he announced that before the Germans would be expected to sign they would have two weeks to examine the terms of the peace. The Allies would provide explanations, if requested, but substantial changes were unlikely.

For his response, the German representative remained seated. It was taken at the time as a mark of disrespect, but may well have been the result of his simply being too nervous to stand. Whether intentionally insulting or not, the speaker proceeded with words unlikely to appease his audience. Choosing from the more aggressive of two prepared texts, Brockdorff-Rantzau argued that Germany was not solely responsible for the war and that the peace terms were incompatible with the Fourteen Points. There was justification for both positions, but coldly set forth in the tense atmosphere of the Petit Trianon his statements, far from creating an atmosphere favorable to negotiation, seemed but one more proof of German insensibility.

Presentation to the Germans of the preliminary terms of the peace treaty marked the beginning of the end of the conference. During the next two months, until June 28, the Big Four continued to meet each morning and afternoon. But the pressures were somewhat relieved, and in the conversations as recorded by Mantoux one catches the tone of weary men who talked endlessly, sometimes about scattered details. Two major tasks confronted them: to frame a peace treaty with Austria, next to Germany the major belligerent among the Central Powers; and to pursue with Brockdorff-Rantzau and his colleagues negotiations leading to a final treaty.

In addition was the wide range of questions left by the defeat and dissolution of the Ottoman Empire. The chief European powers whetted their knives at the prospect of dividing up the rich spoils of the Middle East, seeing in the system of mandates a means by which England could confirm its long-standing influence in Persia, and the French theirs in Syria. Wilson was powerless to avert the dangers he foresaw, and the debates on these issues continued long after he had returned to the United States.

The treaty with Austria, which consumed much of Wilson's last month abroad, confronted the statesmen with nothing less than the need to construct a new political order for central Europe. The breakup of the Habsburg Empire had left a debris of peoples intent on self-determination. How were the boundaries of these new states to be guaranteed? How was their economic life to be fostered and peace among them provided for? To say that Wilson, or any of the leaders of 1919, had answers to these questions would be to exaggerate their wisdom. But the American President was aware of the questions and he did seriously seek solutions. The fragility of the liberated countries of eastern Europe, and the shallowness of their democratic roots, he apprehended fully. He considered indispensable prerequisites to the viability of the new states to be such factors as disarmament; guaranteed protection of minorities, especially Jews; internationalization of waterways; and the maintenance of Fiume as a free port feeding from the deep interior of the region. All these, with the notable exception of Fiume, Wilson managed to incorporate into the treaty. Finally the League of Nations was, in his mind, the essential overarching element in keeping the new countries at peace among themselves and out of the clutches of the old type of imperialism.

More clearly than most statesmen of his day he saw the need for a stable, self-governing Russia at the eastern limits of the region. He viewed the absence of Russia from the conference as a grave defect in the peacemaking process; in vain he had taken the lead in trying to remedy it. A Europe without Russia was a house divided, notwithstanding the fierce, but he believed temporary, aberration of Bolshevism. If the eastern colossus could not be involved directly in the creation of a new order, it could at least be confronted with a situation inviting its ultimate participation. "We cannot rescue Russia," Wilson said prophetically, "without having a united Europe."[10]

The President argued insistently for the various items of this program for the reconstruction of central and eastern Europe. Lloyd George, however, was more concerned with getting reparations from the fragments of the former Austro-Hungarian Empire than he was with their economic health. And Clemenceau cared mostly that the Bolsheviks be left to stew in their own juice. The Italians, first and last, wanted their own territories augmented. Perhaps the wisest of men, in accord on the wisest of measures, could in the end have done little to control a situation so volatile and passion-ridden as existed in the central states and in Russia. From an afternoon session of the Council of Four, on May 30, Mantoux records a conversation perfectly conveying the multiplicity of problems with which the statesmen were dealing, and their inability to make their will prevail.

Wilson opens the conversation by remarking that the fighting between Slovenes and Austrians in the Austrian state of Carinthia seems to be taking a serious turn. Clemenceau interjects that it is necessary to stop the Yugoslavs who are in the process of seizing Klagenfurt (a city in Carinthia near the Yugoslavian border). Furthermore, the Romanians are advancing in a zone which has not been assigned to them. "I wonder," the French leader asks plaintively, "whether the Greeks should not also be asked not to advance far from Smyrna." Perhaps a commission, Orlando suggests, should be sent to Carinthia to interpose themselves between the combatants. Wilson proposes that a message of warning can be sent more rapidly to the Yuogoslavs; at least their delegation can be found in Paris. "We should send them a note," he states, "to remind them to resort to arms is to challenge the authority of the [peace] conference."[11] Clemenceau thinks this is a good idea, and indicates his willingness to sign. No one, however, seems to have the least illusion that the note will have an effect.

Thus, central Europe, deaf to warnings and imprecations, brought itself day by day closer to chaos.

While preoccupied with the Austrian peace treaty, the statesmen in Paris were also engaged in serious exchanges over final terms of the German treaty. German thoroughness, combined with German diplomatic skill, characterized the memoranda that messengers carried daily from the headquarters of the enemy delegation. These argued that Germany was not solely responsible for the war. They maintained that the peace violated the Fourteen Points and the terms set forth in the armistice agreements. In the east, indisputably German territories had been given to the Poles. In the west, the occupation of the left bank of the Rhine had been granted under conditions that left open the possibility of indefinite extensions. Arrangements in the Saar, it was claimed, paved the way for a permanent French presence. Reparations denied Germany the means to reconstruction and recovery. As a final blow, the Germans were kept from early admission to the League of Nations.

Each of these memoranda was rejected by the Allied statesmen. They admitted that the terms imposed on Germany were harsh, but the nation had to bear the responsibility for a war that had been begun and carried through with utmost ruthlessness. However, when the full German case was summed up, and was presented in a weighty document on May 29, it was viewed as something more than a series of self-pitying complaints. In many quarters the Germans were felt to have made a solid case against the Allied leaders.

If a breach was to open within the Council of Four, it might have been thought that Wilson would be the one to waver. It was he who had originally had doubts about Germany's exclusive responsibility for the war, who had shaped the Fourteen Points and had stood against abridgments of the armistice agreements. But Wilson had never been a man to back down in a fight. Besides, he had been deeply angered by German conduct at the close of the war and offended by Brockdorff-Rantzau's behavior. It was Lloyd George, taken aback by the softening of anti-German feeling in Britain, who caved in before the German counterattack. Hastily summoning his cabinet and representatives of the empire to Paris over the weekend of May 30, he conferred with them all at length. Their almost unanimous recommendations were for drastic concessions. If such concessions were not granted, the Prime Minister was authorized to refuse the participation of British forces in any further military or naval actions against Germany.

When at the morning session of June 2 Lloyd George revealed these developments to his colleagues, Clemenceau responded with emotions of alarm and despair. Seeing his program for French security jeopardized, he made it plain that he would not retreat or concede. The situation, he said, was "extremely grave"; indeed "it could not be more grave."[12] Wilson kept his silence, saying only that he would have to consult with his associates.

In a meeting in Lansing's office at the Hôtel Crillon, he put the question of treaty changes before his peace commissioners, advisers, and experts, some fifty people in all. The President, noted one of the younger members present, was "as usual very genial"; he "came around the small circle shaking hands with each of us and saying some words to everyone on his particular work."[13] After setting forth the German case for revision, he asked for an expression of opinions. The general feeling was that the President should support the treaty as written; it was too late and too dangerous to unravel it. Wilson's own disposition was to accept the correction of "injustices" where they were found to exist; but he was not willing to surrender any points merely to gain the Germans' signature. At issue was not whether the peace was hard—"the Germans earned that"—but whether the terms were, or were not, "essentially unjust."[14]

As for the British, "from the unreasonable to the reasonable, all the way around," they were "unanimous . . . in their funk." "Now that makes me very tired," the President asserted.[15]

A new situation was thus created among the Four. For the next weeks Lloyd George dominated the proceedings. Changeful and verbose, he was pitted against the unyielding Clemenceau, with Wilson acting as mediator between them. It was not an easy role for him to play. Much of what Lloyd George was proposing he had himself sought to write into the treaty. If he was tempted to reverse positions that had been forced upon him, he realized the treaty could not be undone without exposing to the Germans a dangerously divided front. If his principles had been compromised, they could not be reclaimed without submitting to the vacillations of the unpredictable Prime Minister. And so he went on from session to session, holding the conference together, picking out here and there points where improvements could be made with the agreement of all.

Changes conforming to some of the German demands were accomplished by this process. Admission to the League was eased; civilian administration of the Saar was defined; possibilities were indicated for an abbreviated occupation of the left bank of the Rhine. On reparations the setting of a fixed sum (which Wilson had steadfastly advocated) was adopted, but was to be set by the Reparation Commission only in 1921. Very important, from the German point of view, the Four agreed that the fate of Upper Silesia, provisionally included in the new Poland, should be determined by plebiscite. These significant changes made it possible for Germany ultimately to sign the peace. They do much, in retrospect, to allay the charge that no serious negotiations with Germany were carried on.

Within the American delegation wholesale resignations were rumored through the month of May. In fact only the disgruntled Bullitt and the youthful idealists Adolf A. Berle, Jr., and Samuel E. Morison broke with the President. Most younger members of the delegation, in spite of their disappointments with the peace treaty, stood loyally by, then and later. Yet virtually no one was ready to acknowledge that the treaty was one embodying reasonable compromises. Herbert Hoover saw it as an economic disaster; Lansing thought that its concessions to the Japanese were "iniquitous." Smuts wrote Wilson privately that in his judgment the treaty did not square with the Fourteen Points. "There will be a terrible disillusion," he said, "if the peoples come to think that we are not concluding a Wilson Peace, that we are not keeping our promises to the world or faith with the public."[16] Wilson admired Smuts and his letter must have touched near the quick.

Adding to the President's burden at this time was the worsening situation at home. Tumulty cabled grim news of the partisan bitterness in the Senate and the growing demand for amendments as the price of the treaty's ratification. Wilson was withholding the text of the treaty, on the grounds that its terms were still under negotiation. This course was diplomatically and constitutionally sound, but it increased the Republicans' frustration and sense of grievance.

In an attempt to focus attention on postwar reconstruction—it would be his last such attempt before the treaty fight absorbed all his energies—Wilson called in a message to Congress for basic changes in the relationship between capital and labor. "We cannot go any further in our present direction," he declared. "We cannot live our right life as a nation or achieve our proper success as an industrial community if capital and labour are to continue to be antagonistic instead of being partners." The object of all reform must be "the genuine democratization of industry, based upon a full recognition of the right of those who work, in whatever rank, to participate in some organic way in every decision which directly affects their welfare or the part they are to play in industry."[17]

Wilson typed away with the vigor of style that had marked proposals of earlier days. But his message, suggestive of what might have been a culminating version of the New Freedom, was scarcely noted by the Republican-dominated Congress.

Through the late Paris spring, isolated from his natural constituency and compelled to back aspects of the treaty to which he had originally been opposed, Wilson managed to keep a surprisingly hopeful outlook. He remained convinced that things would have been worse had he not kept the watch, and that the whole, as he said of the Japanese settlement, was the best that could be got "out of a dirty past."[18] He played down the importance of strict adherence to the Fourteen Points, seeing the more questionable parts of the treaty—in particular the reparation clauses—as certain to be modified by later agreements. The treaty was born of postwar hates; the League would be born of its better hopes. With such arguments, and with a stubborn faith in the ultimate good sense of the people, Wilson managed to avoid depression or despair.

An impromptu speech to a small group of lawyers shows him coming to terms with the disappointments felt by so many. He had been disturbed in recent months, he said, by "the unqualified hope that men have entertained everywhere of immediate emancipation from the things that have hampered them and oppressed them." He was not himself, he declared, of so utopian a frame of mind. "You cannot in human experience rush into the light. You have to go through the twilight into the broadening day before the noon comes and the full sun is upon the landscape."[19]

A major address on Memorial Day, delivered in the cemetery at Suresnes, reveals Wilson's unshatterable idealism in the face of harsh facts. The graves of six thousand Americans, mostly men who had died in the advance on Château-Thierry, stood in rows upon the hillside where he spoke. The ground was bare and dust-covered, except where the resting places of individual soldiers were surrounded by flowers tended by French women living nearby. The day was bright and hot, and the scent of acacias was in the air. The President had attended a brief session of the Four before driving out; he was nervous and preoccupied, as he had confessed to being before an extemporaneous address. Yet, when he spoke, he was at the top of his form—"so sure, so musical," Baker described it: "never did an orator have more perfect command of himself, and without palpable effort, either in voice or movement, infuse his audience with his very spirit."[20]

The opening sentences may be quoted as an example of Wilson's eloquence, worthy of standing with the most memorable in the American experience:

> No one with a heart in his breast, no American, no lover of humanity, can stand in the presence of these graves without the most profound emotion. These men who lie here are men of unique breed. Their like has not been seen since the far days of the Crusades. Never before have men crossed the seas to a foreign land to fight for a cause which they did not pretend was peculiarly their own, but knew was the cause of humanity and of mankind. And when they came, they found fit comrades for their courage and their devotion. They found armies of liberty already in the field—men who, though they had gone through three years of fiery trial, seemed only to be just discovering, not for a moment losing, the high temper of the great affair, men seasoned in the bloody service of liberty. Joining hands with these, the men of America gave that greatest of all gifts, the gift of life and the gift of spirit.

Wilson concluded with words that were to give meaning to his ill-fated struggle to win America's acceptance of the League: "Here stand I," he said, "consecrated in spirit to the men who were once my comrades and who are now gone, and who have left me under eternal bonds of fidelity."[21]

The Wilson who spoke at Suresnes was the pure idealist. On the very day of the address he took a stand against a major item of Lloyd George's liberal revisionism, his effort to secure a plebiscite in the Polish corridor and Upper Silesia. The next day, moreover, in a secret plenary session, Wilson made one of the strongest of his speeches, insisting on the right of the big powers to intervene in the affairs of the smaller ones. The big powers, he argued, had borne the chief burden of the war; they were now prepared to guarantee the peace: it was essential, therefore, that the small powers do nothing by which that peace might be broken. "Where the great force lies," Wilson concluded, "there must be the sanction of peace."[22] The argument shocked Baker. "It appears," he wrote, "that the world in future is not to be governed by a democratic society of equal nations."[23] House saw a gaping discrepancy between these words and "the nobility of his Memorial Day Address."[24]

There was perhaps a discrepancy; but it was like Wilson to combine the loftiness of idealism with his own brand of worldly-wise realism. His statesmanship was compounded of the two, to the point where less friendly observers held him guilty of hypocrisy or self-delusion. "Wilson talks like Jesus Christ and acts like Lloyd George" was a *mot* House confided to his diary.[25] Yet at his best, and through the last period in Paris, Wilson managed to keep these two forces in a workable equilibrium. He played as a statesman the role both of the biblical serpent and the biblical dove; and as a human being he remained detached and integrated, hopeful but not quite fooled, either by himself or by others.

The German plenipotentiaries, having received the modified terms of the treaty, continued to leave doubt as to whether they would sign. The Allies set a deadline and devoted several sessions to discussing what should be done in case the Germans failed to meet it. A march to Berlin with occupation of the country seemed the inescapable course, and Foch was summoned to receive orders. But the general had his own ideas. He did not command enough troops, he asserted, to get more than halfway to Berlin; to limit the forces required he proposed dividing Germany and making a separate peace with Bavaria. The Big Four were infuriated by this transparent attempt of the military to dictate the political terms of the peace. Yet they were plainly unable to raise more troops. Fortunately, a march to Berlin was not to prove necessary.

On the night of June 21 the Berlin government fell, to be replaced by one headed by the socialist Gustav Adolf Bauer. The new government requested a forty-eight-hour delay before being called to sign the peace treaty. In the Council of the Four the following morning Wilson drafted a stern ultimatum. The Allied and Associated powers, it declared, "can accept or acknowledge no qualification or reservation, and must require of the German representatives an unequivocal decision."[26] Along the Rhine, Allied troops (as many as were available) were prepared to march, and at sea the navies waited for orders to prolong the blockade.

Tension mounted in Paris and when in the late afternoon of June 23 word came that the Germans would sign without reservation or delay, crowds gathered and cheered. Sirens screeched, guns boomed, church bells rang out. Men and women danced in the streets.

In front of Wilson's residence a policeman had been observed to jump from a speeding car. Rushing up the steps, he delivered the good news. The President broke what must have been a profound strain by going for a drive, and that night at dinner he called for champagne. His toast was "to the Peace, an enduring Peace, a Peace under the League of Nations."[27] Afterwards he went down to the headquarters of the American commission at the Crillon, where he received what was described as "quite an ovation."

Five days elapsed before the final ceremony. The Austrian treaty was not completed; a treaty with Hungary waited on the formation of a stable government; the disposition of Turkish territories remained undetermined. On June 19 Orlando's government had fallen—first of the overturns that by 1922 would have cast all the Big Four from power—leaving the Adriatic settlement still beyond reach. Amid the unfinished business, thoughts of the American delegation turned irresistibly toward home. Lansing would return, to be replaced in Paris by the Undersecretary of State, Frank Polk; Colonel House would go to London to work with Cecil on the organization of the League; Henry White would remain to deal with various diplomatic issues. Baker, to his great relief, would retreat to his hillside in Amherst. It began to be a time of farewells and of last-minute reappraisals.

For the President, a promise had remained unfulfilled, a visit to Belgium. In the days of waiting for a final German reply to the revised peace terms, he made the trip, long deferred by the unremitting grind of the conference. It turned out to be a happy experience. The young King Leopold proved an enthusiastic host, diverting and congenial, given to driving his own car at extravagant speeds. The fact that the schedule had to be compressed from three days to two seemed to bother him not at all. Rather than shorten the route he drove at higher speeds, forcing the official cavalcade to keep up. Proceeding at fifty or even sixty miles an hour the President was carried across the war-damaged countryside, to be given glimpses of damaged villages and factories systematically denuded of all vestiges of machinery. In formerly rich industrial cities, chimneys stood smokeless. The President shed his business suit for a long white duster, and at lunch on the first day of the trip was almost devoured by mosquitoes.

He had brought with him on the journey his chief economic advisers. The addresses he made at various stops showed the influence of their views, though touched by Wilson's own idealism and magnanimity. The Belgians were less moved by visions of international peace than by assurances that their economic needs were fully recognized. Wilson told them what they wanted to hear, that they would be given priority in receiving credit and raw materials necessary for their industrial revival. They would then become, said Wilson, "our generous and dangerous rivals."[28] That rivalry he welcomed. The image of a Europe restored by American aid, standing on its own feet economically and in vigorous competition with the new world, is another example of Wilson being ahead of his time—or of having too little time to achieve his aims.

The tour concluded on the second day with a lunch given by the American minister; a convocation of the Belgium chamber of deputies; an appearance at the Brussels town hall; and finally the king's farewell dinner. In between was the presentation of an honorary degree by the University of Louvain, in a setting particularly dramatic. In the roofless, half-ruined library of the university Wilson recalled the enormity of the crime against civilization and humane learning inflicted by the Germans early in the war. Afterwards he drove to Malines to meet Cardinal Mercier, the famous churchman known for his defiance of the Germans. In his address to the Belgian parliament Wilson had referred to him grandly as "the true shepherd of his flock, the majesty of whose spiritual authority awed even the unscrupulous enemy."[29] Throughout the tour, indeed, Wilson had spoken with entire felicity, with an almost perfect choice of word and phrase. It was late at night, after a farewell to the king, that his train pulled out from the Brussels station. The next morning Baker, expecting to find him exhausted at the end of the strenuous journey, noted that, on the contrary, he was wearing a new straw hat and looked particularly fit.

Among the events decreed by protocol before his final departure was a dinner tendered by the president of the French Republic. Wilson took it into his head not to go. He did not like Poincaré. He particularly resented his having been the source of many hostile rumors and having allied himself with Foch against Clemenceau. Nevertheless one would have assumed that, having borne so much under the guise of duty, Wilson would willingly have taken on a last official chore. House pleaded with him in vain. The President, House recorded in his diary, had "no notion of eating with Poincaré, . . . he would choke if he sat at the table with him." When House continued, no doubt too insistently and to the point of provoking Wilson's annoyance, "He looked at me," House added, "but made no reply."[30] Wilson's behavior appears odd, but it speaks suggestively of his gradually losing patience with a busy-minded counselor.

In the end, of course, he did go. Jusserand, very probably prodded by House, came to the Paris residence to make the case. The diplomatically sensitive Henry White put in his oar. On the grounds that the German delegation had postponed the actual signing by two days, Wilson declared he could attend the Poincaré dinner and still arrive on time at the waiting *George Washington*. The dinner was a grand affair when it came off on June 26, such an event as the French knew how to prepare brilliantly. Tables were set for three hundred at the Élysée Palace; as the guests crossed the brightly lit courtyard the Garde Républicaine rolled out a salute on the kettle drums. The French president said the right things, and Wilson responded, some thought a little stiffly, but with words of apt simplicity. "We shall continue to be comrades," he said of the Americans and the French. "Though the ocean is broad, it will seem very narrow in the future."[31]

The concluding ceremony, marking the signing of the peace, was played out on a low key, with little of the drama that had marked the presentation of peace terms to the Germans in the Petit Trianon. Though the famous Hall of Mirrors glittered and shone, the peace delegations had abandoned formal dress and wore ordinary black afternoon clothes. Officials, representatives of the press, and a carefully selected group of guests crowded to overflowing the long narrow room. But this time there were no breathlessly awaited declarations, no real uncertainty as to the outcome. A plain business was accomplished by successive strokes of the pen. The Chinese refused to come, and a protest by General Smuts against the harsh terms of the treaty was the only other indication of tensions lying below the surface. Afterwards the Big Four walked together in the square before the palace, where crowds cheered them and photographers recorded the scene. Wilson found the route back to Paris lined with people shouting his name.

At nine-thirty in the evening he was driven to the Paris railway station where he had first arrived just six months before. He was given a fitting farewell by men with whom he had worked and struggled in daily conference; by aides and advisers left on the scene to finish the remaining details; by milling onlookers, curious and grateful, who had never quite lost faith in the tall, serious American now turning homeward. Clemenceau showed visible emotion at the parting. Colonel House, bidding Wilson good-bye, could scarcely have imagined that he would never see again this friend of past days.

CHAPTER ELEVEN

Fighter for the League

◆

SUMMER OF DISCONTENT

Wilson returned to the United States prepared to fight seriously and hard to gain ratification of the treaty by the Senate. The sea voyage had refreshed him. On board were his economic advisers, Baruch, Frank William Taussig, Lamont, Norman Davis, and McCormick. He enjoyed talking with them, while Baker and Grayson, inveterate diarists, recorded lively conversations on education and politics, along with the humorous stories of which the President had an endless supply. "Mrs. W. hauls him out every day to walk," noted Edith Benham, "which he despises but does meekly."[1] The Fourth of July was celebrated in mid-passage, with games and ceremonies, and an address by the President to the soldiers and crew assembled on deck.

His main work on board was to write the address laying the treaty before the Senate. It would be the first time a President had submitted a treaty in person, and he recognized the historic significance of the occasion. The opening day's draft was discarded, probably the only time in Wilson's life, Grayson remarked, when his disciplined mind had fallen short of the desired result.[2] Despite his appearance of well-being, he was suffering from the fatigue of the long Paris debates and from the aftermath of his small stroke in April, together with increasing hypertension. Moreover he was turning from one area of struggle, one mode of discourse, to another. In a phrase he often used, he was like a ship "in irons." The disdain with which he regarded Republican Senate leaders made it the more difficult for him to find the right tone. But on July 5 he summoned his shipboard advisers and read them a draft, accepting their comments good-naturedly.

Anxious to make his appearance before the Senate a first priority, he discarded plans for a formal welcome and resolved to get to the capital at the earliest moment. The *George Washington* landed at Hoboken, New Jersey; the President and his party went by ferry to Twenty-third Street in Manhattan, where they were greeted by New York's governor, Alfred E. Smith, and the mayor, John Hylan. From here the motorcade, on its way to Carnegie Hall, turned into a triumphant procession, with crowds estimated at 100,000 lining the streets. The exchange of official welcomes gave the President opportunity for some agreeably sentimental remarks on his pleasure at being back—and for some relatively mild gibes at his political opponents. At midnight he arrived in Washington. He was again welcomed by large crowds, gathered around the Union Station. The reception, Wilson told Grayson, was "one of the greater surprises in his life"; and when he at last crossed the threshold of home, "This house never looked so beautiful,"[3] he said.

Two days later, with the treaty under his arm and accompanied by Lodge, he walked down the Senate aisle. The galleries were crowded to the last seat, while outside, under a pelting rain, thousands waited in the vain hope of gaining entrance. All sensed the opening of a great contest. And yet the speech did not go well. Reading from small cards, Wilson stumbled several times in a way unusual for him, and only when he reached passages expounding the League did his voice gain its familiar timbre. He was followed attentively, but in a silence unbroken by applause until the end.[4]

Republicans, most of whom had refrained from taking part in the opening ovation, were obviously withholding applause. Others listened undemonstratively to a measured exposition of the long process of peace-making; while an appreciation of American fighting men, coming near the start of his address, was too poignant to invite applause. "They were the sort of men ... every American would wish to claim as fellow countrymen and comrades in a great cause," Wilson said in a moving tribute. "They were terrible in battle, and gentle and helpful out of it, remembering the mothers and the sisters, the wives and the little children at home. They were free men under arms, not forgetting their ideals of duty in the midst of tasks of violence." At the end, when it appeared he had finished, Wilson looked up from his manuscript, and his concluding words echoed through the hushed chamber. They were words which might be taken as an epitome of his career as a statesman: "The stage is set, the destiny disclosed. It has come about by no plan of our conceiving, but by the hand of God who led us into this way. We cannot turn back. . . . The light streams upon the path ahead, and nowhere else."

Wilson praised his colleagues at the peace table (some of his intimates thought overenthusiastically); but he drew on deep strains of historical realism in describing the conditions that had shaped, and so often misshaped, the results. "It was not easy," he said, "to graft the new order of ideas on the old, and some of the fruits of the grafting may, I fear, for a time be bitter." In regard to the immediate political situation he was not, however, realistic at all. Failing to acknowledge the concerns of the opposition, he described the peace treaty and the League in general terms, without clarification or defense of controversial features long under debate. "I was petrified with surprise," confided one friendly senator to his diary. Having hoped for political sustenance he got something (he complained) like Longfellow's "Psalm of Life."[5]

It was not that Wilson was averse to discussing details. In a press conference attended by a hundred reporters just after the Senate speech he dealt frankly with Article X and other disputed clauses (though in words not subject to quotation); and he lingered in the President's Room to discuss the treaty with senators who came by. In the central address he appears simply to have misjudged the occasion, an error rare for him, and thus to have lost the supreme opportunity to get his points of view before the lawmakers and the public in their most effective and authoritative form.

At the same time he ignored one of the most pregnant passages in his earlier writings. In *Constitutional Government in the United States*, his crowning work as a political scientist, he had maintained that, while the Senate traditionally gives way on appointments, the President, just as certainly, leaves with the Senate a large measure of discretion in the consideration of treaties.[6] His memory, or his judgment, failed because he had already conceived such disdain for Lodge and other members of the Senate Foreign Relations Committee that he could not imagine bringing himself to defer to them. For the same reason he could not imagine his own well-formed views being successfully challenged.

Beyond the first, flawed opening of his campaign for the treaty, Wilson had a number of stratagems he was prepared to put into effect. He would be conciliatory with Republicans who were offering so-called mild reservations, meeting with them individually to present the case for ratification. He would work strenuously with Hitchcock, the Senate minority leader, to hold his party in line against amendments which would require renegotiation of the treaty. He would meet with members of the Senate Foreign Relations Committee as a whole, responding candidly to their questions. Finally, kept in reserve, was the possibility of an appeal to the people.

Wilson pursued these various tactics during the summer of 1919, endeavoring to put together a majority sufficient for ratification. Each could be criticized as being not enough in itself, but taken together they appeared to afford a real chance of success. Two major factors, however, conspired to diminish the effect of his efforts. In the first place he tended to misread the attitudes and current opinions of his countrymen. The League was popular, as he believed it to be—it had widespread editorial support, had been endorsed by a vast majority of state legislatures and state governors, as well as by most public-spirited citizens; but the intensity of feeling for the League had fallen off as the war receded into the distance. Economic difficulties, highlighted by strikes and by a steadily rising cost of living; racial tensions spurred by population shifts and new social pressures in wartime; above all a desire to get back to private enjoyments—all these diverted the country from idealistic efforts.

Second, Wilson underestimated the force of the partisan passions opposed to him. He had himself done much to inject the League into party politics, but the Republicans, and especially the Senate leadership, fully shared the blame. The Republican editor William Allen White put the matter fairly. The trouble, he wrote in the *Emporia Gazette*, arose not because of Wilson's performance at Paris. The President "really did strive sincerely and well for genuinely wise things"; and as for faults in the treaty, they could be remedied later by amendment, as the American constitution had been. "The real danger in the situation is a political danger."

The Republicans, White continued, could not get together on a program of social, industrial, and economic reconstruction. But they could get together on beating the Democrats on foreign policy. "They want an issue and they are jeopardizing the peace of the world to make it. It is small business."[7]

The political danger was personified by Lodge, whose chances of success Wilson underestimated, though not for that reason mollifying his hatred for the man. Lodge was mortally afraid that the Democrats would forge a popular record as peacemakers and that Wilson would march into a third term. Within his sphere Lodge was experienced and supremely skilled. Indeed in Taft's administration he had already shown how to kill treaties—in this case treaties of arbitration—by tacking on dubious amendments until the then-President felt compelled to shelve them without action. Through most of the early battles of the New Freedom he had been ill or absent from the Senate, but he drew aim on

Wilson after the Fourteen Points address, and thereafter he never wearied, and never wavered, in his determination to humiliate the President and to defeat his party.

Nevertheless the situation within the Senate did not give Lodge any real assurance of success. He had packed the Republican side of the Foreign Relations Committee with diehard opponents of the League; here he could wield power by instigating delays and promoting destructive amendments. But Lodge did not control the Republican moderates in the Senate as a whole. These could be expected to vote with the Democrats in favor of an unamended treaty, though not one without reservations. Assuming Wilson could hold all the Democrats in line, the votes of only nineteen Republicans needed to be added to assure ratification.

The Wilson of an earlier time, the shrewd and practiced politician, would certainly have found it possible to forge a coalition from among the differing elements to put the treaty across. But Wilson in the summer of 1919 was a depleted man. Exhaustion, recurrent illnesses, the steady drain of untreated hypertension had taken their toll. Ike Hoover, who watched the President closely, remarked on the apparent energy, the strong determination, that marked him on first returning from Europe. Yet Hoover adds ominously that something did not appear quite right. He tells how the President seemed increasingly to harbor his strength, taking frequent rests and conducting his business, not in the Executive Office, but in the residential quarters of the White House.[8]

Mrs. Wilson and Grayson were certainly apprehensive; they combined their forces to try to forestall at all costs the proposed western speaking tour. Underscoring their concern was, as will be seen, a brief but serious incident in early July which may well have been a forerunner of the massive stroke of early October. Thus difficulties Wilson was having with his memory, and also certain ingrained faults of temperament, were intensified at a time when circumstances called him to be at his most astute and clearheaded.

The President's efforts to reach and conciliate the opposition began immediately after his Senate address. He had always been chary of opening himself to extended interviews with congressmen, but on July 15 he announced that he would welcome them, without appointment, any morning between 10:00 A.M. and noon. The following day he specifically invited eight Republican senators, those who favored reservations but were basically supportive of the League, to come individually for extended talks. These conferences began July 17.

Avoiding anything that might be taken for pressure, Wilson explained at length the significance of various aspects of the treaty, and his reasons for not wanting them to be changed. He was open to reservations expressed separately from the act of ratification, but feared that anything of a substantive nature, requiring renegotiation of the terms of the treaty, would lead to endless delays and would open the floodgates of further demands by European countries. He knew how precariously the various portions of the document had been stitched together in Paris, and how easily the whole fabric could be torn apart, now that earlier pressures were being relaxed. The senators listened, put their questions, and went out, usually to assert that their minds had not been altered by the interview.

Wilson was fortunate in having for his chief representative in the Senate Gilbert M. Hitchcock of Nebraska, the minority leader. The two men had differed on policies leading up to the war and Wilson had done his best to deny him the chairmanship of the Foreign Relations Committee. But in 1919 Hitchcock's genuine enthusiasm for the League put him squarely on the President's side. They cooperated closely during the early struggle for ratification. Later, when Wilson was incapacitated by illness, Hitchcock often acted on his own, but always with the President's interests in mind. He was now ideally suited by disposition and experience for the task in hand, that of building up a coalition and getting the League through—if not unchanged, at least with reasonable reservations.

On July 18 Sir William Wiseman visited the President, and his account, cabled to the Foreign Office, gives what is probably an accurate picture of Wilson's state of mind at this time. He looked tired, but he was, wrote Wiseman, confident that the treaty would be ratified. He had abandoned, "for the time being at any rate," his defiant attitude and was dealing with the Senate opposition "seriously and patiently." The next several days, Wilson told him, would reveal when ratification might be expected. Meanwhile he was resolved to hold the line on substantive amendments, standing with the other Great Powers for the League and the treaty as they had been written. If he did not, he said, the newly created states would make extravagant demands, and Bolshevism would present a grave danger to Europe.[9]

The day after this interview Wilson boarded the *Mayflower* for a weekend cruise. Prolonged heat had lain over Washington, and he was anxious to get away. Under heavy showers the party proceeded to the Navy Yard, and boarded the Presidential yacht as storms broke. Lightning and thunder followed them down the Potomac. The President was not feeling well and remained in bed for the two days of the cruise. On the return to Washington Grayson told the press that Wilson was suffering from dysentery, that he had had an uncomfortable day, and that his condition, while not serious, might require his remaining in bed for several additional days. Coming from Grayson, these were strong words. They almost certainly masked one more small stroke, which affected Wilson's capacity to operate at optimal efficiency and was a warning of events to come.

As he so often did, Wilson showed remarkable powers of recuperation. After one day of rest in the White House he insisted on resuming his conferences with the Republican senators. It was clear, however, that he was not making progress. Approval of the treaty without reservations was not within the range of political realities; and he was not ready to define those that might prove acceptable. The Senate Foreign Relations Committee was doing everything possible to postpone a settlement. It considered outlandish amendments, prepared to hear a long list of witnesses, and even listened, more or less intently, as Lodge consumed two weeks of precious time reading out loud the entire text of the treaty. In London Colonel House, assisted by Raymond B. Fosdick, worked to prepare for the first meeting of the League, scheduled for the autumn. Meanwhile much of the world's business—its economic reconstruction and its political pacification—waited on the treaty's approval and the League's establishment.

To break the deadlock, Wilson decided to send a public letter to Senator Lodge, stating that he would not oppose interpretive reservations embodying America's understanding of the League, but that he remained unalterably opposed to anything that would require a new round of negotiations with other powers. Before he could issue the letter, Lodge responded to an offer Wilson had made earlier, to put his full knowledge of the treaty before the committee at any time, either informally or in formal session. Taking up the offer, Lodge requested a meeting of the committee with the President. Wilson jumped at the opportunity and arrangements were promptly made.

He proposed that the committee, meeting in the White House, set up their own stenographers in the mansion's basement. Filling it to capacity, the operation came as near as was possible to the live broadcasts of a later day. Working in brief relays, five Senate stenographers typed up the discussion verbatim and released it in sections to the waiting press. Nothing was confidential. Meanwhile Swem alone recorded for the White House the whole three-and-a-half-hour meeting.

Addressing the lawmakers gathered in the East Room on August 19,[10] Wilson began with a prepared statement (substantially the same as the aborted letter to Lodge) embracing a plea for swift action and a willingness to accept interpretive reservations. The senators then began the questioning. They had done their homework and were armed with technical and often tricky points. Wilson responded with confidence and with apparent mastery of detail, sailing successfully between the twin dangers of claiming too much power for the League and offending the senators, and too little power, offending Europeans counting on it for their defense. On numerous, mostly technical, questions, his memory failed, and he got himself bogged down in a long and confusing discussion of the difference between "legal" and "moral" obligations. Puzzling, though little noted at the time, was his repeated insistence that he had not known of the secret treaties until his arrival in Paris.* If the performance was not vintage Wilson, it was a Wilson overcoming to a convincing degree the handicaps of fatigue and recent illness, a Wilson who remained controlled and affable throughout.

As the discussion dragged through an interminable morning, the President expressed regret at trespassing on the senators' usual lunch hour. He had arranged for some food to be prepared and he invited them all to remain. "It would be very delightful," he managed to say, notwithstanding his evident dislike of the company.

The points of difference between the President and the senators were, in the main, the same as had been voiced from the time of the Covenant's first draft. The senators wanted special recognition of the Monroe Doctrine; an unambiguous right to withdraw; explicit exclusion of domestic issues from the League's jurisdiction; and protection of Congress's constitutional authority to declare war. Wilson had accepted the need to clarify these points while in Paris and had fought long battles to amend the text. At the time he had every reason to believe that he had satisfied the opposition and gained assurance of ratification.

The one issue on which real differences of opinion existed (and the one upon which the League ultimately foundered) was Article X. This

---

*Wilson's knowledge of the secret treaties, prior to the opening of the peace conference, has been much debated. In fact, his statements on the subject at the White House conference are in general supported by the most recent scholarly research. (For a full discussion of how for so long, despite many appearances to the contrary, he managed to ignore the details of these treaties see the discussion by the Editors of the Woodrow Wilson Papers, in note 27 to "A Conversation with Members of the Senate Foreign Relations Committee," PWW, 62:365–66.)

embodied an obligation on the part of all members of the League to defend the political independence of its member states and to preserve them against external aggression. Whatever might be said or done, this concept of collective security drew a line between parties and men, between internationalism and the various shades of antiinternationalism. For Wilson it was, and remained, the heart of the League, and for the most extreme of his opponents it remained the reason for their determination to kill it.

By the time the senators met with Wilson in the White House, the treaty as a whole had been scanned and fresh issues of controversy had been defined. Among Americans of German extraction the harsh economic and territorial claims were considered opprobrious. The Shantung settlement provoked violent hostility, particularly in the West. In constituencies where Irish-Americans predominated, vigorous objections were raised to the fact that in the League assembly the participation of the British Empire was swelled by admission of India and the dominions. Dissent on these specific points was fanned by the diehards into a growing, but still controllable, flame of general opposition.

From another source, American liberals and intellectuals, came opposition hardly less pronounced. Disappointed by the treaty's failure to follow more narrowly the Fourteen Points, they maintained that the League would have the effect of solidifying and guaranteeing a basically unjust order. Article X of the charter, protecting the territorial integrity of its member states, was as strongly opposed by them on the ground that it would prevent change, as it was opposed, for quite different reasons, by isolationist senators.

Among younger liberals, Fosdick and Seymour argued that the League—born, as Wilson had said, "to be a living thing"—would rectify boundaries and modify injustices. In a different camp was Walter Lippmann who, after being a strong supporter of the League, swung to the opposite pole. Turning the *New Republic* into a violently anti-League organ, he argued that the peace treaty was essentially unsound and that Article X would freeze its injustices beyond any hope for change. Lippmann embraced the isolationists in the Senate, even going so far as to provide Hiram W. Johnson of California, a leader of the opposition, with a line of questioning to be used against the President in the White House meeting.[11]

The anti-League and anti-Wilson intellectuals found their case summed up, and served with an irresistible relish, when in October 1919, John Maynard Keynes published his *Economic Consequences of the Peace.* The British financial expert argued with what at the time seemed unassailable logic that the treaty would subject Germany to total economic devastation. He also created the image of Wilson, and to a lesser extent of his colleagues at the peace table, as doddering or Machiavellian. For a generation or more the brilliance of Keynes's rhetoric determined the way the sophisticated public judged the peace conference.

Two issues of foreign policy, not directly related to the League, agitated the Senate at this same time. The first was the security treaty with France, guaranteeing that the United States would come to its defense in the case of unprovoked aggression by Germany. A promise to submit the treaty to the Senate had been won from Wilson at Paris as the price of French renunciation of claims to the left bank of the Rhine. In the best of circumstances this would have been a sensitive issue; now in the troubled atmosphere of Washington it was an embarrassment and one to which Wilson faced up reluctantly. The Senate committee pressed him to submit the treaty; he acquiesced, after intending to postpone it, and then did so tentatively and inconclusively. He never pushed for ratification, an indication of his own crumbling leadership and of the confusion into which the fight for the League had deteriorated.

The administration's Russian policy was the second area of concern and disagreement. American troops remained in Siberia and the Foreign Relations Committee, not unreasonably, wanted to know what they were doing there. In reply to a Senate inquiry of July 22 Wilson stated the simple facts. Two companies of American railway troops, all volunteers, remained temporarily around Vladivostok to keep open the Tran-Siberian Railway. A local population that had fought effectively with the Allies while Russia was in the war now found itself in desperate need of food, medicines, and other supplies. To aid them was a humanitarian obligation and the sole purpose for the deployment.

Beneath the surface, however, was a highly complex situation. It went back to the spring of 1918, when the President had made his decision to give support to the Czech troops stranded in Russia. There was not only confusion as to the precise situation of these Czechs, but, as the months passed, there were questions about the mission of the Americans. Were they merely aiding the Czechs? Or were they opposing the Bolsheviks, or counterbalancing Japan's military presence in the area?

The major anti-Bolshevik figure in the field was Admiral Alexander Kolchak. Seeing him as a possible winner in the civil war, the Allies backed him militarily; but Wilson was not drawn into this trap. The commander of the American expedition forces in Siberia, General William S. Graves, was, fortunately, a man to observe strictly the President's policy of nonintervention. Wilson joined the British and French in endeavoring to elicit from Kolchak an understanding as to his views, in case he should establish himself in political power. But Kolchak was a military man whose views on democracy were vague at best; moreover, he failed to win decisive victories. The U.S. senators had reason to be puzzled by the situation in Siberia, and to be concerned that American forces were not more rapidly withdrawn. The anticipated limit of "a few weeks" was, in fact, stretched repeatedly; not until October 1920 did the last U.S. contingent leave Russian soil.

The urgency of domestic problems also intruded upon Wilson's fight for the League. Having disbanded the war agencies in haste, he was shorn of powers that might have enabled him to deal effectively with postwar reconstruction. Moreover, he had little in the way of reforms to suggest. Traces of the old progressivism might appear now and then, as when on the journey home he stated that necessities like water, electricity, and railways, "which are now a part of our national life as air for our lungs,"[12] should be managed by government. The time for well-worked-out schemes, he said, would soon be ripe. On issues of civil rights he was, moreover, still the liberal; and on these he was determined to act.

Before leaving Paris he cabled the Attorney General and the Postmaster General, asking that they arrange for complete pardon of U.S. citizens convicted of antigovernment expressions in speech or print during wartime. This was followed by a message to the Secretary of War calling for as wide an amnesty as possible for conscientious objectors. Baker responded promptly with a measured program, which Wilson accepted *in toto*. Burleson and Palmer, however, did not share Wilson's sense of urgency. The former advised his chief that there had been no wartime convictions for mere expression of opinion: all convictions had been made under statutes—a distinction undoubtedly lost on some of those suffering from imprisonment. Palmer advised that he would be ready to recommend an amnesty only after the peace treaty had been ratified.

The summer of 1919 was not, at best, conducive to the kind of magnanimity that Wilson was prepared to practice. Severe race riots broke out; lynchings occurred across the country. In Washington that July the Secretary of War, after consulting with the President, called up troops to maintain civil peace, and the imposition of martial law was narrowly averted. Popular passions that were to ignite the red scare and the wholesale arrests of aliens were already smoldering.

Meanwhile, a wide range of economic problems, crystallized in a concern for the high cost of living, confronted the President. For a time he called off the meetings with Republican senators and devoted himself to the growing internal crisis. Hoarding and racketeering were seen to be the major factors driving up food prices. Unions reacted by demanding an increase in wages, while industrial leaders were quite ready to prolong restrictions imposed on labor during the war. Wilson saw his task to be that of maintaining industrial peace and, at the same time, of halting the upward spiral of prices.

As often in the past he set himself to mobilizing opinion by an address to Congress. He called on cabinet members to make recommendations, and the message as delivered was in large part a collage of their separate contributions.[13] A wide-ranging program against racketeers and others abusing the system was to be enforced by severe penalties, with the separate departments taking action within their fields. Unlike most of Wilson's messages it lacked a central theme and seemed meandering and overlong.

The most immediate threat of a devastating strike came from the railwaymen who were still under wartime restrictions and felt themselves gravely disadvantaged by the rise in food prices. On August 25, Wilson met with the shopmen, delivering a strong plea for patience and restraint, and issued a formal message (written by the director general of railroads, Walter D. Hines) to the public at large. The administration had apparently carried the day. The President, wrote Justice Brandeis to a friend, "seems to have grappled effectively with domestic labor outbreaks, and will doubtless secure ratification of the treaty."[14]

The course of the treaty was not, however, at all reassuring. Wilson waited for a favorable turn after his conference with the Senate committee on August 19; it was difficult to discern one. On the day following the meeting Senator Key Pittman, apparently with White House approval, introduced four interpretative reservations following the President's views as stated at the conference and also embodying the substance of seven mild reservations submitted earlier by Republicans. It looked as if the moment of compromise had arrived. "I can only hope, and hope without confidence," Wilson wrote to a friend on August 21.[15] But the moment passed. The committee under Lodge showed little interest in the Pittman proposal. After hearings bringing forth hostile witnesses, votes were taken on amendments so irresponsible and often so preposterous as to infuriate the President. On August 25 an amendment was considered that would have directly reversed the Shantung settlement. This was rubbing salt into an open wound, and in a state of cumulative anger Wilson took one of the fateful decisions of his career.

He decided, finally, that he would embark on the long-contemplated (and often deferred) western tour. To bring the cause of the League before the people was one of the weapons he had held in reserve through-out the trying summer of 1919. It was one, moreover, he had often used in the past and that was deeply embedded in his ideas of statesmanship. At Princeton he had gone to the alumni as to his constituents; his term as governor was one long series of appeals from the stump. When the issue of preparedness arose, he made a wide swing around the country. He had frequently mentioned the possibility of a western tour on behalf of the League, and on shipboard coming home he had drawn up a list of topics to discuss. But he was not anxious to take the personal and political risks involved. He canceled the project more than once, and then embarked on it against opposition and in the face of warnings as to the possible cost.

The most consistent opposition came from Edith Wilson and Dr. Grayson. Wilson's wife and his doctor saw at close hand what others could only infer from the President's often disappointing and unchar-acteristic public performances—his fumbling with the typed cards in presenting the treaty to the Senate; his inability to control his own administration so as to gain amnesty for wartime offenders; his lack of intellectual drive in formulating an economic program; his memory lapses when he met with the Senate committee. They saw that he was a man of diminished force, heading—unless he conserved his strength —for a certain breakdown.

Other reasons than health militated against the trip. In Washington public business had accumulated, some of it left over from his long absence abroad, some arising out of new developments both domestic and international. It would prove impossible to deal with these problems amid the confusions and the gargantuan efforts of the speaking tour. Even more serious was the question of whether the trip could accomplish anything tangible. As a politically astute journalist warned Wilson, Sen-ator Reed Smoot (one of the League's arch-opponents) was hardly likely to change his votes because the President talked to his constituents out in Utah, while he might be impressed if the President talked to him in Washington.[16] Reaching over the heads of the senators might, indeed, do positive harm. An appeal to the nation might work with House members, as Wilson himself had long since pointed out, but "the Senate is not so immediately sensitive to opinion and is apt to grow, if anything, more stiff if pressure of that kind is brought to bear upon it."[17]

Yet another aspect of the projected tour was, it seems clear, influencing Wilson. He had almost invariably shown himself prepared to face reality when the showdown came. It was in the nature of his leadership to stand upon a principle, but in its application, after marshaling and consolidating his forces, to take circumstances into due account. In Princeton, in the struggles for the New Freedom, in Paris, Wilson fashioned compromises without feeling himself defeated. But like a skillful player he made sure before the final settlement that his own base was as secure as possible. When he toured the country on the issue of preparedness, it was to return, his popularity and authority enhanced, to hammer out a reasonable policy. When he ordered the *George Washington* sent full steam to Brest, it was to permit him to bargain from a strong hand. Now, as the month of August waned in Washington, Wilson was certainly aware that he could not get the League passed without some changes. He was aware, also, that he would need to command the full resources of his office when he entered into the critical negotiations.

Two days before the date set for his departure, the White House staff was informed that the President wanted to see Senator Hitchcock on the morrow "as long before seven o'clock, his leaving time, as possible."[18] When Hitchcock came, the President presented him with a memorandum containing reservations on the four disputed League articles. A suggested preamble read: "The Senate of the United States advises and consents to ratification of said treaty with the following understanding of the said treaty . . . and requests the President of the United States to communicate these interpretations to the several [European] States."[19] Hitchcock was not permitted to identify these reservations as coming from the White House. They were to remain in his keeping, the basis for later negotiations and for final agreement. Meanwhile, the President would go off on his own journey, confirming his political strength, testing the opinion of the American people.

Besides instructing Hitchcock, there were other matters to be taken care of, as the President cleared his desk like any other man facing an imminent long voyage. On August 29 he wrote his daughter Jessie not to delay the christening of young Woodrow because of the vagaries of her "incalculable father": "He goes where he must, not where he would, though he prays some day to be free again."[20] To Charles Shinn, his friend from Johns Hopkins days, now a forester living in the West, he wrote about the forthcoming San Francisco visit: "I am going to beg that you will not hesitate to invade my hotel and demand to see me. . . . I shall look forward with genuine pleasure to seeing my old classmate."[21] On public matters he framed instructions for the Secretary of Labor to summon a major industrial conference to meet on his return in October;

and he cabled House that he expected to see the League ratified at about the same time.

The member of a group which had appealed for amnesty and for a full pardon of Eugene V. Debs (on the ground of the latter's advanced years and high moral character, notwithstanding his violation of law) received encouraging words.* To the petitioner, John Spargo of Vermont, the President expressed "nothing but thanks" for his "candid letter." The letter, he said, "concerns a matter that I have more nearly at heart, I think, than I have been able to make evident. I assure you that I am going to deal with the matter as early and in as liberal a spirit as possible."[22] At the same time he dispatched a note to his attorney general. "Spargo is right," he said, and he ordered that action be "promptly formulated and taken."[23]

In this spirit, and with these hopes, Wilson set out upon his westward trip.

WESTERN TOUR

On the evening of September 2, 1919, in Washington's Union Station, the President boarded his private car, named (like the Presidential yacht) the *Mayflower*. Tumulty had planned the trip carefully. It would bring the President over the next twenty-seven days as far as the Pacific Coast, passing through the western and midwestern states where isolationist sentiment was strong. It called for more than thirty major speeches, with stops in the hometowns of some of the League's most convinced detractors. The South, firmly Democratic territory, would in the main be bypassed, as would the Northeast, which was strongly Republican. On board, in addition to a large representation of the press, would be Tumulty, master political tactician; Grayson, keeper of the President's health; and Swem, the indefatigable stenographer. And of course there would be Mrs. Wilson, overseeing every detail of her husband's comfort and adding a particular element of crowd appeal. What was not planned in advance was the grim drama created by Wilson's growing symptoms of debility, concealed through the early stages of the trip and contrasting sharply with the public excitement, the cheering crowds, the parades and ovations.

---

*Debs had been sentenced to ten years imprisonment for speaking in violation of the wartime Espionage Act.

To reporters, as he boarded the train, he gave the impression of being "in excellent health," in "good trim."[1] Fortunately, for it required all of his natural resiliency to make the best of an inauspicious beginning of the tour in Columbus, Ohio. The meagerness of the crowds in the streets could be explained by a local trolley strike or by bad weather, but nevertheless to the newspapermen the reception appeared almost an insult—a "painful anticlimax,"[2] wrote one, to the demonstrations that had greeted the President in Europe. At the state capitol only a fifth of the two thousand seats in the reviewing stand were full.

But that evening, at least from the point of view of numbers, things went better; the hall where he delivered his first scheduled address was crowded. Wearing a dark grey business suit and a comfortable, turned-down collar, the President spoke slowly for the first few minutes, seeming to choose his words carefully. He had left the confinement of Washington, he said, to report to his fellow countrymen "concerning those affairs of the world which now need to be settled."[3] Then, as it appeared to one observer, he switched to the tone of the schoolmaster: "It was a rare treat to see him become the punctilious pedagogue again."[4] But Wilson was lecturing a class which had no pressing interest in the facts he was trying to convey. To Ohioans the Covenant and the details of the treaty were remote subjects. Though they listened politely, they did not appear eager to obey his injunction to read for themselves the text of the peace—if indeed they could have imagined where to look for it. Wilson nevertheless appeared in good spirits to the newspapermen who questioned him afterwards, expressing himself as satisfied with his reception.

At Indianapolis, the next stop, organized Republican efforts to obstruct the President were evident. The spirit of the old campaigner was awakened, and the crowds responded eagerly. But it was in St. Louis, where Wilson appeared jauntily in a straw hat (everyone else was wearing sober felts) that the tour began to hit its stride. Large crowds were out in the streets as the President toured the city for two and a half hours, halting his caravan to greet old academic friends at Washington University. Edith Wilson came in for special attention. Her dress of navy blue satin, with short sleeves and a rather low neckline, was thought to reveal a distinctly Parisian touch.[5]

That night at the Coliseum, where Wilson had been nominated for a second term, he received what was considered one of the greatest ovations in the history of the city. This was enemy country; Republicans calling themselves a "truth squad" were following with meetings of their own. After the relatively tepid atmosphere elsewhere, electricity was in the air, and Wilson knew well how to stir passions and to lift them into the service of an ideal. After that the excitement was repeated in Kansas City, and it reached new heights in Des Moines. There the streets overflowed with a surging mass that repeatedly broke through the police lines. Touring the city, the President stood up the whole way in his automobile, smiling and waving greetings.

By now the newspapermen, both the local press in the cities through which the train passed and the correspondents aboard, were beginning to make favorable assessments of the tour. Wilson was careful to avoid partisanship; but, as the Washington *Post* observed, the crowds were delighted to hear him "lambaste" obstructionist senators.[6] They were keyed up to battle; they were clearly for the treaty and the League, yet they were not insisting that one man receive all the credit. Some mild reservations, quickly assented to, seemed to them the best way out of the growing stalemate. Wilson, as the press noted, steered a course between subservience to his opponents and outright defiance, often giving credit to those with honest doubts. Though ready to predict a dire fate for anyone who insisted on altering the treaty, he would almost invariably add the saving words "in any important respect."

The New York Times reported on September 8 that the President was enjoying every minute of the trip, and that instead of being wearied by the strenuous schedule he appeared to be "refreshed as he goes along." His voice was holding out well. Despite the need to reach audiences of fifteen thousand or more, without means of amplification, it faltered only once, for a moment, in Kansas City, a lapse which he attributed to "an old Paris cold." When the train stopped overnight at Des Moines, to give the President and his party a first night of rest in a hotel, one phase of the tour had been successfully accomplished. Ahead, over the next week, were to be stops leading to the Pacific Coast, through states often sparsely populated but the seat of some of the League's most fervent opponents. Eleven major addresses were scheduled.

The addresses delivered on this part of the tour, often two a day, often lasting more than an hour in length, are on the whole remarkable for their cogency and force. There was almost no time for preparation. The President had left Washington with what long ago, as a young professor, he had called "an empty barrel." One reporter recorded a last glimpse of the President at his typewriter, "pounding the keys strenuously" as the train pulled out from Kansas City.[7] But mostly there were not even typewritten notes. Wilson spun his speeches on the spot, out of firm convictions, out of a deeply ingrained knowledge of events, out of his passion for a cause that he felt could be lost only at peril to the whole civilized world. A lifetime of training marshaled and fired the apparently casual words. Sometimes he repeated himself; sometimes he strayed as he forced himself to go through a labored explanation yet once again. (When this happened Swem, from his stored-up knowledge, would patch up the text that was given out to the public.) But mostly, through all the difficulties—of physical weariness, of overcrowded halls and noisy audiences—he rose to the challenge of the historic debate.

His speaking style was generally colloquial and expository. He could let short sentences fall with the effect of blows. "I would a great deal rather be put out of the world than live in a world boycotted and deserted," he declared at St. Louis in describing League sanctions. "The most terrible thing is outlawry. The most formidable thing is to be absolutely isolated."[8] Or the sentences would take off into flights of unexpected eloquence. Speaking of his "mortification and shame" if unable to fulfill his promises to American servicemen, he would feel compelled to say to them:

> You are betrayed. You fought for something that you did not get. And the glory of the armies and navies of the United States is gone like a dream in the night, and there ensues upon it, in the suitable darkness of the night, the nightmare of dread which lay upon the nations before this war came; and there will come some time, in the vengeful Providence of God, another war in which not a few hundred thousand men from America will have to die, but as many millions as are necessary to accomplish the final freedom of the peoples of the world.[9]

"I have it in my heart," he said, "that if we do not do this great thing now, every woman ought to weep because of the child in her arms."[10] And on another occasion: "There is little for the great part of the history of the world except the bitter tears of pity and the hot tears of wrath."[11]

Moving westward he dealt increasingly with the relation of the peace treaty to the development of a stable and prosperous economy at home. "You have heard so many little things about the treaty," he challenged one audience, "that I thought you might like to hear some big things."[12] Leaving aside the specific clauses under dispute he pictured in broadest terms the disadvantages of isolation as opposed to the advantages of taking part in a new worldwide economic order. "If you want to talk business, I am ready to talk business,"[13] he declared at Des Moines. And so he did—linking America's domestic problems of industrial reconstruction and the high cost of living to sociopolitical reforms on a world scale.

As he developed these themes, the treaty in Wilson's mind became

Henry Cabot Lodge

The return: Union Station, Washington, D.C., September 28, 1919

Starting out: at Columbus, Ohio, September 4, 1919

more and more beneficent and all-encompassing. The struggles in Paris receded into the distance. The agony of compromise was assuaged, and personal differences with his European colleagues dimmed. He had gotten the best he could, and these results he seemed ready to equate with the best that in any circumstances might have been imagined. In general his audiences seemed to agree with him. They were not so much looking for flaws in the treaty as hoping that the whole thing might be settled quickly, once and for all—preferably with a few bones thrown to the troublesome senators, and with some concessions wrung from this proud man whose visions could at the same time arouse them and make them uneasy.

After Des Moines the tour moved farther west, with stops in Nebraska, Minnesota, in the Dakotas and Montana, in Idaho, and then on to Oregon. The President was now in alien country, in cities and regions where isolationist sentiments lay deep, as in Coeur d'Alene, Idaho, where the irreconcilable Senator Borah had his home. He continued to expound in his addresses the mixture of idealism, hard-headed economics, and controlled polemics which had already won him respectful hearings. He added to earlier themes expressions of concern for the lawlessness of radical unions and took favorable note of the distant governor of Massachusetts, Calvin Coolidge, who had put down without equivocation a strike of the Boston police. All troublesome or evil things seemed to spring from uncertainty over the outcome of the League struggle; all good things, from the prospect of its favorable conclusion.

In Seattle, as if struck by the light of the Pacific, he found a new mood. It was to last throughout the week the Presidential party traveled on the West Coast. "The spirit of the crowd seemed at times akin to fanaticism," reported *The New York Times*. "The throngs . . . joined in a continuous and riotous uproar."[14] The police were forced to use harsh measures, and memories of Wilson's reception in Italy were again recalled, this time without reflection upon the American public. Patriotic fervor reached a climax as Wilson reviewed the Pacific fleet, standing bareheaded on the forward turret of the *Oregon*. The next day he was in Portland for what citizens of that city considered a more dignified and appropriate (but no less friendly) welcome.

As another Sunday of comparative rest came around, Wilson could take satisfaction in the fact that he had completed some four thousand miles of the projected ten-thousand-mile trip, and that eighteen of the planned thirty-three speaking engagements had been fulfilled. Newspapermen took stock of where things stood. "The opinion is generally held," said *The New York Times*, "that the President has steadily advanced his cause since he started out on his nationwide tour. . . . It seems a safe assertion that the ten states through which he has passed believe with him that the Treaty of Peace should be ratified without delay and that they are willing to bring the United States into a League of Nations. . . . The President everywhere has received a most generous reception and very attentive hearers."[15] A reporter for a Portland paper spoke of his "evident vigor" and his enjoyment of the welcome in that city.[16] He looked "little older," it was said, than when he had last visited Oregon, in his primary campaign for the Presidency in 1911.

Thus on the surface all seemed to be going well. Another and more somber side of the story, however, was apparent to those who were closest to the President and were watching him closely day and night. His health was plainly deteriorating. Despite all the external signs of success—the enthusiastic crowds, the effective speeches, and the cheerful steadfastness of Wilson's behavior—the walls of the inner citadel had started to crumble. Early in the tour, to minimize the strain, Grayson had forbidden addresses to the crowds that gathered around the rear platform at each stop of his train. On leaving St. Paul, the physician noted in his diary that the President was "very tired" and had suffered a recurrence of the headaches that often troubled him. By the time the tour reached Seattle, he was "not feeling very well . . . the strains of the last days being evident." The night of September 14 at Portland found a sleepless President afflicted by an "extremely troublesome" cough and again suffering from a headache.[17]

Ahead lay what were to be the most challenging and taxing days of the tour, the invasion of California, where he would take issue with Senator Hiram Johnson, intransigent critic of the League. Here Wilson would face a volatile and uncertain public, one that in 1916 had given him the decisive votes necessary to his second-term election, but whose varied passions were now deeply stirred. Not only was the test to be between loyalty to the President and to a popular state leader; in two crucial aspects the peace affronted widely held sentiments. The first was the Shantung settlement, appearing outrageously favorable to Japan; the second, anathema to the state's Irish-Americans, was the charter provision giving votes in the League assembly to the British dominions. That Wilson made of the California incursion what was judged a turning point in his fortunes, that he managed (at least in contemporary journalistic opinion) to neutralize a leading member of the League's Senate death squad, must be put down as a triumph of the spirit over the weakening flesh.

The Presidential train moved down from Oregon through the Siskiyou mountain range, drawn by three huge oil-burning engines, stopping at isolated settlements where the calm was as that preceding a storm. Arriving in San Francisco on September 17, he found the weather hot and the crowds tumultuous. A luncheon address to a large audience of women gave Wilson the opportunity to identify himself with the progressive movement and to stress his efforts to get support for the woman-suffrage amendment. It was remarked that he seemed nervous before an audience of females. In fact a splitting headache made it almost impossible for him to speak.

That night the huge civic auditorium was overcrowded and overheated, the audience was unruly, and Wilson had trouble making himself heard. Yet he persisted, and he presented his case convincingly. Among the press corps, which had begun to see through Grayson's optimistic public statements, there was (according to one of the chief reporters) "universal admiration for the President's qualities as a stayer. . . . His gameness was the more remarkable when it is known, as all of us know, that he had had a splitting headache for two days. To master a crowd twice as big as the hall could accommodate was a performance that rallied his train-mates in fresh admiration."[18] The following day he made another luncheon address as well as talks in Berkeley and Oakland.

In the midst of these public events Wilson made determined efforts to revive links with his past. He managed to see his old classmate Shinn. He dined with the Edward Elliotts—with Madge, Ellen's younger sister who had been so much a part of Princeton days and in later years had receded from the family circle. A little later, in Los Angeles, he lunched with Mary Hulbert at his hotel.

Edith Wilson was present throughout the meeting. In her memoir she refers to the afternoon's guest by her earlier name of Mrs. Peck. She was someone, she states, whom Woodrow "had known in Bermuda many years before . . . a faded sweet-looking woman who was absorbed in an only son."[19] As for Mary Hulbert, she describes the President's wife as being "without question, a woman of strong character."[20] She adds that Edith Wilson was "much more junoesque" than in her photographs.

"All through the long afternoon we talked," Mrs. Hulbert recalls. More acidly Edith states that "darkness had fallen when she finally rose to go." It was obviously not, for any one of the three present, an agreeable occasion. Mary Hulbert is forgivably catty in saying of Mrs. Wilson that "she played well that most difficult role of being the third party to the reunion of two old friends endeavoring to relive the incidents of years." Might not Edith after all have left the two alone together? For Mary the meeting was a last chance to converse with a man she had loved, and by whom she felt she had been harshly let down. Woodrow Wilson had given her much; he had supported her in many troubles; but when the collapse of her spirit and her fortunes came, he was far away and unapproachable. Desperately tired though he was now, she need hardly have been begrudged a little time before the final adieu.

Moving on down the coast to San Diego Wilson spoke at the municipal stadium to a crowd estimated at between thirty and forty thousand people. On this occasion he had the use of a primitive system of amplification, "an electrical device," it was reported, by which "the carrying power of [his] voice was increased."[21] He spoke for an hour and ten minutes, but he was suffering from a slight cold and Grayson secured an extra day's rest by reducing the schedule from two days to one in the city. Los Angeles was ahead, where the largest ovation of his trip awaited him. The city was in a holiday mood, with an estimated 100,000 people in the streets and a tumultuous welcome for his speech in the Shriners Auditorium. He was in his best debating form, and made a full-scale defense of those aspects of the treaty still being subjected to attack. He went into the background of the Shantung settlement, declaring that Japan had given him its word that it would withdraw from the peninsula (she would indeed withdraw in 1922); he belittled the British Empire's extra votes by showing them to be merely advisory.

"This is Woodrow Wilson country now,"[22] *The New York Times*'s reporter summed up the situation, as the President ended the California phase of his trip.

The train turned eastward on September 22, with everyone relieved and yet with dark clouds gathering. In his diary Grayson expressed mounting fears for the President's health. In Salt Lake City he was "suffering very serious fatigue. . . . This trip was far too strenuous." The next day, as the train wound through the Rocky Mountains, he was "suffering a great deal and his nervous condition was apparent." Before arriving at Denver, the President had had "a very trying night"; his nerves were "working overtime."[23] Though concealed from the public and from the large audiences that heard him speak, the President's condition was beginning to be apparent to the newspapermen on the train. At Salt Lake City they observed the first signs of real trouble. He had to be helped up the steps when he entered the hall; he faltered in his speech and did not seem to have his usual command over words. After that, in mingled pity and admiration, they watched for telltale slips or hesitations.

Developments in Washington had added to Wilson's problems as the tour progressed. Seeking out hostile witnesses, Lodge followed a suggestion of Walter Lippmann's and called William Bullitt before the committee. An early admiration for the President had been replaced in Bullitt by the most intense and almost pathological hatred, partly because of what he considered Wilson's errors at Paris, and more personally because of Wilson's failure to receive him when he had returned the previous March from his mission to Russia. The senators drew from this arrogant young man a spicy catalogue of dissents and criticisms within the American delegation at the peace conference. Most sensational was his revelation of Lansing's hostility to the President and the League of Nations.

Lansing was starting on a vacation in the northern woods, and used this as an excuse to avoid comment. When he made a statement several days later, it was an evasive and mild repudiation of Bullitt's testimony. In the midst of his tour Wilson found that he had been betrayed from within his own household. He must have added one more to a growing list of reasons for a break with his Secretary of State.

More serious was Lodge's mounting intransigence and the weakening of the President's followers in the Senate. In early September Hitchcock had won Democratic backing for a minority report in favor of the treaty without change. Now he was confronted with the drift of Democrats toward the mild reservationists. He had been playing a waiting game, hoping he could hold the line until Wilson's return, but it began to look as if time was running out. Fearing that the mild reservationists might go over to Lodge, he warned Wilson not to attack them. At the same time Tumulty advised the need for Wilson to explain fully the reasons for opposing a reservation to Article X on which Lodge and the mild reservationists had just agreed.

Exhausted, running on raw nerves, Wilson disregarded the advice and managed to make a bad situation worse. He went further than ever in attacking the moderates. "All the elements that tended to disloyalty are against the League," he cried out in Ogden, Utah: "If this League is not adopted we will serve Germany's purposes."[24] When he tried to explain his objection to the Article X reservation, he confused his audience and evoked applause at the wrong place. Finally, having equated the opposition with pro-Germans, he went on in Salt Lake City to group together all who were not ready to accept the League as it was. "Reservations," he declared flatly, "are to all intents and purposes equivalent to amendments."[25]

This occurred at the time when Wilson should have been considering, not fatal antagonisms, but the start of a crowning attempt to reach accommodation. The situation called for a creative solution—something comparable, perhaps, to the proposal for an eight-hour day that had settled the railway strike of 1916; or the defensive alliance with France that had broken the stalemate on the Rhine provinces. Hitchcock held in his hand the interpretations the President had approved before leaving on his trip, not vastly different from the reservations the Republican moderates supported. His enormous investment in the western tour put the President in a solid position to begin negotiations. Now all must be brought to a head. "If [the President] have character, modesty, devotion, and insight as well as force," Wilson had written in his *Constitutional Government*, "he can bring the contending elements of the system together."[26] It was the hour for Wilson to display all of these qualities. But he mustered only a show of angry force.

Whether on his return he could in fact have worked out a settlement with the Senate remains one of the ifs of history. Wilson in full mental and physical health would surely not have acted so much out of character as to bring down the temple rather than achieve a compromise. The mild reservationists would probably not have proved so consumed by politics as to make concessions an excuse for further, unacceptable demands. It will never be known. The return to Washington was made in circumstances which made impossible the supreme test of Wilson's statesmanship.

In Pueblo, Colorado, on September 25, Wilson spoke at length, ending with words that stand as his testament:[27] "It always seems to make it difficult for me to say anything, my fellow citizens, when I think of my clients in this case. My clients are the children; my clients are the next generation. They do not know what promises and bonds I undertook when I ordered the armies of the United States to the soil of France, but I know. And I intend to redeem my pledges to the children; they shall not be sent again upon a similar errand.

"There seems to me to stand between us and the rejection or qualification of this treaty," he continued, "the serried ranks of those boys in khaki—not only those boys who came home but those dear ghosts that still deploy upon the fields of France." He described in moving terms the scene at Suresnes on Decoration Day, where he had seen French women tending the graves of American soldiers—"putting flowers every day upon those graves, taking them as their own sons, their own beloved, because they had died to save France. France was free, and the world was free because America had come!" If only men now opposing the treaty, he cried, could accept the obligation implied by that scene. But the mists were clearing away.

> I believe that men will see the truth, eye to eye and face to face. There is one thing that the American people always rise to and extend their hand to, and that is the truth of justice and of liberty and of peace. We have accepted that truth and we are going to be led by it, and it is going to lead us, and through us the world, out into pastures of quietness and peace such as the world never dreamed of before.

These were the last words that, as President, Woodrow Wilson was to speak before a public audience.

Twenty miles out of Pueblo the train was brought to a halt. Wilson was suffering acute discomfort and Grayson hoped that a walk in the open air would help him breathe. For almost an hour the two men and Mrs. Wilson walked out across the dry tableland and then up a country road. The President was recognized by an elderly farmer driving along in a small automobile, who stopped to give him a head of cabbage and some apples. On the way back to the train he saw a soldier in a private's uniform sitting on a porch some way back from the road. The youth was plainly ill, and the President, climbing a fence, went over to greet him and to speak with the family that quickly gathered.

A little farther on, at Rocky Ford, the train made another brief stop to change engines. A crowd of five thousand was waiting. A quarrel ensued between Grayson, the protector, and Tumulty, ever anxious to bring his chief before the people. In the end Wilson stepped onto the rear platform. "Then as the car pulled out," Grayson records, "he stood there and waved his hand."[28]

That night was one which those close to the President were never to forget: "the longest and most heartbreaking of my life," Edith later recalled.[29] At first Wilson seemed refreshed by the walk he had taken in the late afternoon. He ate well and withdrew early for what all hoped would be a good night's rest. But he could not sleep. At eleven-thirty he called out to Edith, asking her to come as he was very sick. She sat by him through hours of pain, until at dawn, still sitting upright, he fell asleep.*

The train's next scheduled stop was to be in the morning at Wichita,

---

* What Wilson had suffered at this point was not a stroke but a transient ischemic attack—a warning of a severe stroke to come.

Kansas. A large crowd had gathered at the station and all preparations had been made for a major address. At seven the President awoke, saying he must get dressed quickly so as to be ready. Frantically Edith, Tumulty, and Grayson—the triumvirate that soon would have all matters in their hands—conferred. It was certain the President could not go on with his schedule and that subsequent meetings must be canceled. But how to announce it? How to persuade *him*? In the midst of their discussion Wilson appeared—"freshly dressed," in Edith's words, "shaven, and looking, oh, so piteously ill." He protested strongly, but finally gave in. "He accepted the decree of Fate," Edith wrote, "as gallantly as he had fought the fight."[30]

"I don't seem to realize it," he said pathetically to Tumulty, "but I seem to have gone to pieces."[31]

For fifteen minutes on the station platform at Wichita the large crowd stood waiting. Then a forlorn Tumulty appeared to read a short statement. The President was suffering from "nervous exhaustion." His condition was "not alarming" but he must rest for a considerable time.

With drawn shades, the train was ordered to proceed directly to Washington.

CHAPTER TWELVE

Embattled Invalid

A PRESIDENT DISABLED

In the car reserved for newspapermen the reporters were anxious to get home and relieved to have the long trip ending. They gossiped idly, speculated on the President's condition, played cards, and sang. Tumulty issued soothing bulletins, saying that the President was suffering from exhaustion and would recover after a short period of rest. But the patient himself was undergoing agonies. He could not sleep. His headaches were unremitting. Twice the train was ordered to slow down so that its jolts and swings would not add to the discomfort.

Sunday, September 28, the long journey home ended as the train drew into Union Station. His daughter Margaret was there to greet him, and a crowd of perhaps a thousand people. Steeled by a never-failing will he walked unaided to his car. In that early Sabbath hour the streets were deserted, but at one point, solemnly, very deliberately, Wilson lifted his hat and bowed. It was a pathetic gesture, the last time as President that he would have even the illusion of acclaim.

Over the next four days he kept to the residential quarters of the White House, going out for short drives, playing a little pool. On the evening of October 1 he seemed in the eyes of his physician better than he had been at any time since the breakdown. But the next morning disaster fell. Going into his room, Edith found him on the floor of the bathroom and left to make a frantic call to Ike Hoover, the White House usher. Grayson must be summoned at once, she said; the President was very sick. When she returned, Wilson was unconscious and his face and head were bloodstained. Edith put a pillow under his head and when the doctor arrived helped lift him into his bed. They found that his left side was paralyzed.

To this had come the long decline in Wilson's health, beginning as far back as 1896, when he was forty, with the "neuralgia" that caused Ellen to hurry him off on a vacation in England. It had shown itself more ominously in 1906, when he awoke after what was undoubtedly a stroke to find himself blind in one eye. The remarkable career that intervened between then and his devastating collapse was owed to Wilson's own determination; to the regime of regular rest and recreation which Grayson had mostly succeeded in imposing during the Presidential years, and not least to the good fates' withholding for so long the stored-up blow. Yet the course was marked by accelerating signs of danger. The relatively small strokes, symptoms of increasing hypertension, which he had suffered in Paris and after his return to Washington had left him physically and to some extent mentally diminished. To a surprising degree he recovered from the aftereffects, going on to perform ably in the debates of the late Paris spring, and to achieve the popular successes of the western tour. Yet continued hypertension (with rampant high blood pressure and arteriosclerosis) took its toll of a mind whose resiliency and scope of interest were progressively narrowed, and of a spirit whose earlier generous impulses were damped down.

Now the White House was suddenly filled with doctors and nurses. Grayson issued a bulletin, as he had been doing in recent days, frank to the point of betraying his concern, but unenlightening (as all future bulletins were to be) about the nature of Wilson's affliction. "The President had a fairly good night," it asserted, "but his condition is not at all good this morning."[1] That same day Lansing went to New York to welcome the King and Queen of the Belgians, whose projected state visit had much preoccupied Wilson, and on his return called Grayson to ask whether he could come by. Grayson told him the President's condition was "bad" and that no one could see him. About six on that Thursday, October 2, Ike Hoover was summoned to the sickroom to help move some furniture. As he remembered the scene afterwards, "The President lay stretched out on the large Lincoln bed. He looked as if dead. There was not a sign of life. His face bore a long cut above the temple from which the signs of blood were still evident. . . . He was just gone as far as anyone could judge from appearances."[2]*

---

*A hitherto unknown statement giving clinical details of the result of an examination of the President by Grayson and Dr. F. X. Dercum at four-thirty on the afternoon of October 2 is among the newly disclosed Grayson papers. (It is printed as Enclosure with F. X. Dercum to C. T. Grayson Oct. 20, 1919, PWW, 64 64:500–507.) The statement, in which the two doctors concurred, appears to have been intended to serve in case of a public inquiry. In graphic but technical language it describes the

That night came a second bulletin—once more designed to promote a mixture of alarm and reassurance, and still with no real facts: "The President is a very sick man. His condition is less favorable today and he has remained in bed throughout the day."[3]

The next day Lansing met with Tumulty in the Cabinet Room. Coldly he read the clause of the Constitution which stated that in the event of the President's inability to discharge the powers of his office, these should devolve upon the Vice President. Tumulty asked who should certify to the disability of the President. Lansing replied that it would be up to him, Tumulty, or to Grayson. "You may rest assured," Tumulty replied, "that while Woodrow Wilson is lying in the White House on the broad of his back I will not be a party to ousting him. He has been too kind, too loyal ... to receive such treatment at my hands." At this point Grayson entered the Cabinet Room. "And I am sure," Tumulty added, "that Doctor Grayson will never certify to his disability." Grayson indicated that indeed he would not. In this strange way, and in these few words, the Constitutional provision was disposed of.[4]

The following Monday, at a meeting officially convoked by Secretary Lansing, the cabinet met at its regular hour. Most of those present knew by then that the President's left side was paralyzed (Tumulty had indicated as much by a grim, silent gesture) and Lansing mentioned the question of action by the Vice President. Grayson immediately spoke up. According to Lansing, he "gave a very encouraging report on the President's condition, which, he said, showed decided improvement and seemed to indicate speedy recovery." After that (still according to Lansing), there was no course open but to ask Grayson to "convey to the President our felicitations and best wishes."[5] The cabinet proceeded to a routine discussion of departmental affairs.

Thus began, with the silent assent of some, with the active maneuvering of others, such a cover-up as American history had not known before. Grayson's twice-daily bulletins gave the public no hint that the President had suffered a severe stroke, describing his illness as the result of overwork and exhaustion; Tumulty gave to reporters his own particular version of events. An article in the Washington *Post* published the day the cabinet was meeting stated that the President had had a better day and "might be definitely on the road to recovery." It was said that Dr. Grayson had difficulty in persuading him to remain in bed. Two

---

condition of the President after suffering a massive stroke or (as Grayson tended to say) a clot. Printed together with the Dercum-Grayson memorandum is a commentary by Dr. J. F. Toole and Dr. B. E. Park. (Note 2, PWW, 64:503–505.)

days later the same source reported that "Wilson still gains" and indicated that he might be allowed to do a little work later in the week.[6]

Grayson was, however, aware of the grave nature of the President's illness and correct in his privately expressed prognosis. Undersecretary of State Polk quotes him as saying on November 9 that he did not expect the President to be able to handle any business for at least six weeks. In minimizing in public the extent of Wilson's disability (attributing it to neurasthenia, or simple exhaustion) he was following what was the practice of the day, protecting at all costs the privacy of his patient. He was maintaining a long tradition of keeping confidential the maladies of public figures. But he was responding also to a particular factor: Mrs. Wilson's strong objection to making known the nature of the President's illness.

Grayson relates that by October 4, 1919, two days after the stroke, it was clear that the symptoms would not clear up. "It was then desired by all consultants in the case to make a full statement of the President's condition, but in view of the wishes of [Mrs. Wilson] this was deferred." It was at her insistence, according to Grayson, that the physicians fell back on "general statements." Mrs. Wilson, he adds, "was absolutely opposed to any other course."*

Nevertheless the facts, as facts do, began to circulate, and rumors spread widely. On October 11 the newspapers made much of a letter sent to his constituents by New Hampshire's Senator George H. Moses, no friend of the President's, which indicated the evidence for a cerebral hemorrhage, and stated that although the President might live, he would not again be "a material force or factor in anything."[7] There was no comment from the White House as misleading bulletins and inspired stories in the press continued to indicate the President's recovery. A week later a crisis further strained the situation, when the President suffered a severe urinary blockage. The specialists recommended a prostate operation, at that time considered one of the most difficult of surgical interventions. They warned Grayson that for a man in Wilson's condition the operation would in all probability be fatal. As the fever mounted, as the threshold of irreversible poisoning came dangerously close, Mrs. Wilson took a decisive stand against operating. The blockage dissolved naturally; but of all this the public heard only enough to fuel its wildest suspicions.

The three persons in direct charge of the President—his wife, his doctor, and his secretary—realized that the Vice President, at least,

---

* From an unpublished memorandum by C. T. Grayson, n.d., in Grayson papers, printed in PWW 64:507–10.

would have to be informed of the true situation. They chose for their purpose the Washington correspondent of the Baltimore *Sun*, J. Fred Essary, who, taking great pains to avoid attention, went to Marshall's office. Briefly he told Marshall why he had come and who had sent him. The President, he said, might die at any moment. Marshall sat speechless, staring at his hands on his desk. As his biographer puts it: "Essary finished, hesitated, rose, and went to the door. He looked back, but Marshall never looked up."[8]

Wilson had called him "a small calibre man," and it was indeed easy to belittle him. But he was essentially decent, and he was politically acute. *The New York Times* spoke for many when it said at his death in 1924, "We liked him better than we have liked some greater but less hospitably human persons." Physically small, weighing only 125 pounds and walking with a slight limp, the genial Hoosier was not avid for power; he conceived the Vice Presidency as principally a part of the Legislative rather than of the Executive Branch. The nearest he came to complaining of the inferior place to which Wilson assigned him occurred shortly after the armistice, when he remarked plaintively to his wife that "he thought it was very unkind of President Wilson not to inform him of his plans to leave the country." But publicly he gave assurance that in the President's absence he would not assume any Executive duties. Wilson got the hint, and promptly went to call on his Vice President, asking that he preside at cabinet meetings. Marshall was reluctant to do so, and after a few meetings that found him playing a desultory role, he desisted, indicating that they bored him, and that, besides, he was not drawing any additional salary. In the new, more fateful circumstances he had no inclination to resume the experiment.[9]

For a month after the stroke of October 2 Wilson was totally disabled and was incapable of carrying out his duties. During this period no proclamations were issued, no pardons granted; bills became laws without a signature. The regular meetings of cabinet members gave the country the impression that some matters were being dealt with. They sat, these lieutenants who had once gathered around a formidable chief, discussing for the most part trivial matters, and even then were often unable to make decisions. Lansing, always brusque and with the largest list of questions demanding attention, complained that the government could not cease to act merely because the President was sick. Indeed it came almost to that, except insofar as ways could be found around the roadblock. A letter drafted by Secretary Lane was sent by Tumulty to Wilson's sickroom on October 21, whence it was returned for release without change and undoubtedly without Wilson himself having seen it.

A message vetoing the Volstead Act, providing machinery for the enforcement of Prohibition, was written by Tumulty. The veto was overridden, but at least a sign of life had emanated from the White House.

At some point during this period Edith Bolling Wilson came to define her responsibility. "Madam," said Dr. Dercum, as she later remembered the conversation, "it is a grave situation, but I think you can solve it. Have everything come to you; weigh the importance of each matter, and see if it is possible by consultations . . . to solve it without the guidance of your husband. . . . Always bear in mind that every time you take him a new anxiety or problem . . . you are turning a knife in an open wound." For Edith, it meant putting her husband's life above the effective functioning of the government, and she thought she could manage it. "The only decision that was mine," she declared naïvely, "was what was important and what was not."[10]

Thus unwilled and only half pursued, a major share in the governance of the country fell to this woman of strong natural intelligence (but with no more than two years of formal schooling); of prejudices and preferences deeply rooted in her nature; and, not least, of passionate devotion to her husband. It was often asked, then and later: "Was Mrs. Wilson running the country?" Obviously she was not, at least not in the sense of making decisions on legislative and administrative matters. It would be more accurate to say that the country simply was not running; in Baker's phrase, government was "out of business." Yet her power, derived from determining what issues would come before her husband, and what visitors would be admitted to the sickroom, was obviously very great. It was exercised, on the whole, with single-minded concern for the patient's health.

On matters of personnel, more than on matters of policy, the strength of her hand was visible. She was responsible for keeping Tumulty at bay, and made sure that Colonel House remained in New York. On two major issues, underlying the whole course of government, she was unchallenged. It was she who was responsible not only for keeping from the public the true nature of the President's illness. Also, it will become plain, she prevented serious consideration of the President's resigning.

By the end of the month Wilson began to be a little better. On October 30 Palmer was the first member of the cabinet to confer with him, discussing a threatened nationwide coal strike. The King and Queen of the Belgians made their much-publicized visit to the White House, with hundreds of persons milling outside the gates, while Edith and Margaret sat down alone with them at tea. Afterwards Edith suggested they might like to see her husband. The king was first admitted alone to the bed-chamber where the President he had last seen touring his country, an eloquent towering figure, now lay unmoving, speaking in muffled tones. Two weeks later, in similar hushed circumstances, the youthful Prince of Wales was admitted to the sickroom. About the same time the President was first allowed to sit up, then to be placed in a wheelchair, to be pushed to the south portico, and still later into the White House garden. The cabinet during its sessions could see their chief being wheeled about the grounds, followed in melancholy procession by his nurse, by Dr. Grayson, by Mrs. Wilson, and frequently by his daughter Margaret.

Congress was to reconvene on December 1. Tumulty requested of Mrs. Wilson that she remind the President of the event and that a message from him would be expected. The task of preparing the message fell, as did so much else, to Tumulty. In a press briefing he gave out fanciful background information, adding that the President's shorthand draft was written in "extremely clear and unwavering" strokes.[11] The President was not capable of writing shorthand, or anything else, at this time.

The secretary's draft knit together reports supplied by members of the cabinet, together with lengthy passages of his own on the importance of ratifying the peace treaty. The latter, he assured Mrs. Wilson, were in the spirit of the President's western speeches. When the draft was returned, the passages written by Tumulty were marked for omission, and the final version had no reference either to the treaty or the League. Conceivably Wilson wanted the subject ignored because he interpreted it as one strictly between himself and the Senate, whereas the message was addressed to both houses of Congress. Mrs. Wilson, in any case, must have derived satisfaction from seeing Tumulty's particular contribution excised.

The treaty was, inescapably, the chief issue before the country. Its unresolved questions plagued American as well as European officials, and the "state of the union" depended very largely on their resolution. Here as in all other matters the method of government was by delay. On November 17 the State Department asked if the President could indicate his answer to recent notes on the Turkish treaty and on the settlement of claims concerning various British ships. The President (through Mrs. Wilson) let it be known that he was not ready to consider either question until he was stronger. On December 2, Secretary Lansing made an urgent plea that Assistant Secretary of State William Phillips be relieved for reasons of health of administrative duties and made ambassador to Belgium; the answer, again through Mrs. Wilson, was that "in regard to diplomatic appointments the President is sorry to be obliged to insist that they all wait until his recovery."[12] Many other instances of such prevarication could be cited. The Secretary of State's impatience with this way of doing business is clear in a late November message from Lansing to Tumulty. He would very much appreciate it, he said, if the Secretary would "intimate" to the President that delay— in this case extending recognition to the new Costa Rican government —would "tend to undermine the authority of that government."[13] As Lansing was well aware, Tumulty's "intimations" were not very effective, and the status of the Costa Rican government remained in limbo.

Wilson had not spoken about the League in public, nor taken any action regarding it, since his Pueblo speech. But the reservations he had left with Hitchcock before going West were still held in confidence as the basis of a possible settlement. Hitchcock hesitated to begin the negotiations that even Wilson at his best would have had difficulty in bringing to a conclusion; he continued to hope that the President's health would soon be restored. As this prospect darkened, Hitchcock wrote Mrs. Wilson a long letter setting forth the facts of the political situation.

The reservations agreed to by Lodge and the "mild reservationists" were now, he explained, before the Senate. The Democrats proposed to offer a substitute resolution calling for unqualified acceptance of the treaty. This, too, was bound to be defeated, but the situation would at least have been clarified. Lodge would then offer for final vote a resolution of ratification including all his reservations. The Democrats could prevent the necessary two-thirds majority, and might have a chance to negotiate. The outcome, however, was uncertain, and an indefinite stalemate might ensue.

Would the President, Hitchcock inquired earnestly, consider advising the Democrats to vote for the Lodge resolution on the chance of being able to get the treaty through, even in a form not entirely agreeable to them? Having received no answer, Hitchcock two days later again wrote Mrs. Wilson, saying that the time was at hand when a decision must be made.

From Mrs. Wilson came back a flat no. The President "could not accept ratification with the Lodge reservations."

On November 17 Hitchcock, still hoping for compromise, visited the White House. Wilson was wheeled out onto the lawn. "I beheld an emaciated old man with a thin white beard," Hitchcock recalled. When the Senate leader reported that the Democrats were defeating all amendments as they were presented, the President "brightened up"; but when told that the treaty could not be ratified without reservations—in the outcome only thirty-eight senators were for unqualified acceptance—he "fairly groaned. 'Is it possible? Is it possible?' " he asked.[14] In a letter, drafted by Hitchcock after the interview and submitted to the Democratic senators, Wilson declared the Lodge reservations to be a "nullification" of the treaty.[15] The senators, examining the letter, noted that it did not bear the President's signature, but that the words "Woodrow Wilson" "were affixed thereto by a rubber stamp . . . in purple ink."[16] Nevertheless in the vote on November 19, most of them obeyed their stricken and disabled leader.

The fight for the League had thus come to a stalemate. It could not be ratified without reservations; and Wilson was unwilling, and was indeed physically unable, seriously to consider a compromise. The Republicans marshaled their forces against further motions and the Senate adjourned. It was expected that Wilson would withdraw the treaty.

The President was besieged by advice. The fight was not over, wrote Frank Cobb. Others suggested that he relax his efforts and let the Democratic leaders in Congress carry the ball. From Colonel House in New York came two urgent letters addressed to Mrs. Wilson. In a last effort to cross over the bridge now separating them, House pressed upon his chief the suggestion that without further comment he turn the treaty over to the Senate, letting Hitchcock know that he expected ratification in some form. If, having been passed with reservations, it were rejected by other signatories, Wilson would at least be vindicated. If it were accepted by them, the peace would be validated and the League set in operation.

The advice was sound for it recognized, as few seemed willing to do, the President's incapacity to act as leader in this supreme crisis. "Pitt," the young Wilson had written long ago, "was a noble statesman; the Earl of Chatham was a noble ruin." Wilson, who had been so masterful a statesman, was now himself "a noble ruin"—an "emaciated old man with a thin white beard." He could stand fast. He could, with his one clear eye, behold a visionary future. But he could not lead; he could not mediate; he could not act creatively.

The country in the meanwhile was turning away from the concern with the treaty and the League that had preoccupied it during the summer of 1919. It was surrendering to a frantic scramble to readjust after the war and to make money amid new economic and social conditions. It was also, for a few brief months, surrendering to one of those violent waves of fear that at intervals in a democracy inflame the public mind. Industrial strife had been a growing postwar problem, and radical unions seemed to be at the base of much of the unrest. Ninety percent of the followers of the American Communist and anarchist movements were foreign-born, and a highly vocal cry for deportation of the aliens arose among politicians and in the press. From within the Wilson administration the Attorney General, Mitchell Palmer, was ready to respond with zeal.

Elevation to a major cabinet post had not satisfied Palmer's ambition. His desire to be a candidate in the next Presidential election, combined with a strain of illiberalism in his nature, led him down the politically popular path of wholesale attacks on the radicals. It must be said in his defense that his house in Washington had been bombed in the spring of 1919 and that he had himself narrowly escaped death.

On November 6, which happened to be the second anniversary of the Bolshevik revolution, agents of the Department of Justice swooped down upon the meeting places of Russian-born workers in twelve American cities. In early January another series of spectacular raids was carried out in scattered urban centers. Homes were invaded and arrests made without warrants; individuals were threatened and beaten while being questioned. The press applauded these outrages almost unanimously, and when the transport *Buford* set sail on December 21, carrying 249 anarchists back to Russia, the popular mood was ecstatic.

The so-called Palmer raids stand as a black stain upon the Wilson administration. At the time liberals and defenders of civil rights were close to despair. "It is forever incredible," Walter Lippmann wrote to the Secretary of War, "that an administration announcing the most spacious ideals in our history should have done more to endanger fundamental American liberties than any group of men for a hundred years."[17] Within the administration, Palmer had his supporters—Burleson, Lansing, Tumulty; he also had a strong group of adversaries—Baker, Daniels, Lane, Houston, W. B. Wilson. But without leadership, without a commanding voice, there was little possibility of calling a halt to a course so solidly supported by an overwhelming majority of the people. The absent voice was that of Woodrow Wilson—and no evidence indicates that in his sickroom he learned of the Palmer Raids. Isolated, guarded against anything that might excite or dismay him, receiving only such news as was relayed by his wife, doctor, and Tumulty, he waked and slept, and took his daily ride in a wheelchair, ignorant of the ax that had been laid to the roots of democratic liberties. Later he showed a strong dislike of Palmer, for reasons good and bad, but there is nothing in the record to suggest that he ever discussed the raids with him or with anyone else.

In Congress patience with the White House regimen began to wear thin. Up to a point the Republicans were willing to tolerate a nonfunctioning President; his very impotence gave them scope; and Democrats, out of loyalty or fear, refrained from challenging the stream of optimistic reports. Indeed it is indicative of the immense authority Wilson had long held that even flat on his back he was heeded by his party, and treated with respect (if also with icy hate) by his adversaries. By December, however, stirrings of revolt threatened the fragile balance. "Well, here's another message from Tumulty," was the Senate joke, and "We've a batch of some more of Tumulty's nominations to act on."[18]

Senator Albert B. Fall of New Mexico, one of those most unremittingly hostile to Wilson personally and to the League, became a strong advocate of intervention in Mexico, where the situation was once more in turmoil. Answering a Senate inquiry, Lansing had been so imprudent as to say that he had not discussed with the President the case of a certain American citizen, William O. Jenkins, who was being held by Mexican authorities under Carranza. This seemed to Senator Fall a sufficient reason to probe the President's competence, and he got himself appointed a delegation of two, along with Senator Hitchcock, ostensibly to discuss the Mexican situation.

Of those near the throne, Lansing was the most skeptical of the President's capacities. "Someone as a rule is acting for him and thinking for him too," he confided to a private memo. "If ever it gets out it will make a fine scandal." However, he added, "I believe that Fall and Hitchcock will see the President and that his strong will will be able to stand the test."[19] Lansing proved to be right on both counts.

The request for the interview was made to Tumulty, and referred to Grayson, who consulted with Mrs. Wilson. On the appointed day, December 6, 1920, Wilson was placed, stretched out, upon his bed, his shoulders lifted slightly by a pillow, his left arm concealed beneath a blanket. A single light was placed so as to cast a shadow where he lay. The State Department had provided a brief summary of the main features of the Mexican situation as they appeared at that time, with particular reference to the Jenkins case. The two senators arrived promptly at two-thirty, and stayed for forty minutes. Mrs. Wilson sat by the bedside and took notes.

Senator Fall did most of the talking, his vanity proving superior to his desire to quiz the President. In the midst of his exposition, Grayson, having left the room, reappeared to announce dramatically that word had just been received of Jenkins's release. When the President responded, Hitchcock later wrote, his articulation was "somewhat thick [but] I could understand perfectly every word he said."[20] Some of it was indeed worth hearing. "We've been praying for you, sir," Senator Fall declared unctuously. To which the President replied, "Which way, Senator?"

Next day *The New York Times* summed up the effect of the interview: the senators' report, it said, was "accepted as silencing for good the many wild and often unfriendly rumors of Presidential disability."[21]

AGITATIONS AND DELUSIONS

The visit of the two senators was a turning point in the slow and painful history of White House developments after Wilson's stroke. Encouraged by the success of his camouflage, and indeed growing slightly stronger, Wilson began to assert himself. Early in February he first started dictating to Swem, with results that were often unfortunate or embarrassing. Meanwhile the public, with its apprehensions of the President's physical disability somewhat allayed, and ready to believe White House statements about his continuing improvement, judged his actions (and inactions) the more harshly. Had they been able to know the depression and the physical tortures from which he suffered they might have been more charitable, or at least more comprehending. As it was, what should have been sympathy turned to bitterness.

Wilson's determination to act on his own produced a bog of administrative contradictions and confusions. To take a single example: On December 9 it turned out in the cabinet meeting that Wilson had on his own approved the position of Harry Garfield, the acting fuel administrator, in a labor dispute involving the coal miners. The Secretary of Labor, the invaluable William B. Wilson, threatened to resign. Queries to the sickroom were dispatched, whereupon a note in Mrs. Wilson's handwriting withdrew the President's support of Garfield. At that point the latter resigned.[1]

A pileup of unsettled business also ensued. In a memorandum of this time Tumulty submitted to the President a sobering list of matters needing to be dealt with. These included a message in regard to the return of the railroads to private owners, recognition of the new government of Costa Rica, selection of a commission to settle the miners' strike, and many appointments—a Secretary of the Treasury, a Secretary of the Interior, envoys to Holland and Italy and numerous other diplomatic posts.[2] In addition, the Senate was getting ready to take up the peace treaty for final disposition, and difficult negotiations on the Adriatic were in train.

As if these were not enough, Wilson was meditating a curious and disturbing plan of his own. Around the middle of December he discussed with Tumulty a scheme to get the League before the voters for a direct and unqualified referendum. Several themes came together in what, if it had not been aborted, would surely have been one of the most fantastic procedures ever considered by a President. With recollections of his earlier advocacy of a parliamentary form of government for the United States, and of his advocacy in the 1912 campaign of direct forms of democracy, he got Tumulty to draft a proposed letter to the American people. This challenged a list of more than twenty senators opposed to the League to resign their seats and immediately run for reelection. If the majority were defeated, a "great and solemn referendum"[3] would have been achieved; if a majority were elected, he, the President, would resign along with the Vice President, after appointing a Republican Secretary of State to succeed him under the constitution.

Fortunately the plan died aborning, when its total impracticality became clear. But the idea of a "solemn referendum" persisted, and would presently reveal itself in different forms. The first occurred in January, when the Democrats were to assemble in two simultaneous Jackson Day dinners in Washington. Wilson promised them a message, and Tumulty was again summoned for its drafting. From the earlier, incompleted letter he drew crucial passages, this time proposing that the "solemn referendum" on the League be carried out by means of the forthcoming Presidential elections.

The intervention of Houston and others eliminated certain absurdities and gross factual misstatements in the message, but the core of the idea remained. As was quickly pointed out, the concept of a referendum was unrealistic in view of the nature of American presidential campaigns, and the possibility of enforcing its results would in any case be slim. Worst of all, at a time when the American public was clearly in favor of ratification with some form of reservations, the President was trying to commit the Democratic Party to a wholly intransigent position.

Mention has been made of the Adriatic negotiations in train; these must be looked at not only because they are important in themselves but as illustrating Wilson's state of mind in these months. On December 9, 1919, the governments of Britain, France, and the United States had come to an agreement on the long-vexed issue of Italian claims, the essence of which was to make Fiume a free city under the League, while according the Yugoslavs sovereignty over the part of the city containing the harbor and railway facilities. Between these two areas would be a strip of land given to the Yugoslavs as a form of protection against future Italian expansion. During subsequent talks, at which Wilson forbade American representation, the agreement was modified in ways that might seem reasonable but which Wilson vehemently refused to accept.

His smoldering animosities toward Italy, his increasing mistrust of the French and British, gelled into a frozen determination not to budge. On January 28, when Lansing inquired of him whether any further conferences looking for terms of settlement "different in any material aspect" from his solution would be "useless and undesirable," the letter came back with the single word "Yes" inscribed in Mrs. Wilson's hand.[4] A week later came a note from her: "He considers the Italian claims in the Adriatic unjust . . . and means to resist them to the end, no matter what the consequences are."[5]

With the threadbare power that was left to him, Wilson instructed Polk and Lansing specifically to restore a concluding paragraph in a note to the Allies, which he had drafted and which they had discreetly omitted. "If it does not seem feasible to obtain the acceptance of the generous and just concessions" offered to Italy in the note of December 9, the paragraph read, "he [the President] must seriously consider withdrawing the treaty with Germany and the agreement between the United States and France of June 28, 1919."[6]

The British and French Prime Ministers were aghast, and in a long answer insisted that the changes had been agreed to by all and represented no more of a capitulation to Italy than to Yugoslavia. The Prime Ministers declared themselves "reluctant to believe that the President can consider that the modifications which they have made in the memorandum of December ninth can constitute in themselves a justification for withdrawal from all further cooperation with them. . . . [They] cannot believe that it is the purpose of the American people to take a step so far-reaching and terrible in its effects on a ground which has the appearance of being so inadequate."[7]

Wilson at another time would perhaps have thundered, as he did now in reply to the Allies, that Italy's material sacrifices in the war, great as they were, could not be "made the reason for unjust settlements which will be provocative of future wars."[8] Yet at other times he had also known how to balance and mediate. In such a case as the Adriatic settlement he would have weighed the fact that Italy had surrendered much—virtually all its claims under the Treaty of London, including most of the Dalmatian islands and coast; that it was not pressing any claims in Asia Minor; and he would have helped find an acceptable solution to Fiume. But that Wilson was gone, and in his place was the shell of a man who could only brandish threats and say no.

In Washington, during these grim winter months, another drama was unfolding, with its somber as well as ludicrous overtones. Lord Grey, the aged and greatly respected English statesman, now ailing and half blind, had been sent on a last diplomatic mission to the United States as ambassador. In his entourage was Major Charles K. Crauford-Stuart, a figure who liked to shine at social gatherings and who was undeniably a gossip. Wilson got wind of some disparaging remarks he was reported to have made about his wife, and demanded that the man be sent back by Grey. The old diplomat, feeling he could not dispense with his services, demurred. From then on Grey was *persona non grata* at the White House. That he was not formally received by the President was perhaps not surprising given Wilson's physical condition; but not even a polite nod was given by his wife; and when the Prince of Wales visited the White House, Grey was not in attendance.

The attitude toward the ambassador was more complex than mere pique over Crauford-Stuart. That he was House's friend undoubtedly put Mrs. Wilson on edge. Moreover Grey, a man of immense charm, representing the cream of English breeding and tradition, found himself naturally at home with Anglophiles in American public life, including Lodge. They gathered in his home for good conversation and worldly-wise comment, as men like John Hay and Henry Adams had formed a familiar circle around Spring Rice. This was enough to irritate the President. Even his Assistant Secretary of the Navy, Franklin D. Roosevelt, sinned in warming to Lord Grey's hospitality; relations between Wilson and Roosevelt were strained until paralysis had made the younger man, like the elder, its prisoner.

Grey returned to England in December, after paying a last call on House in New York. His eyesight had improved and on the whole he kept a good impression of America. But that was not the end of the matter. On January 31 the *Times* of London carried a long letter from Lord Grey, immediately reprinted in *The New York Times*, implying that the British government was quite ready to tolerate the so-called Lodge reservations. This cut to the heart of the President's position, that such amendments betrayed America's promises to the Allies. As a result of the letter, commented the influential Springfield *Daily Republican*, "Mr. Lodge cannot conceal his pleasure." Lord Grey had become "in effect an ally of Lodge."[9] Wilson had the last word in a White House statement which he drafted himself: "If Lord Grey had ventured on any such statement while in Washington, his government would have been asked to withdraw him."[10] Thus ends the story of the relationship be-

tween two men who, in better circumstances, would have enjoyed being
together and appreciated each other's qualities.

These events strained another relationship, that between the President
and his Secretary of State. In Paris Lansing had felt ineffectual and
humiliated, and he was unsympathetic to Wilson's concept of a peace
rationalized and made viable by the League. Lansing's halfhearted disavowal of the Bullitt testimony drove the wedge deeper between them.
After his stroke Wilson never saw his Secretary of State, and as he grew
stronger his letters were polite, but phrased in such terms as scarcely to
warm the heart of a man so little characterized by warmth as Lansing.
Direct evidence attesting to Wilson's feelings is lacking; but Polk, in a
conversation with House, described Mrs. Wilson as "white-hot with
indignation" and wishing the Secretary would resign.[11] In his private
diary Lansing poured out his increasingly bitter despair. "My intense
desire is to retire from the cabinet," he wrote on December 10; "the
irascibility and tyranny of the President . . . cannot be borne much
longer." And a month later: "The situation is unbearable. I am at my
wits' end. It is only a question as to when I should send in my letter of
resignation. I cannot wait much longer."[12]

So things stood in early February, and it would not have seemed too
difficult for Wilson to gain his Secretary's resignation on grounds of
basic incompatibility, in a period when he especially needed complete
understanding and full sympathy with his policies. The country would
certainly have understood that need. Instead, he wrote a letter on February 7, precipitating the break in the worst possible way. "Is it true,
as I have been told," he wrote, "that during my illness you have frequently called the heads of the executive departments into conference?"
The suggestion that Wilson had not known the cabinet was meeting
regularly was patently absurd; or, if true, fatally revealed his incapacity
to function. Lansing answered that indeed he had called the cabinet
together, with the approval of its members. To this Wilson replied, "This
affair, Mr. Secretary, only deepens a feeling that was growing upon me."
He accepted the Secretary's invitation to relieve him of "any embarrassment" and took up the resignation which had been placed in his
hands.[13]

"Thank God," wrote Lansing in his desk diary, "an intolerable situation has ended." He had a last moment of gloating, as he contemplated
the effect on the public when all the facts were made known. "I never
for a moment imagined that such an opportunity as this would ever be
given me. . . . The President delivered himself into my hands and of

course I took advantage of his stupidity."[14] Lansing was right about the subsequent public uproar. The Democratic *World* commented on "the virtual unanimity of the American press in expressions of amazement and regret." As for Wilson, he bore the outcry (insofar as it was permitted to reach him) with the disdain for popularity or unpopularity he had always affected. "Well, Tumulty," he remarked a week afterwards to his faithful aid, as he sat having his hair cut, "have I any friends left?" "Very few, Governor," was the reply; and for once Tumulty was admitting the truth.[15]

Wilson's actions in the Lansing dismissal, his extreme obduracy on the Adriatic issue, and his continuing inability to secure ratification of the treaty revived the question of his physical and mental condition. The country continued to be fed false reports about his recovery—that he was rising from his bed and walking unassisted; that his eyes were bright; that his complexion showed the glow of health. Only those who knew he had had a severe stroke realized that he had suffered permanent damage to his left side and that, what was worse, he was afflicted by symptoms typical of such cases—depression, paranoia, rigidity of mind, brief attention span, and loss of control over the emotions. Gregory, former Attorney General, visited Colonel House in December: "He believes," House reported, "like every sensible friend of the President, that he has been crucified by trying to perform the functions of his office when totally unfit to do so."[16]

Early spring found the invalid undertaking the excruciatingly difficult task of learning to walk again. Heavily supported, dragging his left leg, he took one agonizing step at a time; he then forced himself over and over to climb three wooden steps that Grayson had had constructed in the basement. The progress of this rehabilitation was dishearteningly slow. Wilson never managed to rise unassisted from a chair. When in March he met with a small delegation of railway unionists they found him seated, wrapped in a blanket, a golf cap pulled down over his eyes. Ambassadors waited months to present their credentials. The Swiss minister, given an audience on May 28, reported to his foreign office the grim details of the event.

He had been warned that the ceremony must be brief. Wordlessly he presented an address (the text of which had been communicated two months earlier to the State Department); again wordlessly, and without rising, the President handed over the text of his reply. After a few formal words of welcome the minister took his leave. He was struck by the President's aged appearance: "His mouth, which he left open . . . gives

him an air of senility."[17] Polk, the Undersecretary of State (who had
served as acting Secretary after Lansing's dismissal and yet had not been
received by the President since his illness), "appeared to be painfully
afflicted by the sight." Polk commented that he got the impression "of
a very sick man, greatly emaciated, with a droop to his jaw and staring,
almost unseeing, eyes." He was in doubt as to whether the President
recognized him; and he added, significantly, that throughout the interview he never smiled.[18]

Early in his illness Wilson had developed a taste for movies. The
flickering images were first displayed across a suspended sheet in his
sickroom, and by the spring of 1920 they had become a daily feature
of his routine. Shown in the East Room, regularly at noon, they were
often embarrassingly poor in quality. Even so, Ike Hoover was hard
beset to find a new one every day. A solution of sorts was provided
when the Signal Corps sent over films taken of the President during his
triumphant tours abroad. These he would see over and over. He dragged
in guests (Hoover complained) ostensibly for their amusement, but in
fact to immerse himself again in departed glories.

Ray Stannard Baker, invited to one of these sessions, left a vivid
impression of the contrast between the broken President, slumping im-
mobile in his seat, and the filmed images of the erect, smiling figure
acclaimed by unprecedented crowds in Europe. All the while Mrs. Wilson
and her sister—there were always extra Bollings about—talked together
in loud tones. The magic display ended, the lights went up, and the last
image was the President shuffling down the White House corridor, on
a marble floor laid bare so that his left leg could slide behind him; and
the last sound was the tapping of his cane.[19]

On March 3 he went out for the first time for an afternoon drive. The
day before, the car had been kept waiting at the door of the White House
while some difficulty kept him from emerging as planned. But this time
he was lifted into his seat, heavily wrapped. No photographers were
present, but an amateur recorded in a snapshot, published in all the
newspapers, the President's pitifully changed aspect.

"It is an uphill work and the hill is very steep," Wilson said of his
physical struggles at this time.[20]

Such was the man—or rather the shadow of a man—who now faced
the supreme challenge of his career, the test by which the success of his
Presidency would be judged and his place in history largely determined.
Wilson's final efforts to secure ratification of the League of Nations in
a form which he considered valid are usually described as having taken
place when Wilson was more or less his normal self; his shortcomings

are judged in relation to the person he had once been. In fact the stroke had made him incapable of acting as the situation required. "He cannot have lost all of his old suppleness and dexterity," remarked a friendly observer.[21] But in fact he had lost it, as irretrievably as he had lost his physical strength. He could be silent, or he could say no. Beyond that his physical and mental condition had rendered him impotent.

After the deadlock of November, when both the "naked" treaty and the treaty containing the Lodge reservations were voted down, the President was expected to withdraw and then resubmit it. Instead he let it languish in the Senate Foreign Relations Committee, preferring that his Republican opponents live with the situation they had created. Nevertheless the opening of the new Congress in December provided opportunity for getting the issue looked at afresh and settled once and for all. The country was impatient with the long delay in establishing peace; the technicalities of the League reservations seemed unimportant. Even the League's strong supporters felt that the reservation to Article X (assuming the other signatories went along) would affect the working of the League but slightly, once the United States had joined.

In a talk with Wilson, Hitchcock had earlier been given the impression that he "should go on and do the best he could" to work out a compromise.[22] If the President had indeed said that he quickly withdrew it. A White House statement of December 14 declared that the President "has no compromise or concession of any kind in mind."[23] Mrs. Wilson repeated to Hitchcock two days later that her husband intended to propose nothing, nor would he accept any changes beyond such interpretations of the treaty as he had set forth in his meeting with the Foreign Relations Committee the previous summer.

Without encouragement from the White House a bipartisan group in the Senate began negotiations running from January 15 to January 30. By January 22 the conference seemed close to an agreement. Only the substance of Article X was unresolved. On this rock the negotiations foundered. As the weeks wore on Democrats hitherto strongly anti-Lodge began slipping over to his side, indicating a readiness to vote for the treaty with his reservations rather than have it go down to certain defeat. Hitchcock warned the President that without some strong intervention the cause was lost. At this, Wilson roused all his latent energies and framed a public letter which was to have fateful and irreversible results.

Wilson himself (not Tumulty) appears to have made the first draft of the famous Hitchcock letter of February 28. It was revised on March 1 and shown to Hitchcock and Houston, but to no one in the State Department.[24] Its release on March 8, after further revisions, caused a furor rarely exceeded even in Wilson's most combative days. In it he took an inflexible stand on Article X, raising it to a significance far beyond what had been previously envisaged or had been broached in Paris. The guarantee of territorial integrity to League members had been originally understood as a way of protecting the new and fragile states carved from the ruins of the Austro-Hungarian Empire. But "it must not be forgotten, Senator," Wilson now wrote, "that this Article constitutes a renunciation of wrong ambition on the part of powerful nations with whom we were associated in the war. . . . For my own part, I am as intolerant of imperialistic designs on the part of other nations as I was of such designs on the part of Germany."

The choice, he went on, was between two ideals: "democracy, which represents the rights of free people everywhere to govern themselves; and . . . the ideal of imperialism, which seeks to dominate by force and unjust power." The latter is an ideal, he added, as if to twist the knife thrust in the side of former allies, which "is by no means dead and is earnestly held in many quarters still."

The first reaction to the letter was one of outrage at its domestic implications. It threw the League squarely into the midst of partisan politics, where it could only be decided in a national campaign; and it made Wilson himself the logical candidate for that campaign. As for the upcoming Senate vote, it put the final nail in the League's coffin. The second reaction was from abroad. The British and French professed to be appalled at these suggestions that their motives were impure and their designs imperialistic. Jusserand demanded an audience, and Polk was at a loss as to what he should be told.

"You might tell him," Wilson wrote, "that I was fully cognizant while I was in Paris of the constant militaristic intrigues which were going on against Monsieur Clemenceau under the leadership of Marshal Foch and with the countenance and encouragement of President Poincaré."[25] Polk said as much when he saw Jusserand on March 15, adding that the French attitudes on the Reparation Commission and the Rhineland Commission indicated "a military spirit." Within a few weeks, amid threats of revolution, German troops advanced to occupy Frankfurt. When the French responded with military displays across the Rhine, Wilson and Polk were prepared to find their worst suspicions justified.

On March 19 the Senate voted on the treaty. By then, emboldened by the disarray into which Wilson had thrown his supporters, Lodge had strengthened his crucial reservation to Article X. Not only did it specify that no military action could be taken under the League without explicit authorization of Congress, but also no action of any kind, including economic boycott. Nevertheless almost half the Democrats, many of them former Wilson supporters, voted with the Republicans in favor of the amended treaty. Together, however, they were not enough to form a two-thirds majority. Unable to get a sufficient majority, either for the treaty with amendments or for the treaty without amendments, it was in effect declared dead.

Wilson received the news with apparent equanimity. But the night, Grayson tells us, was a restless one. Several times he was called into the bedroom of the President. "Doctor," said he at about three o'clock, "the devil is a busy man." He asked that a passage from St. Paul's Epistle to the Corinthians be read to him: "We are troubled on every side, but not distressed; we are perplexed, but not in despair." "If I were not a Christian," he said, "I think I should go mad, but my faith in God holds me to the belief that He is in some way working out His own plans."[26] Afterwards Wilson never faltered in his position that no further efforts at compromise be attempted.

On April 14 Wilson attended his first cabinet meeting since his departure for the West, held in his study in the residential quarters of the White House. He was placed in his chair before the cabinet members started arriving and the name of each was announced as they came in. They found him there, prematurely old as others had described him, but ready with a story to break the awkward silence.

He was meeting for the first time with new members. Bainbridge Colby he had called from a New York law office to become, unexpectedly to the nominee as to everyone else, Lansing's successor. Wilson admired Colby's literary skills, trusted him to be faithfully subservient, and felt indebted because he had broken with the Bull Moose party to become a supporter in the 1912 campaign. Edwin T. Meredith, a Democrat from Iowa, he had brought in to replace Houston as Secretary of Agriculture, when the latter took the place of Carter Glass at the Treasury. (Glass was now a senator from Virginia.) Joshua W. Alexander had been picked more or less at random—after being interviewed by Mrs. Wilson—to replace Redfield at Commerce. Finally John Barton Payne, of Illinois, had gone to Interior on Lane's resignation. It was not altogether a happy team. Seeing Colonel House in New York, Houston told him that he did not like Meredith, that Alexander was "totally unfit"; and he expressed, added the Colonel, "even stronger feelings as to the unfitness of Colby."[27]

In the middle of the meeting, Mrs. Wilson and Grayson appeared. "This is an experiment, you know," Mrs. Wilson said. The cabinet understood that they were not to stay too long.

Nevertheless the discussion at that first meeting was revealing. Palmer blamed the Bolsheviks for the anthracite coal strike then in progress. The Secretary of Labor demurred. Palmer excoriated an official for having released "alien anarchists" who should have been deported. Again the Secretary of Labor demurred. Aliens might be deported who committed overt acts, not those who went over to the Communists in a body. Woodrow Wilson must have appeared far off, but somewhere in the depths the soul of the old liberal flickered—the Wilson who had sought a general amnesty, who had planned to free Debs, who had suffered for the crimes against civil liberties which he knew must be the bitter fruits of war. According to Daniels, "Wilson told Palmer not to let the country see red."[28] It was a feeble rebuke, by a man too feeble to make it count; yet Daniels did well to inscribe it on the record.

One day that April, according to Grayson's *Intimate Memoir*, Wilson dismissed his nurse, and calling his physician to his side, told him that he was contemplating resignation—if, he said, "I become convinced that the country is suffering any ill effects from my sickness."[29] He would call Congress into session and get Grayson to wheel his chair into the House of Representatives. He would have his address prepared and would try to read it, but if his voice was not strong enough he would ask the Speaker to take over. Then, he concluded, "I shall be wheeled out."

These melodramatic musings are not the first time the question of the President's resignation had come up. Grayson later told John W. Davis (and repeated to Ray Stannard Baker) that he had reluctantly advised Wilson to resign in January.[30] He added that Mrs. Wilson objected. His wife's attitude would have been decisive with the doctor, and it must have been very persuasive to the patient. Nevertheless Wilson apparently continued to brood on the possibility until April, and then, after the painful show of bravado related above, dismissed it permanently from his mind.

It must seem extraordinary that a man who had since student days argued in favor of resignation after a leader's loss of parliamentary support, and who in 1916 had prepared his own immediate resignation if defeated at the polls, should have clung to office after a debilitating stroke. In the first phase of his illness Wilson was, understandably, not able to act; and even then he was under the illusion, persistently fostered by those around him, that he was on the way to recovery. A strong conviction, moreover, was at work within the recesses of his mind. He kept the extraordinary belief that he might again go before the American people as a candidate for the Presidency, seeking final, popular vindication for his unyielding stand on the League. Without such a thought to sustain him, he could hardly have endured the dark night of the peace treaty's apparent defeat, or held with such tenacity to the shreds of power.

Far from entertaining thoughts of resignation, Wilson meditated and schemed to prolong his days in office. In vain Tumulty pleaded with him to declare publicly that he had no third-term ambitions. With his hopes of being a candidate, McAdoo lay siege to the White House, looking eagerly for assurances that his father-in-law would not run. Palmer pushed his own preconvention campaign, to find himself ostracized from the Presidential circle. By May, Ike Hoover was telling Swem that Wilson himself fully expected to be the nominee; cabinet members who sought to supersede their chief were considered to be "lacking in character."[31] In the famous Hitchcock letter, the President had paved the way for his own third-term campaign. Now he bided his time; he watched the changing political scene, as he watched for signs of returning health.

No one, however, would tell the President that his candidacy was an utter impossibility. Neither his wife nor Grayson, both fearing to see him fall back into his poststroke depression, told him the truth plainly. As Ike Hoover describes the charade within his official family, one or more cabinet members would lag behind after a cabinet meeting had ended, suggesting that they would go to San Francisco, seat of the upcoming national convention, and have him nominated. Whatever the degree of seriousness lying behind the charade—only Colby seems to have been unrealistic to the end—these men, who should have known better, played shamelessly upon the President's weakness and ambition.

Undated rough notes in longhand reveal that at some time during this spring Wilson drafted a document entitled: "3rd Inaugural." The people were thanked for the "overwhelming honor" they had conferred. The duties of the United States were defined as first, "to lead by moderation and constructive plans," and second, "to fight and defeat . . . all Reaction." A last, feeble flourish evoked the image of a torch which "our fathers lighted," and which they placed "at the front of the nation."[32]

So pathetic a gesture would not be worth noting except that it affords insight into the mood of the wounded fighter as the Democratic chieftains made preparations for the national convention to gather in early July at San Francisco. The national chairman, Homer S. Cummings, was received by the President to discuss the keynote address. He was glad, he said, that Cummings would be representing him at San Francisco, but was ominously silent when other names were mentioned. Together the two men worked out a code to be used in messages to and from the convention. Then Cummings was invited to stay for the inevitable movie show.

Senator Glass was next enlisted, with Mrs. Wilson sending word that the President would like him to come to the White House at 2:00 P.M. on June 12. It turned out that the President could not see him; he had forgotten he had an appointment at that hour with his masseur. But he had commissioned her to say he wanted Glass to be chairman of the platform committee. "In her usual womanly way," Glass added revealingly—for Edith Wilson was never quite as innocent as she appeared—"she professed ignorance of the convention processes." Stopping at the Executive Offices on the way out, Glass found Grayson waiting for him. The latter expressed the "greatest anxiety about the President's third-term thoughts"; it would be "literally impossible" for him to measure up to the exactions of the campaign.[33] Tumulty also showed concern. Glass assured them that there was no way the convention would nominate a man in the President's physical condition.

Within this same week an extraordinary interview, covering most of the front page, appeared in the New York *World*. Written by a friendly journalist, Louis Seibold, it sought to assure the public that the President was fit for any duties. Seibold reported that during a three-hour visit he had found the President moving freely about the White House, showing only "a slight limp," scarcely noticeable. A long discussion of the President's routine indicated that he was functioning better than before his illness, having more time to study matters in depth. The interview gave every evidence of having been carefully arranged, and it was widely interpreted as being a bid for a third-term nomination. Shortly after its publication McAdoo, convinced that his father-in-law would run, formally withdrew from the race.

The genesis of the interview, not known to the public until years later, reveals Wilson, abetted by his wife, being deliberately artful in seeking to become a candidate. Tumulty, though unwilling to tell the President to his face that a third term was hopeless, made plans for Seibold to come on two consecutive days to the White House. It was Tumulty's idea that the long interview would give Wilson the opportunity for a definitive withdrawal; it was Seibold's idea that Wilson would have a chance to explain fully his stand on the League of Nations. They both failed to take Mrs. Wilson into account. She acquiesced in the interview, but declared in a letter (filed away by Tumulty with an expletive penciled in the margin) that no political questions could be asked. Its only purpose, she averred, was to "exalt" her husband.[34] As for Wilson himself, he seized the occasion to put on the kind of act that, at another stage of his illness, had fooled Senators Fall and Hitchcock.

Just before leaving for San Francisco, on June 19, Glass again stopped at the White House, this time being received for tea on the south portico. Wilson was outspokenly harsh in his judgment of the three leading candidates, expressing mistrust of McAdoo, dislike of Palmer, disdain for Ohio governor James M. Cox. After an appropriate farewell, Glass was accompanied by Grayson and Tumulty to the train. They were particularly anxious to know if the President was still thinking of a third term. Glass assured them that he had made no mention of it. The train was pulling out as Grayson made a last plea. "If anything comes up," he said, "save the life and fame of this great man from the juggling of false friends."[35]

From the convention floor on July 1 Cummings wired the President that the League plank was "entirely in accord with your views" and that the platform committee was "in the hands of your friends." The next day, Wilson wired Cummings: "We are in fighting trim and in winning mood, why should we concede anything?" And a day later, a mimic general brandishing a wooden sword, Wilson wired again: "We are following the vision of the founders [with] a conquering purpose and nothing can defeat it."[36] These messages were encoded by the President and Mrs. Wilson working together with the aid of Swem; Tumulty was not aware of their contents, nor, for that matter, did he know the code.

Far more serious was a message from Colby on July 2 showing the Secretary's political naïveté and his shocking sycophancy. To the man waiting hungrily for good news in the White House he sent a message asserting that a "unanimity and fervor of feeling for you" prevailed at the convention; he declared it to be the "consensus . . . that no one who has been named can command sufficient votes for nomination." Colby went on to state that "I propose, unless otherwise definitely instructed, to take advantage of the first appropriate moment to . . . place your name in nomination."[37]

This was going beyond White House playacting, to risk humiliation for the President and reduction to absurdity of the convention procedures. As Cummings described the situation some years later, he was horrified when he learned of Colby's message. It had been sent without consultation with anyone in San Francisco though not, it appears, without having been discussed by telephone between Colby and the White House. At a conference in San Francisco attended by all the President's friends, Colby found himself to be in a minority of one. On July 4 he informed Wilson that although his message had been sent "in all sincerity" it had been overruled.[38]

Meanwhile at the convention a boom for McAdoo was started. He climbed in the balloting but fell short of a two-thirds majority; John W. Davis was promoted as a dark horse. On July 6 the deadlock broke. Cox was nominated, with Franklin D. Roosevelt as the Vice-Presidential candidate.

Wilson sent congratulatory messages to them both, but made little effort to conceal his disappointment. When cabinet members returned from San Francisco they were treated coolly. Daniels, for whom Grayson intervened, was restored first into the President's good graces; Colby was readmitted under Mrs. Wilson's aegis. To make matters worse, Wilson found his friend Cummings excluded from the chairmanship of the National Committee. Under pressure, Cox had surrendered to the choice of the political regulars, who named George White of Ohio. When Cummings visited the White House on July 26 he found the President affable, beginning the interview with a few golf stories, but bitter over the White appointment. "It is a terrible mistake," he said. "If Governor Cox . . . continues that course . . . his administration will be a failure, and will end in a guffaw." Then, after a pause: "You know, I would rather be hated than be the object of derision."[39]

The Democratic candidate received conflicting advice upon the degree to which it might be politically helpful, or harmful, to receive a Presidential blessing. To his credit, he decided upon a visit to the ailing chief. Franklin Roosevelt accompanied him, and left his account for history. The two were kept waiting as Wilson was rolled out to his habitual place on the south portico. Looking up as they approached, in "a very low, weak voice [he] said: 'Thank you for coming. I am very glad you came.' " His feebleness startled both men, and the younger saw tears in the eyes of his running mate. "Mr. President," Cox said, "we are going to be a million per cent with you . . . and that means the League of Nations." On the way out Cox asked Tumulty for paper, and then and there wrote out the statement committing them both to making the League the paramount issue of the campaign.[40]

For Wilson, however, this was scant satisfaction, after the large ambitions he had held. His interest in the campaign became limited at best. Cox was faithful to his pledge of support for the League; he drew good crowds, but behind him was an apathetic organization and a demoralized party. The Republicans nominated the handsome, blustering senator from Ohio, Warren G. Harding, who responded to the mood of the country with his promise of a return to "normalcy."

In this interval Wilson can be seen with painful detail in the distressing imprisonment of mind and body to which his illness confined him, sometimes accepting his fate passively, sometimes surmounting it by a steely act of will. "Our beloved sufferer," Edith called him in a letter to a friend; yet her watchfulness over every act, private and public, must sometimes have been galling. "Just a word in your ear," Wilson wrote late in August 1920 to Josephus Daniels. "I received recently a number of messages about departmental business through third persons . . . and I write to beg that you will communicate with me directly whenever there is anything that it is necessary for me to decide." Yet another letter a few weeks later gives a sad picture of the President's lack of conviction in trying to cope with affairs. "The suggestion made by Mr. Tumulty," he advises the Secretary of State (in regard to a statement on Panama Canal tolls), "seems to me to have a good deal of merit. I submit it to your judgment so that my own may be corrected if I am in error. If you agree with me that it is a good suggestion, will you not be good enough to draft and forward the message suggested."[41] A journalist meeting Wilson at this same time commented in a confidential memorandum on "a timidity, almost an apologetic effect in President Wilson's manner."

"For the first time," Wilson told the journalist, "I have a man who can write a [diplomatic] note for me." He was very pleased with a note to Poland that Colby had just written. "But of course it was your note just the same,"[42] said Mrs. Wilson with a smile, knitting nearby.

Swem, who was taking the President's dictation, began making diary notes. In their sessions Wilson would fall into "a sort of coma." He refused to answer letters he did not like. He was "too ill to do that sort of thing," he told his stenographer.[43] Such letters would be filed away unless Mrs. Wilson, who was usually keeping watch, prodded him.

Yet on some days he seemed to enjoy the dictation, as if it were the one way he could make himself heard. His letters could become imperious, or wittily sardonic. He was asked by the head of the International Labor Office of the League for a statement on its functions. "My own judgment," he stated, "is that the Labor Office should show what functions it ought to perform by performing them, and by feeling its way from experience to experience." The same morning he was asked for a statement endorsing a new Presbyterian college in Memphis, Tennessee.

"I must frankly say," he replied, "that I do not believe in denominational colleges, and I think that their multiplication would be a very serious mistake." A memorial to him had been proposed: he expressed an "entire unwillingness to have my effigy mounted as is suggested. Moreover I don't like the partner they offer me." (The "partner" was Jefferson Davis, president of the Confederate States during the Civil War.[44])

To the Attorney General he dashed off an inquiry wanting to know precisely what powers he held under his title of "Chief Magistrate." He would like to hold up some "scoffing automobilist," he told Swem, "and sit by the roadside and fine him about a thousand dollars." The Attorney General replied gravely that he was a chief magistrate, but not a magistrate in the ordinary sense, and that he held only such powers as were enumerated in the Constitution.[45]

If a man is not a hero to his valet, Wilson—though much liked by him—was not a hero to this stenographer. A certain individual had been hurt by one of the President's actions and wanted a long letter of explanation. "I wish," said the President, "people wouldn't have *feelings* in politics." Asked why he would not himself write the story of the peace conference, "He would have to fill it too full of acid," he replied. "It would be as bitter as the memories of John Adams." (The President, added Swem, "has often commented on J. A. and his 'acidity.' ") He was annoyed by a request from Tumulty to prepare a line of condolence for someone who was dying. "The President said that the people the secretary said were dying never turned out to die. One case he cited was Theodore Roosevelt, another was Cardinal Gibbons, both of whom revived." (Swem seemed to have the distinct impression that the President wished they hadn't.) The secretary, Wilson added, was always going off "half-cocked."

Again, there was the case of the "very bad portrait," with a letter asking whether it had been received. "The President," said Swem, "told me to reply: 'Unfortunately it had been received in good shape.' " Mrs. Wilson suggested some word of appreciation. "He said, 'No, I will not lie to these people. They ought to do something honest like digging.' "[46]

By Labor Day the campaign was clearly getting nowhere. "The truth is that at the present moment we are licked to a frazzle," wrote one informed observer to Tumulty.[47] The secretary wanted Wilson to put his "laboring oar" into the debate; he wanted the release of cables showing that Wilson had been receptive to Republican advice while he was shaping and reshaping the covenant in Paris. "No answers to Harding of any kind will proceed from the White House with my consent,"[48] was the President's dictum. He was, however, ready to issue an appeal on behalf of the League, and in early October toiled over its composition.

In its language and in the force of its argument it was a pale imitation of Wilson's earlier state papers. He went back to notes he had kept on hand for a "3rd Inaugural," eliminating references to his proposed candidacy and using sentences calling for a national popular referendum on the League. Seeing a draft, Tumulty ventured to object to the idea of a referendum, and to the statement that the election was "not to be left to groups of politicians of either party, but is to be referred to the people themselves for a sovereign mandate." Tumulty argued that many other issues besides the League were being played up in the campaign and that no one was being given the real facts about it. A penciled note came back: "I am sorry, but I cannot agree with you. W. W."[49] And so W. W. drove obstinately on, demanding the impossible, inviting defeat.

The month of October dragged by. "I hobble from one part of the house to the other," he wrote Jessie, "and go through the motions of working every morning, though I am afraid it is work that doesn't count very much." And to his old friend Lucy Smith: "Nothing changes very much with us. I am said to be making progress towards health, but it is slow and by force of will rather than anything else, and I can only try to be patient."[50] Yet there was to be one more major effort, an address in the White House to twenty Republicans favorable to the League. He apologized for having to deliver it sitting down, and for reading from a manuscript. As invariably with those who saw the President for the first time after his illness, they were shocked by his appearance.

In the same week Tumulty made a campaign speech in Bethesda, Maryland, drawing a picture of Wilson the human being. "I modestly step out from my obscurity in the wings," he began, "and tell the audience a few things about the leading actor in this great drama of the past eight years."[51] The audience warmed to it, and the speech was widely reprinted, but the man in the White House was not pleased.

LEAVING THE WHITE HOUSE

Election day saw Cox defeated in a Republican landslide, his popular vote being nine million to Harding's sixteen million. Only those close to the President seemed surprised at the outcome. "I am bowed under the weight of disappointment and discouragement," Colby wrote. Tumulty confessed to his old friend Jim Kerney, "I never thought we could live through these melancholy days."[1] Wilson himself took the election calmly, as he had always taken the popular verdict. Instead of being knocked out, Grayson reported, he accepted the situation, and after the first period of dismay, actually improved in health. Visiting the White House in mid-December, Cleveland Dodge was surprised to find him "generally in good spirits and [he] cursed out his enemies in grand form."[2]

Wilson wrote a graceful letter to Cox, and immediately offered Harding the use of a warship for a proposed trip to Panama, adding that he would be welcome to sail down the Potomac on the *Mayflower* to meet his ship.[3] Considering how much Wilson cherished the *Mayflower*, both for the sake of the good trips he had made upon her and as a crowning prerogative of the Presidency, his offer to the President-elect was no mean courtesy.

For the man who in health and sickness had borne through what seemed a lifetime the inescapable burden of power, the end of the road was now in sight. Early in December an annual message to the Congress had to be assembled. Tumulty drafted it once more, but Wilson made extensive emendations. He had little reason to believe that anything he proposed would be acted on. Diffidently, he suggested that aid be sent to Armenia in its struggle for freedom; he proposed that, a stable government having been established in the Philippines, the islands be given their independence. Mostly the message went over ground already familiar and much was repeated from earlier statements.

As the year ran out he learned that he had been awarded the Nobel Peace Prize for 1919. The pleasure he might have received from the honor was diminished by the fact that the prize for 1920 went to Léon Bourgeois, who had represented France on the League of Nations Commission in Paris. Bourgeois had bored the President with his long, technical speeches, and outraged him by efforts to convert the League into a military alliance against Germany.

Diminished, too, was another event that might have provided the great triumph of his career—a "midday hour of the world's life," in an earlier Wilson phrase.[4] On November 15, the League of Nations held its first meeting in Geneva. The absent President was acclaimed as the League's spiritual father; but everyone present knew that the international institution was seriously handicapped by uncertainties regarding America's role. Wilson himself was in a bitter frame of mind. He was unrelenting toward his Senate foes, telling Colby a few days after the Geneva meeting that he was "entirely against" resubmitting the treaty to the Senate: "the so-called reservations proposed in the last Senate were not drawn in good faith," but were "nullifications" of the treaty itself.[5]

To no less a degree he was angry and vindictive toward the major powers on whose conduct the future of the League rested. Since his return from Paris he had fumed against renewed militarism in France, outcroppings of British imperialism, and what seemed the utter irresponsibility of the Balkan countries. Three times he had told Lansing that he felt like having the United States withdraw from participation in European affairs. He would not, he said, join a League aimed at guaranteeing unjust settlements. To Colby as the first Geneva meeting approached he wrote that he did not want an American observer to be present, among "other great powers . . . now mismanaging the world."[6]

By December 1920, business at the White House came to a virtual standstill. A friend of the President's, dropping by at the Executive Offices, found all "very quiet, serene, here, in your former haunts."[7] "Another, and our last Christmas in the White House," Edith Wilson noted; "a family dinner party but further than that . . . little celebration."[8]

The President and his wife turned to their private concerns. They needed to settle, first of all, on a place to live after March 4. Considering various possibilities, mostly in the South, they rated each according to such factors as climate, friends, and nearness to libraries. In the end their choice fell on Washington. They looked at sites where they might build, keeping an architect busy making and revising plans. Finally, after several building lots proved unsuitable, Mrs. Wilson found a recently constructed house on S Street which was entirely to her liking. In her memoir Edith recounts that Woodrow presented her with the deed one December afternoon at tea. In fact the arrangements for the purchase (the house cost $150,000) seem to have been carried on between Grayson and several of Wilson's friends who contributed the necessary funds, while Wilson himself was kept in ignorance. Very probably it was Edith, that December afternoon, who presented the deed to him.

In any case, various changes and additions had to be made: an elevator for the ex-President's use, a side entrance from which he could slip into his car, a garage that would shelter the White House Pierce Arrow, now purchased for his private use (also by friends). When the plans were completed, only twenty-eight days remained to accomplish the work and to get the furniture and household goods moved in.

Frank Sayre and Jessie went to Princeton to oversee the packing and shipment of furniture long in storage. Wilson canvassed the navy to locate the desk he had used on his crossings on the *George Washington*, and he wrote Hibben requesting a large table—which he had purchased privately—from the study at Prospect. (Hibben offered to have Princeton pay the freight; Wilson insisted on paying it himself.) He also coveted a chair from his White House office. Colonel Clarence S. Ridley of the Corps of Engineers wrote that he saw no objection to the removal of such chairs. Mr. Roosevelt had removed one; Mr. Taft three, and each had provided a similar replacement. In fact, the colonel added, this procedure was a benefit to the United States, "inasmuch as it practically avoids the expense of maintenance of these chairs."[9]

Meanwhile Mrs. Wilson, like any good housewife, was going through the White House closets. There she found two suits left by Colonel House in the days—before her marriage to Woodrow—when he was a constant visitor. She had the suits packed up and sent to New York. Considering the high cost of living, she wrote House, they might prove useful. House acknowledged the favor with every appearance of being exceedingly glad to have his old suits back.[10]

There were also papers to be dealt with. Ray Stannard Baker told the President of his ambition to write a book on the Paris peace conference—one that "would exhibit America in contact with Europe for the first time . . . the clash of character, ideals, method." One day in January 1921, Wilson agreed to give him first access to the papers and documents he had brought with him from the peace conference, and to let him interpret them with complete freedom. Going upstairs to the President's study, Baker saw before him the steel box he had often observed on the desk of his study in Paris. "I recalled," Baker later wrote, "just how he shut and locked it every night."[11] There were in addition three trunkfuls of papers, besides a cabinet and a smaller box shortly removed from a local bank.

In a third-floor White House bedroom, with Margaret practicing her singing in an adjoining room, Baker set up his workshop, starting what were to become three major volumes on the peace conference. Mrs. Wilson would often invite him down to lunch, and the President would help decipher shorthand comments or clarify the meaning of the documents for the journalist-scholar. When the Wilsons moved to S Street these papers (along with Baker) were given a place in a reception room on the first floor, and later were removed to Baker's home in Amherst.

As the last days drew near, Wilson observed the amenities of parting. He accepted routine resignations with a few words of gratitude. He wrote personal letters to members of the White House Secret Service, and he and Mrs. Wilson made gifts to the whole staff. A major indebtedness, such as his to Tumulty, he did his best to take care of, in this case with a judgeship. (Tumulty declined, feeling the need to make money in the practice of law.) But one act of generosity that Wilson might have performed, one last humane and liberal step, he sternly refused. This was the granting of a pardon to Debs.

It will be recalled that, just before going West, Wilson had promised to deal with the Debs case "in as liberal a spirit as possible." But the Wilson who returned from the West, and who emerged enfeebled from his struggle with death, was a different Wilson, and he had a different view about a pardon. Through 1920 the issue was kept alive, in the press, and in private communications to the President from his official family and from civil rights advocates. To restore a conviction that justice was being done after the fevers of the war years, to atone for the excesses of the red scare, seemed to many something that only a general amnesty could accomplish; and at the very least—because his case had become a symbol—a pardon granted to Debs. After the November elections, as the President's term drew to a close, pressure for the pardon increased.

Wilson remained adamant. Palmer's assurances that Debs's health was excellent and that in prison he was being humanely treated strengthened the President's resolve not to act. When in the postelection period William B. Wilson, Secretary of Labor, urged a pardon the President responded, "I am sorry that my judgment differs from yours. . . . I always differ from you with hesitation and regret, greatly trusting your judgment."[12] It must be said that Newton D. Baker, the most sensitive in the cabinet on issues of civil rights, found reasons for continuing to hold Debs in prison. He was there because of offenses committed in wartime, Baker argued, under statutes unanimously approved by the Supreme Court; merely because peace had come was no reason for releasing him. But this was unlike Baker, as Wilson's position was unlike that which he had taken in better days.

Finally, two weeks before the close of the administration, the Attorney General sent a recommendation of pardon.[13] In a single penciled word, "Denied," Wilson barred the last chance to end his term on a healing and magnanimous note.*

Palmer had been "coaxed" by Tumulty into making the recommendation, Ike Hoover thought; and the President's abrupt refusal was

---

* Debs was finally released with twenty-three other political prisoners by President Harding on December 23, 1921; their sentences were commuted to time already served.

directed as much against Palmer as against Debs. But there were deeper reasons at work. In the murky universe of the ailing leader, with depression and helplessness clouding his judgment, he had developed a mystical identification with the American soldiers who had fought and died at his command. In the western speeches the theme of their utter self-sacrifice (and of his own) had been expounded; and in afteryears he never lost an opportunity to show toward any soldier whose path he crossed a gentle and almost worshipful respect. He became convinced that to grant amnesty to any who had impeded the war was to betray a holy cause. Sinking into this emotional quagmire, he betrayed himself.

The last cabinet meeting, best recorded in Houston's diary, fell on March 1. Along with Daniels and Burleson, Houston had been present at the first cabinet meeting eight years before. The contrast between the hope of that occasion and the overwhelming sadness of this one—between the Wilson of 1913 and the Wilson of 1921—weighed heavily. Houston arrived early at the Cabinet Room in the Executive Wing, and taking his seat could see the President making his way slowly, tortuously, from the elevator that descended from the residential quarters—a distance, it had been figured earlier, that required 170 steps, and took him seven minutes to cross. Houston, unable to bear the pain of watching, withdrew and returned with the others when the President had been seated.

After some cursory remarks, Colby undertook to express on behalf of his colleagues the admiration in which the President was held. Following Colby, Houston began a tribute of his own. But he paused; he saw that the President could no longer contain his emotions. "Gentlemen," Wilson said weakly—and such a confession did not come easily from one who had lived by an ironbound discipline—"it is one of the handicaps of my physical condition that I cannot control myself as I have been accustomed to do. God bless you all."[14] The men around the table rose silently and shook his hand as they went out. Later the cabinet members joined in a letter: "Mr. President: the final moments of the Cabinet on Tuesday found us quite unable to express the poignant feelings with which we realized that the hour of leave-taking and official dispersal had arrived. Will you permit us to say to you now, and as simply as we can, how great a place you occupy in our honor, love, and esteem."[15]

In a letter to a friend written at about the same time, Wilson's old associate of scholarly days summed up succinctly the emotion that all were attempting to express. "Fate has dealt hardly with him," wrote Frederick Jackson Turner; "but Time, the great restorer, and, let us believe, History, will do him justice."[16]

CHAPTER THIRTEEN

Into History

———◆———

THE HOUSE ON S STREET

At precisely eleven o'clock on March 4, the inaugural procession reached the Capitol where Wilson debarked at the freight entrance. Declining a wheelchair he walked slowly on the arm of his attendant to the elevator and then to the President's Room where so often in the past he had come to marshal and persuade the lawmakers. Now, carrying out the last rituals of office, he signed a few remaining bills. Senator Lodge entered. The sixty-eighth Congress, he announced, was ready to adjourn. For just a moment the old man glared at his adversary. "Tell them I have no further communications to make," he said. And then, the words scarcely audible in the hushed chamber: "I thank you for your courtesy."[1]

To join the outdoor ceremony where Harding took the oath of office was obviously too much for the invalid. Unobserved, virtually alone, he made his way to the side door of the Capitol where an autombile awaited him. Cheers could be heard echoing from the west front as Woodrow Wilson, now Mr. Wilson, ex-President, passed through deserted streets into what seemed certain oblivion and the darkness of defeat.

Quitting office, he had been punctilious to leave no duty unfulfilled. Yet in the official silence that had wrapped him during his last months in office, and that now was unbroken by any words to the nation of summary or farewell, he appeared a forlorn, forgotten figure. He was hated by many. He had asked for no pity and had received none. From the common people in whom he had so often expressed his faith he had withdrawn in his weakness and spiritual agony. "Today," confided one friendly senator to his diary, "he is bereft of popularity."[2]

His automobile, passing in front of the White House grounds, turned

645

off Massachusetts Avenue into S Street, to stop before number 2340. A crowd waited to watch him enter.

The brick and limestone residence, set back from the street by a shallow drive, was modest compared to the house he had lived in during the past eight years; but it was substantial and handsome, suitable for a President in retirement. Up three steps, a white door gave into a marble-floored hall; to the left, warmed by an open fire, was the room that served as an office. A large billiard room stretched behind it. On the second floor a living room extended across most of the street side, while looking out over the garden, facing south, were the dining room and library, separated by a small solarium. Wilson's bedroom, on the third floor, was quiet and capacious, distanced from his wife's by a small room, intended for a children's nanny, now prepared for a nurse. Here the ex-President was to live for two years and eleven months.

Those years and months were important in Wilson's life, for they were more than the record of an old man's decline. They tested his faith; they showed his emergence from despair into something like hope and into a growing recognition that his life had not been in vain. They reveal, also, a people's slowly maturing sense of what this gaunt man had meant to them. Had Wilson died at Pueblo he would have been remembered as a martyr, and his life would have held something of the mystery and awe that surrounded Lincoln's. Instead, Wilson was compelled to suffer through the unraveling of his hopes and the harrowing diminution of his stature. When he retired to S Street the question could well be put whether he would not go to his grave a forgotten man. Yet by 1924, in part because of the way he conducted himself as an ex-President, in part because of a slow but profound change in public opinion, the answer to that question was clear. Popularity might never return; but fame would endure.

On that first arrival at S Street he found everything not only in order, but arranged so as to ease the transition. Mrs. Wilson, the White House staff, and his own intimate circle had worked through the previous day and night to make his surroundings appear familiar. A bed specially made to equal in size the so-called Lincoln bed had been installed; the large oak table and desk from Princeton days had their place. Over the bedroom mantel hung the painting of a young girl in a blue mandarin coat, which he had bought after Ellen's death.* The first shell fired in

---

* Edith Wilson could never bring herself to admit that over her husband's bedroom mantel in his last years hung a painting vividly reminiscent of his first wife. In her memoir she states that it was a portrait of herself which hung there. (E. B. Wilson, *My Memoir*, p. 306.)

the American offensive in the Argonne recalled a more recent past. A favorite White House nurse was on duty, as well as Scott, a lithe, small black man who was to prove the most sensitive of personal attendants.

Complete rest was ordered, and it seemed to be everyone's conviction—including that of the patient himself—that his condition would rapidly improve. Wilson followed what he called "a routine of convalescence"; it was more nearly a routine of complete invalidism. No visitors were allowed; his meals were taken in his bedroom; if he went into the garden in the spring sun it was to lie stretched out in a chair, wrapped in blankets. Meanwhile the impression was carefully cultivated that with the laying down of public duties his strength was returning. "In an effort to secure a complete rest Mr. Wilson is seeing no one at present," his secretary, John Randolph Bolling, would write. "The rest is doing him a world of good—and he shows an almost daily improvement in health." Even his daughter Jessie was misled, thinking it possible that he might come up to Cambridge for the christening of her little son Woodrow. "I could not without folly undertake a journey yet a while,"[3] he wrote her, in an awkwardly scrawled pencil note. One who was admitted for a short visit on April 25 found him in bed, "more depressed than I had ever known him." However, he added, "the family told me he was very much better and did a great deal of work."[4] In fact, he suffered during this period several setbacks, including digestive disorders not improbably the consequence of small strokes.

In June Stockton Axson visited S Street, reporting to Hibben, who had shown himself "so solicitous" about his "old friend."[5] (Axson was always trying to effect a reconciliation between the two men.) His report would be brief, Axson said, because in effect there had been almost no change since the autumn of 1920, when he had last reported to Hibben. Wilson was no more active physically than on that occasion—in fact, he was less so, since he did not have the long halls of the White House to traverse and refused to walk in the street or the garden of the new residence. Yet he had recovered from the "bad upset" of the previous week and showed himself "intermittently jocose."

"All agree," Axson concluded, "that what he most needs now is systematic mental occupation." He could not get interested in writing. But Colby had been there: "Maybe he will get interested in *that*—God grant it!"

"*That*" was nothing less than the practice of law, and Colby's visit had been to discuss arrangements (first broached while Wilson was still President) for a partnership between the two men. Now the idea appealed increasingly—and, considering his condition, with increasing lack of realism—to the ex-President. "I am looking forward to my new career as a lawyer,"[6] Wilson wrote as early as mid-March to his old friend Charles W. Eliot. He and his former Secretary of State soon began elaborate preparations to open a Washington office. In this they had an enthusiastic ally in John Randolph Bolling, his secretary, who not only shared in the general concern to keep Wilson busy, but for himself wanted at least a modest role in the new enterprise.

Bolling—Edith's brother, one of nine children in the family and two years younger than she—was a hunchback, crippled in youth. He never married and was of delicate health. "Every time it rains," he told a correspondent, "I get as hoarse as a frog."[7] A happy inspiration induced Edith to prevail on her husband to take him as secretary, a post in which, despite his disabilities, he did heroic work, either answering on his own or following Wilson's explicit and carefully nuanced instructions—"Mr. Wilson asks me to say," "Mr. Wilson directs me to say," etc.—the growing volume of mail arriving at S Street. He had, besides, a primitive shorthand system of his own which permitted him to take down the boss's dictation. It was, however, the prospect of having a desk in the new, prestigious law firm that chiefly excited his interest. A correspondence, from most of which the senior partner was happily spared, detailed the search for suitable office space and furniture, and traced the vicissitudes of remodeling and decorating.

All the possible mishaps of such an undertaking befell Colby and his ardent lieutenant. The construction workers put up the walls in the wrong place; then they went on strike. The wiring in the building was condemned as unsafe and all of it had to be replaced. Meanwhile such seemingly important details as choosing the right text for the announcement, and selecting the paper, the type, and the printer, kept the mails busy between Washington and New York.

Not least of the problems was to secure admission to the bar for a man who, even though he had been President of the United States, could boast neither long-standing nor recent legal experience. Colby undertook this politically sensitive task. Seeking passage of a special bill in the legislature of New York State, where his own political base was strong, he secured the unanimous vote of both houses. The District of Columbia bar came next. On one of his rare sorties Wilson made a ceremonial visit to the judge's chambers of the supreme court of the District. The required formal motion in the appellate division was moved by a friendly senator; and for the final step the clerk of the D.C. supreme court visited the applicant in his home. After administering the oath he rushed back to the courthouse to affix the seal, which was too big to be transported to S Street.

Finally in mid-August 1921, several weeks later than had been anticipated, the founding of the firm of Wilson & Colby—"Attorneys and Counsellors at Law"—was announced. For the second time in his life Wilson hung out his shingle as a practicing attorney. This venture, for quite different reasons, was to prove as short-lived as his practice at the start of his career in Atlanta. For different reasons, too, business proved as difficult to get. Wilson went down to inspect the offices on the opening day; he did not visit them again. Bolling had his desk conveniently set up, accessible to the three phones and the three buzzers whose installation he had carefully overseen, and daily visits provided for him a welcome relief from the close atmosphere of S Street.

A first case was presented by a seemingly uneducated man who had made a disastrous investment in a Haitian-American sugar company. The papers were sent down to Washington, but Wilson wrote Colby that he was unable to give them proper attention because when he "settled down to their perusal . . . my one good working eye (I have only one such) threatened to give out."[8] Neither the case itself, nor the senior partner's capacity to deal with it, promised well for the firm. Colby, who turned out to be unfailingly kind in his dealings with Wilson, sent him a check for $5,000 as his share in the partnership; Wilson accepted it somewhat reluctantly, and with the pleasant windfall he bought a small electric car for his wife. By the end of 1921 business was still not coming in, and Colby found fewer reasons for journeys to Washington. "When things go better and I have heartening results to report," Colby wrote in December, "I will come over oftener. They will go better—I know it. Please believe it."[9] Wilson begged Colby not to worry; he shared the belief that business "will come along in great fashion after the first of the year."[10]

Besides the will-o'-the-wisp of the law, literary possibilities haunted the sick man. He lay "propped against a huge pile of pillows . . . bitter at heart," the mind "still working with power, but with nothing to work upon but memories and regrets."[11] Yet he was constantly asked to write something—from a life of Jesus to a review of the best-seller of the day, Lytton Strachey's *Eminent Victorians*. Even had the topics been congenial he knew he did not have the strength for literary composition. To all suggestions the answer came over Bolling's signature, stating that Mr. Wilson was not contemplating any writing for the present.

A request for an inscription for a war memorial in Chickamaugua seemed especially daunting. An inscription "is the most difficult of all forms of literary work," Bolling was instructed to reply; Mr. Wilson "does not feel he can undertake to write it."[12] Pleas for prefaces to books, for articles on current affairs, for comments on this or that were peremptorily turned down. Wilson's frail body and shattered nerves made it impossible for him to concentrate; besides, he was genuinely anxious not to say useless things—"merely to beat the air,"[13] as he told one correspondent.

Yet he lived in the midst of books—reminders of old ones he had written long ago (royalty statements still came in regularly showing slow but steady sales of, among others, *The New Freedom, Congressional Government, The Life of George Washington, A History of the American People*), or new books that his friends and enemies were publishing. The day Wilson left the White House, Lansing's unflattering account of the peace negotiations was published. "It comes to this," Lansing declared self-righteously in the preface. "Was I justified then? Am I justified now?"[14] But Wilson did not let old disagreements trouble the airs of his sickroom. He had not read the book, he told a caller; "I can stand it, if Lansing can."[15]

Other writers were seeking to present Wilson's achievements in a favorable, or in a reasonably objective form. William E. Dodd, a professor at the University of Chicago, published a second edition of his *Woodrow Wilson and His Work*. In Amherst, Ray Stannard Baker was completing *Woodrow Wilson and World Settlement*, soon to be published in three volumes and widely syndicated. Based on primary sources, this work gave authoritative underpinning to the American point of view, with emphasis on the forces and personalities that had opposed a Wilsonian peace. It did much to correct the image of a President who had surrendered weakly or been "bamboozled" by more wily statesmen. Meanwhile Tumulty, with ineffable Irish sentiment, was preparing a book, also destined to circulate widely, showing the President's human side.

Believing that history would vindicate him, Wilson never contemplated writing anything about himself. But as the days in S Street lengthened, his mind turned to nebulous schemes for returning to his old fields of scholarship. A single undated page, apparently from this period, carries the dedication of a volume, *The Philosophy of Politics*, which he was preparing to write when he was elected to the Princeton presidency. The few words of tribute to Edith are all that exist of the once grandly conceived *magnum opus*.

At another time he formed the intention to write a study of the effect on European nations of the successful establishment of a sovereign government by the United States. His old professor at Johns Hopkins, John Franklin Jameson, was asked to indicate materials necessary for such a study. Jameson was puzzled as to the scope and import of the proposed work; he suggested that perhaps the establishment of a government in America was not, after all, considered very important by the Europeans. He produced, nevertheless, a bibliography showing his own remarkable grasp of historical sources. A few pages of Wilson's typewriting remain, the outline for a volume to be called *The Destiny of America*. But the flame of his interest flickered out and by the time Jameson's bibliography arrived at S Street, his febrile mind had turned in other directions.

In his confinement, when health and spirits were at their lowest, came the first intimations of a tide of opinion growing in Wilson's favor. It had begun in the colleges, among the young who were ready to do battle for the League of Nations. The first Woodrow Wilson Club was set up at Harvard, and over fifty colleges later joined the movement. In May 1921, Princeton formed its own group, with more than six hundred undergraduate members. The lonely figure in S Street acknowledged these touching signs of interest and confidence, and occasionally received the leaders for brief interviews.

The founding of the Princeton club had a particular significance. "This is," wrote Wilson's former student, Lawrence C. Woods of Pittsburgh, "the beginning of the honor which Princeton will ultimately pay to its greatest son."[16] Only eleven years had passed since his departure from Princeton in bitterness, amid furious controversy. It seemed an age, given the length of the journey, and given the rapid turnover of student generations. Despite their interest in the League, the young could no longer imagine the spell he had cast in the lecture room and across the campus; older alumni and some faculty members, their hatreds congealed by time, preferred to recall nothing of the good he had done. Wilson was unprepared to take any step to break the official silence lying between him and the university. In vain some of his friends discussed the possibility of a reconciliation. Yet things were bound to change, and now time was beginning, very slowly, to heal the wounds.

His classmates, and especially the old Witherspoon Gang, remained dear to him. In the spring of 1921 Robert Bridges and Hiram Woods managed a small reunion and hoped their "Tommy" might be with them. Wilson had to write that the degree of his recovery had been exaggerated. Afterwards the gang reported—"with love"—that "all the old jokes had been recalled and some new ones devised."[17] "It seemed very strange not to be part of such a re-union," Wilson replied, promising to seek some occasion "to recover the lost ground."[18]

From the faculty a number of letters arrived to assure him he was not forgotten. Dean Fine headed the list of the faithful. George McLean Harper wrote him: "It has at times been hard to live at Princeton amid the memories of great hopes unfulfilled and thinking constantly of what might have been. I see a ghostly group of colleges here which were never built, and am haunted by a vision of that intellectual preeminence which Princeton was on the point of attaining." "Those ghostly colleges," Wilson answered, "will haunt some trustees to their graves."[19]

Meanwhile a plan to embody Wilson's ideals in some form of ongoing organization was making progress. Spearheaded by Wilson's former Assistant Secretary of the Navy, Franklin D. Roosevelt, a group of friends conceived of raising funds by popular subscription to perpetuate the fight for liberalism and internationalism. A good deal of discussion ensued about how the organization should be characterized. Wilson objected to the word "memorial." It made it seem as if he were no longer around, and "I hope in the near future," he said, "to give frequent evidences that I am not dead."[20] The word "endowment" was suggested; but this might indicate to the malevolent that the honoree had endowed himself. Finally "The Woodrow Wilson Foundation" became the name, over Wilson's mild protest that Mr. Rockefeller and Mr. Carnegie had foundations very different from what he wanted his to become.

Roosevelt visited S Street early in June, when the plans were first discussed. Later that summer, in the icy waters off Campobello, he went for the fateful swim that brought on polio. On learning that he was hospitalized, Wilson telegraphed his good wishes, having no conception of how seriously his once-vigorous lieutenant had been afflicted. Later there were other messages between them, the old leader cheering on the young, and being cheered in turn by Roosevelt's characteristically ebullient assurance that, with him, everything was going along "famously." To this, Wilson sent a sad reply. "I shall try and be generous enough, not to envy you," he wrote.[21]

Meanwhile, with Roosevelt's name on the letterhead as national chairman, others took up the work of getting the foundation under way. Cleveland Dodge was chairman of the executive committee (the board of trustees was to be formed later) containing such names as Carrie Chapman Catt, Frank I. Cobb, Henry Morgenthau, Adolph S. Ochs, and Rabbi Stephen S. Wise. The executive director was Hamilton Holt, editor of *The Independent*. In January 1922, the drive for one million

The stricken President

Armistice Day, 1921

S Street: at the front door

To the church on the hill, February 6, 1924

dollars was launched, and committees across the country began soliciting funds in small amounts from the plain people in whom Wilson had always trusted.

For Armistice Day, 1921, President Harding made plans to bury in the national cemetery at Arlington the remains of an anonymous soldier killed in the world war. A longhand letter from the President came to S Street, inquiring discreetly whether Wilson would desire to take part in the ceremonies. (The President, ready to show courtesy to his predecessor, was not anxious to invite a public rebuff.) Wilson replied that he would indeed want to honor the unknown soldier and asked that, in view of his disability, he and Mrs. Wilson be permitted to ride in a carriage. This was granted, but to his chagrin, despite a personal appeal to the President himself, he was refused a request to have the carriage continue in the procession as far as Arlington. Arriving at the White House promptly on the appointed day, he found himself placed near the end of the line.

Wilson might have spared himself his injured feelings. What happened on that November 11, quite unanticipated and unprepared for, was as remarkable a tribute as has ever been paid to an ex-President. The procession moved down Pennsylvania Avenue in silence, the crowds awed as the caisson of the unknown soldier passed by. But when Wilson's carriage appeared, far down the line and conspicuous in its isolation, a murmur went up; then gathering applause rolled down the length of the avenue as the people recognized the pale face of the stricken old campaigner. In a wave of mass emotion they realized, perhaps for the first time, that he had given all but his life to the country's cause, as unstintingly as the soldier in the flag-drapped coffin.

From that moment Wilson loomed in the public imagination as one more than life-size; he took his place among the myths by which a nation defines its destiny. "The Man They Cannot Forget" was the title of a much-quoted editorial appearing a few months later in *Collier's* magazine: "The persistent, mysterious, unconscious way in which men today draw together around Woodrow Wilson"[22] was explained by the fact that he reminded them of what they had dreamed at their best, of hopes that in their finest moments they had dared believe in and pursue. The change from a figure appearing arrogant and withdrawn to one who seemed to embody a lost idealism occurred on that first Armistice Day after his retirement.

The Wilson carriage peeled off the procession to return to S Street. There he was surprised to find a milling crowd, estimated at twenty thousand persons, waiting to greet him. They stood bareheaded when, several hours later, he appeared on the doorstep, pitifully frail and shaken by the scene. The three steps at the front of the house he descended without assistance, leaning heavily on his cane, to greet a small group of disabled veterans. He withdrew into the house; he reappeared and tried to speak. "I can only say, 'God bless you' "—and the crowd let out a cheer. Tears rolled down his cheeks as he groped for his wife's hand. "The grief of the trembling man," wrote a reporter at the scene, "seemed to reach out into the crowd and men and women also burst into tears."[23] The two figures stood there for a full minute. The strains of "My Country, 'Tis of Thee" sounded in the near distance; and then they turned slowly, and went into the house.

After Armistice Day letters poured into S Street. Soon it was the holiday season, and greetings and gifts supplemented the messages of sympathy and goodwill. Wilson dictated scores of thank-you notes for the flowers, the poems, the candy, the partridges, the ducks, the oysters, the beaten biscuits, and so on, until sometimes the larders of S Street must have been intolerably strained. The Cleveland Dodges arrived for a visit. For the first time since he had been at S Street Wilson sat at lunch with guests. He looked well, Mrs. Dodge thought; he laughed heartily and took a keen interest in what was going on.

Afterwards Cleveland Dodge went up alone to converse with Wilson in his bedroom, and at three o'clock they all went out for one of the long motor rides which, with improvement in his health, Wilson was once more enjoying regularly. They climbed into the Pierce Arrow, formerly the White House car, now with his monogram painted over the official seal and a small Princeton tiger upon the radiator. Wilson wore a grey cape he had bought years ago on a walking trip in Scotland—he liked old things, and besides, it was easy to wear over his helpless arm.

They motored out toward Mount Vernon, stopping on the way to pick up a serviceman seen hobbling along on crutches. Hundreds of cars had passed him by, but Wilson never observed a serviceman without saluting him—"I regard all servicemen as my comrades," he wrote more than once—and on this occasion took the veteran into the car. He had been an aviator in France; he was a Virginian, and he was trying to get to Norfolk to spend Christmas with his mother. They left him at the railroad station, the beneficiary of a small supply of cash.[24]

His interest in affairs returning, Wilson began at this time to give much attention to framing a statement of principles generally referred to as The Document. Colby was his chief assistant in this endeavor, but before long Justice Brandeis became an accomplice; Frank Cobb, Norman Davis, and David F. Houston were regular contributors. Wilson himself was not up to efforts of composition or editing; but he prodded his friends and occasionally supplied brief passages. Indeed, he told Brandeis apologetically, "I am firing these things at you ... with inconsiderate frequency and rapidity"; but "they form themselves somewhere in the hidden recesses of my system and I am uneasy until I get them out."[25]

The Document, as it took form, was a somewhat helter-skelter assemblage of liberal and internationalist ideas. The question naturally arose as to what purpose it might serve. Wilson never indicated the answer to his collaborators. They assumed it might be useful as a confidential guide to candidates in the next year's congressional races; or, more generally, as a test of liberal orthodoxy. What they could not have known was that in Wilson's mind it was to be used as the Democratic platform when Wilson himself ran for a third term in 1924. He never abandoned the belief that he would recover his health and that he would run. Meanwhile, The Document's authors were content to keep the sword, such as it was, in its shield. But it gave to its chief perpetrator a sense of being in the midst of things; and when the following spring he called his fellow drafters together for a conference in the library at S Street, he found himself not wearied but considerably invigorated by the discussion.

So it was that as the year 1921 drew to a close, with The Document being shaped, the cheers of Armistice Day still echoing, with good hopes for the law firm, and the Woodrow Wilson Foundation taking form, the mood at S Street brightened. It would not last. In the new year hopes would be disappointed, and politics and personalities, on at least one occasion, would intrude unpleasantly.

The opening of what is usually called "the Tumulty affair" was simple enough. The ex-President's former secretary wrote to inquire whether his chief might not send a message of greeting to a New York Democratic Club dinner. The party henchmen of the Empire State would be on hand, including Colby, Morgenthau, and Polk; Cox was billed as the principal speaker. The ex-President was not favorably inclined. "I feel a message to the New York dinner which you suggest," he wrote Tumulty, "would be quite meaningless unless I made it a serious expression of my views and feelings about the present national situation, and I do not feel that the occasion is a specially appropriate one for breaking my silence."[26]

Tumulty must have been puzzled by this response. He had asked only for a message which "could take the form of an acknowledgment of the invitation and an expression of regret at not being able to attend."[27] Moreover he knew that Wilson had been making it a practice to send messages to party conclaves. "The party represents the things that are permanent and which no human force can defeat," he had wired the Democrats of Allentown, Pennsylvania, not long before. "It stands with those who think justly and plan righteously everywhere in the world, and the future belongs to these."[28] Indeed at the very time he was writing Tumulty, Wilson was sending a message to the Woodrow Wilson Foundation: "I have the assured faith that the ideals with which we entered the war are still consciously held . . . by the whole body of our people and that we are upon the eve of a notable reassertion of the principles for which we sacrificed so much."[29] How Tumulty's heart would have leaped up to receive a message like this!

The next day Tumulty asked to see Wilson. Apparently he had the discretion not to question the ex-President's decision against a message to the New York dinner. But in general conversation he thought he heard words which, without harm, could be transmitted to his fellow diners. And so at his seat during the dinner he wrote out on yellow paper a few words and passed them on to the toastmater. "Ex-President Wilson says," it read, "that he will support any man who will stand for the salvation of America, and the salvation of America is justice to all classes." The sentiments seemed harmless enough. Unfortunately they were read just before Cox's speech. The diners, as one of those present remarked, had by then reached a state of "spirituous exuberance,"[30] and they were quick to interpret the words as the launching of a Cox boom for a second try at the Presidency.

Wilson was furious when he read in the papers next day of the purported "message" from him and of its interpretation as an endorsement of Cox. Apart from a sense of confusion and betrayal, he was convinced that a second run by the party's defeated standard-bearer would be "suicide" for the Democrats. Incredible as it seems, moreover, he was planning to run again in 1924. Apparently not suspecting Tumulty of being the author, he wrote asking him to find out who was responsible. The contrite Tumulty confessed. In vain seeking an interview with his old chief, he declared himself ready to accept any rebuke without complaint.

Wilson was unrelenting. Undoubtedly encouraged by Edith, who saw the opportunity to satisfy a long-standing prejudice, he dispatched to *The New York Times* a statement that he had not sent "any message whatever" to the dinner, "nor authorized anyone to convey a message."

Tumulty stood discredited. Certainly he had erred, but the punishment was out of all proportion to his indiscretion. Despite his pleas, he never saw the President again. To the list of broken associations in Wilson's life, the name of the doughty Irishman who had served him throughout his political career, the incarnation of loyalty and of an almost fawning adoration, now had to be added.*

The law business was not progressing favorably. From New York came sad little notes from Colby. The office had received the case of an action for personal injuries: "This is not a case for us,"[31] he advised. A woman who claimed lands in England provided "no clue upon which any rational investigation could even be started." Another woman, this time from Kentucky, felt herself to have been cheated by a Boston publisher. Colby made a trip to Boston, finding the publisher to be a man "shifty, nervous and unprepossessing"; his reputation was bad, but undoubtedly the woman had urged him on, wanting to be published at any price.[32] More distressing, however, were cases which might have been interesting and which promised lucrative fees—except that the ex-President would not touch them because in some degree they involved past actions of his administration.

A request came for aid in securing a loan to build railways in Ecuador. An oil corporation sought counsel in congressional investigations. These cases, among others, were rejected as a result of Wilson's scruples. "It makes one a little dizzy sometimes," wrote Colby, "to toss away business which one's professional brethren are bending every energy and resource to get. But it's a fine game . . . as long as we can hold out."[33]

Hold out was precisely what the fledgling firm could not do indefinitely. In the summer of 1922 Wilson suggested to Colby that the partnership be dissolved: "I cannot . . . in conscience," he wrote, "go on putting my personal limitations upon your activities."[34] By autumn it seemed the only course. The Washington office, Bolling wrote Colby, "is absolutely a dead expense . . . the only people who come are curiosity seekers."[35] The end came handsomely. Colby put out a press release stating that as a result of the "steady gain in Mr. Wilson's health" he was turning increasingly to other matters. He added that "Mr. Wilson's

* Nevertheless (and happily) this was not quite the end of the "Tumulty affair." Among Wilson's last letters is one recommending Tumulty as a candidate for the U.S. Senate, calling him "a redoubtable debater" and one "whose political training has been more varied than that of any man I know." (WW to J. Kerney, Oct. 30, 1922.)

disciplined power and effectiveness as a lawyer have been a veritable revelation. . . . He has taken a most active interest in the affairs of the firm."[36] "True or not," wrote Wilson of this statement, "I thank you for it with all my heart."[37]

Colby might be blamed for having embraced so uncritically the idea of a partnership with the ex-President, perhaps seeing in it a means to wide publicity and ample financial rewards. But he was largely innocent of such calculations. He was too naïvely idealistic, and besides, he was genuinely grateful to Wilson for having made him Secretary of State. Although the failure must have gone hard with this foolish man, he never faltered in his generosity to the ex-President. As for Wilson, the ending of his second brief legal career was only one more sorrowful reminder that the spirit was more adventurous than the ailing flesh.

That spring Wilson was well enough to set his mind upon going South. In Asheville, North Carolina, an accommodating innkeeper assured him of a cottage with the conveniences he required: among them room for two or three servants, an entrance at ground level, and (not least) a Pierce Arrow available for afternoon drives. Negotiations were progressing satisfactorily when the doctor put his foot down. Other reasons apart, Mrs. Wilson would scarcely have wanted to spend summer months in an area recalling Wilson's youth and first courtship; and now his old friend from Philadelphia, Dr. E. P. Davis, advised firmly that the President should remain at home. "You are gaining steadily there . . . so we would avoid risk."[38]

As is often the case with the advice of doctors, this seems to have been unduly restrictive. The patient could hardly have been worse for a change from the tedium of the Washington house. Yet he had no choice but to give in, which he did with relative cheerfulness. He said he liked the hot days; they were "his" weather. Mail and visitors fell off, but occasionally would come such an invitation as that to be an honorary member of the Order of Merrymen, which evoked from him a latent good humor. He accepted—whereas he had turned down almost everything else. "I grieve as you do," he told his young companions, "at the barbarous destruction of trees which seems to be going on in almost every direction. . . . It looks as if a great many vandals were loose."[39]

By autumn there was a definite improvement in health. Though still dreadfully handicapped and with his nerves on edge, he appeared more ready to take the initiative than at any time since his 1919 stroke. At the same time public recognition of his services, and sympathy for his plight, were growing. His Saturday night visits to Keith's Vaudeville were taking on the character of a public ritual. He would find hundreds waiting as his car drove up, ready to cheer as he made his way laboriously to his box at the back of the theater. The audience would rise as one. Afterwards another crowd would be waiting outside as he left; often members of the cast would gather around his car to pay their respects.

The famous, along with the curious and the unknown, made their way into S Street. Wilson would agree to an admirer's coming for a handshake before he set out on his afternoon drive; he would permit a group of schoolchildren to stand on the opposite side of the street while he emerged from the front door, promising to wave in silent greeting. Old associates were admitted with increasing frequency. They would be entertained at a brief tea, or would join him for a talk while he ate his solitary lunch, afterwards going down to the dining room where Mrs. Wilson and members of the family were having theirs. On these occasions Mrs. Wilson appeared invariably elegant and gracious; the conversation would be gossipy and cheerful, in contrast to the somber atmosphere surrounding the invalid upstairs.

A notable visitor that fall was Clemenceau. Wilson had deep affection for the old tiger of France, despite their antagonisms in Paris. Clemenceau had compromised, as Wilson had, and had fallen from power in the nationalistic excesses of the post-Versailles period. The anger Wilson felt at militaristic tendencies of subsequent French policy only enlarged his tolerance for Clemenceau's undeviating but comprehensible concern for French security. From S Street, on the latter's arrival in the United States, went a telegram assuring the visitor that he would find "none but friends," and the greatest applause during Clemenceau's Metropolitan Opera House speech came with the evocation of Wilson's name. The reunion of the two men provided a touching footnote to history. "We didn't discuss the future—only the occasional good moments of the old days," Clemenceau later reported (his sardonic realism summed up in the word "occasional"). "We fully forgave each other for our bitter quarrels at Versailles. That was all in the past; and both of us had lost."[40]*

November brought mid-term elections. Wilson had set his heart on a Democratic victory; he was, he wired one senator, "breathlessly awaiting"[41] the results of the voting. The outcome was indeed favorable

---

* Lloyd George had also made a visit to S Street, in December 1920. Wilson told a caller the following day that he was depressed because the former Prime Minister had seemed interested only in hearing limericks. (J. Kerney, *The Political Education of Woodrow Wilson*, p. 471.)

to the Democrats, although in Massachusetts Lodge and in Missouri Reed—opponents of the League and men whom Wilson especially longed to see defeated—came through as winners. The election was decided on issues other than the League; but Wilson was prepared to find comfort in the crumbs. Still looking forward to vindication, "We shall complete in [nineteen] twenty-four," he wired one supporter, "what is now so well begun."[42]

Armistice Day, following immediately after the elections, again brought a crowd of thousands into S Street, awaiting the ex-President as he emerged for his afternoon drive. Wilson paused in the doorway, and then standing, bent over but unassisted, and with his enunciation clear, delivered the best speech since his stroke. Cheers filled the autumn dusk as with grim humor he excoriated his erstwhile Senate foes. "They do not represent the United States," he said, "because the United States is moving forward and they are slipping backward. Where their slipping will end, God only will determine." With his good arm he lifted his high silk hat to his head: "If you will pardon an invalid for putting on his hat," he continued, "I will promise not to talk through it." Laughter and applause were stilled as he moved into a gentle peroration. "I think, then, we may renew today our faith in the future, though we are celebrating the past. The future is in our hands, and if we are not equal to it the shame will be ours."[43]

He paused again. "I thank you from a very full heart, my friends, for this demonstration of kindness by you and bid you and the nation Godspeed." Afterwards he appeared with Edith at an upstairs window of the house. The cheering was resumed and a band (arranged for by the faithful Tumulty) led the crowd in song. It was "an exciting day for us and also a very happy one," Wilson wrote afterwards to a friend. "It left me limp but content."[44]

The Woodrow Wilson Foundation announced that it had achieved its fund-raising goals and was now fully established. "A private citizen who but yesterday was rejected of men" (so Creel described Wilson at the foundation's celebratory dinner) would see men and women working across the decades to perpetuate his ideals. "A bed of pain," he said with pardonable hyperbole, "has become the shrine of our country's faith."

Christmas brought the usual stream of gifts and greetings, except that this year they seemed even more plentiful than before, and were acknowledged by the ex-President in letters freshly and often touchingly phrased. A fat opossum, sweet potatoes, partridges, quail, oysters, clams—each received its word of praise and gratitude; and the messages brought together names from different parts of his life, Princeton friends, political associates from the New Jersey and Washington years, unknown people who had shared his vision and been shaken by his fall. The family gathered. Jessie and Frank Sayre; Eleanor and McAdoo; Margaret, her singing career abandoned and now looking rather forlornly for something to do—all came and went at this season. The anniversary of Wilson's marriage to Edith, and then his own birthday, were duly marked. "My dearest husband," Edith wrote him that Christmas Eve (they made it a habit of leaving handwritten notes of endearment about the house), "the chimes are ringing out . . . and I am sending you this little Christmas message . . . with the tender hope that the coming year may bring you the deepest happiness and the return of all the health and vigor you so long for."[45]

In that hour, with a benign, almost mellow light settling over S Street, with the depressed and tortured invalid seeming more nearly reconciled than at any other time to his fate, even the impossible seemed possible.

TO THE END

Wilson's intransigence in regard to the League never altered. Under Harding and Secretary of State Charles Evans Hughes, various efforts were made to bring the United States into some form of relationship with the new international organization, then struggling to establish itself in Geneva. Arguments were made that it was different in operation from what the founders had conceived—less involved with questions of collective security than of mediation and accommodation—and that in these circumstances the dreaded Article X was not essential to its constitution. Conceivably the United States could become an associate member, accepting responsibilities except those where the use of force might be invoked. As the harsh spirit of partisanship receded, efforts were launched to establish on a bipartisan basis renewed efforts to end American isolation.

For Wilson, brooding in his enforced retreat, such schemes were anathema. "I do not believe there can be any settlement of the question [of the League] except by party action,"[1] he wrote to a political associate; and the only party that could act was the Democratic. Norman Davis, a frequent S Street visitor, was warned against suggesting "any detour from the straight road." Convinced that time was on the side of his program, Wilson was prepared to wait out the delay until entrance into the League would come in the wake of a Democratic victory, on the terms he had originally fought for, and (as he still hoped) under his leadership.

While expressing himself freely in private, Wilson maintained throughout this period a public silence often galling to his followers. Could it be that he was indifferent to the fate of the country? Did he enjoy in his grim and bitter retirement the prospect of general confusion? In fact he was not physically or mentally able to inject himself into the political scene. Yet he kept the illusion that at some point he would speak out decisively; at moments he even persuaded himself that the vague and inadequate formulations of The Document would, upon their release, provide a rallying cry. Spurred on by vague ambitions and perhaps taunted by the disappointment of his friends, he began in 1923 to work on a statement that he believed would be worthy of the widest possible circulation—the end of his silence, the restoration of his intellectual and spiritual authority.

The composition of the work was infinitely painful. A sentence at a time was shaped, in penciled notes transmitted to Edith for transcription, or in disorderly lines upon his own typewriter. Days went by with only fragmentary additions to the text. Failing eyesight, physical weakness, and incapacity for mental concentration contributed to the agony of the writing. Finally, early in April, he read a first draft to Edith, and next day he sent off the manuscript to Creel. It was an essay, fifteen hundred words in length, entitled "The Road Away from Revolution."

Creel was appalled. This was not the manifesto he had anticipated; it was brief to the point of superficiality and open to ridicule if it was circulated as a major statement. He wrote Edith, who seemed ready to look at the situation realistically. "I so fully agree with you that his literary reputation must be safe-guarded," she responded, "and feel at the moment that the whole facts should be laid before him."[2] Creel came to S Street for a consultation and wrote afterwards to Edith that he had pointed out to the ex-President "as delicately as I could, what the article lacks is *body*." Under different circumstances he would have advised instantly and with all his power against publication. But such a course might have crushed his confidence, "restoring all of the old depression."[3]

He suggested *Collier's* as a possible publisher, but Mrs. Wilson objected to the low price (two thousand dollars), and Wilson himself came up with the idea of submitting the piece quietly to the *Atlantic Monthly*. Rather than lengthening the article, as had been suggested, he decided to make it even shorter, describing it as "an essay in the form of a challenge." On May 2 he sent it off, unsolicited, to the editor. "In former years," he wrote, "whenever I happened to have produced an essay, it used to be my preference and pleasure to send it to the *Atlantic*." He reserved the right to publish the essay separately, he concluded, "in case you should accept it."[4] The editor, Ellery Sedgwick, was understandably delighted by this windfall, and promptly wrote that it was an article "which, brief as it is, will set the nation thinking."[5] He enclosed a check for two hundred dollars, a sum to which no one seems to have objected.

It was not, in fact, a bad article, nor inappropriate to the time; and it drew upon layers of Wilson's thinking that had not for some time been raised to the level of conscious thought. If this was to be a last word—as in effect it was—he could have done far worse. The cause of the present unrest, he began, was not to be found in superficial politics or mere economic blunders: "it probably lies deep at the sources of the spiritual life of our time."[6]

With historical acumen he went straight to the Russian Revolution as "the outstanding event of its kind in our age." But it was not to raise fears or to denounce horrors. So great and widespread reactions against capitalism, he argued, do not occur without cause or provocation. "Are we to say that the blame for the present discontent and turbulence is wholly on the side of those who are in revolt?" It was a disturbing question, and Wilson faced its ultimate depths. In American capitalism he saw "offenses against high morality and true citizenship"; capitalists had too often "seemed to regard the men whom they used as mere instruments of profit." In the end only justice could bring social peace; and justice "must include sympathy and helpfulness and a willingness to forgo self-interest in order to promote the welfare, happiness and contentment of others and of the community as a whole."

The sum of the matter, Wilson concluded, is that "our civilization cannot survive materially unless it be redeemed spiritually."

The essay was printed in the August 1923 issue of the *Atlantic Monthly*, and immediately, at Wilson's request, reprinted as a small (almost a miniature) book. It was well accepted by the public, which raised no questions about the author's competence—and certainly was without conception of the agony in which it had been produced. No public comment was made upon the extreme radicalism of the argument, nor upon the fact that in this final effort Wilson had assumed the burden of being the West's spokesman against Leninism.

It would have appeared the height of fantasy if anyone had proposed on the March day Wilson rode to the Capitol to turn over power to Warren G. Harding—the one worn out and hated, the other in his prime and the darling of the crowds—that Harding should be the first to die. Yet on July 31 the ex-President wired his successor in California that he had learned with concern of his illness, and three days later, shocked by Harding's death, expressed his "profound sympathy"[7] to the widow. In private, Wilson could be contemptuous of Harding (he was incapable of thought, he told a caller, because he had "nothing to think with"[8]); but in public the two men kept a polite—and even a considerate—relationship. Wilson respected profoundly the office of the Presidency; moreover he was resolved to set an example as ex-President. He let it be known that he would attend the funeral. In formal mourning attire, in the Pierce Arrow that had served him in office, he drove with Mrs. Wilson and Grayson to the White House. Members of his old staff came out to greet him; troops saluted. But Wilson was not up to the ordeal of getting out of the car before the public gaze or of mounting the White House steps. In silence he waited in the parked car while the funeral service unfolded within.

As another summer passed, with the confinement and routine beginning to affect her health, Edith realized the necessity of her getting away. In August, for the first time since her husband's illness, she was absent for more than a brief foray, going to visit for a week her friends the Charles S. Hamlins in Mattapoisett, Massachusetts. Grayson was left in charge at S Street. Edith found herself the center of attraction in a busy, social summer colony, and enjoyed the experience fully. She did not forget the ill man languishing in Washington's heat. "Dear Heart," she wrote, "remember that I love you—and that I want to come whenever you want me." A few days later: "Three years and eleven months today since you were taken ill—but the end of the road is in sight and we are going to have lots of lovely times together."[9] Woodrow bore the separation with some fretfulness. "Not the house inly [only] but the world als [also] itself has been empty since you left,"[10] he told her. A few days later he found the effort of using the typewriter too much for him.

On her return Edith sensed that her husband's condition had deteriorated subtly—or perhaps she saw it for the first time with an outsider's perspective. More frequently now his dictation would fade off during the morning's session with Bolling; or letters would lie unsigned for days upon his bedroom table. Edith had long kept a close watch on his outgoing mail, censoring judgments that appeared extreme or bitter, often allowing her own prejudices to show through. "Dictated but not sent; friend of Col. House" stands at the top of a letter of thanks for a gift of leaves from the churchyard in Columbia where Wilson's family was buried. Bolling was instructed to write instead a routine acknowledgment. On another occasion, on Edith's order, Bolling's formal acknowledgment was substituted for an affectionate letter Wilson had dictated to a friend of his first wife. Now, increasingly, letters would not be mailed "on account bad signature."

Wilson himself was sometimes discouraged but was far from being ready to concede any hopelessness in his condition. "There is so much to fight for," he wrote a correspondent in November, "that ill health must if possible be got out of the way."[11] But a letter to Dr. E. P. Davis that same month perhaps gives a truer picture of his state of mind. He was "ashamed," he wrote, when given credit for patience. "I have been anything but patient, and have repeatedly thrown myself against the bars of my cage. I wish the doctors could tell me what is going to happen to me, but they do not seem to know, and I have to grope along in the dark."[12] Putting the best possible face on things, "Yes, I am growing better," he said at about the same time in a handwritten note to his old friend Mrs. Reid—"too, too slowly, but still noticeably."[13]

The approach of Armistice Day caused a special stir in the S Street household. Two young women, one of them Belle, the flamboyant daughter of Bernard Baruch, had taken Mrs. Wilson's fancy. They were devoted to the cause of the League and were very up to date in their manners and dress. The ex-President seems not to have been entirely immune to their charms, and he consented—as it was most unlikely that he should have done—to their plea that he broadcast an Armistice Day address. Radio was still in its infancy; its capacity to reach huge audiences was untested, and Wilson hated in any case to speak into mechanical contraptions. Once having given his word, however, he set himself to the painful task of preparation. He went through three drafts; the last, done on his own typewriter and exceedingly rough in form, bore corrections in Edith's handwriting.

On Armistice Day eve a single truck parked itself in the S Street drive; one cable reached indoors to the ex-President's library where a microphone was set up. Wilson insisted on standing for the delivery, an uncertain bent figure leaning on a cane, reading haltingly, with his wife close at his side. For most of his listeners the reception was too poor to allow more than his own faint voice to be made out; but in a few places Edith's promptings could be plainly heard, as he groped pathetically to read the written words.

Briefly, he expressed a profound disillusionment: "We turned our back on our associates; refused to bear any responsible part in the administration of peace . . . and withdrew into sullen and silent isolation." More noteworthy than the words was the seeming miracle that brought them into hundreds of thousands of homes. The mails next day were freighted with letters from men and women expressing naïve astonishment at the clarity with which the voice came through. Thus only at the end, when Wilson was too feeble to make it count, did the scientific marvel of mass communication come to his aid. The last years of his life present fateful examples of time being "out of joint." He should have died earlier; and certainly he should have had radio at his disposition in the climactic struggle to make the League understood. Indeed this master of style could more than any public man of his day have unlocked the magic of the new techniques. But his chance came too late, when mind and body were broken.

The next day's ceremonies were an anticlimax. Crowds gathered as they had for two years past in front of the house; the grey worn figure appeared at the door, and his ardent supporter Carter Glass made a brief address. But Wilson's response could scarcely be heard, and when he endeavored to pay tribute to the armed forces which he had served as Commander-in-Chief, sobs shook the exhausted frame. "Your gentleness and sympathy when I broke down touched me very deeply and made me very grateful,"[14] Wilson wrote the next day to Glass. Yet even from this sad end of things something unforgettable emerged. He had finished, it seemed; he turned to reenter the house. Then he paused, and in a voice now clearly carrying to those crowded before him, he cast into the teeth of fortune a last, a lovely and forlorn and essentially Wilsonian, defiance:

> Just one word more. I cannot refrain from saying it. I am not one of those who have the least anxiety about the triumph of the principles I have stood for. I have seen fools resist Providence before, and I have seen their destruction, as will come upon these again, utter destruction and contempt. That we shall prevail is as sure as that God reigns.[15]

That autumn a small group of Wilson's friends—Cleveland Dodge, Jesse H. Jones, Thomas D. Jones, and Cyrus McCormick—combined to provide for him an annuity of ten thousand dollars. Congress at that time made no allowance for ex-Presidents; the group of friends wanted to fill the gap, but even more they wished to pay tribute (as Jesse Jones wrote Wilson) to "the great and useful life that you have lived," and to provide "a slight reward and . . . a slight token of our love and admiration for you." It was a generous and fortifying gesture. "My heart is full to overflowing," Wilson responded. "I am deeply proud that such men should think me worthy of such benefits."[16] He accepted the annuity not as an acquittance but as a new challenge to action. "As I see it," he told Dodge, "the greatest fight of all lies immediately ahead of the liberal forces of this country and of the world—the fight to conquer selfishness and greed and establish the rule of justice and fair play."[17] The defeated warrior was still not giving up.

Nevertheless the year's end was marked by portents, by remembrances of past things, and the vague sense of dissolution. In his correspondence are references to the house at Glencove, Bermuda, where he had spent days of rest after his 1912 victory: he hoped that the pleasure of occupying the house again "is only postponed and not entirely foregone."[18] He dreamed of the island he still owned on Muskoka Lake. ("Do you remember our picnics there," he said softly one day to Eleanor, "and your mother reading poetry under the pines? I wish I could hear her voice."[19]) But the "wished-for time" when he might "build on and occupy his little estate"[20] he now supposed never would come. Meanwhile the news arrived that the house where the family had stayed in Cornish, New Hampshire, had been destroyed by fire, reviving memories and at the same time leaving a void.

Going far back to his youth, he wrote to the man who in Augusta, just after the Civil War, had been his first teacher. A letter to Professor Joseph T. Derry is signed by Wilson as "your pupil and friend."[21] An acceptance of mortality begins to show. He had been elected president of the American Historical Association; in early January he accepted, but not without adding that he "cannot be sure that he will be fit for the duties that fall to the occupant of that office."[22] To a treasured colleague of his administration he sent simple words which could not be taken otherwise than as a farewell. "I only hope that our association with one another," he wrote Newton D. Baker, "has been as satisfying to you as it has been to me."[23]

The sadness of parting found expression when the Sayre family left for Siam. Wilson had urged his son-in-law to take the diplomatic assignment offered him, arguing that it would advance his academic standing. Yet it was hard to see them go. The Sayre children—Francis Jr., Eleanor, and Woodrow—were favorites; and Jessie, with her particular sweetness and her feelings close to adoration for her father, was a presence he could hardly bear to lose. "Good-bye," he wired them early in November. "May God keep you all and vouchsafe you every blessing and happiness."[24] He must have known that he would not see them again.

Nevertheless the old fires burned, often expressing themselves in touching forms. The first payment on the annuity provided by his "incomparable friends" was acknowledged when it was paid in January as having provided him not with the assurance of repose but rather with "the most powerful additional reasons for continuing to try to be what they have in their generosity believed me to be."[25] But in plans laid before his younger friend, Raymond Fosdick, the unquenchable drive led to what seemed almost ludicrous results. Fosdick had returned from Geneva where he observed the League at work, and had established connections with the Rockefeller Foundation. Urgently Wilson asked him to come down to S Street, where he arrived for an interview on October 30. Fosdick was astonished to find Wilson meditating plans to put into effect educational theories he had developed at Princeton. He wanted the Rockefeller trustees to finance a new college, with himself as president, where small groups of students would work in close personal contact with instructors.

Fosdick returned to New York embarrassed by the implausible proposal. He talked to some of the trustees and with utmost tact wrote that they were reluctant to finance an experimental venture. Wilson would not be satisfied, replying that a great opportunity would be lost forever if the trustees refused to aid him. "I can honestly say," he concluded, "that my plans are so thoroughly thought out in detail that there is nothing experimental about them."[26]

The sands were running out now. On January 16 Cordell Hull, chairman of the Democratic National Committee, brought the members of the committee to pay their respects. Wilson sat in the library on S Street hunched in his favorite chair before the fire, barely lifting his right hand as more than a hundred men passed, barely audible as he mumbled a greeting to each. Four days later Fosdick made one more visit. The conversation, to his relief, dealt with other than educational plans. Wilson quoted John Quincy Adams when asked about his health—"Mr. Adams is all right, but the house he lives in is dilapidated, and it looks as if he would have to move out." He went back over the League fight, and when Fosdick, on leaving, promised that the younger generation would see it through to success, the old man lost control of his emotions. "My last impression of him," Fosdick recalled, "was a tear-stained face, a set, indomitable jaw, and a faint voice whispering 'God bless you.' "[27] With his white hair and grey, lined face, he seemed to his visitor like a reincarnation of the prophet Isaiah. This was just two weeks before death came.

A last letter, left unsigned, was dictated on Saturday, January 25, to Ray Stannard Baker. The next day Grayson was planning to leave for a shooting trip in South Carolina. Wilson had suffered an attack diagnosed as a "digestive upset," but he seemed to be recovering, and with the patient's reluctant consent the doctor went forward with his plans. The denouement now unfolded rapidly, within the length of a long week.

For several days Wilson continued to go over his mail as usual with Bolling,[28] although too tired to dictate replies or to indicate what the response should be. To Edith's eye the decline in his condition was clear. In the early morning hours of Wednesday, she woke Bolling, saying that she wanted a telegram sent immediately asking Grayson to return. He came on Thursday, still ready to insist that Wilson was suffering from one of his "old indigestion attacks" and that, "while he seemed very unwell, he did not regard his condition as alarming." Edith wanted to call the children, but Grayson demurred. "It would," he said, "only alarm the children and start a lot of wild reports."

The optimism Grayson had long practiced could no longer serve. Edith insisted that Dr. Sterling Ruffin, her physician, be summoned for a consultation, and that Grayson spend the night at S Street. On Friday she was convinced that her husband was in fact dying and called Margaret to the bedside. (Jessie, in Siam, could not be reached; Eleanor would not arrive from California until the day of the funeral.) By then the press had gotten wind of the crisis and newsmen gathered, grimly hungry for news, before the house. A bulletin was issued: "Mr. Wilson has suddenly taken a decided turn for the worse and his condition [is] very serious." Saturday the bulletins, signed by three doctors, were issued almost hourly. The ex-President continued gradually to lose ground; he recognized those about him but was too exhausted to speak; he was "profoundly prostrated" but was not in pain.

Meanwhile Wilson lay upstairs on the great bed, as large as Lincoln's. Edith was there all day and most of the night, with Margaret sharing the vigil. To Grayson, before unconsciousness set in, the dying man had spoken his last connected sentence: "The machinery is worn out. I am ready."[29]

On Sunday, February 3, 1924, there was a bright sun and Washington was bathed in the airs of premature spring. Joined to the newspapermen keeping their unbroken watch were now hundreds of people who knelt in the street and prayed for the man whose life was ebbing away. At eleven-fifteen in the morning the end came, announced by Grayson in a few words from the doorstep. Across the country, as men and women emerged from church services they learned the news. Flags dropped to half mast; bells tolled, and the great and the plain people began making their way to the house on S Street, to leave cards, or flowers, or simply to stare at the brick dwelling that suddenly seemed empty. Woodrow

Wilson was gone—the Woodrow Wilson who had fought, bravely but too stubbornly, for high ends; who had served them, no doubt less than perfectly, but with all his mind and heart.

The funeral was very much Edith's. She had earned the right to manage its details. Her husband had said one day that in the Arlington cemetery he would rest uneasily; they had both favored a private funeral. For practical reasons Staunton, his birthplace, and Columbia, where his parents were buried, were ruled out. In any case Edith would have been reluctant to give Woodrow back to his own past, to the life she had not shared with him. On Mount St. Alban, the highest point in Washington, the vast structure to become the Washington Cathedral was then being constructed, and Edith decided that her husband would lie there, in the crypt. There would be two services, at the S Street house and in the Bethlehem Chapel; she would herself issue the invitations to both. The funeral would be held on Wednesday, February 6.

Calvin Coolidge, who as Vice President had succeeded Warren Harding, had established with Wilson a relationship of close respect. A sprig of spring flowers had scarcely been placed on the door at S Street, signifying the ex-President's death, before he and Mrs. Coolidge arrived to express their condolences. Now he offered to the widow all the grand perquisites the nation could provide. "Anything that the State, War and Navy Departments can do," he wrote Grayson, "I should be glad to have done, if you will let me know."[30] But Edith remained determined there would be no lying in state, no military displays. Nevertheless government offices closed for three days, and the Senate adjourned. An official Senate delegation, with Lodge among them, was appointed to be present at the funeral. Hearing of this, Edith sent off a handwritten note: "Realizing your presence would be embarrassing to you and unwelcome to me I write to request that you do not attend."[31] Lodge responded with courtesy, chilled and succinct.

Sunday's signs of spring had vanished and the cold grey of winter lay over the capital when silent crowds gathered to watch the funeral party, led by the Coolidges, enter the ex-President's home. Colonel House was not there. Tumulty was admitted only as a result of last-minute arrangements made by McAdoo. At the brief ceremony the ministers of the Presbyterian churches Wilson had attended in Princeton and in the capital officiated. The body was borne to the cathedral along streets lined by the public, accompanied by a small detachment of soldiers, sailors, and marines. The unfinished cathedral permitted the attendance of only four hundred persons, led by the President and his wife, members of the Supreme Court, of the cabinet, ambassadors and ministers of foreign governments. Close to the family and intimate friends was a delegation from Princeton, including several of Tommy's old classmates.

With its twenty-four choirboys and thirty-two acolytes the service was not the austere ceremony Wilson the Presbyterian would have chosen; but it suited Edith. Familiar passages of Scripture that Wilson had read daily through his life were now spoken over his last remains; "The strife is o'er, the battle done" were words sung for the recessional. When everyone had left, Edith waited and watched the casket prepared for lowering into the crypt.* Taps sounded in the winter dusk. Upon the casket Edith placed a spray of orchids, one last memorial, peculiarly her own.

The stone flooring of the Bethlehem Chapel bore only the words "Woodrow Wilson, Born December 28 1856 Died February 3 1924."

---

* Wilson's body was later moved to the nave of the cathedral, where Edith, who lived on in the S Street house for thirty-seven years, until 1961, was finally entombed beside him.

Acknowledgments

My publisher, Charles Scribner III, first suggested that I undertake a one-volume life of Wilson, based on all the sources then being brought together and edited at Princeton University. I went naturally for counsel to Professor Arthur S. Link, editor of the Woodrow Wilson Papers. Without Professor Link's encouragement I would not have begun; and I certainly could not have concluded the work without his support and friendship. He has put every needed resource at my disposal; he has patiently answered my questions, discussed my bewilderments, and, with an unfailing eye for errors, has read the complete manuscript.

To others connected with the Woodrow Wilson Papers, especially David W. Hirst, senior associate editor emeritus, I am also greatly indebted. Dr. Hirst has been indispensable in helping get my notes straightened out and verifying my quotations, besides contributing generously from his rich store of knowledge. Members of the team that is now bringing the Wilson papers to completion have been invariably helpful and welcoming. These include John E. Little, Manfred F. Boemeke, L. Kathleen Amon, and Ilse Mychalchyk. Among those active earlier as editors, I think with particular gratitude of Margaret D. Link, L. Denise Thompson, Fredrick Aandahl, and the late John Wells Davidson.

Thomas H. Wright, vice president of the university, has personified Princeton's kindness to a footloose scholar. Through Professors Aaron Lemonick and Robert C. Gunning, deans of the faculty, I have twice held visiting fellowships in the Department of History. These have provided the researcher with invaluable privileges.

Jacques Barzun read the entire manuscript with his acute sense of style and accuracy. Phyllis C. Robinson, who collaborated with me on earlier books, gave me the benefit of her trained editorial judgment on this one. Michael Mayer was a much appreciated assistant in the early stages of the work.

In the Firestone Library at Princeton I have enjoyed the courtesy of the staff, especially that of the Division of Manuscripts and its curator, Jean Prescott. In the Library of Congress I was given a good start by the acting chief of the Manuscript Division, Paul T. Heffron, and by the subsequent chief, James Hutson.

Andrew and Margaret Hofer, installing themselves in Princeton at a critical juncture of my research, generously lodged their great-uncle on his many visits. Others I might mention have been generous in offering moral and material support.

For the last I have left the expression of an indebtedness, very great and going back a long way, to Pendleton Herring. A Wilsonian and a scholar, he has been a constant and encouraging resource. Besides, he and his wife, Jill, sheltered me in baronial splendor during intervals of an academic year. As if this were not enough, they put up my small Honda for several seasons afterwards.

There remains only the formal assurance that none of the above, however responsible they may be for what merits this biography possesses, are responsible for its mistakes. And finally (not formal at all) is the assurance to my wife that I appreciate her careful reading of the manuscript and the patience with which she tolerated innumerable absences.

AUGUST HECKSCHER
"High Loft," Maine
October 1990

Notes

———◆———

Abbreviations used in correspondence:

BC	Bainbridge Colby
EAW	Ellen Axson Wilson
EBG	Edith Bolling Galt
EBW	Edith Bolling Wilson
ELA	Ellen Louise Axson
EMH	Edward Mandell House
HAW	Harriet Augusta Woodrow
JPT	Joseph Patrick Tumulty
JRB	John Randolph Bolling
JRW	Joseph Ruggles Wilson
JWW	Janet Woodrow Wilson
MAH	Mary Allen Hulbert
MAHP	Mary Allen Hulbert Peck
RB	Robert Bridges
RL	Robert Lansing
RSB	Ray Stannard Baker
WHP	Walter Hines Page
WW	Woodrow Wilson

Other abbreviations used:

LC	Library of Congress
PUL	Princeton University Library
PWW	*The Papers of Woodrow Wilson*
WP,PUL	Wilson Papers, Princeton University Library
WWLL	*Woodrow Wilson, Life and Letters*, by Ray Stannard Baker

Full citations of books mentioned in the notes are found in the bibliography.

1. Youth

PRINCETON, 1875

1. From a Wilson notebook, Sept. 7–Dec. 18, 1875, PWW 1:74.
2. Interview with Robert H. McCarter, July 15, 1940, quoted in Bragdon, *Woodrow Wilson*, pp. 21, 22.
3. Minutes of the American Whig Society, Sept. 24, 1875, PWW, 1:75.
4. M. H. Thomas, "Princeton in 1874." *Princeton Historical Review*, V (1971), 72ff.; with engraving by H. H. Bailey.

LANDSCAPE WITH FIGURES

1. After-dinner remarks in New York to the Friendly Sons of St. Patrick, PWW, 9:103. See also C. A. Spring Rice to W. Tyrrell, Dec. 22, 1913, PWW, 29:60.
2. Quoted in R. S. Baker, WWLL, *Youth*, p. 12.
3. *Ibid.*, pp. 11–12.
4. Account of Thomas Woodrow's journey is from a handwritten biography of James Woodrow by Marion Woodrow, in R. S. Baker Papers, LC.
5. For the best account of Wilson's midwestern relatives, from which much of the information presented here is taken, see Francis P. Weisenberger, "Middle Western Antecedents of Woodrow Wilson," *Mississippi Valley Historical Review*, XXIII (Dec. 1936), pp. 375–90.
6. JWW to WW, Jan. 4, 1886. WP,PUL.

GROWING UP

1. WW to EAW, July 20, 1902, PWW, 14:29.
2. This and preceding quotation from JWW to Thomas Woodrow, April 27, 1857, in WP,PUL.
3. Quoted in F. F. Corley, *Confederate City*, p. 8.
4. See J. M. Mulder, *Woodrow Wilson: Years of Preparation*, p. 9.
5. JRW in "Memorial Addresses," cited by Mulder, *ibid.*, p. 11.
6. "Abraham Lincoln, Man of the People," PWW, 19:33.
7. Baccalaureate Address, June 12, 1904, PWW, 15:365–66.
8. See Editorial Note, "Wilson's Imaginary World," PWW, 1:20–22.
9. "The Young People and the Church," Oct. 13, 1904, PWW, 15:510.
10. WW to MAH, July 30, 1911, PWW, 23:240.
11. See A. L. George and J. L. George, *Woodrow Wilson and Colonel House*, pp. 14–19.
12. E. A. Weinstein, *Woodrow Wilson: A Medical and Psychological Biography*. pp. 14–19.
13. J. M. Cooper, Jr., *The Warrior and the Priest: Woodrow Wilson and Theodore Roosevelt*, p. 3.
14. Helen Woodrow Bones to RSB, July 2, 1925, R. S. Baker Papers, LC.
15. Interview with Jessie Bones Brower, Oct. 25, 1925, R. S. Baker Papers, LC.
16. Interview with James Wilson Woodrow, Feb. 10, 1926, R. S. Baker Papers, LC. Facts in the above paragraph taken from this source.

17. *Memorial . . . of the First Presbyterian Church, Augusta, Georgia.* Quoted in J. M. Mulder, *op. cit.*, p. 45.
18. R. S. Baker, WWLL, *Youth*, p. 62.
19. WW to J. G. Hibben, Jan. 26, 1907, PWW, 17:17.
20. Remarks in his grandfather's church in Carlisle, Dec. 29, 1918, PWW, 53:541.
21. J. Woodrow to J. W. Woodrow, Feb. 24, 1873, R. S. Baker Papers, LC.
22. Editorial Note, "Wilson's Study and Use of Shorthand, 1872–1892," PWW, 1:8–19.
23. Interview with Jessie Bones Brower, Oct. 5, 1925, R. S. Baker Papers, LC.
24. Minutes of Session, First Presbyterian Church, July 5, 1872, PWW, 1:22–23.
25. Diary of N. S. Toy, Jan. 3, 1915, PWW, 32:8–9.
26. J. D. Hoeveler, Jr., *James McCosh and the Scottish Intellectual Tradition*, p. 3.
27. From a notebook, Sept. 29–Oct. 3, 1873, PWW, 1:30–31.
28. R. S. Baker, WWLL, *Youth*, p. 74.
29. A memorandum, June 1, 1873, PWW, 1:53.
30. W. B. Hale, *Woodrow Wilson*, pp. 40, 41.
31. JWW to WW, May 20, 1874, PWW, 1:50.
32. Mulder, *op. cit.*, p. 16.
33. R. S. Baker, WWLL, *Youth*, p. 84.
34. Quoted in "Wilson's Imaginary World," Editorial Note, PWW, 1:21–22.
35. WW to A. J. Graham, Apr. 24, 1875, PWW, 1:62; A. J. Graham to WW, Apr. 30, 1875, PWW, 1:63.
36. J. Dooley to WW, July 22, 1875, PWW, 1:71.
37. WW to J. W. Leckie, July 4, 1875, PWW, 1:70.
38. J. W. Leckie to WW, May 7, 1875, PWW, 1:75.
39. WW to J. W. Leckie, May 28, 1875, PWW, 1:65.
40. D. McKay to WW, June 25, 1875, PWW, 1:66.

"MAGICAL YEARS"

1. This and following quotations from Wilson's shorthand diary, June 3–12, 1876, PWW, 1:132–40.
2. This and following quotations from Wilson's commonplace book, Feb. 22–Nov. 15, 1876, PWW, 1:87–127.
3. Wilson's shorthand diary, June 27, 1876, PWW, 1:146.
4. Ibid. June 20 and July 24, 1876, PWW, 1:159.
5. "To the Editor," July 8, 1876, PWW, 1:150–51.
6. "Work-Day Religion," PWW, 1:176–78.
7. "One Duty of a Son to His Parents," Oct. 8, 1876, PWW, 1:205–207.
8. Wilson's shorthand diary, Nov. 8, 1876, PWW, 1:22.
9. JWW to WW, Nov. 8, 1876, and Nov. 15, 1876, PWW, 1:223.
10. Wilson's shorthand diary, Nov. 23, 1876, PWW, 1:231.
11. Baccalaureate address, June 12, 1910, PWW, 2:521.
12. H. Woods to RSB, Mar. 16, 1928; also conversation with R. S. Baker, Dec. 9, 1928, R. S. Baker, Papers, LC.
13. *The Princetonian*, May 2, 1878, PWW, 1:369.
14. *Ibid.*, Sept. 26, 1878, PWW, 1:406.

15. "The Ideal Statesman," Jan. 30, 1877, PWW, 1:242, 244.
16. JRW to WW, Mar. 27, 1877, PWW, 1:254.
17. JRW to WW, Jan. 25, 1878, PWW, 1:342.
18. JRW to WW, May 27, 1877, PWW, 1:255.
19. JWW to WW, Jan. 22, 1878, PWW, 1:332.
20. JRW to WW, Jan. 25, 1878, and Dec. 22, 1877, PWW, 1:345–46 and 1:332.
21. WW to JRW, May 23, 1877, PWW, 1:265. (The letter may not have been mailed.)
22. "Prince Bismarck," Nov. 1877, PWW, 1:307–14.
23. "William Earl Chatham," Oct. 1879, PWW, 1:407–12.
24. "Cabinet Government in the United States," Aug. 1879, PWW, 1:493–510.
25. WW to ELA, Oct. 30, 1883, and WW to C. A. Talcott, July 7, 1879, both in PWW, 2:449–50 and 1:487.
26. WW to A. M. Palmer, Dec. 22, 1920, and Jan. 19, 1921, PWW, 64 (forthcoming).
27. Marginal note, PWW, 1:485.

LAW AND LOVE

1. WW to RB, July 30, 1879, and Sept. 4, 1879, PWW, 1:490 and 1:541.
2. WW to RB, July 7, 1878, and July 30, 1879, PWW, 1:386 and 1:490.
3. "Self Government in France," Sept. 4, 1879, PWW, 1:515–39.
4. WW to RB, Sept. 4, 1879, PWW, 1:540.
5. "The Ideal Statesman," Jan. 30, 1877, PWW, 1:242.
6. WW to C. A. Talcott, Dec. 31, 1879, PWW, 1:59.
7. WW to RB, Feb. 25, 1880, and Nov. 7, 1879, PWW, 1:604, 606; and 1:581–82.
8. JWW to WW, Nov. 18, 1879, and Oct. 6, 1879, PWW, 1:584 and 1:575.
9. H. Bragdon, interview with R. H. Dabney, Mar. 22, 1941, Bragdon Papers, PUL.
10. JRW to WW, Apr. 2, 1879, PWW, 1:646.
11. JRW to WW, Dec. 22, 1879, and Jan. 27, 1880, PWW, 1:589 and 1:596–97.
12. JRW to WW, Jan. 27, 1880, PWW 1:597.
13. WW to RB, Feb. 25, 1880, PWW, 1:607.
14. "John Bright," Mar. 6, 1880, PWW, 1:618, 619.
15. News item, Apr. 1880, PWW, 1:646. (The debate was held on April 2, 1880.)
16. Newspaper report, June 30, 1880, PWW, 1:661–63.
17. JRW to WW, June 7, 1880, and JWW to WW, June 18, 1880, PWW, 1:660 and 1:661.
18. WW to RB, Sept. 4, 1879, PWW, 1:541.
19. WW to HAW, Dec. 30, 1879, PWW, 1:590.
20. JWW to WW, Nov. 5 1880, PWW, 1:686.
21. JWW to WW, Dec. 9, 1880, PWW, 1:700.
22. JWW and JRW to WW, Dec. 14, 1880, PWW, 1:701.
23. JWW to WW, Dec. 21, 1880, PWW, 1:702.
24. WW to HAW, Jan. 15, 1881, PWW, 2:15.
25. WW to RB, May 24, 1881, PWW, 2:70.

26. WW to RB, Nov. 7, 1879, PWW, 1:583.
27. M. W. Kennedy to WW, Apr. 15, 1880, PWW, 1:650.
28. WW to RB, Aug. 22, 1881, PWW, 21:79.
29. WW to C. A. Talcott, Sept. 22, 1881, PWW, 2:82.
30. WW to HAW, Sept. 26, 1881, PWW, 1:86. Details of the episode are from Helen Wells Thackwell, "Woodrow Wilson and My Mother," *Princeton University Library Chronicle*, XII (Autumn 1950), pp. 6–18; also editorial note, PWW, 2:84.
31. WW to HAW, Oct. 3, 1881, PWW, 2:89.
32. JRW to WW, Aug. 28, 1882, PWW, 2:138.
33. WW to RB, Mar. 15, 1882, PWW, 2:108.
34. WW to ELA, July 4, 1883, PWW, 2:381.
35. JWW to WW, June 13, 1882, PWW, 2:133.
36. J. R. Wilson, Jr., to WW, May 15, 1882, PWW, 2:129.
37. Editorial Note, "Wilson's Practice of Law," PWW, 2:144–45.
38. New York *World*, Sept. 24, 1882, cited in PWW, 2:148, n. 3.
39. WW to RB, Jan. 4, 1883, and Apr. 29, 1883, PWW, 1:281 and 2:343.
40. JRW to WW, Aug. 14, 1882, Aug. 20, 1882, and Dec. 15, 1882, PWW, 2:135, 1:135–36, and 2:277.
41. WW to R. H. Dabney, Jan. 11, 1883, PWW, 2:285.
42. JRW to WW, Mar. 13, 1883, and Oct. 21, 1882, PWW, 2:316 and 2:147.
43. JWW to WW, Apr. 11, 1877, and Oct. 26, 1877, PWW, 1:257 and 1:306.
44. JWW to WW, Dec. 24, 1882, PWW, 2:278.
45. WW to RB, Jan. 10, 1883, PWW, 2:284.
46. WW to ELA, July 4, 1883, PWW, 2:381.
47. K. D. M. Simons to WW, Aug. 11, 1918, quoted in PWW, 49:306, n. 2.
48. ELA to WW, July 12, 1883, PWW, 2:383.
49. WW to RB, Apr. 29, 1883, PWW, 2:343.
50. JRW to WW, Feb. 13, 1883, PWW, 2:304.
51. WW to ELA, Oct. 11, 1883, PWW, 2:468.
52. Significant new material on Ellen Axson's early life and friendships, including her attitude toward men and marriage, is in F. W. Saunders, *Ellen Axson Wilson*, pp. 20–25.
53. WW to ELA, May 28, 1883, and June 25, 1883; ELA to WW, June 25, 1883. In PWW, 2:363, 2:371, and 2:372.
54. JWW to WW, June 7, 1883, and June 21, 1883, PWW, 2:365 and 2:370.
55. WW to RB, July 26, 1883, PWW, 1:393.
56. ELA to WW, Sept. 1, 1883, PWW, 2:416–17.
57. ELA to WW, Sept. 21, 1883, PWW, 2:435.
58. WW to ELA, Aug. 12, 1883, PWW, 2:411.

2. Scholar, Teacher

BALTIMORE/NEW YORK

1. WW to ELA, Mar. 9, 1889, PWW, 6:139.
2. WW to R. H. Dabney, Feb. 17, 1884, PWW, 1:26.

3. WW to ELA, Jan. 8, 1884, and Nov. 20, 1883, PWW, 1:653 and 1:536 (italics omitted).
4. WW to ELA, Feb. 21, 1884, PWW, 3:38.
5. WW to ELA, Dec. 11, 1883, PWW, 2:578.
6. ELA to WW, Dec. 14, 1883; July 12, 1883; Nov. 28, 1883. In PWW, 2:583, 385, and 556.
7. WW to ELA, Feb. 5, 1884, and Nov. 27, 1883, PWW, 3:10 and 2:551.
8. "President Eliot's Views," New York *Evening Post*, Feb. 2, 1884, PWW, 3:42.
9. WW to ELA, Sept. 22, 1883, PWW, 2:597.
10. WW to ELA, Jan. 1, 1884, PWW, 2:641.
11. WW to ELA, Feb. 9, 1884, PWW, 3:36.
12. WW to RB, May 31, 1884, PWW, 3:199.
13. JRW to WW, Mar. 10, 1884, PWW, 3:74.
14. C. H. Shinn to WW, Jan. 22, 1884, PWW, 2:662.
15. R. Bridges, interview with R. S. Baker, Feb. 10, 1926, R. S. Baker Papers, LC.
16. ELA to WW, Nov. 19, 1884, PWW, 3:463.
17. WW to ELA, Oct. 8, 1884, PWW, 3:339.
18. ELA to WW, Feb. 12, 1884, and Feb. 12, 1885, PWW, 4:244 and 4:241.
19. WW to ELA, Feb. 14, 1885, PWW, 4:251.
20. F. W. Saunders, *Ellen Axson Wilson*, pp. 21–22, 29.
21. ELA to WW, Mar. 28, 1885, PWW, 4:429.
22. ELA to WW, Feb. 15, 1885, and Mar. 28, 1885, PWW, 4:261 and 4:431.
23. *Ibid.*, Mar. 28, 1884, and Mar. 29, 1884, PWW, 4:236.
24. Reviews of *Congressional Government*, by Gamaliel Bradford, in the New York *Nation*, XL (Feb. 12, 1885), PWW, 4:236, 240; and by Albert Shaw, in the Minneapolis *Daily Tribune*, Feb. 13, 1885, PWW, 4:284.
25. JWW to WW, Mar. 23, 1885, PWW, 4:399.
26. WW to ELA, Oct. 30, 1883, PWW, 2:502.
27. WW to RB, Nov. 19, 1884, PWW, 3:465.
28. WW to ELA, Feb. 27, 1885, PWW, 4:305.
29. JRW to WW, Jan. 15, 1885, PWW, 3:612.
30. WW to ELA, Feb. 27, 1885, PWW, 4:305.
31. *Ibid.*, Mar. 28 and Apr. 17, 1885, PWW, 4:427 and 496.
32. ELA to WW, Apr. 18 and Apr. 13, 1885, PWW, 4:497 and 481.
33. WW to ELA, May 22, May 26, May 28, May 29, and May 22, 1885, PWW, 4:616, 664, 668, 671, and 617.
34. WW to ELA, June 16, 1885, PWW, 47:20.

BRYN MAWR

1. E. Finch, *Carey Thomas at Bryn Mawr*, p. 1.
2. "Objects and Methods of Study," Sept. 24, 1885, PWW, 5:20.
3. *Ibid.*
4. Notes for classroom lectures, c. Apr. 14, 1887, and c. Feb. 8, 1887, in PWW, 5:490, 459.
5. The text of "The Modern State," Dec. 18, 1885, is in PWW, 5:61–92. The quotation is from JRW to WW, PWW, 5:92.

6. "Responsible Government under the Constitution," Feb. 10, 1886, PWW, 5:107, 124.

7. JRW to WW, Feb. 17, 1886, PWW, 5:125.

8. "The Study of Administration," Nov. 1, 1886, PWW, 5:361.

9. JRW to WW, Feb. 17, 1886, PWW, 5:125.

10. WW to H. B. Adams, Apr. 2, 1886, PWW, 5:151; Apr. 7, 1886, PWW, 5:154.

11. WW to H. B. Adams, Apr. 8, 1886, PWW, 5:155; WW to EAW, May 27, 1886, PWW, 5:263.

12. M. A. Elliott, *My Aunt Louisa and Woodrow Wilson*, p. 7ff.

13. JRW to WW, Apr. 5, 1886, WP,PUL; and JWW to WW, Jan. 4, 1886, PWW, 5:98.

14. JRW to WW, Feb. 17, 1886, WP,PUL.

15. This and following quotation, WW to EAW, Apr. 22 and Apr. 24, 1886, PWW, 5:167, 169.

16. Quoted in PWW, 5:170, n. 2.

17. WW to EAW, May 8, 1886, PWW, 5:205.

18. Quotations from EAW to WW, May 8 and June 6, 1886, PWW, 5:209, 292.

19. WW to EAW, June 4 and June 6, 1886, PWW, 5:263, 283; and EAW to WW, June 7, 1886, PWW, 5:295.

20. WW to H. B. Adams, Dec. 5, 1886, PWW, 5:416–17.

21. R. H. Dabney to WW, Jan. 25, 1887, PWW, 5:434–35.

22. JRW to WW, Jan. 12, 1887, PWW, 5:431.

23. "An Old Master," Feb. 1, 1887, PWW, 5:444–55, quotations from pp. 452 and 454.

24. WW to RB, Nov. 5, 1887, PWW, 5:623.

25. JRW to WW, Sept. 12, 1887, PWW, 5:588.

26. JWW to WW, Sept. 12, 1887, PWW, 5:500.

27. For example, see M. E. Hoyt to EAW, Mar. 17, 1886, WP,PUL.

28. JRW to WW, June 11, 1887, PWW, 5:516.

29. JRW to WW, Mar. 12, 1887, PWW, 5:467.

30. N. A. Thorsen, *The Political Thought of Woodrow Wilson*, p. 9, n. 17.

31. EAW to WW, June 4, 1886, and Oct. 6, 1887, PWW, 5:284 and 610.

32. WW to EAW, Apr. 19, 1888, PWW, 5:719.

33. WW to EAW, Apr. 22, 1888, PWW, 5:468–69.

34. "Confidential Journal," Oct. 20, 1887, PWW, 5:619.

35. For text of the agreement, see Mar. 14, 1887, PWW, 5:468–69.

36. J. Woodrow to WW, Aug. 15, 1888, PWW, 5:761.

37. For facts as agreed on, see "Minutes of the Executive Committee," June 27, 1888, PWW, 5:739–40.

38. J. E. Rhoads to WW, June 27, 1888, PWW, 5:742.

39. *Ibid.*, July 6, 1880, PWW, 5:749.

40. WW to President and Trustees of Bryn Mawr College, June 29, 1888, PWW, 5:746.

"A VIVID MIND"

1. WW to A. Shaw, May 5, 1890, PWW, 5:742.
2. Quotations in this paragraph from Bragdon, *op. cit.*, p. 168; news items from the Wesleyan *Argus*, Oct. 12, 1888, PWW, 6:24.
3. Quoted in Bragdon, *op. cit.*, p. 166; see also J. F. Jameson to WW, Nov. 20, 1888, PWW, 6:24.
4. EAW to WW, Feb. 17, 1889, PWW, 6:139.
5. WW to EAW, Mar. 9, 1889, PWW, 6:139.
6. "A Commemorative Address," PWW, 6:179.
7. *The State*, PWW, 6:303; see also editorial note, 6:244–52.
8. "Leaders of Men" is in PWW, 6:646–71; quotations are from PWW: 650, 652, 654, 663.
9. JRW to WW, May 9, 1889, PWW, 6:218.
10. EAW to WW, May 22, 1886, PWW, 5:251.
11. "Of the Study of Politics," Nov. 25, 1886, PWW, 5:395–406; quotation from p. 403.
12. JRW to WW, July 25, 1889, PWW, 6:358.
13. RB to WW, July 30, 1889, PWW, 6:360.
14. F. L. Patton to WW, Feb. 18, 1890, PWW, 6:257.
15. WW to RB, Nov. 6, 1889, PWW, 6:412.
16. F. L. Patton to WW, Mar. 5, 1890, PWW, 6:543.
17. J. McCosh to WW, Feb. 17, 1890, PWW, 6:526.
18. WW to JRW, Mar. 20, 1890, PWW, 6:544.
19. Wesleyan *Argus*, June 28, 1890, PWW, 6:680.
20. "Confidential Journal," Dec. 28, 1889, PWW, 6:462.

IN ARCADIA

1. F. L. Patton to J. W. Alexander, Apr. 20, 1891, PWW, 7:192.
2. WW to A. Shaw, Nov. 3, 1890, PWW, 7:62–63.
3. F. J. Turner to C. M. Sherwood, Feb. 13, 1889, PWW, 6:88.
4. C. T. Winchester to WW, Oct. 24, 1891, PWW, 7:315.
5. JRW to WW, Sept. 2, 1891, PWW, 7:285.
6. WW to EAW, Feb. 1, 1895, PWW, 9:149.
7. EAW to WW, Apr. 27, 1892, PWW, 7:596.
8. JRW to WW, Mar. 7, 1891, PWW, 7:174.
9. WW to ELA, Mar. 15, 1892, PWW, 7:487.
10. EAW to WW, Mar. 20, 1892, PWW, 7:498, and WW to EAW, Feb. 14, 1895, PWW, 9:195–96.
11. EAW to WW, Mar. 27, 1892, PWW, 7:522.
12. EAW to WW, Apr. 3, 1892, PWW, 7:541.
13. EAW to WW, Apr. 15, 1892, PWW, 7:602.
14. WW to EAW, Apr. 30, 1892, PWW, 7:602.
15. EAW to WW, May 6, 1892, PWW, 7:620.
16. WW to EAW, May 9, 1892, PWW, 7:628.
17. See PWW for the texts of "Mere Literature," June 17, 1893, 240–52; "A

Calendar of Great Americans," Sept. 15, 1893, 8:368–80; "The Course of American History," May 16, 1895, 9:257–74.

18. "Should an Antecedent Liberal Education Be Required of Students in Law, Medicine, and Theology?," PWW, July 26, 1893, 8:285–92; quotation is on p. 289.
19. "University Training and Citizenship," PWW, 8:593.
20. WW to EAW, Jan. 27, 1895, PWW, 9:133.
21. EAW to WW, Jan. 28, 1895, PWW, 9:138–39.
22. JRW to WW, Apr. 16, 1896, PWW, 9:498.
23. WW to EAW, Jan. 24, 1895, PWW, 9:124.
24. B. Perry, *And Gladly Teach*, p. 158.
25. *Ibid.*, p. 133.
26. E. W. McAdoo, *The Woodrow Wilsons*, p. 23.
27. *Ibid.*, p. 10.
28. EAW to WW, Feb. 16, 1895, PWW, 9:202.
29. McAdoo, *op. cit.*, p. 30.
30. Elliott, *op. cit.*, p. 114.
31. Interview with Mrs. Bradford Locke, July 13, 1939, Bragdon Papers, PUL.
32. Elliott, *op. cit.*, p. 119.
33. WW to ELA, Apr. 5, 1885, PWW, 4:455.
34. McAdoo, *op. cit.*, p. 6.
35. WW to EAW, July 23, 1894, PWW, 8:623.
36. WW to EAW, PWW, 8:627. Subsequent quotation in this paragraph is from WW to EAW, July 20, 1894, *ibid.*, 632.
37. WW to L. M. Smith, Sept. 15, 1897, PWW, 10:316.
38. WW to A. W. Corwin, Sept. 10, 1900, PWW, 11:573; also, JRW to WW, Feb. 13, 1901, PWW, 12:367. The project was outlined in "A Memorandum," Aug. 29, 1900, 11:572.
39. B. Perry, *op. cit.*, p. 134.
40. H. Craig to RSB, Mar. 4, 1927, R. S. Baker Papers, LC.
41. H. M. Alden to WW, June 28, 1895, PWW, 9:311.
42. Jan. 28, 1897, PWW, 10:123.
43. WW to J. F. Jameson, Nov. 11, 1895, PWW, 9:348.
44. "Preparatory Work in Roman History," *Wesleyan University Bulletin*, Oct. 15, 1889, PWW, 6:404.
45. "On the Writing of History," *Century Magazine*, Sept. 1895, PWW, 9:304.
46. T. W. Hunt to WW, Feb. 6, 1896, PWW, 9:417.
47. See n. 2 to WW to Harper and Brothers, May 27, 1896, PWW, 9:507.
48. WW to EAW, June 21, 1896, PWW, 9:523.
49. *Ibid.*, 9:527.
50. This and other quotations in this paragraph are from WW to EAW, Aug. 4, 1899, 206; July 12, 1899, 161; July 17, 1899, 173; all in PWW, 11.
51. This and the following three quotations are from EAW to WW, June 22, 1899, 131; July 10, 1899, 161; Aug. 3, 1899, 201; all in PWW, 11.
52. EAW to WW, July 24, 1899, PWW, 11:188.
53. EAW to WW, Aug. 6, 1896, PWW, 9:558.
54. WW to EAW, Aug. 24, 1896, PWW, 9:575.

3. Educator

TOWARD POWER

1. EAW to M. E. Hoyt, Oct. 27, 1896, PWW, 10:37.
2. "Princeton in the Nation's Service," Oct. 21, 1896, PWW, 10:23, 24.
3. EAW to WW, Jan. 31, 1897, PWW, 10:134–35.
4. F. L. Patton to C. H. McCormick, Apr. 4, 1898, PWW, 10:498.
5. WW to F. J. Turner, Mar. 31, 1897, PWW, 10:201.
6. WW to EAW, Jan. 29, 1897, PWW, 10:123.
7. WW to EAW, Feb. 4, 1897, PWW, 10:144.
8. "When a Man Comes to Himself," Nov. 1, 1899, PWW, 11:268.
9. "What Ought We to Do?," Aug. 1, 1898, PWW, 10:575–76.
10. A report of a speech on patriotism, Dec. 14, 1899, *Waterbury* (Conn.) *American*, PWW, 11:298.
11. A news report of a lecture on constitutional government, Nov. 2, 1898, Richmond *Times*, PWW, 11:66.
12. Preface to the fifteenth edition of *Congressional Government* (1900), pp. v–xiii.
13. "Mr. Cleveland as President," Jan. 15, 1897, PWW, 10:102, 103, 119.
14. WW to EAW, Feb. 4, 1898, PWW, 10:374–75.
15. C. H. McCormick to WW, Apr. 2, 1898, PWW, 10:493.
16. WW to F. J. Turner, Dec. 27, 1894, PWW, 9:120.
17. F. J. Turner to WW, Dec. 24, 1894, PWW, 9:118.
18. WW to J. F. Jameson, Feb. 21, 1900, PWW, 11:431.
19. See N. A. Thorsen, *The Political Thought of Woodrow Wilson*, pp. 150–51.
20. WW to R. W. Gilder, Jan. 6, 1901, PWW, 12:68.
21. WW to F. J. Turner, Feb. 4, 1901, PWW, 12:240.
22. WW to J. Woodrow, Feb. 4, 1901, PWW, 12:89.
23. D. B. Jones to WW, Mar. 17, 1902, PWW, 12:296.
24. C. H. McCormick to C. C. Cuyler, Apr. 7, 1902, PWW, 12:319–20.
25. J. W. Alexander to C. H. McCormick, Apr. 7, 1902, PWW, 12:321.
26. C. C. Cuyler to C. H. McCormick, Apr. 3, 1902, PWW, 12:316.
27. D. B. Jones to C. H. McCormick, May 31, 1902, PWW, 12:385.
28. A. B. Perry to EAW, June 10, 1902, PWW, 12:405–406.
29. T. Roosevelt to WW, June 23, 1902, PWW, 12:454.

TIME OF ACCOMPLISHMENT

1. WW to E. G. Reid, July 12, 1902, PWW, 14:3.
2. WW to EAW, July 20, 1902, PWW, 14:29.
3. WW to EAW, Aug. 9, 1902, and WW to EAW, Aug. 10, 1902, PWW, 14:67, 70.
4. WW to EAW, Aug. 17, 1902, PWW, 14:90.
5. WW to J. D. Hibben, Aug. 31, 1902, PWW, 14:121.
6. To the Board of Trustees of Princeton University, Oct. 21, 1902, PWW, 14:150.
7. Quoted in S. Kiceluk, "Revising the Two Cultures in Medical Education," *Texas Studies in Language and Literature*, 26 (Summer 1984), pp. 242–62.

8. A news report of Wilson's inauguration, *Princeton Alumni Weekly*, III (Nov. 1, 1902), 83–86, PWW, 14:194.
9. An Address to the Princeton Alumni of New York, Dec. 9, 1902, PWW, 14:268–76; quotations are from p. 275.
10. D. C. Gilman to WW, Nov. 2, 1902, PWW, 4:197.
11. Memorandum of conversation with Stockton Axson, R. S. Baker Papers, LC.
12. WW to E. G. Reid, Feb. 3, 1903, PWW, 14:347.
13. WW to T. Roosevelt, Feb. 1, 1903, PWW, 14:337.
14. "Trust in the Lord," sermon quoted in Mulder, *op. cit.*, p. 28.
15. From reviews by G. McL. Harper, Jan. 1, 1903, PWW, 14:309–10, and by C. M. Andrews, Dec. 11, 1902, PWW, 14: 280–81.
16. C. W. Eliot, *Educational Reform*, pp. 132–33.
17. "The Statesmanship of Letters," Nov. 5, 1903, PWW, 15:41.
18. *Ibid.*, p. 36.
19. To the Board of Trustees of Princeton University, Dec. 10, 1903, PWW, 15:72.
20. An address on education, Dec. 12, 1903, PWW, 15:89.
21. To the Board of Trustees of Princeton University, Dec. 14, 1905, PWW, 16:259.
22. "The Statesmanship of Letters," Nov. 5, 1903, PWW, 15:33–46; quotations are from pp. 37 and 35.
23. This and the following two quotations are from "Baccalaureate Address," June 12, 1904, PWW, 15:366.
24. M. A. Elliott, *op. cit.*, pp. 175–76.
25. WW to A. G. Cameron, Nov. 18, 1903, PWW, 15:152, n. 1.
26. WW to EAW, July 16, 1899, PWW, 11:171, and see again *ibid*.
27. E. W. McAdoo, *op. cit.*, p. 82.
28. WW to A. Carnegie, Apr. 17, 1903, PWW, 14:412; and "The Formal Opening of Lake Carnegie," *Princeton Alumni Weekly*, VII (Dec. 8, 1906), 182–86.
29. EAW to WW, Apr. 26, 1904, PWW, 15:298.
30. "An Address to the South and the Democratic Party," New York *Sun*, Nov. 30, 1904, PWW, 15:547, 548.
31. An address on Thomas Jefferson, Apr. 16, 1906, PWW, 16:364.
32. EAW to M. E. Hoyt, June 12, 1906, PWW, 16:423, and EAW to F. S. Hoyt, June 27, 1906, PWW, 16:430.
33. E. W. McAdoo, *op. cit.*, p. 94.
34. Idem.
35. WW to H. A. Garfield, Sept. 3, 1906, PWW, 16:450.
36. WW to C. H. Dodge, Sept. 16, 1906, PWW, 16:453.

GATHERING CLOUDS

1. WW to J. G. Hibben, June 4, 1906 (draft), PWW, 16:413–14.
2. A resolution, Oct. 20, 1906, PWW, 16:467.
3. A. F. West to WW, Oct. 30, 1906, PWW, 15:478.
4. M. W. Jacobus to WW, Nov. 4, 1906, PWW, 16:480.
5. M. W. Jacobus to WW, Nov. 6, 1909, PWW, 16:484.
6. See note 1, *supra*; italics added.
7. "A Supplementary Report to the Board of Trustees," Dec. 13, 1906, PWW, 16:525.

8. M. W. Jacobus to WW, Dec. 13, 1906, PWW, 16:528.
9. C. H. Dodge to WW, Dec. 19, 1906, PWW, 16:535.
10. EAW to A. Harris, Mar. 11, 1905, PWW, 16:28.
11. WW to RB, Apr. 8, 1905, PWW, 16:86, n. 1.
12. WW to EAW, Jan. 15, 1907, PWW, 16: 6, 7.
13. WW to EAW, Jan. 26, 1907, PWW, 16:11.
14. *Ibid.*, p. 14.
15. *Ibid.*, p. 15.
16. Notes for a sermon, Feb. 3, 1907, PWW, 17:27.
17. WW to EAW, Jan. 30, 1907, PWW, 17:15.
18. *Ibid.*, p. 26.
19. WW to MAHP, Feb. 6, 1907, PWW, 17:29; Feb. 20, 1907, PWW, 17:48.
20. MAHP to WW, Feb. 25, 1907, PWW, 17:50.
21. *Constitutional Government in the United States*, PWW, 18:114, 115.
22. Andrew Fleming West to the Board of Trustees Committee on the Graduate School, May 13, 1907, PWW, 17:143.
23. A. F. West to WW, July 10, 1907, PWW, 17:271.
24. WW to J. G. Hibben, July 10, 1907, PWW, 17:268.
25. WW to A. H. Osborn, July 17, 1907, PWW, 17:286.
26. WW to M. W. Jacobus, July 1, 1907, PWW, 17:241.
27. Speech to the faculty: abstract by A. F. West, Oct. 7, 1907, PWW, 17:424.
28. WW to J. G. Hibben, July 10, 1907, PWW, 17:268.
29. Address at Harvard University, June 26, 1907, PWW, 17:226, 227; news report of an address to the Philadelphian Society, *Daily Princetonian*, Oct. 25, 1907, PWW, 17:455.
30. R. S. Baker, WWLL, *Princeton—1890–1910*, pp. 256–57.
31. From the minutes of the Board of Trustees, Oct. 17, 1907, PWW, 17:442.
32. Report of an interview, Oct. 18, 1907, PWW, 17:445.
33. M. T. Pyne to A. C. Imbrie, Oct. 23, 1907, PWW, 17:454.
34. WW to M. W. Jacobus, Oct. 23, 1907, PWW, 17:451.
35. News report of an address to the Philadelphian Society, *Daily Princetonian*, Oct. 25, 1907, PWW, 17:455.
36. WW to EAW, Jan. 26, 1908, PWW, 17:608.
37. *Ibid.*, p. 607.
38. "A Salutation," Feb. 1, 1908, PWW, 17:611.
39. Baccalaureate Address, June 7, 1908, PWW, 18:326.
40. WW to EAW, Aug. 3, 1908, PWW, 18:387.
41. WW to EAW, June 26, 1908, PWW, 18:343.
42. WW to EAW, July 2, 1908, PWW, 18:350.
43. WW to EAW, July 16, 1908, PWW, 18:365.
44. WW to EAW, July 6, 1908, PWW, 18:352.
45. Wilson's description of his visit to Skibo is in WW to EAW, Aug. 13, 1908, and WW to EAW, Aug. 16, 1908, PWW, 18:398, 399–402.
46. WW to EAW, Aug. 23, 1908, PWW, 18:409.
47. R. A. Cram to WW, Apr. 8, 1908, PWW, 18:326.
48. WW to EAW, June 29, 1906, PWW, 18:346.
49. WW to MAHP, July 18, 1909, PWW, 19:312.
50. "Abraham Lincoln: A Man of the People," Feb. 12, 1909, PWW, 19:44.

51. "The Spirit of Learning," July 1, 1909, PWW, 19:285–89; quotations from 279, 282, 285.
52. WW to MAHP, July 3, 1909, PWW, 19:290.

THE END AT PRINCETON

1. WW to M. W. Jacobus, Mar. 17, 1909, PWW, 19:124.
2. WW to R. Garrett, Apr. 19, 1909, PWW, 19:166.
3. W. C. Procter to A. F. West, May 8, 1909, PWW, 19:190.
4. WW to C. H. McCormick, May 15, 1909, PWW, 19:196 (emphasis added).
5. For a description of life at Merwick see Willard Thorp (ed.), "When Merwick Was the University's Graduate House, 1905–1913," *Princeton History* (Nov. 1, 1971), p. 55; and E. Capps *et al.* to WW, Jan. 10, 1910, n. 2, PWW, 19:755.
6. H. B. Fine to WW, Apr. 1, 1909, p. 141; E. Capps to WW, Mar. 30, 1909, p. 133; W. M. Daniels to WW, Mar. 31, 1909, pp. 135–36, and also E. Capps *et al.* to WW, Jan. 10, 1909, p. 754; all in PWW, 19.
7. "Princeton Ideals," *Princeton Alumni Weekly* (Dec. 13, 1902), pp. 199–204.
8. From A. F. West, Oct. 19, 1909, with enclosure, "Report of the Faculty Committee . . . ," PWW, 19:421–33.
9. From the minutes of the Board of Trustees, Oct. 21, 1909, PWW, 19:435–39.
10. WW to MAHP, Apr. 13, 1909, PWW, 19:162.
11. An outline and two drafts of statements, Sept. 30, 1915, PWW, 34:496.
12. WW to EBG, Sept. 19, 1915, PWW, 34:491–92.
13. WW to EBG, Sept. 21, 1915, PWW, 34:500.
14. See E. A. Weinstein, *Woodrow Wilson*, especially pp. 188–91 where the same hypothesis is set forth. For another description of the Peck affair, see F. Saunders, "Love and Guilt: Woodrow Wilson and Mary Hulbert, *American Heritage*, XXX (Apr.–May 1979), pp. 68–77.
15. M. A. Hulbert, *The Story of Mrs. Peck*, pp. 224–25.
16. *Ibid.*, p. 226.
17. MAHP to WW, Feb. 15, 1910, PWW, 20:127; Feb. 18, 1910, PWW, 20:142.
18. "An Outline . . . ," Sept. 20, 1915, PWW, 34:496 (Wilson's emphasis).
19. Elliott, *op. cit.*, p. 198.
20. *Ibid.*, pp. 199–200.
21. WW to MAHP, May 31, 1909, PWW, 19:224.
22. Baccalaureate Address, June 19, 1909, PWW, 19:247.
23. WW to MAHP, Sept. 12, 1909, PWW, 19:382.
24. WW to MAHP, Sept. 12, 1909, PWW, 19:382.
25. WW to MAHP, Sept. 19, 1909, PWW, 19:385.
26. WW to MAHP, June 19, 1909, PWW, 19:262.
27. WW to MAHP, July 11, 1909, PWW, 19:309.
28. *Ibid.*, pp. 309.
29. "What Is a College For?," *Scribner's Magazine*, XLVI (Nov. 1909), pp. 570–577, and "The Tariff Make-Believe," *North American Review*, CXC (Oct. 1909), pp. 535–56. (Dates of composition given in Wilson's drafts in Library of Congress are, for the former, Aug. 18, 1909; for the latter, Sept. 5, 1909.)
30. WW to M. T. Pyne, Dec. 22, 1909, PWW, 19:620.

31. WW to M. T. Pyne, Dec. 25, 1909, PWW, 19:628.
32. *Ibid.*, p. 630.
33. D. B. Jones to WW, Dec. 29, 1909, PWW, 19:656.
34. Editorial note: Wilson at the meeting of the Board of Trustees of January 13, 1910, PWW, 20:6.
35. *Ibid.*, p. 8, and M. W. Jacobus to H. B. Thompson, Jan. 22, 1910, PWW, 20:46.
36. WW to C. H. Dodge, Feb. 7, 1910, PWW, 20:83.
37. WW to MAHP, Feb. 18, 1910, PWW, 20:140.
38. WW to EAW, Feb. 21, 1910, PWW, 20:146.
39. Interview with Booth Tarkington, Nov. 27, 1940, Bragdon Papers, PUL.
40. WW to H. B. Brougham, Feb. 1, 1910, PWW, 20:69–71.
41. "Memorandum of conversation between President Wilson and Prof. Paul van Dyke," Mar. 16, 1910, PWW, 20:249–51.
42. W. O. Inglis, "Helping to make Woodrow Wilson President," *Collier's Weekly*, LVIII (Oct. 7, 1916), p. 37. Quoted in A. S. Link, *Wilson: The Road to the White House*, p. 142. See also D. W. Hirst, *Woodrow Wilson: Reform Governor*, pp. 6–9.
43. News report of an address to New York bankers, Jan. 18, 1910, PWW, 20:24, 25.
44. WW to MAHP, April 13, 1909, PWW, 19:162.
45. W. A. White, *Woodrow Wilson: The Man, His Times, and His Task*, p. 179, n. 1.
46. An address to the Princeton Club of New York, Apr. 7, 1910, PWW, 20:337, 341, 342.
47. H. B. Thompson to C. H. Dodge, Apr. 15, 1910, PWW, 20:361.
48. See, for example, a news report of an address to the Princeton Club of Philadelphia, Mar. 20, 1909, PWW, 19:112–13.
49. A news report of the Pittsburgh speech, Apr. 20, 1910, PWW, 20:375; see also two other news reports, Apr. 17, 1910, PWW, 363–68.
50. WW to I. H. Lionberger, Apr. 28, 1910, PWW, 20:399.
51. McAdoo, *op. cit.*, p. 101.
52. A. F. West to M. T. Pyne, May 22, 1910, PWW, 20:465.
53. A baccalaureate sermon, June 12, 1910, PWW, 20:520, 521.
54. J. M. Harlan to WW, June 11, 1910, PWW, 20:520, and WW to J. M. Harlan, *ibid.*, p. 540.
55. For description of Wilson's trip from Old Lyme and the dinner, see Hirst, *op. cit.*, pp. 15–24.
56. Interview with Robert S. Hudspeth, Nov. 3, 1927, R. S. Baker Papers, LC.
57. A statement, July 15, 1910, PWW, 20:581.
58. White, *op. cit.*, p. 204.
59. McG. Bundy, *An Atmosphere to Breathe*, p. 11.

4. Politician

NEW JERSEY TRIUMPHS

1. W. O. Inglis, "Helping to Make a President," *Collier's Weekly*, LVIII (Oct. 14, 1916), pp. 12–14, 46, quoted in D. W. Hirst, *Woodrow Wilson Reform Governor*, p. 4.
2. Inglis, quoted in Hirst, *ibid.*, p. 47.
3. News report of a campaign address in Camden, N. J., Oct. 25, 1910, PWW, 21:420.
4. WW to G. B. M. Harvey, July 26, 1910, PWW, 21:24.
5. WW to E. Williamson, Aug. 23, 1910, PWW, 21:60.
6. J. Kerney, *The Political Education of Woodrow Wilson*, p. 51.
7. *Ibid.*, p. 52.
8. *Ibid.*, p. 53.
9. WW to MAHP, Aug. 16, 1910, PWW, 21:38.
10. Descriptions of this scene appear in Kerney, *op. cit.*, pp. 54–55 and in J. P. Tumulty, *Woodrow Wilson as I Know Him*, pp. 19–22.
11. For the text see PWW, 21:91–94 and 118–20.
12. An excellent account of Tumulty as a New Jersey politician is in John M. Blum, *Joe Tumulty and the Wilson Era*.
13. For this meeting, see Kerney, *op. cit.*, pp. 62–64.
14. A news report of a religious address, PWW, 21: 62–64.
15. Tumulty, *op. cit.*, p. 28.
16. J. L. O'Connell to WW, Oct. 3, 1910, PWW, 21:240.
17. "A Proposed Resolution," PWW, 21:353.
18. WW to L. C. Woods, Oct. 29, 1910, PWW, 21:444.
19. M. T. Pyne to W. C. Procter, Oct. 25, 1910, PWW, 21:434.
20. This and following quotes are from WW to G. L. Record, Oct. 24, 1910, PWW, 21:406–11.
21. The final address of the campaign, Nov. 5, 1910, PWW, 21:576.
22. Kerney, *op. cit.*, p. 22.
23. *Newark Sunday Call*, Nov. 13, 1910, quoted in Link, *The Road to the White House*, p. 12, n. 28.
24. Quoted in Hirst, *op. cit.*, p. 126.
25. WW to G. B. M. Harvey, Nov. 15, 1910, PWW, 22:47.
26. Address to the Conference of Governors, Nov. 29, 1910, PWW, 22:103–104.
27. W. B. Hale, *Woodrow Wilson: The Story of His Life*, p. 181.
28. WW to MAHP, Dec. 7, 1910, PWW, 22:141.
29. A statement on the senatorship, Dec. 8, 1910, PWW, 22:153.
30. A statement by James Smith, Jr., Dec. 9, 1910, PWW, 22:166.
31. See "A Statement," Dec. 23, 1910, PWW, 22:248–52.
32. "The Law and the Facts," Dec. 27, 1910, PWW, 22:263–72; quotations from pp. 264 and 271.
33. F. W. Saunders, *op. cit.*, p. 213.
34. WW to MAHP, Jan. 3, 1911, PWW, 22:329.
35. Address in Jersey City, Jan. 5, 1911, PWW, 22:306. The scene is well described in Tumulty, *op. cit.*, pp. 61–62.

36. WW to MAHP, Jan. 22, 1911, PWW, 22:363.
37. WW to O. G. Villard, Jan. 2, 1911, PWW, 22:288.
38. Inaugural address, Jan. 17, 1911, PWW, 22:345–54; quotations from p. 353.
39. A statement on the Geran bill, Feb. 15, 1911, PWW, 22:431.
40. "A Statement about an Altercation," Dec. 20, 1911, PWW, 22:512–13; see also WW to MAHP, Mar. 26, 1911; *ibid.*, p. 518; and Trenton *Evening Times*, Mar. 21, 1911.
41. Report of a conference with Democratic assemblymen, Mar. 14, 1911, PWW, 22:504. For a moving account of this meeting see B. J. Hendrick, "Woodrow Wilson: Political Leader," *McClure's Magazine*, XXXVIII, Dec. 1911, pp. 229–230.
42. WW to MAHP, Mar. 5, 1911, PWW, 22:477.
43. "An Astonishing Legislature," *Jersey Journal*, April 22, 1911, quoted in full in Hirst, *op. cit.*, pp. 197–98.
44. WW to MAHP, Apr. 23, 1911, PWW, 22:582.

TOWARD THE PRESIDENCY

1. WW to MAHP, Jan. 10, 1911, PWW, 22:324.
2. WW to MAHP, Mar. 5, 1911, PWW, 22:478.
3. WW to MAHP, Mar. 12, 1911, PWW, 22:500.
4. *Ibid.*, p. 501.
5. WW to MAHP, Apr. 30, 1911, PWW, 22:598.
6. News report of an address in Norfolk, Virginia, from the Norfolk *Virginia-Pilot*, Apr. 30, 1911, PWW, 22:598.
7. WW to MAHP, May 7, 1911, PWW, 23:11.
8. "The Bible and Progress," May 7, 1911, PWW, 23:12, 20.
9. A news report of an address in San Francisco, May 16, 1911, PWW, 23:58.
10. WW to MAHP, May 21, 1911, PWW, 23:80–81.
11. WW to WHP, June 7, 1911, PWW, 23:135.
12. See J. E. Martine to WW, July 28, 1911, PWW, 23:234, n. 1.
13. News report of a speech to the Warren County Farmers' Picnic, Aug. 17, 1911, Newark *Evening News*, PWW, 23:270.
14. See W. F. McCombs to WW, Aug. 4, 1911, PWW, 23:252, n.1.
15. C. Seymour, ed., *The Intimate Papers of Colonel House*, I, p. 46.
16. *Ibid.*, p. 45.
17. *Ibid.*, p. 49.
18. See A. S. Link, "The Wilson Movement in Texas, 1910–1912," in *The Higher Realism of Woodrow Wilson*, pp. 178–79.
19. WW to G. B. M. Harvey, Dec. 21, 1919, PWW, 23:603 and n. 1 thereto.
20. "Woodrow Wilson Sought a Pension," New York *Sun*, Dec. 5, 1911, PWW, 23:564–65.
21. A statement about the Cleveland letter, PWW, 24:3–4.
22. WW to A. H. Joline, Apr. 29, 1907, PWW, 17:124.
23. Address to the Jackson Day Dinner, Jan. 8, 1912, PWW, 24:16.
24. For Bryan's reaction to Wilson's speech, see Link, *op. cit.*, p. 356–57.
25. Tumulty, *op. cit.*, p. 98.
26. A. S. Link, *Wilson: The Road to the White House*, p. 422.

27. "To the Democrats of New Jersey," May 24, 1912, PWW, 24:433.
28. EAW to J. W. Wescott, Feb. 3, 1912, PWW, 24:190.
29. WW to MAHP, May 11, 1912, PWW, 23:392.
30. WW to MAHP, Oct. 8, 1911, PWW, 23:425.
31. WW to MAHP, Jan. 7, 1912, PWW, 24:6.

THE BALTIMORE CONVENTION

1. A news report, July 1, 1912, PWW, 24:519.
2. WW to MAHP, June 17, 1912, PWW, 24:482.
3. E. A. McAdoo, *The Woodrow Wilsons*, p. 153.
4. Baker, WWLL, *Governor, 1910–1913*, p. 339.
5. WW to W. J. Bryan, June 22, 1912, PWW, 24:493 (italics added).
6. Official Report of the Proceedings of the Democratic National Convention of 1912, p. 160, quoted in Link, *op. cit*, p. 447.
7. Quoted in Baker, *op. cit.*, p. 348.
8. Quoted in *ibid.*, p. 350.
9. Press interview with Ellen Axson Wilson, related in *ibid.*, p. 350. On the controversial question of whether Wilson ordered his delegates to be released, see Tumulty, *op. cit.*, p. 120 for what appears to be the most convincing account.
10. "Official Report," quoted in R. S. Baker, *op. cit.*, p. 355.
11. Link, *op. cit.*, p. 441, reveals that the Sullivan switch was more immediately the result of a deal with Wilson strategists by which Sullivan's Chicago delegates were recognized by the credentials committee.
12. Memorandum of a conversation with A. S. Burleson, Mar. 17–19, 1927, R. S. Baker Papers, LC.
13. WW to MAHP, July 21, 1912, PWW, 24:561.
14. WW to MAHP, Aug. 25, 1912, PWW, 25:56.

THE GREAT CAMPAIGN

1. S. E. Morison, *The Oxford History of the American People*, p. 840.
2. B. Whitlock to N. D. Baker, Sept. 28, 1912, quoted in A. Nevins, ed., *The Letters of Brand Whitlock*, p. 154.
3. A talk to Democratic leaders in Syracuse, Sept. 12, 1912, PWW, 25:144, 145.
4. From the Newark *Evening News*, Sept. 13, 1912, quoted in J. W. Davidson, ed., *A Crossroads of Freedom*, p. 149.
5. L. D. Brandeis to D. S. Miller, Sept. 4, 1912, quoted in A. T. Mason, *Brandeis: A Free Man's Life*, p. 377.
6. L. D. Brandeis to WW, Sept. 30, 1912, PWW, 25:289.
7. See Thorsen, *op. cit.*, pp. 21–25.
8. WW to L. D. Brandeis, Sept. 27, 1912, PWW, 25:272.
9. A Labor Day address in Buffalo, Sept. 2, 1912, PWW, 25:75.
10. Newark *Evening News*, Aug. 9, 1912, quoted in Davidson, *op. cit.*, p. 37.
11. An address to the New York Press Club, Sept. 9, 1912, PWW, 25:119.
12. Remarks from the rear platform in Union City, Indiana, Sept. 16, 1912, PWW, 25:148.

13. Address at Tremont Temple, Boston, Sept. 27, 1912, quoted in Davidson, *op. cit.*, pp. 284–96.
14. T. Roosevelt to A. W. Cooley, July 10, 1912, quoted in E. E. Morison, *et al.*, eds., *The Letters of Theodore Roosevelt*, VII, p. 575.
15. T. Roosevelt to H. Plunkett, Aug. 12, 1912, *ibid.*, p. 592; and T. Roosevelt to A. H. Lee, Aug. 14, 1912, *ibid.*, p. 598.
16. An address to the New York Press Club, Sept. 9, 1912, PWW, 25:124.
17. Afternoon address in Minneapolis, Sept. 18, 1912, PWW, 25:177.
18. Address in Columbus, Sept. 20, 1912, PWW, 25:212.
19. A campaign address in Indianapolis, Oct. 3, 1912, PWW, 25:327.
20. *Ibid.*, p. 327.
21. *New York Outlook*, 102 (Oct. 26, 1912), pp. 360–62.
22. Remarks to students and neighbors, Nov. 5, 1912, from the Brooklyn *Eagle*, Nov. 6, 1912; quoted in Davidson, *op. cit.*, 525–26.

5. Emerging Statesman

PRESIDENT-ELECT

1. New York *World*, Nov. 7, 1912.
2. WW to W. J. Bryan, Nov. 12, 1912, PWW, 25:240.
3. Newark *Evening News*, Nov. 2, 1912. The *News* carried the Bermuda story in detail. See especially Nov. 18, 22, 26; and Dec. 3, 5.
4. New York *World*, Dec. 18, 1912.
5. Address at the Mary Baldwin College, Dec. 28, 1912, PWW, 25:639.
6. Address at a birthday banquet, Dec. 28, 1912, PWW, 25:639.
7. Quotations from *New York Times*, Jan. 13, 1913; and New York *World*, Jan. 15, 1913.
8. New York *World*, Dec. 17, 1912.
9. "Mr. Cleveland's Cabinet," Mar. 17, 1893, PWW, 28:160–78; quotations are from pp. 173, 177, 178.
10. Diary of E. M. House, Dec. 19, 1912, PWW, 25:614.
11. Quotations in this paragraph from *New York Times*, Feb. 1, 1913, and the *Nation*, Feb. 13, 1913.
12. New York *World*, Jan. 31, 1913.
13. Diary of E. M. House, Jan. 15, 1913, PWW, 27:57.
14. Diary of J. Daniels, March 6, 1913, PWW, 27:157.
15. *Boston Journal*, Nov. 21, 1912.
16. New York *World*, March 4, 1913.
17. Address to the New York Southern Society, Dec. 17, 1912, PWW, 25:597.
18. WW to MAH, Feb. 23, 1913, PWW, 27:128.
19. Remarks to Princeton neighbors, Mar. 1, 1913, PWW, 27:143.
20. For full account of inaugural events see *New York Times* and New York *World*, Mar. 4 and 5, 1913.
21. Inaugural address, Mar. 4, 1913, PWW, 27:148–52.
22. *Outlook*, Mar. 15, 1913.

THE WILSON WHITE HOUSE

1. C. Seymour, *Woodrow Wilson and the World War*, p. 19.
2. "Leaders of Men," June 17, 1890, PWW, 6:663.
3. Remarks to the National Press Club, Mar. 20, 1914, PWW, 29:362.
4. Diary of E. M. House, Dec. 18, 1912, PWW, 25:610.
5. Interview with C. L. Swem, July 16, 1929, R. S. Baker Papers, LC.
6. W. B. Hale, "Watching President Wilson at Work," *World's Work* (May 1913).
7. C. T. Grayson, WW: *An Intimate Memoir*, p. 12.
8. *Ibid.*
9. WW to MAH, Apr. 13, 1913, PWW, 29:298.
10. H. W. Bones to J. W. Bones Brower, Apr. 12, 1913, PWW, 29:557. Weinstein states that Wilson had suffered at this time "a probable stroke." E. Weinstein, *Woodrow Wilson*, p. 251.
11. Diary of E. M. House, Mar. 25, 1914, PWW, 29:377.
12. F. W. Saunders, *Ellen Axson Wilson*, pp. 244–47.
13. R. S. Baker, *WWLL President, 1913–1914*, p. 465.
14. F. W. Saunders, *op. cit.*, pp. 242–44; also S. G. Blythe, "Record of a Conversation," *Saturday Evening Post*, Apr. 17, 1914, PWW, 29:517.
15. Diary of E. M. House, Apr. 28, 1914, and Dec. 22, 1914, Yale University Library.
16. H. W. Bones to J. W. Bones, May 3, 1913, PWW, 29:357.
17. D. F. Houston to E. M. House, Mar. 19, 1914, Houston Papers, LC.
18. R. V. Oulahan to RSB, Mar. 15, 1929, R. S. Baker Papers, LC.
19. Remarks at a press conference, Jan. 15, 1917, PWW, 34:471.
20. Quotations in this paragraph from press conference remarks, Feb. 9, 1914, Mar. 14, 1914, Feb. 5, 1914; all in PWW, 29:242, 334, 225.

APPOINTMENTS AND PATRONAGE

1. "Interview with Albert S. Burleson, Mar. 17, 1927," R. S. Baker Papers, LC.
2. *New York Times*, Nov. 5, 1913.
3. S. G. Blythe, "A Talk with the President," Dec. 5, 1914, PWW, 31:399.
4. WW to A. S. Burleson, Mar. 30, 1913, PWW, 27:239.
5. WW to J. R. Wilson, Apr. 22, 1913, PWW, 27:346.
6. Diary of E. M. House, Apr. 18, 1913; see also *New York Times*, July 19, 1916: "Diplomatic Posts Ranked as Spoils."
7. W. J. Bryan to WW, June 22, 1914, Wilson Papers, PUL.
8. WW to C. W. Eliot, Sept. 17, 1913, PWW, 28:230.
9. WW to H. B. Fine, Apr. 11, 1913, PWW, 27:290.
10. A statement, Mar. 23, 1913, PWW, 27:217.
11. *Ibid.*
12. WW to J. B. Clark, May 4, 1914, PWW, 29:543.
13. WW to J. S. Williams, Apr. 2, 1914, PWW, 29:394.
14. J. S. Williams to WW, Apr. 13, 1913, Williams Papers, LC.
15. J. P. Gavit to O. G. Villard, Oct. 1, 1913, PWW, 28:349.
16. *Ibid.*, p. 350.

17. "The Politics and Industries of the New South," Apr. 30, 1881, PWW, 2:54. See "Woodrow Wilson, The American as Southerner," in A. S. Link, *The Higher Realism of Woodrow Wilson*, p. 21ff.

18. WW to O. G. Villard, Aug. 21, 1913, and Sept. 22, 1913, both in PWW, 28:202, 316.

19. New York *World*, Nov. 13, 1914.

20. Diary of J. Daniels, Apr. 11, 1913, PWW, 27:291.

21. *New Republic*, VII (June 24, 1916), p. 185.

22. Remarks to a delegation, and a dialogue, Nov. 12, 1914, PWW, 31:301–308; quotation on p. 301.

FIRST TESTS IN FOREIGN POLICY

1. To E. G. Conklin of Princeton University. See Baker, WWLL, *President*, p. 55.

2. For a summary of these ideas see essays published in *The New Freedom: A Call for the Emancipation of the Generous Energies of a People* (1912).

3. W. H. Taft to G. J. Karger, Sept. 17, 1913, Taft Papers, LC.

4. London *Daily Express*, Apr. 25, 1913.

5. *New York Times*, Apr. 23, 1915.

6. WW to W. L. Marbury, Feb. 5, 1914, PWW, 29:220.

7. Statement on relations with Latin America, Mar. 12, 1913, PWW, 27:172.

8. Statement on the pending Chinese loan, Mar. 18, 1913, PWW, 27:193.

9. Diary of J. Daniels, Apr. 4, 1913, PWW, 27:262.

10. WW to L. M. Garrison, Aug. 8, 1914, PWW, 30:262.

11. Address on Latin American policy, Oct. 27, 1913, PWW, 28:448–53; quotation on p. 450.

12. Memorandum enclosed in J. B. Moore to WW, May 15, 1913, PWW, 27:438, 439.

13. WW to MAH, Aug. 24, 1913, PWW, 28:217.

14. Diary of J. Daniels, May 16, 1913, PWW, 444–45.

15. B. A. Fiske to J. Daniels, May 14, 1913, appended to Daniels Diary, May 15, 1913, LC.

16. W. H. Taft to E. Root, May 5, 1913, Taft Papers, LC.

6. National Leader

THE NEW FREEDOM ENACTED

1. *Constitutional Government in the United States*, PWW, 18:105.

2. An address on tariff reform, Apr. 8, 1913, PWW, 27:269–72.

3. A public statement on tariff lobbyists, May 26, 1913, PWW, 27:473.

4. WW to MAH, June 29, 1913, PWW, 28:13.

5. WW to EAW, June 29, 1913, PWW, 28:11.

6. An address at Gettysburg, July 4, 1913, PWW, 28:23–26; quotations from p. 25.

7. WW to EAW, June 29, 1913, PWW, 28:12; WW to MAH, June 29, 1913, PWW, 28:13.

8. EAW to WW, July 30, 1913, PWW, 28:99.
9. WW to EAW, Sept. 7, 1913, PWW, 28:261; WW to MAH, July 27, 1913, PWW, 28:86.
10. WW to MAH, July 27, 1913, PWW, 28:86.
11. WW to EAW, Sept. 28, 1913, PWW, 28:335.
12. EAW to WW, Oct. 5, 1913, PWW, 28:364.
13. EAW to WW, July 20, 1913, PWW, 28:55; WW to EAW, July 27, 1913, *ibid.*, p. 84; Oct. 5, 1913, PWW, 28:364.
14. WW to EAW, Sept. 3, 1913, PWW, 28:249.
15. EAW to WW, Sept. 4, 1913, PWW, 28:256.
16. WW to EAW, Sept. 21, 1913, PWW, 28:310; WW to EAW, Oct. 12, 1913, *ibid.*, p. 394.
17. Remarks upon signing the tariff bill, Oct. 3, 1913, PWW, 28:352.
18. Remarks to the Class of 1879, June 13, 1914, PWW, 30:177.
19. *Nation* (XCVII), Aug. 14, 1913.
20. Address on banking and currency reform, June 23, 1913, PWW, 27:570–71.
21. *Ibid.*, pp. 572–73.
22. H. C. Lodge to H. L. Higginson, Apr. 7, 1914, Higginson mss., Harvard University Library.
23. WW to MAH, Sept. 28, 1913, PWW, 28:336–37.
24. *Ibid.*, p. 336.
25. New York *World*, Oct. 8, 1913.
26. *New York Times*, Dec. 24, 1913.
27. *Saturday Evening Post*, 186 (Dec. 22, 1913).
28. C. Seymour, ed., *The Intimate Papers of Colonel House*, I, p. 120.

COMPLEXITIES AND TRAGEDY

1. WW to MAH, Dec. 23, 1913, PWW, 29:60.
2. WW to JPT, Dec. 27, 1913, PWW, 29:77.
3. Grayson, *WW: An Intimate Memoir*, pp. 31–32.
4. WW to J. H. Neville and S. H. Neville, Jan. 3, 1914, PWW, 29:99.
5. WW to MAH, Jan. 9, 1914, PWW, 29:114.
6. WW to MAH, Feb. 1, 1914, PWW, 29:211.
7. Diary of T. W. Brahany, Mar. 17, 1917, PWW, 41:424.
8. WW draft of "An Address on Antitrust Legislation," Wilson Papers, LC; see also full text in PWW, 29:153–58; the quotation is on p. 154.
9. WW to MAH, Mar. 15, 1914, PWW, 29:346.
10. J. Bryce to WW, March 6, 1914, PWW, 29:320; and, in this paragraph, H. C. Lodge, speech of Feb. 19, 1914, quoted in J. A. Garrety, *Henry Cabot Lodge*, p. 300.
11. WHP to WW, May 8, 1914, PWW, 30:9.
12. "Annual Message to Congress," Dec. 2, 1913, PWW, 29:5.
13. *Ibid.*, p. 4.
14. C. Spring Rice to E. Grey, Feb. 7, 1914, PWW. 29:229.
15. An Address to Congress on the Mexican Crisis, Apr. 20, 1914, PWW, 29:471–74.
16. *The Economist*, LXXVIII (Apr. 18, 1914), pp. 906–907.

17. A memorial address, May 11, 1914, PWW, 30:13–15; quotations from p. 15.
18. For a full discussion of this lamentable episode see G. M. McGovern and L. F. Guttridge, *The Great Coalfield War*, pp. 210–40; also M. F. Boemeke, "The Wilson Administration, Organized Labor, and the Colorado Coal Strike," Ph.D. diss. in the Princeton University Library.
19. Remarks at a Press Conference, Mar. 19, 1914, PWW, 29:353.
20. Remarks to the National Press Club, Mar. 20, 1914, 29:361–66.
21. Remarks to the Class of 1879, PWW, 30:176–80; quotations from p. 177.
22. Remarks to the Princeton Alumni Association of the District of Columbia, May 29, 1914, PWW, 30:103–108; quotations from p. 107.
23. WW to E. G. Reid, Apr. 15, 1914, PWW, 29:439.
24. WW to MAH, May 10, 1914, PWW, 30:13.
25. WW to MAH, June 7, 1914, PWW, 30:158.
26. WW to MAH, Aug. 2, 1914, PWW, 30:328.
27. WW to E. P. Davis, July 28, 1914, PWW, 30:312.
28. WW to MAH, Aug. 7, 1914, PWW, 30:357.
29. Interview with C. T. Grayson, Feb. 18–19, 1926, R. S. Baker Papers, LC.

THROUGH THE SHADOWS

1. J. Buchan, *A History of the Great War*, I, pp. 5–6.
2. WHP to WW, Sept. 6, 1914, PWW, 31:6–7.
3. WW to E. M. House, May 29, 1914, PWW, 30:109.
4. Remarks at a press conference, Aug. 3, 1914, PWW, 30:332.
5. WW to WHP, Oct. 28, 1914, PWW, 31:243.
6. J. J. Jusserand to Foreign Ministry, Aug. 28, 1914; quoted in Link, *Wilson: The Struggle for Neutrality*, p. 50, n. 132; C. Spring Rice to E. Grey, Sept. 3, 1914, PWW, 30:472. See also House Diary, Aug. 30, 1914, PWW, 30:462.
7. D. Lloyd George, *The War Memoirs of David Lloyd George, 1915–1916*, II, p. 117.
8. "An Appeal to the American People," Aug. 18, 1914, PWW, 30:393, 94.
9. Remarks to the Belgian Commissioners, Sept. 16, 1914, PWW, 31:34.
10. S. Axson, "Memoir," ms. in the possession of A. S. Link.
11. C. T. Grayson to EBG, Aug. 25, 1914, PWW, 31:564.
12. WW to MAH, Oct. 11, 1914, PWW, 31:141.
13. WW to N. S. Toy, Nov. 9, 1914, PWW, 31:289.
14. Secretary to Mrs. Wilson to J. F. T. O'Connor, unsigned, Dec. 7, 1932. Papers of E. B. Wilson, LC.
15. WW to MAH, Sept. 20, 1914, PWW, 31:60; WW to N. S. Toy, Sept. 6, 1914, PWW, 31:5.
16. Diary of E. M. House, Nov. 6, 1914, PWW, 31:274, and *ibid.*, Nov. 14, 1914, PWW, 31:319–20.
17. H. W. Bones to E. T. Brown, Mar. 12, 1915, R. S. Baker Papers, LC.
18. WW to N. S. Toy, Dec. 23, 1914, PWW, 31:515.
19. WW to N. S. Toy, Dec. 12, 1914, PWW, 31:456.
20. WW to MAH, Jan. 17, 1915, PWW, 32:83.
21. WW to O. W. Underwood, Oct. 17, 1914, PWW, 31:168–74.
22. *New Republic*, I (Nov. 21, 1914), p. 7.

23. Diary of E. M. House, Nov. 4, 1914, PWW, 31:264–65.
24. "A Jackson Day Address," Jan. 8, 1915, PWW, 32:29–41; quotations from pp. 30–31, 33.
25. WW to N. S. Toy, Jan. 31, 1915, PWW, 32:165–66, and Feb. 4, 1915, PWW, 32:191.
26. An unpublished statement on the ship-purchase bill, Mar. 4, 1915, PWW, 32:313–16; quotation is from p. 316.
27. A statement, Mar. 4, 1915, PWW, 32:316.
28. WW to N. S. Toy, Mar. 7, 1915, PWW, 32:334–35; see also n. 1 thereto.
29. WW to J. W. Sayre, Mar. 14, 1915, PWW, 32:370.

ENTER EDITH BOLLING GALT

1. C. T. Grayson, op. cit., pp. 50–51; see also EBW, My Memoir, p. 56.
2. E. W. Starling, Starling of the White House, p. 49.
3. WW to EBG, Apr. 28, 1915, PWW, 33:87; EBG to WW, Apr. 28, 1915, PWW, 33:87.
4. EBG, op. cit., pp. 60–61, and EBG to WW, May 5, 1915, PWW, 33:108–10.
5. WW to EBG, May 5, 1915, PWW, 33:111–12.
6. EBG to WW, May 11, 1915, PWW, 33:164.
7. WW to EBG, July 20, 1915, PWW, 33:539, 541, and WW to EBG, Oct. 7, 1915, PWW, 35:40.
8. WW to EBG, May 28, 1915, PWW, 33:278.
9. EBG to WW, May 28, 1915, PWW, 33:279.
10. WW to EBG, May 29, 1915, PWW, 33:284.
11. EBG to WW, May 28, 1915, PWW, 33:279.
12. E. Jaffray, Secrets of the White House, p. 36.
13. MAH to WW, June 10, 1915, PWW, 33:382.
14. EBG, "A Pledge," June 29, 1915, PWW, 33:458.
15. J. Daniels, The Wilson Era: Years of Peace, pp. 452–54.
16. For what appears to be a straightforward account of the affair, see Diary of E. M. House, Sept. 22, 1915, PWW, 34:506–508. Contrary to this, Mrs. Wilson says it was the joint idea of House and McAdoo; while McAdoo told her it was entirely House's! E. B. Wilson, op. cit., p. 78.
17. WW to EBG, Sept. 18, 1915, PWW, 34:489; EBG to WW, ibid., p. 490.
18. WW to EBG, Sept. 19, 1915, PWW, 34:489; EBG to WW, ibid., p. 490.
19. WW to MAH, Oct. 4, 1915, PWW, 35:23; MAH to WW, Oct. 11, 1915, PWW, 35:53.
20. MAH to WW, Nov. 22, 1915, PWW, 35:237.
21. E. T. Brown, M. C. M. Brown, Sept. 24, 1915, R. S. Baker Papers, LC; and interview with S.. Axson, Sept. 25, 1915, ibid.
22. Starling, op. cit., p. 56.
23. WW to L. M. Smith and M. R. Smith, Dec. 27, 1915, PWW, 35:399.

7. Diplomatist

DIPLOMACY OF NEUTRALITY

1. WW to J. W. Gerard, Feb. 10, 1915, PWW, 32:207–10; especially p. 209; see also WW to W. J. Bryan, Mar. 24, 1915, *ibid.*, 424–25.
2. Quoted in *Literary Digest*, L (Apr. 10, 1915), pp. 789–91.
3. R. Lansing to W. J. Bryan, May 1, 1915, PWW, 33:92.
4. *New Republic*, II (Mar. 6, 1915), pp. 113–14.
5. WW to EMH, May 18, 1915, PWW, 33:217.
6. New York *World*, May 2, 1915.
7. From Captain Otto Schwieger's logbook of the U-20; translation in A. S. Link's notes in PUL.
8. *New York Times* and New York *World*, both May 8, 1915; the incident is also summarized in Link, *Wilson: The Struggle for Neutrality*, pp. 370–72.
9. Statement to the American people, May 8, 1915, PWW, 33:154, n. 1; see also *New York Times*, May 9, 1915.
10. WHP to WW, May 8, 1915, PWW, 30:133.
11. W. H. Taft to WW, May 10, 1915, PWW, 33:151–52.
12. WW to EBW, May 11, 1915, PWW, 33:160–61.
13. An address in Philadelphia, May 10, 1915, PWW, 33:147–50; quotation from p. 149.
14. Remarks at a press conference, May 11, 1915, PWW, 33:154.
15. For the advice of Wilson's mother see JWW to WW, Nov. 15, 1876, PWW, 1:228.
16. The text of the note is printed in an enclosure in WW to W. J. Bryan, May 12, 1915, PWW, 33:174–78.
17. The debate within Germany as well as the German response to the note is described in Link, *op. cit.*, pp. 397–409.
18. W. H. Page memorandum, Aug. 30, 1916, quoted in Link, *Wilson: Campaigns for Progressivism and Peace*, p. 72.
19. Diary of E. M. House, June 24, 1915, PWW, 34:449.
20. EMH to WW, July 17, 1915, PWW, 35:387.
21. WW to EMH, Dec. 24, 1915, PWW, 35:387.
22. Diary of E. M. House, Feb. 7, 1916, as quoted in C. Seymour, ed., *The Intimate Papers of Colonel House*, II, p. 163.
23. EMH to WW, Feb. 15, 1916, PWW, 36:180, n. 2.
24. J. H. von Bernstorff to the German Foreign Office, June 2, 1915, PWW, 33:318.
25. Devlin, *Too Proud to Fight*, p. 149.
26. WW to RL, Oct. 21, 1915, PWW, 35:91–92, n. 1.
27. New York *Tribune*, Dec. 29, 1916; *World's Work*, XXXII (Oct. 1916), pp. 600–601.

1916: DIPLOMACY PURSUED

1. Annual message to Congress, Dec. 8, 1914, PWW, 31:243.
2. *New Republic*, III (June 19, 1915), pp. 162–63.
3. Address in Cleveland, Jan. 29, 1916, PWW, 36:47.

4. Address in St. Louis, Feb. 3, 1916, PWW, 36:120.
5. Diary of E. M. House, Sept. 24, 1915, PWW, 34:514.
6. WW to L. M. Garrison, Feb. 10, 1916, PWW, 36:164.
7. Enclosure II, Jan. 25, 1916, in RL to WW, PWW, 35:534.
8. C. Spring Rice to E. Grey, Jan. 27, 1916, is cited and summarized in Link, *Confusions and Crises*, pp. 153–54; see also Enclosure I, in RL to WW, Jan. 27, 1916.
9. *New York Times*, Feb. 14, 1916.
10. *Ibid.*, Feb. 24, 1916.
11. WW to W. J. Stone, Feb. 24, 1916, PWW, 36:213–14.
12. Quoted in R. S. Baker, WWLL, *Facing War*, p. 185.
13. *Ibid.*, p. 185.
14. Diary of E. M. House, Apr. 2, 1916, PWW, 36:402.
15. Address on Abraham Lincoln, Sept. 4, 1916, PWW, 38:144.
16. For the debate in Germany see Link, *Confusions and Crises*, pp. 256–74.
17. R. Lansing to WW, May 6, 1916, 36:620.
18. W. J. Ferguson to WW, Oct. 27, 1915, WP,PUL.
19. Memorandum for the Adjutant General, Mar. 10, 1916; Enclosure III in N. D. Baker to WW, Mar. 10, 1916, PWW, 36:285–86.
20. The punitive expedition was closely followed by *The New York Times*, Mar. 17 to Apr. 11, 1916, and its dispatches form the basis for the following account.
21. *New York Times*, Apr. 15, 1916.
22. H. L. Scott to J. T. Dickman, Apr. 8, 1916, Scott Papers, LC.
23. E. Grey to EMH, Apr. 8, 1916; Enclosure II in EMH to WW, April 8, 1916, PWW, 36:444.
24. WW to EMH, May 16, 1916, PWW, 37:57.
25. F. L. Polk to WW, May 22, 1916, PWW, 37:93.
26. E. Grey to EMH, June 18, 1916; Enclosure in EMH to WW, July 12, 1916, PWW, 37:412.
27. WW to EMH, May 18, 1916, PWW, 37:68.
28. An address to the League to Enforce Peace, May 27, 1916, PWW, 37:113–16; quotations from 113, 115–16.
29. *New Republic*, VII (June 3, 1916), pp. 102, 104.

TOWARD A SECOND TERM

1. WW to C. A. Culberson, May 5, 1916, PWW, 36:609–10.
2. EMH to WW, Apr. 21, 1916, PWW, 36:523 (the second of three letters on same date).
3. WW to EMH, June 6, 1916, PWW, 37:103.
4. T. Roosevelt to H. W. Coe, July 5, 1916, and T. Roosevelt to W. D. Foulke, Aug. 1, 1916, both in Roosevelt papers, LC.
5. A Flag Day address, June 14, 1916, PWW, 37:223.
6. This account of the convention is based largely on coverage in *New York Times*, June 15 and 16, 1916.
7. *New York Times*, June 16, 1916.
8. Quoted in R. S. Baker, *WWLL: Facing War*, pp. 252–53.
9. *Ibid.*, p. 254.

VICTORY AT THE POLLS

1. WW to EMH, June 22, 1916, PWW, 37:281.
2. To the British Foreign Office, July 26, 1916, 37:478.
3. WW to EMH, July 23, 1916, PWW, 37:466–67; also manuscript in C. L. Swem papers, PUL, cited in A. S. Link, *Wilson: Campaigns for Progressivism and Peace*, p. 73, note 106.
4. F. L. Polk to WW, July 11, 1916, PWW, 37:401.
5. WW to EMH, July 23, 1916, PWW, 37:466–67.
6. WHP to A. W. Page, Aug. 26, 1916, and Diary of W. H. Page, n.d., both in Houghton Library, Harvard University.
7. WHP to A. W. Page, Aug. 26, 1916, Houghton Library, Harvard University.
8. WW to EMH, June 22, 1916, PWW, 37:281.
9. Remarks to the New York Press Club, June 30, 1916, PWW, 37:333.
10. C. Kitchin to W. R. Capehart, Sept. 6, 1916, Kitchin Papers, University of North Carolina Library.
11. A statement, Aug. 19, 1916, PWW, 38:49.
12. *New York Times*, Aug. 30, 1916.
13. WW to H. Bittner, Aug. 30, 1916, PWW, 38:117.
14. *New Republic*, VIII (Sept. 2, 1916), pp. 100–101.
15. WW to C. R. Holcomb, Sept. 6, 1916, Wilson Papers, LC.
16. *New York Times*, Oct. 1, 1916. See campaign speech to Young Democrats at Shadow Lawn, Sept. 30, 1916, PWW, 38:307; and a speech in Long Branch, New Jersey, Sept. 2, 1916, PWW, 38:131.
17. WW to J. A. O'Leary, Sept. 29, 1916, PWW, 38:286.
18. *Nation*, CIII (Oct. 5, 1916), p. 312.
19. Remarks at a press conference, Sept. 29, 1916, PWW, 38:289.
20. *Nation*, CIII, (Oct. 5, 1916), p. 367.
21. Quoted in R. Steel, *Walter Lippmann and the American Century*, p. 106.
22. Remarks at a press conference, Sept. 29, 1916, PWW, 38:287.
23. The final campaign address, Nov. 4, 1916, PWW, 38:615.
24. WW to J. R. Wilson, Jr., Nov. 27, 1916, PWW, 38:90.
25. EBW, *My Memoir*, p. 118.
26. *New York Times*, Nov. 9, 1916.
27. A news report, Nov. 10, 1916, PWW, 38:626–27; *New York Times*, Nov. 11, 1916.
28. F. L. Polk to WHP, Nov. 23, 1916, Polk Papers, Yale University Library.
29. Diary of E. M. House, Apr. 6, 1916, and Nov. 15, 1916, Yale University Library.
30. *Ibid.*, Jan. 12, 1917.
31. *New York Times*, Dec. 18, 1916.

WHEN THERE IS NO PEACE

1. An unpublished prolegomenon to a peace note, Nov. 25, 1916, PWW, 40:67.
2. The full text of Lansing's statement to the press is quoted in n. 1 to the Enclosure in JPT to WW, Dec. 21, 1916; Enclosure and n. 1, PWW, 40:306–309.
3. WHP to RL, Dec. 22, 1916, PWW, 40:319.

4. WHP to RL, Dec. 26, 1916, PWW, 40:332 (italics mine).

5. An appeal for a statement of war aims, Dec. 18, 1916, PWW, 40:273–76; quotations from p. 274.

6. WW to L. M. Smith and M. R. Smith, Dec. 27, 1916, PWW, 40:336.

7. C. H. Dodge to WW, Dec. 27, 1916, PWW, 40:338.

8. W. G. Sharp to RL, Jan. 10, 1917, PWW, 40:439–42; quotation from p. 441.

9. WW to EMH, Jan. 16, 1917, PWW, 40:491.

10. An address to the Senate, Jan. 22, 1917, PWW, 40:533–39; quotations from pp. 534, 536, 538.

11. See F. C. Penfield to RL, Feb. 5, 1917, PWW, 41:129–30.

12. WHP to WW and RL, Feb 11, 1917; enclosed in RL to WW, Feb. 13, 1917, PWW, 41:210–42; also see WHP to WW, Feb. 22, 1917, PWW, 41:270–73.

13. For the text of the Zimmerman telegram, see WHP to RL, Feb. 24, 1917, PWW, 41:280–82. For the story of its interception by the British and new light on its origin in the German Foreign Office, see Link, *Wilson: Campaigns for Progressivism and Peace*, pp. 342–346, 433–36.

14. Diary of E. M. House, Feb. 1, 1917, PWW, 41:87.

15. Lansing recorded the gist of this conversation and of follow-up discussions with the President in "Memorandum on the Severance of Diplomatic Relations with Germany," Feb. 4, 1917, PWW, 41:120–24.

16. Diary of E. M. House, Feb. 1, 1917, PWW, 41:88.

17. An address to a joint session of Congress, Feb. 3, 1917, PWW, 41:108–12; quotations from pp. 111–12.

18. A statement, Mar. 4, 1917, PWW, 41:320.

19. The second inaugural address, Mar. 5, 1917, PWW, 41:332–36; quotations from pp. 333, 335.

20. Diary of E. M. House, Mar. 5, 1917, PWW, 41:341.

8. War Leader

DECISION FOR WAR

1. T. Roosevelt to H. C. Lodge, Mar. 13, 1917, in E. Morison, *et al.*, eds., *The Letters of Theodore Roosevelt*, VIII, p. 1162.

2. Diary of J. Daniels, Mar. 24, 1917, PWW, 41:466.

3. "A memorandum of the Cabinet meeting, 2:30–5 P.M., Tuesday, March 20, 1917," PWW, 41:436–44; quotations from pp. 442, 443–44.

4. Diary of T. W. Brahany, Mar. 21, 1917, PWW, 41:449.

5. *Ibid.*, p. 474.

6. Diary of J. Daniels, Mar. 24, 1917, PWW, 41:466.

7. RL to WW, Mar. 26, 1917, PWW, 41:466, and Mar. 22, 1917, PWW, 41:455.

8. Diary of T. W. Brahany, Mar. 30, 1917, PWW, 41:515.

9. Diary of J. Daniels, Mar. 30, 1917, PWW, 41:506.

10. W. Lippmann to WW, Apr. 3, 1917, PWW, 41:537–38; Lippmann was quoting from his editorial, "The Great Decision," in the *New Republic*, X (Apr. 7, 1917), pp. 279–80.

11. Address to a joint session of Congress, Apr. 2, 1917, PWW, 41:519–27; quotations are from pp. 521, 522–23, 525, 526–27.
12. J. M. Cooper, *The Warrior and the Priest*, pp. 321–22.
13. The scene is described in the diary of T. W. Brahany, Apr. 6, 1917, PWW, 41:557.

AT THE SIDE OF THE ALLIES

1.   Diary of T. W. Brahany, Apr. 22, 1917, PWW, 42:121.
2.   *Ibid.*, Apr. 24, 1917, p. 125.
3.   Diary of E. M. House, Apr. 26, 1917, PWW, 42:142.
4.   Diary of T. W. Brahany, Apr. 23, 1917, PWW, 42:123.
5.   J. J. Jusserand to the Foreign Ministry, May 25, 1917, PWW, 42:403.
6.   E. Hovelaque, *Les États-Unis et la Guerre—de la Neutralité à la Croisade* (Paris, 1919), pp. 227–30, quoted in n. 1 to J. J. Jusserand to the Foreign Ministry, May 25, 1917, PWW, 42:403.
7.   T. H. Bliss to N. D. Baker, May 25, 1917, enclosed in N. D. Baker to WW, May 27, 1917, PWW, 405–10.
8.   A proclamation, May 1, 1917, PWW, 42:180–82. Prepared by Baker and edited by WW, it was issued on May 18, 1917.
9.   A statement on volunteer divisions, May 18, 1917, PWW, 42:325.
10. Diary of T. W. Brahany, Apr. 10, 1917, PWW, 42:31–32.
11. J. J. Pershing to N. D. Baker, July 9, 1917, enclosed in N. D. Baker to WW, July 24, 1917, PWW, 43:262–265.
12. F. Frankfurter to RL, Aug. 7, 1917, enclosed in RL to WW, Aug. 13, 1917, PWW, pp. 442–48; see especially p. 446.
13. S. E. Morison, *The Oxford History of the American People*, p. 826.
14. Address to the officers of the Atlantic Fleet, Aug. 11, 1917, 43:427–31; quotations from pp. 428, 430.

THE HOME FRONT

1.   J. L. Heaton, *Cobb of "The World,"* pp. 268–70. Cobb later believed he had spoken with Wilson in the early morning of Apr. 2. But Arthur Link argues persuasively that the interview took place in late afternoon on Mar. 19, 1917. See Link, "That Cobb Interview," *The Journal of American History*, 72 (June 1985), pp. 7–17. The exchange rings true, as Link maintains.
2.   WW to W. B. Munson, Apr. 22, 1918, PWW, 47:395.
3.   WW to JPT, Apr. 10, 1918, PWW, 47:311.
4.   WW to H. Froelicher, May 6, 1918, PWW, 47:536.
5.   WW to A. E. M. Blaine, Apr. 22, 1918, PWW, 47:394.
6.   WW to T. W. Gregory, July 7, 1917, PWW, 43:116.
7.   WW to EMH, July 29, 1917, PWW, 43:314.
8.   A statement to the American people, July 26, 1918, PWW, 49:97–8.
9.   WW to M. Eastman, Sept. 18, 1917, PWW, 44:210–11.
10. Diary of E. M. House, July 4, 1917, PWW, 43:99–100.
11. Telephone message from F. I. Cobb, Jan. 17, 1918, PWW, 46:16.

12. Telegram from the National Association of Manufacturers, Jan. 17, 1918, PWW, 46:18.
13. Diary of E. M. House, Jan. 17, 1917, PWW, 46:23–24.
14. Chamberlain's speech, with the critical paragraph in boldface, appeared in the New York *World*, Jan. 20, 1918.
15. A press release, Jan. 21, 1918, PWW, 46:55.
16. Diary of J. Daniels, Jan. 22, 1918, PWW, 46:78.
17. A memorandum by Sir William Wiseman, Jan. 23, 1918, PWW, 46:85.
18. To the Democrats of New Jersey, Mar. 20, 1918, PWW, 47:84.
19. *New Republic*, XIV (Mar. 30, 1918), pp. 246, 248.
20. Diary of E. M. House, Feb. 24, 1918, PWW, 46:436.
21. The draft is enclosed in WW to EMH, Aug. 23, 1917, PWW, 43:33–36. The reply, as sent, is WW to His Holiness Benedictus XV, Aug. 27, 1917, PWW, 44:57–59.
22. Diary of E. M. House, Sept. 10, 1913, PWW, 44:185.

THE FOURTEEN POINTS

1. D. Lloyd George to WW, Sept. 3, 1917, PWW, 44:125–30.
2. W. Wiseman to E. Drummond, Oct. 13, 1917, PWW, 44:374.
3. Address to the American Federation of Labor, Nov. 12, 1917, PWW, 45:14.
4. WW to F. Clark, Nov. 13, 1917, PWW, 45:39.
5. Lord Reading to A. J. Balfour, Mar. 19, 1918, PWW, 47:79.
6. W. Wiseman to E. Drummond, May 30, 1918, PWW, 48:204.
7. S. Vaughan, *Holding Fast the Inner Lines*, p. 141.
8. *Ibid.*, p. 21.
9. E. N. Hurley, *The Bridge to France*, pp. 320–21.
10. A. W. Lane and L. H. Wall, eds., *The Letters of Franklin K. Lane*, p. 267.
11. WW to L. S. Overman, Mar. 21, 1918, PWW, 47:94.
12. WW to H. B. Swope, Mar. 21, 1918, PWW, 47:93.
13. WW to M. E. Hoyt, Mar. 25, 1918, PWW, 47:140.
14. J. W. W. Sayre to WW, Mar. 26, 1918, PWW, 47:154.
15. P. W. Wilson to the London *Daily News*, April 8, 1918, PWW, 47:297–98.
16. WW to H. B. Swope, Mar. 27, 1918, PWW, 47:159.
17. Annual message on the state of the Union, Dec. 4, 1917, PWW, 45:194–202; quotations from pp. 195, 196, 197, 198.
18. Diary of E. M. House, Jan. 9, 1918, PWW, 45:550–59; quotation from p. 555. In this entry, House tells the story of the drafting of the address in great detail.
19. An address to a joint session of Congress, Jan. 8, 1918, PWW, 45:534–39.
20. An address on the opening of the Third Liberty Loan Campaign, Apr. 6, 1918, PWW, 47:270.

THE WAR'S END

1. W. Wiseman to E. Drummond, May 30, 1918, PWW, 48:205.
2. WW to RL, June 26, 1918, PWW, 48:435; see also RL to WW, June 27, 1918, PWW, 48: 447–48.

3. N. D. Baker to WW, Nov. 27, 1918, PWW, 53:227.
4. Diary of EMH, May 17, 1918, PWW, 48:52–53.
5. *Ibid.*, Sept. 10, 1917, PWW, 44:186.
6. Address on behalf of the American Red Cross, May 18, 1918, PWW, 48:53–57; quotation from p. 54.
7. E. von Ludendorff, *Ludendorff's Own Story: August 1914–November 1918*, II, pp. 326, 332.
8. Address on behalf of the Fourth Liberty Loan in the Metropolitan Opera House, Sept. 27, 1918, PWW, 51:127, 133, n. 2.
9. *Ibid.*, pp. 128, 131.
10. Max, Prince of Baden, to WW, Oct 6, 1918, enclosed in F. Oederlin to WW, Oct. 6, 1918, PWW, 51:252–53.
11. The subsequent German peace notes are printed in PWW, 51 at Oct. 12, 1918, p. 317, and Oct. 20, 1918, p. 402. Wilson's replies, beginning with the German note of Oct. 6, are also in PWW, 51 at Oct. 8, 1918, pp. 268–69; Oct. 14, 1918, pp. 33–34, and Oct. 23, 1918, pp. 417–19.
12. Enclosure with J. J. Jusserand to C. A. deR. Barclay, Oct. 11, 1918, PWW, 51:307.
13. The diary of J. Daniels, Oct. 23, 1918, PWW, 51:416.
14. The various Wilson drafts of the appeal appear in PWW, 51 at Oct. 13, 1918, p. 317; Oct. 15, 1918, pp. 343–44; Oct. 17, 1918, pp. 353–55. The final draft, which was issued on Oct. 25, 1918, is printed at Oct. 19, 1918, pp. 381–82. Italics added.
15. WW to J. W. W. Sayre, Nov. 13, 1918, 53:68; and a memorandum by H. S. Cummings, Nov. 8, 1918, PWW, 51:646–47.
16. EMH to WW, Oct. 30, 1918, PWW, 51:512.
17. EMH to WW, Oct. 29, 1918, PWW, 51:495–504.
18. WW to EMH, Oct. 30, 1918, PWW, 51:513.
19. WW to EMH, Oct. 31, 1919, PWW, 51:533.
20. WW to EMH, Oct. 28, 1918, PWW, 51:473.
21. EMH to WW, Nov. 5, 1918, PWW, 51:594.
22. A statement, Nov. 11, 1918, PWW, 53:34.
23. Address to a joint session of Congress, Nov. 11, 1918, PWW, 53:35–43.
24. N. D. Baker to WW, Nov. 11, 1918, PWW, 53:46; C. H. Dodge to WW, *ibid.*; and George V to WW, Nov. 12, 1918, PWW, 53:53.
25. A memorandum by Robert Lansing, Nov. 12, 1918, PWW, 53:66.
26. Confidential memorandum by F. I. Cobb for Colonel House, Nov. 4, 1918, PWW, 51:590–91. This memorandum is now in the Wilson Papers, LC, indicating that House must have passed it on to the President.
27. WW to EMH, Nov. 18, 1918, PWW, 53:109.
28. Annual message on the state of the Union, Dec. 2, 1918, PWW, 53:274–86.

9. World Spokesman

ODYSSEY

1. Diary of J. Daniels, Dec. 2, 1918, PWW, 53:301.
2. Diary of C. T. Grayson, Dec. 4, 1918, PWW, 53:314.
3. Diary of E. Benham, Dec. 5, 1918, PWW, 53:319.
4. Diary of R. B. Fosdick, Dec. 8, 1918, PWW, 53:340.
5. Diary of E. Benham, Dec. 10, 1918, PWW, 53:357–58.
6. Diary of R. B. Fosdick, Dec. 5, 1918, PWW, 53:322.
7. C. Seymour to his family, Dec. 12, 1918, PWW, 53:377.
8. H. Nicolson, *Peacemaking, 1919*, p. 27.
9. C. Day to E. D. Day, Dec. 10, 1918, PWW, 533:49. For the substance of this talk see the diary of W. C. Bullitt, Dec. 10, 1918, and the memorandum of I. Bowman, same date, both in PWW, 53:350 and 353, respectively.
10. Diary of R. B. Fosdick, Dec. 11, 1918, PWW, 53:366.
11. *Ibid.*, Dec. 14, 1918, PWW, 53:385.
12. Diary of E. M. House, Dec. 14, 1918, PWW, 53:389.
13. A reply to President Poincaré, Dec. 14, 1918, PWW, 53:386.
14. Diary of E. Benham, Jan. 10, 1914, PWW, 53:707.
15. An address at the Guildhall, Dec. 28, 1918, PWW, 53:531, 532.
16. D. Lloyd George, *The Truth about the Peace Treaties*, I, pp. 228, 230.
17. Minutes of a meeting of the Imperial War Cabinet, Dec. 30, 1918, PWW, 53:559, 560, 564–65.
18. Diary of C. T. Grayson, Dec. 30, 1918, PWW, 53:544, n. 1.
19. Remarks in his grandfather's church in Carlisle, Dec. 29, 1918, PWW, 53:541.
20. An address to the Italian parliament, Jan. 3, 1919, PWW, 53:598.
21. Remarks at the Royal Palace in Milan, Jan. 5, 1915, PWW, 53:617; remarks at the capital, Jan. 3, 1919, PWW, 53:603.
22. R. S. Baker, *WW: World Settlement*, I, p. 104.

PEACE CONFERENCE: FIRST PHASE

1. Hankey's notes of a meeting of the Supreme War Council, Jan. 12, 1919, 2:30 P.M., PWW, 54:7–12. (Lt. Col. Sir Maurice Hankey was secretary-general of the British delegation. Hereinafter these "notes" or minutes will be referred to by the short title, "Hankey's notes," with the time of the meeting given in each case, whether they be from a meeting of the Supreme War Council, the Council of Ten, or the Council of Four. The author's text and the time cited will indicate which body is being referred to. Similarly, the short title "Mantoux's notes" will be applied to accounts made by Paul Mantoux, the French interpreter and unofficial reporter of the meetings of the Council of Four.)
2. Diary of E. Benham, Jan. 2, 1919, p. 4, and diary of C. T. Grayson, Jan. 12, 1919, p. 5, both in PWW, 54.
3. C. Seymour to his family, Jan. 30, 1919, PWW, 54:383, and *ibid.*, Feb. 8, 1919, PWW, 55:35.
4. Memorandum by Isaiah Bowman, PWW, 53:355.
5. Hankey's notes, Jan. 20, 1919, 10:30 A.M., PWW, 54:155.

6. Hankey's notes, Jan. 22, 1919, 3:15 P.M., PWW, 54:205–206.
7. Hankey's notes, Jan. 12, 1919, 4 P.M., PWW, 54:14.
8. See H. B. Swope and others to WW, Jan. 14, 1919, enclosed in RSB to C. T. Grayson, Jan. 14, 1919, PWW, 54:59–60; and WW to JPT, Jan. 16, 1919, PWW, 54:105.
9. Hankey's notes, Jan. 15, 1919, 2:30 P.M., PWW, 54:73.
10. Protocol of a plenary session of the Inter-Allied Conference, Jan. 18, 1919, PWW, 54:131.
11. Hankey's notes, Jan. 24, 1919, 10:30 A.M., PWW, 54:242.
12. *Ibid.*, Jan. 28, 1919, 4 P.M., PWW, 54:325.
13. *Ibid.*
14. *Ibid.*, Jan. 30, 1919, 3:30 P.M., PWW, 54:363–64 and n. 3 thereto.
15. *Ibid.*, Jan. 30, 1919, 11 A.M., PWW, 54:357.
16. *Ibid.*, Jan. 28, 1919, 4:00 P.M., PWW, 54:326.
17. JPT to WW, Jan. 13, 1919, PWW, 54:53–54.
18. W. C. Bullitt to WW and others, Mar. 16, 1919, PWW, 55: 540–545 and n. 1 thereto.

WHITE HOUSE IN THE RUE MONCEAU

1. For description of the Hôtel Murat see EMH to WW, Nov. 23, 1918, PWW, 53:180–81, and a news report of an interview with Wilson printed in the London *Times*, Dec. 21, 1918, PWW, 53:429–30.
2. EBW to her family, Dec. 15, 1918, PWW, 53:398.
3. W. Lippmann to S. E. Mezes, Sept. 5, 1918, quoted in R. Steel, *Walter Lippmann and the American Century*, p. 148.
4. Diary of C. T. Grayson, Mar. 18, 1919, PWW, 56:62, and diary of E. Benham, April 19, 1919, PWW, 57:502.
5. Diary of C. T. Grayson, May 27, 1919, PWW, 59:527.
6. H. White to H. C. Lodge, Feb. 10, 1919, quoted in A. Nevins, *Henry White: Thirty Years of American Diplomacy*, p. 398.
7. C. Seymour, *Letters from the Paris Peace Conference*, p. 10.
8. A. Nevins, *op. cit.*, p. 378.
9. C. Seymour, *op. cit.*, p. 16; and C. Seymour to his family, Jan. 30, 1919, PWW, 54:383.
10. Diary of E. Benham, Jan. 12, 1918, PWW, 54:34.
11. Diary of R. S. Baker, Mar. 8, 1919, PWW, 55:464–65.
12. WW to T. W. Gregory, Feb. 26, 1919, PWW, 55:276.
13. JPT to WW, Jan. 30, 1919, PWW, 54:390.
14. N. D. Baker to WW, Jan. 1, 1919, PWW, 53:583.

THE LEAGUE OF NATIONS

1. From "Leaders of Men," June 17, 1890, PWW, 6:663.
2. Protocol of a Plenary Session of an Inter-Allied Conference, Jan. 25, 1919, PWW, 54:264–71. Wilson's speech is reported on pp. 365–68.
3. An address in Free Trade Hall, Dec. 30, 1918, PWW, 53:551.

4. Diary of C. T. Grayson, Jan. 26, 1919, PWW, 54:278–81; Wilson's comment is on p. 281.
5. From Wilson's confidential journal, Dec. 28, 1889, PWW, 6:462.
6. Minutes of a meeting of the Commission of the League of Nations, Feb. 11, 1919, PWW, 55:70–80.
7. News report of a press conference, Feb. 14, 1919, PWW, 55:161–63.
8. An address to the Third Plenary Session of the Peace Conference, Feb. 14, 1919, PWW, 55:164–78.
9. Hankey's notes, Feb. 14, 1919, 6:30 P.M., PWW, pp. 178–83.
10. Diary of E. M. House, Feb. 14, 1919, PWW, 55:196.

10. Peacemaker

POLITICS AT HOME

1. Diary of C. T. Grayson, Feb. 19 and Feb. 23, 1919, PWW, 55:207 and 229.
2. An address in Boston, PWW, 55:238–45; the quotation is on pp. 241–42.
3. WW to A. S. Burleson, Feb. 28, 1919, PWW, 55:327, and n. 1.
4. Schenck v. United States (249. U.S. 47).
5. WW to A. M. Palmer, Mar. 12, 1919, PWW, 55:482.
6. A news report of a press conference, Feb. 14, 1919, PWW, 55:163.
7. A full report on the meeting is in New York Times, Feb. 27, 1919, printed in PWW, 55:268–76.
8. Remarks to members of the Democratic National Committee, PWW, 55:323.
9. An address at the Metropolitan Opera House, PWW, 55:413–21; quotations are from pp. 418, 415.
10. Diary of R. S. Baker, Mar. 13, 1919, PWW, 55:490.

PEACE CONFERENCE: SECOND PHASE

1. Diary of C. T. Grayson, Mar. 14, 1919, PWW, 55:497.
2. Remarks at the Royal Palace in Milan, PWW, 53:617.
3. Diary of E. M. House, Mar. 14, 1919, PWW, 55:499.
4. EBW, My Memoir, pp. 245–46.
5. WW to EMH, Feb. 23, 1919, PWW, 55:230.
6. Diary of V. C. McCormick, Mar. 2, 1919, 55:387.
7. EMH to WW, Mar. 4, 1919, PWW, 55:423.
8. Diary of R. S. Baker, Mar. 27, 1919, PWW, 56:338.
9. Ibid., Mar. 31, 1919, PWW, 56:441.
10. Diary of E. M. House, Mar. 22, 1919, PWW, 56:180.
11. Ibid., Mar. 14, 1919, PWW, 55:500.
12. Ibid., 499.
13. Diary of R. S. Baker, Mar. 15, 1919, PWW, 55:531, and n. 1 thereto.
14. Mantoux's notes, Mar. 24, 1919, 3:00 P.M., PWW, 56:208.
15. Quoted in A. Lentin, Lloyd George, Woodrow Wilson, and the Guilt of Germany, p. 121.

16. A memorandum by David Lloyd George and others, Mar. 25, 1919, PWW, 56:259–79; quotations are from pp. 260, 263.
17. Mantoux's notes, Mar. 27, 1919, 11:00 A.M., PWW, 56:316, 320.
18. Diary of E. M. House, Mar. 16, 1919, PWW, 55:538.
19. W. H. Taft to WW, Mar. 21, 1919, PWW, 56:159.
20. Minutes of a meeting of the League of Nations Commission, Mar. 26, 1919, PWW, 56:302.
21. Address to the Senate, Jan. 22, 1917, PWW, 40:539.
22. Mantoux's notes, Mar. 28, 1919, 4:00 P.M., PWW, 56:360–71; quotations are from pp. 365, 366, 368.
23. Diary of E. M. House, Mar. 28, 1919, PWW, 56:349.
24. Diary of R. S. Baker, Apr. 2, 1919, PWW, 56:542.
25. Ibid., Apr. 3, 1919, PWW, 56:578.
26. Diary of C. T. Grayson, Apr. 3, 1909, PWW, 56:554.
27. Ibid., pp. 556, 557; also Apr. 4, 1919, p. 584, and Apr. 5, 1919, 57:3.
28. Diary of R. S. Baker, Apr. 7, 1919, PWW, 57:68.
29. See n. 2 to the Grayson diary for April 3, 1919, PWW, 56:544, for a discussion by several medical authorities of Wilson's attack and the editor's inference that "acute respiratory illness" is probably the correct diagnosis. For a discussion of the influenza hypothesis and of Wilson's general health problems while in Paris see the essays by B. E. Park, M.D., "The Impact of Wilson's Neurologic Disease During the Paris Peace Conference"; E. A. Weinstein, M.D., "Woodrow Wilson's Neuropsychological Impairment and the Paris Peace Conference"; and J. F. Toole, M.D., "Some Observations on Wilson's Neurologic Illness," in "Appendix: Wilson's Neurologic Illness at Paris," PWW, 58:607–40.
30. Diary of C. T. Grayson, May 1, 1919, PWW, 58:275–76.
31. Ibid., Apr. 5, 1919, PWW, 57:4.
32. JPT to C. T. Grayson, Apr. 9, 1919, PWW, 57:177.
33. Mantoux's notes, Apr. 9, 1919, 3:30 P.M., PWW, 57:163–64.
34. Hankey's notes, Mar. 19, 1919, 3:00 P.M., PWW, 56:88–95; the quotation is from p. 94.
35. Important new evidence regarding Wilson's state of health at the end of April 1919 has colored and given form to the author's narrative. For highly suggestive medical discussions see again "Appendix: Wilson's Neurologic Illness at Paris," especially the "Editor's Introduction," pp. 607–11, and "Editor's Commentary," pp. 638–40, all in PWW, 58, as well as, more generally, the accompanying essays cited in n. 29 above.

A JUST PEACE?

1. Enclosure in WW to RSB, Apr. 14, 1919, PWW, 57:336.
2. Hankey's notes, Apr. 19, 1909, 11 A.M., PWW, 57:483.
3. WW to N. H. Davis, Apr. 19, 1919, PWW, 57:495.
4. Hankey's notes, Apr. 19, 1919, 11 A.M., PWW, 57:489.
5. T. H. Bliss to E. A. Bliss, May 1, 1919, PWW, 58:320.
6. Diary of C. T. Grayson, Apr. 25, 1919, PWW, 58:113.
7. Diary of R. S. Baker, Apr. 25, 1919, PWW, 58:142–43.

8. Diary of C. T. Grayson, May 3, 1919, PWW, 58:367.
9. Diary of E. Benham, May 7, 1919, PWW, 58:530.
10. Remarks to the Democratic National Committee, Feb. 28, 1919, PWW, 55:320.
11. Mantoux's notes, May 30, 1919, PWW, 59:613.
12. Hankey's notes, 4:00 P.M., June 3, 1919, PWW, 60:28.
13. C. Seymour to his family, June 3, 1919, PWW, 60:76.
14. A discussion with the American delegation, June 3, 1919, PWW, 60:45–71; quotation from page 67.
15. *Ibid.*, p. 71.
16. J. C. Smuts to WW, May 30, 1919, PWW, 59:618.
17. A special message to Congress, May 20, 1919, PWW, 59:290–91.
18. Diary of C. T. Grayson, Apr. 30, 1919, PWW, 58:244–45.
19. After-dinner remarks, May 9, 1919, PWW, 58:598.
20. Diary of R. S. Baker, May 30, 1919, PWW, 58:622.
21. Remarks at Suresnes cemetery on Memorial Day, May 30, 1919, PWW, 59:606–10; quotations are from pp. 606, 610.
22. Minutes of a plenary session of the Inter-Allied Conference, May 31, 1919, PWW, 59:630.
23. Diary of R. S. Baker, May 31, 1919, PWW, 59:646.
24. Diary of E. M. House, May 31, 1919, PWW, 59:644.
25. *Ibid.*, May 30, 1919, p. 624.
26. Reply to German note, June 22, 1919, PWW, 60:76.
27. Diary of E. Benham, June 24, 1919, PWW, 61:135.
28. Remarks at a dinner in the Royal Palace in Belgium, June 19, 1919, PWW, 61:25–26.
29. An address to the Belgian parliament, June 19, 1919, 61:17.
30. Diary of E. M. House, June 23, 1919, PWW, 61:114.
31. After-dinner remarks, June 26, 1919, PWW, 61:190–91.

11. Fighter for the League

SUMMER OF DISCONTENT

1. Diary of E. Benham, July 2, 1919, PWW, 61:370.
2. Diary of C. T. Grayson, July 1, 1919, PWW, 61:360.
3. *Ibid.*, July 8, 1919, PWW, 61:401.
4. Address to the Senate, July 10, 1919, PWW, pp. 426–36; quotations in the following paragraphs are from pp. 428, 436, 429.
5. Diary of H. F. Ashurst, July 11, 1919, PWW, 61:445.
6. *Constitutional Government in the United States*, PWW, 18:160–61.
7. W. A. White, "The President and the Peace," *Emporia* (Kansas) *Daily Gazette*, July 11, 1919; quoted in PWW, 61:507.
8. "A Memoir by Irwin Hood Hoover," longhand manuscript, quoted in Appendix I, PWW, 63:632.
9. W. Wiseman to A. J. Balfour, July 18, 1919, PWW, pp. 541–43.

10. Conversation with members of the Senate Foreign Relations Committee, Aug. 19, 1919, PWW, 62:339–411.
11. See R. Steel, *Walter Lippmann and the American Century*, pp. 162–63.
12. Diary of V. C. McCormick, July 1, 1919, PWW, 61:366.
13. Address to a joint session of Congress, Aug. 8, 1919, PWW, 62:209–19.
14. N. Hapgood to WW, Aug. 20, 1919, PWW, 62:427.
15. WW to E. P. Davis, Aug. 21, 1919, PWW, 62:437.
16. H. H. Kohlsaat to WW, July 25, 1919, Wilson Papers, PUL.
17. *Constitutional Government in the United States*, PWW, 18:161.
18. G. F. Close to the White House staff, Sept. 2, 1919, PWW, 62:615.
19. A memorandum, Sept. 3, 1919, PWW, 62:621.
20. WW to J. W. Sayre, Aug. 26, 1919, PWW, 62:516.
21. WW to C. H. Shinn, Aug. 29, 1919, PWW, 62:554.
22. WW to J. Spargo, Aug. 29, 1919, PWW, 62:559.
23. WW to A. M. Palmer, Aug. 29, 1919, PWW, 62:555.

WESTERN TOUR

1 *New York Times*, Sept. 3, 1919; St. Louis *Post-Dispatch*, Sept. 4, 1919.
2. St. Louis *Post-Dispatch*, Sept. 5, 1919.
3. Address in Columbus, Ohio, Sept. 4, 1919, PWW, 63:7.
4. New York *World*, Sept. 5, 1919.
5. St. Louis *Post-Dispatch*, Sept. 5, 1919.
6. Washington (D.C.) *Post*, Sept. 6, 1919.
7. St. Louis *Post-Dispatch*, Sept. 6, 1919.
8. Address in the Indianapolis Coliseum, Sept. 4, 1919, PWW, 63:24.
9. Luncheon address in St. Louis, Sept. 5, 1919, PWW, 63:42.
10. Address in Tacoma, Wash., Sept. 13, 1919, PWW, 63:248.
11. Address in Oakland, Sept. 13, 1919, PWW, 63:353.
12. Address in Minneapolis, Sept. 9, 1919, PWW, 63:131.
13. Address in Des Moines, Iowa, Sept. 6, 1919, PWW, 63:80.
14. *New York Times*, Sept. 14, 1919.
15. *Ibid.*, Sept. 17, 1919.
16. Portland *Oregonian*, Sept. 16, 1919.
17. Diary of C. T. Grayson, Sept. 10, 1919; Sept. 13, 1919; Sept. 15, 1919; in PWW, 63:152, 240, 275, respectively.
18. *New York Times*, Sept. 22, 1919.
19. E. B. Wilson, *My Memoir*, p. 281.
20. M. A. Hulbert, *The Story of Mrs. Peck*, pp. 271–72.
21. *New York Times*, Sept. 20, 1919.
22. *Ibid.*, Sept. 22, 1919.
23. Diary of C. T. Grayson, Sept. 23, 1919; Sept. 24, 1919; Sept. 25, 1919; in PWW, 63:446, 467, 487, respectively.
24. From the rear platform, Ogden, Utah, Sept. 23, 1919, PWW, 63:448.
25. Address in Salt Lake City, Sept. 23, 1919, PWW, 63:451.
26. *Constitutional Government in the United States*, PWW, 18:162.
27. Address in Pueblo, Colorado, Sept. 25, 1919, PWW, 63:511, 512, 513.
28. Diary of C. T. Grayson, Sept. 25, 1919, PWW, 63:488–90.

29. E. B. Wilson, *My Memoir*, p. 284.
30. *Ibid.*, p. 285.
31. Related in diary of C. T. Grayson, Sept. 26, 1919, PWW, 63:519.

12. Embattled Invalid

A PRESIDENT DISABLED

1. Grayson bulletin, 11:00 A.M., Oct. 2, 1919, quoted in the Washington *Post*, Oct. 3, 1919, PWW, 63:544.
2. "Memoir of I. H. Hoover," PWW, 63:Appendix I, p. 634.
3. Grayson bulletin, 10:00 P.M., Oct. 2, 1919, quoted in Washington *Post*, PWW, 63:544.
4. J. P. Tumulty, *Woodrow Wilson As I Know Him*, p. 444.
5. R. Lansing, "Cabinet Meetings During the Illness of President Wilson," Lansing papers, Feb. 3, 1920, PWW, 64:456–57 (volume forthcoming).
6. Washington *Post*, Oct. 6 and 7, 1919.
7. Quoted in *New York Times*, Oct. 12, 1919.
8. C. M. Thomas, *Thomas Riley Marshall—Hoosier Statesman*, p. 258. The account of Essary's visit to Marshall is based on letters by Essary and by Marshall's private secretary written twenty years later. No other documentary evidence exists; but the story rings true. It was undoubtedly Tumulty who picked Essary for the mission.
9. *Ibid.*, pp. 219, 258.
10. E. B. Wilson, *My Memoir*, p. 289.
11. *New York Times*, Dec. 3, 1919, PWW, 64:106.
12. EBW to RL, Dec. 2, 1919, PWW, 64:119.
13. RL to JPT, Nov. 26, 1919, PWW, 64:94–95.
14. Related in Note 1 to "Memorandum by C. T. Grayson," Nov. 17, 1919, PWW, 64:45.
15. WW to G. M. Hitchcock, Nov. 18, 1919, PWW, 64:58.
16. Diary of H. F. Ashurst, Nov. 19. 1919, PWW, 64:63.
17. W. Lippmann to N. D. Baker, Jan. 17, 1920, quoted in R. Steel, *Walter Lippmann and the American Century*, p. 167.
18. *New York Times*, Dec. 5, 1919, PWW, 64:133.
19. R. Lansing, "A Memorandum," Dec. 4, 1919.
20. E. B. Wilson, *op. cit.*, p. 299. Mrs. Wilson is the sole source for Wilson's classic rejoinder; on this point one does not wish to doubt her!
21. *New York Times*, Dec. 7, 1919.

AGITATIONS AND DELUSIONS

1. Diary of J. Daniels, Dec. 9, 1919, PWW, 64:166.
2. JPT to EBW, Dec. 18, 1919, PWW, 64:204–206.
3. Draft of a public letter, Dec. 17, 1919, PWW, 64:199–202.
4. RL to WW, Jan. 28, 1920, PWW, 64:341.
5. EBW to RL, Feb. 3, 1920, PWW, 64:352–53.

6. RL to H. C. Wallace, Feb. 10, 1920, PWW, 64:402.
7. Prime ministers of France and Great Britain to WW, Feb. 17, 1920, and Feb. 20, 1920, PWW, 64:441, 442.
8. For the reply agreed upon, see F. L. Polk to H. C. Wallace, Feb. 24, 1920, PWW, 64:459–63.
9. Springfield (Mass.) *Republican*, Feb. 3, 1920. The Grey letter appeared in the *New York Times*, Feb. 1, 1920.
10. White House press release, Feb. 5, 1920, PWW, 64:363–64.
11. Diary of E. M. House, Jan. 11, 1920, PWW, 64:270.
12. Memorandum by R. Lansing, Dec. 10, 1919, PWW, 64:179, 256.
13. WW to RL, Feb. 7, 1920, and Feb. 11, 1920, PWW, 64:383, 404.
14. Desk diary of R. Lansing, Feb. 11, 1920, PWW, 67:405; memorandum by R. Lansing, Feb. 13, 1920, PWW, 64:415.
15. J. P. Tumulty, *op. cit.*, p. 445.
16. Diary of E. M. House, Dec. 22, 1919, PWW, 64:217.
17. M. Peter to G. Motta, May 28, 1920, WP,PUL.
18. Desk diary of R. Lansing, May 29, 1920, WP,PUL.
19. R. S. Baker, *American Chronicle*, pp. 481–82.
20. WW to E. M. House, June 10, 1920, WP,PUL.
21. Springfield (Mass.) *Republican*, quoted in n. 1 to JPT to EBW, Feb. 3, 1920.
22. JPT to EBW, Dec. 18, 1919, PWW, 64:203.
23. White House statement, Dec. 14, 1919, PWW, 64:187.
24. WW to G. M. Hitchcock, Feb. 28, 1920, and Mar. 8, 1920. (From here on, unless otherwise noted, copies of all documents referred to or cited are in WP,PUL. They are in the process of being edited for use in the final volumes of the *Papers*.)
25. WW to F. L. Polk, Mar. 15, 1920.
26. C. T. Grayson, *Woodrow Wilson: An Intimate Memoir*, p. 106.
27. Diary of E. M. House, Mar. 2, 1920.
28. Diary of J. Daniels, Apr. 14, 1920.
29. Diary of J. W. Davis, Dec. 6, 1920, Yale University Library.
30. Notes for a "3rd Inaugural," n.d.
31. Shorthand diary of C. L. Swem, May 17, 1920.
32. Notes for a "3rd Inaugural," n.d.
33. Memorandum by C. Glass, June 12, 1920, and June 16, 1920.
34. The Seibold interview is in the New York *World* for June 18, 1920. Mrs. Wilson's instructions to Tumulty and the latter's expletive in the margin are described by J. M. Blum in *Joe Tumulty and the Wilson Era*, pp. 242–44. (At that time these items were noted as being in the Tumulty papers, but they have since been misplaced.)
35. Memorandum by C. Glass, June 19, 1920.
36. H. S. Cummings to WW, July 1, 1920; WW to H. S. Cummings, July 2, 1920 (two telegrams).
37. BC to WW, July 4, 1920, and memorandum by H. S. Cummings, Jan. 18, 1929.
38. Memorandum by H. S. Cummings, Jan. 18, 1929. (Original in R. S. Baker Papers, LC.)
39. *Ibid.*, July 26, 1929.

40. J. M. Cox, *Journey Through My Years*, pp. 241–44, contains F. D. Roosevelt's account of the meeting as written by him to Claude G. Bowers.
41. WW to J. Daniels, Aug. 28, 1920; and WW to B. Colby, Sept. 24, 1919.
42. Report of an interview by William W. Hawkins, Sept. 27, 1920. Original of this document is in the B. Colby Papers, LC.
43. Shorthand diary of C. L. Swem, July 26, 1920, and May 17, 1920.
44. WW to R. Meeker, Sept. 27, 1920; WW to S. W. McGill, Sept. 27, 1920; and WW to A. S. Burleson, Nov. 15, 1920.
45. WW to A. M. Palmer, Sept. 9, 1920; shorthand diary of C. L. Swem, Sept. 9, 1920; A. M. Palmer to WW, Sept. 14, 1920.
46. Memoranda of C. L. Swem: Feb. 26, 1921; Dec. 18, 1920; Jan. 5, 1921.
47. R. W. Wooley to JPT, Sept. 30, 1919.
48. WW to JPT, Sept. 26 1920.
49. JPT to WW, Oct. 1, 1920.
50. WW to J. W. Sayre, Oct. 25, 1920; and WW to L. A. Smith, Oct. 25, 1919.
51. The Tumulty speech, Oct. 28, 1919, is in WP,PUL.

LEAVING THE WHITE HOUSE

1. BC to WW, Nov. 3, 1920, and JPT to J. Kerney, Mar. 2, 1921, Tumulty papers, LC.
2. C. H. Dodge to B. Dodge and M. B. Dodge, Dec. 16, 1920.
3. In a letter to J. Daniels, Nov. 5, 1920.
4. Annual message on the state of the Union, Dec. 4, 1917, PWW, 45:198.
5. WW to BC, Nov. 20, 1920.
6. *Ibid.*, Nov. 15, 1920.
7. J. H. Eagle to WW, Dec. 28, 1920.
8. E. B. Wilson, *My Memoir*, p. 307.
9. C. S. Ridley to WW, March 2, 1921.
10. EBW to EMH, Nov. 15, 1920; EMH to EBW, Nov. 16, 1920.
11. R. S. Baker, *American Chronicle*, p. 488.
12. W. B. Wilson to WW, Dec. 18, 1920; WW to W. B. Wilson, Dec. 20, 1920.
13. A. M. Palmer to WW, Jan. 29, 1921.
14. D. F. Houston, *Eight Years with the Wilson Cabinet*, p. 149.
15. Members of the cabinet to WW, Mar. 3, 1921.
16. F. J. Turner to W. E. Dodd, Feb. 19, 1921.

13. Into History

THE HOUSE ON S STREET

1. Diary of H. F. Ashurst, Mar. 4, 1921.
2. *Ibid.*
3. WW to J. W. Sayre, Apr. 22, 1921.
4. Diary of H. S. Cummings, Apr. 25, 1921.
5. S. Axson to J. G. Hibben, June 11, 1921.
6. WW to C. W. Eliot, Mar. 15, 1921.

7. JRB to G. Creel, Jan. 19, 1921.
8. WW to BC, Aug. 18, 1921.
9. BC to WW, Dec. 5, 1921.
10. Quoted in JRB to BC, Dec. 6, 1921.
11. Diary of R. S. Baker, Mar. 22, 1921, quoted in R. S. Baker, *American Chronicle*, pp. 492–93.
12. JRB to G. Lee, May 25, 1921.
13. Quoted in J. C. Redfield to JRB, Oct. 5, 1921.
14. R. Lansing, *The Peace Conference: A Personal Narrative*, p. 13.
15. Diary of R. S. Baker, Mar. 22, 1921, quoted in *American Chronicle*, p. 493.
16. L. C. Woods to WW, June 6, 1921, and L. C. Woods to WW, June 29, 1921.
17. RB *et al.* to WW, May 30, 1921.
18. WW to RB, June 3, 1921.
19. G. M. Harper to WW, Oct. 8, 1921, and WW to G. M. Harper, Oct. 10, 1921.
20. WW to F. D. Roosevelt, July 4, 1921.
21. F. D. Roosevelt to WW, July 7, 1921; JRB to F. D. Roosevelt, July 9, 1921; WW to F. D. Roosevelt, Sept. 16, 1921, and Apr. 30, 1922.
22. *Collier's*, Feb. 18, 1922. This editorial was written by the noted journalist Ida M. Tarbell.
23. New York *World*, Nov. 18, 1921.
24. C. H. Dodge to E. D. Huntington, Dec. 15, 1921.
25. WW to L. D. Brandeis, Dec. 6, 1921.
26. WW to JPT, Apr. 6, 1922.
27. JPT to WW, Apr. 5, 1922.
28. A message to Democrats, Allentown (Pa.) *Record*, May 7, 1921.
29. WW to H. Holt, Apr. 7, 1922.
30. S. N. Warren to WW, Apr. 4, 1922.
31. BC to JRB, May 11, 1922.
32. BC to WW, Sept. 2, 1922.
33. BC to WW, Nov. 24, 1922.
34. WW to BC, Nov. 24, 1922.
35. JRB to BC, Nov. 24, 1922.
36. Press release, Dec. 1, 1922.
37. WW to BC, Dec. 14, 1922.
38. E. P. Davis to WW, May 25, 1922.
39. WW to W. Safford, Sept. 19, 1922.
40. W. Williams, *The Tiger of France*, p. 234.
41. WW to C. A. Swanson, Nov. 6, 1922.
42. WW to F. A. Walker, Nov. 8, 1922.
43. *New York Times*, Nov. 12, 1922.
44. WW to M. and B. King, Nov. 13, 1922.
45. EBW to WW, Dec. 24, 1922.

TO THE END

1. WW to J. H. Clarke, Jan. 19, 1923.
2. EBW to G. Creel, Apr. 30, 1923.

3. G. Creel to WW, Apr. 19, and EBW to G. Creel, Apr. 24, 1923.
4. WW to E. Sedgwick, May 2, 1923.
5. E. Sedgwick to WW, May 16, 1923.
6. "The Road Away from Revolution," *Atlantic Monthly*, Aug. 1923.
7. WW to F. K. DeW. Harding, Aug. 3, 1923.
8. Ida Tarbell, "Memorandum of a Visit to Woodrow Wilson," May 5, 1922.
9. EBW to WW, Aug. 27, 1923, and Aug. 28, 1923.
10. WW to EBW, Aug. 29, 1923.
11. WW to C. Ford, Nov. 26, 1923.
12. WW to E. P. Davis, Nov. 18, 1923.
13. WW to E. G. Reid, July (n.d.) 1923.
14. WW to C. Glass, Nov. 12, 1923.
15. *New York Times*, Nov. 12, 1922.
16. J. H. Jones to WW, Oct. 2, 1923; and WW to C. H. Dodge and to J. H. Jones, Oct. 4, 1923.
17. WW to C. H. Dodge, Oct. 4, 1923.
18. WW to A. H. Lightnow, Nov. 21, 1923.
19. Told to J. Daniels by E. W. McAdoo; see J. Daniels, *The Wilson Era: Years of Peace*, p. 488.
20. WW to B. Johnson, Sept. 14, 1923.
21. WW to J. T. Derry, Jan. 2, 1923.
22. WW to J. B. Bassett, Jan. 2, 1924.
23. WW to N. D. Baker, Dec. 29, 1923.
24. WW to J. W. Sayre, Oct. 5, 1923.
25. WW to C. H. Dodge *et al.*, Jan. 20, 1924.
26. WW to R. B. Fosdick, Nov. 28, 1923.
27. R. B. Fosdick, *Chronicle of a Generation*, p. 232.
28. Details in following paragraphs are largely from J. R. Bolling, "A Brief History of the Last Illness of Honorable Woodrow Wilson."
29. C. T. Grayson, *Woodrow Wilson: An Intimate Memoir*, p. 139.
30. C. Coolidge to C. T. Grayson, Feb. 4, 1924.
31. EBW to H. C. Lodge, Feb. 4, 1924.

Bibliography

———◆———

NOTE

A full bibliography for Wilson's life would be far longer than I could present here. The following list of books contains the ones that have been most helpful or interesting to me, and I have made comments on a few of them. This list also contains full titles of books cited in the text or notes. Beyond these, and unfortunately beyond acknowledgment or listing, are what E. B. White called those "thousand unremembered and mysterious sources" upon which the mind of the writer feeds.

A word needs to be said on the principal source of this biography, the *Papers of Woodrow Wilson*, running when completed to some fifty thousand pages in sixty-eight or sixty-nine volumes, published by the Princeton University Press. It is now nearing final form after more than thirty years under the editorship of Arthur S. Link and a group of dedicated coworkers. This unprecedented compendium not only brings together in authoritative form Wilson's personal and official correspondence, speeches, interviews, diplomatic notes, etc., but adds much significant collateral material, as well as hitherto unknown Wilson texts, many of them translated from his shorthand or the shorthand of stenographers. No biographer could by himself have found access to this vast body of material, and I have been at every turn the grateful beneficiary of the work of others. The completion of my own text was timed so as to coincide with the editing, at least in preliminary form, of documents covering all but Wilson's final four years. In this way I have been able to include new material that otherwise would have been missed.

I have, of course, read widely in other materials, in newspapers, in documents not qualifying as primary sources and therefore omitted from the *Papers*, as well as in the works of previous biographers and scholars. But the *Papers* remain the foundation stone, as it will be in the future to all who work in this field.

In my Notes, above, where the *Papers* include material that has appeared in some other place (and which I may originally have found elsewhere), I have cited the *Papers* as my source. This will undoubtedly be a convenience to readers, and it assures the authenticity of the texts.

List of Books

Ambrosius, Lloyd E. *Woodrow Wilson and the American Diplomatic Tradition* (Cambridge; New York, 1987).

Axson, Stockton. "Memoir" (typed manuscript in the possession of Arthur S. Link). Rich in insights; by a man who admired Wilson and knew him intimately.

Bailey, Thomas A. *Woodrow Wilson and the Great Betrayal* (New York, 1945).

———. *Woodrow Wilson and the Lost Peace* (New York, 1944).

Baker, Ray Stannard. *Woodrow Wilson, Life and Letters: Youth 1856–1889; Princeton 1890–1910; Governor 1910–1913; President 1913–1914; Neutrality 1914–1915; Facing War 1915–1917; War Leader 1917–1918; Armistice* (Garden City, N.Y., 1927–1939). This pioneer work is still valuable, especially the earlier volumes. Baker interviewed virtually everyone who knew the young Wilson, and his memoranda and correspondence are preserved in the Library of Congress. Not being considered primary sources, these interviews are not included in the *Papers*.

———. *Woodrow Wilson and World Settlement*, 3 vols. (Garden City, N.Y., 1923). Also valuable, although Baker in telling the story of the peace conference aimed to show the wickedness of the Old World as contrasted with the virtue of the New.

———. *American Chronicle* (New York, 1945).

Bartlett, Ruhl J. *The League to Enforce Peace* (Chapel Hill, N.C., 1944).

Bell, Herbert C. F. *Woodrow Wilson and the People* (Garden City, N.Y., 1945).

Berle, Beatrice Bishop, and Travis Beal Jacobs, eds., *Navigating the Rapids: From the Papers of Adolf A. Berle* (New York, 1973).

Billington, Ray Allen. *Frederick Jackson Turner—Historian, Scholar, Teacher* (New York, 1973).

Birdsall, Paul. *Versailles Twenty Years After* (New York, 1941). An early attempt to look with perspective and common sense on the shaping and the results of the peace.

Blum, John M. *Joe Tumulty and the Wilson Era* (Boston, 1951).

———, ed., *Public Philosopher: Selected Letters of Walter Lippmann* (New York, 1985).

———. *Woodrow Wilson and the Politics of Morality* (Boston, 1956). A sympathetic and enlightening account.

Boemeke, Manfred F. "The Wilson Administration, Organized Labor, and the Colorado Coal Strike," Ph.D. dissertation, Princeton University, 1983.

Bragdon, Henry W. *Wilson: The Academic Years* (Cambridge, Mass., 1967). Especially useful for information gathered on the Bryn Mawr and Wesleyan years. Bragdon, like Baker, kept records of his interviews, which are now in the Firestone Library at Princeton.

Buchan, J. *A History of the Great War*, 2 vols. (Boston, 1922).

Buehrig, Edward H. *Wilson's Foreign Policy in Perspective* (Bloomington, Ind., 1957).

————. *Woodrow Wilson and the Balance of Power* (Bloomington, Ind., 1955). Shows an aspect of Wilson's foreign policy not always sufficiently emphasized.

Bundy, McGeorge. *An Atmosphere to Breathe: Woodrow Wilson and the Life of the American University College* (New York: The Woodrow Wilson Foundation, 1959).

Calhoun, Frederick S. *Power and Principle, Armed Intervention in Wilsonian Foreign Policy* (Kent, Ohio, 1986).

Clements, Kendrick A. *Woodrow Wilson, World Statesman* (Boston, 1987). A current brief, authoritative biography.

Coben, Stanley. *A. Mitchell Palmer: Politician* (New York, 1963).

Cooper, John Milton, Jr. "The Irony of Fate," from *A Commemorative Celebration, The Woodrow Wilson Center for Scholars* (Washington, D.C., 1982).

————. *The Warrior and the Priest: Woodrow Wilson and Theodore Roosevelt* (Cambridge, Mass., 1983).

————. *Walter Hines Page: The Southerner as American 1885–1918* (Chapel Hill, N.C., 1977).

Corley, Frances F. *Confederate City, Augusta, Georgia: 1860–1865* (Columbia, S.C., 1960).

Cox, James M. *Journey Through My Years: An Autobiography* (New York, 1946).

Craig, Hardin. *Woodrow Wilson at Princeton* (Norman, Okla., 1960).

Creel, George. *Rebel at Large—Recollections of Fifty Crowded Years* (New York, 1947).

Daniels, Jonathan. *Washington Quadrille—The Dance Beside the Documents* (Garden City, N.Y., 1968).

Daniels, Josephus. *The Life of Woodrow Wilson* (Chicago, 1924).

————. *The Wilson Era: Years of Peace, 1910–1917; Years of War and After, 1917–1932* (Chapel Hill, N.C., 1944 and 1946).

Davidson, John Wells, ed. *A Crossroads of Freedom—The 1912 Campaign Speeches of Woodrow Wilson* (New Haven, 1956). A ground-breaking work, now superseded by the texts in the *Papers* but still useful for its comments.

Devlin, Patrick. *Too Proud to Fight: Woodrow Wilson's Neutrality* (New York, 1974). The point of view of a witty and learned Britisher.

Dodd, William E. *Woodrow Wilson and His Work* (New York, 1920).

Doerries, Reinhard R. *Imperial Challenge—Ambassador Count Bernstorff and German American Relations 1908–1917.* Trans. by Christa D. Shannon (Chapel Hill, N.C., 1989).

Egerton, George W. *Great Britain and the Creation of the League of Nations* (Chapel Hill, N.C., 1978).

Eliot, Charles W. *Educational Reform—Essays and Addresses* (New York, 1901).

Elliott, Margaret Axson. *My Aunt Louisa and Woodrow Wilson* (Chapel Hill, N.C., 1944). A delightful book, important in its recollections of Wilson's middle years.

Ferrell, Robert H. *Woodrow Wilson and World War I—1917–1921* (New York, 1985).

Finch, Edith. *Carey Thomas at Bryn Mawr* (New York, 1947).

Floto, Inga. *Colonel House in Paris: A Study of American Policy at the Paris Peace Conference of 1919* (Princeton, 1981). Authoritative study of the peace conference.

Fosdick, Raymond B. *Letters on the League of Nations* (Princeton, 1966).

———. *Chronicle of a Generation* (New York, 1958).

Foulke, C. Pardee. "Woodrow Wilson: A Projected Biography." Unfinished typescript, PUL.

Fowler, Wilton B. *British-American Relations 1917–1918: The Role of Sir William Wiseman* (Princeton, 1969).

Freud, Sigmund, and William Bullitt. *Thomas Woodrow Wilson: A Psychological Study* (Boston, 1967). A misleading book, written out of hatred; an embarrassment to students of Freud.

Gardner, Lloyd C. *Safe for Democracy: The Anglo-American Response to Revolution, 1913–1923* (New York, 1984).

Garrety, John A. *Henry Cabot Lodge—A Biography* (New York, 1953).

George, Alexander L. and Juliette L. *Woodrow Wilson and Colonel House: A Personality Study* (New York 1956). A psychological interpretation of Wilson's personality.

Grayson, Cary T. *Woodrow Wilson: An Intimate Memoir* (New York, 1960). Highly discreet but informative, now supplemented by Grayson material in the *Papers*.

Griswold, A. Whitney. *Far Eastern Policy of the United States* (New York, 1938).

Gwynn, Stephen, ed. *The Letters and Friendships of Sir Cecil Spring Rice*, 2 vols. (London, 1929).

Hale, William Bayard. *Woodrow Wilson: The Story of His Life* (Garden City, N.Y. 1912). A campaign biography, unexpectedly useful because Wilson talked with the author about his early life.

Hatch, Alden. *Edith Bolling Wilson—First Lady Extraordinary* (New York, 1961).

Heaton, John L. *Cobb of "The World"* (New York, 1924).

Hendrick, Burton J. *The Life and Letters of Walter Hines Page*, 3 vols. (Garden City, N.Y., 1924–1926).

Hirst, David W. *Woodrow Wilson: Reform Governor—A Documentary Narrative* (Princeton, 1965).

Hoeveler, J. D., Jr. *James McCosh and the Scottish Intellectual Tradition* (Princeton, 1981).

Hofstadter, Richard. *The Age of Reform: From Bryan to FDR* (New York, 1953).

Holton, Gerald, and Yehuda Elkana, eds. *Albert Einstein: Historical and Cultural Perspectives* (Princeton, 1982).

Hoover, Herbert. *The Ordeal of Woodrow Wilson* (New York, 1958).

Hoover, Irwin H. *Forty-two Years in the White House* (Boston, 1934). Revealing when supplemented by Hoover's manuscript memoir in the *Papers.*

House, Edward Mandell. *The Intimate Papers of Colonel House,* 4 vols. Charles Seymour, ed. (Boston, 1926–1928).

————, and Charles Seymour, eds. *What Really Happened at Paris: The Story of the Peace Conference* (New York, 1921). Both House books are vital documents; must be read against the complete House manuscript diary.

Houston, David F. *Eight Years with the Wilson Cabinet—1913–1920* (Garden City, N.Y., 1926).

Hulbert, Mary Allen. *The Story of Mrs. Peck: An Autobiography* (New York, 1933).

Hurley, Edward N. *The Bridge to France* (Philadelphia, 1927).

Jaffray, Elizabeth. *Secrets of the White House* (New York, 1927).

Kennan, George F. *Russia Leaves the War* (Princeton, 1956).

————. *The Decision to Intervene—Soviet-American Relations, 1917–1920* (Princeton, 1958).

Kennedy, David M. *Over Here: The First World War and American Society* (New York, 1980).

Kerney, James. *The Political Education of Woodrow Wilson* (New York, 1926).

Keynes, John Maynard. *The Economic Consequences of the Peace* (New York, 1919).

Lane, Anne Wintermute, and Louise Herrick Wall, eds. *The Letters of Franklin K. Lane, Personal and Political* (Boston, 1922).

Lansing, Robert. *The Peace Conference: A Personal Narrative* (Boston, 1921).

Lawrence, David. *The True Story of Woodrow Wilson* (New York, 1924).

Leitch, Alexander. *A Princeton Companion* (Princeton, 1978).

Lentin, A. *Lloyd George, Woodrow Wilson, and the Guilt of Germany, An Essay in the Pre-History of Appeasement* (Baton Rouge, La., 1985).

Leopold, Richard W. *The Growth of American Foreign Policy: A History* (New York, 1962).

Levin, N. Gordon, Jr. *Woodrow Wilson and World Politics* (New York, 1968).

Link, Arthur S. *Wilson,* 5 vols.: *The Road to the White House* (1947); *The New Freedom* (1956); *The Struggle for Neutrality, 1914–1915* (1960); *Confusions and Crises, 1915–1916* (1964); *Campaigns for Progressivism and Peace, 1916–1917* (1965); all published at Princeton. These monumental volumes are essential to any study of Wilson and his times, a blend of history and biography, based upon meticulous and wide-ranging scholarship. It would be excessive to list all of Link's other studies in the field, but the following have been most valuable to the author:

————, ed. *The Papers of Woodrow Wilson,* 63 vols. published to date (Princeton, 1966–1990).

————, ed. *Woodrow Wilson and a Revolutionary World, 1913–1921* (Chapel Hill, N.C., 1982).

————. *The Higher Realism of Woodrow Wilson* (Nashville, Tenn., 1971).

———. *Woodrow Wilson and the Progressive Era* (New York, 1954).

———. *Woodrow Wilson—Revolution, War, and Peace* (Arlington Heights, Ill., 1979).

Livermore, Seward W. *Politics Is Adjourned: Woodrow Wilson and the War Congress, 1916–1918* (Middletown, Conn., 1966).

Lloyd George, David. *The Truth About the Peace Treaties*, 2 vols. (New Haven, 1939).

———. *The War Memoirs of David Lloyd George, 1915–1916*, 2 vols. (New Haven, 1939).

Ludendorff, Erich von. *Ludendorff's Own Story: August 1914–November 1918* (New York and London, 1920).

Mantoux, Etienne. *The Carthaginian Peace, or, The Economic Consequences of Mr. Keynes* (London, 1946). A useful antidote to Keynes, by a brilliant young French economist.

Mantoux, Paul. *The Deliberations of the Council of Four, March 24–June 28, 1919: Notes of the Official Interpreter*, trans. and ed. by Arthur S. Link and Manfred F. Boemeke (Princeton, forthcoming). This complete text, with notes and a new translation, will be a major contribution to the literature of the peace conference.

Mason, Alpheus T. *Brandeis, A Free Man's Life* (New York, 1946).

Mayer, Arno J. *Politics and Diplomacy of Peacemaking: Containment and Counterrevolution at Versailles* (New York, 1967). Significant because of its emphasis on the importance of the Bolshevik Revolution in the making of the peace.

McAdoo, Eleanor Wilson, ed. *The Priceless Gift—The Love Letters of Woodrow Wilson and Ellen Axson Wilson* (New York, 1962).

———. *The Woodrow Wilsons* (New York, 1937).

McAdoo, William G. *Crowded Years—The Reminiscences of William G. McAdoo* (Boston, 1931).

McCombs, William F. *Making Woodrow Wilson President* (New York, 1921). A bitter, untrustworthy book.

McGovern, George S., and Leonard F. Guttridge. *The Great Coalfield War* (Boston, 1972).

McMillan, Lewis. *Woodrow Wilson of Princeton* (Narberth, Pa., 1952).

Morison, Elting E., *et al.*, eds. *The Letters of Theodore Roosevelt*, 8 vols. (Cambridge, Mass., 1951–1954).

Morison, Samuel Eliot. *The Oxford History of the American People* (New York, 1965).

Mulder, John M. *Woodrow Wilson: Years of Preparation* (Princeton, 1978). An important contribution to understanding Wilson's father, and the whole religious background.

Munro, Dana G. *Intervention and Dollar Diplomacy in the Caribbean, 1900–1921* (Princeton, 1964).

Murray, Robert K. *Red Scare—A study in National Hysteria* (Minneapolis, Minn., 1955).

Myers, William S., ed. *Woodrow Wilson: Some Princeton Memories*, (Princeton, 1946). These essays throw much light on the Princeton controversies.

Nevins, Allan. *Henry White: Thirty Years of American Diplomacy* (New York, 1930).

Nicolson, Harold. *Peacemaking, 1919* (London, 1933).

Palmer, Frederick, *Newton D. Baker, America at War*, 2 vols. (New York, 1931).

Park, Bert Edward. *The Impact of Illness on World Leaders* (Philadelphia, 1986).

Perry, Bliss. *And Gladly Teach* (Boston, 1935).

Powell, Lyman P., ed. *Historic Towns of the Southern States* (New York, 1900).

Rappard, William E. *Quest for Peace* (Cambridge, Mass., 1940).

Reid, Edith Gittings. *Woodrow Wilson: The Caricature, the Myth, and the Man* (New York, 1934).

Salvatore, Nick. *Eugene V. Debs—Citizen and Socialist* (Urbana, Ill., 1982).

Saunders, Frances Wright. *Ellen Axson Wilson: First Lady Between Two Worlds* (Chapel Hill, N.C., 1985). Especially noteworthy for its new information on the background and youth of Wilson's first wife.

Schlesinger, Arthur M., Jr., et al., eds. *The Coming to Power—Critical Presidential Elections in American History* (New York, 1971).

Schwabe, Klaus. *Woodrow Wilson, Revolutionary German, and Peacemaking—Missionary Diplomacy and the Realities of Power, 1918–1919* (Chapel Hill, N.C., 1985). Massive, with unique material on the German side of the peacemaking process.

Seymour, Charles. *Letters from the Paris Peace Conference*. H. B. Whiteman, ed. (New Haven, 1965).

———. *Woodrow Wilson and the World War* (New Haven, 1921). A remarkably perceptive small volume, considering it was written immediately after the events it recounts.

———, ed., *The Intimate Papers of Colonel House*, 4 vols. (Boston, 1926–1928). (See above, under House.)

Simons, J. K., *A Guide to Columbia, S.C.* (Columbia, S.C., 1943).

Smith, Gene. *When the Cheering Stopped: The Last Years of Woodrow Wilson* (New York, 1964). Journalistic, but important in being a first effort to relate a hitherto untold story.

Smythe, Donald. *Guerrilla Warrior: The Early Life of John J. Pershing*; and *Pershing, General of the Armies* (Bloomington, Ind., 1973 and 1986).

Starling, Edmund W. *Starling of the White House*, as told to Thomas Sugrue (New York, 1946).

Steel, Ronald. *Walter Lippmann and the American Century* (Boston, 1980).

Thomas, Charles M. *Thomas Riley Marshall—Hoosier Statesman* (Oxford, Ohio, 1939).

Thompson, John M. *Russia, Bolshevism and the Versailles Peace* (Princeton, 1966).

Thorsen, Niels Aage. *The Political Thought of Woodrow Wilson—1875–1910* (Princeton, 1988). A first-rate study, with fresh interpretations, particularly of Wilson's concept of the American nation.

Tillman, Seth. *Anglo-American Relations at the Paris Peace Conference of 1919* (Princeton, 1961).

Tribble, Edwin, ed. *A President in Love—The Courtship Letters of Woodrow Wilson and Edith Bolling Galt* (Boston, 1981).

Tumulty, Joseph P. *Woodrow Wilson as I Know Him,* (Garden City, N.Y., 1921).

Unterberger, Betty Miller. *America's Siberian Expedition, 1918–1920. A Study of National Policy* (Durham, N.C., 1956).

———. *The United States, Revolutionary Russia, and the Rise of Czechoslovakia.* (Chapel Hill, N.C., 1989).

Vaughn, Stephen. *Holding Fast the Inner Lines—Democracy, Nationalism, and the Committee on Public Information* (Chapel Hill, N.C., 1980).

Walworth, Arthur. *Wilson and His Peacemakers—American Diplomacy at the Paris Peace Conference* (New York, 1986).

———. Woodrow Wilson, 2 vols.: *American Prophet; World Prophet* (New York, 1958).

Weinstein, Edwin A. *Woodrow Wilson: A Medical and Psychological Biography* (Princeton, 1981). Ground-breaking appraisal of the course of Wilson's illnesses up to his massive stroke of 1919.

White, William Allen. *Woodrow Wilson: The Man, His Times, and His Task* (Boston, 1924). An early work by the noted journalist, interesting in its account of Wilson's youth based on contemporary interviews; my first introduction, as a boy of fourteen, to the subject.

Williams, Wythe. *The Tiger of France—Conversations with Clemenceau* (New York, 1943).

Wilson, Edith Bolling. *My Memoir* (Indianapolis, 1938). Mrs. Wilson's memory is often faulty, colored by her preconceptions; but an essential document.

Wilson, Woodrow. *Congressional Government,* 1885; *The State* (1889); *Division and Reunion* (1893); *George Washington* (New York, 1896); *A History of the American People* (1902); *Constitutional Government in the United States* (1908); *The New Freedom: A Call for the Emancipation of the Generous Energies of a People* (1912); *The Road Away from Revolution* (1923). These are the books by Wilson discussed in the text.

Wimer, Kurt. "Woodrow Wilson's Plan for a Vote of Confidence," *Pennsylvania History,* v. 28 (1961); "Woodrow Wilson Tries Conciliation: An Effort that Failed," *Historian,* v. 25 (1963); "Woodrow Wilson's Plans to Enter the League of Nations Through an Executive Agreement," *Western Political Quarterly,* 11 (1958).

Index